Standard Albanian

STANDARD
ALBANIAN

A REFERENCE GRAMMAR FOR STUDENTS

LEONARD NEWMARK

PHILIP HUBBARD   PETER PRIFTI

STANFORD UNIVERSITY PRESS   STANFORD, CALIFORNIA

Published with the assistance of the
ANDREW W. MELLON FOUNDATION

STANFORD UNIVERSITY PRESS
Stanford, California
© 1982 by the Board of Trustees of the
Leland Stanford Junior University
Printed in the United States of America
ISBN 0-8047-1129-1
Original printing 1982
Last figure below indicates year of this printing:
08 07 06 05 04 03 02 01 00 99

Preface

This book is intended as a reference grammar for English-speaking students who are learning present-day Albanian. It is not a linguist's grammar, not a scientific study of the language for the purpose of advancing our theoretical understanding of language, nor a scholar's grammatical compendium for the purpose of interpreting documents from the historical period preceding the present decade.

A large part of the book is in fact an adaptation (in part, a straight translation) and reworking of A. Dhrimo, E. Angoni, E. Hysa, E. Lafe, E. Likaj, F. Agalliu, and Sh. Demiraj, **Morfologjia**, Tiranë: Akademia e Shkencave e RP të Shqipërisë, Instituti i Gjuhësisë dhe i Letërsisë, 1976, under the editorship of Sh. Demiraj, which was published as the second volume of a planned larger work **Fonetika dhe Gramatika e Gjuhës së Sotme Letrare Shqipe** under the general editorship of Mahir Domi. This work constitutes an important step in the establishment of a modern standard Albanian language, part of a larger undertaking of the Academy of Sciences of the People's Republic of Albania and more particularly of its Institute of Linguistics and Literature.

One of the other works already published as part of this attempt to establish a standard Albanian language was a set of orthographic rules by a commission headed by Androkli Kostallari, and composed of Mahir Domi, Eqrem Çabej, and Emil Lafe, entitled **Drejtshkrimi i Gjuhës Shqipe;** we have made use of the edition published by the Albanian Institute of Prishtinë (Yugoslavia) in 1974. Much more than a set of prescriptive spelling rules, this work reflects a number of popular and scientific decisions over the past twenty-five years determining which forms out of the multitude of regional, generational, and social dialects of Albanian are to be considered to belong to present-day *standard* Albanian. The Albanians refer to this as the **gjuha letrare**, or 'literary language', but since the intention is to establish a general language for popular use throughout the Albanian-speaking community, much more than a language for literature, we have chosen to call it in this book by the broader title "standard."

The third important reference work published in the standardization process is the "orthographic dictionary" **Fjalori Drejtshkrimor i Gjuhës Shqipe,** also published by the Instituti i Gjuhësisë dhe i Letërsisë in 1976, the work of a commission consisting this time of Androkli Kostallari (editor-in-chief), Mahir Domi, Emil Lafe, and Nikoleta Cikulli. In this work too, much more than individual spellings of words have been decided: the inflectional forms of thousands of words are indicated, so that our own reference grammar need no longer provide the numerous alternative grammatical forms that G.Pekmezi felt bound to include in his great *Grammatik der Albanesischen Sprache,* published in Vienna in 1908. Indeed, we have often deliberately made no mention of common variants used in the colloquial language when the **Fjalori Drejtshkrimor** has chosen another variant, as we would have felt required to do in a descriptive grammar, because we accept the standardizing goals of the new prescriptive sources.

In writing this book we have tried to keep in mind its probable audience: we assume our readers will be familiar with many basic grammatical terms and concepts but may need to be refreshed on how they are used, particularly since we occasionally use ordinary terms in a special technical way in this book. We assume that where our explanation of grammatical terms in the body of the book is insufficient, the student will find help in a dictionary. In most cases, the meaning of special terms will be clarified by the examples we give. However, in our attempt to guarantee the currency and authenticity of our examples (by taking them directly from the **Morfologjia**, written for people who already speak Albanian), we recognize that the relevance of some examples may not be immediately transparent to beginners in the language.

This book is not a complete textbook for learning Albanian -- it is not meant to be read and studied cover to cover -- but is rather a book to be consulted for clarification and amplification of matters raised during one's study of the language by other means. The student who wants to learn to use the language should also have access to a textbook and a dictionary. As basic textbooks, students who know English might try: Fehime Pipa, *Elementary Albanian: Filltar i shqipes*, Rome: Vatra, n.d. (lessons in Albanian culture and language aimed primarily at American children of Albanian heritage), Nelo Drizari, *Spoken and Written Albanian: A Practical Handbook*, New York: Frederick Ungar, 1947 (3rd printing 1975; sketchy and out-of-date), or Leonard Newmark, Ismail Haznedari, Peter Prifti, & Philip Hubbard, *Spoken Albanian*, Ithaca, N.Y.: Spoken Language Services, 1980 (with accompanying cassette recordings, can be used for self-instruction in the conversational language). To develop reading skill in Albanian, those students may use Leonard Newmark, Peter Prifti, & Philip Hubbard, *Readings in Albanian*, Washington: ERIC, 1980 (1600 pages; designed for self-instruction; includes a short recognition grammar).

Usable dictionaries exist for both English-to-Albanian and Albanian-to-English: Nelo Drizari, *Albanian-English and English-Albanian Dictionary*, Enlarged edition, New York: Frederick Ungar, 1957 (5500 headwords, 135 pages in Albanian-English section; its small size makes it popular, but undependable); Gaspar Kiçi, *Albanian-English Dictionary*, privately printed in Italy, 1976 (27,000 headwords, 447 pages); and Gaspar Kiçi and Hysni Aliko, *English-Albanian Dictionary*, privately printed in Italy, 1969 (26,000 headwords, 627 pages; designed for the Albanian user). The two Kiçi dictionaries are available only by writing to Gaspar Kiçi, at P.O. Box 1855, Washington, D.C. 20013.

The serious student of Albanian may wish to know of other dictionaries and textbooks, listed below with an indication of their particular value. The student should be warned that finding copies is not likely to be easy.

Oda Buchholz, Wilfried Fiedler, and Gerda Uhlisch, *Worterbuch Albanisch-Deutsch*, Leipzig: VEB Verlag Enzyklopadie Leipzig, 1977, (27,000 headwords, 739 pages; the most recent and best bilingual dictionary of Standard Albanian).

K. Cipo et al., *Fjalor i gjuhës shqipe*, Tirana: Institute of Sciences, 1954 (27,000 headwords, 648 pages; the predecessor of the Kostallari dictionary listed below).

M. Domi, Sh. Demiraj, A. Dhrimo, et al., **Morfologjia**, Tiranë: Akademia e Shkencave e RP të Shqipërisë, Instituti i Gjuhësisë dhe i Letërsisë, 1976, (400 pages; the most recent prescriptive and descriptive account of standard Albanian for Albanian users; the book from which the present book has been adapted, as mentioned above).

D. Nikollë Gazulli, *Fjalorth i ri*, Tirana: Shtypshkroja "Gurakuqi", 1941 (5,000 headwords, 527 pages; contains Gheg forms not found in other dictionaries).

Androkli Kostallari, et al., Tirana: Instituti i Gjuhës Shqipe, 1981 (41,000 headwords, 2273 pages; the largest, most up-to-date dictionary for establishing standard forms, collocations, and meanings).

Angelo Leotti, *Dizionario Albanese-Italiano*, Rome: Istituto per L'Europa Orientale, 1937, (26,000 headwords, 1708 pages; before 1954, the largest and most reliable dictionary of Albanian; exclusively Tosk forms; contains many contextual examples).

Stuart E. Mann, *An English-Albanian Dictionary*, Cambridge: Cambridge University Press,

1957 (21,000 headwords, 434 pages; especially rich in bird and plant names; Albanian forms in central Gheg dialect).

Stuart E. Mann, *An Historical Albanian-English Dictionary (1496-1938)*, Cambridge: Cambridge University Press, 1938-48 (27,000 headwords, 601 pages; contains many historical and dialectal variants).

L. Radovicka, Z. Karapici, A. Toma, *Gjuha shqipe*, Tirana: Shtëpia Botuese e Librit Shkollor, 1975 (graded lessons for foreigners learning Albanian in Albania; has many illustrative pictures, but not designed for self-instruction).

For an excellent summary and lengthy bibliography of scholarship on Albanian, the student should see Eric Hamp, "Albanian", *Current Trends in Linguistics*, Vol. 9, part 2, The Hague: Mouton, 1972, pp. 1626-92.

The authors wish to thank the MIT Press for permission to reprint here "A Sketch of the Country and the People" from Peter R. Prifti's *Socialist Albania Since 1944: Domestic and Foreign Developments* (1978). We owe special thanks to our helpful editors at Stanford University Press, William W. Carver and J.G. Bell, for their help in reading our manuscript so sensitively and making such reasonable suggestions for improving it. Some of the physical characteristics of the book -- for example, the rather cumbersome, inelegant numbering system used for identification of sections and hence referencing of locations -- reflect constraints of the computer hardware and software used to produce it, rather than editorial judgments made with a free hand. Other defects and inconsistencies are attributable to the authors themselves; in defense, we offer to incorporate improvements suggested by observant readers in a future edition, if one is desired.

This work was produced under contract number 300-76-0136 with the International Studies Branch, Division of International Education, of the United States Office of Education.

Contents

Contents

Contents

CHAPTER 3
NOUNS AND NOMINAL PHRASES

CHAPTER 4
ADJECTIVES AND ADJECTIVAL PHRASES

CHAPTER 5
ADVERBS AND ADVERBIALS

Contents

CHAPTER 6
GRADATION, COMPARISON AND QUALIFICATION

Contents

INDEX

Charts and Tables

Abbreviations

1st = First Person
2nd = Second Person
3rd = Third Person
Abl = Ablative
Acc = Accusative
Act = Active
AdjP = Adjectival Phrase
Adm = Admirative
AdvP = Adverbial Phrase
Cond = Conditional
ConjP = Conjunctional Phrase
Dat = Dative
Def = Definite
Fem = Feminine
Fut = Future
Gen = Genitive
Ger = Gerundive
IjP = Interjectional Phrase
Imp = Imperative
Imperf = Imperfect
Inch = Inchoative

Ind = Indicative
Indef = Indefinite
Inf = Infinitive
Jus = Jussive
Masc = Masculine
Mid = Middle
NP = Nominal Phrase
Nom = Nominative
Non-act = Non-active
Opt = Optative
Part = Participle
Pass = Passive
Pl = Plural
Pres = Present
Recip = Reciprocal
Refl = Reflexive
Sg = Singular
Sub = Subjunctive
Sub-Adm = Subjunctive-Admirative
VP = Verbal Phrase

Standard Albanian

CHAPTER 1
Introduction

1.1 A Sketch of the Country and the People

Albania has a reputation as a land of great natural beauty and romantic remoteness. These two characteristics have made it all the more attractive, mysterious, forbidding, challenging, or exasperating to outsiders, be they travelers, scholars, diplomats, or merchants. For example, in a work he published in 1913, the Croatian scholar Milan von Sufflay called Albania *regio mirabilissima*, "a most singular country" or "a most marvelous country." Others have referred to it as the "Switzerland of the Balkans" or as the "rock garden of southeastern Europe." On the other hand, the country's uncommon isolation from the world, arising generally from its rugged, mountainous terrain, has led foreigners to speak of it as "the Tibet of Europe" or as a country more mysterious than central Africa. It is an attitude that has had currency for centuries. We find it, for instance, in the writings of Edward Gibbon, the great eighteenth-century British historian. Speaking of Albania, Gibbon said that it is "a country within sight of Italy, which is less known than the interior of America."

The remoteness and isolation of the country became practically legendary and all too frequently gave rise to reports and descriptions of the land and the people--even in books and encyclopedias--that were closer to legends than to reality. Perhaps because of its romantic remoteness and other reasons, Albania has exerted a continuous fascination on artists, including poets, playwrights, composers, and more recently film makers and producers of television programs. Shakespeare set his comedy *Twelfth Night* in Illyria--a common name for Albania in former times. Lord Byron, who visited southern Albania in 1810, wrote some stirring lines about her landscape in his poem *Childe Harold*:

Morn dawns and with it stern Albania's hills...
Robed half in mist, bedewed with snowy rills.

In Mozart's comic opera *Cosi fan tutte* the principal male characters, Ferrando and Guglielmo, appear for the most part in disguise as two "Albanian noblemen" in a clever scheme to test the love of their fiancées. (The women fail the test when they succumb to the charms of the Albanians but succeed nevertheless in winning back the love of their men.) In our own time, we find that Peter Ustinov--taking a cue from Shakespeare--set one of his comedies, *Romanoff and Juliet*, in post-World War II Albania. Ustinov's Albania is a somewhat fanciful land but serves him well as a neat laboratory to grapple with and overcome the Cold War enmities between American and Soviet diplomats stationed in that country. Three films dealing with Albania and Albanians are *Five Fingers; Action of the Tiger*, and *The President's Analyst*. All three are action films involving intelligence operations, but the last two lack artistic merit and--as is so often the case where Albania is concerned--tend to give a misleading picture of the country.

What then, are the "basic facts" about Albania, as far as we have knowledge of them? The smallest country in the Balkan Peninsula, Albania is bordered on the north and northeast by Yugoslavia, on the southeast by Greece, and on the west and southwest by the Adriatic and Ionian seas. It lies less than 100 km (60 mi) from Italy at the nearest point of the Strait of Otranto. In area, the country encompasses 28,000 sq km (11,000 sq mi), yet it is bigger than Massachusetts (8,200 sq mi) or any other state in New England except for Maine. Its population in 1976 was about 2,500,000; again, not large at all, yet larger than the combined populations of the three New England states of Vermont, New Hampshire, and Rhode Island, which totaled 2,130,000. The capital of Albania, Tiranë, had a population of 190,000 in 1973; all the rest of the nation's cities had populations under 60,000.

For a small country, Albania has a remarkably diverse climate: a semi-tropical zone along the seacoast, warm enough to grow oranges and other citrus fruit, eucalyptus and palm trees; and a hinterland region that is subject to cold, Continental weather patterns, including heavy snowfalls and blizzards in the winter. Most of the country is mountainous, with some of the mountains reaching altitudes of 2,700 m (over 8,000 ft.). The mountain ranges that cover the land have served as a protective shield for the preservation of the nation's ethnic integrity for centuries.

Albania is an unusually homogeneous nation, from the viewpoint of the ethnic composition of her population. According to the 1961 census, slightly over 95 percent of the population consists of ethnic Albanians. The remainder included 40,000 Greeks (2.4 percent), 15,000 Macedonians and Montenegrins (0.9 percent), 10,000 Vlachs (0.6 percent), and about 10,000 Gypsies. In terms of their physical characteristics, most Albanians are said to belong to the Dinaric group, which is found on the western part of the Balkan Peninsula. As such, they are generally tall, have dark eyes and dark hair and straight or curved noses. These traits are found especially among northern Albanians, generally referred to as Ghegs; they are less common among southern Albanians, generally referred to as Tosks. Before the Second World War, the northern part of the country was very backward compared with the southern part, which, owing in some measure to wider contacts with the outside world, stood at a higher social and economic level. Since the war, however, Albania has made progress in eradicating the imbalance in the development of the two regions.

The Albanians are believed to be the descendants of the Illyrians, who inhabited the Balkans as far back as the second millennium B.C. Many scholars affirm that the Albanians are the oldest of the Balkan peoples and that their ancestors, the Illyrians, were in the Balkans centuries before the Slavs began to migrate into the area. The consensus of scholars at present is that the Illyrians were indigenous in the Balkans and not--as some writers have argued in the past--a people who migrated there from another part of the world. Ethnically, the Albanians are neither Slavs nor Greeks but a distinct ethnic group, although like their neighbors they are a part of the larger family of European peoples.

A curious item about Albania is her very name, that is, the etymology of the word "Albania." The country was known as Illyria in ancient times and until the eleventh century A.D. Since the name "Albania" appears in thirteenth-century Latin dictionaries, the term probably was in use even earlier. During the Middle Ages the Albanians called their country Arbër or Arbën and referred to themselves as Arbëresh or Arbënesh. To this day, there are communities of Albanians who migrated to Greece and Italy, in the wake of foreign invasions and pressures, who know themselves by those names. According to the Albanian scholar Konitza, the term "Albania" did not displace "Illyria" completely until the end of the fourteenth century. The term is believed to derive from "Albanoi," the name of an Illyrian tribe in what is now north-central Albania, which was first mentioned in the second century A.D. by Ptolemy, the Alexandrian astronomer. The term slowly spread to other Illyrian tribes until its usage became universal among all the Albanian people.

Still more curious is the fact that the Albanians today call themselves Shqiptarë rather than Albanians, and their country Shqipëri rather than Albania. The two terms came into use following Albania's occupation by the Turks in the fifteenth century, but why and in what manner this occurred is still a mystery.

The Albanian language is a part of the Indo-European family of languages. It is not a Slavic, Latin, or Germanic language, nor is it Hellenic. It forms instead a subgroup of its own, in the same manner as the Armenian and Iranian languages constitute subgroups of their own, within the larger, all-inclusive Indo-European group. Opinions vary concerning the exact origin of the Albanian language, but there is practically no dispute over the thesis that it is related to the Illyrian and Thracian languages.

Until late in the nineteenth century, the teaching and publication of the Albanian language were forbidden by the Turkish authorities and Greek ecclesiastics who collaborated with them during the Turkish occupation of the country. As a consequence, most outsiders, including some respected authors in the West, had the mistaken notion that the Albanian people lacked a literary tradition; in other words, that they had no written language. But in fact the Albanian language has a literary history that goes back to the Middle Ages. A fourteenth-century Dominican friar, Father Brocardus, noted in a pamphlet he published in 1332 that "the Albanians have a language quite other than the Latins," but "they use the Latin letters in all their books." Apart from a fragmentary document in Albanian, published in 1462 by Pal Engjëlli (Paulus Angelus), archbishop of Durazzo (Durrës), the first book in the Albanian language--as far as we know--was published in 1555. Its author was Dom Gjon Buzuku, and it bears the title **Meshari** (Missal). The book is a compendium of church rituals. A copy of it is housed in the Vatican Library in Rome. In 1635, Frang Bardhi (Franciscus Blancus) published in Rome his *Dictionarium latino-epiroticum*, the first known Latin-Albanian dictionary (the term ifIepiroticum, from Greek *Epirus* "mainland", referred to the southern part of Illyria, an area including what is now southern Albania and northwestern Greece). The evidence shows, moreover, that the "study of Albanian grammar has a tradition of 350 years" and includes works by Bardhi (1606-1643), Andre Bogdani (1600-1685), Nilo Katalanos (1637-1694), and others.

Writings in Albanian were scanty in the eighteenth century but increased considerably in the last century with the advent of the national awakening among the Albanians in Italy, Egypt, Romania, Greece, and Bulgaria. Until the twentieth century, this literature was published in a variety of foreign scripts, most of it in Latin and Greek. In 1908, however, leaders of the Albanian national and cultural revival held a congress in Monastir--now Bitola in the Yugoslav part of Macedonia--that laid the basis for the adoption of the Roman alphabet currently in use in Albania.

Like her language and people, a number of Albania's cities and towns bear witness to the antiquity of the country. For example, the nation's leading seaport, Durrës, was founded in 627 B.C. Known in antiquity as Dyrrachium (Dyrrahion) or Epidamnos, the town was the site of the decisive battle in 48 B.C. between Julius Caesar and Pompey. It is alleged, moreover, that Saint Paul preached there in the course of his missionary work in the Balkans. Two other very old towns are Shkodër (Skodra in antiquity) in northern Albania, which dates from the fourth century B.C. and was at one time the capital of Illyria; and the seaport of Vlorë in the south, whose bitumen mines have been in operation since the days of the Roman Empire, when the town was known as Aulon. Pojan, a mere village today near Vlorë, was an important center of culture and education in pre-Christian Albania. A city-state, it had then a population of some 40,000. Apollonia, as Pojan was known in its days of power and renown, was founded in 588 B.C. in honor of Apollo, god of beauty, poetry, and music. Aristotle mentions in it his *Politics* (book 4, chapter 4), saying that in Apollonia "the freemen...rule over the many who are not free"; in other words, the city had an oligarchic form of government.

In their long history the Albanians and their Illyrian ancestors were victims of numerous invasions and occupations by foreign armies. The Romans conquered Illyria in 167 B.C. and ruled it for over five and a half centuries, until A.D. 395, when the Roman Empire was partitioned into East and West, and Illyria became a part of the Byzantine Empire. The consequences of Roman rule are evident in the Albanian language, which was strongly influenced by Latin, and in the traces of the celebrated Via Egnatia that extended from Durrës to Ohrid, then to Salonika, Byzantium (Istanbul), and finally to Jerusalem. A few miles of this road reportedly are still in use in modern Albania, a testimony to the engineering genius of Rome. On the other hand, the Illyrians, too, exerted their influence on the Roman Empire. For nearly one hundred years (A.D. 247-361), emperors of Illyrian origin, among them Claudius II, Aurelian, Diocletian, and Probus, ruled the empire.

For an interval between the fall of the Roman Empire in A.D. 476 and the fall of the Byzantine Empire in 1453, Albania gained recognition for the first time in her history as a distinct political entity under her own name. This happened in the thirteenth century, when Charles I of Anjou (1227-1285), king of Naples, took an army across the Adriatic and occupied Durrës in 1272. He then formed the "Regnum Albaniae" (kingdom of Albania) and assumed for himself the title of "Rex Albaniae" (king of Albania). His kingdom lasted for nearly a century.

The most brilliant chapter in the history of Albania was written in the middle of the fifteenth century, when Gjergj Kastrioti Skënderbeu (George Castrioti Scanderbeg, 1405-1468), Albania's national hero, waged a successful 25-year-long struggle against the Ottoman Turks. Rebelling against the Turkish occupation of Albania, Skënderbeu seized power in 1443 and with the combined support of the nobility and the peasants, plus foreign aid, kept Albania largely free of Turkish control until his death in 1468. The foreign aid came from "the Papacy, the Kingdom of Naples, the Venetian Republic and the City of Ragusa--in short, the entire Catholic world whose cause he championed." During this period, he repulsed two major expeditions that were led in person by two great sultans: the first, by Murad II in 1449-1450; and the second by Mehmed II--the Conqueror of Constantinople (1453)--in 1466-1467. The heroic resistance of the Albanians attracted widespread attention in Europe and led Pope Nicholas V (1447-1453) to call Skënderbeu "Champion of Christendom." The admiration of the Vatican for Albania's brilliant soldier-statesman is reflected also in the remark by Pope Calixtus III (1453-1458) that "...he stopped the fury of the Turkish tide and prevented it from overrunning Christian Europe."

The high estimation of Skënderbeu by Catholic Rome was not without foundation. For after crushing organized Albanian resistance in 1479, "about 10 thousand Turkish soldiers started from Vlorë and landed in Italy, where they captured the citadel of Otranto" in the kingdom of Naples. The Turks were driven out of Otranto in 1481.

During the nearly five centuries of life under the Turks, the Albanian people continued to take up arms from time to time against the occupiers. At the same time, many Albanians took advantage of opportunities available to them to rise to positions of great power and influence in the administration of the Ottoman Empire. At least twenty-seven grand viziers or "prime ministers" of the empire were of Albanian origin--a remarkably large number in proportion to the size of the Albanian population when measured against the total population of the empire.

The modern Albanian state dates from 1912, when the venerable aristocrat Ismail Qemal Bey proclaimed Albania independent from the Turks in the city of Vlorë on November 28 of that year. A stirring cry went up from the delegates who had assembled there from all parts of the country as Qemal raised Albania's flag, the same flag under which Skënderbeu had fought the Turks nearly five centuries earlier. Following recognition of the new state by the Great Powers of Europe in 1913, Wilhelm Wied, a German prince and Prussian army captain, was installed as Albania's ruler, a move intended to orient Albania toward western Europe and western civilization, in an attempt to overcome Albania's image abroad as an oriental country. The prince arrived in Albania in March 1914 but left six months later in the wake of the turmoil created in the Balkans and Europe by the outbreak of the First World War. The new nation experienced the trauma of the invading armies of Serbia, Greece, Italy, and Austria during the war and threats of dismemberment after the war.

In June 1924, roughly ten years after Prince Wied quit his throne, Bishop Fan S. Noli, an American-educated clergyman from Boston and founder of the Albanian Orthodox Church in America, was proclaimed prime minister of Albania. But like Wied's, Noli's reign came to an end six months later (December 1924) when Ahmed Zog, a tribal leader from the Mat region in north-central Albania, drove the bishop out of the country. In 1928 Zog proclaimed himself king of Albania and ruled the country until 1939. On April 7, 1939, Benito Mussolini, to whom he had become increasingly indebted economicaly and militarily, ordered Italian troops into Albania and forced King Zog into exile. He died in Paris in 1961, leaving behind Queen Geraldine and their only heir, Leka, who is currently the pretender to the Albanian throne.

We will conclude this sketch of Albania and her people with a note on the religion and character of Albanians. Christianity appeared on Albanian soil about the second century, when mention is made of the existence of underground Christian groups in Dyrrahion (Durrës) and Aulon (Vlorë). It was therefore "during the Roman rule that Christianity was introduced into Albania." For a while, the new religion had to compete with the cult of Mithra, the Persian god of light, which had spread into Albania. By the fourth century, however, Christianity emerged victorious and became the official religion of the land. The event reflected the triumph of the Christian faith over all the Roman Empire, in consequence of Emperor Constantine's proclamation of Christianity in 313 as the official religion of the empire.

Although Albania became a part of the Eastern (Byzantine) Roman Empire in 395, it belonged to the Roman see until 734 when Leo I, emperor of Byzantium, detached it from Rome and gave it to the patriarchate of Constantinople. In the course of the centuries that followed, Constantinople's hold on Albania weakened progressively, with the result that by the fifteenth century "Albania was preponderantly Roman Catholic." In other words, when Skënderbeu rebelled against the Turks, Albania was a Catholic country. During the Ottoman occupation of their country, Albanians turned increasingly to the Islamic faith. By the twentieth century, the majority of the Albanian population had become Moslem, a condition that is unique among the nations of Europe. According to the 1945 census in Albania, 72.8 percent of the country's population was Moslem, 17.1 percent Orthodox Christian, and 10.1 percent Catholic.

The character of the Albanian people is the product, of course, of many forces: historical, political, geographic, social, and economic. The mountain fastness of their land tended to isolate them from social and commercial intercourse with the outside world. This, plus the fact that they lived largely free of control by a central government through most of their history, helped to breed in them a strong spirit of independence and individualism. According to Konitza, individualism is "the most conspicuous characteristic of the Albanians, and one without the knowledge of which their history remains a mystery." The fact, too, that Albania has experienced waves of conquests and domination by foreign powers through many centuries has made Albanians highly suspicious of neighboring states and sensitive to the slightest threats to their independence and ethnic identity.

Yet, on a person-to-person level, Albanians are known for their hospitality to strangers, as well as to one another. Edith Durham, an English author, illustrates this character trait of the Albanians with a story from personal experience. While traveling in northern Albania in the early part of our century, she visited the mud hut of a poor mountaineer. She was greeted with courtly grace by her ragged host, who said to her: "We are poor. Bread, salt, and our hearts is all we can offer, but you are welcome to stay as long as you wish."

A century earlier, another English author, the poet Lord Byron, wrote from southern Albania to friends back home that he found Albanians to be "brave, unquestionably honest and loyal," and that the Albanian women were "very beautiful." Indeed, Albanians have a reputation for their sense of loyalty, as well as of pride and honor. It was not by chance that Albanians were chosen to serve as the bodyguards of the sultans of Turkey. This refined sense of honor of the Albanian people, which they call **besa**, is rooted in the customs and traditions of their society. It is based on the Code of Lek Dukagjin, a fifteenth-century Albanian feudal lord and contemporary of Skënderbeu, who formulated the body of unwritten, customary laws that governed the lives of Albanian highlanders until recent times.

To be sure, Albanians are afflicted with vices as well, as their detractors have been quick to point out. The late Soviet leader Khrushchev, for example, complained of the stubbornness of the Albanians, using as evidence his dealings with Albania's communist leaders. Others have accused them of being a mercenary people, quick-tempered, violent, ruthless, boorish, and unforgiving toward those who offend or injure them.

Whatever the accuracy or validity of this tableau of Albanian character traits, the significant fact is that, despite their small numbers, they have managed to preserve their language, culture, and ethnic identity; in short, to survive as a distinct ethnic group in the face of overwhelming odds. If survival is a virtue, that is no small achievement. In any case, it is probably just this particular mixture of attractive and unattractive qualities, of virtues and vices, in the makeup of their character that makes the Albanians a people of more than usual interest and fascination to the outside world.

1.2 The Albanian Language

Albanian is the language spoken by approximately five million people, the majority of whom identify themselves as **shqiptarë** who speak a language they call **shqip**, a word which is also an adverb meaning '(to speak) clearly'; the Albanian speakers of Italy and Sicily refer to themselves as **arbëreshë**, and they call their language by the same name. There are some two and a half million Albanian speakers in the present country of Albania proper and almost two million more in adjacent areas of Yugoslavia: a million and a half forming the majority population of the Socialist Autonomous Province of Kosovo, which forms part of the Socialist Republic of Serbia, and half a million more in Macedonia and Montenegro. There are estimated to be an additional third of a million identifiable Albanian speakers in southern Italy (80,000) and in southern Greek villages (50,000), as well as small enclaves in Bulgaria (1000), the Ukraine (perhaps 5000), Romania, and Turkey; in the United States there are some tens of thousands of Albanian speakers, mostly centered in and around the cities of Boston, New York, Philadelphia, Detroit, and Chicago.

Like Greek and Armenian, Albanian forms an independent branch of the Indo-European language family, coordinate with the Germanic, Italic, Balto-Slavic (with which it has some special genetic affinities), Celtic, and Indo-Iranian sub-families. Scholars have argued at various times for its Thracian, Phrygian or Illyrian ancestry, but only the last of these is still advanced by serious scholars. Because the language shares so many structural and lexical features with other Balkan languages, and because its lexicon has so many elements borrowed from Turkish (during the 454-year domination of the area by the Turks), Latin, and Romance languages, its identity as an independent branch of Indo-European is not immediately apparent to an observer, and its identification as Indo-European was not established until relatively late (1854) in the nineteenth century search for European language affinities. For more information about the genetic and areal relationships of Albanian, and for an extensive bibliography pertaining to the language, see the article by Eric Hamp, "Albanian," in Volume 9, *Linguistics in Western Europe,* of the series *Current Trends in Linguistics* under the editorship of Thomas A. Sebeok, published by Mouton in the Hague, 1972.

1.2.1 Dialects and Standard Literary Albanian

Albanian is spoken in a large number of varieties, conventionally and roughly divided into two chief dialect groups: a group north of the river Shkumbini called Gheg and a group south of the Shkumbini called Tosk. In general the two groups can be distinguished by pervasive differences in phonology (e.g., Gheg speakers employ phonological distinctions of vowel length and nasality while Tosk speakers do not; Ghegs preserve **n** in many words in which Tosks have introduced **r**; Ghegs have monophthongs in many cases where Tosks have diphthongs), morphology (e.g., Ghegs use imperfect tense forms ending in **-sha** and **-she** where Tosks have **-nja** and **-nje**), syntax (e.g., Ghegs form infinitives with the preposition **me** while Tosks use the preposition **për**), and lexicon (Gheg dialects have relatively more Turkish and Slavic and fewer modern Greek borrowed words than Tosk dialects do). The dialects of Albanian spoken in Italy, Sicily, and Greece reflect the Tosk origin of their speakers centuries ago, whereas the dialect of Borgo Erizzo on the Dalmatian coast of Yugoslavia reflects the Gheg origin of that Albanian enclave. In other parts of the world where Albanian is still spoken it is still possible to discern whether the speakers are of Gheg or Tosk origin.

Since the second World War, numerous attempts have been made in Albania--and supported by Albanian speakers in other countries--to agree on a single variety of the language to serve as a standard language for the country, and those attempts have had a considerable amount of success, judging from the attempts made by speakers in and out of Albania proper to follow the norms prescribed for this standard. Of course, no language ever achieves perfect standardization, and speakers and writers of Standard Albanian (called by the Albanians themselves "Literary Albanian") display considerable variety in their interpretation of what the standard is. The movement towards greater standardization, however, continues on a massive scale. In the early 1970's the publication in Tiranë, the capital of Albania, followed by republication in Prishtinë, the capital of Kosovo (in Yugoslavia), of a book of orthographical rules, **Drejtshkrimi i gjuhës shqipe,** followed by a widely distributed, authoritative orthographic dictionary in 1976, **Fjalori drejtshkrimor i gjuhës shqipe,** created (and reflected) a considerable degree of phonological normalization as well as spelling reform. The possibility of attaining a standard language with a degree of dialectal uniformity at least as great as for the other European languages now seems well within sight.

1.2.2 Phonology and Orthography

As for all other languages with a written literary tradition, the relationship between the way Albanian is written and the way it is spoken is quite complex. It is quite old-fashioned in language teaching to present the sounds of a language as if they were oral representatives of the "true" language, which is itself something written down and hence visual. Linguists have stressed for almost a century now that language is something spoken, that what is written down is only a partial representation of the "true" spoken language. Thus it smacks of archaic and ignorant confusion to say that a letter or group of letters "has" a particular sound in a language, rather than saying that a given sound or phoneme (a sound unit distinct from other sound units in the language) has a particular traditional visual representation among certain users of the language over a particular expanse of time and space.

Nevertheless, because of special conditions applying to the Albanian language at this moment in its history and to the needs of the student of the language now, it will be convenient in this book to suspend our sophistication about language a bit and to pretend that Standard ("Literary") Albanian is primarily a written language and only secondarily a spoken one. The special conditions calling for this special treatment are these:

Albanian has been spoken for many hundreds of years over an area and under political conditions that precluded easy and frequent communication among large numbers of its speakers. As a result, as local differences arose in one area in pronunciation, grammar, and vocabulary use, those differences were not shared by speakers in other areas. Normalization of these differences and development of a naturally dominant single variety of the language that might have taken place in a dominant cultural center was not possible because no such center could form, given the unfavorable political conditions in Albanian-speaking areas through the centuries. The present system for writing Albanian, an orthography using a homogeneous, phonetically based, Latin alphabet, dates only from 1908 when a group of influential Albanians meeting in the so-called Congress of Manastir (now Bitola in the Yugoslav part of Macedonia) adopted it as one of two acceptable ways of writing the language (the other was a Turkish-based alphabet). In 1916-1917 the Literary Commission of Shkodër (Komisia Letrare e Shkodrës) codified the main conclusions of language scholars formulated during the period of national awakening. The Commission reiterated the cardinal principle of the Congress of Manastir, that the orthography of the language be as phonetic as possible, and thus in effect sanctioned different orthographies for the two sets of dialects spoken by the Ghegs and Tosks--roughly speaking, Albanians living north and south of the Shkumbini River, respectively. On the other hand, the Literary Commission proposed that a national literary language be adopted preserving as much as possible of what was common to the various literary variants of Albanian, while discarding as much as possible features that stigmatized the more aberrant variants. Their proposal was that the dialect of Elbasan be adopted, with some refinements, as the basis of the new standard language. That proposal, approved by the Kongresi Arsimor i Lushnjës (Educational Congress of Lushnjë) in 1920, became the basis of Albanian orthography until the early years of postwar Albania. The Commission did not, however, succeed in creating the uniform orthography, inasmuch as the mechanisms available were insufficient to put the decisions into effect. While the southern Gheg of Elbasan was officially taught as the standard in the only teacher's training school in Elbasan, the school did not have sufficient influence to induce Albanians in general to give up their own varieties of the language in their public use of Albanian; as a result, before the 1950's the prevailing practice was for each writer to spell

Albanian words as he pronounced them, partially modified by his memory of spellings by writers he respected and by what he may have been taught in school.

When the present government of Albania came into power in the 1940's, no one natural variety of the language could be found to be the obvious choice as the standard which every educated user of the language should strive to master. There had been no clear domination of the literary, commercial, or political life of Albanians by speakers of any distinct variety or varieties which would form a natural base for standardization. It was realized early in the regime that no single variety of Albanian then spoken naturally by some group of Albanians could simply be adopted as *the* standard variety without antagonizing speakers of other varieties. As time passed, Tosk (southern Albanian) varieties predominated in official and semi-official publications; by the time formal decisions were made governing official standardization, the *de facto* general public usage had already established that the new standard language would contain individual elements from several dialectal varieties, with some features shared among both Tosk and Gheg (northern Albanian) dialects, many features common to most Tosk varieties, and a few features (mostly individual words and morphemes [=word constituents]) from Gheg. In 1952 the Albanian Writers' Union resolved henceforth to use Tosk in publications rather than to maintain two standard literary dialects as before. While this had an important effect on publications in Albania itself, it was not accepted by the almost equal number of Albanians outside the country; furthermore, the decision was sometimes honored merely by using Tosk spellings to write blatantly Gheg sentences. In 1956 an orthography (**Ortografia e gjuhës shqipe**), treated in some detail the problems of unification or standardization of the literary variants in existence at the time.

Since the late 1960's efforts have increased to establish formally and in detail what the standard language should be. The most effective step toward standardization was taken in 1967, with the publication of a set of orthographic rules: **Rregullat e drejtshkrimit të shqipes.** The completion of this project served as the foundation for drafting in the definitive form the orthography of a uniform national standard language. In 1968 the Linguistic Conference of Prishtinë (Konsulta gjuhësore e Prishtinës) in Kosovo, Yugoslavia, officially adopted the "literary language" in use in Albania at the expense of their own regional standard Gheg.

From November 20 to 25, 1972, the Congress of Albanian Orthography (Kongresi i Drejtshkrimit të Gjuhës Shqipe) convened in Tiranë under the auspices of the Institute of Linguistics and Literature and the State University of Tiranë. The Congress formulated the principles and rules of standard Albanian orthography as developed up to that time. The conclusions and guidelines of the Congress were subsequently published and widely distributed in a volume under the title **Drejtshkrimi i gjuhës shqipe** (The Orthography of the Albanian Language). The year 1976 marks the publication of **Fjalori drejtshkrimor i gjuhës shqipe** (Dictionary of Albanian Orthography), under the auspices of the Albanian Academy of Sciences and the Institute of Language and Literature. The dictionary contains some 32,000 entries, not only establishing standard forms for those entries, but deciding their grammatical inflections and, to a certain extent, their syntactic uses as well.

The effects of all the moves towards standardization are now evident throughout the Albanian-speaking world. However, as with standard languages established for a far longer time than Albanian, it is still often the case (almost always in speech) that an Albanian's local provenience is evident when he writes or speaks at some length. The language editorship (even to the extent of censorship) of public language in all the media in both Albania and the adjacent Albanian-speaking areas seems to be more effective than many students of human culture imagined was possible in such a previously linguistically tolerant society. People who use Albanian self-consciously--teachers, radio announcers, actors, editors, etc.--use the standard variety now in official activities to the utmost of their abilities. Local and regional varieties survive, of course, in intimate conversation and unpublished writing, but that is not so different from the situation in other, well-established standard languages in the world.

For Albanian the pattern of creating a standard language is being shortened in comparison with the pattern that has obtained in other European languages, in which a dominant spoken variety determined a written variety which in turn influenced new spoken standards. In Albanian we are seeing the promulgation of a somewhat artificial (in the sense that it represents the speech of no particular group of speakers) written standard in the process of influencing speakers of the language both in their written and oral uses of the language. For that reason we cannot say, for instance, that the sound [θ] (represented by *th* in the English word *ether*) is represented by **dh** in the Albanian word **madh**, because there is no general agreement among Albanian speakers about the pronunciation of that word. For the practical purposes of this reference book, we shall therefore use the old-fashioned device of saying that **dh** at the end of syllables "is pronounced" by southern Albanians as [θ] or by northern Albanians as [ð] (the sound of *th* in the English word *either*). Such a description will be an oversimplification of the actual complex facts of the matter, but will allow the student to assign some phonetic value to the written symbols. As in other old-fashioned accounts, the student is advised here that the best way of learning to pronounce the language is to listen to the way educated speakers of the language pronounce it. While that advice may lead to confusion in many details--since at present, "educated" speakers of Albanian will display sharp differences in their pronunciations-- as time passes and broad expansion of communication among people from different areas increases (it has already increased enormously through radio, television, and the simple move- ment of large numbers of people created by industrialization and urbanization), we can expect that eventually standard spoken Albanian will be as clearly defined as standard written Albanian is now. That is not to say that differences in speaking and writing the language will eventually disappear in Albanian--we have no evidence in *any* language that such ever happens with real languages--but only that it will be easier to distinguish standard pronunciations from non- standard. To a small extent that can be done already in Albanian (e.g., speakers who use strongly nasalized vowels can be identified by other speakers as using non-standard pronuncia- tions), but without a solid empirical basis for determining how Albanian speakers actually judge phonetic realizations different from their own.

The Albanian alphabet uses Latin letters singly and in combination to represent the 36 Albanian phonemes, i.e., the 36 distinctive sound units that compose all the words of the language. The alphabetic order of the letters of the 36 alphabetic units is as follows: A B C Ç D Dh E Ë F G Gj H I J K L Ll M N Nj O P Q R Rr S Sh T Th U V X Xh Y Z Zh Each letter may appear in upper or lower case (capital or small letter) form; digraphs (**Dh, Gj, Ll, Nj, Rr Sh, Th, Xh, Zh**) may be capitalized by making both components capitals or only the first ones.

The sound units represented by the letters can be roughly characterized as follows. In pronouncing the name of the letter, as in spelling a word out loud, vowel letters are pro- nounced with the value of the vowel they denote, while consonant letters are pronounced as a syllable beginning with the consonant phoneme followed by the sound represented by the letter ë. Table 1.1 provides a rough characterization of the phonetic values of the Albanian letters, in terms of some of their correspondences with English spellings and with IPA (International Phonetic Alphabet) symbols.

Table 1.1 Some Albanian-English Spelling Correspondences			
Albanian letter	Approximate English spelling	English examples	IPA symbol and brief phonetic description
A a	a	m<u>a</u>ma	[a] low, central, unrounded vowel
B b	b	<u>b</u>a<u>b</u>y	[b] voiced bilabial stop
C c	ts	ra<u>ts</u>	[ts] voiceless apicoalveolar groove affricate
Ç ç	ch	<u>ch</u>ur<u>ch</u>	[tʃ] voiceless laminopalatal groove affricate
D d	d	<u>d</u>i<u>d</u>	[d] voiceless apicodental stop
Dh dh	th	ei<u>th</u>er, <u>th</u>y	[ð] voiced apicodental slit fricative

Albanian letter	Approximate English spelling	English examples	IPA symbol and brief phonetic description
E e	e	p<u>e</u>t	[ɛ] mid front unrounded vowel
Ë ë	u, a	m<u>u</u>st, sof<u>a</u>	[ɜ] or [ə] mid central vowel
F f	f	<u>fif</u>e	[f] voiceless labiodental slit fricative
G g	g	<u>g</u>a<u>g</u>	[g] voiced dorsovelar stop
Gj gj	gue y	lea<u>gue</u> <u>y</u>ear	
	g	fi<u>g</u>ure	[ɟ] voiced dorsopalatal stop
H h	h	<u>h</u>istory	[h] voiceless laryngeal glide
I i	e	r<u>e</u>act	[i] high front unrounded vowel
J j	y	<u>y</u>ell	[j] voiced high front glide
K k	k	<u>k</u>i<u>ck</u>	[k] voiceless dorsovelar stop
L l	l	be<u>l</u>ief	[l] voiced lowered-dorsal lateral liquid
Ll ll	ll	hi<u>ll</u>	[ɫ] voiced raised-dorsal lateral liquid
M m	m	<u>m</u>ap	[m] voiced bilabial nasal
N n	n	<u>n</u>ap	[n] voiced apicodental nasal
Nj nj	ny	can<u>y</u>on	[ɲ] voiced laminopalatal nasal
O o	o	m<u>o</u>re	[o] mid back rounded vowel
P p	p	<u>p</u>i<u>p</u>e	[p] voiceless bilabial stop
Q q	cu	<u>cu</u>te	[c] voiceless dorsopalatal stop
	ky	bi<u>ki</u>ni	
R r	t	ci<u>t</u>y	[ɾ] voiced apical flap liquid
Rr rr	rr	va<u>r r</u>oom!	[r] voiced apical trill liquid
S s	s, ss	<u>si</u>s<u>s</u>y	[s] voiceless apicoalveolar groove fricative
Sh sh	sh	<u>sh</u>u<u>sh</u>	[ʃ] voiceless laminopalatal groove fricative
T t	t	<u>t</u>oo<u>t</u>	[t] voiceless apicodental stop
Th th	th	e<u>th</u>er, <u>th</u>igh	[θ] voiceless apicodental slit fricative
U u	oo	p<u>oo</u>r	[u] high back rounded vowel
V v	v	re<u>v</u>i<u>v</u>e	[v] voiced labiodental slit fricative
X x	dz	a<u>dz</u>e	[dz] voiced laminopalatal groove affricate
	ds	hea<u>ds</u>	
Xh xh	j, dge	<u>j</u>u<u>dge</u>	[dʒ] voiced laminopalatal groove affricate
Y y	u	f<u>u</u>ture	[y] high front rounded vowel
Z z	z	ma<u>z</u>e	[z] voiced apicoalveolar groove fricative
	s	ri<u>s</u>en	
Zh zh	z	a<u>z</u>ure	[ʒ] voiced laminopalatal groove affricate
	s	vi<u>s</u>ion	

Table 1.1 (cont.)

A. Vowels

Present-day Standard Albanian has six simple vowels, arranged in Chart 1.1 according to the position of the highest point of the tongue during articulation. Each of the simple vowels is pronounced as a monophthong--unlike English--with the same phonetic value from beginning

Chart 1.1 The Albanian Simple Vowels				
	Front		Central	Back
	Unrounded	Rounded	Unrounded	Rounded
High	i	y		u
Mid	e		ë	o
Low			a	

to end. Each vowel is of somewhat longer duration:

1) when stressed (marked in this book, for clarity of discussion only, by an accent mark ´ over the vowel letter: **á, é, ë́, ó, ú, ý**;

2) when stressed and followed in the same word by another vowel preceded by a single consonant: the **u** is thus somewhat longer in **drúri** than in **dru, plúmbi, thúa, byréku, pus;**

3) when it bears the phrase accent (marked in this book, for clarity of discussion only, by a double accent mark ") which marks the focus of attention in a spoken phrase: the **i, ó** and **ú** are thus longer than any of the other vowels, in the phrases **I tháshë se kisha mysafirë atë mbrémje.** 'I told him that I had guests that evening.' **Po të dóni, jua jàp únë.** 'If you like, I'll give it to you.'

The Albanian vowel **i** is higher and more tense than the corresponding English vowel in *pit*, but lower than the vowel in *peat*.

The vowel **e** is higher and more tense than the corresponding English vowel in *pet*, but lower than the vowel of *pate*.

The vowel **u** is higher and more tense than the corresponding English vowel in *put*, but lower than the vowel in *boot*.

The vowel **o** is higher and more tense than the corresponding English vowel in *bought*, but lower than the vowel in *boat*.

The vowel **a** is more fronted and more tense than the corresponding English vowel in *pot* (unrounded variety), but far less fronted than the vowel in *pat*.

The vowel **y** is lower and less tense than the corresponding French vowel in *du*, but higher than the vowel of *deux*. For English speakers who have no experience in producing rounded front vowels, the sound may be made by starting to say *future*, but prolonging the vowel sound that is heard just before the first *u* is actually made.

The letter **ë** represents a wide range of sounds. First, for many speakers in ordinary speech it will not be pronounced at all when it comes after a single consonant at the end of a word and is not stressed. For other speakers, in the same position it will be a signal that the vowel in the preceding syllable is pronounced long--something like the "silent" e of English *ride*. In the same position, it will be pronounced by some speakers (particularly older ones from southern Tosk areas) like the *i* in English *capital*. In other unstressed positions, speakers often pronounce it (like the *i* in *capital)*, but the further north the speaker, the more likely the letter will be silent. Even in positions where the **ë** is normally not pronounced, a speaker may pronounce it when trying to speak particularly distinctly, for example, in reciting poetry or when speaking to a foreigner.

The pronunciation of stressed **ë** often reflects the area of provenience of the speaker. It ranges from a nasalized, rounded, mid back vowel (like the vowel in French *bon*) in Gheg regions to an oral unrounded, low front vowel (like the vowel in English *pat*) in some southeast Tosk regions. The pronunciation that is least distinct in identifying dialectal provenience--and therefore the one most eligible to be called "standard"--is an oral unrounded (or very slightly rounded) mid central vowel, so that a southern British or southeastern United States pronunciation of the English word *burn* sounds very much like a standard pronunciation of the Albanian word **bën**.

In reading pre-standard Albanian texts, the variation in the way words are spelled is greater in respect to ë than for any other single letter.

NOTE

Gheg speakers of Albanian continue to make a distinction between long and short simple vowels in stressed syllables, although the standard orthography has not adopted the distinction directly. In most cases, however, where the standard orthography spells a word with a final -ë, a Gheg speaker will not pronounce that ë, but will make the preceding stressed vowel long: thus **plak** 'old man' is pronounced with a short vowel by both Gheg and Tosk speakers, while **plakë** 'old woman' will be pronounced without the final ë by all Gheg and most Tosk speakers, but most Gheg and some Tosk speakers will say the word with a distinctively longer **a** vowel than that in **plak**.

When they are speaking their own dialects Gheg speakers also use a whole set of simple nasalized vowels, both long and short, but these have not been adopted in the standard orthography and are avoided when speaking Standard ("Literary") Albanian.

In addition to simple vowels Albanian has many words with vowel clusters: sequences of two vowels not separated by consonants. To understand the problem of pronunciation of such sequences, it is necessary first to keep in mind the distinction between high vowels (**i, u, y**) and non-high vowels (all the others) and second to be aware that the letter **i** and the letter **j** represent the same sound, except that **i**, a vowel, is somewhat longer and more prominent than **j**, a consonant. Now in vowel clusters containing no high vowels, the number of syllables in the cluster is the same as the number of vowels, and the degree of prominence of each vowel is determined by its stress: **teori** has three syllables, of which the first two, both unstressed, are equal in prominence and the third, being stressed, is more prominent; **poét** has two syllables, with the second, stressed syllable more prominent than the first.

The clusters **ie, ua, ye,** and **ue** are diphthongs in Albanian; each cluster counts as a single vowel (in determining stress placement, for example) and bears a single peak of prominence. While speakers from different dialect areas vary and individual speakers may vacillate in locating a peak of prominence within the diphthong, the following general tendencies can be observed among speakers of Standard Albanian:

1) When the diphthong is the last syllable of a word, its first element is likely to be more prominent than its second: **shpíe, përzíen, grúa, dúar, arsýe, përkthýes.**

2) When the diphthong is not the last syllable of the word, speakers are likely to give the first element less or equal prominence in respect to the second; the diphthong **ue**, however, always gives its first element more prominence than its second: **diellór, ziéja, kryenéç, rryéshëm, buallícë, druánim, pastrúese, i vashdúeshëm.**

It should be noted that in certain words and classes of words the standard orthography now represents what were formerly sometimes written as diphthongs with **i** as one element, as sequences of **j** plus vowel or of vowel plus **j**, deciding the question of location of the center of prominence by making the vowel **i** into the consonant **j**: **bjer, përzjéva.** In other words and classes of words, in order to preserve certain morphological identities, the standard orthography represents the glide **j** as if it were the vowel **i**: **ia dha, dhënie, kuptoi.** However, the **i** in the standard orthography of the word **ai** 'he, that' indicates that the word is pronounced with two syllables, with the normal stress on the final vowel.

B. Consonants

In Chart 1.2 the consonants of Albanian are arranged according to the distinctive manner in which they are produced by the vocal apparatus ("manner of articulation") and the moveable part of the articulatory mechanism that is most characteristically involved in producing them.

Chart 1.2 The Albanian Consonants

	Labial	Apical	Laminal	Dorsal	
STOPS Voiceless	p	t	q	k	
Voiced	b	d	gj	g	**LIQUIDS**
					Lateral l ll
FRICATIVES Slit					Central r rr
Voiceless	f	th			
Voiced	v	dh			
Groove Voiceless		s	sh		
Voiced		z	zh		**GLIDES**
					Voiced j
					Voiceless h
AFFRICATES Voiceless		c	ç		
Voiced		x	xh		
NASALS	m	n	nj		

STOPS are sounds made by interfering with the airstream passing through the mouth by closing the oral passage. LABIAL stops close the passage by moving the lower lip in a position to block the air passage at the lips, as in the English sounds *p* and *b*. APICAL stops use the tongue tip (apex) and sides to close off the passage beginning just in back of the teeth; the corresponding stops **t** and **d** in English are typically pronounced with the tongue tip closing the passage further back, on the alveolar ridge (the bumpy ridge felt as one moves one's tongue along the roof of the mouth from front to back). LAMINAL stops use the middle section of the tongue and sides to close off the passage beginning at the hard palate (the smooth, hard part of the roof of the mouth); a similar tongue position is used in English just at the beginning of words like *cue* or *cute*, except that in Albanian the tongue tip is not lowered in the mouth as it is in the English words. DORSAL stops use the rear section of the tongue against the soft palate (velum) to close off the passage beginning there. VOICED stops are produced while the air is being forced through loose flaps (the vocal cords) in the larynx to produce regular vibrations in the air stream, while VOICELESS ones are produced with those flaps open so that the air stream is not affected in the larynx. In Albanian, voicing for a stressed vowel after a voiceless stop begins more quickly than in English, so that the characteristic "aspiration" of English voiceless stops is absent in Albanian. On the other hand, many Albanian speakers, especially those from Tosk areas, end the voicing of voiced stops (also fricatives and affricates) at the end of words much earlier than English speakers do, so that word-final voiced stops, fricatives, and affricates may sound partially or totally voiceless to an English listener.

Albanian FRICATIVES are quite similar to their English counterparts: as in English, they are made by moving the appropriate articulators into a position that leaves only enough space for the air to move with noisy friction through the oral passage. If the passage is relatively longer than it is wide, a GROOVE fricative is produced; if wider than it is long, a SLIT fricative. The labial fricatives are produced by creating air friction between the lower lip and upper teeth, apical fricatives by air friction between the apex of the tongue and the back of the upper teeth, and laminal fricatives by air friction between the middle of the tongue and the hard palate.

AFFRICATES are formed by closing the air passage as for a stop and releasing it through a narrow space as for a fricative. In Albanian the apical affricates **c** and **x** (like English *ts* and *dz*, respectively) are not very frequent, but unlike their English counterparts, they may appear at the beginning of syllables as well as at the end.

NASAL consonants are produced by closing the oral passage as for a stop but opening the nasal passage (by lowering the velum) to allow the voiced air stream to resonate in the nasal passage as well as in the part of the mouth behind the closure. The single laminal nasal **nj** is distinguished in spelling from the sequence of apical nasal **n** plus **j** by writing the sequence as **n** plus **i**: compare **shkronjë** 'of writing' with **dhënie** 'giving.'

In LIQUID consonants the voiced air stream is partially blocked in the oral passage but not in such a way as to create the noise of a fricative. In the LATERALS **l** and **ll**, an apical closure is made (as for **d**) but with one or both sides of the tongue lowered to allow the air stream to flow freely around and out of the mouth. For **l**, the laminal (middle) section of the tongue is more or less raised toward the palate (depending on the dialectal provenience of the speaker) but the dorsal (rear) section of the tongue is lowered; for **ll** the dorsal section is raised. The effect of the difference is to reduce the size of the resonating cavity behind the tongue for **l** and to increase it for **ll**, yielding the typically "light" or "palatal" sound of the first and the "dark" or "velar" sound of the second. English speakers, particularly those with British accents, use something like the Albanian **l** at the beginning of syllables, particularly before a high front vowel or glide, and something like the Albanian **ll** at the end of syllables. In the CENTRAL liquids **r** and **rr**, the voiced air stream is blocked momentarily by holding the apex of the tongue loosely near the alveolar ridge and allowing the voiced air stream to set it in motion, alternately sucking it toward the ridge and blowing it away from it. For **r**, a single or double flapping sound is thus heard, while for **rr** three or more flaps (trills) will be heard. While some British speakers use a *r* pronunciation much like the Albanian one, American speakers make their *r* in a very different way; for them an approximation of Albanian **r** may be heard in casual pronunciations of *t* or *d* between two vowels, the second of which is unstressed: *pity, biddy, Betty,* etc. The trilled **rr** is sometimes approximated by children imitating the sound of a motor: *varroom!* or *prrr.* Unlike English, the Albanian central liquids are not made with rounded lips at the beginning of words.

The Albanian glides **j** (like the English consonant *y*) and *h*, are produced like their English counterparts. For **j** the tongue moves quickly to or away from a high front unrounded vowel position in respect to the neighboring vowel, depending on whether that vowel precedes or follows it, respectively. It is the consonantal (short duration) counterpart of the vowel **i**, and in appropriate rythmic environments (before or after a vowel) actually has been used interchangeably with that vowel. Variant spellings of many words reveal that the interchange has had a long history in Albanian, although the standard orthography now has consistent provisions for distinguishing the two. For **h** the neighboring vowel is simply continued or begun, but without the voicing in the larynx that all vowels otherwise have. As in English, there is variation in the degree to which the written letter **h** is pronounced. Some speakers pronounce it only before stressed vowels, while others pronounce it or feel they pronounce it as the standard orthography indicates it should be pronounced.

C. Intonation and Punctuation

In general, the basic intonation of Albanian phrases is similar to that of American English phrases. In both languages, the most neutral intonation for a sentence-final phrase is one in which the pitch of the voice is highest on the stressed syllable of the last word in the phrase or the word that the speaker presents as the most important, perhaps in order to contrast it with another or simply to identify it as containing new information for the listener. Immediately after this PHRASE STRESS, the pitch falls to a low level: if the phrase-stressed syllable is final in the sentence, the pitch fall will occur in that syllable, and that syllable will be lengthened so that the pitch change can be heard; if other syllables follow the phrase-stressed one, they are all uttered on a low pitch until the end of the phrase. In non-final sentence positions, the most neutral intonation of a phrase also has the phrase-stressed syllable at the highest pitch up to that point in the phrase, but if there are other syllables following the phrase they will remain at that high pitch.

In both English and Albanian, questions which ask the listener for a "*yes*" (**po** in Albanian) or "*no*" (**jo** in Albanian) response use the same intonation as for a non-final phrase, except that in English the very last syllable of such a question has a short, quick rise in the pitch.

A most striking difference between Albanian and English intonation is in phrases in which the pitch falls from a high to a mid-level on the phrase-stressed syllable and remains at that level till the end of the phrase. Such an intonation is quite neutral in Albanian and may be used both for phrases in non-final positions in sentences and in final phrases in questions asking for information other than "yes" or "no". In corresponding English sentences the intonation would not be neutral, but would signal the speaker's feeling of frustration or boredom.

Punctuation marks are used in conventional Albanian orthography largely as they are in conventional English. Stress is normally not marked at all, and intonation is only hinted at by punctuation and underlining. Periods are used to mark sentence ends, abbreviations, and sentence interruptions. Question marks are used to mark the end of queries, whether the intonation actually rises or falls. Exclamation points usually mark emotional expressions, but unlike in English, in Albanian exclamation points are conventionally also used to indicate unemotional imperative commands (**Shko drejt!** 'Go straight ahead.'). Colons precede a set of examples. Semicolons separate coordinate sentences or word-groups which contain internal commas. Commas separate items in a series, non-essential sentence elements like phrasal parentheses, modifiers, and appositives from the rest of the sentence, and sentences introduced by a conjunction from the preceding sentence. Hyphens are used to separate elements in certain compounds and to indicate word continuation at the end of a line. Quotation marks are usually in the form of double angles << >> going in different directions at the beginning and end of the quoted material, but raised commas are also used for this purpose in Albanian as they are in English; because of typographical limitations, wherever the original examples had the double angles, they will usually be replaced in this book by " ". Dashes are also commonly used to separate the speeches of participants in direct quotation. Standard punctuation practices have yet to be established in Albanian, so that a great deal of fluctuation can be observed in the use of commas (sometimes used, contrary to standard English practice, between a long subject and its predicate, before or after dashes, to separate two full sentences), semicolons (sometimes intermixed with colons), spacing before and after punctuation marks, and in the use of various competing devices for indicating direct quotation. The variety of punctuation conventions embodied in the examples of Albanian sentences throughout this book serves to illustrate this point more eloquently than any set of artificial examples.

D. Stress

In general, the main stress in an Albanian stem falls on its last syllable, the main stress of an Albanian word (for compound words with more than one stem) falls on its last stem, and the main stress of an Albanian phrase falls on its last word.

Dictionaries of Albanian differ in how they represent the location of word stress: some do it by marking the stressed syllable, some by indicating where the stem of the word ends, but most do not mark it at all. In this grammar we mark stem end (by a hyphen) and word stress (by an accent mark over a vowel) in general only as relevant to the subject at hand.

Table 1.2 illustrates the effect of various factors in determining word-stress placement.

In compound words, the last stem in the compound has the main word stress (marked here by an acute accent ´); stressed syllables in words before the final one are reduced to secondary (marked by a grave accent `) weak stress (unmarked).

Table 1.2 Examples of Stress Placement		
	STRESS	
	On last syllable	Before last syllable
COMPLEX STEM With		
inflectional suffix		**mál-i** 'the mountain' **lúle-ve** 'of flowers' **kuptó-nim** 'we understood' **punúa-këshit** 'you really worked'
non-verbal, non-inflectional suffix ending in **a, e, o, ë**, or **ë** plus consonant (except **-llḗk**, plural **-llḗqe**)	**budallallḗk** 'foolishness'	**qínd-ra** 'hundreds' **prít-je** 'reception' **plák-ë** 'old woman' **i shíj-shëm** 'tasty' **unáz-a** 'rings' **pállto** 'overcoat'
-thi, -as, -azi		**práp-thi** 'reversed' **májt-as** 'to the left' **fshéhur-azi** 'secretly'
other non-inflectional suffixes	**hekur-ós** 'I iron' **shqip-tár** 'Albanian' **fill-ím** 'beginning' **lumtur-í** 'happiness' **krahin-ór** 'provincial' **angl-ísht** 'English'	
SIMPLE STEMS		
	dembél 'lazy' **qytét** 'city' **shtëpí** 'house' **kalá** 'fortress'	
COMPOUND STEMS		
	kù-dó 'wherever' **megjìth-atḗ** 'however' **krỳe-qytét** 'capital city' **vagòn-restoránt** 'dining car' **bùkur-shkrím** 'calligraphy (fine writing)'	

In a phrase, one syllable bears the main phrase accent (which may be marked by a double accent "), phonetically marked by lengthening the syllable and beginning any pitch change called for by the intonation. The normal place for this phrase stress is on the stressed syllable of the last word in the phrase; any other position of the phrase stress indicates that the phrase-stressed word is being emphasized or contrasted.

When a stressed derivational suffix is added to form a different stem, the main word stress moves to the last syllable of the new stem: **i várf-ër** 'poor,' **vàrf-ër-í** 'poverty,' **vàrf-ër-ím** 'impoverishment,' **vàrf-ër-ísht** 'poorly.'

All inflectional suffixes are unstressed, as are all other suffixes ending in **e, a, o** (except in verb stems), **ë**, or ending in **ë** plus a consonant (except **-llḗk**, plural **-llḗqe**). In many cases, the particular grammatical function of these suffixes is no longer clear, but the lack of stress indicates that they are still suffixes. While some derivational suffixes, such as **-shëm, -thi, -as,** and **-azi**, are unstressed, most others are stressed.

Stems which terminate in a consonant plus a liquid (**r, rr, l,** or **ll**) with or without a final -**ë** have citation forms with an unstressed -**ë**- between the consonant and the liquid, and without a final -**ë**. Citation forms which terminate in a consonant plus **ë** plus a liquid (**r, rr, l, ll**) may thus reflect:

1) a stem whose stem-vowel is **ë**, which is then stressed by the ordinary rule above: **çakërr**;

2) a stem without the **ë**; the **ë** is inserted in the citation form by a rule that prevents syllable-final consonant clusters ending in a liquid: **vjetr-** 'old';

3) a stem ending in the consonant plus a suffix terminating in **ë** plus a liquid: **mbret-ër** 'kings' (cf. **mbret** 'king').

Citation forms terminating in a consonant plus -**ull** may reflect:

1) a stem ending in -**ull**, in which case the **u** is stressed by the general rule above: **fodúll** 'vain person';

2) a stem ending in the consonant plus -**ll**, which first inserts **ë** in the citation form by the same rule cited above, and then converts an unstressed **ë** before **ll** to **ull** by another rule: **shembll** > **shembëll** > **shembll** 'example' (cf. **shembëllej** 'exemplify').

1.2.3 Syntactic and Morphological Constructions

Albanian SENTENCES, the constituent elements of discourse--represented in writing by an initial capital letter and a final punctuation mark (.?!) followed by another sentence or by nothing--are syntactically structured sequences of words. WORDS are marked off in writing by spaces around them. FULL WORDS may appear as utterances in their own right, while CLITICS are always attached grammatically to another part of the sentence.

NOTE

In Albanian all clitics are thus PROclitics. Many other languages have ENclitics, which are attached to a word that precedes them. In Albanian, when a clitic is attached after a word, it becomes suffixed to that word and is no longer separated off by a space: e.g., **më sillni** 'you bring to me'/ **sillmëni** 'bring to me!' show the clitic **më** 'to me' in both positions.

Considered grammatically, every word is constituted of one or more MORPHEMES; considered phonologically (i.e., in terms of their sound), of one or more PHONEMES; considered orthographically (i.e., in terms of their spelling), of one or more GRAPHEMES (we will call them LETTERS in this book).

On the basis of their morphological structure and range of syntactic functions, full words are classified into various PARTS OF SPEECH, described in later chapters of this grammar: nouns, verbs, adverbs, adjectives, prepositions, conjunctions, proforms, determiners, and particles.

In this book we will distinguish between the words *noun, pronoun, adjective, verb, adverb, number, preposition,* and *conjunction,* which are names of parts of speech defined as single words with a characteristic set of syntactic functions, and the words *nominal, pronominal, adjectival, verbal, adverbial, numerical, prepositional,* and *conjunctional,* which are the names of the respective syntactic roles played by these parts of speech, but may also be played by other words or combinations of words. For example, nouns may be used, among many other uses, as the subject of a verb, but other parts of speech may under certain conditions also serve that function (e.g., **Dy erdhën nga Berati.** 'Two came from Berat'); in such a case we could say that the number **dy** 'two' here has a nominal use, is used nominally, has been nominalized, or even *is* a nominal.

A PHRASE is a sequence of one or more words in a sentence which form a syntactic unit in relation to the rest of the sentence. A CLAUSE is a phrase containing a finite verb (a verb whose ending reflects the person and number of its subject). A COMPLETE SENTENCE contains at least one clause not introduced by a conjunction, but unlike edited English sentences, edited Albanian sentences are often not complete in this sense.

Albanian sentences are made up of various combinations of verbal, nominal, adjectival, adverbial, conjunctional, and interjectional phrases and particles.

1.2.4 Words and Morphemes

A number of words consist of a single morpheme. For the most part these Albanian words (and their English counterparts) belong to such invariable parts of speech as adverbs, prepositions, and conjunctions: **lart** 'high,' **drejt** 'straight,' **afër** 'near,' **në** 'in,' **me** 'with,' **e** 'and,' **por** 'but,' **se** 'that,' **unë** 'I,' **ti** 'thou,' **ju** 'you,' **ne** 'we,' **kush** 'who'.

The citation forms of a number of nouns and verbs also consist of a single morpheme called a ROOT: **mal** 'mountain,' **mik** 'friend,' **punë** 'work,' **hap** 'open' **pi** 'drink,' **shes** 'sell,' etc. The root is the lexical nucleus of the word, the carrier of the basic lexical meaning of the word. In terms of its grammatical function, the root acts as the central STEM of the word, i.e., that part to which affixal morphemes (=AFFIXES), if any, may be attached. So in **larg-o-j** 'remove,' **larg-im** 'removal,' **larg-esë** 'distance' **i larg-ët** 'distant,' **larg-as** 'indirectly,' the root **larg-** 'far' contributes the core lexical meaning in all these words. In words of one morpheme, the root is equal to the word itself: e.g., the root of the adverb **larg** 'far' is **larg-**.

The morphemes in a word that are attached to stems are AFFIXES--PREFIXES if they precede the root, or SUFFIXES if they come after it. Affixes which create new stems are called DERIVATIONAL or WORD-FORMING; affixes which mark the syntactic function of a word are called INFLECTIONAL. Inflectional suffixes are called ENDINGS. Words or stems which contain a single root, with or without inflectional endings, are called SIMPLE; words or stems with more than one root are called COMPOUNDS; and words or stems with one or more derivational affixes are called DERIVED.

Words formed from a stem by inflectional suffixes are said to belong to the INFLECTIONAL PARADIGM of that stem. Inflectional paradigms of verbs are called CONJUGATIONS while those of nouns, pronouns, and adjectives are called DECLENSIONS. In most conjugations and declensions the word forms are analyzable into morphemes whose occurrence is predictable in that form given just the citation form of the word and its general grammatical category. But in some paradigms, particularly those of very frequently used words, some forms are not so predictable. In such cases, a good dictionary will specially list and identify the aberrant forms, in addition to giving enough synonyms or descriptions of the meaning(s) of the word and supplementary grammatical information to allow the user to understand how the word is used in most cases.

A. Allomorphs

A morpheme may not always appear in the same phonetic form. Depending on what affixes it is used with, the root morpheme of the verb **djeg** 'burn,' for example, appears in different parts of its conjugation in the form **djeg-, digj-,** or **dogj-**. These are not three different morphemes, but rather different ALLOMORPHS of the same morpheme. The root morpheme of this verb is really the set of its allomorphs **djeg-/digj-/dogj-**. In the same way, the endings **-i** and **-u** that mark the indefinite genitive, dative, and ablative singular or the nominative definite singular cases of certain nouns will be considered to be two different representations of the same morpheme, since the difference between them rests on differences between the phonemes that precede them rather than on a difference in grammatical or semantic function. If the preceding phoneme is **g, k, h, i, é,** or **á** (in monosyllables), the morpheme will have the allomorph **-u**; otherwise the allomorph is **-i**: **zogu** 'the bird,' **shoku** 'the comrade,' **ahu** 'the beech,' **njeriu** 'the person,' **dhéu** 'the earth,' **káu** 'the ox'; but **lisi** 'the oak,' **mësimi** 'the lesson,' **kali** 'the horse,' **përrói** 'the creek,' **vëllai** 'the brother'. The same rule applies to the ending **-i/-u** of the past definite tense of certain verbs: **lagu** 'he moistened,' but **hapi** 'he opened'.

B. General Processes that Create Allomorphs in Albanian

When two or more morphemes are joined to form a word, as happens in forming compound stems, in forming derived stems with prefixes and suffixes, in forming inflected words with inflectional endings, and in attaching clitics to verb forms, the morphemes may take on shapes determined by certain quite general rules.

1) In all combinations, if two vowels, one of which is unstressed **ë**, come together, the **ë** drops:

báshkë + atdhetár = bashkatdhetár
báshkë + -ím = bashkím
shtëpí + -ësë = shtëpisë
xhaxhá + -ënë = xhaxhánë

2) At the end of a word, unstressed **ë** will drop if the word stress is not on the preceding syllable. Thus, many suffixes and endings which have allomorphs ending in **ë** will have other allomorphs without that **ë**, depending on whether they follow a stem with an unstressed or stressed final syllable, respectively:

lúle + -ënë = lúlen
vájzë + -ësë = vájzës
márr + -i- + -më = márrim
gjúhë + -ëzë = gjúhëz
njérëz + -i- + -të = njérëzit
i + hékur + -të = i hékurt

3) When a stem ending in a vowel is followed by a suffixed element (a derivational suffix, inflectional ending, or bound clitic) beginning in an identical vowel, one of them is dropped--an unstressed one, if there is one:

batërdi + -ís = batërdís
lajthí + ishtë = lajthíshtë
fatbárdhë + -ësi = fatbardhësi

But notice that if the second vowel does not begin a suffix, no contraction takes place:

krýe + éngjëll = kryeéngjëll
pa- + anësí = paanësí
jó- + organík = joorganík
anti- + imperialíst = antiimperialíst

4) In combinations of **ç** with a following voiceless consonant, the **ç** becomes **sh**:

ç- + faq = shfaq
ç- + prish = shprish
ç- + këput = shkëput

Followed by a voiced stop or fricative, **ç** becomes **zh**:

ç- + bllokoj = zhbllokoj
ç- + duk = zhduk
ç- + vesh = zhvesh

The particle **ç'** 'what' maintains its status as a proclitic rather than prefix, and is always separated from the following word in the orthography by an apostrophe. In pronunciation, however, it is voiced before voiced stops or fricatives, so that it has the sound of **xh** or **zh** before words beginning with such consonants:

ç' + bukë = ç'bukë (pronounced **xhbukë**)

ç' + do = ç'do (pronounced **xhdo** or **zhdo**)

ç' + verë = ç'verë (pronounced **xhverë**)

5) In combinations of **s** with a following voiced stop or fricative, **s** becomes voiced **z**:

s + bardh = zbardh

s + gjat = zgjat

s + vogël-oj = zvogëloj

The particle **s'** 'not' maintains its constant spelling in the orthography, but in pronunciation it follows the same rule:

s' + bie = s'bie (pronounced **zbie**)

s' + gjendet = s'gjendet (pronounced **zgjendet**)

s' + vras = s'vras (pronounced **zvras**)

CHAPTER 2
Verbs and Verbal Phrases

2.1 Basic Grammatical Categories in Verbs

A VERBAL PHRASE (abbreviated VP) is a word or sequence of words serving in typical functions of a verb, such as forming the nucleus of a clause (the PREDICATION) or of a participial phrase. Every VP must contain a verb as its nucleus, which in turn may be preceded by verbal proclitics and followed by one or more complements. VERBAL PROCLITICS may mark negation, mood, aspect, or tense. Complements may be verbal, adverbial or nominal.

The VERB is that part of speech which forms the nucleus of a predication, exhibiting grammatical distinctions in person, number, mood, tense, and voice. The verb typically denotes an action, state, or changed state in a subject, although verbs used as auxiliaries or semi-auxiliaries have largely lost such a direct semantic connection with the subject, and other verbs are used without any external subject at all.

FINITE verbs exhibit the characteristic grammatical distinctions of person, number, voice, mood, and tense that typify verbs. The form of a finite verb itself reflects the distinctions in person and number of its subject. In addition, pronominal clitics attached to a verb, finite or non-finite, may indicate the person and number of its object (for transitive verbs only) or referent (for any verb).

Table 2.1 Verb Grammatical Categories and their Abbreviations		
FINITE	**PERSON** 1st 2nd 3rd	
	NUMBER S(in)g(ular) Pl(ural)	

	VOICE
	Act(ive)
	Non-act(ive)
	  Pass(ive)
	  Mid(dle)
	  Refl(exive)
	  Recip(rocal)	

	MOOD
	Ind(icative)
	Sub(junctive)
	  Cond(itional)
	  Jus(sive)
	  [Sub(junctive)-Adm(irative)]
	Opt(ative)
	Adm(irative)
	Imp(erative)	

	TENSE	
	ASPECT Com(mon) Perf(ect) Prog(ressive) Inch(oative) Def(inite) Imperf(ect)	**TIME** Pres(ent) Past Fut(ure)
NON-FINITE	**PART(ICIPLE)** Inf(initive) Ger(undive) Abs(olutive)	

The CITATION FORM of a verb is normally its first person, singular number, active voice, indicative mood, present time, common aspect form. In discussing a verb form that form is assumed to have these same grammatical values, except as specified otherwise. Thus if the form **thua** 'you say' is identified just as 2nd person, the implication is that it is also active, indicative, present, and common; the form **u bëftë** 'may it be done', must be specified as 3rd Non-Act Perf, but we may leave unspecified that it is also Sg Ind Pres.

NOTE

Although the citation form for verbs is generally its first person singular present active indicative form (e.g., **shkoj** 'I go'), verbs that occur only in non-active forms are cited in the first person singular present non-active indicative form (e.g., **kollem** 'I cough'). A few verbs occur only in third person forms and they are cited in the third person singular present indicative (active or non-active, depending on the verb) form.

Time and aspect are conventionally treated together as TENSE; **po pres** 'I am waiting' is thus said to be in the present progressive tense. Since the English and Albanian verbal systems do not correspond point by point, the English gloss (given between ' ' following the Albanian form) is, of course, always approximate at best. For example, **shkoje** may be glossed as 'you used to go', but the gloss does not indicate that the "you" here is singular, that the imperfect tense form could just as well be translated as 'went' or 'were going' or 'would go' in the proper context, or that the verb itself could in context be more accurately translated as 'pass' or 'leave' or 'go away'. The reader cannot be guaranteed consistency in the glossing for any particular word, therefore, since the context in which it is used or imagined may change during the discussion.

Verbs are typically thought of as single words, but in Albanian one or more proclitics and auxiliaries may precede the main verb and the whole sequence is then still referred to as "the verb"; many of the conjugational forms of a verb are thus formed with proclitics and/or auxiliaries:

> Future: **DO TË shkoj** 'I shall go'
> Progressive: **PO shkoja** 'I was going'
> Subjunctive: **TË shkoj** 'that I go'
> Conditional: **DO TË shkoja** 'I would go'
> Perfect: **KAM shkuar** 'I have gone'
> Non-active Past Definite: **U lava** 'I was washed'
> Infinitive: **PËR TË shkuar** 'to go'
> Jussive: **LE TË shkojmë** 'let's go'
> Gerundive: **DUKE shkuar** '(while) going'

Sometimes the action of a clause is expressed by means of a locution, or word sequence, generally consisting of a verb and another full word (usually an adverb or a noun in a frozen form): e.g., **bëj ballë** 'I face ("I make forehead")', **bëj pallë** 'I relax ("I make a sword")', **bëj zë** 'I make sound', **bie fli** 'I sacrifice myself', **(ma) ka ënda** 'I like ("pleasure has it for me")', **marr parasysh** 'I consider ("I take before eyes")', **marr pjesë** 'I participate ("I take part")', **marr vesh** 'I understand ("I take ear")', **ngre krye** 'I rebel ("I raise head")', **ngre lart** 'I lift up', **ngre peshë** 'I raise up ("I lift weight")', **vë re** 'I notice ("I put new")', **vë dhjamë** 'I put (on) weight ("fat")', **vë mish** 'I put (on) weight ("meat")', **zë besë** 'I pledge ("I grasp faith")', etc. Such word sequences are equivalent to a single word, and on occasion they can be replaced by one: **zë besë = besoj, bëj ballë = përballoj, vë re = vërej**, etc. Such locutions are grammatically fixed. While the verb itself varies to indicate grammatical distinctions for the locution, the other element, which provides most of its lexical meaning, is grammatically frozen.

2.1.1 Person

The grammatical category of person distinguishes between the speaker of an utterance, those spoken to, and those spoken about. Albanian verbs, like English ones, distinguish three persons--FIRST (= I/we), SECOND (= you), THIRD (= he, she, it, they)--and two numbers--SINGULAR and PLURAL (= we, you, they). The ending of a FINITE verb reflects the person and number of the subject of the verb, and the verb is said to be in the person and number of its SUBJECT. In addition, a TRANSITIVE verb may have a clitic attached that indicates the person and number of its OBJECT (= direct object); and any verb, finite or non-finite, transitive or intransitive, may have a clitic attached that indicates the person and number of a REFERENT (approximately = indirect object). Certain verb forms may have the REFLEXIVE object clitic **u** attached, which indicates that the subject and object of the verb are not distinguished from each other. The specific endings used in Albanian to indicate the person and number of verb subjects will be discussed below in the sections treating the conjugation of verbs.

As in other European languages, second person plural forms may be used in addressing a single person, if the speaker wishes to express politeness. Such use would normally be inappropriate, for example, to address intimate friends or relatives, children or animals.

A. Pronominal Clitics

While endings on the verb indicate the person and number of the subject of the verb, unstressed PRONOMINAL CLITICS are used to indicate the person and number of the object and/or referent of a verb. Even non-finite verbs (those that do not indicate a subject) may have pronominal clitics. In Table 2.2 notice that in the third person, referents are distinguished from objects, while for the first and second persons the same form is used for both referent and object clitic.

Table 2.2 Pronominal Clitics		
	Referent	Object
Singular		
1st person	**më**	
2nd person	**të**	
3rd person	**i**	**e**
Plural		
1st person	**na**	
2nd person	**ju**	
3rd person	**u**	**i**
Reflexive		
Any person and number	**u**	

Often two clitics are used together, the first denoting the referent, the second denoting a third person object. Most of these combinations have undergone phonetic and orthographic changes, resulting in the dropping of the **ë** in **më** and **të**, the appearance of **a** instead of **e** (and **i**) in some forms, and certain other changes (see Table 2.3).

Table 2.3 Combination of Pronominal Clitics		Object		
	Referent	Singular 3rd person **e**	Plural 3rd person **i**	Reflexive **u**
1st Sg	**më**	**ma**	**m'i**	**m'u**
2nd Sg	**të**	**ta**	**t'i**	**t'u**
3rd Sg	**i**	**ia**	**ia**	**iu**
1st Pl	**na**	**na e**	**na i**	**na u**
2nd Pl	**ju**	**jua**	**jua**	**ju**
3rd Pl	**u**	**ua**	**ua**	**ju**

NOTES

1. Similar changes occur when pronominal clitics follow the conjunctive clitic **të**. The combination **të** + **e** becomes **ta**; before any other clitic beginning in **j** or a vowel, **të** becomes **t'**. **TA mësosh mirë** 'that you learn IT well', **T'I shkruash letër familjes** 'that you [TO THEM] write to the family', **T'U thuash që jemi mirë** 'that you tell THEM we're fine', **do T'JU shkruaj letër** 'I will write TO YOU', **M'U lavdërua** 'he bragged ("praised himself") TO ME', **T'U lavdërua** 'he bragged TO YOU'. Other combinations of **të** with pronominal clitics and their combinations are:

Conjunctive Clitic	+	Pronominal Clitic(s)	=	Combination
të		më		të më
		ma		të ma
		m'i		të m'i
		të		të të
		ta		të ta
		t'i		të t'i
		e		ta
		i		t'i
		ia		t'ia
		na		të na
		na e		të na e
		na i		të na i
		ju		t'ju
		jua		t'jua
		u		t'u
		ua		t'ua

2. In colloquial Albanian, the non-standard form **i** is often used instead of the standard form **u** to mark a third person plural referent:

Pionierët I (instead of **U**) **dhuruan miqve buqeta me lule.** 'The pioneers [i.e. boy scouts] presented bouquets of flowers TO their friends.'

Similarly, the non-standard form **u** is used in place of the standard form **ju** to mark a second person referent:

Juve U dhashë të drejtë. 'I agreed with YOU.' in place of **Juve JU dhashë të drejtë.**

U mblodhëm dhe, si diskutuam, vendosëm t'U (instead of **t'JU**) **shkruajmë me shpresë se do t'U** (instead of **t'JU**) **vijë pak keq.** 'We convened and, after discussing things, decided to write to YOU, in the hope that YOU will feel some slight compassion.'

3. The combinations **i** + **e** and **i** + **i** are written **ia** in proclitic position. But in enclitic positions **ia** is written with **j** instead of **i**: **jepja, merrja.**

4. Especially in colloquial narrative, a verb may be preceded by the frozen proclitic form **më** or the frozen clitic combination **më të** to signify the approval or interest of the speaker in what is sometimes called the "ethical dative" relation). Since the verb itself may be preceded by other pronominal clitics in such cases, the effect may be to produce a sequence of two or three apparent referent proclitics:

Pas tij, MË T'IU përvesh prapë Vasili ynë. 'After him, our Vasil really ("FOR ME FOR YOU FOR HIM") went at him again.

Po të paskan tharë krahët që MË IU thaftë ajo gjuhë M'IU thaftë! 'May that tongue of his shrivel up, for they have beaten you black and blue. ("But they have really dried up your arms, so may that tongue FOR ME FOR HIM be dried up").'

A.1 Clitic Position

Pronominal clitics may appear before verb forms of any tense and mood (for the special position with imperative verbs see below):

Unë i them se MË MERR malli dhe ajo MË VËSHTRON me dhëmshuri dhe tund kokën. 'I tell her that I get nostalgic ("nostalgia TAKES ME"), and she LOOKS AT ME with compassion and shakes her head.'

MË PAÇ në qafë, po MA PUNOVE si radhën e parë. 'I'll be damned if I'll let you do that to me again ("MAY YOU HAVE ME in neck if YOU WORKED ME like the first time").'

Mos më vono se po MË PRET im atë. 'Don't make me late because my father is EXPECTing ME.'

When a pronominal clitic or combination of clitics is used with verb constructions with the formative particles **të** 'to', **do të** 'will', **për të** 'to', **duke** 'by', **pa** 'without', etc., it appears between the particle and the verb:

> **Stavri shtriu krahët për t'IU hedhur t'et në qafë dhe u mat të thërriste.** 'Stavri stretched out his arms to embrace ("throw HIMSELF TO HIM in the neck") his father, and almost cried out.'
>
> **Pa E bërë të gjatë, shpalosi tantellën e përthyer të këmishës.** 'Cutting it short ("without making IT long"), he unfolded the pleated lace of his shirt.'

With imperative mood verbs, however, pronominal clitics have two possible positions. When the verb is in the negative imperative, the pronominal clitics always appear between the negative particle and the verb:

> **-- Mos MË shiko ashtu sikur nuk kupton, -- foli Argoni, -- po hajde ta tokim, se kemi qenë miq dhe miq e shokë do të jemi gjer në fund.** '"Don't look AT ME as if you do not understand me," Agron spoke, "but let's shake hands, for we've been friends, and friends and comrades we shall be to the end."'
>
> **Mos MA thuaj atë fjalë, Bardha.** 'Don't say that word TO ME, Bardha.'

With imperative verbs, only pronominal proclitics and combinations of the first, third, and reflexive persons are used. In the positive imperative these proclitics may appear before or after the verb (except for the clitic **e**, which rarely precedes the verb stem in positive imperatives). In the positive plural imperative they usually precede the stem; but they may also appear as enclitics, coming between the stem and the ending, and that whole sequence is written as a single word: **NA thoni** 'tell US', **NA shkruani** 'write US', **MË shkruani** 'write ME', **shkruaMËni** 'write ME'; **MË thuaj** 'tell ME', **thuajMË, të lutem** 'tell ME, please'; **MA hap derën** 'open the door for ME', **hapMA derën** 'open the door for me ("open IT FOR ME the door")'.

A.2 Uses of Pronominal Clitics

In general, the appearance of a pronominal clitic indicates that the verb has a direct or indirect object. Whenever the verb has an indirect object, a referent clitic in the same person and number as that object must appear, whether or not that indirect object is present in the sentence.

> **Kur t'I skruash (atij) I bëj të fala.** 'When you write TO HIM, give HIM my regards.'
>
> **-- Kjo, -- tha, MA mbush zemrën me gëzim të madh.** '"This," he said, "fills MY heart with great joy."'
>
> **Tani në fillim do të TË dhembë pak, njësoj sikur të pritesh padashur me brisk, po pastaj do ta kesh më lehtë se vendi do të mpihet vetvetiu.** 'At first it will hurt YOU a little, just like cutting yourself unwittingly with a razor, but later it will be easier on you, because the place will become numb automatically.'
>
> **Kështu na kishte ndodhur edhe në Zgërdhesh, me të vetmin ndryshim se atje, kur pushonin, fshatarët NA sillnin grushte me kumbulla, kurse këtu nisën të NA sjellin grushte me mana.** 'This is what happened to us in Zgërdhesh as well, the only difference being that over there, when the peasants took a break, they would bring US handfuls of plums, whereas here they began to bring US handfuls of mulberries.'

If the indirect object is present in the sentence, it is expressed as a noun or pronoun in the dative case. In Albanian, indirect objects indicate the involvement of the noun or pronoun with the clause in some relation other than as subject or object. It thus has a far wider use than indirect objects in English:

> **-- E ç'më duhet! -- ia priti Blerta, SË CILËS, në atë gjendje shpirtërore që ishte, nuk mund t'I pëlqente një gjë e tillë.** '"What use is it to me!" shot back Blerta, TO WHOM, considering the spiritual state she was in such a thing could not be pleasing (FOR HER).'
>
> **KËTYRE, xha Vangjel, -- iu përgjegj Viktoria, U lipsen shumë dërrasa, jo vetëm një.**

'"FOR THESE, uncle Vangjel," replied Viktoria, "many slabs, not just one are needed (FOR THEM)."'

The referent clitics of the first and second person singular and first person plural are also used, especially in colloquial Albanian, to indicate the emotional involvement of the speaker in the action of the clause, rather than a syntactic relationship to the verb:

Pa MË T'u bë ai fiku sa një shtëpi e madhe e pa MË T'I bënte ato kokrrat na...sa një ftua. 'That fig tree just grew ("FOR ME FOR YOU") as big as a house, and produced ("FOR ME FOR YOU THEM") figs, wow...the size of a quince.'

Nëno moj, mbaj zi për vëllanë/ me tre plumba NA I ranë/ Na e vran e na e shanë/ Na i thanë tradhëtar. 'Mother/ mourn for our brother/ with three bullets they felled him ("FOR US TO HIM they fell")/ They killed him and insulted him/ They called him traitor.'

The pronominal clitics of the first and second person must be used when the verb has a first or second person direct or indirect object, whether or not that object is also expressed elsewhere in the sentence:

Unë i them se MË merr malli dhe ajo MË vështron me dhembshuri dhe tund kokën. 'I tell her that I become nostalgic ("nostalgia takes ME"), and she looks at ME with compassion and shakes her head.'

When the speaker wants to emphasize the object, a pronoun in the appropriate case is used, usually either before the pronominal clitic or after the verb:

Përse i bën të gjitha këto? Sepse koha NA mësoi NE e TË mësoi TY shumë gjëra. 'Why are you doing all these things? Because time taught US and taught YOU many things.'

Fundja, NA ke dhe NE këtu. 'After all, you have US too here.'

The pronominal third person object clitics may or may not appear when the verb has a third person direct object expressed by a noun, pronoun or dependent clause, but must appear if the verb has an object otherwise unexpressed. In general, the presence of a third person object clitic **e** or **i** implies that the identity of the direct object is known to the audience:

Shumë nga kooperativistët E dinin që ishte njeri i mirë prandaj E donin. 'Many of the cooperativists knew (IT) that he was a good man, so they liked HIM.'

Ç'kërkoni? -- E pyeti përsëri burri me gjyzlykë duke i hedhur të porsaardhurit një vështrim të dyshimtë. '"What do you want?" the man with eyeglasses asked HIM again, casting a suspicious glance at the newcomer.'

Sikur të mos ishte përzhitja e zjarrit, që IA pati bërë FAQET lulukuq, as ajo vetë s'do të dinte ku TA fuste FYTYRËN. 'Were it not for the scorching fire, which had made [THEM FOR HER] HER CHEEKS red as poppies, she herself wouldn't have known where TO hide [IT] HER FACE.'

Ti e di SE PËR KU ËSHTË NISUR NËNA, ndaj mos pyet. 'You know WHERE MOTHER IS HEADED FOR, so don't ask.'

SE ÇKA ME MUA, as unë s'E di. 'WHY HE IS PEEVED AT ME, even I don't know [IT].'

When a form of **të gjithë** 'all' or **të tërë** 'all' is the direct object, an object clitic is required:

Dajë Kurti I di TË GJITHA. 'Uncle Kurti knows EVERYTHING ("knows THEM ALL").'

Pastaj partizanët I nxuarrën TË TËRA. 'Then the partisans brought THEM ALL out.'

Ja I ke TË GJITHË nëpër tavolina, në valle, te banaku i bufesë. 'There, THEY are ("you have THEM") ALL at the tables, dancing, at the buffet counter.'

Note that the third person object clitic is not used when the direct object, bearing the phrase accent to indicate that it conveys new information, is not expected to be identifiable to the audience:

Ngjarja është kaq domethënëse, kaq intersante dhe kaq për të qeshur, saqë dua të jap këtu jo RRËFIMIN e saj, po PËRFYTYRIMIN tim, aq e gjallë më ka mbetur në mendje. 'The event is so significant, so interesting, and so funny that I want to give here not its NARRATION, but my VISION of it, so vivid has it remained in my mind.'
Ke thënë taman MENDIMIN, që kam edhe unë. 'You have expressed exactly THE OPINION that I [too] have.'
S'jemi parë, qëkur thanim KËNETËN e Maliqit. 'We haven't seen each other since we were draining THE Maliqi SWAMP.'

B. Unipersonal Verbs

The majority of verbs may be used in all three persons, but there are also quite a few which are used only in the third person.

B.1 Verbs Designating Animal Action

Verbs that name an action characteristic of a particular animal are normally used only in the third person: **hingëllin** 'neighs' (horse), **hungron** 'growls' (wolf or dog), **kakarit** 'cackles' (chicken), **mjaullin** 'meows' (cat), **pëllet** 'brays' (donkey).

B.2 Impersonal Verbs

Verbs that indicate natural or atmospheric phenomena have a third person subject either expressed or understood: **bie** 'falls' (e.g.,rain, snow), **fryn** 'blows' (e.g.,wind, blizzard), **bleron** 'sprouts, turns green' (e.g.,field, meadow), **gjelbëron** 'turns green' (e.g.,grass), **ushton** 'rumbles, echoes' (e.g.,canyon).

Several verbs (in the singular only) or verbal expressions which name atmospheric phenomena have the third person subject neither expressed nor understood: **vetëtin** 'it flashes, it lightens', **bubullin** 'it thunders', **veson** 'it dews', **bën ftohtë** 'it is ("makes") cold', **bën freskët** 'it is cool', **bën ngrohtë** 'it is warm', etc.

B.3 Verbs with Pseudo Subjects

Verbs with a pseudo third person singular subject have their underlying subject expressed, if at all, in the dative case: **(s'më) besohet** '(I don't) believe (it)', **(më) bëhet** 'it makes (me)', **duket** 'it seems', **(s'më) kujtohet** '(I don't) recall ("it is not recalled to me")', **ndodh** 'it happens', **(më) pëlqen** 'it is pleasing (to me), (I) like (it)', **qëllon** 'it happens', **rastis** 'it chances, it happens':
   KISH QËLLUAR që ish ngritur edhe nga dasma, kurse sot s'po luante nga vendi. 'IT HAD HAPPENED that he had even left the wedding, whereas today he was not budging from his place.
   Nganjëherë NDODH që njerëzit të njihen aty për aty e të lidhen me njëri-tjetrin. Sometimes IT HAPPENS that people become acquainted right away and create a bond'.
   Tashti jam si në ëndërr, S'MË BESOHET që po shetit me ty e po flas. 'It's as if I am dreaming now, I CAN'T BELIEVE that I am strolling with you and talking.'
   Pa dale, pa dale: M'U DUK se pashë një cep gune, M'U DUK se nga driza kërceu diçka e zezë. 'Wait, wait! I thought ("IT SEEMED TO ME") I saw the corner of a cloak, I THOUGHT something black jumped out of the brush.'

Several transitive verbs, such as **di** 'know', **lejoj** 'permit', **ndaloj** 'forbid', **them** 'say', may also occur with pseudo third person singular subjects, when used in non-active forms:
   DIHET që pengesa e papritur është gjithmonë e keqja. 'IT IS KNOWN that the unexpected obstacle is always the bad one.'

FLITET se ato do t'i nxjerrin jashtë përdorimit armët e tjera. 'IT IS SAID that they will make all other arms obsolete.'

Atëherë MERRET ME MEND se kjo do të jetë më tepër një kacavjerrie e mundimshme se sa një fluturim i rrufeshëm. 'Then it is obvious (IT IS TAKEN WITH MIND) that this will be more of a laborious climb than a lightning flight'.

Nuk KUPTOHEJ nëse ata sprapseshin apo pregatiteshin të sulmonin. 'One could not tell (THERE WAS not UNDERSTANDING) whether they were retreating or preparing to attack.'

PARASHIKOHET që sulmet e tyre të ardhshme të jenë akoma më të egra dhe më të dëshpëruara. 'IT IS EXPECTED that their future assaults will be even fiercer and more desperate.'

The verbs **jam** 'I am', **vij** 'I come', **shkoj** 'I go', **dal** 'I emerge', etc., are used with pseudo third person singular subjects in expressions like **(s') është mirë** '(no) good! ("is(n't) well")', **(s') është keq** '(not) bad! ("is(n't) bad")', **(s') është e arsyeshme** '(that's) (not) reasonable', **(s') është e udhës** '(that's) (not) proper ("of the road")', etc.; **më vjen mbarë** 'suits me ("to me it comes prosperous")', **më vjen mirë (keq)** 'I'm glad (sorry) ("to me it comes good (bad)")', **(s') më shkoi ndër mend** 'it did(n't) occur to me ("not to me went through mind")', **më doli nga mendja** 'I forgot ("to me went out from the mind")':

Pastaj ktheu mendje dhe instinktivisht e ndjeu se ISH E UDHËS ta merrte me të mirë. 'Then he changed his mind and instinctively sensed that IT WAS APPROPRIATE to be nice to him.'

MË VJEN KEQ të ta them, shoku Rakip, por ti po bëhesh pengesë për realizimin e planit. 'I REGRET to tell you, comrade Rakip, but you are becoming an obstacle to the realization of the plan.'

Dhe në përgjithësi atij NUK I ERDHI MIRË që u ngjitën në mes të fshatit. 'And in general he did not like it ("NOT CAME TO HIM GOOD") that they ascended to the midst of the village.'

Atyre NUK U SHKONTE KURRË NDËR MEND se ky do të ishte shoku i tyre dhe do të qeshte e do të bënte potere si ata. 'It never occurred to them ("NOT to them WOULD IT NEVER GO THROUGH MIND") that this would be their comrade, who would laugh and get into brawls just like them.'

Duhet and **do** when used as modals have only their third person singular forms, as if they had a pseudo subject.

B.4 Existential Uses of **kam**

The verb **kam** 'I have' is used only in third person singular forms to give the sense of the existential *there is, there are, there were, etc.* in English:

Ata nuk e kuptojnë se politikë KA kudo, në çdo punë e në çdo sektor, se NUK KA kuadro e punë ekonomike, administrative, kulturale e ushtarake të shkëputura nga politika e jashtë politikës së diktaturës së proletariatit. 'There is ("HAS") politics everywhere, in every job and in every sector, that there is NO ("HAS NOT") cadre and economic, administrative, cultural, and military work divorced from politics, and apart from the politics of the dictatorship of the proletariat.'

KA e S'KA fshatra me kroje, po kroje si ato të Voskopojës s'gjen gjëkundi. 'There are villages with fountains and without ("THERE ARE and THERE ARE NOT villages with fountains"), but fountains like those of Voskopojë you can't find anywhere.'

B.5 Impersonal Non-active Intransitive Verbs

Intransitive verbs in third person singular non-active forms are often accompanied by some indication of negation (**s'shkohet** 'there's no going', **s'rrihet** 'there's no staying', **s'hyhet** 'there's no entering', **s'rrohet** 'there's no living', **s'flihet** 'there's no sleeping', etc.) or interrogation. They not only represent the action in a general way without specifying a particular subject, but also express modal nuances of possibility or even necessity. Thus **këtej s'kalohet** means basically the same thing as the sentence **Këtej s'mund** (or **s'duhet**) **të kalojë njeri**. 'No one can (should) pass this way'.

> **Edhe pa këmbë JETOHET. Kështu S'ECET përpara.** 'Even without feet THERE'S LIVING; THERE'S just NO GOING forward that way.'

Note that a pronominal referent clitic may be attached to verbs of this type to designate obliquely the underlying subject of the verb:

> **Mirëpo mua S'MË IKET, kemi shkuar një jetë të tërë këtu, u mësuam.** 'Nevertheless, I can't go ("NOT FOR ME IS THERE GOING"), we have lived our whole life here, we've gotten used to it.'
>
> **Nga miniera kishte ikur, kurse në fshat e ndjente se NUK I VEHEJ.** 'He had left the mine, yet he felt that he could not go ("NOT FOR HIM WAS THERE GOING") to the village.'
>
> **Rustemit e mësuesit U FLIHEJ.** 'Rustem and the teacher were sleepy ("FOR THEM THERE WAS SLEEPING").'
>
> **Në kalibe NUK I RRIHEJ vetëm dhe bariste me duar në xhepat e kapotës së gjatë.** 'He did not feel like staying ("NOT FOR HIM WAS THERE STAYING") alone in the tent; and (so) he strolled with his hands in the pockets of his long cape.'
>
> **Atij atë ditë NUK I PUNOHEJ.** 'He did not feel like working ("NOT FOR HIM WAS THERE WORKING") that day.'
>
> **Kamarierit NUK IU DURUA më dhe erdhi bashkë me ndihmësin e filloi të mblidhte pjatat dhe gotat bosh.** 'The waiter could not stand it ("FOR HIM THERE WAS NO ENDURING") any longer, and he came over with his helper and began to pick up the empty plates and glasses.'

NOTE

In the phraseological expression **s'i bihet murit me kokë** 'one can't bang one's head against the wall', the verb similarly expresses the action in an impersonal manner:

> **Na thoshit se NUK I BIHET MURIT ME KOKË, por ne i ramë dhe muri zuri të lëkundej.** 'You used to tell us that one can't bang one's head against the wall ("THERE IS NOT HITTING THE WALL WITH HEAD"), but we did it, and the wall began to shake.'

2.1.2 Number

By the NUMBER of a verb we mean the number of its subject, expressed or understood. A verb in the plural thus does not indicate plurality of the action, but rather plurality of the subject.

If the subject is a singular collective noun (see Section 3.2.1.B.1), the verb may appear in the third person plural, if the speaker desires to emphasize the semantic plurality indicated by such nouns.

> **Bota THONË ashtu se KANË inat.** 'People ("the world") talk ("SAY") like that because they are spiteful ("HAVE spite").'
>
> **-- E ç'inat DO TË KENË bota? -- pyeti Hakiu.** 'But why should people be spiteful ("And what spite WILL the world HAVE")? asked Hakiu.'
>
> **Di unë ç'inat KANE?** 'How do I know why they are spiteful? ("Know I what spite THEY HAVE?")'.

In these sentences **bota** is a singular collective subject, and the verb **kam** appears in plural forms.

When the action named by the verb does not have a designated actor, then the verb is usually used in the third person singular (see previous section), or in the second person singular with a generalized meaning:

Po të hash perime, do të rrosh për gjithmonë. 'If you eat vegetables, you will live forever.'

2.1.3 Voice

Grammatical voice expresses the agentive relation between the verb and its subject (overtly present or understood). This relation is signalled morphologically in Albanian by selecting one of two groups of verbal forms: ACTIVE or NON-ACTIVE. On the basis of which of these groups is used and depending on the agentive relationships that obtain between the verb and its subject, we may distinguish four voices in Albanian: active, middle, passive, and reflexive (and reciprocal, as a special case of the latter).

A. Active Voice

A verb is in the ACTIVE voice when it has an active form and its subject is itself the AGENT, that is, the performer of the action designated by the underlying verb. On the basis of whether they may or may not take a direct object, active voice verbs are labeled transitive or intransitive, respectively.

A.1 Transitive Verbs

A TRANSITIVE verb represents an action as directed upon an object in the accusative case. Among the transitive verbs in Albanian are: **dua** 'want', **hap** 'open', **kërkoj** 'seek', **marr** 'take', **mbyll** 'close', **nderoj** 'honor', **përshëndet** 'greet', **qep** 'sew', etc.

Afërdita, pasi MBAROI letrën, HODHI vështrimin jashtë nga dritarja dhe sytë i ranë mbi kodrën, ku ngrihej shkolla e re. 'After she FINISHED the letter, Aphrodite CAST a look out the window and her eyes rested ("fell") on the hill, where the new school was being built.'

A.2 Intransitive Verbs

INTRANSITIVE verbs designate actions centering on the subject, such as **fle** 'sleep', **dremit** 'doze', **rri** 'stay', **dal** 'emerge', **eci** 'walk', **hyj** 'enter', **shkoj** 'go', **vij** 'come', **vrapoj** 'run', etc.:

Në qepalla u RËNDONTE gjumi e megjithatë nuk FLININ; nuk FLININ e nuk BISEDONIN, po RRININ të shtrirë rrëzë dy mureve të kasolles, që binte erë kashtë e bar të thatë. 'Sleep WEIGHED DOWN on their eyelids, but in spite of that they did not TALK, but REMAINED lying down by the two walls of the hut, which smelled of straw and dry grass.'

Nga TË KISH ARDHUR ky emër i ri "komisar" që e mbanin këta dy veta, që nuk i zinte gjumi? 'Where HAD this new title, "commissar", COME from, that these two people who could not sleep held?'

Some verbs which are intransitive in Albanian correspond to verbs which are transitive in English. For example, to say 'He entered the room.' Albanian has **Hyri në dhomën,** literally 'he entered in the room'. In a number of such instances, the Albanian intransitive verb will have an indirect object in the dative case, indicating that while the action is centered on the subject, it is directed toward the indirect object:

Korieri u përkul me nderim dhe I HIPI përsëri kalit. 'The courier bowed respectifully and mounted ("CLIMBED TO") the horse again.'

Ai I RA daulles një copë herë. 'He played ("FELL TO") the drum for a while.'

Among verbs in this category are **bie** 'I hit', **hipi** 'I climb', **flas** in the sense 'I scold', **thërras** 'I call', and **besoj** 'I believe'.

Whether a verb is transitive or intransitive depends on its lexical meaning. Since many verbs have more than one meaning, it often happens that a single verb will sometimes be transitive and sometimes intransitive:

Këtë pranverë mezi u ngrit më këmbë, se iu bë djepi varr. Rrinte gjithmonë shtrirë e atje QANTE dhe e QANIM. 'This spring he was barely able to get on his feet, because the cradle had become a grave (to him). He stayed in bed and there he WOULD WEEP and we would weep for him ("and we WEPT HIM").'

Pranë tij SHKOI e ndenji edhe Flamuri. SHKOI dhe një herë pëllëmbën mbi fytyrë e sikur u qetësua. 'Flamuri, too, WENT and stayed by him. He PASSED his hand once more over his face, and seemed to relax.'

Më merret fryma, më ndalet zemra, mundohem të kapem pas ajrit, THËRRES. 'I gasp, my heart stops, I try to clutch at air, I scream ("CALL").'

PO më kot! Zaharia THIRRI të vetët, por s'pati nevojë t'i THËRRISTE, se të gjithë iu gjendën aty. 'But in vain! Zaharia CALLED his own, but he had no need to CALL them, because all of them were there.'

Pse S'FLE nga pak tani në vapë? 'Why don't you SLEEP a bit now at the peak of the day's heat?'

Eh, more djem, ruajuni, bre, nga ata që fshihen në hendekë e në driza, mos E FLINI, bre, mendjen! 'Hey boys, just watch out for those who hide in the ditches and the shrubs; now don't get complacent ("SLEEP THE MIND")!'

Some intransitive verbs in Albanian (as in English) -- **jetoj** 'I live', **fle** 'I sleep', and a few others -- are sometimes used with a 'cognate' object, i.e., a direct object that has the same root as the verb or has a meaning synonymous with that root:

Që të gjitha KISHIN JETUAR JETËN e tyre, kishin ardhur nga kontinente e shtete të ndryshme dhe ja tashti po preheshin e po ruheshin të sistemuara e të regjistruara nga dora e një mjeshtri... 'All of them HAD LIVED their LIFE, had come from different continents and states, and now were quietly being preserved in a manner systematized and registered by a master hand...'

Në dhomën e madhe të hanit dëngjet e mbështetur kurriz më kurriz dukeshin sikur po FLININ edhe ata GJUMIN e rëndë të natës. 'In the large room of the inn, the bales piled up back to back, seemed as if they too WERE SLEEPING the heavy sleep of the night.'

B. Non-active Voices

Many Albanian verbs have both active and non-active forms. A non-active form may represent action in three voices, depending on the relationships between the underlying agent and object of the verb.

B.1 Middle Voice

A verb is in the MIDDLE voice when it has a non-active form and its subject is the underlying agent. In terms of meaning, a verb in the middle voice is similar to an intransitive verb in the active voice.

Verbs in the middle voice include:

1) Verbs that denote movements, like **hidhem** 'I jump', **kapem** 'I grasp at, I am seized', **kthehem** 'I return', **mbahem** 'I hold on', **mbështetem** 'I lean', **ngrihem** 'I get up', **nisem** 'I set

out, I leave', **përdridhem** 'I twist', **përpiqem** 'I struggle', **rrotullohem** 'I rotate', **sulem** 'I attack', **vërsulem** 'I rush forward', **vërtitem** 'I whirl, dash, throw myself at', etc.:

U PËRPOQ TË NGRIHEJ e të kapte armët dhe dha urdhër t'i gatitnin kalin. HE TRIED TO GET UP and grasp his weapons, and ordered that they ready his horse.'

Dhe duhej TË NISEJ sa më shpejt. 'And he had TO LEAVE as soon as possible.'

M'U QEP ky e s'më NDAHET, mendoi Memoja. 'He sticks to me like glue ("TO ME THIS IS SEWN and not from me SEPARATES"), Memo thought.'

2) Verbs that denote psychological actions, such as **dëshpërohem** 'I become disappointed, I get sad', **gëzohem** 'I rejoice', **hidhërohem** 'I become bitter', **kollem** 'I cough', **krenohem** 'I take pride', **mendohem** 'I think', **mërzitem** 'I get bored, annoyed', **pendohem** 'I regret', **pezmatohem** 'I become irritated, I chafe', **pikëllohem** 'I am mortified',

Ai nuk MËRZITEJ duke dëgjuar ngjarje nga jeta e njeriut të derdhur në bronx. 'He did not GET BORED listening to tales about the life of the man cast in bronze.'

-- Me qaramanë nuk bëhet lufta! -- U ZEMËRUA Memoja me të vëllanë. 'You can't fight a war with crybabies--(said) Memo angrily ("Memo BECAME ANGRY") to his brother.'

3) Verbs that denote changes in the state of the subject such as **bëhem** 'I become', **egërsohet (deti)** '(the sea) gets rough', **fishkem** 'I wither', **mvrehem** 'I become sullen, I frown', **nxihem** 'I become black', **përtërihem** 'I recover', **plakem** 'I grow old', **qetësohem** 'I grow calm, I relax', **rritem** 'I grow up', **skuqem** 'I redden, I blush',

Memoja e kish kuptuar që tipi i Rrapos në fillim NXEHET e mund të flasë fjalë të pakontrolluara, por pastaj QETËSOHET e ZBUTET. 'Memo had understood that Rrapo's type BECOMES INFLAMED in the beginning, and may utter careless words, but afterward they CALM DOWN and BECOME MILD;'

U TKURR, U MBLODH kruspull dhe zgjati duart drejt plagëve për të ndaluar gjakun. 'HE SHRANK, curled up ("COLLECTED HIMSELF into a heap"), and stretched his hands toward the wounds to stop the bleeding.'

NOTES

1. The majority of verbs in the middle voice are derived from corresponding active forms: **hidhem** from **hidh**, **kapem** from **kap**, **mbahem** from **mbaj**, **skuqem** from **skuq**, **zverdhem** from **zverdh**, etc. But there are also some verbs in the middle voice that do not have a corresponding active form: **kollem, pendohem, sulem, vërsulem,** etc.

2. There are several verbs in the middle voice whose meaning is identical with or similar to the active voice used intransitively. Compare:

    Ndjente se po e linte fuqia, se po i AFROHEJ vdekja dhe nuk donte të jepej. 'He sensed that his strength was leaving him, that death was APPROACHING, and he did not want to give in.'

    Po AFRONTE koha e drapit të parë dhe e shtegtimit të bagëtive. 'The time of the first harvest and of the migration of the sheep was GETTING CLOSER.'

    Memoja U MENDUA. 'Memo THOUGHT'.

    E zuri për krahu komandantin Rrapo e i tha: -- Të dëgjojmë Zarikun. -- Nuk MENDON keq -- tha Rrapoja dhe i thirri Fatës: -- Zariku atje është? 'He grabbed commander Krapo by the arm and said to him: "Let's listen to Farik." "Not a bad idea ("you don't THINK badly")," said Rrapo, and he called out to Fate: "Is Farik there?"'

B.2 Passive Voice

A verb is in the PASSIVE voice when it has a non-active form, which would be the object of the corresponding active verb and names an action experienced by its subject. The passive voice may thus occur only with transitive verbs. The performing agent of a passive verb may or may not be expressed overtly.

> **Sultan Mehmeti II pas betejës së Pollogut, duke parë që nuk e thyente dot Skënderbeun me forcën e armëve, nisi të përdorte të tjera mjete dhe shpesh thoshte që Skënderbeu DO TË MUNDEJ prej shokëve, të cilët e bënin bë pamundshëm.** 'After the battle of Pollog, Sultan Mehmet II, seeing that he could not defeat Scanderbeg by the force of arms, began to use other means, and often said that Scanderbeg WOULD BE BEATEN by comrades who made him out to be invincible.'
>
> **Komandanti iu afrua partizanëve të mbledhur dhe tha: -- Nuk kam se ç't'ju mollois. E shihni edhe vetë si mbaroi përpjekja. U DOGJËN dhe U THYEN. Ca U VRANË, ca shpëtuan. Prapë, po të kalojnë këtej, DO TË DIGJEN e DO TË THYHEN.** 'The commander approached the assembled partisans and said: I have nothing to tell you. You can see for yourself how the clash ended. THEY WERE BURNED and BROKEN. Some WERE KILLED, some escaped. THEY WILL BE BURNED and BROKEN again, if they come by this way.'

B.3 Reflexive Voice

A verb is in the REFLEXIVE voice when it has a non-active form and denotes an action that is both performed and experienced by the subject of the clause. Only active transitive verbs may have a reflexive voice. When the subject of the clause represents an agent (or several agents) who performs the action on himself (or themselves), then the verb is in the PROPER REFLEXIVE voice, as in **krihem** 'I comb myself', **lahem** 'I wash myself', **mburrem** 'I boast', **vishem** 'I dress up myself', **zhvishem** 'I undress myself', etc.:

> **Kurrë s'mund ta ngatërroja atë me ndonjë tjetër, megjithëse të gjithë ISHIN VESHUR njësoj, me kominoshe dhe çizme.** 'I could never mistake him for someone else, even though all of them WERE DRESSED alike, in overalls and boots.'

But, when the action requires two or more agents acting reciprocally on one another, then the verb is in the RECIPROCAL REFLEXIVE voice, as in **fejohemi** 'we become engaged (to each other)', **hahem (me dikë)** 'I quarrel (with someone)', **kapem (me dikë)** 'I grapple (with someone)', **martohemi** 'we get married', **përqafohen** 'they embrace', **përshëndetem (me dikë)** 'I exchange greetings (with someone)', **piqeni** 'you run into (one another)', **takohemi** 'we meet (one another)', **zihem (me dikë)** 'I quarrel (with someone)', etc.:

> **Ai e ndjente që ISH PRISHUR keq me Memon e me të tjerët.** 'He sensed that he HAD BROKEN UP badly with Memo and the others.'
>
> **Edhe ti, Genci, ZIHESH me shokët ndonjëherë -- tha Demka.** '"You, too, Genci, QUARREL with your comrades sometimes", said Demka.'

> NOTES

1.   Verbs used only in the third person may be in the Active, Middle or Passive voice:

    Active

> **ndodh** 'it happens'
> **ngjan** 'it happens (it resembles)'
> **qëllon** 'it happens (it strikes)'
> **rastis** 'it happens (it chances)'

    Middle

> **do** and **ka** in their modal uses (see Sections in 2.3.7).
> **duhet** 'ought, must'
> **(s'më) duket** 'it (doesn't) seem(s) (to me)'

> **(s'më) iket** '(I don't feel like) going'
> **(s'më) rrihet** '(I don't feel like) staying'

Passive

> **lejohet** 'it is allowed'
> **ndalohet** 'it is forbidden'
> **thuhet** 'it is said'

2. The formation of non-active forms, which are common to the middle, passive, and reflexive voices, will be discussed in Section 2.2.4.

2.1.4 Mood

The speaker's stance towards the relation between the action named by the verb and objective reality is expressed by the grammatical MOOD of the verb. The mood chosen by the speaker expresses his attitude toward the predicated matter, presenting it as an assertion, a possibility, a wish etc. In Albanian only those verb forms which vary according to person and number of the subject--i.e., FINITE forms--exhibit distinctions of mood. Non-finite forms (participles and gerundives) are thus not included.

The Albanian verbal system can be divided into five moods, each with a characteristic set of inflected verb forms: INDICATIVE, ADMIRATIVE, SUBJUNCTIVE, OPTATIVE, IMPERATIVE. In addition, two or three more inflected sets using subjunctive forms are sometimes included as moods on the basis of their modal meanings: CONDITIONAL, JUSSIVE, and less commonly, a so-called SUBJUNCTIVE-ADMIRATIVE mood. These seven (or eight) moods may be divided into three groups:

The first group includes the indicative and admirative moods, by which the speaker expresses an attitude of reality towards the predication made by the verb. By means of the admirative, the speaker adds a sense of surprise as well.

The second group includes the subjunctive (and subjunctive-admirative) and conditional moods which primarily express the modality of potentiality or possibility.

The optative, jussive, and imperative moods, which comprise the third group, are most commonly used to express the modality of desirability, the first in the form of a wish or a curse, the second in the form of a suggestion or proposal, and the third in the form of an order or a demand. The three moods of this third group have close ties to those of the second, because through the moods of desire and command, a future proposition is expressed, the outcome of which is possible but uncertain.

As will become apparent later in the relevant sections, in particular instances, verbal forms of a given mood are sometimes used with secondary modal meanings far removed from their basic meaning.

The grammatical forms of the various moods will be discussed in detail in later sections.

2.1.5 Tense

The relation between the time of the action denoted by the verb and an assumed temporal base point for a clause is expressed by the grammatical category of TENSE. For the spoken language, the base point is assumed to be the moment of speaking, whereas for the written language, the base may either be the moment of writing or some other posited point.

An action occupying some period of time that includes the moment of speaking is expressed by a present tense of the verb. Actions which occur before the moment of speaking are in a past tense, while those which are to occur after the moment of speaking are in a future tense. The basic TIME categories for verb tenses then, are PAST, PRESENT, and FUTURE.

Grammatical tense distinctions are made chiefly in the indicative, subjunctive, admirative, and optative moods, each of which has both present and past tense forms. In the subjunctive, there is a future tense as well. As for non-finite forms of the verb, the temporal meanings of the verb phrases of which they are a part are determined by the tense of the finite verbs that complement them (see Section 2.3.7).

2.1.6 Aspect

The Albanian language is rich in verbal grammatical forms through which various aspectual distinctions, as well as temporal ones, are expressed. The term ASPECT in this text is used to indicate the manner of development of the action designated by the verb. The principal distinction in aspect is based on the contrast between completed and incomplete action, as expressed by corresponding grammatical forms in the verbal conjugation. The grammatical category of aspect is not quite so basic in the verbal system of Albanian as it is, for example, in some Slavic languages, but certain tense forms of this verbal system must be distinguished by their aspectual differences. For example, there are five past tenses of the indicative mood; : IMPERFECT, PAST DEFINITE, PRESENT PERFECT, PAST PERFECT, and PLUPERFECT. Some of these (the present perfect versus the past perfect and the pluperfect) are distinguished from each other by temporal differences; but the distinction between the imperfect, past definite, and perfect is aspectual. The imperfect represents a general, habitual, or repeated action, or an action in progress at a particular time in the past; the past definite represents a particular action carried out at a given moment in the past; and the perfect tenses represent a general or particular action that is prior to the point of temporal reference: the present moment for the present perfect, a past moment for the past perfect or pluperfect.

> **Kamioni e LA pas bërrylin e rrugës dhe U NDAL atje ku kodra SHTRINTE gjunjët e saj në luginë.** 'The truck LEFT [past definite] the shoulder of the road behind and HALTED [past definite] there where the hill STRETCHED [imperfect] her knees into the valley.'
>
> **TË parët ZBRITËN shoferi dhe një grua me një fëmijë nja shtatë a tetëvjeçar.** 'The chauffeur and a woman with a child of about seven or eight DESCENDED first.'
>
> **Gjashtë burra QËNDRONIN ende në karroceri dhe FLITNIN me njëri-tjetrin me zë të lartë.** 'Six men WERE still REMAINING in the carriage station and WERE TALKING to one another in a loud voice.'

As will be explained in the relevant sections, a formal distinction may be made between two aspects of the present and imperfect indicative, one to indicate a momentary action, the other an action which is repeated time after time. When the verb denotes a general or repeated action, it appears in the appropriate one-word form for these two tenses: **laj** 'I wash', **laja** 'I used to wash'; whereas when the verb denotes a momentary action in progress, the emphatic particle **po** is placed before the verb form: **po laj** 'I am washing', **po laja** 'I was washing'. For action already in progress, an alternate progressive form, constructed with the verb **jam** in the present or imperfect followed by a gerundive introduced by **duke**, is also possible:

> **PO ZBRES gjer në fermë, mësues, dhe PO MARR një karrocë! -- tha Rustemi.** '"I am going ("I AM DESCENDING") as far as the farm, teacher, and I AM TAKING a carriage!", Rustem said.'
>
> **Dini qëndroi e mbajti vesh. Matanë avllisë në rrugën e tij dikush PO ECTE me vrap.** 'Dini halted and listened. Behind the wall on his street someone was running ("WAS WALKING hurriedly").'
>
> **Kur i huaji ISHTE DUKE KALUAR kafshën në katoqet e konakëve, djali u ngrit lart e na lajmëroi ≪ PO VJEN kapedani! ≫** 'While the stranger WAS MOVING the beast to the stables of the lodges, the boy got up and informed us, "The chief IS COMING!"'

2.2 Conjugation of the Verb Core

At the core of any VP is a conjugational form of a verb. A conjugational form consists of a verb stem together with its affixes, as well as any auxiliary word that is inseparable from the stem and any verbal clitics attached to either the stem or to the auxiliary. This VERB CORE in a verb phrase may mark person and number of a subject, as well as mood, and tense, in which case we call the verb FINITE, or it may leave those categories unmarked, in which case we call the verb NON-FINITE. The totality of the verb core forms of a particular verb is called its CONJUGATION. The forms that a verb takes in the course of its conjugation may be simple or complex; every conjugational form contains a stem of the given verb, but may or may not contain affixes, auxiliaries, and verbal clitics. In the following discussion the verb stem is marked off from its affixes by a hyphen.

A simple form consists of a verb stem and its ending. The grammatical function of such a form may be marked:

1) By person endings (including the zero-ending): **la-J** 'I wash', **la-N** 'he washes, you (Sg) wash', **la-JMË** 'we wash'. As will be seen, the chief clue to the conjugational forms of most verbs are the STEM VOWEL and STEM CONSONANT. The stem vowel is the stressed vowel or vowel cluster of the stem, which is always the last vowel (or vowel cluster) of the stem (the ONLY one in a monosyllabic stem). The stem consonant is the last consonant or consonant cluster of the stem, if the stem does not terminate in its stem vowel: **la-NI** 'you (pl.) wash', **la-JNË** 'they wash', **la-JA** 'I used to wash', **la-JE** 'you (Sg) used to wash', **la-NTE** 'he used to wash', **la-NIM** 'we used to wash', **la-NIT** 'you (pl.) used to wash', **la-NIN** 'they used to wash', **hap** 'I open', **hap** 'you (Sg) open', **hap** 'he opens', **hap-IM** 'we open', **hap-NI** 'you (pl.) open', **hap-IN** 'they open'.

2) By verb stem modifications:

a) Changing the stem vowel **-a-** to **-e-** or **-o-** to **-e-** in the second and third persons singular of the present indicative of certain verbs: **dal** 'I emerge', **del** 'you emerge', **marr** 'I take' **merr** 'he takes, you take', **jap** 'I give', **jep** 'he gives, you give', **rrah** 'I beat', **rreh** 'he beats, you beat', **njoh** 'I know (recognize),' **njeh** 'he knows, you know,' **shoh** 'I see', **sheh** 'he sees, you see';

b) Changing the stem consonant **-s-** to **-t-** in the same persons as in: **pres** 'I cut', **pret** 'he cuts, you cut', **shes** 'I sell', **shet** 'he sells, you sell', **zbres** 'I descend', **zbret** 'you descend, he descends';

c) Changing both stem vowel **-a-** to **-e-** and stem consonant **-s-** to **-t-** in the same persons as (a) and (b): **flas** 'I speak', **flet** 'he speaks, you speak', **përkas** 'I belong', **përket** 'he belongs, you belong', **vras** 'I kill', **vret** 'he kills, you kill'.

3) By both endings and stem changes:

a) Changing stem vowel **-a-** to **-o-** and **-e-** or **-je-** to **-o-** in the past definite of such verbs as: **dal** 'I emerge', **dol-a** 'I emerged', **marr** 'I take', **mor-a** 'I took', **nxjerr** 'I take out', **nxor-a** 'I took out', **bredh** 'I roam', **brodh-a** 'I roamed', **dredh** 'I twist', **drodh-a** 'I twisted', **heq** 'I pull, remove', **hoq-a** 'I pulled, removed', **mbjell** 'I sow, plant', **mboll-a** 'I sowed, planted', **pjell** 'I give birth', **poll-a** 'I gave birth', **vjel** 'I reap', **vol-a** 'I reaped'. (For verbs with the stem consonant -rr, in the past definite the change of -rr to -r- accompanies the vowel change.)

b) The change of stem vowel **-e-** or **-je-** to **-i-** in the second person plural of the present indicative, in all persons of the present non-active, in the imperfect, and for some verbs in the past definite as well. For a number of verbs, this change is accompanied by some other phonetic change: **heq** 'I pull', **hiq-ni** 'you (pl.) pull', **hiq-em** 'I am pulled', **hiq-ja** 'I was pulling, used to pull', **hiq-esha** 'I used to be pulled', **mbjell** 'I plant, sow', **mbill-ni** 'you sow', **mbill-et** 'it is sown', **mbill-ja** 'I used to sow', **mbill-ej** 'it was sown', **pjek** 'I meet', **piq-ni** 'you meet', **piq-em** 'I meet up', **piq-ja** 'I used to meet', **piq-esha** 'I used to meet up', **djeg** 'I burn', **digj-ni** 'you burn', **digj-em** 'I am burned', **digj-ja** 'I used to burn', **digj-esha** 'I used to be burned', **shes** 'I sell', **shit-ni** 'you sell' **shit-em** 'I am sold', **shit-ja** 'I was selling, used to sell',

shit-esha 'I used to be sold', **shit-a** 'I sold', **përket** 'he belongs' (**përkas** 'I belong'), **përkit-ni** 'you belong', **përkit-ja** 'I used to belong', **përkit-a** 'I belonged'.

c) The expansion of stem vowel -o- into -ua- and -e- into -ye- in the plural past definite and in the participle, or conversely, the collapsing of -ua- into -o- and -ye- into -e- in the singular past definite: **puno-j** 'I work', **puno-va** 'I worked', **punua-m** 'we worked', **punua-t** 'you worked', **punua-n** 'they worked', **punua-r** 'worked'; **rrëfe-j** 'I tell', **rrëfe-va** 'I told', **rrëfye-m** 'we told', **rrëfye-t** 'you told', **rrëfye-n** 'they told', **rrëfye-r** 'told'; **blua-j** 'I grind', **blo-va** 'I ground', **blo-ve** 'you ground', **blo-i** 'he ground'; **thye-j** 'I break', **the-va** 'I broke', **the-ve** 'you broke' **the-u** 'he broke'.

4) By stem-deriving suffixes followed by person endings, as in the synthetic forms of the optative or participles: **la-fsh-a** 'may I wash', **hap-sh-a** 'may I open', **la-rë** 'washed', **lë-në** 'left'.

5) By suppletion of the verb stem followed by person endings or inflectional suffixes: **jam** 'I am', **qe-shë** 'I was', **qe-në** 'been', **jap** 'I give', **dha-shë** 'I gave', **dhë-në** 'given'.

6) By compounding with special forms of **kam** as the second element (the present and imperfect forms of the admirative are formed in this way): **hap-kam** 'I actually open', **hap-kësha** 'I actually opened', **qen-kam** 'I actually am' **qen-kësha** 'I actually was, etc.

2.2.1 Verb Stems

The majority of verbs have a single basic stem upon which all its conjugational forms are built: **hap** 'I open', **mbyll** 'I close', **qep** 'I sow', **mat** 'I measure', etc. Thematic verbs like **puno-j** 'I work' and, **rrëfe-j** 'I tell', which regularly expand their stem vowels into **ua** and **ye** in the plural of the past definite and in the participle, respectively, are also included in this group. Similarly, verbs of the type **shkrua-j** 'I write', **thye-j** 'I break', which regularly collapse **ua** and **ye** into **o** and **e**, respectively, in the singular forms of the definite past are included in this group.

However, a large number of verbs utilize two or more stems in the course of their conjugation.

Verbs of the type **mbaj** 'I hold' or **bëj** 'I make' have an extended stem for the past definite and participles: **mbajt-a** 'I held', **mbajt-ur** 'held',; **bër-a** 'I made', **bër-ë** 'made', and a non-extended stem for the present and imperfect, for both active and non-active forms: **mba-j** 'I keep, hold', **mba-ja** 'I used to hold', **mba-hem** 'I am held', **mba-hesha** 'I used to be held' etc., **bë-j** 'I make', **bë-ja** 'I used to make', **bë-hem** 'I become', **bë-hesha** 'I used to become', etc.

Verbs of the type **heq** 'I pull', **mbjell** 'I sow', **vjel** 'I harvest', **nxjerr** 'I take out' have three stems which are used in the course of their conjugation.

1) One stem is used for the majority of persons in the present tense and in the participle: **heq** 'I pull', **heq-im** 'we pull', **heq-in** 'they pull', **heq-ur** 'pulled'; **mbjell** 'I sow', **mbjell-im** 'we sow', **mbjell-in** 'they sow', **mbjell-ë** 'sown'.

2) A second stem is shared by the second person plural in the present, all persons in the imperfect, all imperative forms, and all non-active forms in the present and imperfect: **heq** 'pull', **hiq-ni** 'you pull', **hiq-ja** 'I used to pull', **hiq-em** 'I am pulled'; **mbill-ni** 'you sow', **mbill-ja** 'I used to sow', **mbill-et** 'is sown'.

3) A third stem is used for the past definite: **hoq-a** 'I pulled', **mboll-a** 'I sowed'.

A few verbs utilize four distinct stems in their conjugation. These are:

A) The verbs **dal** and **marr**: 1) **dal** 'I come out', **dal-im** 'we come out', etc.; 2) **del** 'he comes out', 3) **dil-ni** 'you (pl.) come out', **dil-ja** 'I used to come out', etc.; 4) **dol-a** 'I came out'.

B) The verbs **vras** 'I kill', **ngas** 'I drive', **shkas** 'I slip'; 1) **vras-im** 'we kill'; 2) **vret** 'he kills'; 3) **vrit-ni** 'you kill', **vrit-ja** 'I used to kill', etc.; 4) **vra-va** 'I killed', **vra-rë** 'killed'.

C) Verbs of the type **pëlcas** 'I burst': 1) **pëlcas-im** 'we burst', etc.; 2) **pëlcet** 'he bursts'; 3) **pëlcit-ni** 'you burst', **pëlcit-ja** 'I used to burst', etc.; 4) **plas-a** 'I burst', **plas-ur** 'burst'.

For the stems of irregular suppletive and non-suppletive verbs see Section 2.2.2.D.

2.2.2 Conjugational Types

The problem of classification of verbs into conjugational groups has not found a uniform, generally accepted solution in the study of Albanian grammar. The chief difficulties lie in the Albanian verbal system itself, which reflects the dramatic grammatical and phonetic changes the language has undergone through its history. In addition, the absence of generally accepted criteria for classification has made the solution of this problem difficult. A variety of criteria have been followed in the grammars of Albanian in such matters as the treatment of irregular verbs, the forms which should be considered as basic for classification into conjugational groups and their subdivisions, etc.

For the classification of verbs into conjugational groups, these criteria will be followed:

1. The analysis will be purely synchronic, using present-day standard Albanian forms as the basis.

2. A verb which throughout its conjugation presents irregularities which do not allow it to be grouped with other verbs will be treated separately as an irregular verb and hence left outside of conjugational classifications. This will be the case not only for suppletive verbs, but also for those verbs which exhibit sound changes that appear idiosyncratic in modern Albanian (for a list of irregular verbs, see below).

3. The primary classification of verbs will be based on the citation form, and particularly on the final sound (or sounds, when relevant) of that stem (referred to as the CITATION STEM or simply as "the stem"), as well as on the endings of the present tense indicative of the active voice ending from the citation form.

4. The further division of conjugational groups into classes and subclasses will be based not only on the citation form, but also on the stem of the past definite and sometimes the participle as well.

On the basis of these criteria, regular verbs in contemporary Albanian are divided into three conjugations:

Conjugation I includes verbs whose citation form ends in a vowel or vowel cluster plus the ending -j: **puno-j** 'I work', **rrëfe-j** 'I tell, relate', **shkrua-j** 'I write', **lye-j** 'I paint'. This group includes the majority of verbs and is very productive.

Conjugation II includes verbs whose citation stem ends in a consonant: **hap** 'I open', **mat** 'I measure'. This conjugation contains a large number of verbs, but is no longer very productive of new ones.

Conjugation III includes verbs whose citation form ends in a vowel: **vë** 'I place, I put', **zë** 'I catch', **di** 'I know', **shpie** 'I carry', etc. This conjugational group includes a small number of verbs and is not productive.

A. Conjugation I

Conjugation I is divided into two classes:

CLASS I. This group includes verbs which extend the stem by **-v-** before the person ending in the first and second person singular of the past definite. The class is further divided into two sub-classes:

SUBCLASS 1 includes:

Variety a) Verbs with the stem vowels **-ó-** or **-é-** which in the past definite plural (for all three persons) as well as in the participle are extended to **-úa-** or **-ýe-**:

Pres	Past Def		Participle
1st Sg	1st Sg	1st Pl	
puno-j	**puno-v-a**	**punua-m**	**punua-r**
'I work'	'I worked'	'we worked'	'worked'
rrëfe-j	**rrëfe-v-a**	**rrëfye-m**	**rrëfye-r**
'I tell'	'I told'	'we told'	'told'

Variety b) Verbs with the stem vowel cluster **-úa-** or **-ýe-** which collapse in the singular past definite (for all three persons) into **-ó-** and **-é-**, respectively:

Pres	Past Def		Participle
1st Sg	1st Sg	1st Pl	
shkrua-j	**shkro-va**	**shkrua-m**	**shkrua-r**
'I write'	'I wrote'	'we wrote'	'written'
lye-j	**le-v-a**	**lye-m**	**lye-r**
'I paint'	'I painted'	'we painted'	'painted'

SUBCLASS 2 includes those verbs with stem vowels **-á-, -i,** or **-ý**, which do not change the stem vowel in the past definite and participle:

Pres	Past Def		Participle
1st Sg	1st Sg	1st Pl	
la-j	**la-v-a**	**la-më**	**la-rë**
'I wash'	'I washed'	'we washed'	'washed'
fshi-j	**fshi-v-a**	**fshi-më**	**fshi-rë**
'I sweep'	'I swept'	'we swept'	'swept'

CLASS II. This class includes those verbs with an extended stem in the past definite and participle. The class is divided into three subclasses.

SUBCLASS 1 includes verbs which have an **-i-** or **-e-** stem vowel and which appear with a stem-extension **-t-** in the past definite and the participle: **arrij** 'I attain, I reach', **gjej** 'I find', **mbërrij** 'I arrive'.

Pres	Past Def	Participle
1st Sg	1st Sg	
arri-j	**arri-t-a**	**arri-t-ur**
'I reach'	'I reached'	'reached'
gje-j	**gje-t-a**	**gje-t-ur**
'I find'	'I found'	'found'
mbërri-j	**mbërri-t-a**	**mbërri-t-ur**
'I arrive'	'I arrived'	'arrived'

SUBCLASS 2 verbs with the stem vowel **-e-, -a-, -o-, -ua-** or **-u** have the stem-extension **-jt-** in the same forms: **brej** 'I gnaw', **gjuaj** 'I hunt', **huaj** 'I loan', **kruaj** 'I scratch', **luaj** 'I play', **mbaj** 'I hold', **mbroj** 'I defend', **mbruj** 'I knead', **përbuj** 'I lodge', **quaj** 'I call, I name', **truaj** 'I dedicate', **vërej** 'I notice':

Pres 1st Sg	Past Def 1st Sg	Participle
gje-j	**gje-t-a**	**gje-t-ur**
'I find'	'I found'	'found'
bre-j	**brej-t-a**	**brej-t-ur**
'I gnaw'	'I gnawed'	'gnawed'
mba-j	**mbaj-t-a**	**mbaj-t-ur**
'I hold'	'I held'	'I held'

NOTE

Since verbs of this class end up with a consonant-final stem in the past definite, they take the same person endings in the singular as Conjugation II verbs.

SUBCLASS 3 includes the verbs **bëj** 'I make' and **hyj** 'I enter' and a few others which appear with a stem-extension **-r-** in the past definite (only in the singular) and participle:

Pres 1st Sg	Past Def 1st Sg	Participle
bë-j	**bë-r-a**	**bë-r-ë**
'I make'	'I made'	'made'
hy-j	**hy-r-a**	**hy-r-ë**
'I enter'	'I entered'	'entered'

B. Conjugation II

Conjugation II is divided into two classes.

CLASS I includes those verbs which have a single stem for the present, past definite and participle:

Pres 1st Sg	Past Def 1st Sg	Participle
hap	**hap-a**	**hap-ur**
'I open'	'I opened'	'opened'
vendos	**vendos-a**	**vendos-ur**
'I decide'	'I decided'	'decided'
mat	**mat-a**	**mat-ur**
'I measure'	'I measured'	'measured'

NOTE

Verbs of the type **ik-i** 'I go', **ik-ën** 'he goes, you go', **hip-i** 'I mount, I climb', **hip-ën** 'he climbs, mounts; you climb, mount', are also placed in this class, even though in the present they take the endings **-i**, **-ën**, **-ën** in the singular, unlike the other verbs in the class which exhibit bare stems in the present singular forms.

CLASS II includes those verbs which have different stem forms in different parts of the conjugation. This class has two subclasses:

SUBCLASS 1 is composed of those verbs which have the stem vowel **-e-**, **-je-** or **-a-** in the second and third person singular of the present indicative, but **-o-** in the past definite.

Variety a) verbs have the stem vowel **-e-** in the citation form.

Pres 1st Sg	Past Def 1st Sg	Participle
dredh	**drodh-a**	**dredh-ur**
'I twist'	'I twisted'	'twisted'
heq	**hoq-a**	**heq-ur**
'I pull'	'I pulled'	'pulled'
nxjerr	**nxor-a**	**nxjerr-ë**
'I take out'	'I took out'	'taken out'
vjel	**vol-a**	**vjel-ë**
'I harvest'	'I harvested'	'harvested'

NOTE

The verbs **pjek** 'I roast', **përpjek** 'I impact', **ndjek** 'I follow', and **djeg** 'I burn', which palatalize the final consonant of the stem (**k: q, g: gj**) are included here: e.g., **poq-a** 'I roasted', **dogj-a** 'I burned'.

Variety b) verbs have the stem vowel **-a-** or **-o-** in the citation form:

Pres 1st Sg	Past Def 1st Sg	Participle
dal	**dol-a**	**dal-ë**
'I emerge'	'I emerged'	'emerged'
marr	**mor-a**	**marr-ë**
'I take'	'I took'	'taken'

SUBCLASS 2 includes those verbs whose stem ends in **-ed** in the second and third person singular of the present indicative.

Variety a) verbs of the type **përkas** 'I belong' with a stem extension which has the form **-as** in the citation form.

Variety b) includes the verbs **shkas** 'I slip, **vras** 'I slay', **ngas** 'I drive', and **gërgas** 'I tease', whose citation form ends in **-as** but whose stem in the past definite and in the participle loses the final consonant and ends in a vowel. Because the stem of the past definite ends in a vowel, these verbs take the same person endings as conjugation I, class I, subclass 2 (**laj** 'I wash': **la-v-a** 'I washed'); **vras/vret** 'he kills, you kill', **vra-v-a** 'I slew' (**vra-më** 'we slew'), **vra-rë** 'slain'.

Variety c) verbs **shes** 'I sell', **pres** 'I await' (**prit-a** 'I awaited'), and **zbres** 'I descend' have citation forms ending in **-es** in their conjugation:

	'sell'	'await'	'descend'
Citation Form (1st Sg Pres)	**shes**	**pres**	**zbres**
2nd Sg Pres 3rd Sg Pres	**shet**	**pret**	**zbret**
2nd Pl Pres	**shit-ni**	**prit-ni**	**zbrit-ni**
1st Sg Past Def	**shit-a**	**prit-a**	**zbrit-a**
Participle	**shit-ur**	**prit-ur**	**zbrit-ur**

C. Conjugation III

Conjugation III is divided into three classes:

Class I verbs have the stem extension **-r** in the singular Past definite and change the stem vowel to **-u** in all forms of the past definite. The verbs in this class have citation forms ending in **-ë** or **-ie**, e.g., **vë** 'I put', **zë** 'I catch', **përzë** 'I dismiss', **nxë** 'I learn':

1st Sg Pres	1st Sg Past Def	1st Pl Past Def	Participle
vë	**vur-a**	**vu-më**	**vë-në**
'I put'	'I put'	'we put'	'put'
zë	**zur-a**	**zu-më**	**zë-në**
'I catch'	'I caught'	'we took'	'taken'
shpie	**shpur-a**	**shpu-më**	**shpë-në (shpur-ë)**
'I convey'	'I conveyed'	'we conveyed'	'conveyed'

NOTE

This class also includes the irregular suppletive verb **bie** 'I bring', **prur-a** 'I brought', **pru-më** 'we brought', **prurë** 'brought'.

CLASS II verbs have a consonant-final stem in the past definite. Included here are **di** 'I know', **fle** 'I sleep', and **ngre** 'I raise' which have the stem-extension **-t-** in the past definite:

di	**dit-a**	**dit-ur**
'I know'	'I knew'	'known'
fle	**fjet-a**	**fjet-ur**
'I sleep'	'I slept'	'slept'
ngre	**ngrit-a**	**ngrit-ur**
'I raise'	'I raised'	'raised'

NOTE

The irregular suppletive verbs **ha** 'I eat' and **rri** 'I sit, I stay', are also conjugated according to this paradigm in the present indicative:

ha	**hëngr-a**	**ngrë-në**
'I eat'	'I ate'	'eaten'
rri	**ndenj-a**	**ndenj-ur**
'I stay'	'I stayed'	'stayed'

CLASS III. This class includes the verbs **pi** 'I drink' and **shtie** 'I shoot' which in the first and second person singular of the past definite have the stem-extension **-v-**:

pi	**pi-v-a**	**pi-rë**
	'I drank'	'drunk'
shtie	**shti-v-a**	**shtë-në**
	'I shot'	'shot'

NOTE

The present indicative of the irregular suppletive verbs **lë** 'I let' (**la-shë** 'I let', **lë-në** 'let') and **bie** 'I fall' (**ra-shë** 'I fell', **rë-në** 'fallen') is also conjugated according to the paradigm of conjugation III.

D. Irregular Verbs

Irregular verbs are divided into two main groups: IRREGULAR SUPPLETIVE and IRREGULAR NON-SUPPLETIVE verbs.

a) Irregular suppletive verbs:

ja-m	**qe-shë**	**qe-në**
'I am'	'I was'	'been'
ka-m	**pat-a**	**pas-ur**
'I have'	'I had'	'had'
bie	**pru-r-a**	**pru-rë**
'I bring'	'I brought'	'brought'
ha	**hëngra**	**ngrë-në**
'I eat'	'I ate'	'eaten'
jap	**dha-shë**	**dhë-në**
'I give'	'I gave'	'given'
rri	**ndenj-a**	**ndenj-ur**
'I stay,	'I stayed,	'stayed,
I sit'	I sat'	sat'
shoh	**pa-shë**	**pa-rë**
'I see'	'I saw'	'seen'
vi-j	**erdh-a**	**ardh-ur**
'I come'	'I came'	'come'

b) Irregular non-suppletive verbs:

the-m	**tha-shë**	**thë-në**
'I say'	'I said'	'said'
dua	**desh-a**	**dash-ur**
'I want'	'I wanted'	'wanted'
lë	**la-shë**	**lë-në**
'I leave,	'I left,	'left,
let'	let'	let'
vdes	**vdiq-a**	**vdek-ur**
'I die'	'I died'	'dead'
vete	**vajt-a**	**vajt-ur**
'I go'	'I went'	'gone'

Other particulars about the conjugation of irregular verbs, especially **jam, kam, them, dua,** etc., will be discussed in later Sections.

2.2.3 Construction of Verb Core Forms

Grammatical forms in the verb core are divided into two major groups according to whether or not they reflect the person and number of the subject: FINITE and NON-FINITE forms. To the first group belong the different grammatical forms for the tenses of the indicative, admirative, subjunctive, optative and imperative moods, while the second group includes the invariable participial forms: the participle itself, **larë** 'washed'; the gerundive **duke larë** 'while (or) by washing, washing'; the non-finite negative form (privative) **pa larë** 'without washing'; as well as non-finite forms of the type **për të larë** 'to wash' and the "perfect participle" **me të larë** 'having washed'.

Finite and non-finite forms of verbs have two sets of inflectional forms--one set for the active voice and another for the non-active (passive, reflexive, and reciprocal voices).

A.   Active Indicative Finite Forms

A.1   Present Tense Forms

The verbs of Conjugation I appear with the following person endings in the present tense:

	Sg	Pl
1st	-j	-jmë
2nd	-n	-ni
3rd	-n	-jnë

Verbs of conjugation II, with the exception of **eci** 'I walk', **iki** 'I go', and **hipi** 'I mount' appear with the following endings for the present indicative:

	Sg	Pl
1st	- ∅	-im
2nd	- ∅	-ni
3rd	- ∅	-in

In the singular, the three verbs **eci** 'I walk', **iki** 'I go' and **hipi** 'I mount' appear with the personal ending **-i** in the first person and **-ën** in the other two persons:

	Sg			Pl		
1st	ec-i	ik-i	hip-i	ec-im	ik-im	hip-im
2nd	ec-ën	ik-ën	hip-ën	ec-ni	ik-ni	hip-ni
3rd	ec-ën	ik-ën	hip-ën	ec-in	ik-in	hip-in

Verbs of conjugation III appear with the endings:

	Sg	Pl
1st	- ∅	-më or -m
2nd	- ∅	-ni
3rd	- ∅	-në or -n

For all three persons in both the singular and the plural Conjugation I verbs have a stem that doesn't change. Only the verb **ble-j** 'I buy' changes stem vowel **-e-** to **-i-** in the second person plural: **bli-ni**.

Verbs of class I of conjugation II have an unchanging stem in the singular and plural.

Verbs of class II of conjugation II undergo the following changes in their stem.

Verbs of subclass 1 variety 2 (**dal** 'I emerge', **marr** 'I take', **rrah** 'I beat', **njoh** 'I recognize', **shoh** 'I see'), as well as those of subclass 2 (**përkas** 'I belong', **vras** 'I kill') and the irregular suppletive verb **jap** 'I give' change the stem vowel to **-e-** in the second and third person singular.

Verbs of subclass 2 (**përkas, vras**) change the stem-consonant **-s** to **-t** in the second and third person singular.

Verbs in class II change the stem vowel (or the sequence **-jé-**) into **-i-** for the second person plural (except for the verb **marr** 'I take' and **jap** 'I give' which keep the stem vowel **-e-**; **merr-ni** 'you take' and **jep-ni** 'you give'). The verbs **ndjek** 'I follow, I pursue', **pjek** 'I roast', **përpjek** 'I impact', and **djeg** 'I burn' also change **-k** to **-q** and **-g** to **-gj** for the second person plural.

In Conjugation III, all verbs of class I, the class II verbs **fle** 'I sleep' and **ngre** 'I raise' and Class III verbs with stem vowels **-e-** or **-ie-** (**shtie** and **bie**) change the stem vowel (or vowel cluster) to **-i-** in the second person plural.

1. Several irregular verbs also undergo changes in their stems in the present tense:

The verbs **jam** 'I am' and **kam** 'I have' in the second person singular as well as the first and second person plural change to **-e-** rather than **-a-**. **Jam** has a different stem altogether for the third person singular, **ësh-të**:

2.2.3 A.1 Present Tense Forms   **45**

	Sg	Pl	Sg	Pl
1st	ja-m	je-mi	ka-m	ke-mi
2nd	je	je-ni	ke	ke-ni
3rd	është	ja-në	ka	ka-në

The-m 'I say' has the stem vowel **-e-** in the first person plural as well as in the first person singular. In the second person singular, the stem vowel is **-ua (thua)**, while for the other forms, it is **-o-**:

	Sg	Pl
1st	the-m	the-mi
2nd	thua	tho-ni
3rd	tho-të	tho-në

Vi-j 'I come' in the second and third person singular has the stem **vje-**:

	Sg	Pl
1st	vij	vijmë
2nd	vje-n	vi-ni
3rd	vje-n	vi-jnë

Dua 'I want' has the **-ua** stem in the first and third person plural as well, but in the other forms of the present, has **-o-** instead:

	Sg	Pl
1st	dua	dua-m
2nd	do	do-ni
3rd	do	dua-n

Vete 'I go' in the singular has its stem expanded by **-te**, whereas in the plural, it occurs with an unexpanded stem:

	Sg	Pl
1st	ve-te	ve-mi
2nd	ve-te	ve-ni
3rd	ve-te	ve-në

2. The person endings for the irregular verbs, with the exception of **jam, kam,** and **them**, are in general the same as for verbs of the regular conjugations, and depend on the final sound of the stem. Thus the verb **vi-j** has the same person endings as the regular verb **fshi-j** 'I sweep' (Conjugation I). The verbs **jap, shoh,** and **vdes** (2nd Pl **vdis-ni**) are conjugated according to the paradigm for Conjugation II, while all the other irregular verbs, with the exception of **jam, kam,** and **them**, and in part **vete**, take the endings of Conjugation III.

The verbs **ja-m, ka-m** and **the-m**, in the first person singular take the ending **-m**. In the second person singular, they have a zero ending. In the third person singular, **jam** and **them** take the ending **-të**: **ësh-të, tho-të**, while **kam** has a zero ending **(ka)**. For the first person plural, they all take the ending **-mi**, while for the other two persons in the plural they take **-ni** and **-në** (like verbs of the type **ha** 'I eat' and **pi** 'I drink' of Conjugation III).

The verb **vete** in the first person plural takes the ending **-mi**: **ve-mi**, just like **je-mi, ke-mi, the-mi**, while for the other two persons in the plural it is conjugated according to conjugation III: **ve-ni, ve-në**, like **di-ni** 'you know', **di-në** 'they know'.

Table 2.4 displays the present tense conjugations of a sample verb from each subclass and variety of all three conjugations: **punoj** 'work' (I-I-1/a), **quaj** 'call' (I-I-1/b), **laj** 'wash' (I-I-2), **gjej** 'find'' (I-II-1), **mbaj** 'hold' (I-II-2), **bëj** 'make' (I-II-3), **hap** 'open' (II-I), **heq** 'pull' (II-II-1/a), **dal** 'emerge' (II-II-1/b), **humbas** 'lose' (II-II-2/a), **vras** 'injure' (II-II-2/b), **shes** 'sell' (II-II-2/c), **vë** 'put' (III-1), **fle** 'sleep' (III-II), **shtie** 'insert' (III-III).

Table 2.4 Present Tense Conjugations of Sample Verbs								
	I-I-l/a	I-I-l/b	I-I-2	I-II-1	I-II-2	I-II-3	II-I	II-II-1/a
1st Sg Pres	puno-j	qua-j	la-j	gje-j	mba-j	bë-j		heq
2nd Sg Pres	puno-n	qua-n	la-n	gje-n	mba-n	bë-n	hap	
3rd Sg Pres								
1st Pl Pres	puno-jmë	qua-jmë	la-jmë	gje-jmë	mba-jmë	bë-jmë	hap-im	heq-im
2nd Pl Pres	puno-ni	qua-ni	la-ni	gje-ni	mba-ni	bë-ni	hap-ni	heq-ni
3rd Pl Pres	puno-jnë	qua-jnë	la-jnë	gje-jnë	mba-jnë	bë-jnë	hap-in	heq-in

	II-II-1/b	II-II-2/a	II-II-2/b	II-II-2/c	III-1	III-II	III-III	
1st Sg Pres	dal	humbas	vras	shes			shtie	
2nd Sg Pres	del	humbet	vret	shet	vë	fle		
3rd Sg Pres								
1st Pl Pres	dalim	humbasim	vrasim	shesim	vëmë	flemë	shtiem	
2nd Pl Pres	dilni	humbitni	vritni	shitni	vini	flini	shtini	
3rd Pl Pres	dalin	humbasin	vrasin	shesin	vënë	flenë	shtienë	

A.2 Past Time Tenses

A.2a. Imperfect Tense Forms

The majority of verbs in the imperfect tense have a stem identical to that of the citation form. However, those verbs which change their stem vowel and/or consonant in the second person plural form of the present tense undergo the same change in the imperfect. For example, compare:

	1st Sg Pres	2nd Pl Pres	1st Sg Imperf
'pull, remove'	heq	hiq-ni	hiq-ja
'bake, roast'	pjek	piq-ni	piq-ja
'kill, slay'	vras	vrit-ni	vrit-ja
'catch, take'	zë	zi-ni	zi-ja
'fall'	bie	bi-ni	bi-ja

The verbs **jam, kam,** and **them** have special stems in the imperfect: **ish-a** 'I used to be, I was', **kish-a** 'I used to have, I had', and **thosh-a** 'I used to say, I was saying'.

All verbs, including irregular ones (except **jam** and **kam**) take the following person endings in the imperfect:

	Sg	Pl
1st	-ja	-nim
2nd	-je	-nit
3rd	-te (-nte)	-nin

The third person singular ending **-nte** is taken by verbs with a vowel final stem.

	'pull'	'kill'	'put'	'open'
	heq	**vras**	**vĕ**	**hap**
Sg				
1st	hiq-ja	vrit-ja	vi-ja	hap-ja
2nd	hiq-je	vrit-je	vi-je	hap-je
3rd	hiq-te	vris-te	vi-nte	hap-te
Pl				
1st	hiq-nim	vrit-nim	vi-nim	hap-nim
2nd	hiq-nit	vrit-nit	vi-nit	hap-nit
3rd	hiq-nin	vrit-nin	vi-nin	hap-nin

The verbs **jam** and **kam** take the endings **-a, -e, -te** in the singular and **-im, -it, -in** in the plural:

	'have'	'be'	'wash'	'call'
	kam	**jam**	**laj**	**quaj**
Sg				
1st	kish-a	ish-a	la-ja	qua-ja
2nd	kish-e	ish-e	la-je	qua-je
3rd	kish-te	ish-te	la-nte	qua-nte
	or kish	or ish		
Pl				
1st	kish-im	ish-im	la-nim	qua-nim
2nd	kish-it	ish-it	la-nit	qua-nit
3rd	kish-in	ish-in	la-nin	qua-nin

A.2b. Past Definite Forms

As mentioned earlier, the majority of verbs in the past definite appear with the same stem that they have in the citation form stem, but a number of verbs also appear with an extended stem, such as **di-t-a** 'I knew', **mbaj-t-a** 'I kept, held', **bĕ-r-a** 'I made'; or with a stem minus its citation form extension, such as **plas-a** 'I burst', **nga-va** 'I drove' (whose citation forms are **pĕlc-as** and **nga-s**); or with a stem with vowel or consonant changes, or both, such as **shit-a** 'I sold', **prit-a** 'I waited', **zbrit-a** 'I descended', **ngrit-a** 'I raised' (compare: **shes, pres, zbres, ngre**). These modified stems are often closely related to the participle (see Section 2.2.5.A), but they may also reflect a sound change (as in **hoq-a** 'I removed, pulled', **poq-a** 'I baked', **dol-a** 'I emerged'; compare **heq, pjek, dal**), that is not related to the participial form (**hequr, pjekur, dalĕ**).

The overwhelming majority of verbs (including the majority of irregular verbs) take the person endings **-a, -e, -i/-u** in the singular, and all verbs (including the majority of irregular verbs) take the person endings **-(ĕ)m(ĕ), -(ĕ)t(ĕ),** and **-(ĕ)n(ĕ)** in the plural.

The 3rd Sg ending **-u** appears on verbs whose stem ends in a back consonant (**-k, -g,** or **-h**), such as **prek-u** 'he touched' **lag-u** 'he wetted', **kreh-u** 'he combed', or with the final vowel **-a, -e,** or **-i,** such as **la-u** 'he washed', **ble-u** 'he bought', **fshi-u** 'he swept'. Verbs that have vowel-final stems extend the stem with **-v-** before the person endings for first and second singular: **puno-v-a** 'I worked', **puno-v-e** 'you worked'; **la-v-a** 'I washed', **la-v-e** 'you (Sg) washed'.

In the plural, verbs with a vowel-final stem appear with the allomorph endings **-mĕ/-m, -tĕ/-t, -nĕ/-n,** the initial **-ĕ-** of the ending dropping after a vowel, by the general rule mentioned in Chapter 1. The forms **-m, -t, -n** are the allomorphs of **-mĕ, -tĕ, -nĕ** resulting from the dropping of the final unstressed **-ĕ,** after an unstressed syllable, as happens in all verbs with the vowel cluster **-úa-** or **-ýe-** in the plural. Compare: **la-mĕ** 'we washed', **la-tĕ** 'you (Pl) washed', **la-nĕ** 'they washed', **vra-mĕ** 'we slew', **vra-tĕ** 'you (Pl) slew', **vra-nĕ** 'they slew' on the one hand, with **punua-m** 'we worked', **punua-t** 'you (Pl) worked', **punua-n** 'they worked'; **lye-m** 'we painted', **lye-t** 'you (Pl) painted', **lye-n** 'they painted' on the other.

Verbs with stem-final consonants appear with the allomorph endings **-ëm, -ët, -ën** for the plural of the past definite, the final **-ë-** dropping by the rule just cited: **hap-ëm** 'we opened', **hap-ët** 'you (Pl) opened', **hap-ën** 'they opened'; **plas-ëm** 'we burst', **plas-ët** 'you (Pl) burst', **plas-ën** 'they burst'; **gjet-ëm** 'we found', **gjet-ët** 'you (Pl) found', **gjet-ën** 'they found'; **hëngr-ëm** 'we ate', **hëngr-ët** 'you (Pl) ate', **hëngr-ën** 'they ate'; **desh-ëm** 'we wanted', **desh-ët** 'you (Pl) wanted', **desh-ën** 'they wanted', etc.

The irregular verbs **bie** 'I fall', **jam** 'I am', **shoh** 'I see', **lë** 'I let', **them** 'I say', whose past definite stems are, respectively, **ra, qe, pa, la, tha** take the special ending **-shë** in the first person singular of the past definite: **ra-shë** 'I fell', **qe-shë** 'I was', **pa-shë** 'I saw', **la-shë** 'I let', **tha-shë** 'I said'. In the plural these verbs take the regular endings **-më, -të, -në**, like other verbs with a stem final vowel: **ra-më, ra-të, ra-në**. In the second person singular the result of adding **e** to an irregular stem ending in **-a** is simply **-e**: **re** 'you fell', **pe** 'you saw', **le** 'you le(f)t', **the**, 'you said'. The special third person singular ending with irregular stems is zero.

Below is a sample of verb conjugations in the past definite, including the auxiliaries and a few others:

	'have'	'be'	'wash'	'call, name'
	kam	**jam**	**laj**	**quaj**
Sg				
1st	**pat-a**	**qe-shë**	**la-v-a**	**quajt-a**
2nd	**pat-e**	**qe**	**la-v-e**	**quajt-e**
3rd	**pat-i**	**qe**	**la-u**	**quajt-i**
Pl				
1st	**pat-ëm**	**qe-me**	**la-me**	**quajt-ëm**
2nd	**pat-ët**	**qe-të**	**la-të**	**quajt-ët**
3rd	**pat-ën**	**qe-në**	**la-në**	**quajt-ën**

	'open'	'pull, remove'	'slay'	'put'
	hap	**heq**	**vras**	**vë**
Sg				
1st	**hap-a**	**hoq-a**	**vra-v-a**	**vur-a**
2nd	**hap-e**	**hoq-e**	**vra-v-e**	**vur-e**
3rd	**hap-i**	**hoq-i**	**vra-u**	**vur-i**
Pl				
1st	**hap-ëm**	**hoq-ëm**	**vra-më**	**vu-më**
2nd	**hap-ët**	**hoq-ët**	**vra-të**	**vu-të**
3rd	**hap-ën**	**hoq-ën**	**vra-në**	**vu-në**

A.2c. Present Perfect Tense Forms

The present perfect is a compound tense of a present tense form of **kam** plus a participle; **kam (ke, ka, kemi, keni, kanë) larë** 'I (you...) have washed'; **kam (ke, ka, kemi, keni, kanë) hapur** 'I (you...) have opened'.

A.2d. Past Perfect Tense Forms

The past perfect is a compound tense composed of an imperfect form of **kam** plus a participle: **kisha (kishe, kishte, kishim, kishit, kishin) larë'** 'I (you...) had washed'; **kisha**

(kishe, kishte, kishim, kishit, kishin) hapur 'I (you...) had opened'.

NOTE

In the spoken language and occasionally also in writing, one encounters doubly compounded forms of the perfect and past perfect to form REMOTE perfects and past perfects. These are constructed by placing an older perfect or past perfect form of the verb **kam**--using an alternative participial form **pasë**-- before a participle, e.g., **kam pasë larë** 'I have washed (some time ago)'.

A.2e. Pluperfect Forms

The pluperfect is constructed by placing a form of the past definite of **kam** before the participle: **pata (pate, pati, patëm, patët, patën) larë** 'I (you...) had washed'; **pata (pate, pati, patëm, patët, patën) hapur** 'I (you...) had opened'.

A.3 Future Time Tenses

A.3a. Future Tense Forms

In present day standard Albanian, the future tense is constructed by placing **do** before a present subjunctive verb form (see Section 2.2.3.C.1).

	kam 'have'	jam 'be'	laj 'wash'	hap 'open'	vë 'put'
Sg					
1st	do të ke-m	do të je-m	do të la-j	do të hap	do të vë
2nd	do të ke-sh	do të je-sh	do të la-sh	do të hap-ësh	do të vë-sh
3rd	do të ke-të	do të je-të	do të la-jë	do të hap-ë	do të vër-ë
Pl					
1st	do të ke-mi	do të je-mi	do të la-jmë	do të hap-im	do të vë-më
2nd	do të ke-ni	do të je-ni	do të la-ni	do të hap-ni	do të vi-ni
3rd	do të ke-në	do të je-në	do të la-jnë	do të hap-in	do të vë-në

NOTE

Gheg varieties of Albanian have a future tense composed of **kam** + **me** + *short form of the participle,* e.g., **ka me shkue** 'he will go'. In recent years a hybrid form of the future has developed in standard Albanian on this model. The hybrid construction replaces the Gheg infinitive (**me** + *short form of the participle*) with the Tosk infinitive (**për** + **të** + **participle**), yielding forms like **kam (ke, ka, kemi, keni, kanë) për të larë** 'I (you, he...) will wash'; **kam (ke, ka, kemi, keni, kanë) për të hapur** 'I (you, he...) will open'. For some speakers, this construction has a modal nuance of obligation, similar to English 'I have washing to do', or even 'I have to wash'.

A.3b. Future Perfect Forms

THE FUTURE PERFECT is a compound tense composed of a future tense form of **kam** plus a participle:

	'will have washed'	'will have opened'
Sg	**do të kem larë**	**do të kem hapur**
	do të kesh larë	**do të kesh hapur**
	do të ketë larë	**do të ketë hapur**
Pl	**do të kemi larë**	**do të kemi hapur**
	do të keni larë	**do të keni hapur**
	do të kenë larë	**do të kenë hapur**

A.3c. Past Future Forms

THE PAST FUTURE is a compound tense composed of the particle **do** plus the subjunctive form of the imperfect:

'I (you...) was going to have'	'I (you...) was going to be'
kam	**jam**
do të kisha	**do të isha**
do të kishe	**do të ishe**
do të kishte (kish)	**do të ishte (ish)**
do të kishim	**do të ishim**
do të kishit	**do të ishit**
do të kishin	**do të ishin**

'I (you...) was going to wash'	'I (you...) was going to open'	'I (you...) was going to put'
laj	**hap**	**vë**
do të laja	**do të hapja**	**do të vija**
do të laje	**do të hapje**	**do të vije**
do të lante	**do të hapte**	**do të vinte**
do të lanim	**do të hapnim**	**do të vinim**
do të lanit	**do të hapnit**	**do të vinit**
do të lanin	**do të hapnin**	**do të vinin**

Much less commonly a past future is constructed with the imperfect forms of **kam** and a following non-finite phrase of the type **për të larë: kisha (kishe, kishte,** etc.) **për të larë** 'I (you, he, etc.) was going to wash', **kisha (kishe, kishte,** etc.) **për të hapur** 'I (you, he, etc) was going to open'. (See preceding NOTE.)

A.3d. Past Future Perfect Forms

THE PAST FUTURE PERFECT is constructed by placing a form of the past future of the auxiliary **kam** before a participle: **do të kisha (kishe,** etc.) **larë** 'I (you, etc.) would have washed'; **do të kisha (kishe,** etc.) **hapur** 'I (you, etc.) would have opened'.

B. Admirative Mood Forms

B.1 Present Admirative Forms

This tense of the admirative is constructed by suffixing the person forms of the present tense of the auxiliary **kam** to a short form of the participle, with the forms of **kam** losing their stress. The present tense of the admirative is a synthetic form created by compounding in inverted order the two formative elements of the present perfect tense. In the third person plural, the second element of this form loses its final unstressed -**ë** because it now follows an unstressed syllable:

'I have'	'I am'	'I wash'	'I open'	'I put'
kam (pasur)	jam (qenë)	laj (larë)	hap (hapur)	vë (vënë)
pas-kam	qen-kam	la-kam	hap-kam	vën-kam
pas-ke	qen-ke	la-ke	hap-ke	vën-ke
pas-ka	qen-ka	la-ka	hap-ka	vën-ka
pas-kemi	qen-kemi	la-kemi	hap-kemi	vën-kemi
pas-keni	qen-keni	la-keni	hap-keni	vën-keni
pas-kan	qen-kan	la-kan	hap-kan	vën-kan

B.2 Imperfect Admirative Forms

The imperfect admirative is created by suffixing the imperfect tense forms of **kam** to the short form of the participle. In this construction, these suffixed forms of **kam**, being unstressed, have undergone several phonetic changes: the stem vowel has been reduced to **ë**, and the 3rd Sg ending has been dropped. An alternant 3rd Sg form **-kej** is used in some varieties of Standard Albanian.

'I used to have'	'I used to be'	'I used to wash'	'I used to open'	'I used to put'
kam	**jam**	**laj**	**hap**	**vë**
pas-kësha	qen-kësha	la-kësha	hap-kësha	vën-kësha
pas-këshe	qen-këshe	la-këshe	hap-këshe	vën-këshe
pas-kësh	qen-kësh	la-kësh	hap-kësh	vën-kësh
(pas-kej)	(qen-kej)	(la-kej)	(hap-kej)	(vën-kej)
pas-këshim	qen-këshim	la-këshim	hap-këshim	vën-këshim
pas-këshit	qen-këshit	la-këshit	hap-këshit	vën-këshit
pas-këshin	qen-këshin	la-këshin	hap-këshin	vën-këshin

B.3 Present Perfect Admirative Forms

The present perfect admirative tense is composed of the present admirative form of **kam** plus a participle: **paskam (paske, paska, paskemi, paskeni, paskan) larë** 'I (you...) have actually washed'; **paskam (paske, paska, paskemi, paskeni, paskan) hapur** 'I (you...) have actually opened'.

B.4 Past Perfect Admirative Forms

The past perfect admirative tense is composed of the imperfect admirative forms of **kam** plus a participle: **paskësha (paskëshe, paskësh, paskëshim, paskëshit, paskëshin) larë** 'I (you...) had washed'; **paskësha (paskëshe, etc.) hapur** 'I (you...) had opened'.

NOTE

Occasionally one encounters doubly compounded forms for the admirative remote perfect (of the type **paska pasë larë** 'he had actually washed') and for the future (of the type **do të laka** 'he will actually wash').

C. Subjunctive Mood Forms

The mark of the subjunctive mood is the particle **të** plus the present or imperfect tense forms of the verb.

C.1 Present Subjunctive Forms

After the particle **të** all the present subjunctive plural forms are the same as in the present indicative. In the present subjunctive singular, however, only the first person forms of the subjunctive are identical to those of the indicative. As indicated in Table 2.5, for the second and third person singular of the present subjunctive, the stem used is generally the same as for the citation form of the verb, and thus unlike many of the corresponding 2nd and 3rd Sg stem forms in the indicative.

Table 2.5 Indicative/Subjunctive Stem Differences		
	Ind Sg	**Sub Sg**
1st	**dal**	**të dal**	'emerge'
2nd	**del**	**të dal-ësh**	
3rd	**del**	**të dal-ë**	
1st	**jap**	**të jap**	'give'
2nd	**jep**	**të jap-ësh**	
3rd	**jep**	**të jap-ë**	
1st	**shoh**	**të shoh**	'see'
2nd	**sheh**	**të shoh-ësh**	
3rd	**sheh**	**të shoh-ë**	
1st	**flas**	**të flas**	'speak'
2nd	**flet**	**të flas-ësh**	
3rd	**flet**	**të flas-ë**	
1st	**vras**	**të vras**	'kill'
2nd	**vret**	**të vras-ësh**	
3rd	**vret**	**të vras-ë**	
1st	**zbraz**	**të zbraz**	'descend'
2nd	**zbret**	**të zbraz-ësh**	
3rd	**zbret**	**të zbraz-ë**	

The verbs **jam** and **kam** have the stems **je-** and **ke-** respectively for all persons (singular and plural) in the present subjunctive: **të je-m** 'that I be', **të ke-m** 'that I have', etc.

The verb **ve-te** 'I go' has its stem expansion **-te** only in the first person singular of the present subjunctive: **të vete, të vesh, të vejë**, etc.

The verbs **ngre** 'I lift' and **fle** 'I sleep' (conjugation III, class II), **vë** 'I put', **zë** 'I catch', **nxë** 'I learn', **përzë** 'I dismiss', **shpie** 'I take to, I carry', and **bie** 'I bring' (conjugation III, class I), **shtie** 'I shoot' (conjugation III, class III), as well as the verb **lë**, have their stem extended by **-r** in the third person singular of the present subjunctive: **të ngre-r-ë, të fle-r-ë, të vë-r-ë, të zë-r-ë, të nxë-r-ë, të përzë-r-ë, të shpje-r-ë, të bje-r-ë, të shtje-r-ë, të lë-r-ë**.

For all verbs, the only person endings of the subjunctive which differ from those of the indicative are the ones for the second and third person singular of the present tense: **-(ë)sh** and **-ë**. The form **-ësh** appears after a consonant-final stem. Verbs which have a stem-final vowel in the third person singular add **-j** before the ending **-ë**: **të la-j-ë** 'that he washes', **të shkrua-j-ë** 'that he writes', etc.

The verbs **jam, kam** and **them** also take the normal endings, but for the third person singular, they extend the stem by **-t**: **të je-t-ë, të ke-t-ë, të tho-t-ë**. Compare these with the corresponding forms of the present indicative: **ësh-të, ka,** and **tho-të**. Following are sample paradigms for selected verbs in the present subjunctive:

kam	jam	laj	hap	vë
'have'	'be'	'wash'	'open'	'put'

të ke-m	të je-m	të la-j	të hap	të vë
të ke-sh	të je-sh	të la-sh	të hap-ësh	të vë-sh
të ke-t-ë	të je-t-ë	të la-j-ë	të hap-ë	të vë-r-ë
të ke-mi	të je-mi	të la-jmë	të hap-im	të vë-më
të ke-ni	të je-ni	të la-ni	të hap-ni	të vi-ni
të ke-në	të je-në	të la-jnë	të hap-in	të vë-në

C.2 Past Time Subjunctive Tenses

C.2a. Imperfect Subjunctive Forms

In the imperfect tense, after the particle **të** all verbs have the same forms for the subjunctive mood as they do for the indicative. For example, compare the indicative and subjunctive imperfect forms for 1st, 2nd, and 3rd Sg below:

	'wash'		'open'		'go'	
	Ind	Sub	Ind	Sub	Ind	Sub
1st	laja	të laja	hapja	të hapja	vija	të vija
2nd	laje	të laje	hapje	të hapje	vije	të vije
3rd	lante	të lante	hapte	të hapte	vinte	të vinte

C.2b. Present Perfect Subjunctive Forms

This tense is composed of the present subjunctive forms of **kam** plus a participle: **të kem (të kesh, të ketë, të kemi, të keni, të kenë) larë** 'that I (you...) have washed'; **të kem (të kesh, të ketë, të kemi, të keni, të kenë) hapur** 'that I (you...) have opened'.

C.2c. Past Perfect Subjunctive Forms

This tense is composed of the imperfect subjunctive forms of **kam** plus a participle: **të kisha (të kishe, të kishte, të kishim, të kishit, të kishin) larë** 'that I (you...) had washed'; **të kisha (të kishe**, etc.) **hapur** 'that I (you...) had opened'.

NOTE

The so-called SUBJUNCTIVE ADMIRATIVE MOOD is composed of the admirative preceded by the subjunctive particle **të**. This mood is rarely encountered, and then chiefly in the imperfect or past perfect: **të qenkësha** 'that I actually was', **të qenkëshe** 'that you actually were', etc.

D. Optative Mood Forms

D.1 Present Optative Forms

Present optative forms are constructed by adding the following person endings to the special optative stem:

	Sg	Pl
1st	-a	-im
2nd	- ∅	-i
3rd	-të	-in

The special stem of the optative is constructed with the stem-forming suffix **-fsh/-sh/-f**. This suffix is attached to a verb stem which in the majority of cases is identical to the stem of the past definite, but in some cases to the stem of the participle, where this differs from that of the past definite. When the stem to which this suffix is attached ends in a vowel, the allomorph **-fsh** is used; if it ends in the consonant **n** or **sh**, the allomorph **-ç** is used; otherwise **-sh** is the allomorph chosen.

The allomorph **-fsh** forms the optative stems of:

1. The overwhelming majority of the verbs of conjugation I, with the exception of subclass 1 of class II: **la-fsh-a** 'may I wash', **the-fsh-a** 'may I break', **shkro-fsh-a** 'may I write'.

2. The verbs of subclass 3 of class II of conjugation II (**vras** 'I slay', **shkas** 'I slip', **ngas** 'I drive', **gërgas** 'I tease', and **pres** 'I cut'): **vra-fsh-a, shka-fsh-a, nga-fsh-a, gërga-fsh-a, pre-fsh-a.**

3. The verbs of conjugation III (**pi** 'I drink', **shtie** 'I shoot'): **pi-fsh-a, shti-fsh-a.**

4. The irregular verbs **bie** 'I bring' (**prura** 'I brought'), **bie** 'I fall' (**rashë** 'I fell'), **shoh** 'I see', **vete** 'I go',: **pru-fsh-a, ra-fsh-a, pa-fsh-a, va-fsh-a,** (the last being constructed with the truncated stem of the past definite **vajt-a** 'I went'); as well as **jam: qo-fsh-a,** constructed with the stem of the past definite **qe-shë** 'I used to be', modified to **qo-**.

The allomorph **-sh** forms the optative of stems of:

1. The majority of the verbs of conjugation II, with the exception of those of subclass 3, class II: **hap-sh-a** 'may I open', **heq-sh-a** 'may I remove, may I pull', **mat-sh-a'** 'may I measure', **bërtit-sh-a** 'may I yell', etc.

2. The verbs of subclass 1, class II, of conjugation I, which appear with a consonant final stem in the past definite: **gjet-sh-a** 'may I find', **mbajt-sh-a** 'may I hold', **mbrojt-sh-a** 'may I defend'.

3. The verbs of conjugation III, class II: **dit-sh-a, fjet-sh-a, ngrit-sh-a.**

4. The irregular verbs **ha** 'I eat', **dua** 'I want', **rri** 'I stay', **vij** 'I come', **vdes** 'I die': **hëngër-sh-a, ndenj-sh-a, ardh-sh-a, vdek-sh-a.**

The allomorph **-ç** forms the optative stems of:

1. The verbs of conjugation III, class 1: **vën-ç-a, zën-ç-a, përzën-ç-a, nxën-ç-a, shpën-ç-a** (also **shpu-fsh-a**);

2. Those verbs of conjugation II whose stems end in **-sh**; **qesh-ç-a.**

3. Those irregular verbs whose optative stems end in **-n** or **-sh**: **thën-ç-a** (them), **dhën-ç-a** (jap), **lën-ç-a** (lë), **dash-ç-a** (dua);

4. The irregular verb **kam: pa-ç-a**.

NOTES

1. Verbs of subclass 1, class II, of conjugation I, like **heq** 'I pull'/**hoq-a** 'I pulled', **vjel** 'I harvest'/**vol-a** 'I harvested', **dal** 'I emerge'/**dol-a** 'I emerged' form the stem of the optative from a stem common to the present tense and the participle: **heq-sh-a, vjel-sh-a, dal-sh-a**.

2. Verbs which have a participle that ends in **-në**, with the exception of the verbs **jam, ha**, and **bie** 'fall', construct the stem of the optative from the participle: **vën-ç-a, zën-ç-a, përzën-ç-a, nxën-ç-a, lën-ç-a, dhën-ç-a**.

3.   The verbs **vij, dua**, and **vdes** also form the optative stem from the stem of the participle: **ardh-sh-a (ardhur), dash-ç-a (dashur), vdek-sh-a (vdekur)**.

4.   All other verbs form the optative from a stem identical to that used for the past definite singular.

A sample paradigm of the present optative for selected verbs appears below:

	kam	**jam**	**laj**	**hap**	**vë**
1st Sg	paç-a	qo-fsh-a	la-fsh-a	hap-sh-a	vën-ç-a
2nd Sg	paç	qo-fsh	la-fsh	hap-sh	vën-ç
3rd Sg	pas-të	qo-f-të	la-f-të	hap-të	vën-të
1st Pl	paç-im	qo-fsh-im	la-fsh-im	hap-sh-im	vën-ç-im
2nd Pl	paç-i	qo-fsh-i	la-fsh-i	hap-sh-i	vën-ç-i
3rd Pl	paç-in	qo-fsh-in	la-fsh-in	hap-sh-in	vën-ç-in

D.2 Present Perfect Optative Forms

The forms of this tense are constructed by placing the optative forms of **kam** before a participle: **paça larë** 'I wish I had (may I have, if only I had) washed', **paç larë** 'I wish you had (may you have, if only you had) washed', **pastë larë** 'I wish he had (may he have, if only he had) washed', **paçim larë** 'I wish we had (may we have, if only we had) washed', **paçi larë** 'I wish you had (may you have, if only you had) washed', **paçin larë** 'I wish they had (may they have, if only they had) washed'.)

E. Imperative Mood Forms

This mood has forms only for the second person singular and plural.

The imperative plural for all verbs has the same form as the second person plural of the present indicative (see Section 2.2.3.A.1 for these). These two homonymous forms are distinguished from one another by the contexts in which they appear. In writing, an exclamation point (!) is used in Albanian to mark imperative sentences. Although English does not usually use the exclamation point this way, we will use it here in the glosses to mark the verb as imperative. Compare: **(ju) punoni** '(you) work' vs. **punoni!** 'work!'; **(ju) dilni** '(you) emerge' vs. **dilni!** 'emerge!'; **(ju) vilni** '(you) harvest' vs. **vilni!** 'harvest!'; **(ju) vini** '(you) come' vs. **vini!** 'come!'. Only a small number of verbs have the same form in the second person singular of the present indicative as in the imperative singular. These are:

1.   The verbs of class I of conjugation II: **(ti) hap** '(you) open' vs. **hap!** 'open!', **(ti) mat** '(you) measure' vs. **mat!** 'measure!'.

2.   The verbs of conjugation III (**di** 'I know', **pi** 'I drink'): **(ti) pi** vs. **pi!**, '(you) drink' vs. 'drink!'

3.   The irregular suppletive verbs **ha** 'eat', **rri** 'sit, stay', **jap** 'I give': **(ti) ha** vs. **ha!** 'eat!', **(ti) jep** vs. **jep!** 'give!'.

The verbs which have different forms for the singular imperative from those of the second person singular of the present indicative can be divided into four groups:

1.   Verbs of conjugation I with stems in **-o-, -e-** (except **brej** 'I gnaw', **gjej** 'I find', and **blej**) 'I buy', as well as all those in **-i-**, take no ending in the singular imperative: **mëso** 'learn!', **puno** 'work!', **shko** 'go!', **rrëfe** 'tell!', **shpërble** 'compensate, reward!', **fshi** 'sweep!', **përpi** 'swallow up!'

NOTE

But note that **bre-j** 'gnaw!', **gje-j** 'find!', are like the verbs of group 2 below, and **bli** 'buy!' is like the verbs of group 3 below.

2. All other verbs of conjugation I (with the exception of those of group 1 above, and the verb **hyj** 'I enter') and the irregular verbs **them** and **dua** in the imperative singular have the ending **-j**: **mba-j** 'keep! hold!', **la-j** 'wash!', **mbru-j** 'knead!', **fry-j** 'blow!', **shkrua-j** 'write!', **lua-j** 'play!', **lye-j** 'paint!', **thye-j** 'break!', **përzie-j** 'mix!', **bë-j** 'do!, make!'; **thua-j** 'tell!' **dua-j** 'like!, love!'.

3. Verbs whose imperative plural has the stem vowel **-i-** form the imperative singular by removing the **-ni** suffix from the plural form: **hiq** 'pull!' (**heq**), **vil** 'harvest!' (**vjel**), **mbill** 'plant!, sow!' (**mbjell**), **nxirr** 'take out!' (**nxjerr**), **dil** 'emerge!' (**dal**), **piq** 'bake!' (**pjek**), **digj** 'burn!' (**djeg**), **bërtit** 'yell!' (**bërtas**), **thërrit** 'call out!' (**thërres**), **fli** 'sleep!' (**fle**), (**mos e**) **ngri** '(don't) lift (it)!' (**ngre**), **ji** 'be!' (**jam**), **ki** 'have!' (**kam**), **shih** 'see!' (**shoh**), **vdis** 'die!' (**vdes**), (**mos e**) **vrit**! '(don't) kill (it)!' (**vras**), (**mos e**) **ngit**! '(don't) drive (it)!' (**ngas**), (**mos e**) **gërgit**! '(don't) incite (it)' (**gërgas**), (**mos e**) **prit**! '(don't) cut (it)!' (**pres**).

4. Verbs which have an **-r-** extended stem in the third person singular of the present subjunctive use that same stem for the imperative singular:

a) The verbs of conjugation III: **vë** 'put', **zë** 'catch', **përzë** 'dismiss', **shtie** 'shoot', **shpie** 'take to': **vër, zër, përzër, shtjer, shpjer**;

b) the verb **hyj** 'I enter' of conjugation I, as well as the irregular verbs **bie** 'fall' and **lë** 'let'; **hyr, bjer, lër**.

NOTES

1. The verbs of subclass 3, class II of conjugation II (**vras, ngas, gërgas, pres** 'I cut') have a more common singular imperative form that is identical to the stem of the past definite: (**mos e**) **vra**! '(don't) kill (it)!' (**mos e**) **nga**! '(don't) drive (it)!' (**mos e**) **gërga**! '(don't) incite (it)!' (**mos e**) **pre**! '(don't) cut (it)!'

2. The verb **flas** 'I speak' has **fol** for the singular imperative, but **flit-ni** for the plural, identical to the second person plural of the present indicative.

3. The irregular verb **vij** 'I come' appears in the imperative as **eja, ejani**.

4. The irregular verb **vete** 'I go' does not have a special form in the imperative. The second person singular and plural of the subjunctive are used instead: **të vesh** '(that you) go', **të veni** '(that you) go (pl.)'.

When a singular imperative form ends in a vowel and is followed by a pronominal clitic of a personal pronoun, **-j-** is added to the verb form and the clitic is suffixed after it, as in **mëso-j-e** 'learn it!', **shpërble-j-e** 'reward him!':

Ndihmo-j-e shokun! 'Help (your) comrade!' **Rrëfe-j-u shokëve!** 'Tell (your) comrades!', **Trego-j-i të gjitha me radhë!** 'Show them all one after another!'

However, when an imperative is followed by the clitic form of the third person singular pronoun **i** followed by another short form or the reflexive non-active clitic **u**, a **-j-** is not inserted between the two vowels; rather, the short form **i** is written as **-j-**:

Hapja derën mikut! 'Open the door for your friend!'
Përvishju punës menjëherë! 'Get to work at once!'

This observation is also valid on those occasions where the pronominal clitic is inserted after the stem, but before the person ending for the plural of the imperative:

Ndihmo-j-e-ni shokun! 'Help (your) comrade!'
Trego-ja-ni shokut të vërtetën! 'Tell (your) comrade the truth!'.

After the negative particle **mos**, the pronominal clitic precedes rather than follows the verb stem, and is written with a space before the verb. Compare:

2.2.3 E. Imperative Mood Forms   **57**

	Positive		Negative
	digje 'burn it!'		**mos e digj** 'don't burn it!'
	věreni 'put it!'		**mos e vini** 'don't put it!'
	tregojini 'tell him!'		**mos i tregoni** 'don't tell him!'
	hapja derën mikut		**mos ja hap derën mikut**
	'open the door for (your) friend!'		'don't open the door for (your) friend!'

2.2.4 Non-Active Voice Forms

As was explained in Section 2.1.3.B, non-active verbal forms are used to express the passive, reflexive, and middle voices. What marks a verb form as non-active may be 1) its distinctive endings, 2) the clitic, 3) the auxiliary verb **jam** followed by a participle.

A. Non-Active Forms Marked by Endings

The non-active forms of the present indicative and subjunctive, the imperfect indicative and subjunctive, as well as the future (of the type **do të lahem** 'I will wash myself') and the past future (of the type **do të lahesha** 'I was going to wash myself'), have distinctive non-active endings, following the non-active stem formative **-he-** (after vowel ending stem) or **-e-** (after consonant-ending stem).

A.1 Present Tense Non-Active Forms

The person endings for the present tense of the non-active conjugation are: **-m, -sh, -t, -mi, -ni, -n**. These endings are added to the same verb stem form as used in the second person plural of the present tense active:

		Citation form	2nd Pl Act	3rd Sg Non-Act
'open'		**hap**	**hap-ni**	**hap-e-t**
'wash'		**laj**	**la-ni**	**la-he-t**
'pull'		**heq**	**hiq-ni**	**hiq-e-t**
'sow'		**mbjell**	**mbill-ni**	**mbill-e-t**
'roast'		**pjek**	**piq-ni**	**piq-e-t**
'burn'		**djeg**	**digj-ni**	**digj-e-t**
'kill'		**vras**	**vrit-ni**	**vrit-e-t**
'speak'		**flas**	**flit-ni**	**flit-e-t**

However, verbs whose second person plural present active stem ends in a vowel cluster **-ua-, -ye-,** or **-ie-** drop the second vowel of the cluster:

		Citation form	2nd Pl Act	3rd Sg Non-Act
'call'		**quaj**	**qua-ni**	**qu-he-t**
'break'		**thyej**	**thye-ni**	**thy-he-t**
'sense'		**ndiej**	**ndie-ni**	**ndi-he-t**

Following is a representative sample of present non-active paradigms:

laj	quaj	hap	heq
'I wash'	'I call'	'I open'	'I pull'
la-he-m	qu-he-m	hap-e-m	hiq-e-m
la-he-sh	qu-he-sh	hap-e-sh	hiq-e-sh
la-he-t	qu-he-t	hap-e-t	hiq-e-t
la-he-mi	qu-he-mi	hap-e-mi	hiq-e-mi
la-he-ni	qu-he-ni	hap-e-ni	hiq-e-ni
la-he-n	qu-he-n	hap-e-n	hiq-e-n

mat	vras	vë
'I measure'	'I slay'	'I put'
mate-m	vrit-e-m	vi-he-m
mat-e-sh	vrit-e-sh	vi-he-sh
mat-e-t	vrit-e-t	vi-he-t
mat-e-mi	vrit-e-mi	vi-he-mi
mat-e-ni	vrit-e-ni	vi-he-ni
mat-e-n	vrit-e-n	vi-he-n

These same forms are used for the non-active forms of the subjunctive mood, preceded by the particle **të**:

	1st Sg Non-Act Ind	1st Sg Non-Act Sub
'wash'	la-he-m	të la-he-m
'call'	qu-he-m	të qu-he-m
'pull'	hiq-e-m	të hiq-e-m

A.2 Imperfect Tense Non-Active Forms

The non-active imperfect tense is marked for all forms except (optionally) the 3rd Sg by the stem-formative suffix **-sh-**. Following that suffix are the person endings **-a, -e, -j, -im, -it, -in**. The combination **shj** that would be thus produced in the 3rd Sg is impossible in Albanian; instead, either the **sh** or the **j** is dropped, leaving the other as the ending of the form. The verbal stem to which these endings are added is identical to that of the present non-active stem.

Following is a representative sample of the imperfect non-active paradigms:

laj	quaj	hap
la-he-sha	qu-he-sha	hap-e-sha
la-he-she	qu-he-she	hap-e-she
la-he-j	qu-he-j	hap-e-j
(la-he-sh)	(qu-he-sh)	(hap-e-sh)
la-he-sh-im	qu-he-sh-im	hap-e-sh-im
la-he-sh-it	qu-he-sh-it	hap-e-sh-it
la-he-sh-in	qu-he-sh-in	hap-e-sh-in

heq	vras	vë
hiq-e-sh-a	vrit-e-sh-a	vi-he-sh-a
hiq-e-sh-e	vrit-e-sh-e	vi-he-sh-e
hiq-e-j	vrit-e-j	vi-he-j
(hiq-e-sh)	(vrit-e-sh)	(vi-he-sh)
hiq-e-sh-im	vrit-e-sh-im	vi-he-sh-im
hiq-e-sh-it	vrit-e-sh-it	vi-he-sh-it
hiq-e-sh-in	vrit-e-sh-in	vi-he-sh-in

The non-active imperfect subjunctive (including the future anterior of the type **do të laja** 'I would wash') use these same forms following the particle **të**:

	1st Sg Imperf Non-Act Ind	1st Sg Imperf Non-Act Sub
'wash'	**la-he-sh-a**	**(do) të la-he-sh-a**
'call'	**qu-he-sh-a**	**(do) të qu-he-sh-a**
'pull'	**hiq-e-sh-a**	**(do) të hiq-e-sh-a**

B. Non-Active Forms Marked by the Clitic **u**

For the past definite indicative, the present and imperfect admirative, the present optative, the imperative, and all forms constructed with the participle, including the future of the type **kam për të larë** 'I have washing to do', and the anterior future of the type **kisha për të larë** 'I had washing to do', the corresponding non-active forms are constructed with the clitic **u**.

B.1 Past Definite Tense Non-Active Forms

The non-active past definite is marked by the clitic **u** before the corresponding active forms of the verb: **u lava** 'I washed myself, I was washed', **lave, u lamë, u latë, u lanë** (compare **lava** 'I washed' **lave, lamë, latë, lanë**); **u ktheva** 'I returned, I turned (myself), I was turned', **u ktheve, u kthyem, u kthyet, u kthyen** (compare: **ktheva** 'I turned (something)', **ktheve, kthyem, kthyet, kthyen**); **u hapa** 'I opened up (myself)', **u hape, u hapëm, u hapët, u hapën** (compare; **hapa** 'I opened', **hape, hapëm, hapët, hapën**).

In the non-active third person singular, however, the active person ending **-i** or **-u** does not appear:

	3rd Sg Act Past Def	3rd Sg Non-Act Past Def
'open'	**hap-i**	**u hap**
'hold'	**mbajt-i**	**u mbajt**
'wash'	**la-u**	**u la**
'touch'	**prek-u**	**u prek**
'kill'	**vra-u**	**u vra**

Verbs with a stem in **-o-** or **-e-** (with the exception of **ble-j** 'I buy') appear with the expanded stem vowel clusters **-ua-** and **-ye-** respectively in the third person singular: **shkro-i** 'he wrote'/**u shkrua** 'it was written'; **mëso-i** 'he learned'/**u mësua** 'he was taught'; kthe-u 'he turned'/**u kthye** 'he returned'; **shpërble-u** 'he rewarded'/**u shpërblye** 'he was rewarded', etc.

Those verbs of class II/1 of conjugation II whose stems end in one of the consonants **-l, -ll, -r, -rr** (e.g., **vjel** 'harvest'/**vola** 'I harvested'; **sjell** 'I bring'/**solla** 'I brought'; **nxjerr** 'I take out'/**nxora** 'I took out'; **marr** 'I take'/**mora** 'I took'), also expand the vowel **-o-** into the cluster **-ua-** in the third person singular of the past definite: **voli/u vual** (also **u vol**); **solli/u suall; nxori/u nxuar; mori/u muar;** etc.

The verbs of class II of conjugation III appear in the third person singular without the stem extension, compare: **vur-i** 'he placed'/**u vu** 'he was placed'; **zur-i** 'he caught'/**u zu** 'he was caught'; **përzur-i** 'he dismissed'/**u përzu** 'he was dismissed'; **shpur-i** 'he conveyed'/**u shpu** 'he was conveyed'; **prur-i** 'he brought': **u pru** 'he was brought'.

B.2 Admirative Mood Non-Active Forms

For the non-active present and imperfect admirative, the particle **u** appears before the corresponding form of the active conjugation: **u lakam** 'I actually wash myself', **u lake, u laka, u lakemi, u lakeni, u lakan; u lakesha** 'I actually washed myself', **u lakeshe, u lakesh** (or **u lakej), u lakeshim, u lakeshit, u lakeshin.**

B.3 Optative Non-Active Forms

The present optative non-active has the particle **u** before the corresponding person forms of the active conjugation: **u lafsha** 'may I wash myself', **u lafsh, u laftë, u lafshim, u lafshi, u lafshin.**

B.4 Imperative Non-Active Forms

In the non-active forms of the imperative the clitic **u** (preceded by **-h-** after vowel-ending stems) is suffixe to the corresponding active form of the second person singular, right after the stem (and thus before the person ending of the second person plural): **hap-u** 'open yourself up!', **hap-u-ni** 'open yourselves up!' **la-h-u** 'wash yourself!', **la-h-u-ni** 'wash yourselves!'; **zi-h-u** 'quarrel!', **zi-h-u-ni** 'quarrel (among yourselves)!'.

However, when the non-active imperative is preceded by the negative particle **mos**, the clitic **u** appears directly before the verb: **mos u hap** 'don't open yourself up', **mos u hapni** 'don't open yourselves up'; **mos u laj** 'don't wash yourself', **mos u lani** 'don't wash yourselves'; **mos u zër** 'don't quarrel', **mos u zini.**

B.5 Participial Non-Active Forms

The non-active forms composed of tenses (the hybrid future and past future) that use **kam** plus a participle have the clitic **u** preceding the participle: **kam për të larë** 'I have washing to do', **kisha për të larë** 'I had washing to do', **kam (ke, ka, etc.) për t'u larë** 'I have washing of myself to do'; **kisha (kishe, kishte, etc.) për t'u larë** 'I had washing of myself to do'.

C. Non-Active Forms Marked by **jam** + Participle

In the non-active conjugation, all compound verbal forms constructed with the auxiliary **kam** in the active conjugation are constructed instead with **jam**. In these constructions, the auxiliary **jam** is conjugated for person and number, while the participle remains invariable.

The following non-active tenses, then, are constructed with **jam**:

1. The present perfect, past perfect, pluperfect, past future, and past future perfect of the indicative mood: **jam (je, është, etc.) larë** 'I have been washed' **jam hapur** 'I have been opened'; **isha larë** 'I used to be washed', **isha hapur** 'I used to be opened'; **qeshë larë** 'I had

been washed', **qeshë hapur** 'I had been opened'; **do të jem larë** 'I will have been washed', **do të jem hapur** 'I will have been open'; **do të isha larë** 'I would have been washed', **do të isha hapur** 'I would have been opened'.

2. The present perfect and past perfect of the admirative: **qenkam larë** 'I have actually been washed', **qenkam hapur** 'I have actually been opened'; **qenkësha larë** 'I had actually been washed', **qenkësha hapur**; 'I had actually been opened'.

3. The present perfect and past perfect of the subjunctive; **të jem larë** 'that I have been washed', **të jem hapur** 'that I have been opened', **të isha larë** 'that I had been washed', **të isha hapur** 'that I had been opened';

4. The present perfect of the optative: **qofsha larë** 'may I have been washed', **qofsha hapur** 'may I have been opened'.

2.2.5 Non-Finite Verb Forms

PARTICIPLES are the non-finite forms of verbs in Albanian, that is, the verb forms which do not reflect the person and number of a subject.

The first group of constructions using participles are the COMPOUND TENSES, treated in appropriate places in this chapter. The PERFECT tenses are composed of a finite auxiliary verb--principally a form of **jam** or **kam**--plus a participle. Depending on whether the auxiliary is **kam** or **jam** the compound tense will be active or non-active voice, respectively. Depending on the tense and mood of the auxiliary, the compound tense may be present, past, or future, and indicative, subjunctive, admirative, or optative. In all these compound tenses, the verb aspect is PERFECT, indicating that action is completed at the reference base point assumed in the clause. The PERIPHRASTIC COMPOUND tenses are composed of a form of **kam** or **jam** plus INFINITIVE (see below) or GERUNDIVE (see below) or of a modal auxiliary plus the participle (see Section 2.3.7 A).

The second group includes the participle itself and those non-finite constructions using it as the base: PRIVATIVES (**pa larë** 'without washing'), GERUNDIVES (**duke larë** 'while washing'), and characteristic Gheg forms like **me punue** 'to work') and **me të larë** 'by washing, having washed'.

A. Formation of the Participle

The verbal stem from which a participle is formed is usually the same as the stem of the past definite, although it may instead either be the same as a stem used in the present tense or different from either of these.

1. The following verbs form the participle from a stem like one used for the past definite:

a) All verbs of conjugation I. Verbs with the stem vowel **-o-** or **-ua-** and **-e-** or **-ye-** have participles whose stem vowel is the cluster **-ua-** and **-ye-** respectively, just as in the past definite plural: **la-va** 'I washed': **la-rë** 'washed'; **fshi-va** 'I swept': **fshi-rë** 'swept'; **punua-m** 'we worked': **punua-r** 'worked'; **shkrua-m** 'we wrote': **shkrua-r** 'written'; **rrëfye-m** 'we told': **rrëfye-r** 'told'; **lye-m** 'we painted'; **lye-r** 'painted', etc.: **gjet-a** 'I found': **gjet-ur** 'found'; **mbajt-a** 'I held': **mbajt-ur** 'held'; **bër-a** 'I made': **bër-ë** 'made'.

b) The verbs of conjugation II (except for those of subclass 1 of class II which change their stem vowel to **-o-** in the past definite): **hap-a** 'I opened'/**hap-ur** 'open'; **mat-a** 'I measured'/**mat-ur** 'measured'; **bërtit-a** 'I yelled/**bërtit-ur** 'yelled'; **thirr-a** 'I called out'/**thirr-ur** 'called out'; **fol-a** 'I spoke'/**fol-ur** 'spoken'; **shit-a** 'I sold'/**shit-ur** 'sold'; **vra-va** 'I killed'/-**vra-rë** 'killed'.

c) The verbs of conjugation III (**di** 'know', **fle** 'sleep', **ngre** 'raise', **shpie** 'take to', and **pi** 'drink') **dit-a** 'I knew'/**dit-ur** 'known'; **fjet-a** 'I slept'/**fjet-ur** 'slept'; **ngrit-a** 'I raise'/**ngrit-ur** 'raised'.

d) The irregular verbs **jam** 'I am', **bie** 'I bring', **rri** 'I sit, stay', **shoh** 'I see', and **vete** 'I go', **qe-shë** 'I was'/**qe-në** 'they were'; **pru-ra** 'I brought'/**pru-rë** 'brought'; **ndenj-a** 'I stayed'/-**ndenj-ur** 'stayed'; **pa-shë** 'I saw'/**pa-rë** 'seen'; **vajt-a** 'I went'/**vajt-ur** 'gone'.

2. The following verbs form the participle from a stem like one used for the present tense:

a) The verbs of subclass 1, class II of conjugation II: **heq** 'pull' (**hoq-a** 'I pulled'): **heq-ur** 'pulled'; **vjel** 'harvest' (**vol-a** 'I harvested'): **vjel-ë** 'harvested'; **pjek** 'bake' (**poq-a** 'I baked'): **pjek-ur** 'baked'; **nxjerr** 'take out' (**nxor-a** 'I took out'): **nxjerr-ë** 'taken out'; **dal** 'I emerge' (-**dol-a** 'I emerged'): **dal-ë** 'emerged'.

b) The verbs of class I of conjugation III and the irregular verb **lë** 'leave, let': **vë** 'I put' (**vur-a** 'I put')/**vë-në** 'put'; **zë** 'I catch' (**zur-a** 'I caught')/**zë-në** 'caught'; **përzë** 'I dismiss' (-**përzur-a** 'I dismissed')/**përzë-në** 'dismissed'; **nxë** 'I learn' (**nxur-a** 'I learned')/**nxë-në** 'learned'; **lë** 'I leave, let' (**la-shë** 'I left')/**lë-në** 'I left, let'.

3. The following verbs form the participle from a verbal stem that is different from the stems used for the present or past definite: **bie** 'I fall' (**ra-shë** 'I fell')/**rë-në** 'fallen'; **ha** 'I eat' (**hëngr-a** 'I ate')/**ngrë-në** 'eaten'; **jap** 'I give' (**dha-shë** 'I gave')/**dhë-në** 'given'; **shtie** 'I shoot' (**shti-va** 'I shot')/**shtë-në** 'shot'; **them** 'I say' (**tha-shë** 'I said')/**thë-në** 'said'; **ka-m** 'I have' (**pat-a** 'I had')/**pas-ur** 'had'; **dua** 'I want' (**desh-a** 'I wanted')/**dash-ur** 'wanted'; **vdes** 'I die' (**vdiq-a** 'I died')/**vdek-ur** 'dead'.

The suffixes used to form participles are: **-rë** or **-r, -ur, -e**, and **-në**.

1. The following verbs form their participles with **-rë** (after a stressed vowel) or **-r** (after an unstressed vowel):

a) the verbs in class I of conjugation I: **lá-rë** 'washed', **fshi-rë** 'swept', **punúa-r** 'worked', **lýe-r** 'painted', etc.;

b) the verbs in subclass 3, class II of conjugation II: **vrá-rë** 'slain', **shká-rë** 'slipped, slid', **ngá-rë** 'driven', **pre-rë** 'cut', etc.;

c) the conjugation III verb **pi** 'drink'/**pi-rë** 'drunk', as well as the irregular verb **shoh** 'I see'/**pá-rë** 'seen'.

2. The following verbs form their participle with **-ur**:

a) the verbs in subclass 1, class II of conjugation I: **gjet-ur** 'found', **mbajt-ur** 'held', **mbrojt-ur** 'defended', etc.;

b) the verbs of conjugation II, except for those in subclass 3 of class II (see 1b) and those with stems in **-l, -ll, -r, -rr** (class II/1) which change the stem vowel to **-o** in the past definite (see 3b below): **hap-ur** 'opened', **vendos-ur** 'decided', **mat-ur** 'measured', **rrah-ur** 'beaten', **njoh-ur** 'recognized' (class II/1);

c) the verbs of conjugation III (class II/1): **di** 'I know', **fle** 'I sleep', **ngre** 'I raise'/**dit-ur** 'known', **fjet-ur** 'slept', **ngrit-ur** 'lifted';

d) the irregular verbs **kam** 'I have', **dua** 'I like', **rri** 'I stay', **vdes** 'I die', **vete** 'I go', **vij** 'I come'/**pas-ur** 'had', **dash-ur** 'liked', **ndenj-ur** 'stayed', **vdek-ur** 'dead', **vajt-ur** 'gone', **ardh-ur** 'come, arrived'.

3. The following verbs form their participles with **-ë**:

a) the verbs **bëj** 'I make' and **hyj** 'I enter' (class II/2) of conjugation I: **bër-ë** 'made', **hyr-ë** 'entered':

b) the verbs in subclass 1 of conjugation II, class II which have stems ending in **-l, -ll, -r, -rr**, and which change the stem vowel to **-o-** in the past definite: **vjel-ë** 'harvested', **dal-ë** 'emerged', **mbjell-ë** 'sown', **sjell-ë** 'brought', **nxjerr-ë** 'taken out', **tjerr-ë** 'spun', **marr-ë** 'taken';

c) the verbs **bie** 'I bring' and **shpie** 'I convey' (**prura** 'I brought' and **shpura** 'I conveyed'): **prur-ë** 'brought' and **shpur-ë** (or **shpën-ë**) 'conveyed', respectively.

2.2.5 A. Formation of the Participle   **63**

4. The following verbs form their participle with **-ë**:

a) the verbs in class I of conjugation III: **vë** 'I put', **zë** 'I catch', **përzë** 'I dismiss', **nxë** 'I learn', as well as the class III verb **shtie** 'shoot'/**vë-në** 'put', **zë-në** 'caught', **përzë-në** 'dismissed', **nxë-në** 'learned', **shtë-në** 'shot';

b) the irregular verbs **jam** 'I am', **bie** 'I fall', **ha** 'I eat', **jap** 'I give', **lë** 'I leave, let', **them** 'I say'/**qe-në** 'been', **rë-në** 'fallen', **ngrë-në** 'eaten', **dhë-në** 'given', **lë-në** 'let, left', **thë-në** 'said'.

B. Participial Constructions

B.1 Active Participial Forms

B.1a. Privatives

Non-finite PRIVATIVE forms are constructed by placing the preposition **pa** before the participle: **pa pasur** 'without having', **pa larë** 'without washing', **pa qenë** 'without being', **pa hapur** 'without opening', **pa vënë** 'without putting', **pa ngrënë** 'without eating'.

In Standard Albanian one rarely encounters complex forms of the type **pa pasë larë** 'without having eaten', which use the special short participial form **pasë** (rather than **pasur**) of the auxiliary **kam** before the participle of the main verb. Such complex forms are sometimes called the perfect aspect of the privative; forms like **pa larë** may then be called the common aspect.

B.1b. Gerundives

The GERUNDIVE is composed of the particle **duke** plus the participle: **duke pasur** '(while) having', **duke qenë** '(while) being', **duke larë** '(while) washing', **duke hapur** '(while) opening', **duke vënë** '(while) putting', **duke ngrënë** '(while) eating'.

In Standard Albanian one rarely encounters complex forms of the type **duke pasë larë** 'having washed', with the special short participial form **pasë** of the auxiliary **kam** before the participle of the main verb. Forms of this type **duke pasë larë** are sometimes called the perfect aspect of the gerundive; forms like **duke larë** may then be called the common aspect of the gerundive.

B.1c. Infinitives and Absolutives

So-called INFINITIVES of the type **për të larë** 'to wash' and ABSOLUTIVES of the type **me të larë** 'having washed, upon washing, by washing', are composed of the prepositions **për** and **me** respectively plus **të** plus a participle. The characteristic Gheg infinitive form is composed of **me** plus a short form of the participle, e.g., **me punue** 'to work', but will not be discussed further here because it has not been accepted as belonging to present-day standard literary Albanian.

B.2 Non-Active Participial Forms

The non-finite privative forms, the gerundive, non-finite forms of the type **për të larë** 'to wash' and **me të larë** 'to wash', all have non-active forms as well. In all of these forms, for the common aspect the clitic **u** appears immediately before the verbal stem: **pa u larë** 'without washing oneself', **pa u hapur** 'without opening oneself', **pa u zënë** 'without quarrelling'; **duke u larë** 'while washing oneself', **duke u hapur** 'while opening oneself up', **duke u zënë** 'while quarrelling'; **për t'u larë** 'to wash oneself', **për t'u hapur** 'to open oneself', **për t'u zënë** 'to quarrel'; **me t'u larë** 'having been washed', **me t'u hapur** 'having been opened', **me t'u zënë** 'having been caught'.

Qenë, the participle of **jam**, is used for the perfect aspect of the non-finite privative and gerundive: **pa qenë larë** 'without being washed', **pa qenë hapur** 'without being opened'; **duke qenë larë** '(while) being washed', **duke qenë hapur** '(while) being opened'.

NOTE

In the same way, the non-active Gheg form corresponding to the active infinitive **me la** 'to wash' is **me qenë la** 'to be washed', **me qenë hapun** 'to be opened'.

2.3 Major Uses of Conjugational Verb Forms

2.3.1 Indicative Mood Uses

As mentioned in Section 2.1.4, the speaker may use the indicative mood to present the action named by a verb as real. When the speaker wishes to deny or express uncertainty toward this reality, the verb is accompanied by the negative proclitic **nuk** or **s'** or by a qualifying adverb like **ndofta** 'maybe, perhaps', **mbase** 'perhaps, maybe', **kushedi** 'perhaps ("who knows?")', etc.

Është ora katër pas dreke. 'It is four o'clock in the afternoon.'
Armiku ka diktuar lëvizjen tonë e PO na RREH me artileri e mortaja të rënda. 'The enemy has detected our movement and IS HITTING us with heavy artillery and mortar.'
Mitralozat gjermane PO DËGJOHEN më afër. 'The German machine guns ARE BEING HEARD closer.'
Duhet të shpejtojmë; ndryshe, DO TË na SHPËTOJË zogu nga dora. 'We must hurry; otherwise, the bird WILL GET AWAY from us ("from the hand").'
Batalioni i parë NUK KA ARDHUR akoma. 'The first battalion HAS NOT ARRIVED yet.'
Po e DIMË se pas pak DO TË na VIJË në ndihmë. 'But WE KNOW that in a little while IT WILL COME to our aid.'

Verb forms in the indicative mood, are conventionally divided into TENSES: sets of person-number forms that indicate a particular time and aspect. Besides the present tense forms, Albanian distinguishes five tenses dealing with past time: imperfect, past definite, perfect, past perfect, and pluperfect.

A. Present Tense Uses

The basic use of a verb in the present indicative is to indicate the reality of an action at the moment of speaking. But, as will become apparent below, in particular contexts the action indicated may take place at an indefinite time or even in the future or past.

When used to specify action limited to the present time, present tense verb forms (with a few exceptions--see notes 1 & 2 below) are usually preceded by the momentive proclitic **po**, which signals that a particular action is actually under way or imminent at the moment of speaking. The complex verb form constructed with the present tense of the auxiliary **jam** plus a gerundive can be used with a similar meaning, except that the action it indicates must already be in progress:

JA, PO HESHT. Vetëm ti m'u hiq sysh. 'THERE, I'M SHUTTING UP. Just get out of my sight.'
-- Ç'PO BËN këtu? -- e pyeti kryeveqilharxhi, kur kaloi përbri. 'WHAT ARE YOU DOING here?--the chief attorney asked him, when he passed alongside.'

-- **PO VËSHTROJ si mblidhet këshilli i lavdishëm** -- **tha kronikani.** 'I AM WATCHING how the glorious council convenes, the chronicler said.'

NOTES

1. Several verbs which designate actions or states that normally characterize the subject for an indefinite time are rarely, if ever, accompanied by the particle **po**. Such are the verbs: **dua** 'I want', **di** 'I know', **dashuroj** 'I love', **urrej** 'I hate', **kam, jam, gjendem** 'I am (at)', **ndodhem** 'I happen to be (at)', **nxë** 'I learn', **përmban** 'contains', **ngërthen** 'tightens', etc.

   Dhe tani S'DUA të më shqetësojë njeri. 'And now I DO NOT WANT anyone to disturb me.'

   Ju ADMIROJ! 'I ADMIRE you.'

   Nuk do të harroj kurrë këtë mbrëmje, që po kalojmë me ju. Nuk e DI, kjo s'më ka shkuar ndërmend. 'I shall never forget this evening that we are spending with you. I don't KNOW why I feel like this ("I don't know, this has never crossed my mind").'

2. Several verbs, particularly those indicating physical or physiological actions, are usually used without the particle **po**, especially in questions, even when a specific action is involved. This happens because such verbs normally already indicate specific actions. Nevertheless, to emphasize the momentaneous aspect of the action, **po** may be used with its usual value even with these verbs:

   -- **Pse HESHT? TË paktën ti mos hesht.** KEEP") QUIET? At least you should not keep quiet.'

   Ç'MENDON ti? S'mund të bëj unë një punë? 'WHAT DO you think? I can't handle ("do") a job?'

   -- **PO HABITESH?** -- **tha kryeveqilharxhi.** 'YOU ARE (BEING) SURPRISED?--said the chief attorney.'

   -- **Ti nuk më DËGJON? Ti PO QAN?** 'You are not listening ("DO NOT LISTEN") to me? You ARE CRYING?'

When used with an indefinite temporal meaning, verbs in the present tense are not accompanied by the particle **po**. Used in this way, they may indicate:

a) general actions that are repeated time after time:

   Janë çelur udhë, udhë të gjera, kryq e tërthorë. Traktorët TËRHEQIN rrëshqanë trungjet dhe atje, në të përpjetë, trungjet vërsulen teposhtë, të llahtarshëm, nëpër lugjet e drunjta dhe me potere të hatashme, BIEN tutje në fund të pyllit, ku i PRET sharra. 'Roads have been built, wide roads, all over. The tractors DRAG the trunks and there, on the incline, the trunks dash downward, frightfully, among the wooded valleys, and with a horrible din tumble down ("FALL") way out at the end of the forest, where the sawmill AWAITS them.'

   Sharrat elektrike të dorës UTURIJNË nga të katër anët e pyllit. 'Electric hand saws hum on all ("four") sides of the forest.'

   Ai NGRIHET në mëngjes në orën 5. 'He RISES at 5 o'clock in the morning.'

b) actions which are not bound to a particular time, because they have a timeless value. One such use of the present tense is noticed in popular sayings (proverbs) and in scientific axioms of general truths, when they make assertions that have value for all times, including the moment of speaking:

   Ai që S'PUNON, LËNGON. 'He who DOES NOT WORK, LANGUISHES.'

   GJYKON puna, S'GJYKON guna. 'It's the work that counts ("JUDGES"), not the cloak.'

   UJI që RRI më një vend, qelbet. 'Water that STAYS in one place becomes smelly.'

   Lumi FLE, hasmi S'FLE. 'The river SLEEPS, the enemy DOESN'T (SLEEP).'

   Oksidi i karbonit ËSHTË një gaz pa ngjyrë, pa erë, pak më i lehtë se ajri, nuk TRETET në ujë. 'Carbon monoxide IS a gas without color, without odor, slightly lighter than air, does not DISSOLVE in water.'

Oksidi i Karbonit ËSHTË shumë i helmët. 'Carbon monoxide IS very poisonous.'

Oksidi i karbonit FORMOHET, kur qymyri DIGJET në temperaturë të lartë dhe kur oksigjeni nuk ËSHTË i mjaftueshëm për të oksiduar të gjithë karbonin e qymyrit në gaz karbonik. 'Carbon monoxide IS FORMED when coal BURNS at a high temperature and the oxygen IS not sufficient to oxidize all the carbon in the coal into carbon gas.'

Shqipëria SHTRIHET në bregun lindor të Adriatikut. 'Albania LIES on the eastern shore ("hill") of the Adriatic.'

The present tense of the indicative mood may also be used with a future meaning, when the sentence has an adverbial indicating the future, such as **nesër** 'tomorrow', **pasnesër** 'day after tomorrow', **pas një ore** 'after an hour', etc. In this usage the verb in the present tense is not accompanied by the particle **po**, although it may indicate a specific action:

Dëgjo këtu, NESËR na VJEN uji te dera e do të gëzohemi. 'Listen here, TOMORROW the water COMES to our door and we will rejoice.'

The present indicative is used on two kinds of occasions when the time of the action indicated is in the past:

a) When in order to enliven a past, we pretend that it is happening right before our eyes. This is called the historical or narrative present tense:

Krujë, o qytet i bekuar, / Prite, prite Skënderbenë, / PO VJEN si pëllumb i shkuar / të shpëtojë mëmëdhenë. 'Krujë, oh blessed city / wait, wait for Skënderbeu / HE IS COMING like a friendly swan ("pigeon") / to save the motherland.'

JEMI në Labovën e Poshtme aftër darkës së 19 janarit 1944. 'WE ARE in Lower Labovë near evening of January 19, 1944.'

VJEN një fonogram që THOTË: "Komandanti i Brigadës të niset urgjentisht për Sheper". 'A telephone message COMES that SAYS: the Brigade Commander must set out urgently for Sheper.'

E DËRGON Shtabi i PËrgjithshëm. 'The General Staff SENDS HIM.'

NISEMI menjëherë lart malit. 'WE LEAVE at once [to go] up the mountain.'

Nata na ZË në malin e Labovës. 'The night overtakes ("CATCHES") us on the mountain of Labovë.'

Mezi KALOJMË Çajupin dhe mëngjesi na ZË në kishën e Sheperit, në Zagori. 'We barely CROSS the Çajup mountain and morning finds ("CATCHES") us in the church of Sheperi in Zagori.'

b) When a time adverbial indicates how long an action continuing at the moment of speaking has been going on. In this case, the present is used with the sense of the present perfect (see Section 2.2.3 A.2c). In this usage the verb in the present tense is generally not accompanied by the particle **po**:

Kemi tri net që pothuaj nuk FLEMË. 'For ("we have") three nights we have not slept ("WE almost do not SLEEP").'

Ja se ç'ma HA e ç'ma BREN zemrën këto tre vjet, që kur u bënë fejesat tona. 'This is what has been eating and gnawing ("EATS and GNAWS") at my heart these three years, since our engagement ("since our vows were made").'

NOTE

The first person plural of the present indicative is also used with the sense of the subjunctive jussive mood to express the speaker's advice, encouragement, etc. (see Section 2.3.7 B.2):

-- DALIM në ajër të pastër -- tha kryeveqilharxhi. '"LET'S GET OUT into clean air," said the chief attorney.'

SHKOJMË në çadrën time të pimë ndonjë gjë dhe të çlodhemi pak. 'LET'S GO to my tent to drink something and rest awhile.'

B. Past Tense Uses

Among the five main past tenses, the imperfect, past definite, and perfect forms generally indicate actions concluded prior to the moment of speaking, whereas the past perfect and pluperfect forms indicate actions completed before a particular moment in the past.

B.1 Imperfect Tense Uses

The basic use of the indicative imperfect is to indicate the reality of an action over a period of time in the past.

Tani ato me siguri FLININ, të lodhura e të këputura nga rruga, në çadrën e tyre nyjyrë lila. 'They were now assuredly ASLEEP, tired, and exhausted ("broken") from the journey ("road"), in their lily-colored tent.'

Me hapa të qeta ai u kthye dhe u fut në çadër, pa iu hedhur as sytë dy rojeve, që RRININ si të ngrirë, me heshta në duar, në hyrje të saj. 'With calm steps he turned and entered the tent, without even glancing ("throwing the eyes") at the two guards that STOOD at its entrance, as if frozen, with lances at hand.'

Pastaj ngriti sytë nga adjutanti, që PRISTE në këmbë. 'Then he looked up at the adjutant, who WAITED standing.

To specify continuous actions limited to a specific period in the past, an indicative imperfect form is usually accompanied by the proclitic **po**, which emphasizes that a particular action is actually under way or imminent at a particular moment in the past, often indicated by a temporal adverbial:

Kështu mendonte Dini pa vënë re se PO RËNDONTE me bërryl mbi dorezën e derës së vagonit, ku qe pështetur. 'This is the way Dini thought, not noticing that he WAS PRESSING DOWN with his elbow on the handle of the wagon door (on which) he was leaning.'

Treni PO HYNTE në kthesën e madhe. 'The train WAS ENTERING the big bend.'

The proclitic **po** is less commonly used with the imperfect than with the present tense.

In particular contexts the imperfect indicative may be used with other particular values:

1. It is used to indicate an indefinite action, repeated time after time in the past. In such cases, the verb in the imperfect is often accompanied by an adverbial which indicates the repetition of the action more clearly. The adverbial may be:

a) a temporal expression which indicates a fraction or period of time that is regularly repeated, like: **çdo mëngjes** 'every morning', **çdo ditë** 'every day', **çdo javë** 'every week', **çdo vit** 'every year', **herë pas here** 'time after time, from time to time.'

Jeniçerët i NDËRRONIN çdo dy orë me trupa të freskëta. 'They replaced ("CHANGED") the Janissaries every two hours with fresh troops.'

Herë pas here KTHENTE kokën e shikonte fytyrën e të vëllait dhe sytë i NDALTE në atë të gërvishturën e faqes. 'From time to time he TURNED his head and looked at the face of his brother, and rested ("STOPPED") his eyes on that scratch on (his) face.

Nganjëherë në vendet më të ngushta të saj trupat BLLOKOHESHIN, gjersa xhenierët HAPNIN ndonjë shteg ndihmës për të përballuar dyndjen e paprerë. 'Sometimes the troops WERE BLOCKED at its narrowest places, until the engineers OPENED an auxiliary passage in order to resist the incessant advances.' **Pastaj rruga LIROHEJ përsëri dhe ushtria lëvizte ngadalë përmes pluhurit.** 'Afterward the road WOULD BE LIBERATED again, and the army would move slowly through the dust.'

b) a subordinate clause which also has as its predicate a verb in the imperfect indicative:

Ata heshtën. Sa herë që BISEDONIN për protezat, midis tyre BINTE një heshtje e rëndë. 'They became silent. Whenever THEY DISCUSSED the protheses, a heavy silence FELL between them.'

Shpeshherë ato HIDHESHIN nga shkëmbinjtë dhe COPËTOHESHIN nëpër humnera, kur ushtarët armiq U AFROHESHIN për t'i kapur. 'Often they JUMPED OFF the rocks and SHATTERED THEMSELVES among the ravines, when the enemy soldiers APPROACHED them in oder to capture them.'

2. It may also be used to indicate general action extending over an indefinitely long time in the past:

NË Fushat e bregdetit dhe në krahinat e tjera pjellore të Ilirisë popullsia MERREJ me bujqësi e blegtori dhe me kulturat frutore. 'In the coastal plains and in the other fertile regions of Illyria the population engaged ("WAS TAKEN") in farming and livestock and with fruit cultures.'

NË krahinat e brendshme malore ekonomia e tyre MBËSHTETEJ kryesisht në blegtorinë. 'In the interior mountainous regions their economy DEPENDED chiefly on livestock.'

Veglat, me të cilat PUNOHEJ toka, ishin parmenda e drunjtë dhe kazma e hekurt. 'The implements with which the land WAS cultivated ("WORKED") were the wooden plow and the iron pick.'

3. The imperfect indicative is also used to represent the moment of speaking in the past. This happens when a sentence with a predicate in the present indicative in direct discourse is turned into indirect discourse by being embedded in a clause with a verb of saying (**them** 'I say', **pyes** 'I ask', **përgjigjem** 'I respond', etc.) in one of the past tenses, chiefly the imperfect or past definite. Such a replacement of the present by the imperfect may also occur when sentences describing a landscape become embedded in another clause whose verb is in one of the past tenses. On such occasions the imperfect takes the particle **po** if the verb in direct discourse would have it with the present tense:

Kronikani shkruante se këto ISHIN male të lartë, ku as sorrat nuk fluturoni dot. 'The chronicler wrote that these WERE high mountains where even ravens could not fly.'

Pashai i tha se nuk DONTE të hante. 'The Pasha said to him that he did not WANT to eat.'

As Adili s'po ngopej dot atë mëngjes së shikuari këtë fushë të gjerë, që SHTRIHEJ lirisht në mes dy lumenjve të mëdhenj, Vjosës dhe Semanit, e MBYLLEJ përpara nga një vetull e dëndur dhe e errët pishash. 'That morning, even Adil couldn't have his fill of looking at this broad plain, that SPREAD OUT easily ("freely") between two big rivers, Viosë and Seman, and WAS CLOSED OFF ahead by a dense and dark eybrow of pine trees.'

NOTE

The imperfect forms of the verbs **jam** and **kam** are sometimes used with the value of the past definite.

B.2 Past Definite Tense Uses

The basic use of the past definite is to indicate an action performed and completed at a particular, definite time in the past. Thus, the difference between this tense and the imperfect is essentially aspectual in character (see Section 2.1.6):

-- Po, -- THA me mundim Dini. '"Yes," SAID Dini with effort.'

ERDHI, më PA, QAU, dhe IKU. 'HE CAME, SAW me, CRIED, and LEFT.'

MË PA, siç po më sheh ti. 'He SAW me, as you see me.'

NË të dalë të dimrit, kur delegatët e sulltanit U LARGUAN, ne e KUPTUAM që lufta

ishte e pashmangshme. 'Toward the end ("coming out") of winter, when the Sultan's delegates DEPARTED, we realized ("UNDERSTOOD") that the war was unavoidable.'

Ata na BËNË gjithfarë presionesh që ne të pranonim vasalitetin. 'They exerted ("MADE") all sorts of pressures on us to accept vassalage.'

Past definite forms are often accompanied by a temporal indication that excludes the moment of speaking. Such an indication may be made by a temporal adverb marking a specific moment or period of time in the past: **dje** 'yesterday', **pardje** 'the day before yesterday', **vjet** 'last year', **parvjet** 'the year before last', **atëherë** 'then', etc., or phrases of the type **atë ditë** 'that day', **atë vit** 'that year', **para dy ditësh** 'two days ago', **para një jave** 'a week ago', etc.

If the definite action indicated by the past definite form extended over a period of time, the temporal indication may be an adverbial like **kurrë** 'never', **tërë jetën** 'throughout life, for a lifetime', etc., or may be made by repeating the verb:

Ai PUNOI TËRË JETËN për lirinë e atdheut dhe KURRË nuk U TREMB nga kërcënimet dhe ndjekjet e armiqve. 'He WORKED ALL [HIS] LIFE for the freedom of the country, and WAS NEVER FRIGHTENED by the threats and persecutions of enemies.'

ATË DITË Xha Demi U HËNGËR e U THER me vetveten më shumë se ç'e kish bërë të tjera herë. 'THAT DAY uncle Demi quarreled with ("ATE") and kicked ("PRICKED") HIMSELF much more than he had other times.'

Po THERI e THERI sulltan qeni me dorë të xhelatëve të tij. 'The dog of a Sultan used his executioners to keep up the killing ("SLEW and SLEW by the hand of his executioners").'

The past definite may be used to express thoughts with a timeless value. One such usage is found in popular sayings. In such a case the distinction in meaning between the past definite and present indicative (see Section 2.3.1 A) is inoperative; in some of these cases, the two tenses are thus interchangeable:

Kush MËNGOI, BLOI. 'He who GOT UP EARLY, MILLED.'

Nuk U LODHE sot, do të mundohesh mot. 'If you do not labor ("GOT TIRED") today, you will toil next year.'

PUNOVE? GËZOVE; HËNGRE fikun, vish leshnikun. 'DID YOU LABOR? YOU REJOICED (from the fruit of your labor); [if] YOU ATE THE FIG, put on the woolen cloak (the winter season is upon you).'

The past definite may be used when a future event is involved:
1) When the speaker represents as an accomplished fact some activity that is intended to be realized in the immediate future:

≪ **Largohu, se ti HODHA zorrët në majë të plepit** ≫ **më thotë i paturpshmi.** 'Scram, or I'll SPILL your guts ("or to you I THREW the guts on top of the poplar tree"), the shameless one says to me.'

Herë-herë shoferi e ngadalësonte shpejtësinë dhe bërtiste me të madhe: ≪ **Hapuni, se ju SHTYPA:** ≫ 'From time to time the chauffeur decreased the speed and cried out forcefully ("with the big") "make way ("open up"), or I'll run you over" ("I TRAMPLED you").'

Erdha -- thirri Batoja dhe vrapoi me shishe në dorë. '"I'm coming ("I CAME")!" yelled Bato, and he ran with bottle in hand.'

-- IKA, -- tha mjeku dhe u ngrit -- mund të vij prapë. '"I'm going ("I WENT")", the doctor said, and he got up. "I may come again."'

Do të vij, premtoi TITI, -- sa të mbaroj punë, ERDHA. 'I shall come, Titi promised--as soon as I finish working, I will come ("I CAME").'

2) After the subordinating conjunction **po**, in antecedent clauses of conditional sentences. In this usage it is synonymous with the present subjunctive (see Section 2.3.3 A). In

such cases, the verb in the consequent clause is usually in the imperative or in the present or future indicative, but it may also be in the past definite used with the future sense as above:

> -- **Po S'ERDHE ti, as ne s'vemi -- thanë shokët e tjerë.** '"If you don't ("DID NOT") COME, we don't go either," said the other comrades.'
>
> **Dhe mos kujto se ne do të të lutemi ≪ Aman o Qano, bëhu përgjegjës këshilli, se po S'U BËRE, na mori lumi! ≫** 'And don't think ("recall") that we will beg you, "Please, Qano, be a council supervisor, because if you don't BECOME one, we're sunk ("the river took us")!"'

In some sentences the past definite is interchangeable with the perfect:

> **ERDHA (= kam ardhur) të punoj këtu në Maliq.** 'I CAME (= have come) to work here in Maliq.'
>
> **Më THANË (= kanë thënë) se keni kërkuar një mësues.** THEY TOLD (= have told) me that you have been looking for (= have looked for) a teacher.'
>
> **ERDHA (= kam ardhur) për një punë të ngutshme -- tha mjeku.** '"I CAME (=have come) on urgent business," said the doctor.'

NOTES

1. For the usage of the past definite in place of the pluperfect in dependent temporal clauses conjoined by means of the subordinating conjunctions **si** 'after, since', **pasi** 'since, because, after', see Point 5 below.

2. For the verbs **jam** and **kam**, the imperfect forms are sometimes used in place of the past definite. But it is not uncommon to observe the contrary phenomenon as well:

Imperfect

> **Jam këtu me inxhinier E.D., i cili ka përvijuar projektimin e parkut të Korçës. ISHTE (=QE) puna e tij e parë, mbasi kreu studimet.** 'I am here with engineer E.D., who has outlined Korçë's park project. IT WAS his first job, after he completed his studies.'
>
> **-- ISHE (=QE) ti kur e çau shkëmbin? -- pyet një nga punëtorët dhe ne qeshim.** '"WERE YOU [present] when he split the rock?" asks one of the workers, and we laugh.'
>
> **-- Nuk ISHA (= QESHË) -- përgjigjet. -- Atë s'e kam parë. Por ty dhe Sabriun, ju pashë si e mbyllët grykën.** '"I WAS not", he answers. "I have not seen him. But I saw how you and Sabri closed off the gorge."'

Past Definite

> **QE (= ishte) e thjeshtë ajo odë e vogël, e mësuesit, e lyer me gëlqere.** 'IT WAS simple, that little room of the teacher, white washed ("painted") with quicklime.'
>
> **Shtëpia QE (= ishte) e vogël, me dy të ndara e një çardhak në mes.** 'The house WAS small, with two rooms ("partitions") and a veranda in the middle.'
>
> **Dhoma e zjarrit, ajo ku rrinin dimër e verë, QE (= ishte) me dysheme.** 'The living room ("room of the fire"), the one where we stayed winter and summer, wAS [equipped] with a floor.'

B.3 Present Perfect Tense Uses

The basic use of the present perfect of the indicative mood is to indicate that the scope of time considered by the speaker includes both the past and the moment of speaking. By using this tense the speaker implicitly claims that an action has some connection with the present moment, although it began in the past. This is the basic difference between this tense and the past definite, by which the speaker claims only that the action terminated at a given point in the past. (See point 2. above.) For example, contrast these two tenses in the following sentence:

Dhe kur hapej muhabeti për kurbetin, xha Teloja thoshte: -- Lipsur qoftë, se na HËNGRI gjithë djemtë e na KA DJEGUR zemrën. 'And when the conversation turned to migration abroad, uncle Telo would say, "To hell with it, for it wasted ("ATE to us") all [our] sons, and HAS SCORCHED our hearts."'

The past definite form **HËNGRI** 'he ate' indicates that the action of "eating up" of the boys by immigration had ended at the moment when Uncle Teloja said these words, whereas the perfect form **KA DJEGUR** 'has burned' indicates that the hearts of the people were still burning as a consequence of the immigration.

Specifically, the perfect is used:

1. When the past action is connected to the moment of speaking through its effect at the moment of speaking. In such cases the perfect:

a) May be accompanied by no temporal marker:

-- **Ne KEMI MBETUR edhe pa komisar! -- tha Nurka.** '"We find ourselves ("HAVE REMAINED") even without a commissar!" said Nurka.'

-- **Komandant Rrapoja KA PËRZËNË tre komisarë. -- tha Memoja. Komandant Rrapoja do të përgjigjet për këtë.** '"Commander Rrapo HAS DISMISSED three commissars," said Memo. "Commander Rrapo will answer for this."'

E di që KE ARDHUR për dinamit. Isha në Maliq. 'I know that YOU HAVE COME for dynamite. I was in Maliq.'

-- **Nga lufta e KANË PËSUAR? -- pyeti Vehbiu.** '"Are they suffering because of the war ("From the war THEY HAVE SUFFERED IT")?" asked Vehbi.'

-- **E kush S'E KA PËSUAR nga lufta? -- ia bëri përkthyesi.** '"And who is not suffering ("HAS NOT SUFFERED IT") because of the war?" the interpreter replied.'

b) May be accompanied by a temporal marker that designates a particular period of time that includes the moment of speaking: **sot** 'today', **sivjet** 'this year', **këto ditë** 'these days', **këtë javë** 'this week', **këtë muaj** 'this month', **këtë vit** 'this year', etc.; **që dje** 'since yesterday', **që vjet** 'since last year', **që atëherë** 'since then' **që atë ditë** 'since that day', **që atë javë (e gjer sot)** 'from that week (up to today)'

-- **Tani unë punoj duke kënduar. -- Ndaj KE NXJERRË shumë qymyr këto ditë -- e ngacmoi xha Jorgji, -- duket KE KËNDUAR shumë. KËta dhjetë vjetët e fundit JANË ARRITUR suksese të mëdha.** '"Now I sing as I work." "That's why you have dug ("EXTRACTED") so much coal these days," uncle George teased him, "apparently YOU HAVE SUNG a lot. Great successes HAVE BEEN ATTAINED during these past ten years."'

c) May be accompanied by a temporal marker designating an indefinitely long time: **gjithmonë** 'always', **gjithnjë** 'always', **kurdoherë** 'always, whenever', **shpesh** 'often', **dendur** 'frequently', **herë pas here** 'time after time', **kurrë** 'never', etc.

E në është kështu, në këta damarë, KURRË gjaku i Shqipërisë sonë nuk KA LËVIZUR me një gjallëri dhe vrull si ky që kam para syve. 'And if it is so, NEVER before has the blood of Albania coursed ("HAS MOVED") in these veins with a vitality and drive such as the one I am witnessing.'

Partia jonë e KA PASUR KURDOHERË në qendrën e vëmendjes së saj zhvillimin e shkollës sonë të re. 'Our Party HAS ALWAYS HAD the development of our new school at the center of its attention.'

Ej, dëgjoni këtu: KËto janë sendet e kambialet e dëftesat e borxheve, që KEMI PAGUAR DENBABADEN, janë zgjebja që na KA NGRËNË TËRË JETËN. 'Hey, listen here: These are the things and bank notes and debt certificates that WE HAVE PAID FOR AT SOME TIME; they are the scab that HAS EATEN AWAY at us all [OUR] LIFE.'

2. When an action begun in the past is still continuing at the moment of speaking. This

meaning of the perfect emerges from the context, which may have a temporal marker indicating either the starting point of the action, or the entire period from the beginning of the action up to the moment of speaking. The present indicative may also be used with this meaning (see Section 2.3.1 A).

Duhet ta dish se KA TRE VJET që ma KA MOLEPSUR mola shpirtin. 'You should know that it's been ("IT HAS") THREE YEARS that the moth HAS INFECTED my soul.'

Dhe nëpër hangare të mëdha kombajnat KANË ÇELUR gojën e po gërhasin në vapë. 'And in the big hangars the combines HAVE OPENED [their] mouths and are snoring in the heat.'

In spoken Albanian, and sometimes in writing as well, a perfect form may appear where a past definite form would be expected:

Ç'të duhet ty sot se ku e KAM HEDHUR (= hodha) unë lumin atëherë? 'What does it matter to you today where I crossed ("HAVE THROWN") (=threw) the river at the time?'

I KAM PRERË (=preva) edhe udhën pardje e i JAM LUTUR (=u luta). 'I even STOPPED ("HAVE CUT = I cut") him on the road the day before yesterday, and BEGGED ("I HAVE PRAYED = prayed") him.'

Dhe rrallë na kujton Konstandini, siç e di dhe ti vetë, o Nikodim, ndonëse nëna e tij, Maria, KA VDEKUR (=vdiq) me emrin e tij në gojë, dhe babait tonë iu çel për të një plagë. 'And only rarely does Konstandin remember us, as you yourself know, Nikodim, even though his mother, Maria, died ("HAS DIED = died") with his name on her lips, and a sore broke out on our father on account of him.'

The perfect, like the past definite, is also sometimes used like a future, when the speaker represents as an accomplished fact an action which has not yet begun:

Po e gjete librin që më ka humbur, ta KAM FALUR (=do të fal). 'If you find the book I'm missing, you can have it ("I HAVE OFFERED = I will offer it to you").'

NOTE

The meaning of the doubly-compounded forms of the perfect have a meaning similar to that of the perfect, although they are usually employed exclusively for actions in the distant past:

NË Elbasan u KANË PASË THËNË surreta. 'In Elbasan THEY HAVE called ("SAID") them scarecrows.'

B.4 Past Perfect Tense Uses

The basic use of the past perfect is to indicate an action completed prior to a particular moment in the past. This completed action:

a) may be connected to the particular moment in the past by its results or by its continuation up to that moment:

Vetëm të nesërmen Dini mendoi i qetë për ato që KISHIN NDODHUR. 'Only on the next day did Dini think calmly about what HAD HAPPENED.'

Ai filloi të bindej se ISHTE KTHYER papritur e pakujtuar në një trung. 'He began to be persuaded that he HAD BEEN TURNED suddenly and unexpectedly into a tree trunk.'

b) or it may be disconnected from that particular moment in the past:

Dini provoi të kujtonte se si dikur KISHTE HIPUR në një caracë, se si ISHTE VARUR te një degë dhe ISHTE HEDHUR prej saj e KISHTE RËNË shëndoshë e mirë në tokë. 'Dini tried to recall how at one time he HAD CLIMBED up on a hackberry tree, HAD DANGLED from a branch and HAD JUMPED from it, and HAD FAL-

LEN, sound and healthy, to the ground.'

For both these cases, the meaning of past perfect is determined by context. In the first case, the past perfect has value of a perfect-in-the-past, whereas in the second, it has the value of a past-definite-in-the-past. This difference seems clearer in the two sentences below involving indirect discourse. If it is used in direct discourse, the verb will be in either the perfect or the past definite, depending on the temporal meaning:

> **Pastaj njëri nga adjutantët i solli raportin e komandantit të kampit, që lajmëronte se trupat KISHIN ARRITUR të gjitha sipas parashikimit, se ISHIN VËNË roje kudo sipas rregullave, se ISHIN NXJERRË patrulla zbulimi në gjithë zonën dhe se gjithçka tjetër ishte krejt në rregull.** 'Then one of the adjutants brought to him the report of the camp's commander, announcing that all the troops HAD ARRIVED as foreseen, that guards HAD BEEN POSTED everywhere in accordance with the rules, that reconnaisance patrols HAD BEEN sent out ("BROUGHT OUT") throughout the zone, and that everything else was completely in order.'

It we turn the content of the report of the comandant of the camp into direct discourse, then all of the verbs in capitals above are in the perfect:

> **Raporti i komandantit të kampit njofton: ≪ Trupat KANË ARRITUR të gjitha sipas parashikimit, JANË VËNË roje kudo sipas rregullave, JANË NXJERRË patrulla zbulimi në gjithë zonen dhe gjithçka tjetër është krejt në rregull. ≫** 'The report of the camp's commander notes: "The troops HAVE all ARRIVED as foreseen, guards HAVE BEEN POSTED everywhere in accordance with the rules, reconnaissance patrols HAVE BEEN SENT OUT throughout the zone, and everything else is completely in order."'
> **Mirëpo miqtë e tij të ngushtë KISHIN THËNË se në vendin, ku ai shkonte, ishte vështirë të kapje robina.** 'However, his close friends HAD SAID that in the place where he was going, it was difficult to capture female slaves.'
> **Mirëpo miqtë e mi të ngushtë, MË THANË: -- ≪ NË vendin, ku po shkon, është vështirë të kapësh robina. ≫** 'However, my close friends TOLD ME: "At the place where you are going, it is difficult to capture female slaves."'

In both these uses, the past perfect may be accompanied by a temporal adverbial, such as an adverbial prepositional phrase like **që atë ditë** 'since that day', **në atë kohë** 'at that time'; **gjer atëherë** 'until then'; an adverbial nominal phrase like **atë vit** 'that year', **atë verë** 'that summer', or by an adverbial subordinate clause (usually introduced by the subordinating conjunction **para se** 'before'). But the temporal setting may be implied from what has been said before and then need not be expressed:

> **ATË VERË toka KISHTE MARRË zjarr nga aksionet e njësiteve guerile.** 'THAT SUMMER the land HAD caught ("TAKEN") fire from the actions of the guerrilla units.'
> **Gjithë jetën ISHIN PËRPJEKUR qysh e qysh të copëtonin Shqipërizezën dhe ISHIN BËRË aq të zanatit në këtë punë, sa s'ta priste mendja.** 'All their life THEY HAD TRIED by all means to partition unlucky ("black") Albania, and HAD BECOME so clever at this job that you can't imagine.'
> **Po GJER ATË DITË asnjë kështjellë, që KISHTE SULMUAR, nuk u KISHTE QËNDRUAR artilerisë dhe goditjes së ushtrisë turke.** 'But UNTIL THAT DAY not a single castle that he HAD ATTACKED HAD WITHSTOOD the artillery and attack of the Turkish army.'
> **Kronikanin porsa e KISHTE ZËNË gjumi, KUR U ZGJUA NGA BRITMAT E PARA TË ALARMIT.** 'The chronicler HAD just FALLEN asleep ("the sleep HAD CAUGHT him") when he was awakened by the first cries of the alarm.'

NOTES

1. The past perfect is used occasionally, especially in the spoken language, with the value of the conditional perfect in the consequent clause of conditional sentences:

    TË mos të kisha në vatër time, të KISHA VRARË (= do të të kisha vrarë) 'Were you not living in my home ("if I did not have you in my hearth"), I WOULD HAVE KILLED you ("I HAD KILLED you = I would have killed you").'

2. The doubly-compounded form of the past perfect occurs most commonly in northern dialects; in the standard language it is rarely encountered. It is used to indicate the completion of an action prior to a far distant moment in the past:

    -- Është e vetmja brengë, që më mbetet -- shqiptoi më qartë ai, pasi kishte folur një copë herë, në mënyrë të ngatërruar, për një vajzë të bukur dhe inteligjente, me të cilën e KISHIN PASË FEJUAR prindët qysh në fëmijëri. '"It is the only grief that remains to me," he enunciated more clearly, after talking a while in a confused manner about a beautiful and intelligent girl, to whom his parents HAD ENGAGED him since infancy.'

B.5 Pluperfect Tense Uses

The basic meaning of the pluperfect is to indicate an action completed before a particular point in the past. In this sense it is synonymous with the past perfect:

-- Zeqoja u vra! -- thirri Hodo Allamani. -- Jo more! -- ia bëri komandant Rrapoja dhe psherëtiu ngadalë -- Fli, o Zeqo vëllai! -- Është dragua, -- PATËN FOLUR disa. Nga ata që lindin me fletë dhe ngrihen natën vjedhurazi e luftojnë me kuçedrën. Po, ra kështjella e kështjellave që kurrë s'e PAT SHKELUR këmbë armiku. '"Zeqo has been ("was") killed!" yelled Hodo Allamani. "Oh, no!" Commander Rrapo said, and sighed slowly. "Sleep, brother Zeqo!" "He is a dragon," several HAD SAID, "of the type that are born with wings and arise secretly at night and battle the monster. Yes, the castle of castles fell, that enemy foot HAD never TROD."'

Of these two synonymous grammatical forms the past perfect is much more common in present-day Standard Albanian. This is in accordance with the general displacement of the past definite forms (e.g., **qe** and **pat**) of the verbs **jam** and **kam** by those of the imperfect (e.g. **ishte** and **kishte**). However, as the following examples attest, there is still some vacillation between the two:

Andrea Borova shikonte punën e vet, atë punë për të cilën ishte lodhur e shqetësuar muaj të tërë. NË fillim PAT MARRË një tog me baltë, pastaj e KISHTE HEDHUR (=pat hedhur) atë mbi një skelet të hekurt. 'Andrea Borova tended his job, that job which had tired and preoccupied him months on end. In the beginning he HAD TAKEN a pile of mud, then HAD THROWN it over an iron frame.'
Ishte një ditë e diel. Rrojtorja e Bexhetit QE (=ishte) MBUSHUR plot e përplot me njerëz. 'It was a Sunday. The barber shop of Bexhet HAD BEEN (= was) FILLED to capacity with people.'
E ngashërimi im ishte aq i madh sa fytyra më QE (= ish) NGUROSUR e gjendja ime shpirtërore prej kalamani e kishte kaluar atë cakun e njohur të tronditjes, kur lotët nuk dalin më. 'And my anguish was so great that my face HAD BEEN (= was) PETRIFIED, and my infantile spiritual state had passed that well-known point of agitation when tears no longer flow.'

NOTE

In subordinate temporal clauses, introduced by the subordinating conjunction **si** 'as' or **pasi** 'after', the past definite is not uncommonly used in place of the pluperfect:

Si IKU kamarieri, të dy shokët vazhduan për një kohë të gjatë të qeshnin me njeri tjetrin. 'After the waiter LEFT, the two continued to smile at one another for a long time.'

In current Albanian, the pluperfect is also used, though rarely, like a perfect subjunctive to express an action which *might* have been completed prior to the moment of speaking. With this meaning, it is found in subordinate conditional clauses introduced by the subordinating conjunction **po** 'if' (compare the similar use of the past definite in such constructions, as discussed above):

> **Veç haram e paç gjirin, që të kam dhënë, po u PATE RRËFYER ti.** 'Cursed be the milk I have fed you, if you have told them ("may you have the breast forbidden, which I have given you, if you HAD TOLD them.").'

2.3.2 Admirative Mood Uses

In general, the admirative mood is used to express reality accompanied by the speaker's sense of surprise at an unexpected action which has taken place in the past or is taking place at the moment of speaking. If the speaker wishes to express surprise at the failure of an action to take place in the past or at the moment of speaking, the admirative form is preceded by one of the negative proclitics **nuk** or **s'**:

> -- **Ç' ju PASKA NGJARË, more djem?** '"What [in the world] HAS HAPPENED to you, boys?!"'
> **Dhe unë S'PASKAM DITUR gjë! Na matufespi ky i uruar mulli!** 'And I really didn't know ("HAVEN'T KNOWN") a thing! This blessed mill has benumbed us!'

Through use of the admirative mood, the speaker may also express his doubt or dissent, and sometimes irony as well, related to what someone else says:

> **Ç'janë këto akuza monstruoze, këto trajtime prej tregtari ndaj Partisë sonë, popullit tonë dhe një vendi socialist, i cili U HUMBKA dhe U FITUAKA si një lojë bixhozi? Ç' janë këto konsiderata për një parti motër, e cila sipas jush, QENKA hallkë e dobët në lëvizjen komuniste ndërkombëtare?** 'What kind of monstrous accusations are these, these commercial attitudes toward our Party, our people, and a socialist country, which are now ALLEGEDLY TO BE LOST and WON like a gambling game?! What kind of considerations are these for a sister party which, according to you, IS SUPPOSED TO BE a weak link in the international communist movement?!'

In addition to a present tense the admirative mood has three past tenses: imperfect, perfect, and past perfect. On rare occasions a future form constructed of **do të** plus the present admirative of the type **do të lakam** 'I will actually wash!' may also occur:

> **Gëzimin e fshatarëve ato ditë të vitit 1945 e shtoi edhe një lajm tjetër i madh: Kuvendi Popullor paska dekretuar që në maj reformën e plotë agrare e në vjeshtën e këtij viti DO T'U BËKAN ndarje të reja në Grykas.** 'Another great piece of news increased the joy of the villagers in those days of the year 1945. The People's Assembly actually decreed total agrarian reform since May, and in Autumn of this year will implement ("MAKE TO THEM") new [land] distributions in Grykas!'

A. Present Tense Admirative Uses

The basic use of a verb in the present tense of the admirative mood is to express the surprise of the speaker toward an action that continues to be realized at the moment of speaking. With this meaning, the present admirative may be accompanied by the momentive particle **po**:

> -- **QENKENI invalid, -- ha Sokrati, pasi vuri re të ecurit e rëndë të qytetarit të ri me shkop.** '"YOU REALLY ARE an invalid!" said Sokrat, after he noticed the clumsy ("heavy") gait of the new townsman.'
> **E ky...PO e HËNGËRKA me gjithë tavë.** 'And this one...He IS EATING it with the whole casserole [to boot]!'

The present admirative is also used to express the surprise of the speaker toward an action that is repeated time after time. In such a case, like the present indicative (see Section 2.3.1 A), it is not accompanied by the particle **po**:

Ah! Fiqiri, si NDRYSHUAKA njeriu kaq shpejt! 'Ah, Fiqiri, how quickly a human being DOES CHANGE!'

B. Imperfect Tense Admirative Uses

The imperfect of the admirative is used to express the surprise of the speaker toward a particular action operating at a particular moment in the past. In such cases it may be accompanied (though rarely) by the particle **po**:

Atë ditë astronomët bënin fjalë për një kometë, që PO IU AFRUAKËSH tokës me shpejtësi të madhe. 'That day the astronomers spoke ("were making words") of a comet that SUPPOSEDLY WAS APPROACHING the earth at great speed.'

Like the present admirative, the imperfect may also be used to express the surprise of the speaker toward an indefinite action which is repeated time after time in the past. In such cases the verb is never accompanied by the particle **po**:

Thonë se kishte qëlluar nga vendi i kozakëve dhe kozakët, me ç'më kanë dëgjuar veshët, QËNKESHIN kalorës të prapë dhe e PËRDORKËSHIN lakun për të zënë pela të egra, më keq seç e përdornin turqit në ato kohëra për të varur njerëzinë. 'They say that he had come from the land of the Cossacks, and from what my ears have heard, the Cossacks REALLY WERE cunning horsemen, and ACTUALLY USED the lasso to capture wild mares, worse than the Turks who used it in those days to hang people.'

C. Admirative Perfect Tense Uses

The admirative perfect is used to express the surprise of the speaker toward an action whose time scope includes both the past and the moment of speaking:

-- **QËNKE NGRITUR në këmbë! Po më çudit.** '"You're standing up ("YOU HAVE BEEN RAISED to foot")! You surprise me."'
Këtij paska kohë që i PASKA DALË narkoza. 'It's been quite a while since the narcotic wore off this one ("HAS ACTUALLY COME OUT of him").'
Njeri i çuditshëm! Unë tani dua të shpresoj me gjithë shpirt, për gjithë botën! Zemra nuk më PASKA LËNË! 'A strange man! Now I want to hope with all my soul for the whole world! My heart HAS not LEFT me!'
Paskam fuqi të përpiqem! -- Vërtet? -- pyeti ajo e habitur. -- Po ne si s'e PASKEMI MARRË vesh? '"I do have the strength to try!" "Really?" she asked, surprised. "And how is it that we HAVE SOMEHOW not heard ("TAKEN ear") about it?!"'

D. Past Perfect Admirative Uses

The past perfect of the admirative is used to express the surprise of the speaker toward an action that took place prior to a particular moment in the past:

-- **Po atë Memon e PASKËSHIN PLAGOSUR, se ia pashë emrin në ato afishet.** 'But THEY HAD ACTUALLY WOUNDED that Memo guy, because i saw his name on those posters.'
Tani e kuptonte se e PASKËSH DASHUR minierën me gjithë forcën e zemrës, dhe ndofta, u desh kjo provë e vështirë dhe kjo ndarje që të shkoqiste një gjë kaq të thjeshtë. 'He understood now that HE HAD INDEED LOVED the mine with all the strength of his heart, and perhaps this difficult test and this separation was necessary, [in order for him] to unravel so simple a thing.'

-- **Na PASKËSHIN ZBULUAR** -- **tha dikush.** -- **kurse ne s'dinim gjë.** '"THEY HAD DETECTED us!" someone said. "Whereas we didn't know a thing."'

2.3.3 Subjunctive Mood Uses

The subjunctive mood is basically the mood that indicates dependency of the verb. In most sentences a subjunctive verb form will be preceded by an antecedent modal, verb, adjective, adverb, conjunction, noun, or particle to which it is subjoined. Used without such an expressed antecedent, the subjunctive conveys dependence on the speaker's will, and may thus be used by itself to express the speaker's desire for an action, in contrast with the indicative which affirms the independent reality of the action. Using subjunctive forms, other moods may be formed by using various antecedents to express possibility, desirability, or obligation, for example. In English, when the verb is dependent in this way, an infinitive form, with or without the proclitic **to**, is often used; in Gheg dialects of Albanian similar constructions use the infinitive with the proclitic **me**; but in present-day standard Albanian, finite subjunctive forms of the verb indicating the person and number of the subject are used instead:

Në rendin tonë socialist, ashtu siç organizohen puna dhe riprodhimi i zgjeruar socialist, krahas tyre duhet TË ORGANIZOHEN edhe shkolla dhe edukata, që këto T'U PËRGJIGJEN nevojave objektive të socializmit dhe komunizmit, që eksperienca e prodhimit T'I SHËRBEJË mendimit, që zhvillimi i materies TË SQAROJË mendimin dhe ky TË UDHËHEQË e TË NDIHMOJË zhvillimin e praktikës revolucionare, zhvillimin dhe transformimin e shoqërisë. 'In the same way that labor and expanded socialist reproduction are organized in our socialist order, [so also] must the school and education BE ORGANIZED alongside them, that these MAY ANSWER to the objective needs of socialism and communism, that the experience of production MAY SERVE thought, that the development of matter MAY CLARIFY thought, and that this [i.e. thought] MAY GUIDE and AID the development of revolutionary practice, the development and transformation of society.'

-- **Qoftë jotja, o bir, edhe tjetër herë TË të VEJË trimëria mbarë!** 'May it be yours, son, and MAY valor serve you ("GO FOR YOU") well next time.'

Pa mua plakut le TË më MBETET kjo! -- dhe ngriti xha Miti përpjetë bishtin e qepës. '"Just let this be mine ("THAT IT REMAIN to me") as an old man!" and uncle Miti raised the green part ("the tail) of the onion.'

Following are examples which illustrate the contrast in modality between verbs a) in the indicative and b) in the subjunctive:

a) **Mësuesit i zhurmoi në veshë përsëri ato natë. Dhe sa herë KALON këtej, ajo zhurmon e zhurmon.** 'It buzzed in the teacher's ears again on those nights. And whenever HE PASSES BY this way, it buzzes and buzzes.'

b) **Ne do të bëjmë që, sa herë që TË VIJË koha e korrjeve dhe e ditëve të lëmit, ju të shikoni qiellin sikur të ishte...** 'We will act in such a manner that, whenever reaping and threshing time MAY COME, you will look at the sky as if it were...'

a) **Nganjëherë në vendet më të ngushta të saj trupat blokoheshin për një kohë të gjatë, gjersa xhenierët HAPIN ndonjë shteg ndihmës për të përballuar dyndjen e paprerë.** 'Sometimes in its narrowest places the troops would be blocked for a long time, until the engineers OPENED an auxiliary passage so as to resist the incessant movement [of enemy forces].'

b) **Ai vendosi të qëndronte, gjersa mjeku TA SHIKONTE.** 'He resolved to stay until the doctor WOULD SEE HIM.'

a,b) **Si KAM PIRË e si KAM KËNDUAR atë ditë, or shokëni, s'di TË KEM PIRË e TË KEM KËNDUAR në jetën time.** 'The way I drank ("I HAVE DRUNK") and sang ("I

HAVE SUNG") that day, my friends, I don't know WHETHER I (MAY) HAVE
DRUNK or SUNG [like that] in my life.'

The subjunctive mood has a present tense and three past tenses: imperfect, perfect, and
past perfect. In addition, each of these tenses may be preceded by **do** to form new tenses: future, past future, anterior future, and past anterior future.

A. Present Tense Subjunctive Uses

The present subjunctive is used after a variety of antecedents. After modal verbs it
expresses the modality of possibility when preceded by the modal **mund** 'can, may, could'. To
express obligation or necessity, the subjunctive form may be preceded by the modal **duhet** (or
lipset) 'should, ought, must, have to', or by a word sequence that expresses the modality of
obligation, such as **është e nevojshme** 'it is necessary'.

After other verbs in the present tense as antecedent, the present subjunctive form may
follow directly, or it may be preceded by an elucidating subordinating conjunction **që** 'which,
that', a conative subordinating conjunction **që** or **me qëllim që** 'in order that', a temporal
subordinating conjunction, such as **si** 'as', **pasi** 'after', **kur** 'when', **sa** 'as soon as', **porsa** 'just
as', **para se** 'before', **sa herë që** 'whenever', a locative subordinating conjunction, such as **kudo
që** 'wherever', **ngado që** 'wherever, anywhere', **ku** 'where', **nga** 'from'; a conditional subordinating conjunction, such as **po** 'if', **sikur** 'if'; a concessive coordinating conjunction **sado që**
'however much, no matter how much', **sido** 'no matter how, however', **sido që** 'no matter
how, however', **edhe pse** 'although, even though', **edhe sikur** 'even if', etc.; the oppositional
subordinating conjunction **në vend që** 'instead of'; as well as by relative or interrogative conjunctions, such as **që** 'that', **i cili** 'who, which', **kush** 'who', **ç'** 'what', **cili** 'who', **sa** 'how'.

Vështirë është TË ZBËRTHESH shpirtin e njeriut. 'It is difficult TO UNRAVEL the
soul of man.'
-- Kush je ti, njëherë, se nuk di TË KEM TË BËJ me ty? -- hyri në mes qiraxhiu.
'"Who are you, anyway, because I don't know that I have any business ("THAT I HAVE
THAT I DO") with you?" the tenant interposed.'
-- Sado TË MASKOHESH, të njohin, more byrazer! 'No matter how YOU MAY
MASK YOURSELF, they recognize you, brother.'
Tani është natë dhe njerëzit tanë, të lodhur e të këputur, kanë rënë TË FLENË.
'Now it is night and our people, tired and exhausted, have gone to SLEEP ("have fallen
THAT THEY MAY SLEEP").'
Ti vetë the se karabinieri e bën hesap dy herë, po T'i ZGURDULLOSH sytë. 'You
yourself said that the *carabiniere* will think ("makes a calculation") twice, if you MAKE his
eyes POP OUT.'
**Ata do të na sulmojnë, pasi të na kenë lënë disa javë pa ujë dhe përpara se TË
FILLOJNË shirat e shtatorit.** 'They will attack us, after they have left us a few weeks
without water, and before the rains of September begin ("MAY BEGIN").'
**Detyra jonë është TË MBAJMË në gjendje pune këto mjete që kemi e jo TË BËJMË
eksperimente, që TË na HANË kokën.** 'Our duty is to maintain ("THAT WE MAIN-
TAIN") in a working condition these tools that we have, and not to do ("THAT WE DO")
experiments that would finish us off ("that MAY EAT the head to us")'
E fjalën usta s'ia nxjerr dot goja, sikur TË mos JETË bujku usta në punë e tij. 'You
would not get the word craftsman from his lips at all, if the farmer WERE not a craftsman
in his work.'
Këtu ka qiell sa TË DUASH. 'Here you have all the sky you could ("THAT YOU
MAY") WANT.'
**-- Komandant Rrapoja në vend që TË LAJË hesapet me Salih Protopapën, është
mbyllur në Gur-Kusar!** 'Instead of settling ("THAT HE WASH") accounts with Salih
Protopapa, Commander Rrapo is cloistered in Gur-Kusar!'

2.3.3 A. Present Tense Subjunctive Uses   79

Me cilindo që TË BISEDOSH, do të na flasë për vëllanë e tij... 'Whoever YOU (MAY) TALK to will speak to us about his brother...'

NOTES

1. In contrastive subordinate clauses (whether preceded or not by the clarifying conjunction **që**), the present tense of the subjunctive must be used when the antecedent verb in a present, future, or perfect tense expresses will or desire (**dua** 'I like, love', **dëshiroj** 'I desire', **uroj** 'I congratulate, greet, wish well', **urdhëroj** 'I order, command', **porosit** 'I recommend, I request', **kërkoj** 'I search, ask for', **them** 'I say', **këshilloj** 'I advise', **lut** 'I pray, request', etc.) or the opinion or attitude of a person (**mendoj** 'I think', **preferoj** 'I prefer', **duroj** 'I endure', **lë** 'I let', **lejoj** 'I permit', **ndaloj** 'I forbid', **kundërshtoj** 'I oppose', **dyshoj** 'I doubt', **nuk besoj** 'I don't believe', **pres** 'I wait', **parashikoj** 'I foresee', etc.):

Unë S'DUA T'U BESOJ syve se kam përpara një të ri, që sapo mbushi 6 vjet në kërkimet gjeologjike. 'I DON'T WANT TO BELIEVE [my] eyes that I have before me a young man who just completed 6 years in geological research.'

'Një xhade e posaasfaltuar të FTON TË RRITËSH shpejtësinë. 'A newly asphalted road INVITES you to accelerate ("THAT YOU ACCELERATE") the speed.'

Me të hyrë të Lushnjës, hoteli i ri KËRKON TË të BËJË me zor mysafir. 'On entering Lushnjë, the new hotel SEEKS to make ("THAT IT MAKE") you a guest by force.'

Përmeti i ringjallur gërmadhash nuk të LË TË HARROSH mizoritë naziste të 1944-ës. 'Përmet resurrected from ruins won't LET (THAT) you FORGET the Nazi atrocities of 1944.'

2. Especially in the spoken language, but sometimes also in writing, we find the present subjunctive used in place of the imperfect subjunctive. This occurs when it is used after verbs in the indicative imperfect, past definite, past perfect, or pluperfect, that is, after temporal forms not connected to the moment of speaking:

Me këtë ai i DHA TË KUPTOJË (=të kuptonte) se duhej të hynte në pazarllëk me njerëzit, që kishte lënë pas. 'By this he GAVE him TO understand ("THAT THEY UNDERSTAND=UNDERSTOOD") that he should deal with the people he had left behind.'

Kur nisi lufta, fqinjët, sa herë që kishin ndonjë lajm me rëndësi, SHKONIN te Stefani që TË SHOHIN (=të shihnin) mbi hartat e tij se ku kish hyrë gjermani. 'When the war began, the neighbors, whenever they had any news of importance, WOULD GO to Stefan so as to see ("THAT THEY SEE = WERE SEEING") on his maps where the German [foe] had entered.'

Ai, për çudi, nuk ishte nxehur e nuk PATI DHËNË urdhër T'I MARRIN (=t'i merrnin) e T'I ÇOJNË (=t'i çonin) në postë. 'Surprisingly, he did not get upset, and HAD not GIVEN orders for them to take ("THAT THEY TAKE = WOULD TAKE THEM") and DISPATCH them to the post office.'

Besides such optional cases, there are also occasions when the present subjunctive is obligatory after the past definite: when the time of operation of the action designated by the subjunctive verb lies in the future with respect to the time of action of the antecedent verb, or when the past definite is interchangeable with the present perfect (see Section 2.3.1 B.3):

Mos i THE (=ke thënë) gjë TË SHKOJË sonte me hënë për dru? 'Did'nt you TELL (=have told) him, perhaps to go ("THAT HE GO") tonight to cut wood by moonlight?'

As indicated above, the present subjunctive is also used without an antecedent verb or verb phrase. In such cases it expresses the modality of possibility, obligation, or desirability, usually with a future temporal value. It expresses the modality of possibility or obligation:

1. When it is used in direct interrogative clauses, which may begin with or without an interrogative word (interrogative pronoun, adverb, or particle):

Ku TA VËMË? -- pyeti Rustemi. '"Where shall ("MAY") WE PUT IT?" asked Rustem.'

-- Kush TE JETË kaq vonë? -- pyeti doktori më tepër veten sesa të tjerët. '"Who CAN IT BE this late?" asked the doctor more to himself than to others.'

E, o Sulejman Tafili. Ç'fjalë T'I SHPIE tim eti? 'Eh, Sulejman Tafil. What message am I to take ("MAY I TAKE") to my father?'

2. When it is used in interrogative clauses used as exclamations in which the speaker expresses a feeling of anger, protest, surprise, desire, etc.:

S'ke punë në mbledhje ti, po rri aty e mos luaj nga shtëpia. -- Si? TË mos VETE? -- u kthye ajo me fytyrë nga i ati. 'You've got no business at the meeting, so just stay put at home. "What? (THAT) I not GO?" she replied, with her face toward her father.'

-- Gjer këtu TË ARRIJË njeriu, more vëllezër? -- ai e tundi nagantin në dorë. 'Is it possible, brothers, that man should reach this point ("until here THAT MAN ARRIVE")? He shook the revolver in [his] hand.'

-- I plagosur! Ku TA NJOHËSH! -- i tha mësuesi. '"Wounded! How can one tell ("where do YOU RECOGNIZE IT")!" the teacher said to him.'

JUSSIVE mood is a term that conveys the desirability or obligation expressed by the present subjunctive when it is used:

1. with the value of a mild imperative (to order, incite, urge, advise, propose, etc.) It is used with this value not only in the second person singular and plural, but also with or without a proclitic **le** 'let' in the first person plural ("Let's___," "Shall we___") and the third person singular and plural ("Let her___", "Have them___", etc.) which otherwise have no special imperative forms:

-- Po ç'të bëj tjetër? -- TË KËRKOSH kopertona e T'I GJESH ku të jenë. '"But what else can I do?" "[YOU SHOULD] LOOK for tires and FIND THEM wherever they may be."'

Le TA MARRË vesh Salih Protopapa se cilët jemi ne. 'LET Salih Protopapa find out ("TAKE ear") who he is dealing with ("who we are").'

Është kohë bereqeti, LE TË RRINË ky drapër dhe këta kallinj gruri pranë Memos, se, që thoni ju, Memoja e donte edhe draprin edhe grurin. 'It is harvest time, LET this sickle and these ears of grain REMAIN by Memo, because as you know, Memo loved both sickle and grain.'

-- Po errësohet -- ha Rustemi, TË VENDOSIM se ku do të shkojmë sonte. '"It is getting dark," said Rustem, "LET'S DECIDE where we will go tonight."'

TË RRIMË shtrembër e TË PLASIM drejt. 'LET'S SIT CROOKED(LY) but ("and") SPEAK straight.'

Me veten e tij LE TË TALLET, por Naimin TË mos e PREKË. 'LET HIM KID himself but not TOUCH Naim.'

2. with no antecedent to express a hope or desire of the speaker, with very much the same value as the optative mood:

Po s'ka gajle, TË na RROJNË djemtë, dhe me çupa pas, urova me vete, kur pashë Dafinën e dajë Shahinit. '"But it doesn't matter, [long] LIVE our boys, and with daughters hereafter, I said ("wished") to myself, when I saw uncle Shahin's Dafine.'

Hajt faqebardhë! TË RROJË Partia, shokë! Përpara! 'Well, good luck! MAY the Party LIVE [ON], comrades! Forward!'

B. Past Tense Subjunctive Uses

B.1 Imperfect Tense Subjunctive Uses

Imperfect subjunctive forms are used after the same variety of antecedents as the present subjunctive, except that an antecedent verb must be in a past rather than present tense. Where the English equivalent for the present subjunctive is often **may, can,** or **shall** plus verb, for the past imperfect subjunctive it is often **might, could,** or **should** plus verb. The imperfect subjunctive is used, then, in the majority of those cases where the present subjunctive is used (see Section 2.3.3 A), but only after those temporal forms that are not tied to the moment of speaking; that is, after the past definite, the imperfect, the past perfect, and the pluperfect:

Leksi DESHI TË PËRGJIGJEJ, po s'pati kohë. 'Alex WANTED to reply ("THAT HE WAS REPLYING"), but did not have time.'

S'DONTE gjë tjetër veçse TË ZGJASTE një çikë kjo qetësi e vogël, TË ZGJASTE sa TË MERRTE një herë frymë, TË NGOPEJ me ajër dhe TË VENDOSTE. 'HE DID NOT WANT anything else except that this little quiet MIGHT LAST A bit, LAST until HE MIGHT once TAKE a breath, SATIATE HIMSELF with air and [then] DECIDE.'

Dhe e KISHIN RREGULLUAR ashtu që koka t'i BINTE mbi shpëndrat e rrëzës së fikut. 'And THEY HAD ARRANGED it in such manner that the head MIGHT FALL over the herbs at the foot of the fig tree.'

Piloja shikonte t'ëmën, që VINTE anës nëpër shtëpi, sikur TË mos GJENTE derën nga TË DILTE dhe çaplonte e zbërthente nofullat, pa ditur ku TË FUSTE zemërimin. 'Pilo was watching his mother, who WAS GOING about ("along the side of") the house, as if SHE COULD not FIND the door from which SHE COULD EXIT, and was fuming and clenching her jaws, without knowing where TO VENT ("SHE SHOULD INSERT") her anger.'

Një krismë, para se TË HIQTE këmbëzën e pushkës, buçiti. 'A shot rang out, before HE COULD PULL the trigger of the gun.'

As kosovari s'do të ndihej më, kur TË MERRTE vesh që Vita KISHTE DASHUR TË ARRATISEJ me një të panjohur. 'Even the Kosovar would not stir any more when he learned ("TOOK ear") that Vita HAD WANTED TO escape ("THAT SHE MIGHT ESCAPE") with a stranger.'

Po TË DËGJONTE zemrën, a nuk ISHTE një sikur TË DËGJONTE botën, botën që ndjen e atë që s'ndjen! 'If HE WERE to LISTEN to his heart, WOULD IT not BE the same as if HE WERE LISTENING to the outside world, the world that feels and the one that doesn't feel!'

Bujkut në vend që T'I MERREJ fryma, sikur i ERDHI zemra në vend. 'Instead of the farmer losing his breath, ("the breath WOULD BE TAKEN FOR HIM") [it seemed] as if his heart regained its balance ("to him the heart CAME in place").'

DONTE TË TËRHIQEJ, para se TË BINTE. 'HE WANTED TO WITHDRAW, before HE FELL.'

Por, edhe sikur TA VININ re, nuk DO TË ISHIN në gjendje TË NDIQNIN dot kafshët. 'But even if THEY noticed it ("WOULD PUT attention") they WOULD not HAVE BEEN in a position to pursue ("THAT THEY MIGHT PURSUE") the animals.'

DUHEJ TË NDËRHYNTE ndonjë tjetër, ndonjë që TË ISHTE pak i jashtëm. 'Someone else SHOULD HAVE INTERVENED, someone who MIGHT BE a bit of an outsider.'

The imperfect subjunctive is used with the specific sense of past possibility or obligation:

1. When it is preceded by the modal **mund** (either in its invariable form or in one of its past tense forms (except the perfect) or the modal **duhet** in one of its past tense forms (except the perfect). Its use after the present tense of **duhet** is to be avoided in standard Albanian:

Nuk MUND TË GJEJE shenjë nga trupi i tij dhe nga mitralozi, sepse çdo gjë ishte zhdukur. 'You COULD not FIND a trace of his body and of the machine gun, because everything had disappeared.'

Ne MUNDËM TA KALONIM megjithëse të lodhur, të këputur. 'We WERE ABLE TO CROSS IT, eventhough tired, exhausted.'

Po edhe në vend nuk DUHEJ TË QËNDRONIM. 'But WE SHOULD not HAVE STOOD STILL ("IN PLACE") either.'

Për të arritur në këto fitore të mëdha, popullit shqiptar IU DESH TË BËNTE sakrifica të mëdha. 'In order to achieve these great gains, the Albanian people had to ("TO IT WAS NEEDED") make great sacrifices.'

2. When it is used in direct interrogative clauses, with or without an antecedent interrogative word:

SI TË QËNDRONTE në një shtëpi tok me atë? 'HOW COULD HE STAY ("HOW THAT HE MIGHT STAY") in a house together with him?'

Konxheja nuk foli më. E Ç'TË FLISTE? ''Konxhe did not speak any more. WHAT COULD SHE SAY?'

Po ME SE TË SHKONTE? 'But how ("WITH WHAT") COULD SHE GO?'

3. When it is used in interrogative or declarative exclamatory clauses, expressing anger, protest, surprise, desire, etc.:

E ku T'I SHKONTE asaj në mendje se një ditë do të takohej me të papritur e papandehur! 'And how could she imagine ("where TO HER WOULD IT BE GOING in mind") that one day she would meet him suddenly and unexpectedly!'

Kur Ç'TË SHIKOJE! 'What a sight that was ("When WHAT YOU MIGHT BE SEEING")!'

IU derdh ky Bogdani si qen stani. Mirë nga dera e prindit doli ashtu si doli, po në prak të Adilit si TË SHKELTE kështu! 'This Bogdan guy rushed at him like a sheepdog. Granted he came out of his parent's door as he did, but how COULD HE STEP over the threshold of Adil like this!'

Sikur TË KISHIM proteza! Unë do t'u mësoja se si të ecnin për së dyti. 'If WE [ONLY] HAD the prostheses! I would teach them how to walk again.'

In hypothetical sentences, the antecedent clause, whether introduced by a subordinating conjunction **po** (or **sikur**) 'if' or not, often uses an imperfect subjunctive form to express a counterfactual condition, that is, one which the speaker supposes to have little or no possibility of being realized (see Section 2.3.7 C below).

Unë, o Sulejman Tafili, do t'i duroja më fort, po TË më LËSHOHESHIN pa atë djall pipërimë. 'I, oh Sulejman Tafil, could stand them better, if they WERE TO UNLEASH THEMSELVES ON ME without that devilish squeaking.'

Po hane sa mirë do të na vinte, po TA GJENIN nga ne, bujqëria. 'But how well we would have felt long ago, if they had been punished by ("THEY WERE TO FIND IT from") us, the peasantry.'

Ti ke të drejtë të çuditesh -- tha kryeveqilharxhi. -- Edhe unë, po TË ISHA në vendin tënd, kështu do të çuditesha. "You are right to be surprised," said the chief advocate. "I, too, if I WERE in your place, would be surprised."'

NOTE

Instead of the regular form of the imperfect subjunctive of the verb **jam** (**të isha, të ishe,** etc.), in colloquial and occasionally in written Albanian sub-standard forms like **të qeshë, të qe,** etc., are encountered:

Dhanë e morën, e kthyen mbarë e prapë atë të flamosur gjuhë, sikur TË QE (= të ishte) pe e s'futej dot në vrimën e gjilpërës. 'They tried this tack and that, they turned that unfortunate language forward and backward, as if IT WAS thread that could not go through the eye of the needle.'

2.3.3 B.1 Imperfect Tense Subjunctive Uses   83

B.2 Subjunctive Present Perfect Tense Uses

The perfect subjunctive may be preceded by the modal **mund** in its invariable form (see Section 2.3.7 B.3) to indicate possibility in a way that corresponds to English *may have* + participle. When it is preceded by the modal **duhet** in its present tense form, the verb in the perfect subjunctive may, like English *is* or *(are) supposed to have* + participle, express the modality of surmised obligation (=English *should have* + participle) or surmised probability (=English *must have* + participle):

Një kompani prej 47 vetësh ka ardhur në Malin e Brate dhe MUND TË JETË HEDHUR nga Smokthina. 'A company of 47 persons has arrived on Brat Mountain and MAY HAVE left ("BEEN THROWN") for Smokthine.'

Sot DUHET TA KENË VARROSUR. DUHET TË KETË QENË mbarimi i marsit ose fillimi i prillit 1915. 'Today THEY MUST HAVE BURIED IT. IT MUST HAVE BEEN the end of March or the beginning of April, 1915.'

Skënderi më tha se ata MUND TË KENË ARDHUR për punë të kanalit. 'Skënder told me that they MAY HAVE COME in regard to the canal.'

The perfect subjunctive also occurs without an antecedent: in subject clauses and object complement clauses; after verbs in the present indicative that express the will or attitude of the speaker (see Section 2.3.7 B.3); in subordinate clauses introduced by one of the temporal conjunctions **kur** 'when', **si** 'after', **pasi** 'after', etc.; one of the locative conjunctions **kudo që** 'wherever', **ngado që** 'from all sides, wherever'; clauses introduced by one of the conditional conjunctions **po** 'if', **sikur** 'if'; or by one of the concessive conjunctions **sado** 'no matter how much', **sado që** 'no matter how much', **sido** 'no matter how', **sido që** 'no matter how', **edhe sikur** 'even if', etc:

Ka rrezik që Salih Protopapa TË KETË ZËNË grykat. 'There is a danger that Salih Protopapa MAY HAVE SEIZED the passes.'

Ka mundësi që qysh atëherë ata TË KENË MARRË të dhënat e para për ekzistencën e ujësjellësit tonë. 'There is the possibility that since that time they MAY HAVE GOTTEN the first data on the existence of our aqueduct.'

Pyesin sikur ne TË KEMI ARDHUR këtu për të bërë sehir. 'They ask as if we (MAY) HAVE COME here [just] to watch.'

Kështu kanë thënë e mund të jetë e vërtetë se Zaganj e Mojsinj e Hamzanj ka pasur edhe në shtëpitë e tjera të zotërve tanë, dhe më vjen turp TË KETË DALË dhe një nga shtëpia e mëmës sime. 'This is what they have said, and it may be true that there have been Zaga and Mojsi and Hamza [types of people] even in other houses of our masters, and I feel ashamed tha even one MAY HAVE ARISEN from my mother's house.'

Po, që T'I KETË VAJTUR mendja asaj apo mua se babai do të marrë ndonjë ditë pendën dhe të shkruajë një tregim...kurrë. 'But that IT MAY HAVE CROSSED her mind or mine that father would one day take up his pen and write a story...never.'

Po, kur TË KENI LEXUAR dhe këtë histori të dytë, do të shihni se ai... 'However, when YOU (MAY) HAVE READ this second tale, you will see that he...'

Nën ujë gurët skuqin nga myshqet e leshterikët, sikur T'I KETË NGJYER dikush me bojë të kuqe. 'Beneath the water the stones are red from the moss and seaweed, as if someone HAD PAINTED THEM with red paint.'

Do të bëj një fyell, që TË MOS E KEM BËRË kurrë! 'I will make a flute, such that I HAVE never MADE before!'

In temporal subordinate clauses, the perfect subjunctive may indicate a possible action that is prior to some point in the future, such as one indicated by a future tense verb in the controlling clause or by an adverbial referring to the future. In such a case, it is parallel to the anterior future indicative:

Kur TË KETË HYRË në thellësi, ti do të hapësh zjarr dhe do të zbresësh në bisht të kolonës së tyre. 'When IT HAS ENTERED deep within, you will open fire and descend on the tail [end] of their column.'

Ata do të sulmojnë, pasi të na KENË LËNË disa javë pa ujë. 'They will attack us, after THEY HAVE LEFT us several weeks without water.'

Ai dha urdhër që sonte TË KENË MBARUAR duajt së lidhuri. 'He gave orders that by tonight THEY SHOULD HAVE FINISHED binding the sheaves.'

The perfect subjunctive is also used in interrogative or declarative exclamatory clauses, sometimes with the additional nuance of doubting:

TË KETË QENË Kozmai? 'COULD it HAVE BEEN Kozma?'

Ta kesh kokën tënde dhe TË ta KETË RRËMBYER tjetri?! 'To have your head and [then to have] someone else GRAB IT from you?!'

Thua t'i KETË MARRË malli i nënës, i gruas, i fëmijës? 'Do you suppose ("you say") they BECAME nostalgic ("that nostalgia MAY HAVE TAKEN them") for their families ("mother, wife, children")?'

The perfect jussive tense, formed by the perfect subjunctive with or without the proclitic **le**, is occasionally used to express a mild imperative that is to be executed prior to a particular moment in the future:

Kjo punë TË KETË MARRË fund gjer nesër! 'Let this job be completed ("THAT IT HAVE TAKEN end") by tomorrow!'

B.3 Subjunctive Past Perfect Tense Uses

The past perfect subjunctive, like the present perfect subjunctive, may be preceded by the antecedent modal **mund** in its invariable form, in which case it is equivalent to English *might* (or *could) have* + participle, expressing past possibility; or by the antecedent **duhet** in one of its imperfect forms, in which case it is equivalent to English *was (were) supposed to* or *ought to have* + participle, expressing past obligation:

Lirinë MUND TA KISHIT FITUAR me trimërinë tuaj edhe menjëtjetër çlirimtar. 'With your valor, you COULD HAVE WON liberty with another liberator as well.'

Ai mendoi se ç'arkitekt MUND TA KISHTE PROJEKTUAR këtë kështjellë. 'He pondered what architect COULD HAVE DESIGNED ("PROJECTED") this castle?'

Prapëseprapë dyshimi se MUND TË ISHIN ZBULUAR prej kështjellarëve, u varej mbi kokë. 'Just the same, the suspicion that they MIGHT HAVE BEEN DETECTED by the residents of the castle, hung over [their] heads.

Pat kaluar dreka dhe djaloshi DUHEJ TË KISHTE MARRË nga lengu, që doktori ia pat dhënë kundër malarjes. 'Lunch time had passed, and the boy OUGHT TO HAVE TAKEN of the liquid against malaria that the doctor had given him.'

In the same types of subordinate clauses in which the present perfect subjunctive is used, the past subjunctive is used even more frequently. In conditional sentences the past subjunctive, introduced or not by a subordinating conjunction **po** (or **sikur**) 'if' is particularly common, as well as in subordinate clauses introduced by the subordinating conjunction **sikur** 'as if':

S'e zura dot, ke hak, se, po TA KISHA ZËNË, e dija vetë. 'I didn't catch it at all, you're right, because if I HAD CAUGHT IT, I would know it myself.'

Sikur TË mos e KISHTE PARË Sania, Vita do të kishte rendur andej nga ta çonin jo zemra, po këmbët. 'If Sania HAD not SEEN HER, Vita would have run over to where [her] feet, not heart, would take her.'

U kthye andej vramuz, sikur TA KISHIN LIDHUR A RRAHUR me ata litarë, që po kërkonte, e TA KISHIN HEQUR zvarrë në ca rrugë të panjohura. 'He returned over there scowling, as if THEY HAD TIED OR BEATEN HIM UP with those ropes he was looking for, and HAD DRAGGED HIM along some unfamiliar streets.'

Mimoza uli kokën nga turpi dhe gishtërinjtë, që i punonin shtizat, i pushuan menjëherë, sikur TË ISHTE PARALIZUAR. 'Mimoza bent her head down from embarrassment, and the fingers that worked the knitting needles, stopped all at once, as if SHE HAD BEEN PARALYZED.'

Unë mora në dorë shokun e vrarë, një pionier, që zor T'I KISHTE MBUSHUR të katërmbëdhjetat. 'I took in my arms the slain comrade, a pioneer, who barely HAD completed ("FILLED") [his] fourteenth [year].'

The past perfect is also encountered on rare occasions without an antecedent, espcially to express a desire which can no longer be realized:

-- Si të harroj? Le që do ta gjesh në shkollë. TA KISHA GJETUR këtu! -- tha vajza -- S'më pelqen të mërzis gjithë dynjanë. '"How [can] I forget? Besides you will find it in school. I wish I had ("I SHOULD HAVE") FOUND IT here!" said the girl. "I don't like to bother everybody [about it]."

NOTE

The forms of the so-called subjunctive-admirative, constructed of the proclitic **të** plus the imperfect admirative forms of an auxiliary plus a participle, have a restricted use in both colloquial and literary Albanian. In regard to use, it combines the meaning of the admirative with the syntax of the imperfect subjunctive:

Poshtë tufave të reve ngjyrë plumbi flutorojnë e sillen rrotull ca re të vogla, të zeza pis, sikur TË QENKESHIN tym prej dinamiti. 'Below the lead-colored cluster of clouds, there fly around and roam about a few small clouds, pitch-black, as if THEY ACTUALLY WERE dynamite smoke.'

Ra dhe u ronit e u shkri, sikur TË PASKËSH QENË prej dëbore. 'It fell and crumbled and dissolved, as if IT WERE ACTUALLY [made] of snow.'

Sikur e gjyshja TË mos PASKËSH NXJERRË kokën nga qerrja e TË mos E PASKËSH THIRRUR, kushedi sa gjatë do të kishte mbetur ashtu, më këmbë, në mes të shiut, që ishte shtruar mbi fushë. 'If his grandmother HAD not ACTUALLY STUCK her head OUT of the cart and HAD not ACTUALLY CALLED him, who knows how long he would have remained like that, standing, in the (midst of the) rain that had settled over the plain.'

C. Future Tense Uses

The basic use of future tenses, all constructed with **do** + a subjunctive verb form, is to indicate actions operative sometime after a point of reference. When that reference point is the moment of speaking and no ending time limit is given, the future subjunctive, constructed of **do** + present subjunctive, of the type **do të bëj** 'I will do', is usually used:

Unë ndjej kënaqësinë e rrallë që ta has këtu, majëshkëmbit, tek vërtit në kokë projektidenë, duke soditur gërxhet e greminat, ku DO TË NGJITEN xhade të tjera, DO TË ÇELEN të tjera galeri, DO TË HIDHEN në erë shkëmbinjtë. 'I anticipate the rare pleasure that I may find it here, atop the rock, as I ponder the idea of the project in [my] head, while contemplating the crags and ravines, where other roads WILL CLIMB, other tunnels WILL BE OPENED, the rocks WILL BE blown up ("THROWN into the air").'

Constructions with some form of **kam** + infinitive of the type **kam për të bërë**, literally 'I have for doing', may be used with the same meaning as the future subjunctive, although in many instances they add to that meaning an implication of a present obligation to perform the action: in meaning it is thus either something like English *will* in *will do* or like *have* in *have (something) to do*. In the first case they are then sometimes equivalent to the future subjunctive of the type **do të bëj**, but more often, they are only partly synonymous with such a formation. In Gheg dialects the construction **kam** + infinitive (with **me** rather than **për të**) is used instead of the future composed of **do** + present subjunctive.

a)   **Të jap fjalën e burrit se nuk KAM PËR të KALLËZUAR Adilin.** 'I give you my word
     ("the word of the man") that I WILL not ACCUSE ("I DO NOT HAVE [REASON] TO
     ACCUSE") Adil.'
     **DO TË RRI shtrirë në diell gjithë ditën, DO TË ÇLODHEM e rrobat KANË PËR
     T'U THARË.** 'I WILL lie ("STAY" lying) in the sun all day, I WILL REST and the
     clothes WILL HAVE [TIME] TO DRY.'
     **Shokët KANË PËR TË më KËRKUAR. Me siguri do t'u shkojë mendja se jam në
     lumë.** 'The comrades WILL LOOK for me ("HAVE me TO LOOK FOR"). Assuredly
     they will think ("to them the mind will go") that I am in the river.'

b)   **Gruaja u ul në kolltuk, rregulloi flokët me duar dhe i tha djaloshit: -- Sot S'KE PËR
     TË SHKUAR në shkollë. DO TË MËSOJMË bashkë.** 'The woman sat down in the
     armchair, arranged her hair with her hands and said to the boy: "Today YOU WILL NOT
     GO ("YOU HAVE NOT TO GO") to school. WE SHALL STUDY together.'

The second and third person forms of the simple future are sometimes used with an
imperative meaning, to give an order, a request or instructions, sometimes more categorically
than the imperative mood itself (compare English *Close the door.* with *You will close the door!*):

     Këmbës t'i biesh tashti, atë DO TË MARRËSH se ai qe kismet i yt. 'Do what you
     will, ("however you may strike your foot now"), that is who YOU WILL marry ("TAKE"),
     because that is ("was") your fate.'
     **Nejse, edhe sikur të mos kthehet Guri, ti DO TË SHKOSH vetë në Korçë, Demkë! --
     iu drejtua mësuesi Demkës.** '"No matter, even if Guri does not return, you WILL GO
     to Korçë yourself, Demkë!" the teacher said ("directed himself") to Demkë.'

The future subjunctive of the verbs **jam** and **kam**, mostly in the second and third person
forms, is sometimes used with the evidential sense of 'turn out to...' rather than of a future
'will':

     Apo mos kushedi ka zemër të mirë? E ç'zemër DO TË KETË ai, moj e mjerë! 'Or is
     he after all somehow good hearted ("have a good heart")? And how can he be good
     hearted ("what heart DOES HE TURN OUT TO HAVE"), you poor girl!'
     **Memoja dhe Xhemali shikuan njëri-tjetrin. Ky DO TË JETË Rrapoja menduan dhe e
     lanë trungun e lisit.** 'Memo and Xhemal looked at each other. "This must ("WILL") BE
     Rrapo," they thought and they left the trunk of the oak tree.'
     **-- Kushedi se Ç'DO TË KESH, se dhëmbi pas heqjes s'duhej të të dhimbte -- tha
     Rrapoja.** '"Who knows what's bothering you ("WHAT YOU TURN OUT TO HAVE"),
     because after extraction, the tooth ought not to have hurt you," said Rrapo.'

C.1 Subjunctive Future Perfect Uses

Forms constructed of the future subjunctive of **kam** (**jam** for passives) + participle, of
the type **do të kem punuar** 'I will have worked', are used only rarely in Albanian to indicate an
action which is to be completed before some future point of time:

     **-- Ata do të pendohen për këtë sherr të madh, që nisën me ne, por atëherë do të jetë
     vonë -- tha kronikani. -- Shumë gjak DO TË JETË DERDHUR.** '"They will regret
     this great quarrel they began with us, but then it will be [too] late," said the chronicler.
     "Much blood WILL HAVE BEEN SHED."'
     **-- Këtu -- kryeveqilharxhi, tregoi me dorë tokën -- ata do të shikojnë gjurmët e kampit
     tonë, që shirat e dimrit DO T'I KENË PRISHUR e MBULUAR me baltë, por që nuk
     DO T'I KENË ZHDUKUR dot krejtësisht.** '"Here," the chief advocate pointed to the
     land with his hand, "they will see the traces of our camp, which the winter rains WILL
     HAVE DAMAGED and COVERED with mud, but which WILL by no means HAVE
     ERASED entirely."'
     Nuk ia kam thënë Halilit se sa më është dhimbsur Shkëmbi i Pishkashit, Tryeza e

Skënderbeut, që ai nisi të hidhte në erë sot e dy vjet dhe që, për pak kohë, do të jetë një rrënojë, prej së cilës DO TË KENË NXJERRË mijëra toneleta mineral të kuq. 'I have not told (it to) Halil how hurt I felt about the Rock of Pishkash, the Table of Skënderbeu, which he began to blow up two years ago, and which in a little while will be a ruin, from which they WILL HAVE EXTRACTED thousands of tons of red ore.'

The future perfect is more often used to express the probability that an action is already completed by the time of the moment of reference. In this usage it is like the perfect subjunctive preceded by a verb with the modal value of 'could' or 'might':

A DO TË KENË IKUR ato dallandyshet prej çerdhes në ballkonin e shtëpisë sonë? 'I wonder if ("WILL") those swallows HAVE LEFT the nest on the balcony of our house?'
-- Ku ta dish, mbase edhe kanë ikur. '"Who knows, perhaps they have left."'
-- Me siguri -- MENDOI Memoja -- DO TA KETË MARRË vesh mendimin tonë për Spiron. '"For sure," THOUGHT Memo, he WILL HAVE heard ("TAKEN ear") about what we think of Spiro."'
Edhe fjalët e rënda, që thashë unë për të fejuarin e saj, DO TA KENË DËSHPËRUAR. 'The hard words, too, that I spoke about her fiance probably ("WILL") HAVE DISTRESSED HER.'

C.2 Subjunctive Future Past Perfect Uses

A future past perfect tense constructed of **do** + past perfect subjunctive, of the type **do të kisha larë**, is rarely used to express a future action to be completed before a particular moment in the past. However, like the future perfect, it is used to express the probability that an action has already been completed by the time of the reference moment, in the case of this tense, a moment in the past:

Ata e kishin parë tek ikte kaluar me t'ëmën prapa dhe e morën me mend se këtij njeriu diç DO T'I KISHTE NGJARË. 'They had seen him as he went riding with his mother in the rear, and they understood ("took with mind") that something MUST HAVE HAPPENED to this man.'
Vishej trashë dhe kaq keq i rrinin rrobat në trup, sa menjëherë formoje bindje se këto rroba dikush DO T'ia KISH FALUR. 'He wore heavy clothes, and the garments so ill suited him that at once you became convinced that someone MUST HAVE DONATED these clothes to him.'

C.3 Future Imperfect Tense Uses

The basic use of the future imperfect, constructed of **do** + imperfect subjunctive, is to indicate an action which is to be operative after a reference moment in the past. When a past moment is established as the point of reference, as may happen in consequent clauses of conditional sentences whose antecedent clause is in a past tense, in relative clauses embedded in sentences with past tense main verbs, and in indirect discourse after a verb of saying or thinking (e.g., **them** 'I say', **mendoj** 'I think', **kujtoj** 'I recall', **pandeh** 'I suppose', **shpresoj** 'I hope') in the past definite or imperfect, a future imperfect form may be used to express the future in respect to the past:

Nga ana tjetër, shpresoi se gjithë kujdesi i tepruar, që tregonte nëna për vëllanë e madh, tani DO TË BINTE mbi këtë. 'On the other hand, she hoped that all the excessive care that her mother had shown for her older brother WOULD now FALL upon her.'
Dhe, sa herë që mundohej të përfytyronte atë "burrin", me të cilin pas disa muajve DO TË MARTOHEJ, përpara syve të mendjes, atje pranë tij, i dilte edhe Raifi. 'And, whenever she tried to envisage that "husband" to whom she WOULD BE MARRIED after a few months, in her mind's eye, close to him, there appeared Raifi as well.'

Dulla i tha se atë ditë DO TË PUNONIN me orar të zgjatur, ndaj ata nuk do të bënin gabim, po të kalonin në ndonjë tavolinë tjetër. 'Dulla told him that on that day they WOULD BE WORKING on an extended schedule so that they would not be making a mistake if they moved over to another table.'

2.3.4 Optative Mood Uses

Modality of desire is expressed by the optative mood verb forms as a wish, blessing, or curse:

-- Isha gati për të qarë dhe po qesh si budalla. HË, MOS VDEKSH kurrë, o xha Spiro, dhe ti, o djalë, U BËFSH ç'të them, u mendua i sëmuri. 'I was ready to cry and here I am laughing like crazy. Hey, MAY YOU never DIE, uncle Spiro, and you, son, MAY YOU BECOME, what shall I say, considered the sick man.'

-- Vezir, -- qeshi një tjetër. -- Jo, jo, -- vazhdoi i sëmuri dhe aty për aty shtoi: -- U BËFSH njeri i madh, të NDEROFSHIN të gjithë!' '"Vizier," another joked. "No, no," continued the sick man and right away added, "MAY YOU BECOME a great man, MAY everyone HONOR you."'

"Aj, murgjinjë, të ÇAFTË ujku të ÇAFTË!" '"Oh, dun cow, MAY the wolf CHOP you UP, CHOP you UP."'

Note in the last example how the optative verb is repeated for emphasis. The intonation on the repetition is at a low, unchanging pitch, like an "under the breath" afterthought.

The optative mood has two tenses: present and perfect.

In clauses with negative meaning the proclitic particle of negation **mos** is used rather than **s'** or **nuk,** before the optative.

A. Present Tense Optative Uses

The basic use of the present tense of the optative mood is to express the speaker's wish in respect to an action at the moment of speaking or after it:

-- Dhe ti, o bir, QOFSH i gëzuar e të RROFSHIN djemtë e u HËNGËRSH dasmën, që na bëre të kujtojmë ato kohë të qëmoçme, -- tha plaku e mbushi kupat. '"And you, son, MAY YOU be mirthful and MAY your boys LIVE (LONG) and MAY YOU CELE-BRATE ("EAT") their wedding, (you) who made us recall those old times" the old man said and filled up the glasses.'

Qe stanar Istrefi. Stanar i THËNÇIN, se njëzet krerë s'i kishte në tufë. 'It was the livestock breeder, Istref. Livestock breeder so-called ("MAY THEY SAY to him"), be-cause he didn't have twenty heads in his herd.'

Ju KËNDOFTË zemra, o bijtë e mi! -- uroi xha Miti që nga fundi i zemrës. '"MAY your heart SING, o my sons!" wished uncle Miti from the bottom of his heart.'

However, the present optative may also be used to express a possible future action, without particularly expressing the speaker's wish for that action, when it appears after **në** 'if', or **edhe në** 'even if' in the antecedent clause of a hypothetical sentence. In such a usage, it is synonymous with the present subjunctive preceded by the subordinating conjunctions **po** 'if' and **edhe po** 'even if' respectively:

Atëherë EDHE NË I PUSHTOFSHIM ne, nuk kemi për t'i nënshtruar dot më. 'Then, EVEN IF we OCCUPY THEM, we shall not be able to subdue them any more.'

EDHE NË RËNÇA, do të arrij të mbështetem pas murit. 'EVEN IF I FALL, I will manage to support myself against the wall.'

The third person (and occasionally the second person as well) of the verb **jam** in the present optative is also used synonymously with the present subjunctive after the relative conjunctions **kushdo** 'whoever', and **cilido** 'whichever, whoever,' and the adverbial conjunctions **kudo** 'wherever' and **kurdo** 'whenever':

> **Njeriu, që e mban në duar atë fletë, CILIDO QOFTË, veç armikut, e ndjen menjëherë veten pjesëtar të kësaj lufte.** 'The man who holds that card in his hand, WHOEVER HE MAY BE, except the enemy, feels himself at once to be a participant in this struggle.'
> **Folmë, thuam, CILIDO QOFTË.** 'Speak to me, tell me, WHOEVER IT MAY BE.'

B. Perfect Tense Optative Uses

The perfect tense of the optative, unlike the present tense, has a much more restricted usage in its basic meaning, since only in very special cases can it express the wish of the speaker for an already completed action:

> **E moj Parti, të QOFSHA FALË për këto gëzime që na jep!** 'Oh Party, be thanked ("MAY I HAVE THANKED") for these joys that you give us!

In antecedent clauses of hypothetical sentences the perfect optative is also used very occasionally after the conjunction **në**:

> -- **NË PAÇIM PUNUAR edhe ne kështu për ngritjen e kooperativës, vaj halli.** '"If we too HAD WORKED like this in the setting up of the cooperative, forget it!"'
> -- **Ai sot të ndjek e, po të rrethoi, të vret, si na vrau ca ditë më parë një shokun tonë në Tiranë, Qemal Stafën, NË E PAÇ DËGJUAR.** 'Today he pursues you and, if he surrounds you, he kills you, as he killed a few days ago a comrade of ours in Tiranë, Qemal Stafë, IF YOU HAVE HEARD OF HIM.'

Instead of the perfect optative in antecedent clauses the perfect subjunctive preceded by the conditional subordinating conjunction **po** is more often used.

We occasionally find the perfect optative used in the WHAT IF exclamatory or interrogative clauses: **po në më PASTË PRITUR e pastaj të jetë larguar?!** 'But (what) if he HAD WAITED for me and then had left?!'

2.3.5 Imperative Mood Uses

As indicated in Section 2.1.4, modality of desire in the form of a command, a demand, advice, a request, an appeal, an invitation, permission, etc., is expressed by the imperative mood. To form the negative, the particle **mos** 'don't' is placed before the imperative form:

> -- **LINI pushkët, LINI pushkët e MOS GJUANI më, o gjahtarë -- urdhëron Mark Shalëgjati, i pari i gjahut.** 'LEAVE the guns, LEAVE the guns and DON'T HUNT any more, o hunters, orders Mark Shalëgjati, the leading man of the hunt.'
> -- **DËgjove ti, o Milosh, o bir? ZGJIDH të njëqind kalorësit më të mirë dhe kalorësit e mi dhe NISU.** 'Did you hear, o Milosh, o son? CHOOSE the best one hundred riders and my riders and DEPART.'

This mood has person forms only for the second person singular and plural. If the speaker, through the participants in the conversation, wishes to order one or several persons who are not taking part in the conversation, he uses the third person forms of the present subjunctive in the singular or plural, preceded or not by the particle **le** 'let, leave' (see Section 2.3.7 B.2 on Jussives), with the sense of an imperative. The first person plural of the present subjunctive is also used with an imperative sense when the speaker wishes to motivate a group of persons toward an action in which he will also take part (like English "let's go"). The future subjunctive is also sometimes used with imperative force (see Section 2.3.3 C).

The basic meaning of the imperative is to express the desire of the speaker with nuances of a) ordering, b) inviting, c) advising, d) imploring, e) approving the performance of action at the moment of speaking or after it:

a) ordering:
"MOS U AFRONI te gropa!" "LARGOHUNI nga gardhi!" -- dha urdhër komandanti i
njësitit. '"DON'T GET NEAR the hole!" "GET AWAY from the fence!" ordered the
commander of the detachment.'
b) inciting or inviting:
-- Atëherë ZGJIDHE vetë, hajt, BËHU burrë! 'Then RESOLVE IT yourself, come
on, be ("BECOME") a man!'
-- TË betohem se s'do t'i them kurrkujt, veç BËJI shpejt. 'I swear to you that I won't
tell anyone, just DO THEM quickly.'
c) advising or requesting:
-- QETËSOHU, -- i pëshpëriti infermierja -- MUNDOHU të flesh. '"RELAX" the
nurse whispered to him, "TRY to sleep."'
-- DËGJOMË e mos m'U ZËMËRO, një fjalë do të të them: Mos U DORËZO, mos e
LËSHO veten; e di që je pa këmbë, po mos U DORËZO. Po u dorëzove, humbe fare.
'"LISTEN TO ME and do not BE ANGRY with me. I have but one bit of advice for you:
don't SURRENDER, don't let go ("RELEASE the self"); I know that you lost your legs,
but don't SURRENDER. If you surrender, you're totally lost."'
d) imploring:
-- MË THUAJ të drejtën ç'sëmundje kishin minjtë, që lëshuam ne gjatë sulmit? --
pyeti me zë lutës jeniçeri. '"TELL me the truth, what disease did the mice that we
released during the offensive have?" asked the Jannissary in a pleading voice.'
-- Uh, aman, LERINI këto muhabete -- tha biondja. '"Oh, please, stop ("LEAVE
THEM") these conversations," said the blonde.'
e) approving, allowing:
-- THUAJE të shkretën, -- ndërhyri DINI, -- mos të të vijë zor, THUAJE troç, siç të
ka hije; THUAJE se jam një copë sakat, që kërkon të barazohet me njerëzit normalë.
'"(You may) SAY the worst," intervened Dini, "don't be squeamish, SAY IT bluntly, as it
behooves you; SAY that I am just a cripple, who is trying to be the equal of normal people."

To indicate with special expressive force one or more actions repeated in the past, the
second person singular of the imperative may be used with subjects in all three persons, singular or plural, whether expressed or unexpressed in the sentence. In such cases, the imperative
of a single verb is repeated, or the imperative forms of two or more different verbs may be
used, accompanied by their respective subjects or not, and connected either asyndetically or by
the coordinating conjunction e 'and':

Gjermani HIDH në zjarr një jastëk, xha Mekja HIDH dy. 'The German threw
("THROW!") one pillow into the fire, uncle Meko threw '"THROW!") two.'
PËrpara rendte xhaxhai me "austriakun" në dorë e pas vinim ne. HIDHU e bot nëpër
driza e ferra, RRËSHQIT në hendeqe, bjer në pellgje me ujë! 'Ahead ran our uncle
with the gun ("the Austrian") in his hand, while we followed. We jumped ("THROW
YOURSELF!") like crazy over brush and bramble, slid ("SLIP!") into ditches, fell
("FALL!") into pools of water.'
E të na u bënë, or të keqen, këmbët gjak! Dhe QAJ e IK, dhe QAJ e REND, dhe
QAJ e KLITH, nënëza e vrarë arriti majë çukës më të këndejmë të maleve të
Zavalinës, e thirri e thirri tri herë. 'And our feet, mind you, became bloodied! Thus,
weeping ("WEEP!") and walking ("GO!"), and weeping and running ("RUN!"), and weep-
ing and screaming ("SCREAM!"), the wounded mother reached the nearest peak of the
Zavalinë mountains, and shouted three times.'

2.3.6 Uses of the Participle

The participle is a non-finite verb form with semantic and grammatical qualities that are both verbal and adjectival. In Albanian, the participle is an invariable verb form, which can be turned into an adjective by preposing an adjectival article (see Section 4.7.1 A). When used in a predicative function a participle is similar in meaning to an adjective derived from it.

Compare the predicative
Dritaren e gjeta HAPUR. 'I found the window OPENED.'
with the adjectival
Dritaren e gjeta TË HAPUR. 'I found the window OPEN.'

When used in this predicative function, the participle indicates that the designated action is completed or finished.

The participle as such in Albanian does not reflect differences in voice, aspect, mood, person or number. However, when they appear as independent constitutents, the participles of transitive verbs have a passive perfect sense.

O flamur gjak, o flamur shkabë / O vend e vatër, o nën e bab', / LAGUR me lot, DJEGUR me flakë, / Flamur i kuq, flamur i zi. 'Oh blood flag, o eagle flag / oh country and hearth, oh mother and father, / MOISTENED with tears, BURNED with flame / red flag, black flag.'

The fact that articulated adjectives formed from the stems and participles of these verbs generally have a passive meaning also gives support to the hypothesis that participles of transitive verbs have a basically passive sense: **i vrarë** 'slain', **i shkruar** 'written', **i zbukuruar** 'beautified', **i përkthyer** 'translated', **i hapur** 'open(ed)', **i përhapur** 'spread out', etc. On the other hand, participles of intransitive verbs always have an active sense: **i shëtitur** 'strolling'. A few adjectives formed from participles of transitive verbs may have either an active sense or a passive one, depending on the context: **njeri i ditur** 'a learned man', **fakti i ditur** 'the known fact'.

The participle in Albanian has limited use as a constituent in itself; more often, it serves as a component part of complex verbal forms. It is used, for example, in the formation of the compound tenses of the past (see Sections 2.2.3 A.2 c, d, and e), the present and imperfect of the admirative (see Sections 2.2.3 B.1 and B.2), and the present tense of the optative of some verbs (see Section 2.2.3 D).

It is also a constituent of non-finite constructions of the type **pa punuar** 'without working', **duke punuar** 'working, while working' (and **me punue** 'to work' in the Gheg dialect) (see Section 2.2.5 B.1c).

As an independent constituent the participle serves: a) as a predicate complement of the object; b) in absolute constructions as an independent nominal qualifier; c) as the complement of the modals **do** and **duhet**; d) as a predicate of a copular clause:

a) **Nusja e Leksit e mbajti një copë herë NGRITUR, përgjysmë, për t'ia lehtësuar nxjerrjen e vrerit**. 'Leksi's wife held him up ("RAISED") for a while, bent double, in order to facilitate the expulsion of the bile.'

b) **Qetë e shpiragajve, MËSUAR në rrugë fushore dhe me ngarkesë afife sane, kallinjsh e lëpushkash, po kullonin djersë**. 'The oxen of the Shpiragaj, HABITUATED to plain roads and to loads of hay, grain stalks and mullein, were drenched in sweat.'
ARRATISUR, SYRGJYNOSUR / RASKAPITUR E KATOSUR / Brohorit me besë e shpresë / Anës Elbës, anës Spree-së. 'EXILED, CONFINED / FATIGUED and KNOCKED DOWN / I shout with faith and hope / along the Elbe, along the Spree [rivers].'

Xhaketën -- ç'ka, nuk e kishte të keqe, një kadife kombinati BLERË e QEPUR disa muaj më parë, po pantallona zezat s'mbaheshin më! 'The jacket--so-so, it wasn't bad, a factory velvet, BOUGHT and SEWN several months earlier, but the miserable pants were not worth wearing any more!'

NOTE

In functions a) and b) the corresponding adjective with a preposed article is more common:

Hallati, I TREMBUR nga gjithë ato ngjyra, që i farfurinë befas para syve, u ngrit kas dhe shkrofëtiu me të keq. 'FRIGHTENED by all those colors that radiated suddenly before his eyes, Hallat reared up and snorted threateningly.'

TË TMERRUAR nga trimëria juaj dhe nga shkatërrimi i garnizonit të Krujës, ndofta do të na e lëshojnë fortesën me të mirë. 'TERRIFIED by your valor and by the destruction of the Krujë garrison, they may surrender the fortress peacefully.'

c) **Po unë sillesha në atë mënyrë, se ashtu e donte shpëtimi juaj edhe imi, se puna ishte e atillë që DUHEJ BËRË e jo THËNË.** 'But I behaved in that fashion, because your salvation and mine called for it, because the job was such that IT HAD TO BE DONE and not talked about ("SAID").'

DUHEN BËRË vijat kulluese pa mbjellë, shoqja brigadiere. 'The drainage troughs MUST BE prepared ("MADE") before planting, comrade brigadier.'

Ara DO KORRUR, gruri DO SHIRË, lopa DO MJELË, hajvanët DUHEN GRA-ZHDUAR. 'The field NEEDS REAPING, the wheat NEEDS THRESHING, the cow NEEDS MILKING, the livestock NEED feeding ("STABLING").'

d) **"ZGJUAR qenka", i tha vetes dhe e vështroi përsëri.** '"She has finally AWAKENED," he said to himself, and he looked at her again.'

Participles of transitive verbs used as predicates of copular sentences indicate a temporary state or condition of the subject; they may be replaced by the corresponding adjectives with preposed article:

MBYLLUR (= E MBYLLUR) është dera, apo HAPUR? 'Is the door CLOSED or OPEN(ED)?'

NOTES

1. The participle may also be used predicatively in absolute constructions with the value of temporal dependent clauses: **ARDHUR në kohën kur Vita po zhvaste rrobën nga supet, ato iu sulën përsipër.** 'HAVING ARRIVED at the time when Vita was stripping the garment off her shoulders, they threw themselves at her.'

2. The participle **shkuar** 'gone' followed by a noun in the dative case is used to repeat in a reinforcing way the predicate nominative or predicate complement:

Ky është turp e SHKUAR turpit. 'This is disgrace beyond disgrace ("disgrace and PAST disgrace").'

A. Uses of Participial Constructions

As discussed in Section 2.2.5, PRIVATIVE constructions of the type **pa larë** 'without washing' and GERUNDIVE constructions of the type **duke larë** 'while, by washing, washing' are composed of the participle preceded by **pa** or **duke**.

The observations that follow apply also to the infinitive form of the type **me la** 'washing' of the Gheg dialect, for which see the remarks in Section 2.2.5 B.1c.

These non-finite forms are semantically and grammatically different from the bare participle. Active forms of transitive verbs in these non-finite constructions generally have an active sense, but the bare participle has a passive sense. Transitive verbs used in these non-finite forms may thus take direct objects as well as indirect ones:

Ndofta ju shkoi në mendje që e kisha harruar edhe atdheun, edhe nderin, edhe lirinë, kur ju ktheja prapë të helmuar PA JU DHËNË ASNJË SHPRESË dhe PA JU TREGUAR ASNJË NDJENJË fisnike dhe shpirtmadhe. 'Perhaps you thought that I had forgotten the fatherland, and honor, and liberty, when I turned you back dejected WITHOUT GIVING YOU ANY HOPE and WITHOUT SHOWING YOU A SINGLE noble and magnanimous SENTIMENT.'

S'kam lënë vend PA TË KËRKUAR. 'I have searched for you everywhere ("I have not left place WITHOUT SEEKING YOU").'

Pse? Ç'i ke bërë ti atij që të ka në dorë? -- pyeti gruaja DUKE MOS IA HEQUR dorën e djathtë nga qafa, kurse me dorën tjetër fshinte faqet e lagura. '"Why? What have you done to him that he has you in his control?" asked [his] wife WITHOUT TAKING OFF her right hand from his neck, while with her other hand she wiped off his wet cheeks.'

Active forms of intransitive verbs in these non-finite forms may take indirect objects.

-- Xha Llazari? -- i tha Stavri, DUKE I DALË përpara dhe DUKE VËSHTRUAR i qeshur e i gëzuar fytyrën vrarëlije të mësuesit. '"Uncle Llazar?" Stavri said to him, going over to him ("WHILE EMERGING forward TO HIM") and LOOKING at the pock-marked face of the teacher, smiling and joyous.'

The non-finite constructions under examination here are also distinguished from participles by other grammatical qualities. Whereas the bare participle is grammatically invariable, gerundive and privative constructions do reflect voice distinctions: for transitive verbs these constructions have both an active form and a passive form, the latter constructed with the reflexive particle **u** between the particle **pa** or **duke** and the participle:

Përparojmë në këtë mënyrë PA U DIKTUAR dhe, kur afrohemi 200 m, hapim zjarr mbi ta. 'We advance in this manner WITHOUT BEING DETECTED, and when we approach within 200 m., we open fire on them.'

Por Selamiu, PA U VIZITUAR ende nga mjekët e spitalit, pati ndihmën e komunistëve të spitalit. 'But WITHOUT BEING VISITED yet by the doctors of the hospital, Selami received help from the communists in the hospital.'

Ecte me hap të gjatë, DUKE U PENGUAR nëpër plisa. 'He walked in long strides, stumbling ("WHILE BEING HINDERED") in the turf.'

In contrast to the participle, gerundives and privatives may have a subject that is different from the subject of the controlling clause:

Kuajt, sikur ta dinin sa nxitohej i zoti të mbaronte lëmin PA RËNË muzgu, ia nisën, përsëri, zdrënkthi. 'The horses, as if they knew how their owner was hurrying to finish the threshing before dusk ("WITHOUT dusk FALLING"), began again at a gallop.'

Agimin e gjetën te Çezma DUKE PIRË ujë. 'They found Agim at the Fountain, DRINKING water.'

A.1 Uses of Privatives

Privative constructions express the negative of gerundive constructions. They indicate a condition in which the action designated by the verb is absent. The temporal reference of the privative is tied to the temporal reference of the verb in the controlling clause: in general it expresses the absence of an action at the time of the action named by the controlling verb:

PA LUAJTUR këmbët, nuk luajnë dhëmbët. 'WITHOUT MOVING the feet, the teeth do not move (i.e., he who does not work, does not eat).'

Erdhi PA E FTUAR kush. 'He came WITHOUT BEING INVITED by anybody.'

Mos ik PA na LAJMËRUAR. 'Don't go WITHOUT NOTIFYING us.'

U nis PA ZBARDHUR dita. 'He left before dawn ("WITHOUT the day WHITENING").'

NOTE

On rare occasions in the written language one also encounters a compounded PERFECT PRIVATIVE construction of the type **pa pasë larë** 'without having washed':

Nga sa kam para syve materialin, po PA PASË KRYER ndonjë kërkim të veçantë, mua më del se... 'Judging from the material before my eyes, but WITHOUT HAVING COMPLETED any special inquiry, it appears to me that...'

Privative constructions are chiefly used:

1. With a predicative function, after such verbs as **jam** 'I am', **kam** 'I have', **mbetem** 'I remain, I am left', **rri** 'I sit, stay', **lë** 'I let':

Një herë u tërhoq, por hodhi në sulm rezervat, që ISHIN akoma PA REGJISTRUAR dhe përsëri fitoi. 'Once he withdrew, but threw into the attack the reserves that WERE still UNREGISTERED and again he won.'

Iu kujtua Qemal Orhanaj, me të cilin ajo KISHTE muaj PA U PARË dhe kishte hequr çdo shpresë që të shihej më. 'She recalled Qemal Orhanaj, whom she had not seen for months ("with whom she HAD months WITHOUT BEING SEEN") and had given up any hope of ever seeing again.'

Një copë herë Hajdar beu MBETI si dru më këmbë, PA NXJERRË asnjë fjalë nga goja dhe PA LËVIZUR fare nga vendi. 'For a while Hajdar Bey stood standing ("REMAINED on the feet") like a tree, WITHOUT saying a word ("TAKING OUT any word from the mouth") and WITHOUT MOVING at all from the spot.'

Përveç kësaj KISHTE NDENJUR disa ditë PA DALË në diell dhe as në rërë. 'Besides this, HE HAD REMAINED several days WITHOUT GOING OUT in the sun nor even on the sand.'

QËNDRUAN një copë herë PA FOLUR duke i dëgjuar njëri-tjetrit të rrahurat e zemrës. 'THEY REMAINED a while WITHOUT SPEAKING, listening to each other's heartbeats.'

Dua s'dua, DO TË LË kështu PA THËNË shumë gjëra, të cilat, ndonëse jashtë temës, kanë edhe ato rëndësinë e tyre. 'Like it or not, I WILL thus LEAVE many things UNSAID, which, although not appropriate to the subject, have their own particular importance.'

2. With a temporal function.

When used in this function, the temporal subordinating conjunction **sa** '(even) as much (as)' or the particle **që** '(even) before', may appear before it:

PA MBARUAR mirë këto fjalë, një zë nga mesi i turmës bërtet. 'These words hardly finished ("WITHOUT FINISHING well"), a voice from the midst of the crowd roars.'

PO, PA ARRITUR te selia, pa tek vinte drejt tij Jorgj Borën, të ndjekur nga një çun dhjetëvjeçar. 'But before ("WITHOUT") ARRIVING at headquarters, he saw coming toward him Jorgj Bora, followed by a ten-year-old kid.'

Po kjo duket si një anakronizëm, se më 1444 Skënderbeu nuk ishte mjaft i fortë sa të përvishej për një ekspeditë jashtë Shqipërisë, SA PA MBUSHUR motin, qëkur zaptoi Krujën dhe ngriti krye kundër Sulltanit. 'But this seems like an anachronism, because in 1444 Skënderbeu was not strong enough to mount an expedition outside Albania, not even ("AS MUCH AS WITHOUT FILLING") a year after he captured Krujë and rebelled against the Sultan.'

QË PA DALË nga makina, krushk Vasili hodhi një sy rreth e rrotull për të kërkuar miqtë. 'EVEN BEFORE GETTING OUT of the car, cousin Vasil cast his eyes about in search of his friends.'

3. As a circumstantial adverbial:

Po pashai i Gjirokastrës, me të dëgjuar këtë lajm, mblodhi një ushtri të madhe dhe hyri me tradhti në qytet, kur garnizoni dhe ndënjësit po flinin të qetë, dhe e zaptoi kështjellën pothuaj PA DERDHUR gjak. 'But as soon as he heard this news, the Pasha of Gjirokastër assembled a great army and entered the city by treachery, when the garrison and the inhabitants were sleeping peacefully, and captured the fortress almost WITHOUT SHEDDING blood.'

4. With a conditional function:

Realizimi i boshtit ideologijik marksist-leninist në gjithë punën e shkollës nuk mund të arrihet, PA ZBATUAR parimin e njohur marksist-leninist të lidhjes së mësimit me punën prodhuese, PA e ZBATUAR jo me fjalë dhe në mënyrë akademike, por konkretisht, edhe në mënyrë praktike. 'The realization of the ideological Marxist-Leninist axis in the entire work of the school, cannot be attained WITHOUT IMPLE-MENTING the well-known Marxist-Leninist principle of the link between learning and productive labor, WITHOUT IMPLEMENTING it not with words and in an academic manner, but concretely and in a practical manner.'

PA LUAJTUR këmbët, nuk luajnë dhëmbët. 'Unless the feet move ("WITHOUT MOVING the feet"), the teeth won't move.' (i.e., if you don't work, you don't eat)

PA NGRËNË hudhra, s'të vjen erë goja. 'If you don't eat ("WITHOUT EATING") garlic, your mouth won't smell.'

NOTES

1. In constructions with conditional or adverbial functions, the non-finite negative form is synonymous with the negative gerundive: **duke mos larë** 'by not washing'.

2. In constructions with a predicative function, the privative construction is similar in meaning to the corresponding derived adjective with the prefix **pa-**, the difference residing in whether the characteristic is considered to be a regular characteristic (adjective) or a temporary condition (privative):

a) **Ku e lamë e ku na mbeti / Vaj-vatani e mjer-mileti / Anës detit I PALARË / Anës dritës I PAPARË / Pranë sofrës I PANGRËNË / Pranë dijes I PANXËNË!** 'How we left it and how it stagnated / Sad country and wretched folk / By the sea [and yet] UNWASHED / By the light [and yet] UNSEEN / Near the dining table [and yet] UNFED / Near learning [and yet] UNTUTORED!'

b) **PA NGRËNË e PA PIRË / S'mbetemi, moj Mirë.** 'WITHOUT EATING and WITHOUT DRINKING / We won't remain, oh Mirë.'

-- Ç'më do? -- iu përgjigj Tana e u ngrit duke lënë PA PASTRUAR një panxhar, që kishte në dorë. '"What do you want?" Tana replied to him, and she got up, leaving UNCLEANED a beet she had in her hand.'

A.2 Uses of Gerundives

Verbs in this non-finite form express an action that accompanies the action in the controlling clause, usually occurring at the same time. The temporal reference of the gerundive is thus determined by the tense of the controlling clause. Since the action expressed by it is usually realized at the same time as that of the controlling clause, the gerundive, according to context, may refer to the present, past, or future events:

Një zë, që iu duk tepër i njohur, PO PYESTE DUKE U AFRUAR. 'A voice that seemed very familiar to him, WAS QUESTIONING WHILE COMING NEARER.'

Po vjen një ditë që pjeshka, e pjekur dhe e mbushur plot me lëng, del nga fletët e pemës ku qëndron fshehur e, DUKE ZBULUAR gjithë bukurinë e saj, DUKET sikur i thotë udhëtarit, që kalon aty pranë: këputmë e futmë në gji! 'But a day comes when the peach, ripe and juicy, pops out of the leaves of the tree where it remains hidden, and, UNCOVERING all of its beauty, SEEMS to be saying to the traveler who passes by: Pick me off and put me in your bosom!'

Kur të arrini ju atje do t'i gjeni vullnetarët DUKE PUNUAR. 'When you arrive there, you will find the volunteers WORKING.'

NOTE

In written Albanian, a compounded PERFECT GERUNDIVE construction of the type **duke pasë larë** (see Section 2.2.5 B.1b) is occasionally encountered:

Marrëdhëniet midis qytetit dhe fshatit në vendin tonë janë ndërtuar në baza socialiste, në bazë të shkëmbimit të prodhimeve bujqësore dhe industriale, DUKE PASË LIKUIDUAR me kohë sistemin e dorëzimit të detyrueshëm nga ana e fshatarësisë të të gjithë tepricave shtetit dhe DUKE E PASË ZËVENDËSUAR atë me sistemin e shitjes së lirë të tepricave. 'Relations between the city and the village in our country are built on socialist bases, on the basis of the exchange of agricultural and industrial products, HAVING LIQUIDATED long ago the system of obligatory deliveries by the peasantry of all surplus to the state, and HAVING REPLACED that with the system of the free sale of surpluses.'

As indicated in Section 2.3.7, the gerundive is also used in progressive constructions with the auxiliary **jam** in the present or imperfect indicative.

In addition to this function, the gerundive is used in constructions:

1. with the function of a manner adverbial:

Njeriu po afrohej DUKE ECUR në mënyrë të çuditshme. 'The man was approaching BY WALKING in a strange manner.'

O nëna të shtrenjta, që jeni gëdhirë pa gjumë kushedi sa herë DUKE NDENJUR mbi shtratin tonë e DUKE na LEDHATUAR me duart punëtore, të fishkura e plot damare, faqet, ballin, flokët! 'O dear mothers, who have spent who knows how many sleepless nights STAYING by our bed and CARESSING with your working hands, shriveled and full of veins, our cheeks, forehead, hair.'

2. with the function of a temporal adverb:

Ai e dinte se mbasdite, DUKE DËGJUAR fjalimin e tij, qindra mijëra njerëz do të pyetnin veten: do të ketë vallë bllokadë? 'He knew that in the afternoon, hundreds of thousands of people, LISTENING to his speech, would ask themselves: will there be a blockade?'

DUKE KALUAR përpara Mapos, i ra ndërmend të blinte një suvenir. 'PASSING by the Mapo, it occurred to her to buy a souvenir.'

3. with the function of a causative adverbial:

Gjermanët janë nisur që nga Dibra e Martaneshi, DUKE PANDEHUR se ne do të qëndrojmë atje. 'The Germans have set out all the way from Dibër and Martanesh, IMAGINING that we would remain there.'

DUKE PASUR frikë se mos e diktonte plaku, bëri sikur nuk e vuri re, po në të kthyer të rrugës i bëri shenjë me dorë. 'Fearing that the old man might detect him, he pretended not to notice him, but at the turn of the road he signalled him with his hand.'

DUKE mos DITUR ç'të bënte, nisi të lexonte përsëri automatikisht. 'Not KNOWING what to do, he began to read again automatically.'

4. with a conditional function:

DUKE SHTRËNGUAR radhët tona rreth PARTISË, DUKE FORCUAR vigjilencën, DUKE SHUMËFISHUAR përpjekjet tona për të realizuar me sukses më mirë se çdo herë tjetër detyrat për realizimin e planit të shtetit në të gjitha fushat, ne do të dalim faqebardhë. 'BY TIGHTENING our ranks around the Party, STRENGTHENING our vigilance, MULTIPLYING our efforts so as to realize successfully better than any other time the tasks for the fulfillment of the state plan in all areas, we will emerge victorious.'

DUKE U MARTUAR në këtë rast, i cili pa dyshim nuk ishte për dasmë, Skënderbeu do të fuste zjarrin në shtëpinë e vet. 'BY MARRYING at this time, which undoubtedly was not suitable for a wedding, Skënderbeu would have ignited a fire in his own house.'

5. with a predicative function:

U mësua që, kur vinte në shtëpi, ta gjente DUKE PUNUAR me futë përpara, ose të ulur në tryezë. 'He got accustomed, when he would go home, to finding her WORKING with apron on, or seated at the table.'

M'u duk sikur pashë në rrugë një tufë kalorësish DUKE IKUR me të katra. 'It seemed to me that I saw a bunch of riders galloping ("GOING on all fours") on the road.'

The gerundive is also used relatively often to express a second action whose meaning is coordinated with that of the verb in the controlling clause:

-- Mbaroi edhe Salih Protopapa -- tha Memoja DUKE KTHYER (= dhe ktheu) krahët. '"Salih Protopapa is finished", said Memo, TURNING (= and he turned) his back.'

-- Ti ishe atje -- tha kronikani DUKE ZGJATUR (= dhe zgjati) dorën. '"You were there", said the chronicler, HOLDING OUT (=and he held out) his hand.'

Arkitekti ngrinte vazhdimisht dorën, DUKE TREGUAR (=dhe tregonte) një rreth sipër kokës së tij. 'The architect raised [his] hand continuously, POINTING (=and pointed) to a hoop above his head.'

A.3 Uses of Infinitives

As might be supposed from their form, the non-finite verbal forms of the type **për të larë** 'to wash' and **me të larë** were historically formed with a deverbal neuter noun. The component parts of these constructions lost their grammatical independence, and the constructions have taken on semantic and grammatical qualities characteristic of the infinitive forms of verbs in other languages.

A.3a. Infinitives with **për**

The so-called INFINITIVE in contemporary standard Albanian is used frequently but in a restricted number of functions, unlike the Gheg infinitive (e.g., **me la** 'to wash') which is used in a wide range of infinitival functions. Infinitives of the type **me la** have a dialectal character (they are only used by Gheg speakers) and have not been adopted into the national literary language. The Gheg infinitive is variable in voice (**me la** 'to wash' / **me u la** 'to be washed, to wash oneself') and, more rarely, in tense (**me pasë la** 'to have washed'):

Edhe gjashtë vjet, nanë, ti ME PA' PRITË (=me pasë pritë) / Un vetë kmishën, nanë, kish hjekë. 'Even had you waited ("TO HAVE WAITED") six years, mother / I would have taken off my shirt myself, mother.'

In Gheg, infinitives are also used to form the future indicative or present conditional with the auxiliary **kam** in the present or imperfect indicative, respectively:

Sot i jav (=javë) na si n'kjoshim gjallë/KAM ME DALË te Bregu i Gjatë/e me vedi nusen KAM ME E MARRË. 'A week from today, if we are still alive/I WILL COME OUT to the Breg i Gjatë/and I WILL TAKE the bride with me.'

ME ja PA spatën e tij,/të dyve merak KI'ME NA HI (=kish me na hi). 'If we had seen ("TO SEE") his sword, we would both have been siezed with fear ("to both the fear WOULD HAVE ENTERED").'

In contrast, in contemporary Standard Albanian infinitival forms of the type **për të larë** are used more narrowly in constructions:

1. As clause adverbials indicating purpose, with the sense "in order to".

Dhe i gjori fshatar që me mëngjes, pa hapur grykën e qesesë PËR TË HEDHUR ndonjë lek, detyrohej që ta zgjidhte PËR të PAGUAR tagrambledhësin, se përndryshe e priste burgu. 'And the poor peasant, from morning on, before even opening the neck of his purse TO drop ("THROW") a lek [inside], was obliged to untie it IN ORDER TO PAY the tax collector, because otherwise jail awaited him.'

Aleksi priste me padurim që ta thërrisnin në komitetin e partisë PËR T'I DHËNË përgjigjen. 'Alex waited impatiently to be called to the party committee IN ORDER TO GIVE IT the answer.'

In this function the infinitive form may be preceded either by the particle **si** 'as if' or by the particle **sa** 'as much, sufficient':

Atëherë ngriti sytë, pa kosovarin dhe tundi kokën SI PËR TA FALËNDERUAR. 'Then he lifted his eyes, saw the Kosovar, and nodded his head AS IF TO THANK HIM.'

Fjalët e fundit i tha SA PËR T'I DHËNË zemër djalit. 'The final words he uttered ONLY TO GIVE heart to the boy.'

2. With an adjectival function.

Shqipëria ka NJERËZ TË ZOTËT PËR TË QEVERISUR. 'Albania has PEOPLE CAPABLE of ("FOR") GOVERNING.'

MË ndodhi diçka e papritur, DIÇKA PËR TË QESHUR E PËR TË QARË. 'Something unexpected happened to me, SOMETHING comical and tearful ("FOR LAUGHING AND FOR CRYING").'

DËSHIRA PËR TA TAKUAR i qe shtuar më shumë. 'His DESIRE TO MEET HIM had increased still more.'

In this adjectival function too, infinitive forms may be preceded by the particle **si** or **sa**:

Një qëndrim pak SI PËR TË QESHUR mbante zoti Banka. 'Mr. Banka maintained a somewhat ridiculous ("AS IF TO LAUGH") position.'

I duhet dhënë fund prodhimit SA PËR TË PRODHUAR, me qëllim që të realizohet vëllimi global. 'An end must be put to producing FOR THE SAKE OF PRODUCING in order to satisfy the overall quota.'

3. With an obligational function

Infinitive forms are used after such verbs as a) **jam**; b) **kam**; c) **bëhem** 'I become' to express a modal sense of obligation or expectation. This sense is most pronounced in constructions with **jam**:

a) -- **Dale, bre, dale. Ç'është kështu me ty? Qan, kur ËSHTË PËR TË QESHUR -- i hoqi vërejtjen Zefi, duke u ulur në kanapenë pranë dritares, që shikonte nga oborri.** '"Take it easy, I say, take it easy. Why are you behaving like this? You cry, when one should laugh ("IT is TO LAUGH)," Zef reprimanded him, as he sat down on the sofa near the window that looked out on the courtyard.'

Pastaj i tha: TI JE PËR TË VRARË por nuk të vras. 'Then he said to him: you ought to be shot, ("YOU ARE TO KILL"), but I won't shoot you.'

In predicating strings of this type these non-finite forms may be preceded by the particle **sa** 'just enough':

Po mendimi i mjekut ishte që ky ilaç ISHTE SA PËR TË SHTYRË ditët. 'But the doctor's opinion was that this medicine EXISTED JUST TO PROLONG life.'

b) **Nuk e kupton ai vallë se kush KISHTE PËR TË PRERË dru, i ka prerë prej kohësh? -- mendoi Zana me nervozizëm.** '"Doesn't he understand, perhaps, that whoever was ("HAD") TO CUT wood, did so long ago?" Zana thought nervously.'

KEMI edhe shumë punë PËR TË BËRË. 'WE HAVE much work TO DO yet.'

c) **Atëherë iu kujtua se e bija ISHTE BËRË PËR T'U MARTUAR.** 'Then he remembered that his daughter was old enough to marry ("HAD BECOME FOR GETTING MARRIED").'

TI JE BËRË PËR TË LIDHUR, Gori Pisha. 'YOU are fit to be tied ("HAVE

BECOME FOR TYING"), Gori Pisha.'

4. In emphatic constructions of the type **PËR TË NJOHUR, E NJOH** 'AS FOR KNOWING [HIM], I [DO] KNOW [HIM]', in which the infinitive serves to pull out and accentuate the semantic content of the finite form that follows it:

> **PËR TË DËGJUAR, KAM DËGJUAR që Piloja ka shitur dele në pazar.** 'AS FOR HEARING (things), I HAVE HEARD that Pilo has sold sheep in the market.'
>
> **KËshtu e kanë ata: PËR TË MARRË, MARRIN nga ne; PËR TË DHËNË, S'JAPIN.** 'This is how they are: WHEN IT COMES TO TAKING, THEY TAKE from us; WHEN IT COMES TO GIVING, THEY DON'T GIVE.'

5. In constructions with the function of subjects of clauses.

Infinitives are seldom used as subjects in Albanian; when they are, it is usually after the verb **mbetet** 'is left, remains' (in the third person singular only):

> **I mbetej vetëm PËR të RREGULLUAR çatinë e kosheres.** 'It only remained for him TO FIX the roof of the beehive.'
>
> **Tani na ka mbetur PËR TË KËRKUAR vetëm një ushtar i ditës së parë.** 'Now all that remains for us is to SEARCH FOR a soldier of the first day.'

6. As component parts of future and conditional constructions (see Section 2.3.7 B.1).

7. As terms of comparison, accompanied by the comparative conjunctions **sesa** (or **se**) 'than':

> **Pa humbur kohë, Skënderbeu botoi një manifest, ku deklaronte shkaqet e luftës, duke theksuar veçanërisht pikën që kjo ishte një luftë për të shpëtuar Shqipërinë nga copëtimi më tepër SESA PËR TË MARRË Danjën.** 'Without losing any time, Skënderbeu published a manifesto, where he declared the causes of war, stressing especially the point that this was more a battle to save Albania from dismemberment THAN TO TAKE Danjë.'
>
> **Është më shumë për të qarë SE PËR TË QESHUR.** 'It is more [fitting] to cry THAN TO LAUGH.'

8. Finally, infinitives are used (especially in journalistic style) as objects of certain verbs:

> **I tha se asnjeri nuk kishte menduar PËR TA SHQETËSUAR.** 'He told him that nobody had thought of annoying him ("TO ANNOY HIM").'
>
> **Kjo gjë ndihmon PËR TË SQARUAR më mirë problemin.** 'This thing helps TO CLARIFY the problem better.'

It should be mentioned that it is regularly not used with this function after verbs that express the speaker's will, such as: **dua** 'I want', **dëshiroj** 'I desire', **uroj** 'I greet', **urdhëroj** 'I order, command', **porosit** 'I request', **them** 'I propose, say', **kërkoj** 'I seek', **fut** 'I insert', etc.; or his stance, such as: **preferoj** 'I prefer', **duroj** 'I endure', **lë** 'I let', **lejoj** 'I permit', ndaloj 'I prohibit', kundërshtoj 'I oppose', **dyshoj** 'I doubt', **pres** 'I wait', etc.; nor is it used after the modal **mund**. Finite subjunctive verb forms are normally used after these verbs in contemporary Standard Albanian.

A.3b. Participial Absolutes

PARTICIPIAL ABSOLUTES are participles preceded by **me të** to indicate an action on whose realization the action expressed by the controlling verb is contingent. Such constructions may be marked for passive voice (see Section 2.2.5 A.1b).

The action expressed by participial absolutes may be:

1. An individual action completed in the past or expected to be completed in the future, depending on whether the controlling verb designates a particular action in the past (as it does in a past definite or, more rarely, past perfect tense) or in the future (as it does in the future tense, in a present tense with a future sense, in the imperative mood, or in a present

subjunctive with an imperative sense):

> **ME TË PARË Dekon, ai U NDAL, SHTËMËNGU me njërën këmbë macen dhe ia bëri me kokë shokut që të kthehej.** 'UPON SEEING Deko, he STOPPED, REMOVED the cat with one foot and motioned with his head to his comrade to return.'

> **ME TË RËNË muzgu, ISHIN MBLEDHUR tek fiku njerëzit e Koz Dynjasë e të Pip Kedhit.** 'Dusk HAVING FALLEN, the people of Koz Dynja and Pip Kedhi WERE ASSEMBLED by the fig tree.'

> **Adili KISHTE ZËNË të shtruarat, ME T'U KTHYER nga pazari.** 'Adil had set himself down on the carpet ("HAD CAUGHT the laid down ones"), IMMEDIATELY UPON RETURNING from the market.'

> **Ja, i themi se, ME T'U MARTUAR unë, DO TA PAJTOJMË, vajzën.** 'Well, we [can] tell him that AS SOON AS I AM MARRIED WE WILL HIRE the girl.'

> **Kiu Gremi kishte shkuar në arë tek lëronte e i kishte kërkuar pendenën me fjalën se DO T'IA KTHENTE, ME TË IKUR beu nga fshati.** 'Kiu Grem had gone to the field where he was plowing, and had asked him to give him the team of oxen with the promise that he WOULD RETURN IT TO HIM, AS SOON AS the bey LEFT the village.'

> **Tashti mos vrit mendjen hiç, po, ME TË MBYLLUR dyqanin, m'i SHKO vrap në shtëpi.** 'Now, don't bother your head, at all, but instead AS SOON AS [you] CLOSE the store GO quickly to his house.'

2. An action that has been repeated in the past or that is expected to be repeated in the future. In this case also, the time sense of the non-finite form is determined by whether the controlling verb indicates an action that is repeated in the past (when it is in the imperfect indicative) or is to be repeated in the future (when it appears in a future tense, or less often in the present indicative or subjunctive with an imperative sense):

> **Si duket, ai i uruari kumbare, ME TË DALË jashtë trollit të gjyshes e ME T'I SHKUAR ëmbëlsira e fiqve, HARRONTE sakaq, tek mendonte djersën, që duhej të derdhte për të vënë në vend dëshirën e tij.** 'Apparently, that blessed godfather, HAVING LEFT his grandmother's soil and AS SOON AS the sweetness of the figs LEFT HIM, WOULD immediately FORGET, as he thought of the sweat he would have to expend in order to attain his desire.'

> **Si një merimangë e zezë, ME T'U PREKUR një fijëz ZGJOHET E BËHET GATI të mbrohet a të sulmojë.** 'Like a black spider, [which] AS SOON AS a thread [of its web] is TOUCHED, AWAKENS AND GETS READY to defend herself or to attack.'

NOTE

Instead of the non-finite form constructed of **me të** + participle, one occasionally finds in contemporary Standard Albanian non-finite constructions composed of **një të** + participle, which are used to express a particular action that has taken place or is expected to take place before the action expressed by the verb in the controlling clause. Like non-finite contructions with **me të**, **një të** constructions may be marked for passive voice, and their temporal sense is governed by the controlling verb:

> **TË lumtë, o Leks, NJË të IKUR unë nga shtëpia e NJË T'U SHTHURUR gardhi.** 'Bravo, o Leks, ONCE I am GONE from the house, IMMEDIATELY the fence COMES APART.'

> **NJË TË PARË atë, sakaq, edhe nxënësit e tjerë filluan të lëviznin.** 'Having seen ("ONE SEEING") him, immediately the other pupils as well began to move.'

> **E patë si u dogj mbrëmë depoja e armikut? NJË TË MARRË flakë dhe u bë shkrumb e hi.** 'Did you see how the depot of the enemy burned down last night? Once it caught fire ("ONE TAKEN flame") it was reduced to cinders and ashes.'

2.3.6 A.3b. Participial Absolutes   **101**

2.3.7 Uses of Complex Verb Cores

A. Complex Verb Cores with Auxiliaries and Pseudo-Auxiliaries

The VERB CORE of an Albanian VP may consist of simple (composed of a single word) or complex (composed of more than one word) constructions. Many complex verb cores in Albanian are formed with formative clitics (morphemes written as separate words but which have no use except as part of a construction with other words):

> **të laj** 'that I wash', **të laja** 'that I used to wash', **duke larë** 'while washing', **pa larë** 'without washing', **u lava** 'I washed myself', **u lakam** 'I actually wash myself', etc.

The construction **do** plus **të** plus VERB as in **do të shkoj** 'I will go' has special importance in Albanian, in that it is basic to the most usual expressions of the future tense and the conditional mood.

A verb as first element of a complex construction whose second element is a participle form is called an auxiliary. Complex verb cores are constructed with the auxiliary verb **jam** and **kam**:

> kam larë 'I have washed', **kisha larë** 'I had washed', **pata larë** 'I had washed', **paskam larë** 'I have actually washed', **paskësha larë** 'I had actually washed'; **jam larë** 'I have been washed', **isha larë** 'I used to be washed', **qeshë larë** 'I had been washed', **qenkam larë** 'I have actually been washed', **qenkësha larë** 'I had actually been washed', etc.

A.1 Perfect Tenses

The verb **jam** is most often used in Albanian as a semantically neutral copula to relate a subject to a predicate. As a copula it serves to predicate a quality or characteristic of a subject when the predicate is adjectival (or adverbial), or to identify or equate the subject with a nominal complement:

> **ËSHTË një mjek, plotësoi infermierja.** 'He IS a doctor, the nurse added.'
> **MË vonë do të dalësh një ditë, po së paku TË JESH i shëndoshë.** 'Later you will leave some day, but you should at least BE healthy'.

As we have already seen, however, **jam** also serves as an auxiliary in compound tenses of Albanian, like **kam**, appearing immediately before the participle of the main verb to form the perfect tenses: e.g., **kam larë** 'I have washed ', **jam larë** 'I have been washed', **kisha larë** 'I had washed', **isha larë** 'I had been washed'.

A.2 Obligatives

The verb **dua** 'I want' in third person non-active forms may also be used as an auxiliary to form non-active OBLIGATIVES:

> **Kjo këmishë do** (or **duhet**) **larë.** 'This shirt needs washing'.
> **E po DUHET FILLUAR! tha ai pa lëvizur.** 'Well one must begin! ("IT SHOULD BE STARTED!") he said without moving.'
> **As komandanti Rrapo nuk fliste. Gjer në xhade DUHEJ ECUR një orë.** 'Not even commander Rrapo was talking. One HAD TO WALK an hour to reach the highway.'

When the subject is plural, non-active third person plural forms of **duhet** may occur in such constructions, but the corresponding active third person plural forms of **do** do not so occur:

> **Ata janë djem të mirë dhe DUHEN NDIHMUAR.** 'They are good boys and SHOULD BE HELPED.'

When followed by the perfect subjunctive, the verb **duhet** commonly expresses a supposition.

DUHET TË KEM QENË atëherë nja gjashtë-shtatëmbëdhjetë vjeç. 'I MUST HAVE BEEN then about 16-17 years old'.

NOTE

When it is immediately followed by a noun or pronoun that serves as its subject, the verb **duhet** does not have the same modal value, but instead has the value of a regular verb, usually in the sense 'is needed', rather than the literal 'is wanted'. As such it may be used not only in the third person singular, but also in the other persons.

Domosdo DUHET një njeri që ta mbajë skuadrën me fjalë. 'Of course someone IS NEEDED to amuse the squadron.'

TË rrosh ti sa malet, bir, -i thashë- sepse i DUHESH tërë Shqipërisë, tërë popullit, i DUHESH edhe botës. '"May you live as long as the mountains, son," I said to him, "because all of Albania, the whole population NEEDS you, even the world NEEDS you."'

The auxiliary **do** followed by the participle of a main verb expresses the meaning of non-active necessity (though somewhat milder than **duhet**, and more like English IS TO BE, SHOULD BE or OUGHT TO BE constructions), and is used only in the third person singular of the present tense. This construction is more common in the colloquial language, but does occur in literary Albanian as well:

Vrulli i tyre vetëm DO DREJTUAR, DO MBËRTHYER në vendin e duhur e atëherë ai do të bëjë çudira. 'Their drive only NEEDS DIRECTING, NEEDS NAILING DOWN in the proper place and then it will perform miracles.'

A pseudo-auxiliary is also followed by a non-finite verb construction, but unlike a true auxiliary, other material may intervene. The verbs **jam** and **kam** may both be used as pseudo-auxiliaries followed by infinitive constructions of the type **për të larë** 'to wash', expressing the modal meaning of necessity in a somewhat softer form than with **duhet** and **do**. Note that this is the same construction that is to express future. The strength of its modal sense depends on the context:

Po kjo s'duhet të na bëjë ne të mbyllim gojën edhe kur s'ËSHTË PËr TË MBYLLUR. 'But this shouldn't make us shut our mouth even when it OUGHT not TO BE SHUT.'

MËnyra me të cilën u fitua beteja e Nartës, ËSHTË PËR TË VËNË RE, SE... 'The manner in which the battle of Narte was won, IS TO BE NOTED, BECAUSE..'

Ai psherëtiu sikur të KISHTE përpara një punë PËR TË BËRË. 'He sighed as if he HAD a job TO DO.'

Jam also serves as a pseudo-auxiliary with gerundives to form the present and imperfect progressive as in **jam duke larë** 'I am (in the process of) washing', **isha duke larë** 'I was (in the process of) washing'.

The verbs **bëhem** 'I become' and **mbetet** 'it remains' (**mbetet** only in the third person singular) may also be followed by infinitives of the type **për të larë**:

Kur U BËNË niprit për të martuar, gjyshi mori trastën e mori shkopin dhe u nis për udhë. 'When the nephews were old enough to marry ("BECAME what was required to marry"), the grandfather picked up his bag and walking stick and set off on the road.'

Kur menduan se u KISHIN MBETUR edhe gjashtë të tjerë për të dëgjuar, njerëzit s'u përmbajtën dot më. 'When they realized that there still REMAINED six others to be heard, the people could no longer retrain themselves.'

A.3 Inchoatives

A complex construction expressing an INCHOATIVE aspect is formed with **jam** as a pseudo-auxiliary (in the present or imperfect) plus the preposition **në** or **me** plus the clitic **të** /fRplus the participle, optionally followed by the phrase **e sipër** 'and above, beyond', is used with a kind of inchoative aspectual value similar to English about to...:

Tanush Topia mezi po e mbante ushtrinë e tij, e cila ISHTE MË TË THYER E SIPËR. 'Tanush Topia was barely keeping his army together, which was on the verge of being defeated ("WAS AT BREAKING AND ABOVE").'

Skënderbeu po kthehej në Berat, meqenëse të njëmbëdhjetë ditët ISHIN MË TË MBARUAR E SIPËR. 'Scanderbeg was returning to Berat, being that the eleven days were about to end ("WERE AT FINISHING AND ABOVE").'

A.4 Verbal Augmentatives

In order to express the progressive increase of an action, the verb **vij** 'come' (usually in the third person) is used as a pseudo-auxiliary followed by a gerundive contruction, or is preceded by the conjunction **sa** 'ever, more and more', and followed by a verb coordinated with it by the conjunction **e** or **dhe** 'and':

Ia vuri edhe një herë dorën në ballë e tha se temperature VINTE DUKE RËNË. 'He put his hand once more on his forehead, and said that the temperatura was falling MORE AND MORE.'

NOTE

This idea may also be conveyed by a construction consisting of **sa** 'ever' plus **vij** 'I come' plus an action verb coordinated with **e** or **dhe** 'and':

Buçima SA VINTE E ZGJEROHEJ dhe përrenjtë në të dy anët e xhadesë oshëtinin. 'The roar WAS BECOMING EVER WIDER and the brooks on both sides of the road were echoing.'

A.5 Verbal Limitives

To express termination of (or satiation with) an action, Albanian uses constructions of the type **mbarova së foluri** 'I finished speaking'. The first constituent in this type of sequence is generally a form that denotes actions reaching a limit (including verbs like **mbaroj** 'I finish', **pushoj** 'I stop', **lodhem** 'I get tired', **ngopem** 'I get satiated', **vdes** 'I die', **bie** 'I fall'), followed by an invariable clitic **se** plus a participle with the suffix **i** (originally a deverbal neuter noun in the ablative indefinite).

Profesor Llazari, që e kish zakon të shtonte domosdo diçka, kur MBARONTE SË FOLURI ndonjë tjetër, shtoi. 'Professor Llazar, who had a habit of adding something without fail when omeone WOULD FINISH SPEAKING, added...'

Gjithë atë ditë njerëzit, nuk PUSHUAN SË MBLDEDHURI gjithëfarë materialesh. 'That very day the people, did not stop collecting all sorts of materials.'

Zef Moisui KISHTE MBARUAR SË REFERUARI shkurt mbi situatën politike të brendsme e të jashtme. 'Zef Moisi HAD FINISHED REPORTING briefly on the domestic and foreign political ituation.'

Kur MBAROI Ndoni SË RRËFYERI ato që ngjanë me rosat në grurë, Leksi zuri kokën me duar. 'When Ndoni FINISHED TELLING what happened with the ducks in the wheat, Leki grabbed his head (with his hands).'

Vjen një ditë që ne PUSHOJMË SË EKZISTUARI. 'A day comes when we STOP EXISTING.'

Note that in these limitive constructions the former ablative case noun has lost its nominal functions; like other verbal constructions, this one may take an object (if the underlying participle was formed from a transitive verb) and may be modified by adverbial, rather than adjectival, modifiers. In case form it is invariable, and it has lost the syntactic relations of the noun: it is not accompanied by nominal qualifiers or quantifiers, and can be qualified only by another noun functioning as an object, by an adverb or by a word group with an adverbial function, thus largely taking on the syntactic characteristics of a verb form:

Rruga e shtruar zgjati mjaft dhe Rexha s'pushoi SË HEDHURI herë pas here nga një fjalë. 'The paved road stretched on and Rexha did not cease TOSSING IN a word from time to time.'

As Adili s'po ngopej dot atë ditë SË SHIKURARI këtë fushë të gjerë. 'Even Adili could get his fill of LOOKING at this broad field on that day.'

B. Complex Verb Cores with Semi-Auxiliaries

In certain types of complex verb constructions the first element may be a verb with a specialized function (and in some cases with a specialized form) and the second element is a present or imperfect subjunctive verb form. The first element of such a construction is called a semi-auxiliary. Semi-auxiliaries include: **do** and **le**, specialized third person forms of the verbs **dua** 'I want' and **lë** 'I let', respectively; modal verbs; and verbs which are used to express aspect.

B.1 Future and Conditional

The clitic **do** is used in complex constructions with a following subjunctive form of a main verb as the normal future tense and conditional mood forms of that verb. Note that **do** is invariable in such constructions, and that the person, number, and voice of the construction is determined by the verb in the subjunctive.

a) The FUTURE tense, when the following verb is in a present subjunctive form: **do të shkoj** 'I shall go', **do të qeshin** 'they will laugh', **do të laheni** 'you will wash yourselves', **do të mbajë** 'he will hold', **do të bëhesh** 'you will become', **do të takohemi** 'we shall meet', **do të jesh** 'you will be'. The FUTURE PERFECT TENSE is composed of a future tense form of **kam** (active) or **jam** (non-active) plus the participle of the given verb: **do të kem larë** 'I shall have washed', **do të jem larë** 'I shall have been washed'.

b) The CONDITIONAL mood, when the following verb is in an imperfect subjunctive form: **do të shkoja** 'I would go', **do të qeshnin** 'they would laugh', **do të laheshit** 'you would wash yourselves', **do të mbante** 'he would hold', **do të bëheshe** 'you would become'. The PERFECT CONDITIONAL is a past tense form composed of a conditional form of **kam** (active) or **jam** (non-active) plus the participle of the given verb: **do të kisha shkuar** 'I would have gone', **do të kishin qeshur** 'they would have laughed', **do të ishit larë** 'you would have washed yourselves', **do të kishte mbajtur** 'he would have held', **do të ishe bërë** 'you would have become', **do të ishim takuar** 'we would have met', **do të kishe qënë** 'you would have been'.

B.2 Jussives

The clitic **le** is used in complex constructions with a following first or third person, present subjunctive form of a main verb as the normal JUSSIVE mood of that verb: **le të shkojmë** 'let's go', **le të shkojnë** 'let them go'.

B.3 Modals

Modal verbs express the attitude of the speaker toward the action named by the following in respect to its possibility or necessity. The modals in Albanian are **mund** 'can, could' and **duhet** (or **lipset**) 'should, ought'.

The semi-auxiliary **mund**, when it expresses its modal meaning of possibility or permissibility, has an invariable form for all persons, when used with the meaning of present, imperfect, or future:

Vetëm një pendë poetike MUND të përshkruaj meritat e tyre. 'Only a poetic pen CAN describe their merits.'

E kuptoni sa dëm të madh MUND të kemi? '(Do) you realize what great harm we MAY sustain?'

Lirinë MUND ta kishit fituar me trimërinë tuaj edhe me një tjetër çlirimtar. 'With your bravery you COULD have won freedom with another liberator as well.'

Asnjë forcë nuk MUND të ndalte hovin e partizanëve. 'No force COULD have stopped the drive of the partisans.'

However, when it is used in the past definite or in one of the compound tenses, the modal **mund** varies in form to reflect the subject, as in:

Dy prej tyre, pasi MUNDËN të shpëtonin nepër pyje, u bashkuan me karadakun dhe erdhën në brigadë. 'Two of them, after they MANAGED to survive in the forests, joined with Karadak and came to the brigade.'

Ai nuk KA MUNDUR akoma të diktojë qëllimin tonë. 'He HAS not yet BEEN ABLE to detect our purpose.'

Ne MUNDËM të kalonim, megjithëse të lodhur, të këputur. 'We MANAGED to pass, even though tired, exhausted.'

Atë ditë nuk kishte ngrënë as drekë, sepse ekonomati nuk KISHTE MUNDUR t'i furnizonte me ushqim. 'That day he had not even eaten lunch, because the steward's office HAD not BEEN ABLE to furnish them with food.'

NOTE

When it is not followed by a verb in the subjunctive **mund** does not carry modal value and is used with its full lexical meaning as a regular verb 'I defeat':

Nga koha kur romakët MUNDËN Teutën dhe zotëruan detin, shqiptarët u detyruan të mbështeteshin me shpatulla në male. 'From the time that the Romans DEFEATED Teuta and dominated the sea, the Albanians were forced to fall back on the mountains.'

The semi-auxiliary **duhet**, which expresses the modal meaning of necessity or compulsion, is used chiefly in the present and imperfect, and usually only in an invariable third person singular form, no matter what the person and number of the subject is:

Unë duhet të shkoj. 'I must leave.'

Ju duhet ta mbaroni. 'You should finish it.'

Marrëveshja DUHET TË MBETET midis nesh. 'The agreement MUST REMAIN among us.'

Njeri prej të dyve DUHEJ TË THYEJ. 'One of the two HAD TO BE BROKEN.'

Several verbs are used in complex constructions to express the beginning or continuation of the action named by the following verb.

B.4 Inceptives

In addition to the verbs **filloj** and **nis**, which always mean 'start' or 'begin', the verbs **zë** 'I start' **bëj** 'I make', **marr** 'I take', **vihem** 'I place myself', and others may be followed by a subjunctive form of the main verb to signal the beginning of an action:

HËna e bukur, që sapo FILLOI TË DILTE, shkëlqeu në zallin e PËrroit të Thatë. 'The beautiful moon, which HAD just BEGUN TO RISE, shone on the bed of Dry Brook.'

Armiku FILLOI TË RRIHTE me artileri që nga Greshica. 'The enemy BEGAN TO POUND with artillery all the way from Greshica.'

E mori djalin pranë, i mbështeti kokën në gjunjët e vet e NISI T'I LËMONTE flokët. 'She drew the boy close, rested his head on her lap, and STARTED TO STROKE HIS hair.'

Prandaj, kur FILLOI TË LIDHTE plagën, ZURI TA PADISTE një zë nga brenda.

'That is why, when HE STARTED TO BIND the wound, an inward voice BEGAN TO
ACCUSE HIM.'

BËRI TË IKTE nga dera. 'HE MADE (as if) TO GO through the door.'

Simoni u çua përnjëherë, si i trembur, nga karrikja dhe MORI TË DILTE. 'Simon
got up at once from the chair, as if frightened, and STARTED TO GO OUT.'

Pa humbur kohë, ai U VU TË NDIQTE armikun. 'Without losing any time, he set off
("WAS PLACED") TO PURSUE the enemy.'

In colloquial Albanian, and sometimes in the written language as well, the verb **zë** 'begin'
may be linked to a verb in the indicative mood, by the conjunction **e** or **dhe** 'and':

**Unë akoma qeshja me të madhe, e kur thashë se "mamanë e kam në Elbasan," ZUNË
njerëzit E më VËSHTRONIN me dhemshuri.** 'I was still laughing uproariously, and
when I said "my mother is in Elbasan", the people BEGAN TO LOOK at me with sympathy.' (Compare English *While I was talking, he up and hit me.*)

B.5 Continuatives

The verbs **vazhdoj** 'continue' and **vijoj** 'keep on' followed by another verb in the subjunctive are the chief means of indicating continuation of an action:

**Bile u rrëzua një herë, u rrokullis nëpër bar, por prapë VAZHDOI TË VRAPONTE,
deri sa u zhduk thellë në korie.** 'Indeed, he fell down once, rolled over in the grass, but
still kept ("CONTINUED") RUNNING, until he disappeared deep in the grove.'

**Ai ishte ulur këmbëkryq dhe nuk po vinte re që djali VIJONTE TË RRINTE në
gjunjë.** 'He sat crosslegged and did not notice that the boy CONTINUED TO REMAIN
on his knees.'

C. Complex Verb Cores in Hypothetical Constructions

A full hypothetical sentence consists of an antecedent ('if') and a consequent ('then')
clause. In Albanian (and other languages) the antecedent clause may often be represented by
an adverbial expression (such as the adverb **ndryshe** 'otherwise', a prepositional phrase introduced by **me** 'with' or **pa** 'without'), or may be absent completely. If the hypothesis is absolutely straightforward, that is, if the speaker presents the antecedent and consequent without
reservations, the verb in the antecedent clause will be in the appropriate tense of the indicative
mood following a conjunction like **po** 'if', **nëqoftëse** 'in case', which may be shortened to **në**
'if' or (in particularly laconic language) even nothing, and the verb in the consequent clause
will be in the appropriate tense of the indicative. If the conjunctional phrase is an expression
like **nëqoftëse** or **në**, the clause is called CONDITIONAL; if it is an expression like **edhe në**
'even if', the clause is called CONCESSIVE.

Nëqoftëse vjen ai, unë iki. 'In case he comes, I leave.'
or
NË vjen ai, unë iki. 'If he comes, I leave.'
or
Vjen ai, iki unë. 'He comes, I leave.'

Po erdhi dje, atëhere jemi në bela. 'If he came yesterday, then we are in trouble.'

NOTE

In straightforward antecedents the optative of any verb may appear after **në**. In everyday
speech **qoftë** 'may it be' is the most common optative form so used, so much so that
nëqoftëse has become one of the two most common ways of saying 'if' (the other is **po
të**).

If the speaker recognizes the possibility of some other antecedent, but the hypothesis is
still straightforward, the antecedent verb will be in the present subjunctive or, if the antecedent

is prior to the reference point, will be in the perfect subjunctive, following **po** 'if': **po të mbarojë** 'if he finish', **(po) të vij unë** 'if I come', **(po) të ketë mbaruar** '(if) he have finished', **po të kem ardhur** 'if I have come'.

Other optative forms of **jam** and **kam**, and to a smaller extent the optative forms of other verbs, are also used in straightforward antecedents after **në**, so that hypothetical sentences like the following are encountered not infrequently:

NË paça kohë, do të shkoj. 'If I have time, I'll go.'
NË shkofsha nesër, do të të thërras. 'If I go tomorrow, I'll call you.'

Before verbs in the past definite indicative tense, antecedents presupposed to be completed in the past time may be formed. Note that the conjunction **po** must be used instead of **në** with the past definite. Contrast the following three hypothetical sentences, the first two with indicative verbs, the third with a subjunctive verb:

Po erdhi dje, jemi në bela. 'If he came yesterday, we are in trouble.'
NË vinte dje, duhet të na njoftonte. 'If he was coming yesterday, he should have told us.'
Po të vinte nesër, do të ishim në bela. 'If he were coming tomorrow, we would be in trouble.'

If the speaker recognizes the possibility of another consequence, but the hypothesis is still straightforward, the consequent verb will also be in the present subjunctive or, if the consequent is prior to the reference point, will be in the perfect subjunctive, either following **do** 'will' or not: **do të mbarojë** 'he will finish', **do të vij unë** 'I will come', **do të ketë mbaruar** 'he will have finished', **do të kem ardhur** 'I will have come'.

Putting the antecedent and consequent clauses together, or omitting the antecedent clause as such, the following full or incomplete straightforward hypothetical sentences with minimal doubt about the hypothesis on the part of the speaker, are all possible in Albanian:

Po të mbarojë ai, do të vij unë. 'If he finishes, I will come.'
Do të vij unë. 'I will come.' ('If' clause understood.)
Ndryshe, do të mbaroj unë. 'Otherwise, I'll finish.'
Po të kem mbaruar unë, do të ketë ardhur ai. 'If I have finished, he will have come.'
Po të kem ardhur unë, do të mbarojë ai. 'If I have arrived, he will finish.'
Sidoqoftë, unë do të vij. 'In any case, I will come.'
Po të vijë ai, unë do të mbaroj. 'If he comes, I'll finish.'
NË mbaron ai, unë do të vij. 'If he finishes, I will come.'
Po të vijë ai, do të kem mbaruar. 'If he comes, I will have finished.'

If the hypothesis is not straightforward, that is, if the speaker wishes to express doubt about the realization of the antecedent or consequent clause, the verb appears in the imperfect subjunctive or past perfect subjunctive tense. In the antecedent clause the verb may be preceded by a conjunctional like **sikur** 'if, a if', **po** 'if', **edhe po** 'even if' (for concessive clauses); in the consequent clause the verb may be preceded by **do** (in which case the English equivalent is usually 'would'), **mund** when the English equivalent is 'might' or 'could'), or **duhet** (when the English equivalent is **should**). If the past perfect subjunctive rather than the imperfect is used, the English equivalents in the consequent clause are, respectively, 'would have', 'might have' or 'could have', and 'should have':

"Ah! Sikur TË ISHA gjithnjë kaq i qetë, sigurisht se DO TË BËJA diçka, DO TË DIJA të paktën se çfarë të kuturisja", tha me vete dhe mbylli sytë për të fjetur një minutë pa kurrfarë mendimi në kokë. "Ah! If I WERE always so calm, assuredly I WOULD HAVE DONE something, I WOULD at least KNOW what to venture," he said to himself and closed his eyes in order to sleep a minute without any thought at all in his head.'

Edhe unë, po të isha në vendin tënd, kështu DO TË ÇUDITESHA. 'I, too, if I were in your place, WOULD HAVE BEEN AMAZED in the same way.'

-- **Po pse çuditesh? TË ISHA unë në vendin tënd, Ç'DO TË BËJE ti?** 'But why are you surprised? IF I WERE in your place, WHAT WOULD you DO?'

NDRYSHE DO TË DERDHEJ gjak më kot edhe përfundimi DO TË ISHTE një robëri më e keqe se e para. 'OTHERWISE, blood WOULD HAVE BEEN SHED in vain, and the end result WOULD HAVE BEEN a worse captivity than the first.'

Pa ndihmën tënde, S'DO T'IA KISHA DALË mbanë kësaj pune. 'Without your help, I WOULD NOT HAVE seen this job through ("COME OUT beside this job").'

Dinit iu morën mendtë dhe DO TË KISHTE RËNË, po të mos ishte mbajtur pas pemës së trotuarit. 'Dini became dizzy and WOULD HAVE FALLEN, if he had not held on the the tree on the sidewalk.'

E kuptonte se shumë ditë të tij MUND TË KISHIN QENË më të lumtura, po të kishte punuar më shumë. 'He realized that many of his days MIGHT HAVE BEEN happier, if he had worked more.'

-- **E po ja, nënë, kaloi gjysmë ore që ka dalë Kopani. T'I KISHTE NDODHUR gjë, DO T'I KISHTE NDODHUR. DO TË KISHIM DËGJUAR armë, bomba. Apo jo?** '"But look mother, a half hour has passed since Kopan went out. [IF] something HAD HAPPENED TO HIM, IT WOULD HAVE HAPPENED. We WOULD HAVE HEARD firearms, bombs. No?"'

-- **E pra, TË më KISHTE THËNË mua t'i bëja dy këmbë druri S'DO T'IA KISHA DALË kurrë mbanë, megjithëse druri është i bindur, merr ç'do formë që t'i japësh.** '"Well, HAD HE TOLD me to make him two wooden legs I WOULD never HAVE COME CLOSE even though the wood is obedient; it takes whatever form you give it."'

Pa pritur filloi një zhurmë e gjurulldi, që mbase S'DO TË KISHTE MBARUAR, po të mos ishte dëgjuar përsëri zëri i Dinit, i cili përsëri u bëri aq përshtypje të gjithëve, sa mbyllën gojën. 'Suddenly there began a clamor and dispute, that perhaps WOULD NOT HAVE ENDED, if Dini's voice had not been heard again, who again made such an impression on everybody, that they shut up.'

NOTE

In proverbs and occasionally in ordinary language, the imperfect indicative is used in the consequent clause of hypothetical sentences:

TË mos kisha ata kalamaj, që po më hanë sytë, SHKOJA (=do të shkoja) edhe unë atje. 'If I didn't have those kids, who are killing me ("eating my eyes out"), I would be going ("was going") there, too.'

2.4 Formation of Verb Stems

According to their source of formation, verb stems in Albanian are simple, derived, compound, or agglutinated stems.

Simple stems are those consisting of a single morpheme. In the citation forms of verbs in a) below, the single-morpheme stem ends in a vowel. In the citations forms in b), it ends in a consonant. Irregular verbs with simple stems are listed in Section 2.2.2 D.

a) **la-j** 'I wash', **mba-j** 'I keep, I hold', **tha-j** 'I dry (something')', **ble-j** 'I buy', **rrëfe-j** 'I relate, I tell', **gri-j** 'I mince, I grind', **shi-j** 'I thresh', **mëso-j** 'I learn', **krua-j** 'I scratch', **shua-j** 'I erase, I extinguish', **lye-j** 'I paint', **thye-j** 'I break', **ndie-j** 'I sense, feel'.

b) **hap** 'I open', **mbyll** 'I shut', **prek** 'I touch', **qep** 'I sew', **qesh** 'I laugh', **vesh** 'I wear'; **fut** 'I put, insert', **mat** 'I measure', **qit** 'I expel, I shoot', **rrit** 'I raise (cause to grow)', **shëtit** 'I stroll'; **dal** 'I go out', **marr** 'I take', **heq** 'I pull', **mbjell** 'I plant', **ndjell** 'I entice', **vjel** 'I harvest'; **shes/shet** 'I sell/you sell, he sells'.

All verb stems which are synchronically unanalyzable in contemporary Albanian may be considered to be simple. Thus, the following stems may be considered as simple even though they can be analyzed diachronically: **mburr** 'I praise' (from **m** + **burrë**), **prier** 'I tilt, lean' (from **për + ier**), **mpreh** 'I sharpen' (from **për + eh**), **hartoj** 'I draft' (from **art + o-j**).

The roots underlying the stems from which verbs of this type are formed either no longer exist (e.g., **ier, eh**) or they have a meaning that is far removed from the meaning of the derivational stem (e.g. **burrë** 'man'; **art** 'art').

Similarly, stems borrowed from foreign verbs (e.g., **anulloj, diktoj, procedoj, stigmatizoj, verifikoj**) are considered to be unanalyzable in Albanian, even though they may be derived words in the languages from which they are borrowed.

On the other hand the following verbs are not considered to have simple stems:

a) Antonymic pairs of verbs with partially identical stems, such as **ngarkoj** 'I load', **shkarkoj** 'I unload'; **ngul** 'I thrust in, I implant'; **shkul** 'I uproot', etc. Verbs of this type, whose antonymic sense comes from the contrast of their respective prefixes, can be considered derived words, even though the part of the stem after the prefix does not exist as an independent word in the current language (like English re*ceive*, de*ceive*, con*ceive*, etc.)

b) Foreign loans that are analyzable in Albanian because the root from which they are derived has also been taken into the language. Such are verbs of the type: **autorizoj (autor)**, **industrializoj (industri, industrial)**, **kolektivizoj (kolektiv)**, **kolonizoj (koloni)**, **mikrofilmoj (mikrofilm)**, **neutralizoj (neutral)**, **reklamoj (reklamë)**, etc.

c) Verbs of the type **gëzoj** 'I gladden', **lëmoj** 'I file', **lëvdoj** 'I praise', etc., in which the stressed vowel of the underlying stem has been reduced to **-ë-** with the shift in stress created by the suffix **-ó**. Compare **gaz** 'joy, mirth', **limë** 'file', **lavd** 'praise'.

2.4.1 Derived Verb Stems

Derived verb stems are formed chiefly from nouns, from other verbs, and from adjectives and adverbs. There are also a few verb stems formed from other parts of speech (numbers, pronouns, particles) and by onomatopoeia.

Listed in descending order of productivity, derived verb stems are formed:
1. By suffixation: **pun-o-j** 'I work', **vul-os** 'I seal', **uj-it** 'I water';
2. By prefixation: **për-hap** 'I spread', **për-dor** 'I use', **sh-qep** 'I unravel';
3. By prefixation and suffixation simultaneously: **për-gjithë-so-j** 'I make universal, I generalize', **z-bukur-oj** 'I beautify', **sh-kripë-so-j** 'I desalinate';
4. Without affixation: **krip** 'I salt', **sit** 'I sift', **kyç** 'I lock'.

A. Verb Stems Derived by Suffixation

The suffixes with which the derived verbs are formed are:
1) **-o-, -ro-, -so-, -to-, -zo-, -llo-**, with which verbs of conjugation I are formed;
2) **-os-, -s/-is, -atos, -it**: with which verbs of conjugation II are formed.

Of these, the suffixes **-o-** and **-zo-** are the most productive.

A.1 Derivational Suffixes of Conjugation I

The *suffixes* **-ó-, -lló-, -ró-, -só-, -tó-, -zó-**. The last four suffixes are originally merely extensions of the suffix **-ó-**, but in this section they will be discussed separately. For all verbs formed with these, the stress shifts to the **-ó-** of the suffix.

When these suffixes are added to a non-verbal stem, the resulting verbs have meanings related in an unpredictable variety of ways to the meaning of the derivational stem.

Thus, for example, **nderoj** means 'I do *honor* to someone', **lajmëroj** 'I give *the news* to someone', **arsyetoj** 'I judge by means of *reason*', **pyllëzoj** 'I create new *forests* somewhere', **holloj** 'I make (something) *thin*', **ndryshoj** 'I make (something) *different*', etc.

On the other hand, when these suffixes are added to a verbal stem, they usually give the derived verb an intensive, frequentative, or sometimes causative meaning: **nxir-oj**, 'I blacken', **shtjell-o-j** 'I unfold, I develop', **zbardh-o-j** 'I whiten', **zbut-o-j** 'I soften', **flakë-ro-j** 'I inflame', **shkrif-ëro-j** 'I loosen', **shpesh-to-j** 'I intensify (do something more frequently)', **qelb-ëzo-j** 'I cause to stink', etc.

a) The suffix **-o-**.

This is the most productive suffix in the Albanian verbal system. A large number of verbs have been formed with this suffix from stems of: 1) nouns, 2) adjectives, 3) adverbs, 4) verbs:

1) **arn-o-j** 'I mend', **besoj** 'I believe', **botoj** 'I publish', **cenoj** 'I offend, I touch', **darkoj** 'I dine', etc. (from the nouns **arn** 'patch', **besë** 'faith', **botë** 'world', **cen** 'vice', **darkë** 'dinner', etc.). Some verbs formed with this suffix appear only in non-active forms: **zotohem** 'I promise', **motohem** 'I age', **mrekullohem** 'I marvel'.

2) **çal-o-j** 'I cause to limp, I limp', **fisnikoj** 'I ennoble', **holloj** 'I make thin', **mjeroj** 'I make wretched', etc. (from the adjectives **i çalë** 'lame', **fisnik** 'noble', **i hollë** 'thin', **i mjerë** 'wretched', etc.).

3) **afr-o-j** 'I bring close', **ballafaqoj** 'I confront', **barasoj** 'I make equal', **bashkoj** 'I unite', **dyfishoj** 'I double', etc. (from the adverbs **afër** 'near', **ballafaqe** 'face to face', **baras** 'equal', **bashkë** 'together', **dyfish** 'twofold', etc.).

4) **ndal-o-j** 'I stop', **përdoroj** 'I handle', **shtjelloj** 'I develop', etc. (from the verbs **ndal** 'stop', **përdor** 'use', **shtjell** 'I fling, toss', etc.).

NOTE

The verbs **po-h-o-j** 'I admit' and **mo-h-o-j** 'I deny' (from the affirmative and negative particles **po** and **mo** with an **-h-** inserted) have also been formed with this suffix, as have **dhjetoj** 'I tithe' (from the number **dhjetë** 'ten'), **dyshoj** 'I doubt' from the expression "e kam me dysh", and **shumëfishoj** 'I increase manyfold' (by analogy from **dyfishoj** 'I double', **trefishoj** 'I triple').

The suffix is also found in the verb **falënderoj** 'I thank', which has come from the agglutination of the expression **falem nderit** 'thanks'.

b) The suffix **-ro-**.

A relatively restricted number of verbs have been formed from this suffix, chiefly from noun stems. When the derivational stem ends in a consonant, the vowel **-ë-** is inserted before the suffix:

mish-ë-ro-j 'I embody', **lajm-ë-ro-j** 'I announce', **flakë-ro-j** 'I inflame', **lavdëroj** 'I glorify', etc. (from the nouns **mish** 'meat, flesh', **lajm** 'news', **flakë** 'flame', **lavd** 'praise', etc.).

NOTE

The verbs **shqipëroj** 'I translate into Albanian', **fisnikëroj** 'I ennoble', **shkrifëroj** 'I loosen', and **nxiroj** 'I blacken', are formed from the adverb **shqip** 'in Albanian', the adjective **fisnik** 'noble', and the verbs **shkrif** 'loosen' and **nxij** 'I blacken', respectively.

c) The suffix **-so-**.

With this suffix, which is not very productive, verbs are formed primarily from nouns, adjectives, and adverbs. When the stem ends in a consonant, the vowel **-ë-** is inserted before the suffix:

frikë-so-j 'I frighten', **vleftësoj** 'I evaluate, I value', **vlerësoj** 'I evaluate, I value', (from the nouns **frikë** 'fear', **vleftë** 'value', **vlerë** 'value'); **dendësoj** 'I make dense', **ëmbëlsoj** 'I sweeten' ('from the adjectives **i dendur** 'dense', **i ëmbël** 'sweet'); **ngadalësoj** 'I slow down', **pakësoj** 'I decrease', **plotësoj** 'I fulfill' (from the adverbs **ngadalë** 'slowly', **pak** 'little', **plot** 'full').

NOTE

Asgjësoj 'I annihilate' and **tjetërsoj** 'I transfer property' have been formed from the indefinite pronouns **asgjë** 'nothing' and **tjetër** 'other', respectively.

d) The suffix **-to-**.

With this suffix, which is relatively productive, verbs are formed chiefly from nouns: e.g., **arkë-to-j** 'I deposit funds', **arsyetoj** 'I reason', **betoj** 'I swear in (someone)', **copëtoj** 'I break up into pieces' (from the nouns **arkë** 'cashbox', **arsye** 'reason', **be** 'oath', **copë** 'bit').

NOTES

1. In **treg-ë-toj** 'I trade', the **-ë-** is inserted after a voiced stop.

2. In **pushkatoj** 'I execute (by rifle fire)', **rrezatoj** 'I radiate', **vizatoj** 'I design, I draw', **-a-** appears in place of the final **-ë-** or **-e-** in the underlying stem (compare **pushkë** 'rifle', **rreze** 'beam, ray', **vizë** 'line'.)

3. The verbs **besatohem** 'I pledge my word of honor' and **robtohem** 'I slave, toil' have been formed with this suffix, but are only used in the non-active form. A few verbs have also been formed from other verbs, adverbs and adjectives with this suffix: **njoftoj** 'I notify', **dridh-to-hem** 'I am terrified', (compare **dridhem** 'I shiver'); **miratoj** 'I approve', **shqiptoj** 'I pronounce' (from the adverbs **mirë** 'good' and **shqip** 'Albanian'); **shpeshtoj** 'I cause to happen more frequently, I intensify', (from the adjective **i shpeshtë** 'frequent').

e) The suffix **-zo-**.

With this suffix, which has become quite productive, verbs are formed chiefly from nouns, but in some instances from other parts of speech as well, especially adjectives. When the derivational stem ends in a consonant (except those ending in **-ër**), the vowel **-ë-** is inserted before the suffix: **lëng-ë-zo-j** 'I secrete', but **motër-zo-j** 'I make a sister of'.

    1) **bulëzon** 'it buds', **copëzoj** 'I cut into pieces', **dorëzoj** 'I surrender', etc. (from the nouns **bulë** 'bud', **copë** 'bit', **dorë** 'hand', etc.);
    2) **dyzoj (dy)** 'I double (two)', **njëzoj (një)** 'I unite, join';
    3) **aktivizoj** 'I activate', **centralizoj**, **industrializoj** (from the adjectives **aktiv, central, industrial**). As is apparent from the examples, verbs formed from adjectives with this suffix have their stem extended with the addition of **-i-**.

NOTE

In **lulëzoj** 'I flower' and **ndajfoljëzoj** 'I adverbialize', the final **-e-** of the stem is weakened to **-ë-** because of the stress on the suffix. Similarly, in **rrokëzoj** 'I syllabify', the **-je-** of the noun stem **rrokje** 'syllable' is reduced to **-ë-** in the verb stem.
The verb **belbëzoj**, from the adjective **i belbët** or **i belbër** 'stammerer' have dropped the final consonant of the adjective.
The verb **gjunjëzoj** 'I bring to one's knees' has been formed from the plural stem **gjunj(ë)** 'knee(s)'.

f) The suffix **-llo-**.

A few verbs have been formed from this suffix. Chief ones are (1) onomatopoeic but there are also a few formed from (2) nouns and (3) verbs as well. When the derivational stem ends in a consonant, the unstressed vowels **-u-** or **-ë-** appear before the suffix:

(1) **fërfëlloj** 'I beat the wings, I fly', **gurgullon** 'gurgles', **turfullon** 'snorts' (onomatopeic verbs);

(2) **cungulloj** 'I truncate', **pikëlloj** 'I afflict', **xixëllon** 'twinkles', **(n)gallëzon** 'rejoices' (from the nouns **cung** 'stump', **pikë** 'drop, point', **xixë** 'spark, twinkle' **gaz** 'mirth');

(3) **mbushulloj** 'I fill up', **shkundulloj** 'I shake', **tundulloj** 'I shake', **zbardhëllon** 'dawns' (from the verbs **mbush** 'fill up', **shkund** 'shake', **tund** 'shake', **zbardh** 'whiten, brighten').

NOTES

1. Several verbs with onomatopeic sources, like **bubullin** 'thunders', **hingëllin** 'neighs', **vërshëllej** 'I whistle', etc. have been formed with the suffixes -lli- and -lle-, which may be considered allomorphs of -llo-.

2. A few rare verbs have been formed with the suffix -lo-: **kuqëloj** 'I redden', **shosh-loj** 'I gossip'.

A.2 Derivational Suffixes of Conjugation II

The suffixes from which the derived verbs of conjugation II have been formed include -s/-is, -ós, -atis/-atós, and -it. The most productive of these are -ós and -s/-is. The stress is carried by the -o- or -i- of the suffix; for the -s allomorph, the stress remains on stem final -i.

a) The suffix -os.

A rather large number of active transitive verbs have been formed with this suffix from noun stems: **ajr-os** 'I ventilate', **balsamos** 'I embalm', **baltos** 'I spatter with mud', etc. (from the nouns **ajr** 'air', **balsam** 'balm, salve', **baltë** 'mud', etc.).

NOTES

1. **Rehatos** 'I make comfortable' has been formed from the adverb **rehat** 'comfort'. **Llafos** 'I talk' is most often used as an active intransitive verb.

2. Many of these verbs have doublet forms with the -o- suffix: **ajroj** 'I ventilate', **damkoj** 'I brand', etc.

b) The suffix -s/-is.

This suffix, which no longer seems productive, has two allomorphs. The allomorph -s has been added to noun stems ending in a stressed **i**: **arratis** 'go into exile', **batërdis** 'I ruin', **bezdis** 'I bother', etc. (from the nouns **arrati** 'exile', **batërdi** 'ruin', **bezdi** 'bother'). The verb **praps** 'I repulse' has also been formed with this suffix (from the adverb **prap-a** 'behind').

A limited number of verbs have been formed from nouns with the suffix -is, which is added to nouns not ending in stressed -i; **kallaj-is** 'I coat with tin, I solder', **paj-is** 'I equip', etc. (from the nouns **kallaj** 'solder, tin', **pajë** 'dowery'). **Zvarr-is** 'I drag' has been formed from the adverb **zvarrë** 'dragging(ly)'.

NOTES

1. With the exception of **leverdis** 'it is advantageous', **rastis** 'it happens', and **përrallis** 'I waste time, I dawdle', all the other verbs in this group are transitive.

2. Several -is verbs have doublets with the -os suffix: **pajis/pajos** 'I equip', **përrallis/përrallos**, **vajis/vajos** 'I lubricate'.

3. The suffixes -atis and -atos with which a limited number of verbs have been formed (chiefly from nouns), may be considered as extensions of -os and -is: **armatos** 'I arm', **bojatis** 'I paint', **boshatis** 'I empty out', and **helmatis** (**helmatoj**) 'I poison' (from the nouns **armë** 'munitions, arm(s)', **bojë** 'paint', **helm** 'poison', and the adverb **bosh** 'empty').

c) The suffix -it-.

This suffix, no longer treated as productive, is usually added to noun stems: **darov-it** 'I make a present', **gjobit** 'I fine', **kopsit** 'I button (up)', etc. (from the nouns **darovë** 'present', **gjobë** 'fine (penalty)' **kopsë** 'button', etc.). However, verbs with an onomatopeic source are also formed from this suffix: **çukit** 'pecks', **murmurit** 'murmurs', **nanurit** 'sings a cradle song', as are the particular verbs **çapitem** 'I begin to walk' and **kollitem** 'I cough', which are used only in the non-active form. Finally, the verbs **ngulit** 'I insert, I drive in' and **shkoq-it** 'I explain' have been formed from the derived verbs **ngul** 'I implant' and **shkoq** 'I shuck, detach' by the addition of the -it- suffix.

NOTES

1. The verbs **gati-t** 'I prepare' and **përsëri-t** 'I repeat' have been formed from the adverbs **gati** 'ready' and **përsëri** 'again' by the addition of the suffix **-it** and the elision of one of the **-i-**'s.

2. For verbs with an onomatopeic source, such as **dërdë-llit** 'twaddles', **krakë-llit** 'crackles', and **mjau-llit** 'meows', the suffix **-it** is extended with **-ll-**.

B. Verb Stems Derived by Prefixation

The productive prefixes in verb derivation are **për-** and **sh/ç-/sh-**. Other prefixes include: **s-/z-, n-, m-, më-, mbi-, nën-, stër-, shpër-**; and **de-**.

1) The prefix **për-**

A relatively large number of verbs have been derived with this prefix, chiefly from nouns and other verbs. The prefix may occur before verbs of all conjugations, e.g., **për-caktoj** 'I define', **për-hap** 'I spread', **për-mbyt** 'I flood', etc.

The prefix **për-** gives to verbs derived from verbs:

a) an intensification of the meaning of the non-prefixed form: **përcaktoj** 'I define', **përçap** 'I chew', **përdredh** 'I twist', etc.;

b) a new intensive meaning related to the meaning of the source verb: **për-bluaj** 'I brood over'/**bluaj** 'I mill', **përfitoj** 'I profit'/**fitoj** 'I win', **përfshij** 'I include'/**fshij** 'I sweep', etc.

c) a new meaning more distantly related to the meaning of the source verb: **përçmoj** 'I scorn', **çmoj** 'I value', **përvesh** 'I roll up my sleeves'/**vesh** 'I wear', and **përgjigjem** 'I reply'/-**gjegjem** 'I obey, I listen'.

The prefix **për-** is not and has not been very productive in deriving verbs from noun stems. In verbs with **për-** prefixed to noun stems that otherwise end in an unstressed **-ë**, there is no final **-ë**, since verbs in Standard Albanian canonically may not end in **ë**: compare **buzë** 'lip, brink', **dorë** 'hand' with the verbs **përbuz** '(I) scorn, despise' and **përdor** '(I) use'.

Verbs with the prefix **për-** have been formed:

(1) From nouns that name a part of the human body, such as **ballë** 'forehead', **buzë** 'lip', **dorë** 'hand', **krah** 'arm', **gjunjë** 'knees', **shtat** 'body': **përball** 'I confront', **përbuz** 'I despise', **përdor**, 'I use', **përkrah** 'I support', **përgjunj** 'I cause to kneel', **përshtat** 'I adapt'. The verb **përmend** 'I mention, remind' also belongs to this group (from **mend** 'mind'). These verbs can indicate an action that is completed by activating in one way or another the thing named by the derivational stem. However, they are more commonly used with an extended meaning different from their original meaning;

(2) From nouns that name substances, such as **baltë** 'mud', **gjak** 'blood', **hi** 'ashes', **jargë** 'spittle', **mjaltë** 'honey': **përbalt** 'I soil with mud', **përgjak** 'I cause to bleed', **përhij** 'I spatter with ashes', **përjarg** 'I slobber', **përmjalt** 'I sweeten with honey'. These verbs also indicate an action that is realized by putting into action the thing named by the derivational stem. These actions may also be expressed through the verb **bëj** 'I do, I make', plus an instrumental complement constructed of the preposition **me** 'by, with' and the noun from which the verb is formed: **përbalt = bëj me baltë**; **përmjalt = bëj me mjaltë**, etc.

(3) From nouns with various meanings, such as **fill** 'thread', **shëndet** 'health', **udhë** 'road': **përfill** '(I) consider', **përshëndet** '(I) greet', **përudh** 'I guide'.

NOTES

1.   The verb **përshëndosh** 'I greet' is formed with this prefix from the adjective **i shëndoshë** 'robust, strong'.

2.   **Për-** is also used to form the verbs **për-fyt-em** 'I scuffle', **për-lesh-em** 'I come to blows, I scuffle', **për-lot-em** 'I cry (become tearful)', **për-miell-em** 'I get sprinkled with flour', and **për-ves-em** 'I become wet with dew'. These verbs are only used in the non-active form.

3.   A certain number of verbs apparently derived with this prefix are actually agglutinations of a prepositional phrase with the preposition **për**. Such are, for example, the verbs **përkrah** 'I support' and **përshtat** 'I adjust'.

    b) The prefix **sh-/ç-/zh-**

Verbs are productively formed with this prefix chiefly from other verbs and, to a lesser extent, from nouns. The form **ç-** is used before the sonorant consonants (**-l-, -m-, -n-, -r-, -rr-**) and before vowels: **çarmatos** 'I disarm', **çliroj** 'I liberate', **çmallem** 'I satisfy my longing', **çngjyros** 'I discolor', **çregjistroj** 'I cross out, strike off', **çrregulloj** 'I mess up, disarrange'. The form **zh-** is used after voiced non-sonorant consonants: **zhduk** 'wipe out', **zhvesh** 'lay bare, undress', **zhvleftësoj** 'I degrade, I devaluate'. Before voiceless consonants, the form **sh-** is used: **sh-palos** 'unfold', **shqep** 'unseam, unravel', **shthurr** 'unfence', **shfaq** 'express'.

Verbs derived from other verbs by this prefix have:

(1) A meaning opposite that of the derivational stem, as in verbs of the type **shkarkoj** 'I unload', **shkrij** 'I melt', **zhbrej** 'I unyoke', etc., which form contrastive pairs with their counterparts **ngarkoj** 'I load', **ngrij** 'I freeze', **mbrej** 'I yoke', etc.: **shkombëtarizoj** 'I denationalize', **shkrimb** 'I disinfect'; **çarmatos** 'I disarm', **çënjtem** 'I become unswollen'; **zhburrnoj** 'I emasculate, dishonor', **zhdredh** 'I untwist, unwind', etc.

    NOTE

    Zhduk is a back-formation from **zhdukem** 'I disappear', which itself comes from **dukem** 'I appear'.

(2) An intensifying meaning accompanied at times by some new semantic nuance, as in the verbs **sh-këmbej** 'I exchange', **shkëput** 'I yank', **shndërroj** 'I turn into, I convert', **shpërndaj** 'I disseminate, I scatter', **shpërvjel** 'I tuck up', etc.; **çliroj** 'I liberate', **zhbiroj** 'I pierce, bore'.

    NOTE

    The verbs **shpërngul** '(I) displace' and **shpërthej** 'I erupt' may be considered to have been formed with the compound prefix **shpër-** (from **sh-+për-**).

A few verbs have also been formed from nouns with the prefix **sh-/ç-/zh-**. If the underlying stem ends in an unstressed **-ë** or **-e** (e.g., **pikë** 'point, drop', **faqe** 'cheek, page', **koqe** 'kernel, grain'), this vowel is deleted since polysyllabic verbal stems cannot end in **-ë** or **-e** preceded by a consonant: **shfaq** 'manifest, express', **shkoq** 'detach, shuck', **shpik** 'invent'; **çmend** 'madden', **çmallem** 'I satisfy my longing' (this last verb is used only in the non-active form). With the exception of the verb **shfaq**, the prefix **sh-/ç-** has a privative meaning. Thus, **shkoq** means 'remove the grains from an ear (of cereal)', **shpik** 'drink to the last drop', **çmend** 'drive out of one's mind', **çmallem** 'remove my longing for my family and friends'.

    c) The prefix **z-/s-**.

This prefix, which is not very productive, has two forms, **z-** and **s-**, of which **z-** is more common. The form **z-** is used before voiced consonants, as in **zgjat** 'I lengthen', **zbuloj** 'I discover, I uncover', etc., while the form **-s** is used before voiceless ones, as in **skuq** 'I make red', **spastroj** 'I clean up', etc. Verbs derived chiefly from verbs and adjectives have been formed with this prefix.

The prefix gives verbs derived from other verbs:

(1) An intensive meaning: **skuq, spastroj, spraps** (or **zmbraps**) 'I push back, repulse'.

(2) A meaning opposite that of the verbs with the prefix **m-/n-** which form antonymous pairs with them: **mbath** 'I shoe'/**zbath** 'I unshoe'; **mbërthej** 'I nail'/**zbërthej** 'I solve, I unnail'; **mbuloj** 'I cover'/**zbuloj** 'I uncover'; **ngjesh** 'I gird'/**zgjesh** 'I ungird'.

Verbs formed by this prefix from adjectival stems have a causative sense: **skuq** 'I redden', **zbardh** 'I whiten', **zbut** 'I soften', **zgjat** 'I lengthen', **zverdh** 'I make pale', which can be semantically expanded to 'I make (something) red, white, soft, long, yellow', respectively.

d) The prefix **n-/m-**

This prefix, which is not very productive, has the forms **n-** and **m-**. The form **m-** is used before the labial consonants **-b-** and **-p-**; elsewhere **n-** appears.

A limited number of verbs, the derivational stems of which are not encountered as independent words, have been formed with this prefix. The identification of the prefix in verbs of the type **ngul** 'drive in', **mbuloj** 'I cover,', etc. is thus apparent only through contrast with a corresponding antonym such as **shkul** 'I yank, uproot', **zbuloj** 'I uncover', etc.

Antonymous verb pairs, created by the prefixes **n-/m-** and **sh-/zh-** and **z** are: **ndrydh** '(I) sprain'/**shtrydh** '(I) squeeze', **ngarkoj** 'I load'/**shkarkoj** 'I unload', **ngatërroj** 'I mess up, entangle'/**shkatërroj** 'I destroy', **ngreh** 'I construct'/**shkreh** 'I take apart', **ngrij** 'I freeze'/**shkrij** 'I melt', **ngul** 'I drive in'/**shkul** 'I yank, uproot', **ngjit** 'I glue'/**shqit** 'I unstick', **ngjesh** 'I gird'/**zgjesh** 'I ungird', **mbath** 'I shoe'/**zbath** 'I unshoe', **mbërthej** 'I nail'/**zbërthej** 'I unnail', **mbuloj** 'I cover'/**zbuloj** 'I uncover', **mbrej** 'I yoke'/**zhbrej** 'I unyoke'.

NOTES

1. The verbs **mbruj** 'I knead'/**zbruj** 'I tenderize' are not antonymous.

2. For antonymous pairs of the type **ndrydh/shtrydh**, voicing of the initial voiceless stop of the underlying stem to **-d-, -g-, -gj-** is caused by the preceding sonorant consonant **-n-**.

e) The prefixes **mbi-** and **nën-**

A few verbs derived only from other verbs have been formed with these antonymous prefixes. Verbs formed with the prefix **mbi-** 'over' indicate an action that stands higher, exceeds, or is superior to the action expressed by its underlying derivational stem: e.g., **mbiçmoj** 'I overvalue', **mbingarkoj** 'I overload', **mbikqyr** 'I supervise', **mbivleftësoj** 'I overestimate', **mbivlerësoj** 'I overestimate', **mbizotëroj** 'I predominate'.

On the other hand, verbs formed with the prefix **nën-** 'under' indicate an action that stands lower than, is insufficient, or is subordinate to the action expressed by the derivational stem: **nënçmoj** 'I undervalue', **nënqesh** 'I smile', **nënvleftësoj** 'I underestimate', **nënvlerësoj** 'I underestimate'.

The verbs **nënshkruaj** 'I sign, undersign', **nënshtroj** 'I subdue', and **nënkuptoj** 'I imply' have acquired special semantic connotations: **nënshkruaj** means 'I write my name and surname at the bottom of a document'; **nënshtroj** 'I place under my power'; **nënkuptoj** 'I presume, presuppose'.

f) The prefix **ndër-**

A small number of verbs derived from other verbs have been formed with this prefix, e.g., **ndërhyj** 'I interfere', **ndërlidh** 'I connect', **ndërmarr** 'I undertake', **ndërpres** 'I cut off, disrupt'. This prefix gives verbs various semantic connotations: e.g., **ndërhyj** 'intervene' connotes 'I get mixed up in an affair other than my own'.

g) The prefix **ri-**

This prefix, which has become quite productive in written Albanian, occurs only before verbs. Verbs formed with this prefix designate an action that is being performed again, like the English prefix *re-*: **riarmatos** 'I re-arm', **ribotoj** 'I reprint', **rifilloj** 'I begin anew', etc.

In some cases, the prefix **ri-** also expresses some other semantic nuance, such as **ripunoj** 'I rework = I work at it once more in order to improve it', **rivendos** 'I replace = I put it again in its former place', **rivleftësoj** 'I assign (to money) a new value'.

h) The prefix **stër-**

A few verbs have been formed with this prefix, which expresses semantic enlargement or excess: **stërholloj** 'I go into excessive details', **stërmundoj** 'I exhaust (someone)'.

This prefix is also used in expressions of the type **e mata dhe e stërmata** 'I measured it over and over again', **u njohëm** 'we became acquainted', **dhe u stërnjohëm** 'we got to know each other more and more', etc. to describe an action repeated to excess.

NOTES

1.   There are also other non-productive prefixes, such as: **më-** as in **mëkëmb** 'I cause to recover', **mësyj** 'I attack', **mëkoj** 'I feed (a helpless being)', **shp-** as in **shplaj** 'I rinse'; **tër-** as in **tërheq** 'withdraw'.

2.   In the literary language there are also a number of borrowings of the type **decentralizoj, degradoj, dekompozoj, demaskoj, demoralizoj, deshifroj**, etc., in which we can identify a prefix **de-**, which gives these verbs a meaning opposite to that of the corresponding borrowed derivational stem **centralizoj, gradoj**, etc.

C. Verbs Derived by Simultaneous Prefixation and Suffixation

A number of derived verbs have been formed by simultaneously adding prefixes and suffixes to derivational stems, the majority of which are nouns, but a few of which are adjectives and other parts of speech.

The suffixes that take part in the formation of verbs of this type are mainly **-o-**, **-so-**, and **-zo-**, from which verbs of conjugation I are formed: e.g., **përfundoj** 'I conclude', **përjetësoj** 'I perpetuate, immortalize', **shfrytëzoj** 'I exploit'.

Among verbs of conjugation II we have only **nguros** 'I petrify', **çmorrit** 'I de-lice', and **përtërit** 'I renew, reinvigorate'.

In the formation of verbs of this type, the prefixes **për-** and **sh-/ç-/zh-** are the most common.

1) Verbs of the type **për** + derivational stem + suffix

Two subgroups are distinguished here:

a) **për** + noun stem + **-ó-**: **përfundoj** 'I conclude', **përgënjeshtroj** 'I deny', **përmalloj** 'I move (others) emotionally', **përqafoj** 'I embrace'.

b) **për** + noun stem (pronominal or adjectival stem) + **-só-** **përfaqësoj** 'I represent', **përjetësoj** 'I prepetuate', **përgjithësoj** 'I generalize, universalize', **përvetësoj** 'I appropriate, assimilate', **përmirësoj** 'I improve'.

NOTE

The verbs **përjetësoj, përvetësoj**, and some others, have been formed by agglutination of the prepositional phrase **për jetë** 'for life', **për vete** 'for self' and addition of the suffix **-so-**.

2) Verbs of the type **sh-/ç-/zh-** + derivational stem + suffix:

a) **sh-** + noun stem + **-zó-**: **shfronëzoj** 'I dethrone', **shfrytëzoj** 'I exploit';

b) **sh-/ç-** + noun stem + **-só-/-ó-**: **shkripësoj** 'I de-salinate', **shpronësoj** 'I expropriate', **shfletoj** 'I leaf through', **çlyrësoj** 'I de-grease, remove fat'.

c) **zh-** + noun stem + **-ó-/só-**: **zhdoganoj** 'I clear (at customs)', **zhgjakësoj** 'I reconcile (bloodfeuding parties)', **zgjeroj** 'I broaden'.

NOTE

In addition to these, there are other verbs that have been formed with both prefixes and suffixes, such as: **nënvizoj** 'I underscore, I underline', **pavdekësoj** 'I immortalize', **riatdhesoj** 'I repatriate', **nguros** 'I petrify', **çmorrit** 'I de-lice', **përtërit** 'I renew, rejuvenate', (from the nouns **vizë** 'line', **atdhe** 'fatherland', **gur** 'stone', **morr** 'louse', and the adjectival form **të ri** 'young'). The verb **pavdekësoj** is more directly related semantically to the noun **pavdekësi** 'immortality'.

D. Verb Stems Derived by Conversion

There are also a few verbs in Albanian, for the most part derived from nouns and adjectives, without any derivational affix.

From the structural viewpoint, such verbs may be divided into two groups. The first group includes those verbs that have taken on active forms, such as **krip** 'I salt', **shosh** 'I sift', etc., while the second group includes those verbs that have taken on non-active forms, such as **mykem** 'I become moldy', **kujdesem** 'I take care, I care for', etc.

The majority of verbs derived without affixation belong to conjugation II: **krip** 'I salt, **qelb** 'I stink', **shosh** 'I sift', **ndryshk** 'I rust', **sit** 'I sift' (all from noun stems); **sëmur** 'I make ill', **kuq** 'I redden', **verdh** 'I make pale, yellow' (all from adjectival stems); as well as **përsëdyt** 'I repeat' (from the adverbial locution **për së dyti** 'a second time'). However, there are also a few verbs of the first conjugation, such as **huaj** 'I loan' and **shëllij** 'I salt, I brine' (from the noun stems **hua** 'loan' and **shëlli-rë** 'brine').

2.4.2 Verb Stems Formed by Compounding

Verbs with compound stems in Albanian are not numerous. Chief among them are qualifying constructions of the type adverb + verb. In addition, there are some verbs compounded of a noun and a verb.

The most common compound verb stems are those whose first constituent is the adverb **bashkë** 'together' or **para** 'before': **bashkëbisedoj** 'I converse', **bashkëekzistoj** 'I coexist', **bashkëfjalosem** 'I converse (with)'; **paracaktoj** 'I predetermine', **paralajmëroj** 'I forewarn, notify', **paramendoj** 'I premeditate', etc. In stems of this type, a first constituent **bashkë-** corresponds to English **co-, con-** or **com-**, while a first constituent **para-** corresponds to English *pre-, fore-,* or *ante-*.

In compound verb stems with other circumstantial adverbs as first constituent (e.g., **mirë** 'well', **keq** 'badly', **tej** 'beyond, across'), the meaning of this constituent is an abstract or figurative extension of its meaning in ordinary verb phrases: **mirëpres** 'I welcome', **mirëmbaj** 'I preserve, maintain', **keqkuptoj** 'I misunderstand', **keqpërdor** 'I misuse', **tejkaloj** 'I exceed', etc.

In the compound verbs **buzëqesh** 'I smile', **duartrokit** 'I applaud', **udhëheq** 'I lead, guide', **rrethshkruaj** 'I circumscribe', etc., the first constituent (the nouns: **buzë** 'lip(s)', **duar** 'hands', **udhë** 'road', **rreth** 'ring, hoop, circle') complements the action expressed by the second constituent. Thus, **buzëqesh** means 'laugh with the lips', **duartrokit** 'clap the hands', and **udhëheq** 'lead someone on the road'.

2.4.3 Verb Stems Formed by Agglutination

A small number of verb stems originate as phrase agglutinations. The meaning of these agglutinated verbs can be derived directly or indirectly from the meaning of the phrase from which they have been formed: **bëzaj** 'I call, call out' (from **bëj za** 'I make sound', and **vërej** 'I observe, notice' (from **vë re** 'pay attention'). Also **falënderoj** 'I thank' and **ngjatjetoj** 'I greet' have come from the agglutination of their respective phrases: **falem nderit** 'I pray to the honor, thanks' and **tungjatjeta** (from **t'u ngjattë jeta**) 'may life be lengthened for you', plus the suffix **-ó-**.

CHAPTER 3

Nouns and Nominal Phrases

3.1 The Nominal Phrase

A NOMINAL PHRASE (abbreviated NP) is a word or sequence of words which serves in typical functions of a noun, such as subjects and objects of verbs and objects of prepositions. Every NP has a nominal element or a determiner as its nucleus; this nucleus may be followed by one or more adjectival modifiers and by an appositional phrase (another NP designating the same referent as the nuclear element). Nouns and substantivized adjectives may be preceded by one or more determiners. Charts 3.1 to 3.4 indicate the classes of components that may make up a nominal phrase and show their relative order within the phrase. Those elements listed in a column are mutually exclusive; if more than one element within a class may be present in a given NP, they are listed in left to right order corresponding to their order in the NP.

Chart 3.1: The Nominal Phrase (NP)			
Nucleus			
Determiner	Nominal Element	Adjectival Modifier	Appositional Phrase

Chart 3.2: Determiners	
Selective	
Interrogative	Demonstrative
çfarë 'what'	**ajo** 'that, she'
çfarëdo 'whatever'	**kjo** 'this, she'
ç 'what'	**asaj** 'to that, to her'
cili 'which'	**kësaj** 'to this, to her'
	këtë 'this, him, her'
Quantitative	
Indefinite	Definite (Numerical)
disa 'several'	**dy** 'two'
çdo 'every, all'	**katër** 'four'
një 'a, an'	**një** 'one'
ndonjë 'some'	**dhjetë** 'ten'
	gjithë 'all'
	tërë 'entire'
Pronominal	
im 'my'	
yt 'thy'	
tim 'my'	
tët 'thy'	

A NOUN may be simple, compound, or derived. A PRONOMINAL ELEMENT may be a pronoun, a deictic or a substantivized adjective. A DETERMINER may be interrogative, selective, pronominal, or numerical. A SELECTIVE DETERMINER may be indefinite or definite. The PRONOMINAL DETERMINERS 'my' and **yt** 'thy' appear only with a small number of nouns designating persons intimately associated with the pronominal referent--mostly kinship terms. An ADJECTIVAL MODIFIER may be an articulated or unarticulated adjective, an articulated noun in the genitive case, a predicative adverbial, or a relative clause.

Chart 3.3: Nominal Elements
Nouns
vajzë 'girl'
gjyzlykë 'glasses'
qytet 'city'
Enver Hoxha
lumturi 'happiness'
Pronouns
unë 'I'
ti 'thou'
ne 'we'
ju 'you'
kush 'who'
Substantivized Adjectives
i miri 'the good one'
e shkreta 'the wretched'
të voglat 'the little ones'
të duhurit 'what is needed'
së foluri 'speaking'

Chart 3.4: Adjectival Modifiers				
Articulated Noun	Adjective	Unarticulated Adjective	Predicative Adverbial	Relative Clause
i malit 'of the mountain	**i mirë** 'good'	**formal** 'formal'	**atje** 'there'	**që mbarova** 'that I finished'
e vajzës 'the girl's	**e shkretë** 'wretched'	**bujar** 'generous'	**më afër** 'nearer'	**të cilin e njinim** 'whom we knew'
të Hoxhës 'Hoxha's	**të duhura** 'necessary'	**amerikan** 'American'	**në shtëpi** 'at home'	**që është më i madh** 'which is bigger'
të gjyzlykëve 'of glasses	**i shijshëm** 'tasty'	**përmbldhës** 'comprehensive'	**bosh** 'empty'	
i të voglave 'of the little ones	**më e madhe** 'bigger'	**socialist** 'socialist'	**vetëm** 'alone'	

3.1.1 Predeterminers

PREDETERMINERS have special functions in respect to NP's. NEGATIVE predeterminers such as **jo** 'no' or **as** 'not even, not a, not' may precede a determiner to express the contrary of that determiner: e.g., **jo ai zog** 'not that bird', **as tetë herë** 'not even eight times'. The VOCATIVE determiners **o** 'oh', **ej** (or **hej**) 'hey', **moré** (or **oré**) 'hey' (called to a male) or **moj** (or **moré**) 'hey' (called to a female) may be used before nouns (usually names) only in the nominative case to call out to someone or something. **More, moj** have a somewhat rustic, somewhat old-fashioned stylistic tone and even **o** has a slightly old-fashioned literary poetic feeling. The following noun is usually indefinite unless a following adjectival phrase identifies the noun (see Section 3.2.5 C.1).

3.1.2 Determiners

A determiner may precede a noun in a NP, picking out individuals designated by the noun rather than describing the noun as an adjective would typically do. Except for certain sequences with demonstratives (e.g., **ata dy djem** 'those two boys', **gjithë këto lajme** 'all these reports'), only one determiner may appear in a single NP.

INTERROGATIVE determiners ask for an identification of the noun. The interrogative **cili** 'which' acts syntactically like a substantivized adjective: its definite case ending reflects the gender, number, and case of the NP, and the noun that follows has no case ending. (See Table 3.1.)

Table 3.1 Interrogative Determiner + Noun				
	Sg		Pl	
	Masc	Fem	Masc	Fem
	'which city'	'which girl'	'which cities'	'which girls'
Nom	cili qytét	cila vájzë	cilët qytete	cilat vajza
Acc	cilin qytét	cilën vájzë	cilët qytete	cilat vajza
Dat	cilit qytét	cilës vájzë	cilëve qytéte	cilave vajza
Abl	cilit qytét	cilës vájzë	cilësh qytéte	cilash vájza

Other interrogative determiners are almost all invariable in written form, but **ç'** 'what, what (a)!', prefixed to a following noun stem, sounds like **xh** (that is, it is voiced) if the noun begins in a voiced obstruent (stop, fricative or affricate) and voiceless otherwise: **ç'vajzë** 'what girl', **ç'burrë** 'what man', **ç'qytet** 'what city', **ç'njerëz** 'what people', **ç'emër** 'what name' **ç'rrugë** 'what street'. The exclamatory meaning (corresponding to English 'what___!' or 'what a___!') is marked in Albanian orthography by an exclamation point, as in English: **vajzë e bukur!** 'What a pretty girl!' **njerëz zemërgurë!** 'What cruel people!' In both interrogative and exclamatory meanings, the noun stem after **ç'** has no inflectional ending; to express the same meanings for anything but the nominative or accusative case, a form of **cili** is used for the interrogative and **çfarë** for the exclamatory.

Other interrogative determiners are **çfárë** 'what, which' **çfarëdó** 'whatever, whichever', **çfarëdollój** 'whatever kind of, whichever kind of', all expansions of **ç'** (**fárë** 'seed, ilk'; **do** 'you want'; **lloj** 'kind, type').

Table 3.2 Demonstrative Determiners								
	Sg				Pl			
	Far		Near		Far		Near	
	'that'		'this'		'those'		'these'	
	Masc	Fem	Masc	Fem	Masc	Fem	Masc	Fem
Nom	ai	ajó	ky	kjo	atá	ató	këtá	këtó
Acc	atë́		këtë́					
Dat	atíj	asaj	këtíj	kësáj	atýre		këtýre	
Abl					asósh		kësósh	
Gen	i atíj	i asáj	i këtíj	i kësáj	i atýre		i këtýre	

SELECTIVE DETERMINERS have to do with the identity of the individuals concerned and may be demonstrative or interrogative. A DEMONSTRATIVE determiner consists of an unstressed deictic prefix **a-** 'remote' or **kë-** 'near' plus a third person pronominal stem (See Table 3.2). Demonstratives may be followed by nouns in definite or indefinite forms, the former preferred when the noun is followed by an adjectival modifier that further identifies the noun: **këto vajza** 'these girls' [indefinite], **këto vajza të bukura** 'these pretty girls' [indefinite], **këto vajzat e Agimit** 'these daughters of Agim's' [definite].

INDEFINITE determiners designate non-numerical quantities. The so-called indefinite article **një** (unstressed) 'a, an', **(një) tjetër** 'another', **njëfarë** 'a certain, sort of a', **çdo** 'every, each, all', and **ndonjë** 'some (in the sense of "unidentified" rather than "a positive, but unspecified amount"), any' may be followed by a singular countable noun in an indefinite form. **Disá** 'several, some', may be followed by a plural countable noun in an indefinite form, and some speakers also use it in cases where others use **ca**.

Unstressed before a plural countable noun, **pak** corresponds to English 'a few, some' (indicating a positive, but unspecified amount): **pak njérëz** 'a few people, some people'. Stressed in the same position it corresponds to English 'few = not many': **pák njérëz** 'few people'. Unstressed before a singular mass noun it corresponds to 'a little' or 'some' in the same sense: **pak qúmësht** 'a little milk, some milk'. Stressed in that position it corresponds to English 'little (=not much)': **pák qúmësht** 'little milk'. The negative senses of **pák** 'not many, not much' may be reinforced by preceding it by **vetëm** 'only': **vetëm pak njerëz** 'only a few people, few people', **vetëm pak qumësht** 'only a little milk, little milk'. Some speakers from Tosk areas use **ca** in place of unstressed **pak** to mean 'a little, a few, some'.

The indefinite determiners **gjithfarë** 'all sorts of', **gjithfarëlloj** 'all kinds of', **lloj-lloj** 'various kinds of'.

> **Revizionistët kanë përdorur forma, manevra, taktika e metoda të rafinuara, i kanë vënë vetes GJITHFARËLLOJ maskash...** 'The revisionists have used refined forms, maneuvers, tactics, and methods; they have placed ALL KINDS OF masks on themselves.'
>
> **ATO tregonin GJITHFARË ngjarjesh të vogla.** 'THEY would tell ALL SORTS of little stories.'
>
> **Shikonin LLOJ-LLOJ gjërash.** 'They were looking at VARIOUS SORTS of things.'

Tërë 'entire' or **gjithë** 'all' may be used before definite nouns, corresponding to English 'the whole, the entire, all the ___': **tërë ditën** 'the whole day', **tëre bota** 'the entire world', **tërë qumështi** 'all the milk'. **gjithë dita** 'all the day', **gjithë emri** 'the whole name', **gjithë emrat** 'all the names', **gjithë ditët** 'all the days'. The determiner **gjithë** may also be preceded by an adjectival article; if the following noun is plural the articulated form is preferred; if that noun is feminine, the plural form **të gjitha** is used:

Masc Sg	Fem Sg	Masc Pl	Fem Pl
gjithë emri	gjithë dita	gjithë emrat	gjithë ditët
i gjithë emri	e gjithë dita	të gjithë emrat	të gjitha ditët

The determiners **gjithë** and **tërë** are essentially equivalent in meaning:

> **Në themel vija e Partisë sonë në ndërtimin shtetëror dhe në orientimin e TËRË veprimtarisë së Pushtetit Popullor ka qënë kurdoherë e drejtë.** 'Basically, the line of our Party in state construction and the orientation of ALL of the activity of the People's Power has been always correct.'
>
> **GJITHË Skrapari, që ka zbritur sot në Çorovodë, përqafohet.** 'ALL of Skrapar, which has descended today in Çorovodë, embraces [i.e. all of the inhabitants of Skrapar....embrace one another].'

The determiner **mbarë** 'the whole' has the same meaning as **gjithë** and **tërë**, but has a more limited use. It is used mainly before nouns with a collective sense.

The indefinite articulated adjective **i tillë** 'such a, such' is used as a determiner only before indefinite nouns. Its form reflects the case, number, and gender of the noun:

	Singular		Plural	
	'such a hero'	'such a woman'	'such heros'	'such women'
Nom	i tillë trim	e tillë grua	të tillë trima	të tilla gra
Acc	të tillë trim	të tillë grua	të tillë trima	të tilla gra
Dat	të tillë trimi	të tillë gruaje	të tillë trimave	të tilla grave
Abl	të tillë trimi	të tillë gruaje	të tillë trimave	të tilla grave
Gen	i të tillë trimi	i të tillë gruaje	i të tillë trimave	i të tilla grave

NUMERICAL determiners are phrases consisting of a specific cardinal number or a sequence of cardinal numbers (see Chapter 7). As determiners, numbers do not reflect the case of the NP--that is done by the noun nucleus:

Kam një vajzë. 'I have one girl.'

Ilaçet iu dhanë gjashtë qind e nëntëdhjetë e katër njerëzve. 'Drugs were given to six hundred ninety four people.'

Definiteness may, however, be indicated by an adjectival article before the number:

Të katër vajzat u plagosën. 'The four girls were wounded.'

The only PRONOMINAL DETERMINERS that may appear unstressed before nouns are the various case and gender forms for 'my' and 'thy': 'my'= **im, ime, tim, sime, time;** 'thy'= **yt, jot, tët, tyt, sat.** These may precede an indefinite form of a small number of singular nouns designating persons intimately associated with the possessor, for the most part, kinship terms:

	Male		Female	
atë	'father'		**ëmë'**	'mother'
bir	'son'		**bijë**	'daughter'
vëlla	'brother'		**motër**	'sister'
gjysh	'grandfather'		**gjyshe**	'grandmother'
nip	'nephew, grandson'		**mbesë**	'niece, granddaughter'
kushëri	'cousin'		**kushërirë**	'cousin'
kunat	'brother-in-law'		**kunatë**	'sister-in-law'
vjehërr	'father-in-law'		**vjehërr**	'mother-in-law'
shoq	'husband'		**shoqe**	'wife'
njerk	'step-father'		**njerkë**	'step-mother'
zot	'lord, master'		**zonjë**	'lady, mistress'

The paradigms below indicate the forms of **im** and **yt** used in the two genders and four cases:

	'my father'	'my wife'	'thy son'	'thy daughter'
Nom	im atë	ime shoqe	yt bir	jot bijë
Acc	tim atë	time shoqe	tët bir	tët bijë
Dat	tim eti	time shoqeje	tyt biri	tët bije
Abl	tim eti	sime shoqeje	tyt biri	sat bije
Gen	i tim eti	i sime shoqeje	i tyt biri	i sat bije

An ADJECTIVAL phrase (abbreviated AdjP, see Chapter 4) is a word or sequence of words which serve the typical functions of an adjective, modifying a noun or pronoun either directly as an attributive modifier in the noun phrase or indirectly through a verb as a predicative modifier:

Attributive: **mësuesi i lumtur** 'the happy teacher'
              E gjeti mësuesin e lumtur. 'He found the happy teacher.'
Predicative: **Mësuesi ishte i lumtur.** 'The teacher was happy.'
              E gjeti mësuesin të lumtur. 'He found the teacher (to be) happy.'

Adjectival phrases, listed in the order in which they may appear in the NP, may be: articulated or unarticulated adjectives in any degree, with their modifiers; articulated NP's in the genitive case; predicative adverbials; or relative clauses. ARTICULATED modifiers are those preceded by an adjectival article **i, e, të** or **së**. PREDICATIVE ADVERBIALS are adverbs or adverbial phrases (including prepositional phrases) that may serve as predicative modifiers. A RELATIVE clause is introduced by a relative conjunction such as **që** 'that' **i cili** 'who, which', **ku** 'where', **kur** 'when'.

An APPOSITIVE phrase is itself a NP with the same referent as the NP to which it is adjoined; the appositive phrase is either in the nominative indefinite form or in the same case as the main NP.

3.2 The Noun

Nouns are naming words: they may be particular names of particular people or things (**Gjergj** 'George', **Shqipëria** 'Albania') or generic designations (**lopë** 'cow', **djalë** 'boy', **libër** 'book', **bukuri** 'beauty').

The citation form (the form used to refer to the word itself: for example, the form in which the word is listed in a dictionary) of nouns is said to be in the NOMINATIVE ("naming") INDEFINITE ("non-specific") CASE ("form"). For all but a very few nouns, the citation form is SINGULAR ("referring to something or someone as a single entity", as in the examples above) rather than PLURAL ("referring to something or someone as a collection of entities", **pantallona** 'trousers'). From this form, you can usually predict what the other forms of the noun will be, and what forms adjectives (see Chapter 4, Adjectives and Adjectival Phrases) will have when they refer to the noun. The pattern of formation of the different forms of a given noun is called its DECLENSION; since each different form of a noun is called a CASE of that noun, a declension is thus a set of cases of a noun.

In Albanian there are two major types of noun declension, conventionally called MASCULINE (because most nouns that designate males follow this declension pattern) and FEMININE (because most nouns that designate females follow this declension pattern). To know whether a noun is masculine or feminine there is a simple rule of thumb: Most nouns whose citation form ends in a consonant are masculine; most nouns whose citation form ends in a vowel are feminine. The exceptions are certain masculine nouns ending in **á, é, ë̃,** or **o**, and certain feminine nouns that end in **ë** (or **u**) + **r, l,** or **ll**.

Each case form of a noun has a particular set of functions: the form tells you what role the noun plays in respect to the context in which it is found.

The lexico-grammatical class of NOUNS includes a variety of words that designate: people and animals, such as **njeri** 'human being,' **burrë** 'man', **grua** 'woman', **ka** 'ox', **dele** 'sheep' ; concrete things, such as **gur** 'stone', **dru** 'wood', **shtëpi** 'house', **qytet** 'city', **mal** 'mountain'; natural phenomena, such as **dimër** 'winter', **furtunë** 'storm', **tërmet** 'earthquake', **shi** 'rain', **borë** 'snow'; qualities, sch as **bukuri** 'beauty', **dashuri** 'love', **mirësi** 'goodness', **shkathësi** 'alertness'; actions or situations, such as **ecje** 'walking', **drejtim** 'direction', **përkrahje** 'support', **lodhje** 'tiredness', **tmerr** 'terror'; abstract notions such as, **e mira** 'the good', **e vërteta** 'the truth'.

Qualities designated by nouns are considered in isolation from their carriers, i.e., they are abstracted. Compare **gjatësi** 'length' with **i gjatë** 'long', **trimëri** 'bravery' with **trim** 'brave', **drejtësi** 'justice' with **i drejtë** 'just'. Similarly, the action or situation that the noun may refer to is detached from persons or things that act and from the time in which it occurs. This becomes clear, if we compare a few nouns that designate actions, with their corresponding verbs: **punim** 'work' **punoj** 'I work', **lëvizje** 'movement' **lëviz** 'I move', **mbyllje** 'closure' **mbyll** 'I close', **ndarje** 'division' **ndaj** 'I divide'.

The noun is characterized in its morphology by grammatical categories of gender, number, case, and definiteness. Each noun has a specific gender of its own, in contrast with adjectives whose gender depends on the noun they modify.

A characteristic inflectional category of nouns in Albanian is that of DEFINITENESS (unlike in English, where definiteness is expressed only by a preposed definite or indefinite article separated from the noun itself). When an adjective is converted into a noun, it acquires the capacity to be used in both definite and indefinite forms: **një i ri** 'a youth',x **i riu** 'the youth', **një e drejtë** 'a right', **e drejta** 'the right'.

Syntactically, a noun characteristically functions as subject:

AGIMI po zbardhëllonte dalëngadalë, 'The DAWN was brightening gradually';
object: **Për mua e di gjithë fshati që e kam ndihmuar LUFTËN.** 'The whole town knows that I have supported THE WAR';
a predicate nominative: **Janë NGJARJE të kohës së kaluar këto që po nis t'ju tregoj sot.** 'These are EVENTS of the past that I am beginning to tell you today.'
predicate complement: **Pas kësaj ngjarjeje e kishin bërë ROJTAR të fshatit.** 'After this event they had made him SHERIFF of the Village.'
modifier: **Lart në qiell kryqëzohen shigjeta DRITE.** 'Up in the sky crisscross arrows of LIGHT.'
or the object of a preposition: **Nga FUSHA kishin filluar me KOHË të vinin fshatarët.** 'From THE PLAIN the villagers had LONG BEFORE begun to come.'

Another grammatical trait of the noun is its modification by the adjective, which in its own form and in the form of the adjectival article reflects the noun in gender, number, and case (see Chapter 4).

Nouns are also distinguished from other parts of speech by the particular suffixes that may be used in their derivation. On the other hand, despite their differences, nouns and adjectives share certain common features. Many formations with suffixes function either as nouns or as adjectives: **punëtor** 'worker', **fshatar** 'villager', **malësor** 'mountaineer', **kundërshtar** 'opponent', etc. Among nouns there are also some that are used with preposed articles like those of adjectives. These are called articulated nouns: **i ati** 'the father', **e motra** 'the sister', **e marta** 'Tuesday', **të kuqtë** 'the red', etc. Some of these in fact are simply substantivized adjectives: **e mira** 'the good', **e bukura** 'the beautiful', **të rinjtë** 'the young (men)', **të rejat** 'the young (women)', **të ftohtët** 'the cold', **të errëtit** 'the dark' (as in "come out of the dark"). In some formations the preposed article appears as a derivational device in the conversion of participles into nouns, as in **të ecurit** 'walking', **të folurit** 'speaking', **të ngrënët** 'eating'.

3.2.1 Noun Classes

Nouns in Albanian may be classified as COMMON and PROPER. Common nouns in turn divide into COUNTABLE and UNCOUNTABLE. COLLECTIVE nouns and SUBSTANCE nouns are subclasses of the other classes.

A. Common and Proper Nouns

A common noun designates either an entire class of things or living beings or any member(s) of that class: **dele** 'sheep', **ujk** 'wolf', **nxënës** 'pupil', **nënë** 'mother', **fletore** 'notebook', **traktor** 'tractor', **revolucion** 'revolution', **çlirim** 'liberation', **fitore** 'victory', **urdhër** 'order', **ky plep** 'this poplar', **kjo shkollë** 'this school'.

Proper nouns designate particular people, animals or things. In Albanian orthography the initial letter of words considered to be proper nouns is always capitalized. **Petrit** [man's name], **Agron** [man's name], **Balo** [name of ox], **Berat** [name of city], **Korab** [name of a mountain], **Myzeqe** [name of a plain], **Sazan** [name of an island]. Note that names of languages and nationalities are considered to be common nouns in Albanian: **shqip** 'Albanian (language)' **amerikan** 'American'.

Proper nouns include:

1. names and surnames of people, pseudonyms: **Vjollcë** [woman's name], **Flutur** [woman's name], **Genc** [man's name], **Shpëtim** [man's name], **Kostandin Kristoforidhi** [man's name], **Shkurte Vata** [woman's name], **Migjeni** (pseudonym of Millosh Gjergj Nikollë), **Asdreni** (pseudonym of Aleksandër Stavre Drenovë);

2. names of animals: **Balo, Kuqal, Laro, Murro;**

3. geographic names (of rivers, mountains, seas, plazas, regions, cities, streets, squares, etc.): **Drin** [name of a river] **Tomor** [name of a mountain], **Mesdhe** 'Mediterranean', **Karaburun** [name of a mountain], **Sazan** [name of an island], **Shqipëri** 'Albania', **Azi** 'Asia', **Kurvelesh** [name of a region], **Krujë** [name of a city], the **"Konferenca e Pezës"** street, the **"Skënderbeu"** square etc.;

4. names of historical periods and events: **Rilindja** 'The (National) Reawakening', **Kongresi i Manastirit** 'The Congress of Manastir', **Lufta Nacional Çlirimtare** 'The War of National Liberation', **Revolucioni i Qershorit** 'The June Revolution';

5. names of institutions, organizations, enterprises etc.: **Fakulteti i Historisë dhe i Filologjisë** 'The Department of History and Philology', **Ministria e Arsimit dhe e Kulturës** 'The Ministry of Education and Culture', **Partia e Punës së Shqipërisë** 'The Party of Labor of Albania', **Presidiumi i Kuvendit Popullor** 'The Presidium of the People's Assembly', **Bashkimi i Rinisë së Punës të Shqipërisë** 'The Union of the Labor Youth of Albania', the **Partizani** machine shop etc.;

6. titles of literary works, newspapers, and magazines: **"Lulet e verës"** 'Summer Flowers', Migjeni's **"Vargjet e lira"** 'Free Verses', **"Zëri i popullit"** 'The Voice of the People', the magazine **"Nëntori"** 'November', **"Studime filologjike"** 'Philological Studies', etc. (Notice that the first word only is capitalized in Albanian titles.);

7. names of heavenly bodies: **Arusha e Vogël** 'The Little Bear', **Jupiteri** 'Jupiter', **Marsi** 'Mars', etc. But note that, as in English, **hënë** 'moon', **diell** 'sun', and **dhe** 'earth' are not capitalized in Albanian.

Proper nouns also differ from common nouns grammatically. Proper nouns are generally used in only one number (usually the singular), whereas most common nouns are used in both the singular and the plural. Unlike common nouns, proper nouns are used most often in the definite form.

A proper noun is used in the plural only in special cases to identify by surname a number of people who carry that surname: **KOLGJINAJT** 'the KOLGJINAJS', or certain people and things that have the same name:

Në klasën tonë ka dy PETRITË. 'In our class there are two PETRITS'.
Në rrethin e Tiranës ka dy SELITA: Selita e Madhe dhe Selita e Vogël. 'In the district of Tiranë there are two SELITAS: Big Selita and Little Selita'.

The borderline that separates proper nouns from common nouns is not always closed. Transitions occur frequently from one group to the other. Many proper names of people or places have been derived from common names: **Bukuri** 'Beauty', **Gëzim** 'Joy', **Lule** 'Flower', **Sokol** 'Brave', **Vjollcë** 'Violet'; **Dardhë** 'Pear', **Frashër** 'Ash tree', **Maja e Hekurave** 'The Tip of Irons', **Perëndimi** 'The West', **Lindja e Mesme** 'The Middle East' etc. On the other hand, various proper names have become common nouns, by being used as designations for objects of a class named after people or places connected with them: **lek** ('Albanian coin'), **napolon** ('Albanian gold coin'), **amper** 'ampere', **herc** 'hertz', **om** 'ohm', **rëntgen** 'x-ray'; (from: **Lekë, Napoleon; Amper, Herc, Om; Rëntgen); shampanjë** 'champagne (from the Champagne region of France)'.

B. Countable and Uncountable Nouns

Among common nouns one may distinguish countable nouns from uncountable nouns. COUNTABLE nouns indicate objects that can be separated from other objects of the same class and thereby be counted: **libër** 'book', **lopë** 'cow', **mal** 'mountain', **det** 'sea', **njeri** 'human being', **ligj** 'law', **besim** 'belief', **qytet** 'city', **shkollë** 'school', **shtëpi** 'house', etc.

Syntactically, countable nouns are characterized by the fact that they can be quantified by a cardinal number: **një njeri** 'one man', **dy njerëz** 'two men', **një qytet** 'one city', **katër qytete** 'four cities', and morphologically by the fact that they may have a plural form: **qytet** 'city'/-**qytete** 'cities', **shkollë** 'school'/**shkolla** 'schools', **libër** 'book'/**libra** 'books'. Note that a special small class of nouns, the so-called **pluralia tantum** are used only in a plural form but may not be directly quantified by a cardinal number, as countable nouns may. **pantallona-t** 'pants', **syza-t** 'eye glasses', **gërshërë-t** 'scissors'.

The singular countable nouns considered so far designate individuals. For another group of countable nouns, the singular form designates a collective entity itself composed of many individuals: **popull** 'people', **tufë** 'bunch', **fis** 'clan', **kope** 'herd', etc. The plural forms of such nouns designate the plurality of the collective entity: e.g., **popujt** 'the peoples (of the world', **tufat** 'the bunches', **fiset** 'the clans', **kopetë** 'the herds', and may be preceded by cardinal numbers like any other countable noun: **dy popuj** 'two peoples', **dy tufa** 'two bunches', **katër fise** 'four clans', **njëzet kope** 'twenty herds'; and the singular form may be preceded by the word **një** 'one, a' with the value either of the number 'one' or of the indefinite article 'a': **një popull** 'a people', **i një populli** 'of one people', etc.

Nouns indicating abstracted actions, situations, qualities, traits or notions are uncountable: **lëvizje** 'moving', **vrapim** 'running', **durim** 'patience', **dyshim** 'doubting', **gjelbërim** 'greenness', **trimëri** 'bravery', **art** 'art', **kujtesë** 'memory', **liri** 'liberty'. When used with their uncountable meaning, such nouns cannot have plural forms nor be quantified by cardinal numbers. This is clearly seen especially in nouns that designate abstract qualities or traits: **bukuri** 'beauty', **egërsi** 'fierceness', **krenari** 'pride', **mendjemadhësi** 'conceit', **zemërgjerësi** 'generosity'.

Whereas countable nouns can be accompanied by cardinal numbers to specify quantity, uncountable nouns cannot. Only indefinite quantifiers such as **ca** 'some', **gjithë** 'all', may accompany an uncountable noun: **Vetëm gra dhe ca DJEMURI mund të takoje ato ditë në fshat.**

'In those days in the village you could meet only women and some YOUNG FOLK.'

Some uncountable nouns, however, may take on a special sense, and then be used to designate an instantiation of an action, situation, process, quality or trait. In such a sense the uncountable noun becomes countable, may be used in a plural form, and may be determined by cardinal numbers or other quantifiers: **fatkeqësitë** 'the misfortunes', **tri fatkeqësi** 'three misfortunes'; **kalimet** 'the passages', **tri kalime** 'three passages'; **kokëçarje** 'trouble', **shumë kokëçarje** 'many troubles'; **lëvizjet** 'the movements', **tri lëvizje** 'three movements'; **trimëritë** 'the acts of bravery', **dy trimëri** 'two acts of bravery'; **ushtrimet** 'the exercises', **tri ushtrime** 'three exercises'; **vdekje** 'death', **katër vdekje** 'four deaths'. In such instances considerable concreteness of the meaning may develop: e.g., in the word **kalimet** 'the passages' we may be talking about the actual paths for passing through a place.

B.1 Abstract Nouns

Abstract nouns make up the largest subclass of UNCOUNTABLE nouns. With the exception of a few simple words like **frikë** 'fear', **gaz** 'joy', hare 'gaiety', jetë 'life', kohë 'time', **luftë** 'war', **peshë** 'weight', **punë** 'work', **shëndet** 'health', tmerr 'terror', etc., most abstract nouns are derived words. According to the type of formation, they fall into four groups: a) nouns formed from adjectives, verbs or adverbs by means of suffixes like **-i, -ri, -si, -im, -je, -esë, -atë, -më, -izëm**: e.g., bukuri 'beauty', **trimëri** 'bravery', **thjeshtësi** 'simplicity',

zhvillim 'development', **mbledhje** 'meeting', **kujtesë** 'memory', **uratë** 'blessing', **ndihmë** 'aid', **majtizëm** 'leftism', **marksizëm** 'Marxism'; b) neuter nouns formed by the articulated participle: **të ecurit** 'walking', **të menduarit** 'thinking', **të goditurit** 'hitting'; c) nouns formed by the substantivization of the adjective in the form of the neuter gender: **të ftohtët** 'the cold', **të errëtit** 'the dark', **të ritë** 'the youth'; d) compound nouns: **marrëveshje** 'agreement', **marrëdhënie** 'relationship', **kryengritje** 'uprising'.

B.2 Collective Nouns

Among uncountable nouns, COLLECTIVE nouns in the singular form designate a set of people, animals or objects of a type. Compare the plurals of certain countable nouns with their related collective uncountable nouns: **djemtë** 'the boys', **dy djem** 'two boys', **tre djem** 'three boys'/**djalëria** 'the boyhood'; **gratë** 'the women', **dy gra** 'two women', **tri gra** 'three women'/- **graria** 'the womenhood'; **proletarët** 'the proletarians', **dy proletarë** 'two proletarians', **tre proletarë** 'three proletarians'/**proletariati** 'the proletariat.'

In speech, uncountable collective nouns show their double relationship with the singular and the plural in the inflections of the verb, which sometimes takes the singular and sometimes the plural to agree with a collective uncountable subject:

GJINDJA e RRETHONIN kalin e Skënderbeut, e QUANIN çlironjës, që meritonte të gjitha kurorat e botës. 'THE CROWD SURROUNDED [plural] Scanderbeg's horse, CALLED [plural] him liberator, defender of Albania, who merited all the crowns of the world.'

U NGRITËN PLEQËRIA dhe SHKUAN të PAJTONIN binjakët. 'THE OLD FOLKS AROSE [plural] and WENT OVER [plural] to RECONCILE [plural] the twins.'

DJEMURIA në mur të shkollës darkë për darkë ia THOSHIN këngës. 'Every evening THE YOUNG FOLK WOULD SING [plural] by the wall of the school.'

Oshëtima e lajmit u përhap nëpër fushë ku PUNONTE BUJQËRIA. 'The echo of the news spread over the plain where THE FARM FOLK WORKED [singular].'

Most uncountable collective nouns in Albanian designate animate beings but a few of them designate inanimate objects, e.g., **drizëri** 'bushes'.

As a rule, uncountable collective nouns are derived words; only a few simple nouns have a collective use: **bota** 'the world' and **fëmija** 'the child': thonë BOTA '[THE] PEOPLE say'; qajnë FËMIJA 'The children [as a group] ("The child") are crying'.

There are no special suffixes for the formation of uncountable collective nouns. They are formed with the same suffixes, **-i, -ri, -si, -je** and **-im**, that serve for the formation of other abstract nouns: **beqarI** 'bachelorhood', **parI** 'notables', **punëtorI** 'laboring people', **vegjëlI** 'childhood', **çupëRI** 'girlhood', **djalëRI** 'boyhood', **graI** 'womanhood', **vashëRI** 'maidenhood', **fshatarëSI** 'peasantry', **miqëSI** 'friendship', **gjindJE** 'crowd', **rruzullIM** 'universe', and **njerëzIM** 'humanity'.

Depending on the context, the same word may or may not have the meaning of collective noun: **çupëri** 'girlhood' a) the age when one is a girl; b) all the girls of a particular place taken together. The same is also true for **nusëri** 'bridehood', **vashëri** 'maidenhood' etc.

B.3 Substance Nouns

In certain respects nouns designating substances resemble collective nouns. A SUBSTANCE NOUN designates a homogeneous substance which can be divided into parts and weighed, but which cannot be counted.

In terms of lexical meaning, substance nouns designate food products, crops, metals and minerals, chemical products, etc.: **djathë** 'cheese', **dhallë** 'buttermilk', gjizë 'cottage cheese', hime 'bran', **hirrë** 'whey', **kos** 'yogurt', **mjaltë** 'honey', **qumësht** 'milk', **raki** 'brandy', **verë** 'wine'; **duhan** 'tobacco', **elb** 'barley', **grurë** 'wheat', **kashtë** 'straw', **të lashtat** 'crops', **li** 'flax',

thekër 'rye'; **alkool** 'alcohol', **benzinë** 'benzene', **hekur 'iron'**, **krom** 'chrome', **qymyr** 'coal', serë 'asphalt', **squfur** 'sulfur', **vajguri** 'petroleum'; **kartë** 'paper', **nailon** 'nylon', **nitrat** 'nitrate', **superfosfat** 'super phosphate'.

Substance nouns are used only in one number (except as mentioned below); the majority have only singular forms and a few have only plural. Like uncountable collective nouns, these also generally may not be quantified by a cardinal number, including the number and indefinite article **një** 'one'. Particularly in the spoken language, however, a few nouns designating beverages or food substances may become countable nouns and thus be accompanied by the article **një** 'one', but with the special meaning abbreviated of "a usual portion of__": **më sill NJË VERË, NJË UJË, NJË BIRRË** 'bring me A (glass of) WINE, A (glass of) WATER, A (glass of) BEER.'; **NJË QUMËSHT, NJË KOS, NJË DJATHË** 'A MILK, A YOGURT, A CHEESE' (=a glass of milk, a cup of yogurt, a serving of cheese); **më jep NJË DUHAN** 'give me A TOBACCO (=a cigarette of tobacco).

Substance nouns may be preceded by indefinite quantifiers, such as **shumë** 'much', **pak** 'little', and **ca** 'some' (**shumë qymyr** 'much coal', **ca duhan** 'some tobacco', **pak benzinë** 'a little benzine' etc.).

As in English, substance nouns, normally used only in the singular, in some cases may also be used in the plural (usually with the suffix **-ra**), but with the special function of designating *types* of a substance or things made of it: **djathëra** 'cheeses', **vajra** 'oils', **verëra** 'wines'; **bakëre** 'copper items', **hekura** 'irons'. For details of the meanings of the plural see Section 3.2.4.

In the indefinite singular form, substance nouns characteristically have a partitive meaning, as in: **pi UJË** 'drink WATER', **ha MISH** 'eat MEAT', **pi VERË** 'drink WINE', **një gotë UJË** 'a glass of WATER', **një shishe VERË** 'a bottle of WINE', **një kg GËLQERE** 'a kilogram of LIME', etc.

From the point of view of word formation the majority of substance nouns are simple words, although some ar not: **kafeinë** 'caffeine', **të lashtat** 'crops', manaferrat 'blackberries', qymyrguri 'coal', **vajguri** 'petroleum'.

3.2.2 The Category of Gender

Gender differs from the grammatical categories, case, and definiteness, in being a lexical as well as an inflectional category of the noun. The gender to which a given word belongs is a property of that particular word independent of context. It is the gender of the noun that primarily determines what set of forms will be used to mark its own case and definiteness, as well as the set of forms of the various determining words and pronouns that are associated with that noun:

	Masculine	Feminine
Nom Sg Def	**mal-i** 'the mountain'	**fushë-a** 'the plain'
Dat Sg Def	**mal-it** 'to the mountain'	**fushë-s** 'to the plain'
Nom Sg Indef	**ky libër** 'this book'	**kjo shkollë** 'this school'
Nom Sg Indef	**libër i ri** 'new book'	**shkollë e re** 'new school'

For nouns of animate beings, people, and animals (not plants), the gender is usually determined by the sex of the designated being. As a result the gender of nouns of animate beings is not arbitrarily assigned by the grammar of the language but also reflects the semantic reality.

NOTE

There are, however, some nouns designating animate beings that are exceptions. For the most part, these are nouns of animals whose sexual differentiation is of no special importance to the culture: **mi** 'mouse (m.)', **iriq** 'groundhog (m.)', **flutur** 'butterfly (f.)', **peshk** 'fish (m.)', etc.

It should be also noted that there are certain nouns designating male animate beings like **hoxhë** 'priest' and male names ending in **-o**, such as **Kiço, Kole, Petro, Balo**, etc., which in terms of their form and type of declension appear to be feminine nouns: **Nikoja** '(the) Niko', **Nikos** 'to (the) Niko' just like **trikoja** 'the sweater', **trikos** 'to, of, from the sweater'. By virtue of their lexical meaning, however, they take adjectives and other determining words in the masculine form: **Nikoja është i ri** 'Niko is young', **Nikoja im** 'my Niko'.

In current Albanian, nouns of animate beings are only masculine or feminine. Neuter nouns never designate animate beings. Conversely, for nouns designating inanimate beings the gender usually bears no relation at all to the lexical meaning of the word. Semantically, then, the assignment of gender to nouns of inanimate beings is arbitrary. Thus, no consistent semantic principle will explain why **mal** 'mountain' is masculine while **fushë** 'field' is feminine.

Many inanimate masculine nouns are said to become feminine in the plural, because the form of the adjective associated with these nouns is that also used with feminine nouns: e.g., **mal i lartë** 'high mountain' **male të larta** 'high mountains'. Compare: **kalë i lartë** 'tall horse'/**kuaj të lartë** 'tall horses' and: **godinë e lartë** 'high building'/**godina të larta** 'high buildings'. This feature which is known as **"dygjinishmëri"** 'ambigender' occurs often in contemporary Albanian (see Section 3.2.2 A.2).

A. Gender Marking in Nouns

The genders of nouns in Albanian are marked by:

1. the case endings of the indefinite and definite singular forms;

2. the form of adjectives and other determining words like the pronouns **ky** 'this (m.)', **kjo** 'this (f.)', **ai** 'he', **ajo** 'she', **im** 'my (m.)', **ime** 'my (f.)' etc.;

3. the terminal sounds of the stem.

Thus, in the definite and indefinite declension in the singular, masculine nouns have the endings **-i** or **u** (for indefinite genitive-dative-ablative) and **-i, -it, -in,** (or **-u, -ut, -un**) (for definite nominative, genitive-dative-ablative, and accusative, respectively), and feminine nouns have the endings **-e** (singular indefinite genitive-dative-ablative) and **-a, -s(ë) -n(ë)** (singular definite nominative, genitive-dative-ablative, and accusative, respectively).

Apart from meaning, which plays a role only in determining the gender of animate nouns, the chief determinant of the gender of nouns is the form of the stem, and specifically its terminal sound. Exceptional are those masculine and feminine nouns which now end with the same sounds because of coalescing historical phonetic developments: for example, compare the masculine nouns **pjepër** 'cantaloupe', **kungull** 'pumpkin', **lumë** 'river' with the feminine nouns **shufër** 'rod', **kodër** 'hill', **kumbull** 'plum', **fushë** 'plain'. Note that all nouns formed with the suffixes **-i, -ri, -si, -nje** are feminine, whereas nouns formed with the suffixes **-im, -(ë)s** are masculine.

According to the terminal sound of their stem, the following are all MASCULINE:

1. all nouns that end with consonants (except a few with **-r, -ll, -l** preceded by **-ë** or **-u**; see Point 4 under feminine nouns): **faj** 'fault', **fshat** 'village', **gardh** 'fence', **gëzim** 'joy', **gur** 'stone', **këndim** 'reader (book)', **kos** 'yogurt', **krah** 'arm', **lis** 'oak', **mal** 'mountain', **pleh** 'manure',etc.;

2. all nouns whose citation form ends in a stressed vowel and whose stem in all other forms ends in **-r** (including all citation forms ending in **-u**): **dru** 'wood', **fre** 'rein', **hu** 'stake', **mulli** 'mill', **pe** 'thread', **tra** 'beam', **ulli** 'olive', **zë** 'voice, sound', etc., and **druri** 'the wood', **drurit** 'to the wood', **zëri** 'the sound', **zërit** 'to the sound', **hurit** 'the stake', etc.;

3. certain nouns whose citation form ends in the vowel cluster **-ua** (see Point 6 below for the only two feminine exceptions) which in the other forms changes to **-o-**: **krua** 'fountain', **thua** 'fingernail', **ftua** 'quince', etc., and **kro-i** 'the fountain', **kro-it** 'to the fountain', **fto-i** 'the quince', **fto-it** 'to the quince', etc.;

4. certain nouns that end in the stressed vowels **-i**, **-a**, and **-e**: **mi** 'mouse', **njeri** 'human being, man', **shi** 'rain', **thi** 'pig', **veri** 'north', **baba** 'father', **ka** 'ox', **vëlla** 'brother', **dhe** 'earth', **atdhe** 'fatherland';

5. the following nouns that end in the unstressed vowel **-ë**: **burrë** 'man', **djalë** 'boy', **gjumë** 'sleep', **kalë** 'horse', **lëmë** 'threshing yard', **lumë** 'river'. With the decline of the neuter gender, some new words have been added to this group, like: **ballë** 'forehead', **brumë** 'dough', **djathë** 'cheese', **ujë** 'water', etc., which in present-day Standard Albanian are used chiefly as masculine nouns: **balli** 'the forehead', **brumi** 'the dough', **djathi** 'the cheese', **uji** 'the water', etc.

The following are FEMININE:

1. all nouns whose stem ends in the unstressed vowel **-ë**, with the exception of the ones mentioned above under point 5 for masculine nouns: **bukë** 'bread', **dorë** 'hand', **fushë** 'field', **gjellë** 'meal', **kripë** 'salt', **lugë** 'spoon', **punë** 'work', etc.;

2. all nouns, without exception, that end in the *unstressed* vowel **-e**: **ardhje** 'arrival', **dallëndyshe** 'swallow', **faqe** 'cheek', **gjethë** 'bud', **lule** 'flower', **marrje** 'capture, seizure', **zile** 'bell', etc.; most of the nouns in this category are formed with the abstract noun suffix **-je** and the feminine suffix **-e**;

3. most nouns ending in the stressed vowels **-i**, **-e**, **-a**, **-o**: **bukuri** 'beauty', **dashuri** 'love', **drejtësi** 'justice', **liri** 'liberty', **shtëpi** 'home', **be** 'oath', **nge** 'leisure', **re** 'cloud', **rrëke** 'stream', **rrufe** 'lightening bolt', **kala** 'fortress', **byro** 'bureau', etc. The exceptions are masculine nouns like those mentioned under Point 4, some of which indicate male animate beings: **thi** 'boar, pig', **baba** 'father', **ka** 'ox', **vëlla** 'brother'. The majority of nouns in this category consists of abstract and collective nouns formed with the suffixes **-i**, **-ri**, **-si**;

4. some of the nouns that end in the sound sequences **-ër**, **-ël**, **-ur**, **-ull**: **kodër** 'hill', **lodër** 'boat', **motër** 'sister', **shufër** 'rod', **zemër** 'heart', **pupël** 'calf', **vegël** 'tool', **flutur** 'butterfly', **kumbull** 'plum', **petull** 'pancake', **tjegull** 'tile', **vetull** 'eyebrow'; note that at one time these nouns were written and pronounced with the terminal unstressed vowel **-ë** (**kodërë**, **fluturë**, **vegëlë**, **kumbullë**) which dropped after another unstressed syllable.

5. all nouns that end in the unstressed vowel **-o**: **depo** 'depot', **karro** 'cart', **pako** 'package', **pallto** 'coat', **radio** 'radio'. In proper nouns designating animate beings and ending in unstressed **-o**, the gender in terms of agreement is determined by the sex. Thus the male names **Petro**, **Malo**, **Luto**, **Niko** etc. take masculine modifiers while the female names **Haso** and **Maro** take feminine ones;

6. In the nouns **grua** 'woman' and **hua** 'loan', which end in the vowel group **-ua**.

A.1 Gender Distinctions in Animate Nouns

In nouns that denote human beings and animals whose sex distinction has been of social (usually economic) importance, that distinction is expressed:

1. By means of distinctive lexical roots (suppletive words): **vëlla** 'brother'/**motër** 'sister', **burrë** 'man'/**grua** 'woman', **djalë** 'boy'/**vajzë** 'girl', **baba** 'father'/**nënë** 'mother', **i ati** 'his father'/**e ëma** 'his mother', **nip** 'nephew, grandson'/ **mbesë** 'niece, granddaughter' **kalë** 'stallion, horse'/**pelë** 'mare', **ka** 'ox'/**lopë** 'cow', **dash** 'ram'/**dele** 'ewe, sheep', **cjap** 'billy goat'/**dhi** '(nanny) goat', **gjel** 'rooster'/**pulë** 'hen';

2. By means of a feminizing suffix added to the stem of a noun in the masculine gender:

a) with the suffix **-e**: **gjysh** 'grandpa'/**gjyshe** 'grandma', **mik** 'friend'/**mike** 'friend (f.)', **mjek** 'doctor'/ **mjeke** 'doctor (f.)', **shok** 'companion'/**shoqe** 'companion (f.)' (note the change of **k** to **q**). This is the most widespread suffix, because it operates also in derived words formed with the suffixes **-ak**, **-an**, **-tar**, **-ar**, **-as**, **-ës**, **-ist**, **-or**, **-tor**: e.g., **durrsak** 'inhabitant of Durrës'/**durrsake**, **dibran** 'inhabitant of Dibër'/**dibrane**, **fshatar** 'villager'/**fshatare**, **tiranas** 'inhabitant of Tiranë'/**tiranase**, **nxënës** 'pupil'/**nxënëse**, **artist** 'artist'/ **artiste**, **malësor** 'mountaineer'/**malësore, punëtor** 'worker'/**punëtore**.

b) with the suffix **-eshë** (like English -ess): **doktor** 'doctor'/**doktoreshë**, **drejtor** 'director'/ **drejtoreshë**, **luan** 'lion'/**luaneshë** 'lioness' etc.;

c) with the suffix **-ë**: **plak** 'old man'/**plakë** 'old woman', **kunat** 'brother-in-law'/**kunatë** 'sister-in-law', **zog** 'bird'/**zogë** 'bird (f.)' **kushëri** 'cousin' (m.) /**kushërirë** 'cousin' (f.)'; cousin (f.)' (note **-r-** insertion, cf. **kushëriri** 'the cousin (m.)';

d) with the suffix **-ushë**: **ari** 'bear'/**arushë**; **dre** 'stag'/**drenushë** 'doe';

e) with the suffix **-onjë**: **ujk** 'wolf'/**ujkonjë** 'she-wolf' (the older form is **ulkonjë**);

f) with the suffix **-icë**: **buall** 'buffalo'/**buallicë**.

3. A few masculine nouns have been formed from feminine nouns by masculinizing suffixes (**-ak, -ok**): **mace** 'cat'/**maçok** 'tom cat', **patë** 'goose'/**patok** 'gander', **rosë** 'duck (f.)'/**rosak** 'drake (m.)'.

A.2 Gender Shift in Plural Nouns

The majority of nouns in Albanian have the same gender for singular and plural. However, in certain types of plurals with particular suffixes a shift of gender from masculine to feminine takes place in the sense that the adjectives and other determining words associated with the noun form are in their typical masculine singular form when the noun is singular, but their typical feminine plural form when the noun is plural. The following groups of nouns have such masculine agreement in the singular, but feminine agreement in the plural.

1. Inanimate masculine nouns that form the plural with the suffix **-e**. The shift of gender in the plural for these nouns is quite old. With the exception of certain rare instances of instability, it has been generalized in present-day Standard Albanian and is required now by official orthographic rules, though some dialectal variation remains in practice. Thus, one will say: **këto brigje** 'these hills', **brigje të thepisura** 'steep hills', **këto kanale** 'these canals', **kanale ujitëse** 'irrigation canals', **këto male** 'these 'mountains', **malet tona** 'our mountains', **male të larta** 'high mountains', **këto mendime** 'these thoughts', **mendime interesante** 'interesting thoughts', **qytete të mëdha** 'big cities', **qytetet tona** 'our cities', **vende malore** 'mountainous places', **vendime të drejta** 'correct decisions', etc., with the modifiers in their feminine forms, although all the above words take masculine modifiers, specifiers, and case endings in the singular.

2. Inanimate masculine nouns with the suffix **-ra**. Substance nouns and the noun **mall** 'goods, property', belong in this category: **djathëra të kripura** 'salty cheeses', **ujëra të ftohta** 'cold waters', **leshra të dredhura** 'curly hairs', **vajra të ndryshme** 'different oils', **mallra të mira** 'fine goods'. With the plural of the noun **fshat** 'village', either masculine or feminine determiners are used freely: **fshatra të reja** 'new (f.) villages', **fshatra të rinj** 'new (m.) villages', but the tendency to preserve the masculine gender of this noun in the plural is dominant, especially in the information media.

3. Some inanimate masculine nouns with plurals in **-a**, such as **hap** 'step', **kolektive** 'collective': **hapa të gjata** 'long steps', **kolektivat punonjëse** 'worker's collectives'.

B. The Neuter Gender in Contemporary Albanian

The existence of a neuter gender in contemporary Albanian is becoming increasingly difficult to establish. Formal evidence for the existence of such a gender category has been reduced to a limited number of words that appear morphologically only in the **-t(ë)** suffix of the nominative and accusative singular case forms of four special sets of nouns and to the preposed article **të** (instead of the masculine **i** or feminine **e**) in the singular nominative case of certain substantivized adjectives (see below): **krye-T** 'head', **TË ecur-i-T** 'the action of walking', **TË ri-TË** 'youth'.

Thus the neuter gender in today's Albanian has the decided character of a relic, although it is still preserved in four groups of nouns:

1. Articulated deverbal nouns derived from the substantivization of participles: **të ardhur-i-t** 'arrival', **të ecur-i-t** 'walking', **të folur-i-t** 'speaking', **të menduar-i-t** 'thinking', **të ngrënë-t** 'eating', **të shtypur-i-t** 'crushing', etc. With the general decline of the neuter, however, one encounters more and more alongside deverbal neuter nouns, parallel substantivized formations of the deverbal feminine adjectives like **e bërtitur** '(a) shout', **e klithur** '(a) scream', **e qeshur** '(a) laugh', etc.:

> **Në sallë plasi një E QESHUR e gjatë.** 'A long LAUGH erupted in the hall.'

2. A few articulated nouns derived originally from the substantivization of the adjective of the neuter gender, accompanied by the preposed article and suffixed with the definite nominative or accusative suffix **-(i) + (ë)**: **TË errët-i-T** 'the darkness', **TË ftohtë-T** 'the cold', **TË kuq-TË** 'the red', **TË mugët-i-T** 'the dusk', **TË nxehtë-T** 'the heat', **TË verdhë-T** 'the yellow', **TË zi-TË** 'the black'.

3. A number of substance nouns like **brumë** 'dough', **drithë** 'cereal', **dhjamë** 'fat', **grurë** 'wheat', **gjalpë** 'butter', **lesh** 'wool', **miell** 'flour', **mish** 'meat', **mjaltë** 'honey', **vaj** 'oil', and a few others, the majority of which end in the unstressed vowel **-ë**, were at one time neuter in Albanian. However, at present both in the spoken language (with the exception of certain regional dialects) and in the written language, most of these nouns are being used in the masculine: **leshi** 'the wool', **mishi** 'the meat', **mjalti** 'the honey', **uji** 'the water' etc. Owing to the influence of dialects, however, one does encounter these nouns in neuter form here and there in literary works:

> **Ashtu është, se si të ngjethet MISHTË.** 'That's how it is, somehow your flesh crawls ("to you THE MEAT shudders").'
>
> **Drita na erdhi, xhadeja u asfaltua, vetëm UJËT mungon.** '(Electric) light has come to us, the road has been asphalted, only [THE] WATER is lacking.'
>
> **Vita, si kishte marrë LESHTË e manares së Kilit, e kishte larë, nderur e shkrifur.** 'After getting THE WOOL of Kili's pet, Vita had washed it, spread it out, and loosened it up.'

4. The names of two parts of the body may still be used as neuter nouns: **krye-t** 'head' and **ballë-t** (which appears more often as a masculine noun).

> **Arta rrudhi BALLËT, ktheu rrëmbimthi KRYET nga përkthyesi.** 'Arta wrinkled her FOREHEAD, turned her HEAD rapidly toward the interpreter.'
>
> **Manushaqe bukuroshe, pse s'ngre KRYET përpjetë, po rri e mpitë dhe e qetë, pse s'zbukurohe e shëndoshe?** 'Pretty violet, why don't you raise your ("THE") HEAD, instead of keeping stiff and still, why don't you become beautiful and strong?'

3.2.3 The Category of Case

The noun performs a variety of syntactic functions in relation to the other parts of the sentence, and its form varies accordingly. The forms of the noun which reflect its function in the sentence are called its cases, **rasa** in Albanian. When we speak of cases as grammatical categories, we have in mind both the particular forms of nouns and the grammatical functions reflected by them. The totality of case forms of a noun is called its declension (**lakim**). All nouns in Albanian are declined, regardless of their source.

In contemporary Albanian it is necessary to distinguish five cases: **emërore** 'nominative', **gjinore** genitive, **dhanore** 'dative', **kallëzore** 'accusative', and **rrjedhore** 'ablative'. Since every noun is also marked as definite or indefinite (see Section 3.2.5), a definite declension is distinguished from an indefinite one.

At one time Albanian had a locative case as well (see below). In addition some treatments of the language have identified a vocative case; in this treatment the "vocative" is considered to be a set of uses of nouns in the nominative case.

Albanian does not have distinct forms for each of the five cases, definite and indefinite, singular and plural. In the indefinite singular, for example, nominative and accusative nouns share the same form and the dative and ablative share another. This happens also in the indefinite plural except that here the ablative has a special form (the ending **-sh: malesh** 'from mountains'). In the definite singular the accusative differs from the nominative, whereas the dative and the ablative once again share a single form. The same thing happens in the definite plural as in the singular, i.e., the nominative and accusative share one form, and the dative and ablative another. The basis for saying that the genitive is a distinct case is based not only on its function, but on the presence of the preposed article that always accompanies this case (-**biblioteka e shkollës** 'the school library') and formally distinguishes it from the dative which, otherwise, is the same as the genitive. (For the grammatical characteristics of this article see Section 4.2).

In some grammars of Albanian the vocative (**thirrore**) is admitted as a separate case, by virtue of its meaning, its use with the interjectional particle **o**, which may be placed before or after the noun with vocative function: **O bir!** 'Oh son' and **biro!** 'Oh son', and its occurrence without a preceding indefinite determiner, unlike other nominative case occurrences. However, since it is otherwise always formally indistinguishable from the nominative case except by the presence of the particle **o** (which may even be absent, as in **Dëgjo, BABA! Ne që bëmë luftën vetëm, pa ndihmën e beut e të kapedanit, pa ndihmën e tyre do të ngremë dhe jetën tonë.** 'Listen, DAD! We who fought the war alone, without the help of beys and tribal chiefs, we shall likewise build our new life without their help.'), it will not be treated here as a separate case, but rather as a form of the nominative, with which it is formally identical both in the indefinite and the definite form. Note that while vocatives usually have the nominative indefinite case form, female names ending in **-ë** (e.g., **Dritë**) are normally in the nominative case form (**O Drita!**), as are vocatives followed by a restrictive modifier or appositive (e.g., **O shoku Stefan!** 'Comrade Stephen!').

Neither is there in current Standard Albanian a separate form for the LOCATIVE case. Forms with the ending **-t** (**në malt** 'in *or* on the mountain', **në gropët** 'in the hole') which is always used with locative prepositions have not been standardized in the language and remain only as a dialectal form. Locative meaning in the standard language is expressed by the accusative case with prepositions and by the ablative: **në mal, në fushë, malit, fushës**).

In addition to the accusative and the ablative, the nominative can also be governed by prepositions in Albanian. With regard to certain prepositions and new prepositional locutions that relate to the genitive, see Chapter 9, Prepositions and Prepositionals, Section 9.1.4.

A. Primary Functions of the Cases

A.1 Nominative Case

A NOMINATIVE case form not preceded by a preposition may serve as subject of a sentence, predicate nominative (predicate complement of the subject) appositive, or vocative:

REVOLUCIONARIZIMI i shkollës nuk është NJË DETYRË e përkohshme. 'THE REVOLUTIONIZATION of the school is not A transitory TASK.' (subject, predicate nominative)

Ike, SHOKU KADRI -- foli i mallëngjyer një mesoburrë, KRYETARI i këshillit. 'Are you leaving, COMRADE KADRI--a middle-sized man, THE PRESIDENT of the council, spoke with emotion.' (vocative, appositive)

Dhe tani e kishte përpara tij, të shkathët e të gjallë, dhe i bëhej zemra MAL. 'And now he was in front of him, alert and alive, and his heart swelled WITH PRIDE.' (predicate complement)

After the prepositions **nga** 'from' and **te(k)** 'to' nominative case forms are used; prepositional phrases so formed function like any other prepositional phrase:

Iku nga shtëpia. 'He left home.'
Shkoi te prindërit. 'He went to his parents.'
U sëmur nga gripi. 'He became ill with the grippe.'

Compare:

Erdhi në shtëpi. 'He came home.'
U sëmur prej gripit. 'He became ill with ("from") the grippe.'

The nominative indefinite case form is used as the citation form, for example, in dictionaries and in other instances in which a noun is referred to as a word in its own right.

A.2 Genitive Case

GENITIVE case forms are mainly used for a variety of determining functions expressed in English by prepositional phrases introduced by *of*, by the so-called possessive *'s*, or by nouns used as adjectives. They often follow a referent noun or pronoun, explicit or implicit in the sentence, and indicate:

a) affiliation with or ownership of the referent: **tokat E KOOPERATIVËS** 'the lands of THE COOPERATIVE', **djali i Agimit** 'Agim's son', **libri I BIBLIOTEKËS,** 'the library book', **oborri I SHKOLLËS** 'the SCHOOL yard';

b) a quality, substance, etc. identifying a definite referent (with an indefinte referent an ablative case form may be used instead): **lulet E MAJIT** 'THE MAY flowers', **këngët E DASMËS** 'THE WEDDING songs', **ditët E DJALËRISË** 'THE YOUTHFUL days', **aktet E TRIMËRISË** 'THE acts OF BRAVERY', **buka E GRURIT** 'THE WHEAT bread';

c) a particular quality characterizing the referent: **trimëria E USHTARIT** 'the valor OF THE SOLDIER', **kaltërsia E QIELLIT** 'the blue OF THE SKY', **bukuritë E NATYRËS** 'the beauties OF NATURE', **vështirësitë E PUNËS** 'the difficulties OF THE JOB';

d) the object of a nominalized transitive verb: **ruajtja E MAKINERIVE** 'the preservation OF THE MACHINERY', **ndërtimi I HIDROCENTRALIT** 'the construction OF THE HYDROELECTRIC DAM', **shkelja E RREGULLIT** 'the violation OF THE RULE', **hapja E DRITAREVE** 'the opening OF THE WINDOWS';

e) the subject of a nominalized verb: **ardhja E MIQVE** 'the arrival OF FRIENDS', **kthimi I USHTARËVE nga stërvitja** 'the return OF THE SOLDIERS from drill', **lindja E DIELLIT** 'the SUNrise', **oshëtima E TOPAVE** 'the echo OF GUNS'.

f) the whole of which the referent is some portion (partitive genitive): **gjysma E BUKËS** 'half OF THE BREAD', **shumica E STUDENTËVE** 'the majority OF STUDENTS', **një grup I KOOPERATIVSTËVE të KOOPERATIVËS** 'a group OF COOPERATIVISTS of the COOPERATIVE'. The genitive is often used in this sense with fractions: **një e katërta E PUNËS** 'one fourth OF THE WORK', **dy të tretat E MALIT** 'two thirds OF THE MOUNTAIN';

g) the identity of the referent noun or pronoun: **lumi I DEVOLLIT** 'the river OF DEVOLL', **qyteti I VLORËS** 'the city OF VLORE', **muaji I KORRIKUT** 'the month OF JULY';

h) the predicate adjectival: **është I GOJËS** 'he is ARTICULATE', **të gjithë kishin qenë të NJË MENDJEJE** 'all had been OF ONE MIND';

i) the universe that the referent in the superior degree is being compared to: **më e madhja E VAJZAVE** 'the oldest OF THE GIRLS', **më i vogli I DJEMVE** 'the youngest OF THE BOYS', **më e zorshmja E GJITHË DETYRAVE** 'the most difficult OF ALL TASKS'.

Genitive case forms are used after prepositional locutions like **me anë** 'by means of, through', **nga ana** 'on the part of', **për shkak** 'because', etc., expressing thus a means, cause, etc.

Ne fituam ME ANË TË NDIHMËS së tyre. 'We won BY MEANS OF their HELP.'

NOTE

A noun in the genitive case modifying another noun must either be definite or be indefinite and preceded by a determiner: **një nxënës I SHKOLLËS** 'a pupil OF THE SCHOOL', but **një nxënës I NJË SHKOLLE** 'a pupil OF A SCHOOL'.

A.3 Dative Case

DATIVE case forms are usually used with verbs to mark the referent (indirect object) of a verb. Usually, then, they indicate:

a) the person or thing toward whom the action is directed: -- **Tregoji NËNËS, de!** 'Come on, tell MOTHER!' **Fajin ia vumë PLEHUT** 'We blamed THE MANURE ("We put the guilt TO THE MANURE").' **Iu afrua QYTETIT** 'He approached THE CITY';

b) the person who experiences a state (physiological or psychological) expressed by an impersonal or unipersonal verb:

MANUSHAQES nuk i hahej fare në mëngjes, i trazohej. 'MANUSHAQE was not hungry ("TO MANUSHAQE it was not being eaten") at all in the morning; it upset her.' **PETRITIT s'i rrihej në vend.** 'PETRIT was restless ("FOR PETRIT there was no staying in place").'

c) the appositive of a noun or pronoun itself in the dative case:

Atij t'i thuash, atij GJERGJIT. 'Say (it) to him, to that GEORGE.'

d) the indirect object of the verb underlying the participle, for adjectives formed from participles:

Thirrje e drejtuar FSHATARËSISË kooperativiste. 'An appeal directed TO THE COOPERATIVIST PEASANTRY.'

e) the indirect object of a verb implicit, but not expressed, in appeals and slogans:

Përshëndetje KLASËS punëtore! 'Greetings TO THE working CLASS!'
Lavdi e nder PUNËS! 'Glory and honor TO LABOR!'

A.4 Accusative Case

In contemporary Albanian an ACCUSATIVE case form may indicate:

a) the direct object of a transitive verb:

Lufta jonë çlirimtare e nxori POPULLIN në krye dhe këtu e vetëm këtu qëndron arsyeja e fitores. 'Our war of liberation saw our PEOPLE through, and it is this and this alone that accounts for the victory.'

The direct object may be partitive, in the sense that the action of the verb is distributed over an indefinite part of a general object, rather than concentrated on a particular object: **pi UJË** 'drink WATER', **ha BUKË** 'eats BREAD', **solli MISH** 'he brought MEAT';

b) the predicate complement of the object: **e zgjodhën KRYETAR** 'they chose him PRESIDENT', **e ka VËLLA** 'it's his BROTHER ("he has him brother")';

c) the time of performance of an action:

JAVËN e kaluar organizuam një ekskursion. 'Last WEEK we organized an excursion.'
DITËN e shtunë kishim praktikë. 'On SaturDAY we exercised.'

or its extension,

Gjithë DITËN ra shi. 'It rained all DAY long.'

d) quantity and measure:

Këtë libër e kam blerë dy LEKË. 'I bought this book for two LEKS.'
Ky mall peshon katër KUINTALË. 'This article weighs four QUINTALS.'

e) the object of one of the locative prepositions **në** 'in, at', **mbi** 'on', **përmbi** 'over', **nëpër** 'among', **ndër** 'among', **nën** 'under', **më** 'at, on', **në shtëpi** 'at home', **mbi tavolinë** 'on the table', **nëpër male** 'among mountains'; the focal prepositions **për** 'for, about, of' and **mbi** 'on, about, over':

Mendonte PËR DJALIN e saj. 'She thought OF HER SON.'
Foli MBI DETYRAT që na dalin përpara. 'She spoke ABOUT THE TASKS facing us.'

f) the object of the characterizing preposition **me** 'with' or of the privative preposition **pa** 'without', as in **mur ME GURË** 'STONE wall ("wall with stone")', **njeri ME VULLNET** 'man OF WILL', **gjellë PA KRIPË** 'TASTELESS dish ("dish WITHOUT SALT")'; or the instrumental or comitative preposition **me**, as in: **shkruaj ME STILOGRAF** 'I write WITH A FOUNTAIN PEN', **shkova ME BABANË** 'I went WITH MY FATHER.'

A.5 Ablative Case

ABLATIVE case forms may be used with verbs (and deverbal adjectives), nouns, and after prepositions, expressing various circumstances such as cause, origin, means, place, time, etc., in which the sense of derivation or departure from--from which this case takes its name in Latin--represents only a part of its meaning.

Ablative forms are used after a number of temporal and locative prepositions, such as **prapa** 'behind', **pas** 'after', **afër** 'near', **poshtë** 'below', **jashtë** 'outside', **prej** 'from', etc. With **prej** 'by' the ablative case may in addition mark the agent or instrument of the passive verb or adjective formed from the participle of such a verb:

Vetë Moisiu, i mundur PREJ SKËNDERBEUT, i përbuzur PREJ TURQVE dhe i rrahur PREJ VETËDIJËS iku nga Stambolli. 'Moisi himself, beaten BY SKENDER-BEU, scorned BY THE TURKS, and tortured BY his CONSCIENCE, departed from Istanbul.'

In today's standard language this function is being performed more and more by constructions with the noun in the nominative following the preposition **nga** 'by, from'.

Without prepositions, ablative forms of nouns are most often used after referent nouns to perform functions similar to those of genitive forms:

Këtu ka TRENA MALLRASH. or **Këtu ka TRENA TË MALLRAVE.** 'There are FREIGHT TRAINS here'.

The ablative form may be used in this function only when it immediately follows the referent noun and the referent noun is not inflected for either case or definiteness; otherwise the genitive must be used. Compare: **(një) zog pule** '(a) chick ("bird from hen")' [nominative or accusative indefinite] with **zogu i pulës** 'the chick' [nominative definite] and **i një zogu të pulës** 'of a chick' [genitive indefinite]; **zogj pulash** 'chicks ("birds from hens")' [nom. or accusative indef.] with **zogjtë e pulave** 'the chicks' [nom. or accus. def.] and **të zogjve të pulave** 'of chicks' [gen. def.].

In the Albanian of today ablative forms may occur as independent adverbial constituents to indicate place, cause, and time, as in **shkonte RRUGËs** 'he walked ALONG THE STREET', **plasa VAPE** 'I'm dying FROM THE HEAT', **VERËS këtu bën shumë nxehtë** 'It gets very

hot here IN THE SUMMER.' These constructions as well as corresponding plural ablatives--
MALEVE bie dëborë 'it snows IN THE MOUNTAINS'--are becoming rarer, and being
replaced by prepositional phrases. Like the genitive, ablative forms constructions may indicate:

a. affiliation or possession:

**Shkoi, po mori me vete edhe një zemër MALËSORI, që e deshi me tërë forcën, që i
jepte jeta e ashpër e maleve.** 'He left, but took with him a MOUNTAINEER's heart,
which he loved with all the strength that the rough life of the mountains gave him.'

b. a noun performing the same function as the adjective:

**Tërë pylli mban erë PRANVERE, LULESH e GJETHI, PLISI e KULPRE, KOREJE
të athët GËSHTENJE të lëngëzuar.** 'The entire forest smells OF SPRING, FLOWERS
AND FOLIAGE, TURF and IVY, tart BARK of juicy CHESTNUTS.'

c. the whole of which the referent is some portion, or the substance measured by the
referent: **gjysmë BUKE** 'half A LOAF', **grumbull USHTARËSH** 'gathering of SOLDIERS'.

Binjakët ngjanin me njëri-tjetrin si dy pika UJI. 'The twins resembled each other like
two drops of WATER.'

d. the substance from which an object is made. In this use it is always in the indefinite
form and may or may not be preceded by the preposition **prej** 'of': **lugë druri** 'wooden spoon'
= **lugë prej druri** 'spoon of wood', **shtrat prej hekuri** 'bed of iron', **tuba prej gize** 'pipes of pig
iron', etc. **Prej** is the only ablative preposition which a singular indefinite form may follow
with no intervening determiner.

In contemporary Albanian the indefinite plural ablative is widely used without prepositions only in the attributive functions just described. In circumstantial functions, it is usually
accompanied by prepositions, e.g. **prej vitesh** 'since years ago, for years', pas **disa orësh** 'after
a few hours', **para disa ditësh** 'a few days ago'. Often--particularly in the spoken language--in
place of the ablative, we find the dative, e.g., **para DY DITËVE** 'two DAYS ago', **pas DY
ORËVE** 'after TWO HOURS', in accordance with the confirmed tendency of the Albanian of
recent centuries toward the fusing of the ablative with the dative, at the expense of the purely
ablative forms.

In the definite form, the ablative has become fully fused with the dative in uses both with
(**sipas HARTAVE topografike** 'according to typographical MAPS') and without (**DY javë
rrjesht ishin endur RRUGËVE të Shqipërisë.** 'FOR TWO weeks in succession they roamed
THE STREETS of Albania.') prepositions.

3.2.4 Grammatical Number

The grammatical number of an Albanian noun may be singular or plural. The distinction
may be marked by distinct forms of a same noun (**mal** 'mountain'/**male** 'mountains') or by
different forms of a modifier or determiner: **shtëpi e re** 'new house'/**shtëpi të reja** 'new
houses', **kjo shtëpi** 'this house'/**këto shtëpi** 'these houses'. The grammatical number of a
noun reflects its lexical meaning. Hence, some nouns are used only in the singular or in the
plural (see below).

Many nouns that are used regularly in both numbers and indicate countable objects.
These nouns may be quantified precisely when the determiner is: **një djalë** 'a boy' -- **dy djem**
'two boys', **një fshat** 'a village' -- **katër fshatra** 'four villages', and the difference in meaning
between the singular and plural forms of these nouns is purely quantitative. Certain other
nouns (including many nouns derived from verbs) used in the singular without a determiner
designate abstract processes and do not indicate countable objects. In the plural, however, or
preceded by a determiner, these words take on the sense of the result of the process and as
such are countable: **mendim** 'thinking' /**një mendim** 'a thought'/**dy mendime** 'two thoughts';
pikëpamje 'point of view'/**një pikëpamje** 'a viewpoint'/**tri pikëpamje** 'three viewpoints';
vendim 'deciding'/**një vendim** 'a decision'/**dy vendime** 'two decisions'; and so on.

In the plural, abstract nouns that indicate qualities, actions, or conditions may likewise represent embodiments or instances of the quality, action or condition: **turp** 'shame'/**turpe** 'shameful deeds', **nder** 'honor'/**ndere** 'honors' (expressions of honor and respect)', **gëzim** 'enjoyment'/**gëzime** 'joys (occasions of joy)', **hidhërim** 'embitterment'/**hidhërime** 'sorrows (occasions of sorrow)', **liri** 'liberty'/**liritë** 'freedoms (manifestations of liberty)'.

A plural noun of action *(nomen actionis)* may indicate a repeated action or an action performed by several persons simultaneously: **të qeshura** 'laughs', **të bërtitura** 'shouts', **oshëtima** 'echoes', **klithma** 'screams'. **KLITHMAT zemërçjerrëse dhe të mallëngjyera të popullit e mbuluan mandatën e zezë të Dukagjinit, të cilën e vërtetonin OSHËTIMAT vajtimtare të këmbanave.** 'The heart-rending and touching SCREAMS of the people followed the bad news given by Dukagjin, which was confirmed by the lamenting ECHOES of the church bells.'

One may also use a substance noun in the plural, but in this case, as in English, it takes on the meaning of the different varieties or collections of the substance: **vajra** 'oils', **kripëra** 'salts', **djathëra** 'cheeses', **verëra** 'wines', **miellra** 'flours'. In such use it may indicate a large amount of the substance: **UJËRAT e turbullta të lumit.** 'The turbulent WATERS of the river.'

NOTE

The noun **ujë** in the plural may also denote a location filled with water:
Ramë në një përrua, çamë përmes UJËRAVE të ngrira dhe bëmë përpjetë me një frymë. 'We came to a brook, made our way through the frozen WATERS and headed up hill with one breath.'
The noun **mish** 'meat' in the plural **mishra** 'meats' may also have the meaning either of slain livestock:
Theri dy Mishra. 'He slaughtered two beeves ("MEATS") [including cattle, sheep, etc.]).'
Agimi po gdhendte një copë dru, duke i dhënë formën e hellit për të pjekur MISHRA. 'Agim was hewing a piece of wood, giving it the form of a spit for roasting MEATS.'
or of the fleshy parts of the body:
Njeriu ka eshtrat, kyçet, dejtë, MISHRAT. 'Man has bones, joints, veins, FLESH.'

In abstract nouns the plural is often linked to extended meanings of the word. Thus, the word **mbledhje** 'harvesting' in its primary meaning, the act of gathering, as in the harvesting of olives, does not have a plural; whereas in its extended meaning, **mbledhja** 'the meeting, the gathering (of an organization)', it is used in the plural as well: **mbledhjet** 'the meetings (of an organization)'. The same goes for **zgjedhje** 'choosing, selecting, the process of election' in the singular but **zgjedhjet** 'the elections (in the plural)'; **tmerr** 'terror, fright' in the singular, but **tmerret** 'terrors, horrors (of war)' in the plural.

In certain nouns designating metals the plural has moved away from the singular meaning and may be regarded as a separate word. Thus **argjënde** '("silvers") decorative silver articles', **bakëre** '("coppers") copper utensils' denote objects made of the substance, rather than the substance itself in the plural.

The majority of nouns that denote non-countable objects have only a singular form (-*singularia tantum* see Section 3.2.4 B.1) and make no distinction between singular and plural in meaning: **uthull** 'vinegar', **sheqer** 'sugar', **mendjemadhësi** 'conceit', **errësirë** 'darkness', **vapë** 'hot weather'.

Certain nouns designating objects made up of several parts (usually two) are used only or mainly in the plural number *(pluralia tantum,* see Section 3.2.4 B.2); such a noun may indicate either one object or several objects: **pantallonat** 'pants', **syzet** 'eyeglasses' **darët** 'pliers'. In quantifying several such objects the quantifier is usually followed by the noun **palë** 'pair' as in English: **një palë pantallona** 'a pair of pants', **dy palë pantallona** 'two pairs of pants', **disa palë pantallona** 'several pairs of pants', **tri palë syza** 'three pairs of glasses', **katër palë të mbathura** 'four pairs of footwear', etc.

A. Formation of Plural Noun Stems

Nouns that are used in both numbers, form the plural by means of: a) suffixes, b) changes in stem sounds, c) simultaneous changes in stem sounds and suffixes. (For the distinction between "suffix" and "ending" in this book, see Chapter 1, Section 1.2.4.)

The most common method of plural formation is by adding a plural suffix to the singular stem: **mur** 'wall'/**mur-E** 'walls', **lis** 'oak'/**lis-A** 'oaks', **burrë** 'man'/**burr-A** 'men', **fushë** 'plain'/**fush-A** 'plains', **nip** 'nephew'/**nip-ËR** 'nephews', etc.

In many common words, however, the singular/plural distinction is marked by a different stem vowel or consonant (or both) for the singular and plural stems: **dash** 'ram'/**desh** 'rams', **natë** 'night'/**net** 'nights', **mik** 'friend'/**miq** 'friends', **zog** 'bird'/**zogj** 'birds', **plak** 'old man'/-**pleq** 'old men' etc.

For some nouns the singular plural distinction is marked by both suffixation and difference in stem vowel or consonant: **breg** 'hill'/**brIGJ-E** 'hills', **shteg** 'pass'/**shtIGJ-E** 'passes', **pylle/** 'forest'/**pyJ-E** 'forests', **kunat** 'brother-in-law'/**kunEt-ËR** 'brothers-in-law', **atë** 'father'/**et-ËR** 'fathers' etc. For a few nouns one encounters a plural form with stem changes only and a plural form with stem changes and suffix: e.g., **yll** 'star'/**yj** 'stars' or **yje** 'stars'.

A great number of nouns (including all those that end in unstressed **-e** or **-ës**) have the same stem in the plural as in the singular, i.e. they do not take a suffix, nor do they undergo changes in stem sounds: **rrobaqepës** 'tailor'/**rrobaqepës** 'tailors', **gjykatës** 'judge'/**gjykatës** 'judges', **sy** 'eye'/**sy** 'eyes', **dele** 'sheep'/**dele** 'sheep (pl.)', **lopë** 'cow'/**lopë** 'cows', **shtëpi** 'house'/**shtëpi** 'houses' etc. Since in the plural (as well as in the singular) the indefinite nominative and accusative cases have no ending, it is only the other case forms that overtly mark such noun stems as being plural: **shtëpi** 'house *or* houses' [nom. or acc. indef.], **shtëpi-ve** [dative indefinite plural] **shtëpi-sh** [ablative indefinite plural] **shtëpi-të** [nominative or accusative definite plural].

A.1 Masculine Plural Stems

The formation of the plural of masculine nouns is quite complex, with formation by suffixation the most common method. The suffixes that serve to form the plural of masculine nouns, given roughly in the order of their productivity, are **-e, -ë, -a, -nj, -ër, -enj, -inj, -ra**.

While some general rules work to help predict the plural stem, given the singular one (the citation form), for many words, the plural stem cannot be predicted from the singular. In addition, for a number of words there is considerable fluctuations among competing plural forms, in both the suffix used and the exact form of the stem, created both by wealth of models available for analogy and by the influence of competing dialects during the process of crystallization of the contemporary standard language. This is also why doublets exist for a few nouns, alongside the dominant forms, **-ë/-a, -e/a:** **çorap** 'stocking'/**çorape** or **çorapë** 'stockings'.

a) In general, the plural suffix **-e** is found in abstract nouns. All derived nouns with the suffix **-im**, as well as borrowed words that end in **-ion, -um, -ium**, take **-e** in the plural: **gabim-e** 'errors', **mendim-e** 'thoughts', **përparim-e** 'advances, progress(es), **qëllim-e** 'goals', **vendim-e** 'decisions' etc.; **aksion-e** 'actions', **batalion-e** 'battalions', **disertacion-e** 'dissertations', **divizion-e** 'divisions', **embrion-e** 'embryos', **kampion-e** 'models', **komision-e** 'commissions', **leksion-e** 'lectures', **pozicion-e** 'positions', **profesion-e** 'professions', **revolucion-e** 'revolutions', **stacion-e** 'stations', etc. (but **kamion-a** 'trucks', **kampion-ë** 'champions') **album-e** 'albums', **forum-e** 'forums', **muzeum-e** 'museums', **kalcium-e** 'calciums', **simpozium-e** 'symposiums', **stadium-e** 'stadiums' etc.

The plural of the majority of nouns that end with the consonants **t** and **d** (in all nouns with **-ant, -at, -ent, -id, -it, -ont** that do not indicate animates) is also formed with this suffix: **fakt-e** 'facts', **fakultet-e** 'departments', **inat-e** 'angers', **insekt-e** 'insects', **komitet-e** 'committees', **konvikt-e** 'boarding schools', **kopsht-e** 'gardens', **krevat-e** 'beds', **marifet-e** 'artifices', **mjet-e** 'means', **personalitet-e** 'personalities', **qyetet-e** 'cities', **raft-e** 'rafts', **shtet-e** 'states',

fllad-e 'breezes', **katund-e** 'villages', **vend-e** 'places' etc.; but: **rresht-a** 'lines'; **diamant-e** 'diamonds', **restorant-e** 'restaurants', **aparat-e** 'apparatuses', **atentat-e** 'assassination attempts', **kampionat-e** 'championships', **kat-e** 'floors', **kombinat-e** 'industrial complexes', **pallat-e** 'apartments', **shpat-e** 'slopes', **aksident-e** 'accidents' **argument-e** 'arguments' **dokument-e** 'documents', **eksperiment-e** 'experiments', **element-e** 'elements' (chemical), **pigment-e** 'pigments', **instrument-e** 'instruments', **kontinent-e** 'continents', **metaloid-e** 'metalloids', **oksid-e** 'oxides', **deficit-e** 'deficits', **fosforit-e** 'phosphorites', **pirit-e** 'pyrites', **suficit-e** 'surpluses' (but **shirit-a** 'ribbons');
'**horizont-e** 'horizons' etc.

The plural is also formed with -e in many inanimate nouns that end in **-al, -an, -ar, -el, -er**, and in many that end in **-on**: **festival-e** 'festivals', **hidrocentral-e** 'hydroelectric power stations', **ideal-e** 'ideals', **kanal-e** 'canals', **kristal-e** 'crystals', **mal-e** 'mountains', **material-e** 'materials', **mineral-e** 'minerals'; **duhan-e** 'tobaccoes', **dyqan-e** 'stores', **organ-e** 'organs', **plan-e** 'plans', **vullkan-e** 'volcanoes', **pazar-e** 'markets', **seminar-e** 'seminars', **visar-e** 'treasures', **duel-e** 'duels', **hotel-e** 'hotels', **tunel-e** 'tunnels', **themel-e** 'foundations', **zabel-e** 'groves', **dikaster-e** 'ministries', **kantier-e** 'workshops', **karakter-e** 'characters', **mermer-e** 'marbles', **minder-e** 'couches', **mister-e** 'mysteries', **ciklon-e** 'cyclones', **elektron-e** 'electrons', **fron-e** 'thrones', **hormon-e** 'hormones', **proton-e** 'protons', **shabllon-e** 'patterns', **zakon-e** 'customs' (but **aeroplan-ë** 'airplanes'; **çengel-a** 'hooks', **tegel-a** 'hems', **tel-a** 'wires').

Many inanimate nouns that end in other consonants also form the plural with -e: **cikël** 'cycle', **cikle** 'cycles', **fis-e** 'clans', **idil-e** 'idylls', **kafaz-e** 'cages', **kallëp-e** 'molds', **kamp-e** 'camps', **kanun-e** 'canons', **kotec-e** 'coops', **komb-e** 'nations', **kostum-e** 'costumes', **kurriz-e** 'backs', **lloj-e** 'kinds', **manastir-e** 'monasteries', **mikrob-e** 'microbes', **motiv-e** 'motives', **panair-e** 'fairs', **plazh-e** 'beaches', **pullaz-e** 'roofs', **pus-e** 'wells', **qejf-e** 'pleasures', **shesh-e** 'fields', **tank-e** 'tanks', **triumf-e** 'triumphs', **varr-e** 'graves', **virus-e** 'viruses' etc.

NOTE
Borrowed nouns ending in **-azh** also form the plural with -e **ambalazh-e** 'packagings', **grupazh-e** 'groupings', **homazh-e** 'homages', **plazh-e** 'beaches', **silazh-e** 'silages' etc.
2. Corresponding to the two synonymous singular forms of the noun **frut/fryt** 'fruit' are two plural forms which differ in meaning: the form with -e **frytet** has an abstract meaning (the *fruits* of labor), while the form with -a **fruta** has a concrete meaning (fruits and vegetables).

b) Polysyllabic animate nouns with stress on the last syllable of the singular stem, take the suffix **-ë**.

First, **-ë** forms the plural of derived nouns with the suffixes **-ac, -aç, -ak, -an, -jan, -ar, -tar, -ash, -er, -ier, -ist, -it, -iot, -ok, -or, -tor, -uk**: **tullac-ë** 'baldies'; **gjembaç-ë** 'thistles', **rrugaç-ë** 'loafers'; **durrsak-ë** 'inhabitants of Durrës', **ftujak-ë** 'kids (of goats)', **romak-ë** 'Romans', **rosak-ë** 'drakes'; **dibran-ë** 'inhabitants of Dibër', **korean-ë** 'Koreans', **shkodran-ë** 'inhabitants of Shkodër; **lumjan-ë** 'inhabitants of Lumë', **matjan-ë** 'inhabitants of Mat'; **detar-ë** 'marines', **formular-ë** 'forms', **kolonjar-ë** 'inhabitants of Kolonjë'; **anëtar-ë** 'members', **arsimtar-ë** 'educators', **luftëtar-ë** 'warriors'; **larash-ë** 'birds of prey'; **reshter-ë** 'sergeants', **toger-ë** 'lieutenants'; **karrocier-ë** 'coachmen'; **artist-ë** 'artists', **sportist-ë** 'sportsmen'; **gjirokastrit-ë** 'inhabitants of Gjirokastër'; **mallakastriot-ë** 'inhabitants of Mallakastër', **suljot-ë** 'inhabitants of Suli', **patok-ë** 'ganders'; **dasmor-ë** 'wedding guests', **drejtor-ë** 'directors', **fjalor-ë** 'dictionaries', **lakror-ë** 'pies', **punëtor-ë** 'workers'; **bishtuk-ë** 'oil lamps' etc.

In general other animate nouns and some inanimates which happen to end like the ones above with suffixes, also form the plural with **-ë**: **kovaç-ë** 'blacksmiths'; **dajak-ë** 'clubs, posts', **kapak-ë** 'covers'; **aeroplan-ë**, 'airplanes', **çoban-ë** 'shepherds' (also **çobej**), **gjerman-ë** 'Germans'; **beqar-ë** 'bachelors', **hambar-ë** 'bins', **mercenar-ë** 'mercenaries'; **berber-ë** 'barbers', **fener-ë** 'lanterns', **noter-ë** 'notaries', **oficer-ë, shofer-ë, veteriner-ë; inxhinier-ë** 'engineers', **kamarier-ë** 'waiters'; **afarist-ë** 'businessmen'; **bandit-ë, komit-ë** 'outlaws', **petrit-ë** 'hawks';

patriot-ë; major-ë, doktor-ë, eskavator-ë 'bulldozers', **traktor-ë; buzuk-ë** 'mandolin-like instruments', **kolltuk-ë** 'armchairs' etc.

The plural of animate nouns that end with **-ant, -at, -az, -ent, -ez, -ist**, are formed with **ë: aspirant-ë** 'aspirants', **elefant-ë** 'elephants', **argat-ë** 'hired hands', **delegat-ë, diplomat-ë, kroat-ë** 'Croatians', **vlonjat-ë** 'inhabitants of Vlorë', **matrapaz-ë** 'hucksters'; **agjent-ë** 'agents', **asistent-ë, docent-ë, element-ë, klient-ë, student-ë; anglez-ë** 'Englishmen', **borgjez-ë** 'bourgeois people', **francez-ë** 'Frenchmen', **kinez-ë** 'Chinese', **vietnamez-ë, afarist-ë, komunist-ë, politeist-ë** 'polytheists', **socialist-ë**, etc.

The suffix **-ë** also forms the plural of a) many nouns that end in **-af, -ec, -ek, -et, -ik**; b) a few nouns that end in **-a, -ap, -ec, -el, -il, -ir, -oz**; c) other individual nouns, particularly nouns of animates: **fotograf-ë** 'photographers', **paragraf-ë** 'paragraphs'; **gjyveç-ë** 'copper pans', **kryeneç-ë** 'stubborn people'; **fishek-ë** 'bullets', **dyshek-ë** 'mattresses', **grek-ë** 'Greeks', **mjek-ë** 'physicians'; **atlet-ë** 'athletes', **planet-ë** 'planets'; **bolshevik-ë, ibrik-ë** 'pitchers'; **kolonel-ë**, etc.; **admiral-ë, gjeneral-ë; dollap-ë** 'closets', **mesap-ë** 'Messapians'; **guralec-ë** 'pebbles', **memec-ë** 'mutes'; **kriminel-ë; civil-ë; ilir-ë** 'Illyrians', **zinxhir-ë** 'chains'; **marangoz-ë** 'carpenters', **qeroz-ë** 'smart characters in folk tales', etc.; **agronom-ë** 'agronomist', **alpin-ë** 'Alpinists', **arbëresh-ë** 'Albanians of Italy', **hosten-ë** 'goading sticks', **majmun-ë** 'monkeys', **mareshall-ë** 'marshals', **pinguin-ë** 'penguins', **polic-ë** 'policeman', **poliglot-ë** 'polyglots' etc.

NOTE

1. **-ë** also forms the plural of certain one-syllable nouns, such as **dhëmb-ë** 'teeth', **flok-ë** 'hair', **lek-ë** 'leks (Albanian monetary unit)', **lot-ë** 'tears', **shok-ë** 'comrades'.
2. The nouns **bri** 'horn', **dre** 'deer', **dru** 'tree', **fre** 'rein', **tra** 'beam' have plural stems with an **-r** extension (as in the declension of the singular) and take the plural suffix **-ë**: **brir-ë** 'horns', **drer-ë** 'deers', **drur-ë** 'trees', **frer-ë** 'reins', **trar-ë** 'beams'.
3. A number of Turkish words with the Turkish plural suffixes **-llar** and **-ler** have entered the Albanian language; then following the analogy of the type of plural found in **fshatar-ë** 'villagers' they have added the Albanian plural suffix: **aga-llarë** 'small landlords', **at-llarë** 'fathers', **baba-llarë** 'fathers', **usta-llarë** 'master craftsmen', **xhasha-llarë** 'uncles', **bej-lerë** 'landlords', **dervish-lerë** 'dervishes', **efendi-lerë** 'titled citizens', **kadi-lerë** 'judges'. Many of these words have now become obsolete.

c) Nouns that form the plural with the suffix **-a** all denote concrete objects or beings. The majority of one-syllable words form the plural in this fashion, as do a good many words of two or more syllables.

Among such one and two syllable words are: **bel-a** 'troubles', **brez-a** 'belts', **cep-a** 'beaks', **çun-a** 'lads', **dem-a** 'bulls', **derr-a** 'pigs', **grep-a** 'hooks', **qyp-a** 'jugs', **gjel-a** 'roosters', **gjemb-a** 'thorns', **gjym-a** 'kettles', **kec-a** 'kids (goat)', **krimb-a** 'worms', **plep-a** 'poplars', **plis-a** 'clods (soil)', **man-a** 'mulberries', **plumb-a** 'bullets', **qingj-a** 'lambs', **rremb-a** 'streams', **rresht-a** 'lines', **rrip-a** 'slopes', **spec-a** 'green peppers', **stol-a** 'stools', **tel-a** 'wires', **tip-a** 'types', **top-a** 'balls, canons', **trup-a** 'bodies', **viç-a** 'calves', **vidh-a** 'screws', **xhep-a** 'pockets' etc.; **agrep-a** 'scorpions', **bërryl-a** 'elbows', **bilbil-a** 'whistles', **çingel-a** 'hooks', **fitil-a** 'wicks', **gërshet-a** 'braids', **kandil-a** 'candles', **motor-a** 'motors', **person-a** 'persons', **pëllumb-a** 'pigeons', **qilim-a** 'rugs', **rrogoz-a** 'mats', **vagon-a** 'wagons' etc.

Among polysyllabic nouns, **-a** is the most common plural suffix for nouns that end in **-on** and **-oz**, and designate objects, and of some nouns with other stem endings: **gramafon-a** 'phonographs', **magnetofon-a** 'tape recorders', **mikrofon-a, telefon-a; kavanoz-a** 'jars', **mitraloz-a** 'machine guns', etc.; **karkalec-a** 'grasshoppers', **kastravec-a** 'cucumbers'; **automobil-a, karafil-a** 'carnations', **trëndafil-a** 'roses', etc.

All masculine nouns whose citation form ends in **-ër**, form the plural by dropping the **-ë-** and adding **-a**: **cilindër** 'cylinder' / **cilindr-a, emër** 'name' / **emr-a, kalibër** 'caliber' / **kalibr-a, litër** 'litre' / **litr-a, metër** 'meter' / **metr-a, ministër** 'minister' / **ministr-a, misër** 'corn' / **misr-a, numër** 'number' / **numr-a, pjepër** 'cantaloupe' / **pjepr-a, regjistër** 'register' / **regjistr-a**.

NOTES

1. The noun **zë** 'voice, sound' forms the plural with **-a**, but only after extending the stem with **-r**, as in the oblique cases of the singular: **zër-a** 'sounds'.

2. In the standard language, the use of the suffix **-a** has expanded at the expense of the suffix **-ë** and of forms without suffixes. Such literary forms of the plural as **solista** 'soloists', **fiskulturista** 'physiculturists', **shofera** 'chauffeurs', **oficera, qitësa** 'marksmen', **shitësa** 'saleswomen' are distinguished from the normal forms in the standard language.

d) The suffix **-nj** forms the plural of most masculine nouns that end in a stressed vowel (with the exception of words that take the **-llar** or **-ller** suffix and the words **bri** 'horn', **dre** 'deer', **fre** 'rein', **sy** 'eye', **tra** 'beam', **zë** 'sound'). The majority of these are nouns whose singular stem is extended by the consonant **-r** before an ending with an initial **-i: hu** 'stake' / **huri** 'the stake' / **hunj** 'stakes', **kalli** 'ear of grain' / **kalliri** 'the...' / **kallinj** 'ears of...', etc. The nouns that form the plural with **-nj**, are not many: **bari-nj** 'shepherds', **dru-nj** 'trees', **çilimi-nj** 'kids, children', **fajdexhi-nj** 'moneylenders', **flori-nj** 'gold coins', **gdhe-nj** 'knots (in timber), gnarls', **gji-nj** 'breasts', **hero-nj** 'heroes', **kërci-nj** 'shanks', **kërthi-nj** 'sucklings', **kushëri-nj** 'cousins', **mi-nj** 'mice', **mulli-nj** 'mills', **pe-nj** 'threads', **shalqi-nj** 'watermelons', **turi-nj** 'faces', **zanatçiçi-nj** 'craftsmen', **zotëri-nj** 'sirs', etc.

NOTE

The noun **gju** 'knee' takes an **ë** after the **-nj**: **gjunjë** 'knees'.

The ending **-nj** is also used for most masculine nouns that end with the vowel cluster **-úa** (but not **krua** 'water fountain' / **kro-je** 'water fountains'): **ftua** 'quince' / **fto-nj** 'quinces', **thua** 'fingernail' / **tho-nj** 'fingernails', **patkua** 'horseshoe' / **patko-nj** 'horseshoes', **langua** 'hound (dog)' / **lango-nj** 'hounds'. Note the regular change of **-ua** to **-o** in the plural.

e) The suffix **-enj** is used for the plural of a very small number of nouns including a small group whose singular ends in stressed **-a: lumë** 'river' / **lum-enj** 'rivers', **lëmë** 'threshing floor' / **lëm-enj** 'threshing floors', **përrua** 'brook' / **përr-enj** 'brooks', **budalla** 'fool' / **budall-enj** 'fools', **fukara** 'poor' / **fukar-enj** 'poor people', **maskara** 'knave' / **maskar-enj** 'knaves', **qerrata** 'crafty' / **qerrat-enj** 'crafty people'. Note that in the plural the vowel cluster **ua** and the stressed final vowel **-a** drop before the suffix **-enj**.

f) A few nouns form the plural with the suffix **-inj: drapër** 'sickle' / **drapër-inj** 'sickles', **gjarpër** 'snake' / **gjarpër-inj** 'snakes', **shkëmb** 'rock' / **shkëmb-inj** 'rocks', **shkop** 'stick' / **shkop-inj** 'sticks', **thelb** 'kernel' / **thelp-inj** 'kernels'. The nouns **gisht** 'finger' and **prift** 'priest' take two suffixes **ër + inj** in the plural: **gisht-ër-inj** 'fingers', **prift-ër-inj** 'priests'.

g) The suffix **-ër** forms the plural of a small number of nouns, most of which designate animate beings: e.g., **çam-ër** 'inhabitants of Çamëri', **lab-ër** 'inhabitants of Labëri', **mbret-ër** 'kings', **nip-ër** 'nephews', **princ-ër** 'princes', **prind-ër** 'parents', **rob-ër** 'captives'. A few of these change the vowel **a** to **e** in the plural: **atë** 'father' / **et-ër** 'fathers', **kunat** 'brother-in-law' / **kunet-ër** 'brothers-in-law', **skllav** 'slave' / **skllev-ër** 'slaves', **shtrat** 'bed' / **shtret-ër** 'beds'. Included in this group is the noun **vëlla** 'brother', which in addition has the stem extension **-z**: **vëlle-z-ër** 'brothers'.

h) As noted earlier, the plural suffix **-ra** usually modifies the meaning of the word: for example, the plural **shira** of the noun **shi** 'rain' stresses the repetition or continuation of the phenomenon of raining. It is also found generally in substance nouns like **barë-ra** 'medicaments, grasses', **bulmet-ra** 'dairy products', **gjak-ra** 'bloods', **pleh-ra** 'manures', where it suggests a plurality of types or collections of the substance. With or without a special meaning **-ra** plurals are the normal ones for the nouns **fshat** 'village', **mall** 'merchandise, property', and **shi** 'rain': **fshat-ra** 'villages', **mall-ra** 'goods, possessions', **shi-ra** 'rains'.

i) There are three sub-types: of the plural type formed by the palatalization of the **velar** consonants **g** and **k** into **gj** and **q** respectively:

1. A sub-type in which only the final consonant is palatalized: **murg** 'monk' / **murgj, zog** 'bird' / **zogj, armik** 'enemy' / **armiq, bujk** 'farmer' / **bujq, fik** 'fig' / **fiq, mik** 'friend' / **miq, krushk** 'in-law' / **krushq, peshk** 'fish' / **peshq, turk** 'Turk' / **turq, ujk** 'wolf' / **ujq,** etc.;

2. The largest subtype, in which the final consonant is palatalized and the suffix **-e** is added: **bark** 'belly' / **barqe, bisk** 'twig' / **bisqe, bllok** 'block' / **blloqe, brisk** 'razor' / **brisqe, burg** 'prison' / **burgje, cak** 'limit' / **caqe, deng** 'bale' / **dengje, disk** 'disk' / **disqe, dushk** 'oak' / **dushqe, gjak** 'blood' / **gjaqe, hark** 'arch' / **harqe, lëng** 'juice' / **lëngje, park** 'park' / **parqe, pellg** 'pool (of water)' / **pellgje, prag** 'threshold' / **pragje, qark** 'district' / **qarqe, rrezik** 'danger' / **rreziqe, shelg** 'willow' / **shelgje, shkak** 'cause' / **shkaqe, shtog** 'bourtree' / **shtogje, tog** 'pile' / **togje, treg** 'market' / **tregje, trung** 'trunk' / **trungje, varg** 'range' / **vargje, zverk** 'nape of neck' / **zverqe,** etc.;

3. A small sub-type in which the final consonant is palatalized, the stem vowel is changed and the suffix **-e** is added: **breg** 'hill' / **brigje, lak** 'snare' / **leqe, shark** 'cloak' / **sherqe, shteg** 'pass' / **shtigje.**

NOTES

1. In the plural **pleq** 'old men' (singular **plak**) palatalization of the final consonant and a change of the stem vowel from **a** to **e** occurs.

2. Palatalization does not occur in a large number of masculine nouns that end in **k** or (less often) **g** but form the plural with the suffix **-ë**: **flok-ë** 'hairs', **shok-ë** 'comrades', **byrek-ë** 'pies', **fishek-ë** 'bullets', **lejlek-ë** 'storks', **mjek-ë** 'physicians', **zambak-ë** 'lilies', **ibrik-ë** 'pitchers', etc.

3. For nouns that end in **-ek, -yk, -ik,** or **-ëk** alternate plurals (doublets) are usual. In addition to forms with the suffix **-ë** are forms with a palatalized final consonant and the suffix **-e** as well: **byrek** 'pastry' / **byrekë** or **byreqe** 'pastries', **dyshek** 'mattress' / **dyshekë** or **dysheqe** 'mattresses', **gjyslykë** or **gjyslyqe** 'eyeglasses', **hendek** 'ditch' / **hendekë** or **hendeqe** 'ditches', **ibrik** 'pitcher' / **ibrikë** or **ibriqe** 'pitchers', **jastëk** 'pillow' / **jastëkë** or **jastëqe** 'pillows', **oxhak** 'chimney'/ **oxhakë** or **oxhaqe** 'chimneys'.

4. Turkish words with the suffix **-llëk** take the ending **-llëqe** in the plural: **budallallëk** 'foolishness' / **budallallëqe, hamallëk** 'porter work' / **hamallëqe, matrapazllëk** 'huckstering' / **matrapazllëqe.**

j) Nouns whose consonant ending **-ll** or **-r** palatalizes into **-j** in the plural comprise a separate type. Within this type are distinguished those plurals formed: 1. merely by palatalization of the consonant; 2. by palatalization of the consonant plus suffixation of **-e**, with or without a change in the stem vowel; and 3. palatalization of the consonant and change of the stem vowel.

1. The most usual subtype, marked by the palatalized consonant alone: **akull** 'ice' / **akuj, avull** 'steam' / **avuj, brumbull** '(kind of) beetle' / **brumbuj, buall** 'buffalo' / **buaj, dell** 'vein' / **dej, fshikull** 'lash' / **fshikuj, fyell** 'flute / **fyej, grumbull** 'pile' / **grumbuj, ishull** 'island' / **ishuj, kapitull** 'chapter' / **kapituj, kërmill** 'snail' / **kërmij, popull** 'people' / **popuj, portokall** 'orange' / **portokaj, shekull** 'century' / **shekuj, thëngjill** 'ember' / **thëngjij, bir** 'son' / **bij, lepur** 'rabbit' / **lepuj.** (Note that the noun **flamur** 'flag' has both a palatalized plural form **flamuj** 'flags' and a secondary plural with the suffix **-ë, flamurë** 'flags'.)

2. A number of nouns form the plural by both palatalizing the consonant and adding the suffix **-e**: **fill** 'thread' / **fije, hell** 'spit' / **heje, pyll** 'forest' / **pyje, zall** 'rocky dry river bed' / **zaje.**

3. Certain nouns form the plural by palatalizing the final **ll** into **j** and changing the stem vowel **a** to **e**: **bakall** 'grocer' / **bakej, çakall** 'jackal' / **çakej, hamall** 'porter' / **hamej, mashkull** 'male' / **meshkuj.** (But note that he nouns **hall** 'trouble', **mall** 'article of merchandise', **shall** 'scarf' do not follow this pattern in the formation of the plural: their plurals are, respectively, **halle, mallra,** and **shalle.**) The nouns **huall** 'honeycomb', **shuall**

'(leather) sole', and **truall** 'ground', with the plural forms **hoje, troje,** and **shoje,** respectively. are the only nouns ending in **-ll** whose stem vowel cluster is reduced in the plural.

NOTE

The noun **yll** 'star' has two plural forms, **yj** and **yje,** the second of which is preferred.

k) In the formation of the plural of masculine nouns, other changes of stem vowels and consonants occur, sometimes with the addition of plural suffixes.

The plural of some nouns is marked only by a change in the stem vowel, usually from **a** to **e**, but sometimes from **e** to **a**: **cjap** 'billy-goat' / **cjep, dash** 'ram' / **desh, rreth** 'hoop' / **rrathë, thes** 'sack' / **thasë**. The noun **dhëndër** 'bridegroom' has **dhëndurë** in the plural; in **gardh** 'fence' / **gjerdhe,** we have the suffix **-e** in addition to the change in the initial vowel and consonant.

In a few nouns the plural stem has undergone substantial changes in its phonological evolution and now has a form quite different from its corresponding singular stem: **ka** 'ox' / **qe** 'oxen', **kalë** 'horse' / **kuaj**.

NOTES

1. In the plural the noun **njeri** 'man' drops its **-i** termination and takes the extension **-ëz, njerëz,** with the stress moving to the first syllable. This formation has the **z** extension in common with the plural of the noun **vëlla** 'brother' / **vëllezër,** which also adds the plural suffix **-ër**.

2. For most nouns the stress does not move to the suffix in the formation of plurals. Exceptional are nouns with the plural suffixes **-enj, -llar** and **-ller** which are always stressed, and a very few individual such as **dhëndër**: **lúmë** 'river' / **lumënj, shkëmb** 'rock' / **shkëmbénj, gjárpër** 'snake' / **gjarpërinj, dhëndër** 'bridegroom' / **dhëndúrë**.

1) All nouns formed with the suffixes **-(ë)s** and **-as** have the same stem in the singular and in the plural -- **blerës** 'buyer', **gjykatës** 'judge', **kallëzues** 'accuser', **kalorës** 'rider', **lexues** 'reader', **mbledhës** 'gatherer', **mëkëmbës** 'uplifter', **mësues** 'teacher', **nëpunës** 'functionary', **nxënës** 'pupil', **përkthyes** 'translator', **qitës** 'marksman', **rrobaqepës** 'tailor', **shitës** 'seller', **vendës** 'native', **udhërrëfyes** 'guide', **zgjedhës** 'elector', etc. (but **çelësa** 'keys'); **beratas** 'inhabitant of Berat', **egjiptas** 'Egyptian', **elbasanas** 'inhabitant of Elbasan', **kartagjenas** 'Carthaginian', **maqedonas** 'Macedonian', etc.

A few other nouns have stems identical with their plural singular stem: **qen** 'dog or dogs', **qentë** 'the dogs'; **sy** 'eye or eyes', **sytë** 'the eyes'; **muaj** 'month or months', **muajt** 'the months'; **thi** 'swine', **thitë** 'the pigs'.

A.2 Feminine Plural Stems

The formation of feminine plurals is less diverse and more predictable than the formation of masculine plurals.

Suffixation is the most usual process of formation of feminine plural forms; the suffixes used are **-a** and **-ra**. However, many feminine nouns have the same stem in the singular and in the plural.

a) The following nouns form the plural with the suffix **-a**:

1. More than two-thirds of all feminine nouns that end in the unstressed vowel **-ë**, which drops before the suffix **-a**. (The other one-third, for the most part not determinable by rule -- except as noted below -- have identical singular and plural stems.): e.g., **arkë** 'safe' / **arka, bishë** 'beast' / **bisha, fushë** 'plain' / **fusha, gazetë** 'newspaper' / **gazeta, lopatë** 'shovel' / **lopata, mushkë** 'mule' / **mushka, nënë** 'mother' / **nëna, pulë** 'chicken' / **pula, tufë** 'bunch' / **tufa, vajzë** 'girl' / **vajza**. With rare exceptions, animate nouns with unstressed final **ë** take **-a** in the plural, as do derived words with suffixes that end in the vowel: **dëftesë** 'receipt' / **dëftesa, dorezë** 'glove' / **doreza, egërsirë** 'beast' / **egërsira, ulërimë** 'howl' **ulërima**, etc.

2. All feminine nouns whose citation form ends in one of the sequences **-ër, -ël, -ëz, -ull, -ur** (note that the vowel **ë** between the **r** and **l** drops before a suffix beginning in a vowel): **femër** 'female' / **femra, kapistër** 'halter' / **kapistra, kodër** 'hill' / **kodra, kthetër** 'claw' / **kthetra, letër** 'letter' / **letra, lodër** 'game' / **lodra, lundër** 'boat' / **lundra, motër** 'sister' / **motra, thupër** 'wand, rod' / **thupra, zgavër** 'hollow' / **zgavra**, etc.; **gogël** 'acorn' / **gogla, pikël** 'speck' **pikla, pupël** 'calf (of leg)' / **pupla; mollëz** 'cheekbone' / **mollëza, kumbull** 'plum' / **kumbulla, mjegull** 'fog' / **mjegulla, nofull** 'jaw' / **nofulla, petull** 'fried dough' / **petulla, sqetull** 'armpit' / **sqetulla, sumbull** 'button' / **sumbulla, shpatull** 'shoulder blade' / **shpatulla, tjegull** 'tile' / **tjegulla, vetull** 'eyebrow' / **vetulla; flutur** 'butterfly' / **flutura.**

NOTE

Formerly the nouns in this group were written and pronounced with a final **ë**, but being two syllables away from the accent, it dropped, following a very general phonological rule for modern Albanian. We still find the forms with the final **ë** among the authors of the Albanian National Awakening (1878-1912): **zemërë** 'heart', **kodërë** 'hill', **nofullë** 'jaw', **vegëlë** 'tool', **fluturë** 'butterfly', etc.

b) Plural forms with the suffix **-ra** are quite rare among feminine nouns. Only the noun **gjë** 'thing' / **gjëra** and a few substance nouns -- such as **verë** 'wine' / **verëra** -- have this as their regular plural form. For certain other feminine nouns, secondary plural forms with the suffix **-ra** do appear as specialized stylistic variants, but not as regular forms in the standard language: **kohë** 'time(s)' / **kohëra, gjuhë** 'tongue(s), language(s)' / **gjuhëra, copë** 'bit(s)' / **copëra, stoli** 'decor' / **stolira, kala** 'fortress' / **kalara**, etc.

c) As noted earlier, less than a third of the feminine nouns that end in unstressed **-ë** have the same stem in the plural as in the singular. With the exception of a few nouns like **kafshë** 'animal(s)' / **lopë** 'cow(s)' / **shtazë** 'beast(s)' the majority of these are nouns of inanimate objects: **brinjë** 'rib(s)', **ditë** 'day(s)', **enë** 'utensil(s)', **këmbë** 'foot, feet', **këngë** 'song(s)', **lugë** 'spoon(s)', **mollë** 'apple(s)', **plagë** 'wound(s)', **rrënjë** 'root(s)', **rrugë** 'road(s)', **shkallë** 'step(s)', **udhë** 'road(s)', etc.

All nouns that end in unstressed **-e** or **-o**, or in a stressed vowel -- **-í, -ë́, -á, -ú, -ó** -- have the same stem for singular and plural: **anije** 'boat(s)', **dele** 'sheep', **faqe** 'cheek(s)', **lagje** 'neighborhood(s)', **lutje** 'request(s)', **mace** 'cat(s)', **nuse** 'bride(s)', **qime** 'hair(s)', **shoqe** 'wife, wives', **zile** 'bell(s)', etc.; **ballo** 'ball(s)', **depo** 'depot(s)', **karro** 'carriage(s)', **pako** 'pack(s)', **pallto** 'coat(s)', **radio** 'radio(s)', **torno** 'lathe(s)', **triko** 'sweater(s)', etc.; **kusi** 'pot(s)', **lajthi** 'hazelnut(s)', **mushkëri** 'lung(s)', **parti** 'party, parties', **qershi** 'cherry, cherries', **qeveri** 'government, governments', **shtëpi** 'home(s)', **tepsi** 'pan(s)', etc.; **epope** 'epopee(s)', **re** 'cloud(s)', **rrufe** 'thunderbolt(s)', **ve** 'egg(s)'; **bakllava** 'baklava', **bina** 'building(s)', **kala** 'fortress(es)', **mera** 'pasture(s)', **para** 'money', **shaka** 'joke(s)'; **dru** 'tree(s)', **byro** 'bureau(s)'.

Nouns that end in unstressed **-e** actually constitute the majority of feminine nouns, because in this group are included abstract nouns productively formed with the suffix **-je**, as well as nouns productively formed by the feminizing suffix **-e** from corresponding masculines: **mike** 'female friend', **fshatare** 'villager (f.)' **qytetare** 'citizen (f.)', etc.

d) A very few feminine nouns form their plurals by changing the stem vowel. In addition to the change **a** to **e** in the noun **natë** 'night' / **net** (so frequent among masculine nouns), the change **o** to **ua** and **e** to **ye** is found in the nouns **dorë** 'hand' / **duar** and **derë** 'door' / **dyer** (Note the dropping of the final **ë**.) The noun **grua** 'woman' has the plural form **gra** 'women' reflecting a special phonological change.

A.3 Neuter Plural Stems

Being words that indicate mass substances, abstract operations or qualities, neuter nouns are normally used only in the singular.

Substance nouns that were formerly neuter nouns and that in current standard Albanian have passed over almost entirely into the masculine gender in the singular (see section 3.2.2 B), can form feminine plurals with the suffix **-ra**, indicating different types or collections of a substance: **brumëra** 'doughs', **djathëra** 'cheeses', **miellra** 'flours', **vajra** 'oils', etc.

The handful of abstract neuter nouns that historically have been derived by substantivization of the neuter adjective -- such as **të errëtit** 'the dark', **të ftohtët** 'the cold', **të kuqtë** 'the red', **të mugëtit** 'the dusk', **të zitë** 'the black' -- are used only in the singular.

NOTE

The plural form of the neuter noun **krye** 'head, chief', **krerë** 'heads' (with the change **ye/e** and the suffix **-rë**) also has an extended use in counting animals, as in **krerë bagëtish** 'heads of cattle'.

B. Nouns with Restricted Number

B.1 Nouns Used Only in the Singular

Nouns that do not have a plural form and are used only in the singular, can be grouped as follows:

1. Abstract nouns in the proper sense of the term, such as **dashuri** 'love', **guxim** 'daring', **kolektivizim** 'collectivization', **mbarim** 'conclusion', **nxehtësi** 'heat', **partishmëri** 'partisanship' (see also Section 3.2.1 B.1);

2. Collective nouns like **djemuri** 'youth', **grari** 'women', **gjindje** 'situation', **vëllazëri** 'brotherhood' (see Section 3.2.1 B.2);

3. Nouns that refer to a substance as an indivisible, whole mass: **benzinë** 'benzine', **çimento** 'cement', **dhallë** 'buttermilk', **gëlqere** 'lime', **gjizë** 'cottage cheese', **kos** 'yogurt', **rërë** 'sand', **uthull** 'vinegar', **vaj** 'oil', etc. (but some of these may appear with the **-ra** suffix to indicate different types of the substance) (see also Section 3.2.1 B.3);

4. Most of the names of illnesses, the generalness of whose meaning in Albanian approaches that of abstract nouns: **fruth** 'measles', **li** 'smallpox', **kollë** 'whooping cough', **qere** 'ringworm', **zgjebe** 'itch', etc.;

5. Nouns that indicate all the directions of the compass: **veri** 'north', **jugë** 'south', **lindje** 'east', **perëndim** 'west'.

6. Certain plants, such as, **lëpjetë** 'sorrel', **spinaq** 'spinach', **tallë** 'sorghum', **thekër** 'rye'.

7. Most atmospheric phenomena, such as **brymë** 'frost', **breshër** 'hail', **dëborë** 'snow', **vapë** 'hot weather', **vesë** 'dew', **zheg** 'siesta time';

8. Proper nouns denoting unique objects; (see Section 3.2.1 A);

9. The noun **krye** 'head' when used as a body part.

B.2 Nouns Used Only in the Plural

A number of nouns are used only, or mainly, in the plural form. They generally have a collective meaning, indicating not a simple plurality, but a whole entity in some sense. The difference between collective nouns used only in the singular and nouns used only in the plural is that the latter indicate to a greater degree than the former that it is individual members which form the whole.

On the basis of their meanings, these plural-only nouns can be divided in the following groups:

1. Nouns that refer to a substance, in mass objects fashioned from a particular substance, terms dealing with crops, odds and ends, amounts of money: **hime-t** 'bran', **krunde-t** 'bran', **makarona-t** 'macaroni', **qurre-t** 'snot, nasal mucus'; **qelqurina-t** 'glassware', **bakëret** 'copper goods, utensils', **ergjende-t** 'silver decorations'; **të korra-t** 'harvest', **të lashta-t** 'crops', **të mbjella-t** 'plantings', **të vjela-t** 'reapings', **të vona-t** 'late crops', **farishte-t** 'seeds', **perime-t** 'vegetables'; **të fshira-t** 'sweepings', **të shplara-t** 'rinsing', **të lëna-t** 'remains', **të mbetura-t** 'leftovers'; **të holla-t** 'money', **të holla-t** 'money', **të ardhura-t** 'income';

2. Nouns that indicate objects composed of two or more parts: **benevrekë-t** '(type of) pants', **brekushe-t** '(type of) breeches', **dokra-t** 'the large bones of the body', **hejbe-të** 'saddlebags', **këmbje-t** 'embroidered cuffs of bloomers', **kryqe-t** 'loins', **leqe-t** 'stains', **pantallona-t** 'pants', **pranga-t** 'shackles', **rrathë-t** 'hoops' (fishing tool), **ski-të** 'skis', etc.;

3. Nouns that refer to a quantity of animate beings as an indivisible whole: e.g., **dhen-të** '(flock of) sheep', **shqerra-t** '(flock of) lambs', **shtojzovalle-t** '(host of) fairies', **vetë** 'people, persons';

4. Various nouns that indicate certain affective actions, certain names of illnesses, and names of games: e.g., **lajka-t** 'flatteries', **teka-t** 'whims', **paçe-t** '(an insulting gesture)', **gjepura-t** 'falsehoods', **të palára-t** 'dirty deeds', **vome-t** 'laments', **hoka-t** 'jokes', **plaka-t** (three-day period of time around the end of March and the beginning of April), **prime-t** 'folk remedies'; **ethe-t** 'malaria ("fevers")', **shyta-t** 'mumps', **grykë-t** 'tonsillitis'; **kupa-t** 'hearts (card game)', **pllaka-t** 'tag';

5. Certain proper or common nouns that denote places: e.g., **Alpe-t** 'Alps', **lugje-t** 'valley junction', **mrize-t** 'shady places for cattle', **vise-t** 'places', etc.

3.2.5 The Category of Definiteness

Many languages (including English) use little words called ARTICLES to indicate that the noun they accompany denotes one or more exemplars of the class designated by the noun itself. Articles are included in a class of modifiers called DETERMINERS which also serve to select out individuals from a class: in nominal prases that include the noun they modify, demonstrative pronouns, interrogative pronouns, possessive pronouns, a few indeterminate pronouns, and cardinal numbers also often serve as determiners. Unlike other determiners, the article does not have a lexical meaning independent of the noun to which it belongs.

Two types of articles, definite and indefinite, can be distinguished in other languages. A noun accompanied by the definite article--*the* in English--denotes someone or something assumed by the speaker to be identifiable by his audience; a noun accompanied by the indefinite article *a* or *an* in English denotes an individual person or thing that is not assumed to be identifiable by the audience.

In Albanian, on the other hand, definiteness is not indicated by a separate word, but may be indicated by DEFINITE case endings on nouns (see Section 3.3). The usual indefinite article in Albanian is **një** 'a, an' although the determiners **ndonjë** 'some, any, a certain', **ca** 'some, several', **njëfarë** 'a certain, sort of a', or **disa** 'several' also indicate that the referent of the noun phrase they introduce is not presumed to be identifiable to the audience, that is, that the noun phrase is indefinite. The determiner **njëfarë** is an agglutination of the article **një** 'sort, type'. It differs form the other determiners in that it is always followed by a noun in the indefinite ablative case:

Ai nxjerr në skenë figura të reja, që kanë NJËFARË konsiderate në opinionin publik.
'He presents new figures on the stage that have A CERTAIN standing in public opinion.'

Adjectival articles, a category particular to Albanian, serve in general to indicate that the following word is attributed to a noun, present in the sentence or merely implied (see Section 4.2).

A. Uses of Indefinite Articles

The indefinite article is mainly used when the referent of the noun is a single, unidentified individual, but it is also used when the noun has a generic meaning; in the first instance, the indefinite noun preceded by the indefinite article **një** designates one thing from among all the things that comprise a given class, but the identification of that individual is incomplete. In contrast with the definite form of a noun which designates an identified referent, the indefinite form of the noun preceded by the article **një** designates one individual with the characteristics of the noun, but without stressing which individual. In this sense, **një** and **njëfarë** 'a kind of' are synonymous.

The indefinite noun is accompanied by the article **një** especially when mentioned for the first time in a particular context. In such an instance, the speaker gives notice to the audience that the referent is as yet unknown to the latter:

> **NJË HARABEL u hodh nga çerdhja dhe ra pranë saj në degën e NJË FIKU.** 'A SPARROW jumped out of the nest and fell near her on the branch of A FIG TREE.'
> **Te praku i portës qëndronin dy hije: NJË PLAK dhe NJË PLAKË.** 'At the threshold of the gate stood two shadows: AN OLD MAN and AN OLD WOMAN.'

The article **një** 'a, an' is customarily used when a noun that lacks an identified referent appears as subject or object (direct or indirect) of a verb, (in the genitive case) modifier or appositive in a nominal phrase, or as object of one of the locative prepositions **në** 'in', **nëpër** 'among', **mbi** 'on', **nën** 'under':

> **Në hajat kërceu NJË LEPUR.** 'A RABBIT jumped into the porch.'
> **Tashti kishte në shpinë NJË BRENGË të vazhdueshme.** 'Now he had A continuous WORRY on his back.'
> **Krisma e NJË RRUFEJE u duk sikur e çau tokën dysh.** 'The crack of A THUNDER-BOLT seemed to split the ground in two.'
> **Vështrimi shëtit në NJË AMFITEATËR.** 'Vështrim strolls in AN AMPHITHEATER.'

As objects of these prepositions, removing the article **një** would give the noun a definite or generic meaning: Compare **Hipi mbi çati.** 'He climbed on (the) roof.' with **Hipi mbi një çati.** 'He climbed on a roof.'; **U ndal në stacion.** 'He stopped at (the) station.' with **U ndal në një stacion.' 'He stopped at a station'; I kaloi një e dridhur nëpër trup.** 'A shiver passed thru his body.' with **Rryma elektrike kalon nëpër një trup përcjellës.** 'Electric current passes through a conductor.'

The indefinite noun preceded by the article **një** is used as a predicate nominative only when followed by a modifier:

> **Lugina e Matit është NJË PREHJE dhe NJË GËZIM i rrallë për syrin.** 'They valley of Mat is A RELIEF and A rare JOY for the eye.'
> **Ajo ishte NJË VAJZË me vullnet të fortë.** 'She was A GIRL of strong will.'

When the noun is followed by a possessive pronoun, the article **një** may precede a definite noun to indicate that the noun is semantically indefinite -- in the following example, to indicate that it is *a friend of mine* rather than *my friend*:

> **E mbështolla fëmijën me pelena, e futa nën gunë dhe e shupura në një stan te NJË miku im çoban.** 'I wrapped up the child in baby linen, put him under my cloak and took him over to A shepherd friend of mine at a mountain sheepfold.'

The article **një** may also be used before a noun with a generic meaning to represent the referent of the noun as an indefinite aggregate consisting of individual considered together by virtue of their common traits:

Ata e kuptojnë se sa mund të marrë me vete NJË LIBËR i mirë, por edhe ç'dëm mund të bëjë një LIBËR i keq. 'They understand how many adherents A good BOOK can make, but also the harm that A bad BOOK can do.'

NJË NJERI, sado të mira të ketë për veten e tij, s'mund të jetë fatbardhë, po të ketë kombin e mëmëdhenë e vet fatzi. 'A PERSON cannot be considered fortunate, no matter how many good things he may have for himself, if his nation and motherland are unfortunate.'

In this usage, the article *one* has a function quite similar to that of the determiner **çdo** 'every'.

In contrast with the indefinite article, the cardinal number **një** 'one' has its own word stress; as a number, it may be reinforced by the adverb **vetëm** 'only' and may contrast with the other integers: **Bleu vetëm NJË libër**. 'He bought only ONE book.' (rather than two or three books). The number **një** may also be stressed as a pronominal element or unstressed as an indefinite article. In the following illustration the word *one* appears in three different functions, as indefinite article, as cardinal number, and as indeterminate pronoun:

Bashkimi i i të gjitha forcave kombëtare përpara shekullit të njëzetë ishte NJË çudi, që e bëri në historinë e kombit vetëm NJË njeri: Skënderbeu. Që jo vetëm e bëri, po edhe e mbajti pothuaj njëzet e pesë vjet me radhë, në mes të furtunës së jashtme dhe të brendshme, është NJË nga lavditë e tij më të mëdha. 'The union of all national forces before the twentieth century was A miracle that was performed by only ONE man in the nation's history: Scanderbeg. That he not only brought it about, but preserved it for nearly twenty five years in succession, in the midst of external and internal storm, is ONE of his greatest glories.'

Like the number **një**, the indefinite article **një** is the same with both masculine and feminine nouns. Albanian does not have an indefinite article for the plural.

B. Uses of Indefinite Nouns

An indefinite noun form is usually found when the noun is used:

1. As a predicate nominative.

Unlike English, an indefinite noun form in the capacity of a predicate nominative is normally used without an indefinite article; in that function, the predicate serves to characterize the subject, as a predicate adjective would, rather than to identify it:

Sikur të ishte DJALË, mendonte nganjëherë. 'If only she were (a) BOY, she thought at times.'
Djali im i madh është aviator. 'My oldest son is (an) aviator.'
Gruaja e tij është shqiptare. 'His wife is (an) Albanian.'

2. As a predicate complement.

In Albanian a frequent construction with the verb **kam** 'have' is of the type **E kam mik**. 'He is a friend of mine.' Which is literally "I have him (as) friend", an impossible construction in English. Again the indefinite noun acts like a predicate adjective:

Kam për dëshmitar Hamzën, tim nip, që e kam pasur PËRKRAHËS, KËSHILLTAR dhe SHOK armësh. 'I have as witness my nephew, Hamzë, whom I have had (as) SUPPORTER, ADVISOR and COMRADE-in-arms.'
E zgjodhën Agimin sekretar. 'They elected Agim secretary.'

3. As an ablative case qualifier, after an indefinite noun in the nominative or accusative case, in word groups of the type: **mish VIÇI** 'VEAL meat', **ve PULE** 'CHICKEN egg', **këngë DASME** WEDDING song', **vaj ULLIRI** 'OLIVE oil', **lëvizje TRENASH** 'TRAIN movements' etc. (See Section 3.2.3 A.5)

4. In certain idiomatic verbal constructions consisting of a verb plus a noun: **marr FRYMË** 'breathe ("take BREATH")', **shes MEND** 'pontificate ("sell MIND")', **zë BESË** 'give

one's word ("catch FAITH")', **ngul KËMBË** 'insist ("implant FOOT")', **bëj DËM** 'do HARM', **bëj FJALË** 'gossip ("make words")', **heq DORË** 'withdraw, give up ("pull HAND")', **vë DORË** 'commit oneself ("place HAND")', **më jep DORË** 'helps me ("gives me HAND")', etc. In such expressions, if the noun has any form other than the citation form the idiomatic value of the construction is lost: e.g. **heq dorën** would mean something like 'I pull my hand' rather than 'I give up'.

5. In certain idiomatic adverbial constructions with the noun repeated: **gur mbi gur** 'little by little ("stone upon stone")', **stëpi më shtëpi** 'all over ("house to house")', **fshat më fshat** 'all over ("village to village") etc.

6. In negative generic expressions generally corresponding to English *not a*(...nor), *no, there's no, there's not a*, etc.:

MAL s'të sheh syri, as BREG, as GURË. 'There is not (a) MOUNTAIN in sight, nor HILL nor STONE.'
S'ka mbetur DJALË në fshat, të gjithë ikën në mal me partizanët. 'There is not (a) BOY in the village; all joined the partisans in the mountains.'

7. In its citation form when it indicates quantity of a substance, i.e., when it has a partitive rather than an identifying function. In English such uses are indicated by the overt marker *some*. Albanian uses indefinite partitives in many cases when English would use indefinite generics. **ha BUKË** 'eat (some) BREAD', **pi UJË** 'drink (some) WATER', **pi VERË 'drink (some) WINE'**, **blej DJATHË** 'buy (some) CHEESE', **shet BENZINË** 'sell (some) BENZINE', **nxirret NAFTË** '(some) PETROLEUM is extracted', **prodhohet VAJ** '(some) OIL is produced', **një kg MIELL** 'a kg of FLOUR', **një kv SHEQER** 'a quintal (100 kilograms) of SUGAR', **dy litra QUMËSHT** 'two liters of MILK' etc.

8. In a use related to 7., as a general object of the verb **kam** 'have', often in its third person singular existential sense--translated into English as *there is, there are, there were, there have been, etc:* **kam URI** 'I am HUNGRY ("I have hunger")', **ka NËNË** 'he has (or 'there is') (a) MOTHER', **ka VËLLA** 'he has (a) BROTHER', **kishte SHTËPI** 'there was (a) house'.

Ku ka TYM, ka edhe ZJARR. 'Where there is SMOKE, there is [also] FIRE.'

9. In comparisons, in which a common noun stands for one or more relevant characteristics of the class it names:

Luftoi si LUAN. 'He fought like (a) LION.'
Të veprosh si KOMUNIST. 'Behave like (a) COMMUNIST.'

10. To indicate that certain closely related noun pairs constitute a unity that exhausts the universe of discourse (cf. English *kit and caboodle, man and boy, body and soul*, etc.)

In such pairs, the definiteness of the whole noun phrase is marked in neither noun itself, but in the conjunction of the two nouns into a single, particular whole: **vëlla e motër** 'brother and sister', i.e., all siblings, **atë e bir** 'father and son', i.e., both generations, **atë e bijë** 'father and daughter', i.e., adults and children, **këmbë e duar** 'hands and feet', i.e., all limbs, etc.:

Dhe ashtu, ATË E BIR, këndonin të shoqëruar nga gurgullima e ujit. 'And so everyone ("FATHER AND SON") sang, accompanied by the gurgling of the water.'
Kish çelur në kanatë DYER E DRITARE. 'He had opened the shutters of all the openings ("DOORS AND WINDOWS").'
Ai e shikonte si po e linin KËMBË E DUAR. 'He saw how his limbs ("HANDS AND FEET") were deserting him.'

11. In an appositive function. In this function the noun (sometimes marked in English by a preceding *of*) has its generic meaning and, like an adjective, serves to characterize a preceding definite noun:

Gjithë muajin PRILL lëruan në ara me parmendë e me plug. 'The whole month of APRIL they tilled the fields with the wooden and metal plows.'

Ti, Shqipëri,...më jep emrin SHQIPTAR. 'You, Albania...give me the name ALBANIAN.'

12. After an indefinite determiner (i.e., a word that requires that the following noun be in an indefinite form). Such determiners may be:

a) Cardinal numbers.

With cardinal numbers the noun usually appears in an indefinite form:

Në platformë rrinin më këmbë DY VAJZA dhe DY FSHATARË. 'On the platform stood TWO GIRLS and TWO VILLAGERS.'

Note that cardinal numbers also occur as definite determiners followed by a definite form, in which case they are preceded by the article **të**:

Unë i dua TË SHTATË LIBRAT. 'I want THE SEVEN BOOKS.'

b) Indefinite quantifiers: **një** 'a, an', **shumë** 'much', **ndonjë** 'some, any', **asnjë** 'none, no, not one', **çdo** 'each, every, all', **pak** 'little', **aq** 'that much', **kaq** 'so much', **ca** 'some', **disa** 'a few', **mjaft** 'enough'.

DISA KOOPERATIVISTË po ktheheshin nga puna. 'A FEW COOPERATIVISTS were returning from work.'

Petriti dëgjonte me SHUMË VËMENDJE. 'Petrit listened with GREAT ATTENTION.'

Doli në oborin e madh, po s'pa asgjë, ASNJË REPART, ASNJË SHOK. 'He came out in the great yard but didn't see a thing, NOT ONE DETACHMENT, NOT ONE COMRADE.'

Iu duk sikur NDONJË RRUFE, gjatë natës kishte flakur tej atë kurorë dhe e kishte lënë drurin cung. 'He felt as if SOME THUNDERBOLT had blasted off that crown during the night and left the tree maimed.'

Kaloi një VERË të gëzuar. 'He spent a joyful SUMMER.'

NJË MARS kaq i ftohtë e me shira si ky i sivjetmi s'mbahet mend. 'One cannot recall so cold and rainy A MARCH as this year's.'

c) Demonstrative pronouns.

After one of the forms of the third person demonstrative pronouns **ky** 'this (m.)', **kjo** 'this (f.)', **ai** 'he', **ajo** 'she', **ata** 'they (m.)', **ato** 'they (f.)', a noun in the Albanian language regularly appears in the indefinite form:

Kur më ftuat për KËTË VEPËR nga shërbimi i sulltanit, kisha në zemër ATË DËSHIRË, që kishit edhe ju. 'When you invited me to leave the Sultan's service for THIS ENTERPRISE, I had in my heart THAT (same) DESIRE that you had also.'

When used with a deictic (pointing) function the demonstrative pronoun plays an identifying role like that of the definite article. If the pronoun is not deictic, but rather serves an anaphoric function, i.e., to refer to a previously mentioned referent, then the noun associated with it may be definite:

Qëlloi të ishte mytesarif në Berat një turkoshak me emrin Kadri Pasha. KY PASHAI na kishte bërë para të madhe. 'There happened to be in Berat a pseudo Turk governor by the name of Kadri Pasha. THIS PASHA had accumulated great wealth.'

This usage is common in the spoken language:

Le të hipë edhe KJO SHOQJA me KËTË ÇUNIN. 'Let THIS COMRADE climb in with THIS LAD as well.'

d) Interrogative pronouns: **cili** 'who', **ç'** 'what', **sa** 'how much', **çfarë** 'what kind':

Çudi, Ç'NJERËZ, të gjithë nxitojnë. 'Strange, how ("WHAT") PEOPLE are all running.'

e) Preposed possessive personal pronouns **im (ime** f.) 'my', **yt (jot** f.) 'your':

Ka ardhur YT VËLLA. 'YOUR BROTHER has arrived.'

13. After accusative prepositions, namely, **në** 'in', **mbi** 'on', **me** 'with', **pa** 'without', **nën** 'under', **ndër** 'among, between', **nëpër** 'among', **për** 'for', when the noun is not further specified by modifiers.

In certain prepositional phrases, the noun takes the indefinite form, in some instances even when the noun could be said to have an identifiable referent:

Po ti sa erdhe, O Ylli, ku shkon tashti? -- NË SHTËPI. '"But you just arrived, Ylli, where are you going now?" "Home ("TO HOUSE")."'
Ju ma vutë MBI KRYE këtë kurorë, ju ma dhatë NË DORË këtë shpatë. 'You put this crown ON (my) HEAD, you placed this sword in (my) HAND.'

In these sentences the nouns **shtëpi** 'house', **krye** 'head', and **dorë** 'hand' might be thought to have identifiable referents, but the prepositional phrase with the indefinite noun forms an idiomatic adverbial unit, very much in the way *to school, home* or *by hand* form such units in English.

When the noun is followed by a modifier that identifies its referent, however, it has a definite form even when it follows an accusative preposition. Compare **fluturonte MBI LIQEN** 'it was flying OVER the LAKE' and **fluturonte MBI LIQENIN e Shkodrës** 'it was flying OVER THE LAKE of Shkodër', **hipi NË ÇATI** 'he climbed ON THE ROOF' and **hipi NË ÇATINË e shtëpisë** 'he climbed ON the ROOF of the house'. In the spoken language, and somewhat less in the written language, the tendency to preserve the indefinite form after an accusative preposition, even when followed by a qualifier, has been so strong that to this day, one finds prepositional phrases with the indefinite noun, forming adverbials of circumstance: **NË MAL të Tomorit** 'ON Tomor MOUNTAIN', **NË KOHË të lëmit** 'AT threshing TIME', **NË HYRJE të qytetit** 'AT (the) ENTRANCE of the city'. However, they are being crowded out by the newer constructions: **NË MALIN e Tomorit** 'ON [the] Tomor MOUNTAIN', **NË KOHËN e lëmit** 'AT [the] threshing TIME', etc.

14. As a vocative. In this function titles, names, and epithets regularly appear in the indefinite form:

DOKTOR, jam unë, Lavdia. 'DOCTOR, it's me, Lavdia.'
Pa ngrënë e pa pirë s'mbetemi, moj MIRË. 'We won't be left without food and drink, MIRË.'

When followed by a qualifier, the noun may take the definite form:

O FLUTURA krahëshkruar, që fluturon nëpër erë. 'O dapple-winged butterfly that flies in the air.'
NOTE
Nouns whose citation form ends in **-ë** often take the definite form in the vocative.
DRITA, fol më ngadalë! 'Dritë, talk slower.'

C. Definite Nouns

Definiteness in Albanian is an inflectional category for nouns that corresponds roughly to the definite-indefinite distinction in English realized through the articles **a** and **the**, although as will be seen below there are significant differences between English and Albanian usage. Both common and proper nouns have a full set of definite and indefinite forms, although for proper nouns use of indefinite forms is rather restricted (see Section 3.2.5 C.2). To indicate that a common noun in Albanian has a specific referent, the noun may be used in the indefinite form after a demonstrative pronoun, e.g., **ky djalë** 'this boy', **ajo shkollë** 'that school', or, it may be used in the definite form corresponding to English 'the', e.g., **djali** 'the boy', **shkolla** 'the school'. In general a common noun used in the definite form has a specific referent, thought of as distinct from other members of the same class. (See Section 3.3 for the forms of the definite and indefinite endings for each case, gender, and number.)

C.1 Definiteness in Common Nouns

In general a common noun will be in a definite form to indicate:

a) As in English, that a referent has already been mentioned in a given context.

This type of definiteness is called *anaphoric.* Upon repetition in the same context, the noun is definite, because its reference is now familiar to the audience.

> -- **Ç'ke që shtyn, more djalë, më skele! -- bërtiti NJË GRUA dhe vështroi me inat NJË DJALOSH, i cili u skuq dhe aty për aty i kërkoi ndjesë. GRUAS i erdhi keq, kur pa fytyrën e turpëruar të DJALOSHIT.** '"Why are you pushing, boy, you stepped on me!" A WOMAN shouted, and looked angrily at A BOY, who blushed and immediately asked her pardon. THE WOMAN felt sorry when she saw the shame-faced look of THE BOY.'

> **DY FSHATARË ngarkonin dy mushka me vandakë misri. FSHATARËT, me t'i parë udhëtarët, kthyen kokën.** 'TWO PEASANTS were loading sheaves of corn on two mules. As soon as they saw the travelers, THE PEASANTS turned their head.'

b) That there is a logical relation between the referent and another noun that has been identified in the context, such that the presence of the other noun implies the presence of the referent. A special case of this is to indicate possession when the possessor is obvious in the context:

> **Pastaj ia dha vrapit dhe doli në xhade, se pa që larg NJË AUTOBUS. Autobusi mbërriti në kthesën e parë dhe frenoi pranë tij. SHOFERI dhe PASAGJERËT u çuditën.** 'Then he ran and came to the road, because he saw from afar A BUS. The bus reached the first turn and braked near him. THE DRIVER and THE PASSENGERS were astounded.'

> **Edhe këtë herë, sa shkeli te selishta, u ndal: hoqi QELESHEN dhe fërkoi KOKËN.** 'This time as well he stopped as soon as he set foot in the garden plot: he took off his WHITE CAP and rubbed his HEAD.' (Note the use here of the definite form instead of a possessive pronoun when the owner is known. English in such cases requires that the possessor be specified.)

> **E në mes të bisedës iu bë sikur dëgjoi një të trokitur në portë. Pasi heshtën, ai ndenji të mbajë vesh. E trokitura u përsërit, po kësaj radhe I PANJOHURI po i binte derës me grusht.** 'And in the middle of the conversation, he thought if he heard a knocking at the door. After they became quiet, he sat and listened. The knocking was repeated, but this time THE STRANGER was hitting the door with his fist.'

c) That the referent is in the immediate situation in which the speech act occurs.

In such instances the referent is immediately apparent to the participants in the speech act; they share the perception and hence talk about it as an identified object:

> **Shikoni XHENIERËT, -- tha Anseli.** '"Look at THE ENGINEERS", Anseli said.'

> **U poqën edhe MISRAT, -- tha Rustemi. Burri me mustaqe të zeza i hodhi sytë nga ARAT, po nuk foli.** '"THE CORN is ripe," said Rustem. The black-mustached man looked at THE FIELDS, but did not speak.'

d) That the definite noun belongs to the speaker, to the audience, or to some other obvious possessor:

Mos flitni me zë të lartë se do të më zgjoni DJALIN, -- tha nëna. 'Don't talk aloud, or you will wake up my son ("THE BOY")," the mother said.'

e) That the reader of a literary work, such as a novel or short story already knows the identity of the referent. The writer uses the definite form as a stylistic device to give the impression that the reader is already involved in the situation in the story:

Megjithëse i kishte rënë ziles tri herë, ROJTARI nuk po dukej ende. 'Although he had rung three times, THE GUARD had not yet shown up.'

In this sentence, which happens to be the opening line in the work, the noun **rojtar** occurs in the definite form when the reader does not yet in fact know anything about him.

f) That the referent of the noun can be uniquely identified because of its special status: **dielli** 'the sun', **hëna** 'the moon', **marsi** 'Mars', **toka** 'the earth', etc., used in the definite without other qualification designate the particular heavenly bodies called by those names. As in English, the indefinite form could be used only to mean some other sun, moon, etc., than the one that we normally talk about.

Atë do ta kishte aty mbi krye për sa kohë të shndriste DIELLI e HËNA. 'For as long as THE SUN and THE MOON would shine, it would be there overhead.'

The definite form is also used for the names of the seasons, months of the year and certain winds (e.g., **veri** 'north wind', **jugë** 'south wind', **goren** 'north wind, blizzard') that are considered in Albanian to be unique entities:

VERA kalohej si jo më mirë. 'THE SUMMER couldn't have been spent better.'
DIELLI i MARSIT filloi të digjte. 'THE MARCH SUN began to burn.'
Ulërima e GORENIT zbriste nga pllajat. 'The howling of THE NORTH WIND descended from the plateaus.'

NOTE

Certain compound designations formed of a noun and an adjective also indicate unique referents and are thus also used in the definite form: **gjuha shqipe** 'the Albanian language', **populli shqiptar** 'the Albanian people', **letërsia e vjetër shqipe** '(the) old Albanian literature', **proletariati evropian** 'the European proletariat', etc.

g) That the following qualifier singles out the referent, rather than merely describe it. Such qualifiers are of several sorts:

1. Possessive pronouns.

SHOKU im 'my FRIEND', **SHOQJA jonë** 'our FRIEND (f)', **DJEMTË tanë** 'our BOYS', **QYTETET tona** 'our CITIES', **LIBRI i tij** 'his BOOK', **SHOKËT e tyre** 'their FRIENDS', etc. The presence of a following possessive is so influential that even when the noun is preceded by the indefinite article **një** 'one', it still takes the definite form:

Agimin e shpura në një stan te NJË MIKU IM ÇOBAN. 'I took Agim over to the sheepfold belonging to A SHEPHERD FRIEND of MINE.'
NJË MOTRA IME ishte 70 vjeçe, kur iu vu shkrimit dhe leximit të shqipes. 'A SISTER OF MINE was 70 years old when she set off to learn to write and read Albanian.'

Note that when a possessive **im** 'my', **ime** 'my (f)', **yt** 'your', **jot** 'your (f)' precedes, the noun is indefinite: **im VËLLA** 'my BROTHER', **jot MOTËR** 'your SISTER'. (See Section 3.1).

2. A determining noun in the genitive case.

In terms of function, the genitive case of a noun is like a possessive pronoun:

GJËMIMI i topave dhe KËRCËLLIMI i pushkëve lajmëruan që kufoma e Skënderbeut kishte zbritur në varr. 'THE THUNDER of guns and THE FIRING of rifles announced that the corpse of Skënderbeu had been lowered in the grave.'
KRISMA e një rrufeje u duk sikur e çau tokën dysh. 'It seemed as if THE CRACK of a thunderbolt had split the ground in two.'

3. A denumerative adjective (= ordinal number).

Unlike cardinal numbers, ordinal numbers usually have the function of selecting out, i.e., identifying, rather than characterizing a particular member of a set. Thus, one says **viti i dytë** 'the second year', **takimi i parë** 'the first meeting', **hera e tretë** 'the third time', etc. In the same way, the genitive noun form **i fundit** 'of the end, last' (from **fund** 'end' identifies a definite referent: **dita e fundit** 'the last day', **librat e fundit** 'the final books', etc.

4. Adjectives in the superior degree.

The definiteness of the noun serves to identify the adjective as a superlative in such constructions, in contrast with English, which uses an **-est** ending on the adjective to express the same idea:

Agimi ishte PUNËTORI më gazmor i oficinës. 'Agim was THE CHEERIEST WORKER ("the worker more joyful") in the workshop.'
Ndofta PIKA më e gjetur për të admiruar këtë luginë është vetë Burreli. 'Perhaps the most felicitous VANTAGE POINT for admiring this valley is Burrel itself.'

Alternatively the adjective in the superior degree may be placed before the noun; in that event the noun is indefinite while the adjective takes the definite endings that indicate the uniqueness of the referent. Again the English equivalent is an adjective in the superlative degree, i.e., with the suffix **-est** (or with the quantifier *most*):

Ishte MË I VOGLI DJALË i princ Gjon Kastriotit dhe i princeshës Vojsavë. 'He was THE YOUNGEST SON of prince Gjon Kastrioti and of princess Vojsavë.'

5. That a preceding quantifier, **gjithë** 'all' or **tërë** 'entire' identifies the referent, as in English "all the x" and "the entire x": **gjithë qyteti** 'the whole city', **gjithë nxënësit** 'all the pupils', **tërë bota** 'the entire world', etc.

g) That a preposed article, namely, **i, e, të**, or **së**, has the value of a 3rd person possessive pronoun, with a following kinship noun in a definite form: **i biri** 'his, her, or their son', **e mbesa** 'his, her, their niece', **i kunati** 'his, her, their brother-in-law', **e vjehrra** 'his, her, their mother-in-law', **të bijtë** 'his, her, their sons', **të motrat** 'his, her, their sisters', etc.

h) That a following relative clause identifies the referent:

KAPEDANI që priste populli, erdhi. 'THE LEADER that the people were waiting for came.'
Kjo ishte TOKA ku ranë, mbinë dhe shpërthyen me tërë lulet idetë e komunistëve. 'This was THE LAND where the ideas of communists fell to the ground, germinated and burst in full flower.'

The identifying role may also be played by an adverb or by a prepositional phrase:

Mbasi mori frymë thellë, u lëshua në KOLLTUKUN PRANË. 'After taking a deep breath, he plumped into the ARMCHAIR NEARBY.'
Xha Petriti tërë kohën e shkonte në TENDËN AFËR RRAPIT. 'Uncle Petrit spent his whole time in THE BOWER NEAR THE SYCAMORE TREE.'

In certain idiomatic expressions definite noun forms are fixed, and a change of form in the noun is either impossible or results in the loss of the idiomatic sense. On the whole there seem to be fewer idioms with definite nouns than with indefinite ones: **më merr MALLI** 'I am moved' ("the longing seizes me"), **më zë GJUMI** 'I fall asleep' ("the sleep takes me"), **marr FJALËN** 'I speak' ("I take the word"), **jap FJALËN** 'I promise' ("I give the word"), **vras NENDJEN** 'I ponder' ("I kill the mind"), **më mori LUMI** 'I'm done for' ("the river took me"), **thyej QAFËN** 'I slip badly' ("I break the neck"), **i jap DUART** 'I give him a shove' ("I give him the hands"), **i jap DORËN** 'I shake hands' ("I give him the hand"), **heq UDHËN** 'I lead the way' ("I pull the road"), **mbaj FJALËN** 'I keep my word' ("I hold the word")', **mbyll GOJËN** 'I shut up' ("I close the mouth"), etc.

C.2 Definiteness in Proper Nouns

Proper nouns are declined in the same way as common nouns and are used in both definite and indefinite forms. With proper nouns, definiteness does not have quite the same function as with common nouns, since proper nouns, by definition, inherently identify a particular
referent uniquely. The syntactic function of nouns in the sentence plays an important role with
respect to their definiteness. As subject or object of a verb, a noun--including proper names
and plural nouns, unlike English--must be specified either by a preposed determiner, such as a
number, demonstrative pronoun, indeterminate pronoun, etc., or by putting the noun in the
definite form. The first alternative, however, is in practice quite uncommon with proper nouns
because of their very meaning; for example, it is rarely appropriate to use preposed determiners
before names of cities: **ky Berat** 'this Berat', **një Durrës** 'a Durrës', **çdo Tiranë** 'every Tiranë',
etc. Thus proper nouns, including names of persons, in Albanian are usually used in the definite form:

Agimi e pa Dritën në Tiranë. 'Agim ("the Agim") saw Drita ("the Drita") in Tirana.'

Here we see definite forms of the proper names **Agim** and **Drita** used for the subject and object
of the verb, but an indefinite form of the proper name **Tirana** used as object of a locative
preposition (see Point 5 below). In this regard Albanian differs from many other languages
with definite articles, including English.

In Albanian a proper noun is used in the indefinite form only in a few syntactic functions
(where common nouns also appear in indefinite forms):

1. In apposition with a preceding definite noun:

Në fshatin DUSHK ata arritën në mëngjes. 'They arrived in the village of DUSHK in
the morning.'

2. As predicate complement of the subject or the object:

E quajnë AGIM, -- shpjegoi vajza. '"They call him AGIM," the girl explained.'

3. As a vocative not followed by an identifying word or phrase:

Lamtumirë, PETRIT! 'Goodbye, PETRIT!'
Prit, LUMTË! 'Wait, LUMTË!'

4. When preceded by an adjective in a noun phrase:

I ziu PETRIT ç'pësoi! 'What a bad break for poor PETRIT!'

5. As object of locative prepositions that govern the accusative case, or the ablative
preposition **prej** 'from': **PREJ SKRAPARI** 'FROM SHRAPAR', **PREJ DOBREJE** 'FROM
DOBRE', **PREJ VLORE** 'FROM VLORË', **PREJ MYZEQEJE** 'FROM MYZEQE'. (contrast
nga Vjosa 'from (the) Vjosë', and **nga Devolli** 'from (the) Devoll'), This usage pertains only
to geographic locations:

**Kam vajtur në MAT me qëllim që të dal në MARTANESH dhe së andejmi të zbres në
ELBASAN.** 'I went to MAT in order to go to MATANESH and from there go down to
ELBASAN.'
A mos vjen PREJ MALËSIE? 'Are you coming FROM THE HIGHLANDS?'

6. As ablative qualifiers that characterize ratherthan identify an indefinite noun: **ullinj
BERATI** 'BERAT olives', **djathë GJIROKASTRE** 'GJIROKASTER cheese' **verë NARTE**
'NARTË wine', **mollë KORË** 'KORË apple', **duhan SHKODRE** 'SHKODËR tobacco', etc.
This usage also pertains only to geographic names.

C.3 Definiteness in Generics

A singular definite form of a common noun may be used generically, that is, may be used to designate the whole class named by the noun rather than any individual member or members of that class.

Definite forms are used a great deal as generics in Albanian, not only for countable nouns, as in English ("The dog is man's best friend."), but, unlike English, also with substance nouns, abstract nouns, deverbal nouns, and others. In fact, the generic form *must* be definite in Albanian and *cannot* be in English; that is, while in English 'wheat' can be used generically *(wheat is a cereal)* and 'the wheat' cannot be generic *(the wheat* must refer to a specific referent), in Albanian **gruri** 'the wheat' may be generic while **grurë** 'wheat' cannot be.

Krrut në livadhe shkon KAU. 'Humpbacked goes THE OX to the meadows.'

DHINË e vetme e ha UJKU. 'THE lone GOAT is eaten up by THE WOLF.'

Tek korret GRURI, mbillet TËRFILI, ELBI dhe MISRI, THEKRA, PAMBUKU, dhe dëm e kot s'mundohet bujku. 'Where [THE] WHEAT is reaped, [THE] CLOVER, [THE] BARLEY, and [THE] CORN, [THE] RYE, [THE] COTTON are sown, and so the farmer does not labor in vain.'

PUNA e bën NJERIUN njeri, moj vajzë. 'My girl, it is (THE) WORK that makes [THE] MAN human.'

Së shpejti në male fillon DËBORA. 'Soon in the mountains [THE] SNOWING will begin.'

As in English, there is a similarity between indefinite and definite forms of a countable noun with generic meaning. Compare in English the two generic statements *A dog is a four-footed mammal* and *The dog is a four-footed mammal.* In Albanian, however, the definite form of common nouns refers to an idealized being or abstract class while the indefinite generic is used to pick out certain distinctive traits attributable to members of the class. In that sense the indefinite generic in Albanian functions very much like an adjective. To illustrate the difference in Albanian, compare the two generic occurrences of the noun **njeri** 'man', the first definite, the second indefinite, in this sentence: **Puna e bën NJERIUN NJERI** '(The) work makes [THE] MAN (A) MAN.'

3.3 Noun Declension

The phonetic conditions that determine the appearance of the ending **-u** instead of **-i** in masculine nouns are identical with those that we find in the ending **-u** in the third person singular of the past definite in verbs; that is, following a stem that ends in back consonant **k, g, h** [or a stressed vowel (except **ó**)] as in **prek-u** 'he touched', **lag-u** 'he wetted', **njoh-u** 'he recognized', **la-u** 'he washed', **the-u** 'he broke', **pi-u** 'he drank'. Because they are phonologically conditioned, the endings **-i, -u** are viewed here as two different expressions of the same morpheme, though many Albanian grammars put them in separate declensions.

In the indefinite nominative and accusative cases, all nouns are in their citation forms, i.e., without an inflectional ending (or one may say: with a - Ø ending) on the stem. In the other three indefinite cases masculine nouns in the masculine declension take the ending **-i/-u**. In the definite they take the following endings: Nom **-i/u**, Gen **-it/-ut**, Dat **-it/-ut**, Acc **-in/-un(-në)**, Abl **-it/-ut**. Only a few nouns ending in **-á**, the basic kinship terms **vëllá** 'brother', **babá** 'father' and **xhaxhá** 'uncle (father's brother)' are exceptional in taking the **-i** forms rather than the expected **-u** forms in the singular and form the definite accusative with the ending **-në** instead of the expected **-in** or **-un**.

In dictionaries the nominative definite suffix is normally shown immediately after the citation form, with the whole form written out if any alteration of the stem results from the suffixation: **lis, -i**; **burrë, burri**; **ftua, ftoi**; **mik, -u**; **dhe, -u**; **vëllá, -i**; **zë, -ri**; **libër, libri**. Given these two forms, all the other forms of singular declension of the noun are easily derived.

Table 3.3 The Singular Declension: Masculine				
	Indefinite	Definite	Indefinite	Definite
Nom	lis 'oak'	lis-I	burrë 'man'	burr-I
Acc		lis-IN		burr-IN
Dat	lis-I	lis-IT	burr-I	burr-IT
Abl				
Gen	i lis-I	i lis-IT	i burr-I	i burr-IT
Nom	ftua 'quince'	fto-I	vëlla 'brother'	vëlla-I
Acc		fto-IN		vëlla-NË
Dat	fto-I	fto-IT	vëlla-I	vëlla-IT
Abl				
Gen	i fto-I	i fto-IT	i vëlla-I	i vëlla-IT
Nom	zë 'voice'	zër-I	libër 'book'	libr-I
Acc		zër-IN		libr-IN
Dat	zër-I	zër-IT	libr-I	libr-IT
Abl				
Gen	i zër-I	i zër-IT	i libr-I	i libr-IT
Nom	mik 'friend'	mik-U	ka 'ox'	ka-U
Acc		mik-UN		ka-UN
Dat	mik-U	mik-UT	ka-U	ka-UT
Abl				
Gen	i mik-U	i mik-UT	i ka-U	i ka-UT
Nom	dhe 'earth'	dhe-U		
Acc		dhe-UN		
Dat	dhe-U	dhe-UT		
Abl				
Gen	i dhe-U	i dhe-UT		

NOTE

Besides the dominant accusative definite forms **floririn** 'the gold' and **zërin** 'the voice' (among **-i** ending nouns) and **dheun** 'the earth', **kaun** 'the cow', **bariun** 'the shepherd' etc., (among **-u** ending nouns) the older and decreasingly used forms **florinë** 'the gold' and **zënë** 'the voice', **dhenë** 'the earth', **kanë** 'the ox', **barinë** 'the shepherd' etc., are also found. In certain idioms, however, the form with the ending **-në** is fossilized, e.g., **mori DHENË** '(the news) spread, (he) ran away ("he took THE EARTH")'.

All nouns whose plural stem has the extension **-r** (e.g., **bri** 'horn', **dre** 'deer', **dru** 'tree', **fre** 'rein', **tra** '(wood) beam') and a number of other nouns that end in a stressed vowel (such as **flori** 'gold', **gdhë** 'gnarl', **gji** 'bosom', **gju** 'knee', **kërci** 'shin', **kufi** 'border', **kushëri** 'cousin', **mulli** 'mill', **pe** 'thread', **turi** 'face') are declined like the noun **zë** 'voice', viz., the stem is extended by **-r-** in all cases except the indefinite nominative and accusative.

Following the general rule in Albanian that **-ë** always drops if followed by a suffix beginning in a vowel, a masculine noun whose citation form ends in the vowel **-ë** drops that vowel before indefinite genitive, dative, and ablative case endings and in all definite forms: **kalë** 'horse'/**kali** 'the horse', **lumë** 'river' / **lumi** 'the river', **burrë** 'man'/**burri** 'the man'.

Nouns that end in the vowel cluster **-ua** in the nominative and accusative indefinite singular, convert that cluster into **o** in all other singular case forms: **përrua** 'brook'/**përroi** 'the brook', **thua** 'fingernail'/**thoi** 'the fingernail', **ftua** 'quince'/**ftoi** 'the quince' etc. Nouns that have **-ë-** before a stem final **-r** such as **emër** 'name', **libër** 'book', and **numër** 'number' drop the **ë** before a suffix beginning in a vowel, i.e., in the indefinite genitive, dative and ablative and in all definite case forms.

Table 3.4 The Singular Declension: Feminine					
	Indefinite	Definite		Indefinite	Definite
Nom	**fushë** 'plain'	**fush-A**		**dele** 'sheep'	**del-j-A**
Acc		**fushë-N**			**dele-N**
Dat	**fush-E**	**fushë-S**	**dele-j-E**	**dele-S**
Abl				
Gen	**i fush-E**	**i fushë-S**	**i dele-j-E**	**i dele-S**
Nom	**motër** 'sister'	**motr-A**		**rrufe** 'thunderbolt'	**rrufe-j-A**
Acc		**motrë-N**			**rrufe-SË**
Dat	**motr-E**	**motrë-S**	**rrufe-j-E**	**rrufe-SË**
Abl				
Gen	**i motr-E**	**i motrë-S**	**i rrufe-j-E**	**i rrufe-SË**

As shown in Table 3.4, feminine nouns -- like all other nouns -- in the indefinite singular have no ending for nominative and accusative cases, while for the genitive, dative, and ablative cases they have the ending **-e**.

For the indefinite genitive, dative, and ablative cases and the definite nominative, nouns whose stem terminates in unstressed **-e** or in any stressed vowel except **-i**, insert the glide **j** between the stem vowel and the ending. Before the **-a** marking the nominative definite case, the unstressed stem final **-e** then drops: e.g., **dele** 'sheep'/delja, **nuse** 'bride'/**nusja**, **lule** 'flower'/**lulja**. (Nouns that end in stressed vowel **-i**, are written without **j** between the two vowels; thus, **bukurie** 'to beauty', **bukuria** 'the beauty', **shtëpie** 'to (a) house', **shtëpia** 'the house'.)

For nouns whose citation form ends in the unstressed vowel **-ë**, this vowel is deleted before a suffix beginning in a vowel, i.e., in the genitive, dative and ablative indefinite, as well as in the nominative definite but does appear when no suffix is added or when the suffix begins in a consonant, i.e., in the nominative and accusative indefinite and in all the oblique definite case forms.

In the definite declension, feminine nouns take the following endings: Nom **-a**, Gen **-së**, Dat **-së**, Acc **-në**, Abl **-së**. In accordance with the general rule, the final **-ë** drops when the vowel in the preceding syllable is unstressed, so that it appears only in case endings after noun stems that end in a stressed vowel. Nouns that have **-ë-** before a stem final **-l** or **-r** in their citation form (e.g., **vegël** 'tool', **motër** 'sister') move that **-ë- after the -l** or **-r** before an ending. As usual, if the ending begins in a vowel the **ë** then falls; e.g., **vegle, vegla, veglës, veglën, vegla-t** 'the tools'; **motre** 'sister', **motra, motrës, motrën, motra-t** 'the sisters'.

Similarly, feminine nouns with citation forms terminating in nouns with **-ull, -ur**, whose indefinite singular nominative and accusative forms have lost an earlier **-ë**, show that **-ë** before case endings that begin in a consonant:**flutur** 'butterfly'**/fluturës/fluturën, kumbull** 'plum'**/-kumbullës/kumbullën**.

Table 3.5 The Singular Declension: Neuter				
	Indefinite	Definite	Indefinite	Definite
Nom	**të folur** 'speaking'	**të folur-i-T**	**të ftohtë** 'cold'	**të ftohtë-T**
Acc		**të folur-IT**		**të ftohtë-T**
Dat	**të folur-I**	**të folur-IT**	**të ftoht-I**	**të ftoht-IT**
Abl				
Gen	**i të folur-I**	**i të folur-IT**	**i të ftoht-I**	**i të ftoht-IT**

Neuter noun forms (see Table 3.5) are distinct from masculine ones only for the definite nominative and accusative cases: neuter nouns have the ending **-t** in both cases instead of masculine **-i** and **-n**.

A stem final **-ë** (as in **të ftohtë**) drops, as always, when followed by an ending beginning in a vowel.

Neuter nouns derived from participles formed with the suffix **-ur**, insert the vowel **i** in the nominative and accusative definite between the stem and the **-t** ending: **të ngritur-I-t** 'raising', **të ecur-It** 'walking'.

Plural case forms are all constructed regularly given the plural stem. As is true for all nouns, the nominative and accusative indefinite forms have no endings.

By the general rule a word final unstressed **-ë** drops after a syllable with an unstressed vowel, so that only nouns that end in a stressed vowel, such as **rrufé** 'thunderbolts', **kalá** 'fortresses', **qe** 'oxen', and those that end in a consonant with the stress on the last syllable, as in, **miq** 'friends', **cjep** 'billy goats', **djem** 'boys', are written with a final **-ë** in the definite nominative and accusative cases, thus: **rrufetë** 'the thunderbolts', **kalatë** 'the fortresses', **qetë** 'the oxen', **miqtë** 'the friends', **cjeptë** 'the billy goats', **djemtë** 'the boys'.

After plural noun stems that terminate in two consonants (such as **peshq** 'fish', **tirq** '(type of) pants', **turq** 'Turks', **krushq** 'in-laws') or in **-ëz, -s, -ër** (such as **njerëz** 'people', **mësues** 'teachers', **tiranas** 'inhabitants of Tirana', **prindër** 'parents') **i** is inserted before the **-sh** ending in the indefinite ablative and before **-t** in the definite nominative and accusative.

NOTE

In present-day Standard Albanian, the genitive, dative, and ablative definite are being used without the final consonant **-t** that marked these forms in the past.

3.4 Noun Stem Formation

The principal derivational processes involved in the derivation of nouns are AFFIXAL DERIVATION and COMPOUNDING. Affixal derivation may be: suffixal, prefixal, or prefixal and suffixal together. Compounds may or may not have suffixes. Nouns may also be formed by other processes: CONVERSION of other parts of speech, chiefly SUBSTANTIVIZATION of adjectives; and SEMANTIC EXTENSION, by which a noun becomes so distant in meaning

Table 3.6 The Plural Declension				
	Indefinite	Definite	Indefinite	Definite
Nom	lisa 'oaks'	lisa-T	miq 'friends'	miq-TË
Acc		lisa-T		miq-TË
Dat	lisa-VE	lisa-VE	miq-VE	miq-TË
Abl	lisa-SH	lisa-VE	miq-SH	miq-VE
Gen	i lisa-VE	i lisa-VE	miq-VE	i miq-VE
Nom	peshq 'fish'	peshq-i-T	nxënës 'pupils'	nxënës-i-T
Acc		peshq-i-T		nxënës-i-T
Dat	peshq-VE	peshq-VE	nxënës-VE	nxënës-VE
Abl	peshq-i-SH	peshq-VE	nxënës-i-SH	nxënës-VE
Gen	i peshq-VE	i peshq-VE	i nxënës-VE	i nxënës-VE
Nom	rrufe 'thunderbolt'	rrufe-TË		
Acc		rrufe-TË		
Dat	rrufe-VE	rrufe-VE		
Abl	rrufe-SH	rrufe-VE		
Gen	i rrufe-VE	i rrufe-VE		

from the noun from which it has been extended that the semantic relationship between the two becomes opaque, leading to the birth of a new, homonymous lexical unit.

In productivity and extent, suffixation is the most evident means of forming nouns. Compounding and substantivization occupy second place, while prefixation, prefixation-suffixation, and conversion (other than substantivization of adjectives) are only slightly productive. Nouns formed by suffixes are: 1) agentive and autochthonic nouns, primarily indicating a human performer or an inhabitant of a place; 2) concrete inanimate nouns; 3) abstract inanimate nouns; 4) gerundial nouns and associated deverbal derivates; 5) affective nouns; and 6) nouns designating females.

3.4.1 Noun Stem Derivation with Suffixes

A number of suffixes in Albanian form stems which may serve both as adjectives and as nouns, like the English suffixes -an and -ist in the words *American, socialist*, etc., which may be used either as adjectives *He is American, He is a socialist leader*) or as nouns *(He is an American, He is a socialist)*. As in English, the meanings of the word used as an adjective and used as a noun are often obvious from the meaning of the stem and the function of the suffix, but sometimes the combination has a meaning that is not obvious from the two parts separately (e.g., English *sadist)*. Since with some stems only the noun exists *(columnist)* with others only the adjective *(suburban)*, in this use nouns are treated separately from adjectives derived with the same suffix. Thus -ak is found both in a following section on noun derivation and in a later section on adjective derivation.

After any of these noun-adjective suffixes in Albanian the feminine suffix -e may be added, forming a new feminine (and feminine plural) stem that may again serve either as noun or adjective. The agentive and autochthonic suffixes described in the following section are thus all capable of forming adjectives as well as nouns, all of which in turn may take the feminine suffix **-e**.

A. Agentive and Autochthonic Nouns

a) The agentive suffix **-(ë)s** is primarily used to form nouns designating people classified according to their activity, profession or work, although a few formations with this suffix designate people according to their origin, e.g., **ardhës** 'arrival (one who has come)', **vendës** 'native'. The suffix is added mainly to the participial stem of verbs: e.g., **mbledhës** 'gatherer', **nxënës** 'pupil', **qitës** 'marksman', **shitës** 'salesman', **shkelës** 'violator', **vjelës** 'reaper'. In nouns of the type **dëgjues** 'listener', **hetues** 'coroner', **krijues** 'creator', **mësues** 'teacher', **ndërtues** 'builder', **shkrues** 'writer' etc., the suffix **-s** has been added to the stem form ending in **-ue** (found in the Gheg participle of thematic verbs in **-o-** or **-ua-**): as in **ndërtue** 'built', **mësue** 'taught, learned', etc. Some nouns in **-ës** have been formed instead from the citation form stem. Thus **vrasës** 'killer' is formed from the verb **vras** 'I kill'.

The suffix **-(ë)s** has also been used to form the nouns **gjykatës** 'judge', **lajmës** 'messenger', **mullis** 'miller', **ndihmës** 'helper' etc., from other nouns.

b) The suffixes **-ár, -tár (-atár), -ór, -tór (-atór), -ák, -as, -án (-ján), -it, -iót** have been primarily used to form common nouns designating persons classified according to their activity or work, a characteristic feature, place of residence, or birthplace. All except **-as** carry primary stress.

The suffix **-ár** has served mainly to form agentive-profession nouns from nominal stems that indicate the object of the profession such as **argjendar** 'silversmith', **gazetar** 'journalist', **këpucar** 'shoemaker', **kopshtar** 'gardener', **lopar** 'cowheard'; agentive nouns from verbs, such as **kundërshtar** 'opponent', **(kundërshtoj)** 'I oppose'; and a good many autochthonic nouns (indicating residents of a place) from the name of the place, such as **gjakovar** 'inhabitant of Gjakovë', **kolonjar** 'inhabitant of kolonjë', **korçar** 'inhabitant of Korçë', **kosovar** 'inhabitant of Kosovë', **myzeqar** 'inhabitant of Myzeqe', **pogradecar** 'inhabitant of Pogradec'. The words **fshatar** 'villager' and **qytetar** 'city dweller' generally indicate residents of a village or a city.

The related agentive suffix **-tár** forms, from other nouns, nouns that designate agents (usualy human ones) in accordance with some activity they perform, e.g., **dëshmitar** 'witness', **lajmëtar** 'messenger', **luftëtar** 'warrior', **shkaktar** 'casual agent', **udhëtar** 'traveler', or according to their craft or specialty, e.g., **arsimtar** 'educator', **farkëtar** 'blacksmith', **gjahtar** 'hunter', **këngëtar** 'singer', **lundërtar** 'sailor', **zdrukthëtar** 'carpenter', **gjuhëtar** 'linguist', **shkrimtar** 'writer'. An expanded variant of this is the suffix **-atár** as in **peshkatar** 'fisherman', **pushkatar** 'rifleman'. The suffix **-tar** is productive.

The suffix **-ór**, which is quite productive in other ways, has only a limited use in forming animate nouns, and then mainly in the formation of autochthonic nouns, as in **malësor** 'mountaineer', **mirditor** '(inhabitant) of Mirditë', **zadrimor** '(inhabitant) of Zadrimë', and a few other nouns, such as, **dasmor** 'wedding guest', **drejtor** 'director' **këmbësor** 'infantryman'.

Only a few words have been formed with the related suffix **-tór** and its expanded variant **-atór**: e.g., **fajtor** 'guilty one', **murator** 'mason', **punëtor** 'worker', **vjershëtor** 'verse maker'; **eksplorator** 'explorer', **minator** 'miner'. This suffix has been displaced by the suffix **-tar** for some time and as a result has become non-productive.

Autochthonic nouns have also been formed with the suffix **-ák (-arák)**, as in **austriak** 'Austrian', **gramshak** 'inhabitant of Gramsh', **fierak** 'inhabitant of Fier', **durrsak** 'inhabitant of Durrës', **ulqinak** 'inhabitant of Ulqin'. The suffix is also used to form a few other nouns that characterize humans by properties of the underlying stem, which may come from a) a verb: e.g., **dështak** 'miscarriage' **(dështoj** 'I abort'); b) a noun: **pazarak** 'shopper' **(pazar** 'market'); or c) an adjective: **zezak** 'blackman' **(i zi** 'black'). It is not a productive suffix.

Other autochthonic suffixes are **-án (-ján), -as, -it, -jót (-iót)**; **dibran** 'inhabitant of Dibër', **korean** 'Korean', **pejan** 'inhabitant of Pejë', **shkodran** 'inhabitant of Shkodër', **kuksjan** 'inhabitant of Kukës', **matjan** 'inhabitant of Mat', **shaljan** 'inhabitant of Shalë';

beratas 'inhabitant of Berat', **elbasanas** 'inhabitant of Elbasan', **kavajas** 'inhabitant of Kavajë', **kurveleshas** 'inhabitant of Kurvelesh', **tiranas** 'inhabitant of Tiranë', **tropojas** 'inhabitant of Tropojë; **gjirokastrit** 'inhabitant of Gjirokastër, **libohovit** 'inhabitant of Libohovë'; **himarjot** 'inhabitant of Himarë, **kuçjot** 'inhabitant of Kuçi', **mallakastriot** 'inhabitant of Mallakastër'. The most common of these suffixes is **-as**.

c) Certain new suffixes of foreign origin have also been used in the formation of nouns of persons, such as, **-ist, -ik, -ánt, -ënt, -iér (-ér)**.

The suffix **-ist** has been productive in the Albanian language. Using feminine stems, this suffix forms nouns that refer to people according to their profession, or the work they do: **artist, centralist** 'telephone operator', **elektricist, ekskavatorist** 'steam shovel operator', **futbollist** 'football [soccer] player', **karikaturist, kitarist** 'guitarist', **makinist** 'machinist', **pianist, shahist** 'chess player', **specialist, sportist** 'sportsman, athlete', **violoncelist** 'cellist'.

The suffix **-ist** also forms nouns designating adherents (followers) of a movement or doctrine. Such nouns always correspond to abstract nouns that end in **-izëm**, e.g., **anarkist (anarkizëm), idealist (idealizëm), imperialist (imperializëm), komunist (komunizëm), leninist (leninizëm), marksist (marksizëm), materialist (materializëm),socialist (socializëm)**.

The suffix **-ist** has also been joined to stems of native Albanian words: **ballist** 'Frontist' **(ballë** 'forehead') **majtist** 'leftist', **(i majtë** 'left').

There are a few nouns formed with the suffixes **-ik, -ánt, -ënt, -iér (-ér)**: **alkoolik (alkool), nevrastenik** 'neurotic' **(nevrasteni** 'neurosis'); **diplomant** 'holder of a diploma' **(diplomë), emigrant (emigroj** 'I emigrate'), **kursant** 'a course attendant' **(kurs** 'course'), **muzikant** 'musician' **(muzikë); asistent** 'assistant' **(asistoj** 'I attend'), **referent** 'report complier, reporter' **(referoj** 'I report'); **bankier** 'banker' **bankë** 'bank'), **boksier** 'boxer' **(boks** 'box'), **guzhinier** 'cook' **(guzhinë** 'kitchen'), **karrocier** 'coachman' **(karrocë** 'coach'), **kombajner** 'combine operator' **(kombajnë** 'combine'), **magazinier** 'store worker' **(magazinë** 'shop'), **portier** 'goalie', **(portë** 'gate'). The most productive suffix in this set is **-iér (ér)**, which can even be joined to noun stems that strike Albanians today as native words, such as **karrocë** and **portë**.

NOTE

The suffix **-xhi** or its alternant **-çi** (after a stem ending in a voiceless consonant) is of Turkish origin and was formerly quite productive in forming new agentive nouns. Over a period of time it has come to be replaced by Albanian suffixes. Nevertheless, a number of words formed with this suffix are still in use, although for the most part with an archaic ring: **bojaxhi** 'painter' **(bojë** 'paint'), **fshesaxhi** 'broom maker' **(fshesë** 'broom'), **hallvaxhi** 'halva maker' **(hallvë** 'halva'), **hanxhi** 'innkeeper' **(han** 'inn'), **kallajxhi** 'tinsmith' **(kallaj** 'lead'), **qiraxhi** 'tenant' **(qira** 'rent'), **shakaxhi** 'joker' **(shaka** 'joke'), **sahatçi** 'watchmaker' **(sahat** 'watch'), **teneqexhi** 'tinsmith' **(teneqe** 'tin'), **zanatçi** 'craftsman' **(zanat** 'craft'). In some instances the suffix has acquired, or is in the process of acquiring, a pejorative connotation, as in **kalemxhi** 'scribbler' **(kalem** 'pencil').

Nouns of persons formed with foreign suffixes ending in a consonant have corresponding feminine stems with the suffix **-e** that is used: **asistente, guxhiniere** 'cook', **kursante** 'course attendant', **shahiste** 'chess player', **traktoriste** 'tractor operator'.

B. Concrete Inanimate Nouns

In the formation of concrete inanimate nouns, a number of suffixes are used in today's Albanian. Some of these serve also to form animate nouns **(-(ë)s, -or(e), -ar)** or to form abstract nouns **(-esë** and **-je)**. The suffixes that characteristicaly form concrete inanimate nouns are **-ishte, -urinë, -(ë)sirë**, and **-(ë)tirë**.

The suffix **-(ë)s** has been used to form inanimate instruments, masculine and feminine nouns (with the additional feminine suffix **-e**) that indicate tools, furniture or clothing. Thus, çelës 'key' (çel 'I open'), matës 'measure' (mat 'I measure'), ndezës 'flare' (military term, from ndez 'I ignite'); ndenjës 'seat' (ndenjur 'seated'), petës 'rolling pin' (petë 'thin layer of dough'). Although the underlying stem of such words is generally a verb or a noun, the word përparëse 'apron' is derived from the adverb përpara 'forward'.

The suffix -óre) has also been used in the formation of many inanimate feminine and a few inanimate masculine nouns designating objects according to the substance of which they are made or the function they serve. Thus we have akullore 'ice cream' (food of akull 'ice'), avullore 'steamboat' (boat with avull 'steam'), fletor 'notebook' 'book of fletë 'leaf, page'), gushore 'choker' (jewelry for gushë 'front of neck'), lakror 'vegetable pie' (pie of lakër 'cabbage'), qumështor 'custard' (food of qumësht 'milk'), qafore 'neckwear' (clothing for qafë 'neck'), qarkore 'circular, memorandum' (qark 'circle'), rregullore 'regulation' (rregull 'rule').

The related feminine forms -óre and -tóre have been used to form nouns that indicate a place associated with the object designated by an underlying nominal stem, for example, the place where it is sown, extracted, processed, or sold; or less frequently a place characterized by the referent of an underlying verbal or adjectival stem: elbore 'barley field' (a field that has been sown with elb 'barley'), misërore 'corn field' (misër 'corn'), mëngjesore 'morning service' (mëngjes 'morning'), gurore 'quarry' (gur 'stone'), kripore 'salt-making enterprise' (kripë 'salt'), bulmetore 'dairy store' (bulmet 'dairy'), ëmbëltore 'candy store' (të ëmbla 'sweets'), gjelltore 'eating place' (gjellë 'food'), fjetore 'dormitory' (fjetje 'sleep').

In some words designating places, the suffix -óre usually has a diminutive value: bregore 'knoll' (breg 'hill'), fushore 'small plain' (fushë 'plain'), gropore 'basin, gorge' (gropë 'hole'), lugore 'small valley' (lug 'duct').

Inanimate nouns with the suffix -ar are few: ditar 'diary' (ditë 'day'), koshar 'silo' (kosh 'basket'), vjetar 'annual' (vjet 'year') and, with the feminine suffix -e, dritare 'window' (dritë 'light').

The suffix -esë has been used to form from verb stems of the first conjugation concrete inanimate nouns designating objects created by or used instrumentally for the action expressed by the underlying verb: fërgesë 'frier' (fërgoj 'I fry'), fshesë 'broom' (fshij 'I sweep'), kullesë 'strainer' (kulloj 'I strain'), mbulesë 'lid' (mbuloj 'I cover'), ndërtesë 'building' (ndërtoj 'I build'), shtesë 'addition' (shtoj 'I add'), shtresë 'layer' (shtroj 'I lay out'), shkresë 'writing' (shkruaj 'I write'), urdhëresë 'order' (urdhëroj 'I order').

The suffix -je forms a few feminine nouns designating sets of concrete objects, for the most part objects of clothing: këmbje 'embroidered cuffs of a type of bloomers' (këmbë 'foot'), sheshje 'footware, slippers' (shesh 'flat'), mbathje 'underwear' (mbath 'put on clothes on lower part of the body'), veshje 'clothing' (vesh 'I clothe'). However, as will be seen below, the -je suffix serves mainly to form abstract nouns.

From feminine noun stems, the suffix -ishte and its variant -ishtë have formed words that generally indicate the place where the thing designated by the derivational stem is to be found in quantity: fidanishte 'nursery' (fidan 'sapling'), lulishte 'flower garden, park' (lule 'flower'), misërishte 'corn field' (misër 'corn'), pemishte 'orchard' (pemë 'fruit'), plehrishte 'manure heap' (plehëra 'manure'), ranishte 'sandy place' (ranë 'sand'), thekërishte 'rye field' (thekër 'rye'), ahishte 'beech grove' (as 'beech'), gurishtë 'stony place' (gurë 'stones'), lajthishtë 'hazelnut grove' (lajthi 'hazel nut'), ullishtë 'olive orchard' (ulli 'olive'), zallishtë 'rock-strewn land' (zall 'rock-strewn land'). Some nouns formed with this suffix derive from verb or adjective stems, and indicate places connoted by the derivational stem, as punishte 'workshop' (punoj 'I work'), lirishte 'glade' (i lirë 'free').

NOTE

The dialectal suffix -ájë, (-nájë) is used with the same meaning as that of the suffix -ishte, e.g., dushkajë 'oak forest' (dushk 'oak'), lismajë 'oak forest' lis 'oak'). This suffix has begun to enter the standard language as well, as in akullnajë 'glacier' (akull 'ice').

A few place nouns whose meaning reflects a characteristic of the derivational stem have been formed with the suffix **-inë**: **çmendinë** 'insane asylum' (**çmend** 'drive crazy'), **kthinë** 'room' (**kthej** 'I turn'), **luginë** 'valley' (**lug** 'duct'), **rrafshinë** 'flat country' (**rrafsh** 'level'), **rrethina-t** 'environs' (**rreth** 'circle'). This is a dialectal suffix that has found its way into the standard language as well.

Feminine nouns that are used only in the plural with a collective meaning are formed with the suffixes **-ishte, -urin (a)**. Formations with the suffix **-ishte** are few, e.g., **barishte-t** 'herbs', **farishte-t** 'seeds'. More productive is the suffix **-urin (a)** which forms nouns that usually indicate a quantity of different types of a thing, or things of the same substance, as in **degurina** 'brush (wood)' (**degë** 'branch'), **halurina** 'pins, needles' (**halë** 'pin, needle'), **hekurina** 'scrap iron' (**hekur** 'iron'), **mbeturina** 'leftovers' (**mbetur** 'left'), **pemurina** 'fruits' (**pemë** 'fruit'), **plaçkurina** 'goods, belongings' (**plaçkë** 'thing'), **qelqurina** 'glassware' (utensils made of **qelq** 'glass'), **shpesurina** 'fowl' (**shpes** 'bird'). Note that if the stem already ends in **-ur**, only **-inë** is added: **hekurinë, mbeturinë**.

With the suffix **-(ë)sirë**, nouns characterized by a particular feature have been formed from adjectival stems expressing that feature: **ëmbëlsirë** 'dessert, sweet' (**i ëmbël** 'sweet'), **kalbësirë** 'rottenness' (**i kalbur** 'rotten'), **vjetërsirë** 'antique' (**i vjetër** 'old'). The noun **vogëlsira-t** 'bric-a-brac' is used mainly in the plural.

NOTES

1. A small number of nouns designating inanimate objects have been formed from the no longer productive suffixes **-áç(e), -ashkë, -ác**: **gjembaç** 'thistle' (**gjemb** 'thorn'), **lugaç** 'spout adz' (**lugë** 'spoon'), **furkaçe** 'forked stick' (**furkë** 'spindle'), **ngarkaçe** 'forked stick for loading' (**ngarkoj** 'I load'); **dorashkë** 'glove' (**dorë** 'hand'), **gjurmashkë** 'foot sock' (**gjurmë** 'footstep'); **thumbac** 'tip of a goad' (**thumb** 'sting'), **kupac** 'wooden receptacle' (**kupë** 'glass').

2. In collective plural nouns like **argjende** 'silverware', **argjend** 'silver, **bakëre** 'copperware', **bakër** 'copper', the plural suffix **-e** has in effect taken on a derivational word-forming function, since the collective meaning is not a normal function of the plural suffix.

Less frequent use has been made of the suffix **-(ë)sirë** or **-(ë)tirë** in forming nouns designating places. Thus, **shkretëtirë** 'desert' (**i shkretë** 'desolate'), **zbrazëtirë** 'emptiness' (**zbraz** 'I empty', **zbrazur** 'empty'), **hapësirë** 'open air, space' (**i hapur** 'open').

C. Abstract Nouns

The number of abstract nouns formed by means of suffixes has increased considerably in modern times. This development reflects the modernization of Albanian society, and the need to express abstract concepts in the sphere of politics, science, culture, art, administration, industry, etc. Nouns in this category are used increasingly in the literature in all these spheres. With the passage of time, noun formation by suffix has nearly replaced substantivization of adjectives, which was the most productive method of the abstract noun formation in written Albanian up to the beginning of the Albanian National Awakening in the nineteenth century.

A relatively large number of suffixes is used in the formation of abstract nouns, but not all of them are very productive.

C.1 Feminine Nouns Ending in **i**

Feminine nouns that indicate an abstract trait or quality with the suffixes **-i, -(ë)si, -(ë)ri** are formed--mainly from adjectives and nouns, and less often from verbs, adverbs and pronouns. The suffix **-i** is added to adjective stems (the majority of which are adjectives derived from participles ending in **-ur**) that end with the consonant **-r** as well as to noun stems with the same termination. Thus, **bukuri** 'beauty' (**i bukur** 'beautiful'), **dituri** 'knowledge' (**i ditur** 'learned'), **lumturi** 'happiness' (**i lumtur** 'happy'), **njohuri** 'knowledge' (**i njohur** 'known'), **pasuri** 'wealth' (**i pasur** 'rich'), **varfëri** 'poverty' (**i varfër** 'poor'), **verbëri** 'blindness' (**i verbër** 'blind'), **dhelpëri** 'slyness' (**dhelpër** 'fox'), **kusari** 'banditry' (**kusar** 'bandit'), **mjeshtëri** 'craftsmanship' (**mjeshtër** 'craft'). Formations from adjective and verb stems with other terminations are less numerous: **lagështi** 'dampness' (**i lagësht** 'damp'), **ligështi** 'weakness' (**i ligësht** 'frail'), **liri** 'liberty' (**i lirë** 'free'), **plogështi** 'sluggishness' (**i plogësht** 'sluggish'), **pabesi** 'faithlessness' (**i pabesë** 'faithless'), **kundërsht** 'opposition' (**kundërshtoj** 'I oppose'), **lakmi** 'greed' (**lakmoj** 'I am greedy for'), **dredhi** 'twisting' (**dredh** 'I twist'). The words **befasi** 'suddenness' and **tepri** 'excess' are formed respectively from the adverbs **befas** 'suddenly' and **tepër** 'too much'.

The suffix **-(ë)si** is added mainly to the stems of adjectives that end in the unstressed vowel **-ë** or the unstressed sequences **-ër** or **-ël**, as well as certain adjectives and nouns with final accented syllables ending in a consonant other than **-r**: **ëmbëlsi** 'sweet' (**i ëmbël** 'sweet'), **fatbardhësi** 'good fortune' (**fatbardhë** 'lucky'), **fatkeqësi** 'misfortune' (**fatkeq** 'unfortunate'), **gjakftohtësi** 'composure' (**gjakftohtë** 'composed'), **ligësi** 'evil' (**i lig** 'evil'), **madhësi** 'bigness' (**i madh** 'big'), **mbarësi** 'prosperity' (**i mbarë** 'prosperous'), **gjatësi** 'tallness, length' (**i gjatë** 'tall, long'), **nxehtësi** 'heat' (**i nxehtë** 'hot'), **poshtërsi** 'meanness' (**i poshtër** 'mean'), **rëndësi** 'importance' (**i rëndë** 'important'), **vjetërsi** 'antique' (**i vjetër** 'old'), **zemërgjerësi** 'generosity' (**zemërgjerë** 'generous'), **miqësi** 'friendship' (from the plural of the noun **mik** 'friend'), **armiqësi** 'enmity' (from the plural of the noun **armik** 'enemy'), **vazhdimësi** 'continuity' (**vazhdim** 'continuity').

A small number of words are formed from verb and adverb stems by the suffix **-(ë)si**: **mundësi** 'possibility' (**mund** 'can'), **ngutësi** 'haste' (**ngutem** 'I hurry'), **kënaqësi** 'pleasure' (**kënaq** 'I please'), **bashkësi** 'community' (**bashkë** 'together'), **largësi** 'distance' (**larg** 'far'). The words **cilësi** 'quality' and **sasi** 'quantity' are formed respectively from the interrogative pronouns **cili** 'who' and **sa** 'how much'.

NOTE

In the words **dobësi** 'weakness' (**i dobët** 'weak'), **përzemërsi** 'cordiality' (**i përzemërt** 'cordial'), **pjerrësi** 'slope' (**i pjerrët** 'sloping', **dendës** 'density' (**i dendur** 'dense') the terminal **-t** or **-ur** of the derivational stem have dropped.

For some time the suffix **-(ë)ri** was supplanted in the formation of abstract nouns from adjective and noun stems by the synonymous suffix **-(ë)si**. Only a few older words like **besnikëri** 'loyalty' (**besnik** 'loyal'), **djalëri** 'youth' (**djalë** 'boy'), **fisnikëri** 'courtesy' (**fisnik** 'courteous'), **gjallëri** 'liveliness' (**i gjallë** 'lively'), **nusëri** 'bridehood' (**nuse** 'bride'), **pleqëri** 'old age' (from the plural of the noun **plak** 'old man'), **skllavëri** 'slavery' (**skllav** 'slave'), **trimëri** 'bravery' (**trim** 'brave'), **vajzëri** 'girlhood' (**vajzë** 'girl') still exhibited the **-(ë)ri** suffix. Recently, however, this suffix has come back to life, and so now we have new nouns from adjectives ending in the suffix **-shëm**, as in **domosdoshmëri** 'indispensability' (**i domosdoshëm** 'indispensable'), **ligjshmëri** 'legitimacy' (**i ligjshëm** 'legitimate'), **ndershmëri** 'honor' (**i ndershëm** 'honorable'), **papajtueshmëri** 'irreconcilability' (**i papajtueshëm** 'irreconcilable'), **partishmëri** 'partisanship' (**i partishëm** 'partisan'), **pavdekshmëri** 'deathlessness' (**i pavdekshëm** 'deathless'), etc. In certain formations, like **pjellshmëri** 'fertility' and **gatishmëri** 'readiness', the derivational suffix is actually **-shmëri**, which has emerged on the analogy of words like those above.

NOTE

Doublets formed by the suffixes **-i**, **-ri**, and **-si** from the same stem may have quite different meanings: **liri** 'freedom' and **lirësi** 'cheapness', **madhësi** 'bigness' but **madhëri** 'majesty', **pleqësi** 'council of elers' but **pleqëri** 'old age'.

The suffixes **-i**, **-(ë)ri** and **-(ë)si** are also used to form collective nouns. The same word often has both a collective and an abstract sense, depending on the context. Among these suffixes the most productive as a collective is the suffix **-(ë)si** (see section 3.2.1 B.2 on collectives).

NOTES

1. The suffixes **-(ë)zi** and especially **-(ë)sirë** are also used with the same meaning as the suffixes above: **djallëzi** 'deviltry' (**djall** 'devil'), **marrëzi** 'madness' (**i marrë** 'mad, taken'), **errësirë** 'darkness' (**i errët** 'dark'), **lagësirë** 'wetness' (**i lagët** 'wet'), **shtrenjtësirë** 'expensiveness' (**i shtrenjtë** 'expensive'), **thatësirë** 'drought' (**i thatë** 'dry'), **vranësirë** 'cloudiness' (**i vranët** 'cloudy') etc.

2. Other words with the suffix **-i** designate both a trade (or craft) and the place where the people are engaged in that trade: **argjendari** 'silversmithy', **rrobaqepësi** 'clothing business', **zdrukthari** 'carpentry (shop)'.

C.2 Abstract Nouns with Foreign Suffixes

c) Certain foreign suffixes like **-llék, -izëm, -ázh, -úrë** have been used in the formation of abstract nouns in Albanian.

The Turkish suffix **-llék** was used to form nouns--from Turkish stems and occasionally some others--that indicate an abstract trait or quality, usually with a pejorative stylistic nuance. Thus, **avukatllëk** 'lawyering' (**avukat** 'lawyer'), **batakçillëk** 'swindling' (**batakçi** 'swindler'), **budallallëk** 'foolishness' (**budalla** 'fool'), **fodullëk** 'conceit' (**fodull** 'conceited person'), **fukarallëk** 'poverty' (**fukara** 'poor person'), **hajdutllëk** 'banditry' (**hajdut** 'bandit'), **maskarallëk** 'knavery' (**maskara** 'knave'). These formations now belong mostly to the spoken language, and becoming less and less common in standard writing. In the standard language a considerable number of these nouns have been replaced by new formations with native Albanian suffixes or by other Albanian words. Thus **budallallëk** has been replaced by **marrëzi, fodullëk** by **kryelartësi, hajdutllëk** by **kusari** or **vjedhje**, etc.

The suffix **-izëm**, originally entered the language through borrowed words like **automobilizëm** 'automobilism', **burokratizëm** 'bureaucratism', **fanatizëm** 'fanaticism', **feudalizëm** 'feudalism', **kapitalizëm** 'capitalism', **komunizëm, leninizëm, marksizëm, revizionizëm, socializëm** is also responsible for the new formation of derivative words from stems already in Albanian: **djathtizëm** 'rightism', **majtizëm** 'leftism', **shkollarizëm** 'scholasticism', **zyrtarizëm** 'bureaucracy ("officism")'.

Some stems do not exist in Albanian apart from their occurrence in formations with **-ist** and **-izëm**: **optimizëm / optimist, pesimizëm / pesimist, purizëm/purist, revizionizëm / revizionist, shovinizëm / shovinist, turizëm / turist**.

The suffix **-azh** is only weakly productive, and appears only in words designating actions or abstract qualities, as in **grupazh** 'grouping' (**grup** 'group'), **montazh** 'montage' (**montoj** 'I mount'), **pilotazh** 'piloting' (**pilot** 'pilot'), **sabotazh** (**sabotoj** 'I sabotage'), **spiunazh** 'espionage' (**spiun** 'spy'), **tonazh** 'tonnage' (**ton** 'ton').

Likewise, the suffix **-urë** appears in only a few nouns, as in **agjenturë** 'agency' (**agjent** 'agent'), **arkitekturë** (**arkitekt**), **korekturë** 'proofreading' (**korektor** 'proofreader'), **skulpturë** (**skulptor**).

In certain words of foreign origin we can identify the suffix **-ikë** which indicates a field of learning or activity, as in, **atletikë** 'athletics', **estetikë** 'esthetics', **metodikë** 'methodology', **metrikë** 'metrics'.

C.3 Gerundial Nouns

Gerundial nouns designating actions or states based on stems are formed by the suffixes **-im, -je, -esë, -atë, -imë, -më**. The resultant nouns sometimes develop concrete senses which may in time overshadow or even replace the abstract meaning of the gerundial (compare English *seeing, building, clothing*).

The synonymous suffixes **-im** and **-je** are quite productive in forming gerundial nouns, particularly in literary language; in general, which of the two is used depends on the form of the participle of the underlying verb: **-im** is generally used for verbs whose participle ends in **-uar** and for some whose participle ends in **-yer**; **-je** if the participle has some other form.

The suffix **-im** is joined to a stem formed by subtracting the final **-uar** or **yer** of the participle. The resulting masculine noun designates the action denoted by the verb, usually translatable into English as a gerund ending in *-ing*. Since the gerundial translation (English verb + *-ing*) can be assumed to be available for any noun ending in **-im** or **-je**, there is no need to include it in the glosses after the first few examples below: **besim** 'belief, believing' (**besuar** 'believed'), **dorëzim** 'surrender, surrendering' (**dorëzuar** 'handed over'), **drejtim** 'direction, directing' (**drejtuar** 'directed'), **fillim** 'start, beginning' (**filluar** 'begun'), **gjykim** 'judgement' (**gjykuar** 'judged'), **këmbim** 'exchange' (**këmbyer** 'exchanged'), **kërcim** 'dancing' (**kërcyer** 'danced'), **pëlqim** 'approval' (**pëlqyer** 'approved'), **pranim** 'acceptance' (**pranuar** 'accepted'), **rrëfim** 'tale' (**rrëfyer** 'related'), **rrëmbim** 'seizure' (**rrëmbyer** 'seized'), **shikim** 'look' (**shikuar** 'looked'), **shkatërrim** 'destruction' (**shkatërruar** 'destroyed'). In a few words, the suffix **-im** has been added to a verb whose participle ends in a consonant plus **-osur**, treated as if it ended in that consonant plus **-uar**: **çarmatim** 'disarmament' (**çarmatos** 'I disarm'), **varrim** 'burial' (**varros** 'I bury'), **vendim** 'decision' (**vendos** 'I decide'). It has even been added to a noun stem, as in **terracim** 'terracing' (**terracë** 'terrace') implying a non-existent, but possible verb **terracuar** 'terraced'.

Words formed with the suffix **-im** may also indicate the result of an action, as in **fitim** 'gain' (**fituar** 'gained'), **gatim** 'cooking' (**gatuar** 'cooked'), **shkrim** 'writing' (**shkruar** 'written'), **trashëgim** 'inheritance' (**trashëguar** 'inherited'), **tregim** 'story' (**treguar** 'told'), **vërtetim** 'confirmation' (**vërtetuar** 'confirmed'), etc.

Some nouns with the suffix **-im**, as in **burim** 'source' (**buruar** 'sprung up'), **strehim** 'shelter' (**strehuar** 'sheltered'), have even acquired a concrete meaning designating a place suggested by the action of the verb.

The suffix **-je** forms feminine gerundial nouns designating the action denoted by the verb stem to which it is joined. For verbs whose participle ends in **-ur** or **-uajtur**, that ending is subtracted to form the stem to which **-je** is attached. For all other verbs (other than those which take **-im**), **-je** is added directly to the participle. If the participle ends in **-ë** the ë drops; if the resultant stem ends in **-n**, **-je** takes the form **-ie**. Verbs whose participle ends in **-yer** and whose citation form has **-yej** rather than **-ej**, take the suffix **-je** rather than **-im**. **veshje** 'dressing' (**veshur** 'clothed'), **lindje** 'birth' (**lindur** 'born'), **marrje** 'taking' (**marrë** 'taken'), **njohje** 'recognition' (**njohur** 'recognized'), **përkrahje** 'support' (**përkrahur** 'supported'), **zierje** 'boiling' (**zier** 'boiled'), **lyerje** 'painting' (**lyer** 'painted', **lyej** 'I paint'), **thyerje** 'breakage' (**thyer** 'broken', **thyej** 'I break'), **fshirje** 'sweeping' (**fshirë** 'swept'), **ngrirje** 'freezing' (**ngrirë** 'frozen'), **tharje** 'drying' (**tharë** 'dry'), **qarje** 'complaint' (**qarë** 'complained'), **hyrje** 'entrance' (**hyrë** 'entered'), **dhënie** 'giving' (**dhënë** 'given'), **rënie** 'falling' (**rënë** 'fallen'), **mbrojtje** 'defence' (**mbrojtur** 'defended'), **ruajtje** 'keeping' (**ruajtur** 'kept'), **vuajtje** 'suffering' (**vuajtur** 'suffered'), **blerje** 'purchase' (**blerë** 'brought'), **gjetje** 'finding' (**gjetur** 'found').

With the suffix **-je**, too, some nouns have come to designate the result of an action as well as, or instead of, the gerundial meaning: **humbje** 'loss' (**humbur** 'lost'), **mbetje** 'remnant' (**mbetur** 'left'), **shfaqje** 'presentation' (**shfaqur** 'presented'), **shkrirje** 'melting' (**shkrirë** 'melted').

Since **-je** is used for so many different participial types, it forms gerundial nouns for a more diverse set of verbs than does **-im**. On the other hand, since the class of verbs with citation forms ending in **-oj** is the largest and most productive class of verbs in Albanian and since--with the exception of some older forms with participles in **-uajtur** or **-ojtur**--these all have participles in **-uar**, the majority of gerundial nouns in Albanian end in **-im**.

The great expansion in use of these gerundial nouns in **-je** and **-im** corresponds to the reduction in the use of neuter substantivizing participial forms like **të folurit** 'speaking' which now have a somewhat archaic character. Nevertheless, when a stronger sense of verb process in the noun is desired, the latter construction is still required: compare **të folurit** 'speaking' with **folje** 'verb', **të menduarit** 'thinking' with **mendim** 'thought', **të shkruarit** 'writing' with **shkrim** 'script'.

In the formation of action nouns, use has also been made of the weakly productive **-ësë** and the no longer productive **-átë, -më, -imë** suffixes. Nouns formed with these suffixes are all feminine.

The suffix **-ësë**, like the suffix **-im**, is added mainly to verbs whose citation forms end in **-oj**, as in **jetesë** 'living' (**jetoj** 'I live'), **harresë** 'forgetfulness' (**harroj** 'I forget'), **martesë** 'marriage' (**martoj** 'I marry'), **mungesë** 'absence' (**mungoj** 'I am absent'), **përtesë** 'laziness' (**përtoj** 'I am lazy'). The majority of the nouns formed with this suffix now designate a concrete resultant of the action or process specified by the verb: **krijesë** 'creature' (**krijoj** 'I create'), **ndërtesë** 'building' (**ndërtoj** 'I erect'), **ngarkesë** 'cargo, load' (**ngarkoj** 'I load'), **shartesë** '(tree) graft' (**shartoj** 'I graft'), **shtesë** 'addition' (**shtoj** 'I add'). However, other nouns with the suffix may designate things that perform the function of the verb: **fshesë** 'broom' (**fshij** 'I sweep'), **kullesë** 'strainer' (**kulloj** 'I strain'), **mbulesë** 'lid' (**mbuloj** 'I close').

Differences in meaning between nouns formed with the suffix **-im** and those formed with the suffix **-ësë** are most evident in doublets derived from the same verb: nouns formed with **-ësë** designating a concrete result of the activity, those with **-im** the activity itself. Thus, **ankim** 'complaint, complaining' / **ankesë** 'type of fried food', **krijim** 'creation, creating' / **krijesë** 'creature', **kullim** 'straining' / **kullesë** 'strainer', **ngatërrim** 'disarrangement, confusing' / **ngatërresë** 'mess, tumult', **shartim** 'grafting' / **shartesë** 'graft', etc. For some derivative nouns with the suffix **-ësë** there is no corresponding formation with **-im**; instead the neuter substantivized participle is used: **jetesë** 'livelihood, living' / **të jetuarit** 'living', **mungesë** 'shortage, absence' / **të munguarit** 'lacking, missing'. In these instances and in some others (e.g., the psychological terms **harresë** 'forgetfulness' and **kujtesë** 'memory'), where the word has become a permanent and regular lexical term rather than an *ad hoc* derivation, the original abstract meaning has persisted.

The suffix **-átë** appears in only a few words, some designating the result of an action expressed by the verb stem: **lëngatë** 'suffering' (**lëngoj** 'I suffer'), **lëvdatë** 'praise' (**lëvdoj** 'I praise'), **ligjëratë** 'lecture' (**ligjëroj** 'I speak'), **shtrëngatë** 'hurricane' (**shtrëngoj** 'I squeeze'), **uratë** 'blessing' (**uroj** 'I bless'), **zemëratë** 'anger' (**zemëroj** 'I anger'). Alongside these there have developed formations with the suffix **-im**, as in **lëngatë** / **lëngim**, **zemëratë** / **zemërim**, which have rendered archaic the formations with the suffix **-átë**.

The words **ligjërim** 'speech', **shtrëngim** 'pressure', **urim** 'expression of good will', differ in meaning from the corresponding words formed from the same verb with the suffix **-atë** (**ligjëratë** 'lecture', **shtrëngatë** 'hurricane', **uratë** 'blessing'): the word with **-im** designating the action itself, the one with **-atë** designating a result of that action.

Certain foreign nouns which in English end in *-ation* have taken the form **-átë** instead in Albanian and are used with a more or less concrete meaning: **administratë, konsideratë, organizatë, situatë**. Corresponding to the nouns **administratë** and **organizatë** which designate entities, the words **administrim** 'administration, administering' (**administroj** 'I administer'), **organizim** 'organization, organizing' (**organizoj** 'I organize') designate the action of the verbs from which they are derived.

The suffix **-më / -imë** has been used to form action nouns from verbs. The form **-më** is usually added to the past definite stem of certain verbs: **britmë** 'shout' (**bërtas** 'I shout', **brita** 'I shouted'), **krismë** 'crack' (**kërcas** 'I crack', **krisa** 'I cracked'), **klithmë** 'scream' (**këlthas** 'I scream', **klitha** 'I screamed'). For certain other verbs it is added to the imperative stem, as in **dridhmë** 'shiver' (**dridh** 'shiver!'), **ndihmë** 'help' (**ndih** 'help!'). The suffix **-më** also forms action nouns from certain verbs whose citation forms end in **-ij**, e.g., **angullimë** 'howl' (**angullij** 'I howl'), **blegërimë** 'bleat' (**blegërij** 'I bleat'), **bubullimë** 'thunder' (**bubullij** 'I thunder'), **hingëllimë** 'neigh' (**hingëllij** 'I neigh'), **pipëtimë** 'whisper' (**pipëtij** 'I blow lightly, I breathe'), **psherëtimë** 'sigh' (**psherëtij** 'I sigh'), **sokëllimë** 'yell' (**sokëllij** 'I yell'), **ulurimë** 'wail' (**ulurij** 'I wail'), **vetëtimë** 'lightning' (**vetëtij** 'I shine'). Derivations with the form **-imë** are also found in a very few nouns that derive from verbs ending in **-ój** and **-éj**: **gurgullimë** 'gurgling' (**gurgulloj** 'I gurgle'), **xixëllimë** 'twinkling' (**xixëlloj** 'I twinkle'), **vërshëllimë** 'whistling' (**vërshëllej** 'I whistle').

D. Diminutives and Pejoratives

Certain suffixes affect the emotional and expressive nuances of the stem to which they are attached, without changing their basic lexical meaning. Nouns so formed may have endearing and diminutive, diminutive only, or pejorative nuances.

The most common suffixes used to convey endearment and smallness are **-th** and **-z(ë)**. The suffix **-th** creates diminutive masculine nouns of endearment for masculine noun stems, **-zë** the same for feminine which may then take on ironic, even pejorative meanings: **birth** 'wee son, carbuncle', **djalëth** '(sweet, little) boy', **ishullth** 'islet', **kryeth** '(nice, little) head', **qytetth** '(nice, little) city', **vëllimth** (pleasant, little) volume', **zëth** '(quiet, little) voice', **zogth** 'chick'; **arkëz** '(nice, little) box', **copëz** '(tiny) piece', **folezë** ('warm, little) nest', **foshnjëz** '(sweet, little) child', **lajthizë** '(nice, little) hazelnut', **lulez** '(pretty, little) flower', **portëz** '(inviting, little) gate', **shtëpizë** 'bungalow', **zogëz** '(pretty, little) bird', etc. These two suffixes are especially common in poetic language.

NOTES

1. Certain words with these suffixes have now acquired a lexical meaning quite different from that of the underlying stem: **fikth** 'unripe fig, Adam's apple' (**fik** 'fig'), **këmbëz** 'trigger' (**këmbë** 'foot'), **njerith** 'uvula' (**njeri** 'person'), **qiellzë** 'palate' (**qiell** 'sky'), **zokth** 'fleshy part of the arm' (**zog** 'bird'), etc.

2. Other endearing, diminutive suffixes are less frequently used: **-úsh**, found in words such as, **babush** 'father', **kalush** 'pony', **lepurush** 'female rabbit, doe of hare', **plakush** 'old man', **vogëlush** 'little one'; **-úshkë**, as in **fletushkë** 'leaflet', **llambushkë** 'electric bulb'; **qepushkë** 'seedling onion'; and **-icë**, as in **kokërdhicë** 'small object', **rrugicë** 'alley'.

3. The suffixes **-kë** and **içkë** are limited to particular dialects in colloquial speech. Examples are **çupkë** 'girl', **guriçkë** 'pebble', **deriçkë** 'backdoor', **koriçkë** 'grove'. The suffixes of endearment **-ko** and **-çe**, which are added to masculine nouns, have a restricted dialectal character: **dajko** 'uncle' (**dajë**), **vëllako** 'brother' (**vëlla**); **birçe** 'son' (**bir**), **nipçe** 'nephew' (**nip**).

Suffixes that serve to form nouns with a pejorative meaning are **-ac, -acak, -acuk**, as well as the less common **-alaq, -aluq, -alec, -aman, -arash, -avec**, and certain others that are even more rare. These nouns have been converted into unarticulated pejorative adjectives.

With the suffixes **-ác, -acák** pejorative nouns are formed out of other nouns: **burrac** 'small, homely man', (**burrë** 'man'), **dorac** 'cripple, one-armed' (**dorë** 'hand'); **burracak** 'coward' (**burrë** 'man'), **frikacak** 'coward' (**frikë** 'fear'), **morracak** 'lice-infested one' (**morr** 'louse'), **rrenacak** 'liar' (**rrenë** 'lie'). It also forms nouns from verbs, as in **ngordhacak** 'emaciated one' (**ngordh** 'die'), **rjepacak** 'tattered one' (**rjep** 'to skin'), **vjedhacak** 'thief' (**vjedh** 'steal'). Sometimes **-acák** alternates with the suffix **-acúk**, as in **rjepacuk, verdhacuk** 'pallid one'.

The other pejorative suffixes are less frequently used: we find **-aláq** in words like **ngordhalaq** 'emaciated one', **shkurtalaq** 'shorty'; **-alúq** in **shtrembaluq** 'twisted, one, crooked', **trashaluq** 'fatso'; **-aléc** in **barkalec** 'big-bellied one'; **-amán** in **çalaman** 'lame one', **frikaman** 'coward', **qaraman** 'crybaby'; **-arásh** in **mëngjarash** 'lefty'; **-avéc** in **burravec** 'coward', **grindavec** 'quarrelsome one', **qullavec** 'all wet', **qurravec** 'sniveler'.

E. Nouns with Feminizing Suffixes

Nouns designating females have been formed by adding the feminine suffix **-e** to a corresponding masculine stem that designate males. Thus **mjeke** is a female doctor, while **mjek** is a male doctor; **gjyshe** 'grandmother' corresponds to **gjysh** 'grandfather'; and so on. In addition, for any masculine noun (except for those with special feminine counterparts) formed by adding a suffix ending in a consonant (see following sections) and designating a male, a feminine noun designating a female may be formed by adding the additional feminine suffix **-e**:

The most common ending found on simple feminine noun stems in Albanian is **-ë**. Only in a few cases does this **-ë** seem to be a derivational morpheme: **plakë** 'old woman' (**plak** 'old man'), **pjellë** 'offspring' (**pjell** 'give birth'). In contrast, the suffix **-e** very often appears as a derivational suffix in forming animate feminine nouns: **gjykatës / gjykatëse** 'judge (m.&f.)', **nxënës / nxënëse** 'pupil (m.&f.), **malësor / malësore** 'mountaineer (m.&f.)', **arkëtar / arkëtare** 'treasurer (m.&f.)'. For nouns designating inanimate things, the presence of **-e** after certain suffixes, such as **-ës(e)** seems arbitrary **ndezës** 'flare' (**ndez** 'I ignite'), but **përparëse** 'apron' (**përpara** 'forward').

The suffix **-éshë** is used to form nouns designating females from masculine stems in **-xhi** designating males; the **-i** drops before the feminine suffix: **hanxhi / hanxhésë** 'innkeeper', **qiraxhi / qiraxhésë** 'renter'.

3.4.2 Noun Stem Derivation with Prefixes

Prefixal derivation of nouns is only slightly productive. There are over twenty prefixes, but only a few of them have become productive. Some of these prefixes are originally adverbs used as prepositions.

The most productive prefix is **mos-**, which serves principally to form antonyms of gerundial nouns: **mosbesim** 'mistrust', **mosbindje** 'disobedience', **mosmarrëveshje** 'disagreement', **mospajtim** 'incompatibility', **mospëlqim** 'disapproval', **mospërfillje** 'disregard', **mosplotësim** 'incompletion', **mosveprim** 'inaction'. Synonymous with the prefix **mos-**, but of more limited usage, is the prefix **pa-**, especially for abstract nouns designating abstract qualities, such as **pabarazi** 'inequality', **paburrëri** 'unmanliness', **padije** 'ignorance', **pakënaqësi** 'displeasure', **pasiguri** 'insecurity'. In the word **padurim** 'impatience', the prefix has been attached to a gerundial noun.

Prefixes derived from other prepositions have a more limited use, and are found mostly in literary language, e.g., **nën-** 'sub-, under', in **nëntokë** 'underground', **nënkryetar** 'vice president', **nëndrejtor** 'vice director', **nënoficer** 'non-commissioned officer'; **mbi-** 'on, over' in **mbishkrim** 'inscription', **mbiemër** 'adjective', **mbivlerë** 'surplus value', **mbishtresë** 'overlay'; **për-** 'trans-, through', in **përvojë** 'experience', **përvjetor** 'anniversary', **përmasë** 'dimension'; **ndaj-** 'toward' in **ndajshtim** 'apposition', **ndajfolje** 'adverb'; **prej-** 'from' in **prejardhje** 'derivation'.

The prefix **stër-** is primarily attached to certain nouns of kinship to indicate an increased generational spread, as in **stërgjysh** 'great grandfather, forefather', (**gjysh** 'grandfather') **stërnip** 'great grandson or grand nephew' (**nip** 'grandson, nephew'), **stërmbesë** 'great granddaughter or grand niece ', (**mbesë** 'granddaughter, niece'), but it appears in other nouns as well, e.g., **stërdhëmb** 'crooked tooth', (**dhëmb** 'tooth'), **stërqokë** 'jackdaw' (**qokë** 'brood hen').

NOTES

1. Some words exhibit a foreign prefix before a stem that is an independent word in Albanian: **ultra-** in **ultratingull** 'ultra sound', **a-** in **asimetri** 'asymmetry', **anti-** in **antifashist, super-** in **superprodhim** 'super production', **superstrukturë**.

2. In other borrowed nouns with an international character prefixal elements such as **auto-, poli-, bio-, gjeo-**, and others, appear before stems that may or may not be independent in Albanian: **autobiografi, autodidakt** 'self-taught', **autograf, autokritikë, automjet** 'motor vehicle', **autosugjestion; polifoni, poliglot, poligraf, poligrafi, poligjenezë** 'polygenesis', **poliklinikë, politeizëm** 'polytheism', **politeist** 'polytheist'; **biografi, biokimi** 'biochemistry', **biokimist, biolog** 'biologist', **biologji; gjeofizikë, gjeograf** 'geographer', **gjeografi, gjeolog** 'geologist', **gjeologji, gjeometri**.

3.4.3 Noun Stem Derivation by Double Affixation

The formation of nouns by simultaneous prefixation and suffixation is not productive, even though it has its origin in colloquial speech. The majority of nouns so formed are constructed of a noun stem preceded by a preposition serving as a derivational prefix and followed by a suffix.

The most common prefix so used is **për-**, which occurs with various suffixes: **përqindje** 'percentage' (**qind** 'hundred'), **përjetësi** 'immortality' (**jetë** 'life'), **përdhes** 'ground-floor' (**dhe** 'earth'); **përkrenare** 'helmet' (**krye** 'head'), **përbindsh** 'monster' (**bind** 'miracle'), **përshtypje** 'impression' (**shtyp** 'press').

Other affixes in such constructions seem limited to a few words: **nëndetëse** 'submarine' (**det** 'sea'), **nëpunës** 'office worker, civil servant' (**punë** 'work'), **mëkëmbës** 'sustainer' (**këmbë** 'foot'), **mëditje** 'wage' (**ditë** 'day'), **pakujdesi** 'carelessness' (**kujdes** 'care'), **pagjumësi** 'sleeplessness' (**gjumë** 'sleep'), **sëmundje** 'illness' (**mund** 'can').

3.4.4 Noun Stem Derivation by Conversion

Most nouns formed through conversion come from adjectives, including those derived from participles. The substantivization of participles directly into neuter nouns, as in **të folurit** 'speaking' **folur** 'spoken') has been treated elsewhere (see section 3.2.2 B). The substantivization of adjectives is covered in the chapter on adjectives.

Some masculine nouns have been formed directly from the citation form of certain consonant final verbs. (Note that the nouns in the examples below are given in their citation forms followed immediately by a hyphen and the ending for the nominative singular definite. This accords with normal practice in Albanian grammars and dictionaries as both a way of identifying something as a noun and an indication of what its inflectional forms are. From this one form all the other singular case forms are immediately apparent, as is the gender of the noun.) **hap-i** 'pill' (**hap** 'open'), **mund-i** 'effort' (**mund** 'overcome, be able'), **shkul-i** 'skein of wool' (**shkul** 'I pull out'), **tjerr-i** 'flax yarn' (**tjerr** 'I spin'). Feminine nouns have also been derived by conversion from verb citation forms; the characteristic termination -**ë** of feminine nouns appears on the noun stem. Thus, we have **kullotë** 'pasture' (**kullot** 'I graze'), **dredhë** 'winding road' (**dredh** 'I twist'), **rrjedhë** 'current, flow', (**rrjedh** 'I flow'), **presë** 'blade' (**pres** 'cut'), **mburojë** 'shield' (**mburoj** 'I shield'), **shtrojë** 'pad, mat' (**shtroj** 'I lay out'), **lojë** 'game' (**luaj** 'I play'), **pjellë** 'offspring' (**pjell** 'I give birth'), **ndjenjë** 'sensation' (**ndjenj** 'I feel'), **shkronjë** 'letter (of alphabet), (**shkruaj** 'I write'). In the last two examples, the present standard forms of the verbs are **ndjej** and **shkruaj**, respectively. In **pritë** 'ambush' (**pritur** 'waited') and **plasë** 'fissure' (**plasur** 'exploded'), the noun is derived from the participial stem of the verb.

3.4.5 Noun Stem Derivation by Compounding

Next to suffixation, compounding is the most productive method of formation of new nouns.

The term "compound" here includes simple compounds (union of two stems) as well as compounds with nominal suffixes added, as in **marrveshje** 'agreement' (**marr** 'take' + **vesh** 'ear' + **je**). Compounds of the latter sort are not numerous. Most of them are gerundial nouns resulting from a phraseological construction of verb plus noun plus the suffix **-je**. The noun customarily precedes the verb, which takes its normal gerundial suffix. Such are the nouns **dorëheqje** 'resignation ("hand-withdrawing")', (**heq dorë** 'pull hand'), **frymëmarrje** 'breathing ("breath-taking")' (**marr frymë** 'I take breath'), **këmbëngulje** 'insistence ("foot-implanting")' (**ngul këmbë** 'implant feet'), **kokëçarje** 'headache ("head-splitting")' (**çaj kokën** 'split the head'), **kryengritje** 'rebellion ("head-raising")' (**ngre krye** 'raise head'). In only a few cases the suffix **-je** is added to a nominal component which follows a verb: **marrëveshje** 'agreement' (**marr vesh** 'take ear'), **falënderje** 'thanks' (**falem nderit** 'I pray to the honor'). A special case is **mirëseardhje** 'welcome', from the greeting **mirë se ardhe** 'welcome!, (well) that you came)', plus the suffix **-je**.

The structure compound + suffix also fits the nouns **bashkëkohës** 'contemporary' (**bashkë-koh-ës** 'together-time-agentive'), **zëvendës** 'replacement' (**zë-vend-ës** 'take-place-agentive'). This type of formation has a colloquial origin, as evidenced by the compounds **Lanabregas** 'Hogwash-hill', **Kryezjarth** 'Head-canker' (both place names), **kungullujës** 'water-pumpkin' (pumpkin used to hold water), **breshkujëse** 'water-turtle'.

A. Coordinate Compounds

Depending on the type of syntactic relations among their constituent elements, we may distinguish coordinate compounds from subordinate compounds. Literary Albanian formerly had only a few coordinate compounds, but more and more new ones have now been created, modeled mostly on types in the colloquial language, represented by colloquial words like **deledash** 'hermaphrodite', **gushtovjeshtë** 'end of August and beginning of September', **hyrje-dalje** 'coming and going', **pritje-përcjellje** 'hello and goodbye ("welcoming-seeing off")', **thashetheme** 'gossip', **vajtje-ardhje** 'goings and comings'. But most of such compounds belong to the written language. Thus, **marrëdhënie** 'relationship', **veshmbathje** 'clothing', **shitblerje** 'commerce ("selling-buying")', **juglindje** 'southeast', **veriperëndim** 'northwest', (**miniera**) **e hekur-nikelit** 'iron and nickel (mine)', **ngarkim-shkarkim** 'loading-and-unloading', **kafe-restorant** 'cafe-restaurant', **marksizëm-leninizmi**, **post-telegraf-telefon**, etc.

A few compounds exhibit a combining vowel **o** or **a** between the component stems: **gushtovjeshtë** 'Aug.-Sept.', **peshkaqen** 'shark', **dashamir** 'well-wisher', **dashakeq** 'evil-wisher', **dredhalesh** 'twister'.

B. Subordinate Compounds

The majority of compound nouns consists of those that have one element subordinated to the other. Among such compounds several types may be distinguished:

1. WORDS COMPOSED OF THE STEMS OF TWO NOUNS. These may be divided into several sub-types:

a) Noun + deverbal agentive noun formed with the suffix **-(ë)s**. Most of these nouns designate persons according to their profession or the work they do, but some designate tools or instruments. In this type and the next, the first element serves as complement of the second: **bukëpjekës** 'baker ("bread baker")', **flakëhedhëse** 'flame thrower', **gurskalitës** 'stone cutter, sculptor', **gjellëbërës** 'cook ("food maker")', **këpucëbërës** 'shoemaker', **letërprurës** 'letter carrier, mailman', **orëndreqës** 'watch repairer', **pijeshitës** 'bartender ("drink-seller")', **rrobaqepës** 'tailor ("clothes-sewer")', **ujësjellës** 'aqueduct ("water-conveyor")'. The compound nouns

kryengritës 'rebel ("head-raiser")' and **pjesëmarrës** 'participant ("part-taker")' also belong to this group.

b) Noun + deverbal gerundial formed with the suffixes **-je** or **-im**. In these compounds the first element again serves as complement of the verb underlying the second: **besëlidhje** 'pledge ("faith-binding")', **gjakderdhje** 'bloodshed ("blood-spilling")', **mikpritje** 'hospitality ("friend-receiving")', **mirëdashje** 'good will ("good wanting"), **vëllavrasje** 'fratricide ("brother killing")', **armëpushim** 'armistice ("arms-stopping")', **botëkuptim** 'outlook, worldview ("world-understanding")', **dëmshpërblim** 'compensation ("damage-payment")', **fjalëformin** 'derivation ("word-formation")', **letërkëmbim** 'correspondence ("letter-exchange")', etc.

c) Noun + any noun (simple or derived). These compounds have various meanings. The majority are words in which the second element acts as the modifier of the first. Thus, **bregdet** 'seashore' (**breg deti** 'hill of sea'), **ditëlindje** 'birthday ("day of birth")', **mesditë** 'noon ("middle of day")'; **pikëpamje** 'viewpoint ("point-seeing")', **pikëpjekje** 'appointment ("point-meeting")', **rrugëdalje** 'solution ("road-energing")', **vargmal** 'mountain range ("chain mountain")', **vendbanim** 'residence ("place-living")', **vetëbesim** 'selfconfidence ("self-believing")'. This type of formation has its source in the common colloquial word sequence *noun + indefinite ablative noun*. In some of the new compounds, the ablative case ending **-i** or **-e** is still preserved: **vajguri** 'petroleum ("oil of rock")', **qymyrguri** 'coal ("charcoal of rock")'; **luledielli** 'sunflower ("flower of sun")', **gjeldeti** 'turkey ("rooster of sea")', **pikëvështrimi** 'viewpoint ("point of observation")', **lejekalimi** 'safe-conduct ("permission of passage")', **punëdore** 'embroidery ("work of hand")'. For masculine nouns of this type, the definite nominative form is the same as the indefinite nominative and accusative, and thus it is not surprising to find here and there back-formations, such as **vajgur, qymyrgur** in the indefinite singular nominative and accusative:

Nëntoka është plot minerale të çmuara: VAJGUR e serë, krom e hekur, bakër, QYMYRGUR e sa e sa të tjera 'The underground is full of valuable minerals: PETROLEUM and asphalt, chrome and iron, copper, COAL and so many other things.'

Some toponyms too have been formed in just this way, as in **Balldreni** (**balli i drenit** 'the forehead of the deer'), **Qafëkërrabë** (**Qafa e kërrabës** 'neck of the hook').

Compounds with the modifier as first element are less common, but are found both in words of colloquial origin and in new words: **atdhe** 'fatherland', **mëmëdhe** 'motherland', **hekurudhë** 'railroad ("iron-road")', **babagjysh** 'grandfather', **nënëgjyshe** 'grandmother', **peshkaqen** 'shark', **udhëkryq** 'crossroad'; **kinooperator** 'cinema operator', **postkomandant** 'post commander', **skuadërkomandant** 'squadron commander', **organizatë-bazë** 'base organization', **qen-ujk** 'wolf-dog', **qytet-muze** 'museum city', **qytet-hero** 'heroic city', **shtëpi-muze** 'museum house', **vagoncistern** 'tank car', **vagon-restorant** 'dining car', **vinç-urë** 'traveling crane ("winch-bridge")', etc. In the word **dorëshkrim** 'handwriting', the first element, the qualifier, indicates the instrument.

The majority of words in this group are compounds with the noun **krye** 'head' as first element, with the special meaning 'chief, main, principal': **kryeqytet** 'capital (city)', **kryeartikull** 'editorial', **kryefamiljar** 'family head', **kryekomandant** 'commander-in-chief', **kryellogaritar** 'chief accountant', **kryemjeshtër** 'master craftsman', **kryesekretar** 'chief secretary', **kryetrim** 'top hero', **kryeurë** 'main bridge', **kryevepër** 'masterpiece' etc., as well as a few toponyms such as **Kryevidh** and **Kryezjarth**.

NOTE

In artistic literature one often finds compound words created for the occasion, which neither emerge from nor enter into the permanent lexicon of Albanian. As expressive tools of the poetic vocabulary, they are not in general use. They are generaly written with a hyphen between elements: **dif-dragua** 'giant dragon', **fjalë-flamur** 'word-flag', **flamur-gjak** 'blood-flag', **rrufe-shkabë** 'lightning-eagle'.

2. COMPOUNDS COMPOSED OF ADVERB + NOUN

In most adverb + noun compounds the noun implies some action for which the adverb may serve as a circumstantial modifier: **bashkëbisedim** 'conversation', **bashkëbisedues** 'co-speaker', **bashkëluftëtar** 'co-fighter', **bashkëpunëtor** 'co-worker', **bashkëudhëtar** 'fellow traveler', **bashkëveprim** 'co-action'; **drejtpeshim** 'equilibrium ("straight-balance")', **drejtqëndrim** '(military) attention ("straight-position")', **drejtshkrim** 'orthography', **drejtshqiptim** 'correct pronunciation'; **keqkuptim** 'misunderstanding', **keqbërës** 'malfeasant'; **mirëbesim** 'trust ("good-belief")', **mirëbërës** 'benefactor', **mirëkuptim** 'goodwill'; **mbarëvajtje** 'well-being', etc. There are very few compounds with this structure in which the second stem does not imply an action: **bashkatdhetar** 'fellow countryman', **bashkëfshatar** 'fellow villager', **bashkëshort** 'spouse ("together-luck")'.

In this group formations of the following types may also be included: **parathënie** 'foreword', **parandjenjë** 'premonition', **pararojë** 'vanguard', **pararendës** 'forerunner', etc.; **kundërmasë** 'countermeasure', **kundërmësymje** 'counter offensive', **kundërpeshë** 'counterweight', **kundërthënie** 'contradiction', **kundërvajtje** 'infraction'; **prapambetje** 'backwardness', **prapaskenë** 'behind-the-scene', **prapashtesë** 'suffix', **prapavijë** 'rear line'; **sipërfaqe** 'surface', **sipërmarrës** 'undertaker'; **pasardhës** 'successor', **pasrregull** 'fainting (= a disease), **pasthirrmë** 'interjection'.

3. COMPOUNDS COMPOSED OF PRONOUN OR NUMBER + NOUN. The majority of nouns which form these compounds are deverbal, and are modified by the preceding pronoun or number: **vetëvendosje** 'self determination', **vetëbesim** 'self confidence', **vetëdrejtim** 'self direction', **vetëmbrojtje** 'self defense', **vetëmohim** 'self denial', **vetëqeverim** 'self government', **vetëshërbim** 'self service', **vetëvrasje** 'suicide', **dyluftim** 'duel', **tremujor** 'quarterly (something that appears every three months)' (this last word is a compound with the suffix **-or**).

4. COMPOUNDS COMPOSED OF NOUN + ADJECTIVE. This type has been quite productive in the formation of adjectives, but its use in the formation of nouns is very limited, mostly to toponymic nouns: **Buzëmadh** 'Biglips', **Gruemirë** 'Goodwife', **Gurakuq** 'Redstone', **Gurazi** 'Blackstone', **Kryezi** 'Blackhead', **Qafëzes** 'Blackneck'. But note as well the common nouns **gushëkuq** 'robin' ("red-throat") and **lulëkuqe** 'poppy' ("red-flower").

5. COMPOUNDS COMPOSED OF VERB + NOUN.

This type appears in colloquial speech, but is not productive. It is the structure of such nouns as **dashamir** 'well wisher', **dredhalesh** 'wool-spinning mill', **vëmendje** 'attention', **thithlopë** 'toad' and some other dialectal words such as **djegagur** 'summer heat ("burn-rock")' and **thirravajë** 'complaint', etc.

3.4.6 Acronyms

Acronyms are noun compounds formed by joining together abbreviations of words. Acronyms spread quickly in the Albanian language in response to new needs and phenomena after World War II. It is now quite usual to abbreviate the compound names of organizations, political parties, institutions, enterprises, and certain countries. The majority of acronyms are formed by uniting the capitalized initial letters or of the written words; acronyms formed by joining the initial syllables of words are rare in Albanian.

Acronyms of one type are pronounced as sequences of individual letters of the alphabet, with the stress placed on the end of the sequence, e.g., SMT (së-më-të), NBSH (në-bë-shë), etc.: ATSH (**Agjensia Telegrafike Shqiptare** 'Albanian Telegraphic Agency'), BGSH (**Bashkimi i Grave të Shqipërisë** 'Union of Albanian Women'), BRPSH (**Bashkimi i Rinisë së Punës të Shqipërise** 'Union of the Labor Youth of Albania'), NBSH (**Ndërmarrja bujqësore shtetërore** 'National agricultural enterprise'), NSHN (**Ndërmarrja shtetërore e ndërtimit** 'National Construction Enterprise'), OKB (**Organizata e Kombeve të Bashkuara** 'United Nations Organization'), PPSH (**Partia e Punës e Shqipërise** 'Party of Labor of Albania'), SMT (**Stacioni i makinave dhe i traktorëve** 'Machine and Tractor Station'), etc. Nouns of this type are all feminine: **ATSH-ja, PPSH-ja**, etc.

Other acronyms are formed by pronouncing the whole sequence of initial letters as if they spelled a word: **FUD (Forcat ushtarakodetáre** 'Naval Military Forces'), **NIQ (Ndërmarrja e industrializimit të qumështit** 'Enterprise for the Industrialization of Milk'), etc., and a few abbreviations that have come from other languages, such as, **NATO, SEATO, UNESKO**. When nouns of this type end in a consonant, they are masculine and take masculine case endings; **FUD-i**. When they end in a vowel they are treated as feminine; **NATO-ja, SEATO-s**, etc.

Examples of acronyms which mix the two types above are **NILRG (nil-rë-gë), NTSHAP (në-të-shap), NTSHUS (në-të-shus)**, etc. The gender of these nouns is determined by the way the last part of the word is pronounced. If the acronym is pronounced with a final stressed vowel, the noun is feminine: e.g., **NILRG-ja**. If pronounced with a final consonant, it is masculine: **NTSHUS-i**, etc.

Examples of names of institutions formed by joining together the initial syllables of the component words are the department store **Mapo (Magazina popullore)** '("people's store"), and the pharmacy **Profarma (prodhime farmaceutike)** 'drug products'.

Acronyms in Albanian can be fully inflected. Case endings in writing are separated by a hyphen: e.g., **OKB-ja, OKB-së, OKB-në; FUD-i, FUD-it, FUD-in**.

In accordance with the rules of standard orthograhy, acronyms are written without periods between the letters.

CHAPTER 4

Adjectives and Adjectival Phrases

4.1 Adjectival Phrases

An ADJECTIVAL phrase (abbreviated AdjP) is a word or sequence of words which serve the typical functions of an adjective, modifying a noun or pronoun either directly as an attributive modifier in the noun phrase or indirectly through a verb as a predicative modifier:

Attributive:
> mësuesi i lumtur 'the happy teacher'
> E gjeti mësuesin e lumtur. 'He found the happy teacher.'

Predicative:
> Mësuesi ishte i lumtur. 'The teacher was happy.'
> E gjeti mësuesin të lumtur. 'He found the teacher (to be) happy.'

Adjectival phrases, listed in the order in which they may appear in the NP, may be: articulated or unarticulated adjectives in any degree, with their modifiers; articulated NP's in the genitive case; predicative adverbials; or relative clauses. ARTICULATED modifiers are those preceded by an adjectival article **i, e, të** or **së**. PREDICATIVE ADVERBIALS are adverbs or adverbial phrases (including prepositional phrases) that may serve as predicative modifiers. A RELATIVE clause is introduced by a relative conjunction such as **që** 'that' **i cili** 'who, which', **ku** 'where', **kur** 'when'.

An adjective is a word that designates a feature, that is, a distinguishing quality, trait, or characteristic of a referent; in Albanian, it agrees in gender and number with that referent:

> **Është I RI.** 'He's young'.
> **Është E RE.** 'She's young'.
> **pushka E GJATË** 'the LONG rifle'
> **Ç'u bë vullnetari I PALODHUR i hekurudhës?** 'What's become of the TIRELESS railroad volunteer?'

An adjective implies a noun or pronoun referent (present or understood) in the sentence. In this respect adjectives differ from abstract nouns derived from them. Unlike adjectives, abstract nouns designate a quality that is thought of as being autonomous and abstracted from particular referents:

> **Gjer atë ditë ne kishim qenë shumë TË LUMTUR, por atë LUMTURI, për çudi nuk e kishim ndier.** 'Until that day we had been HAPPY, but strangely we had not felt that HAPPINESS.'

4.2 Adjectival Articles

Adjectival articles are proclitics that indicate that the following adjective, noun, number, or pronoun is attributed to a noun. These preposed articles are connected historically with postposed articles which lost their independence and turned into definite case endings. Note the similarity of form of the proclitics and the definite case endings for the same word in the following examples: **I mir-I** 'the good one (masc.)', **TË mirë-T** 'the good ones (masc.)', **SË mirë-S** 'to the good one (fem.)' **TË miri-T** 'to the good one (masc.)'.

In the nominative case adjectival articles have three forms: **i** for the masculine singular, **e** for the feminine singular, **të** or **e** for the neuter singular as well as for the plural of all three genders.

The adjectival article has become the integral, distinguishing characteristic of ARTICU-LATED ADJECTIVES, whether they are simple like **I bardhë** 'white', **I mirë** 'good', **I hollë** 'thin', **I trashë** 'thick', **I verdhë** 'yellow', **I zi** 'black', or derived words like **I ditur** 'learned', **I dytë** 'second', **I gëzuar** 'glad', **I përkohshëm** 'temporary', **I përpiktë** 'accurate', **I sotshëm** 'today's', **I tretë** 'third'. When they become adjectives, participles take preposed articles, as in **i punuar** 'wrought, worked', **i larë** 'washed', **i shkruar** 'written', **i hapur** 'opened', **i ditur** 'learned', etc.

Possessive adjectives are also articulated, although the article appears as a separate word only for third person and for first and second person forms with plural agreement: **I tij** 'his', **I saj** 'her', **I tyre** 'their', **E mi** 'my (masc. pl.)', **E mia** 'my (fem. pl.)', **E tu** 'your (masc. pl.)', **E tua** 'your (fem. pl.)'.

Adjectival articles also mark nouns in the genitive case, as in **oborri i shkollës** 'the school yard', **fusha e Myzeqesë** 'the plain of Myzeqe', **libra të bibliotekës** 'library books', formally distinguishing the genitive from the dative case and permitting the noun that follows it to serve as attribute to the one that precedes it. It is evident in such constructions that the adjectival article belongs to the antecedent or referent noun in terms of grammatical agreement; in a nominal phrase its form is determined by gender, number, and case of the noun that precedes, rather than on the following noun to which it is attached: **drejtori I shkollës** 'the school princi-pal', **drejtorit TË shkollës** 'to the principal OF the school', **drejtoresha E shkollës** 'the school principal (fem.)', **drejtoreshës SË shkollës** 'to the principal of the school (fem.)', **drejtorët E shkollave** 'the principals OF the schools', **drejtoreshat E shkollave** 'the principals OF the schools.' Here the functional similarity of noun genitives with adjectives is reflected also by their formal similarity since, as with adjectives, the adjectival article agrees with the antecedent noun in gender, number, and case.

The plural adjectival article **të** is used before the integers and the indeterminate pronouns **gjithë** 'all', **tërë** 'all' when they indicate an exhaustive, collective quantity of the (implied) referent as in **të tre** 'all three (masc.)', **të tria** 'all three (fem.)', **të katër** 'all four (masc.)', **të katra** 'all four (fem.)', **të tetë** 'all eight', **të teta** 'all eight (fem.)', **të gjithë** 'all', **të gjitha** 'all (fem.)', **të tërë** 'the whole, entire', **të tëra** 'the entire (fem.)'.

The neuter singular adjectival article **të** is used to form nouns designating action gerunds such as **të ecurit** 'walking', **të menduarit** 'the thinking', **të folurit** 'the speaking'.

The relative pronoun **i cili** 'who, which' is distinguished from the interrogative pronoun **cili** 'who, which' by the adjectival article that precedes it. As with substantivized adjectives, both the article and the endings after the stem mark the case, gender, and number of the referent.

The names of the days of the week are treated as feminine articulated adjectives in Albanian: **e hënë** 'Monday', **e martë** 'Tuesday', **e mërkurë** 'Wednesday', **e enjte** 'Thursday', **e premte** 'Fri-day', **e shtunë** 'Saturday', **e diel** 'Sunday'. They are still occasionally used in their full forms, as in **ditë e hënë** 'Monday (day of moon)'--although the shorter forms are much more com-mon.

When certain kinship nouns (the same ones that may be preceded by a first person possessive **im** 'my' or a second person possessive **yt** 'thy'; see Section 3.1.2) are preceded by an adjectival article, the implication is that they are attributed to another noun, that is, they have a third per-son possessor 'his', 'her' or (less frequently) 'their'. The kinship noun in this construction is always in a definite form and the form of the adjectival article is in the same gender, number, and case as the kinship noun:

	'my'	'thy'	'his/her/their'
'son'	**im bir**	**yt bir**	**i biri**
'daughter'	**ime bijë**	**jot bijë**	**e bija**
'sister'	**ime motër**	**jot motër**	**e motra**
'sisters'	**time motra**	**tët motra**	**të motrat**

'brother'	im vëlla	yt vëlla	i vëllai
'cousin (masc.)	im kushëri	yt kushëri	i kushëriri
'cousin (fem.)	ime kushërirë	jot kushërirë	e kushërira
'brother-in-law'	im kunat	yt kunat	i kunati
'brothers-in-law'	tim kunetër	tët kunetër	të kunetërit
'mother-in-law'	ime vjehërr	jot vjehërr	e vjehrra
'lord,master'	im zot	yt zot	i zoti
'lady,mistress'	ime zonjë	jot zonjë	e zonja

NOTE

In today's literary language the construction using the first and second person pronominal adjectives before plural kinship nouns is disappearing: **TË TU vëllezër** 'YOUR brothers', **TË MI kushërinj** 'MY cousins', **TËT kushërinj** 'YOUR cousins', **TËT vëllezër** 'YOUR brothers', **TË TU motra** 'YOUR sisters', **TË MI motra** 'MY sisters', **TIME motra** 'MY sisters'.

Morphologically (in terms of grammatical form) the adjectival article preceding the relative pronoun **i cili** 'who', the names of the days of the week, and the nouns that indicate kinship relations is the same as the article preceding a substantivized adjective like **i riu** 'the young one' (masc.) or **e reja** 'the young one' (fem.), i.e., it agrees in gender, number, and case with the noun which follows.

4.2.1 Declension of Adjectival Articles

The form of the adjectival article reflects the case, gender, and number of its referent (see Table 4.1).

Table 4.1 Declension of Adjectival Articles				
	Singular			Plural
	Masculine	Feminine	Neuter	any gender
Nom	i	e	të(e)	të
Acc	të(e)			
Gen-Dat-Abl	të	të(së)	të	të

The alternate form **e** instead of **të** is used for the singular accusative and the plural nominative and accusative only when a noun referent in a definite form immediately precedes the adjectival article in a nominal phrase: thus **e** rather than **të** will appear only immediately after a noun ending in **-t(ë)** marking the definite plural (or neuter singular) nominative or accusative, or immediately after a noun ending in **-n(ë)** marking the definite singular accusative; **së** rather than **të** will appear either immediately after or immediately before a noun ending in **-s(ë)** (or deictic determiner ending in **-saj**) marking the definite singular feminine genitive, dative, or ablative. The **e** alternate of **të** is not used before predicate complements:

E kam librin të mirë. 'The book I have is good.' (**E kam të mirë librin.** 'I have the *good* book') vs. **E kam librin e mirë.** 'I have the good book.'
E gjeta vëllanë të sëmurë. 'I found (my) brother sick'. vs. **E gjeta vëllanë e sëmurë.** 'I found (my) sick brother.'

Contrast the alternate forms of the adjectival article with accusative case referents in the following examples: **librin E ri** 'the new book'/ **një libër TË ri** 'a new book'; **shokun E shkollës** 'the schoolmate'/ **një shok të shkollës** 'a schoolmate'; **klasën E parë** 'the first grade'/ **një klasë TË parë** 'a first grade class'; **sekretarin E organizatës** 'the secretary of the organization/ **një sekretar TË organizatës** 'a secretary of the organization'; **librin tim TË ri** 'my new book'/ **librin E ri** 'the new book'; **shokun tim TË shkollës** 'my schoolmate'/ **shokun E shkollës** 'the schoolmate'; **shkollat E qytetit** 'the city schools'; **shokun E mirë** 'the good friend'/ **e ka shokun TË mirë** 'his friend is nice ("he has the good friend"; predicate complement)' **fletoren E pastër** 'the neat notebook'/ **e mban fletoren TË pastër** 'he keeps his notebook neat' (predicate complement); **lisat E gjatë** 'the tall oak trees'/ **ky pyll i ka lisat TË gjatë** 'the oak trees are tall in this forest' ("this forest has its oak trees tall"; predicate complement); **herën E parë** 'the first time'/ **TË parën herë** 'the FIRST time'; **djalin E shkretë** 'the wretched boy'/ **TË shkretin djalë** 'the WRETCHED boy'; **botën E tërë** 'the entire world'/ **TË tërë botën** 'the ENTIRE world'.

> **Qenka e tmerrshme të humbasësh në pranverën e jetës sate ndjenjën MË TË PASTËR që na ka dhuruar natyra.** 'In the springtime of your life it's really terrible to lose THE PUREST feeling that nature has granted us.'

Contrast also the alternate forms of the adjectival article with feminine singular referents in the genitive, dative, or ablative case. Following a definite referent, the form is **së**: **shkollës SË mesme** 'the middle school', **shkollës SË fshatit** 'the village school'. Following an indefinite referent, the form is indefinite **të**: **një shkolle TË mesme** 'of a middle school', **një shkolle TË fshatit** 'of a village school'. In cases where the definite noun is followed by two modifiers, the adjectival article of the second modifier has the form **të**: **shkollës SË mesme TË përgjithshme** 'the general middle school', **jetës SË qytetit e TË fshatit'** 'the life of the city and the village'.

Substantivized articulated adjectives in the genitive, dative, and ablative cases take the preposed article **së** when they are definite and the article **të** when they are indefinite and are preceded by a quantifier: **SË resë** 'of the new one (fem.)', **një (kësaj, çdo) TË reje** 'of a (this; every) new one (fem.)', **e SË ardhmes** 'of the future'/ **i një TË ardhmeje të afërt** 'of a near future'.

> **Diferenca ekzistuese midis pagës MË TË ULËT të punonjësve dhe pagës MË TË LARTË në vendin është nga më të voglat.** 'The existing difference between THE LOWEST and THE HIGHEST wages of the workers in our country is among the smallest.'
>
> **Kafshoi buzën nga dhembja e asaj fjale TË PAMENDUAR.** 'He kicked himself for ("bit his mouth from the pain of") that THOUGHTLESS word.'
>
> **Kjo shënon dhe mbarimin e asaj vepre TË MADHE.** 'This also marks the end of that GREAT work.'
>
> **Ta shikoje kur i jepte asaj SË SHKRETE lopatë si përkulej.** 'You should have seen the way he bent over when he used that WRETCHED shovel'.

Note that the form of the adjectival article with neuter singular noun referents is identical to that with plural referents, except immediately following a definite neuter noun in the nominative or accusative case:

> **I dhimbte koka nga të qarët E SHUMTË.** 'His head ached from TOO MUCH weeping'.
> **S'e duroj dot të folurit E SHUMTË.** 'I can't stand EXCESSIVE gabbing.' vs. **Ai ka një të folur TË NGADALSHËM.** 'He has a SLOW way of speaking.'

The referent of the adjectival article may immediately precede the article, as it does normally for modifiers in a noun phrase (**hera e parë** 'the first time,') **djali i Agimit** 'Agim's son'; follow the article as it does with substantivized adjectives, **i gjithë** 'all', **i cili** 'which, who', articulated kinship terms like **e bija** '(his) daughter', etc.; or be implied in the discourse situation (**Jam i sëmurë** 'I am sick (male speaking)'; **jam e sëmurë** 'I am sick (female speaking)'.

If the adjectival article is followed by a noun in the genitive case (note that substantivized adjectives are also nouns), a determiner may come between the article and the noun: **i çdo kombi** 'of every nation', **të DISA grave** 'of several women', **burri i një bije të atij të shkreti baba** 'the husband of a daughter of that miserable father'. In contrast, nothing may come between an adjectival article and the adjective to which it belongs: **i një të shkreti** 'of a wretch' (and not ***i të një shkreti**).

In the paradigms in Tables 4.2 and 4.3, note how the differences in the form of the adjectival article depend on the definiteness, gender, case, and number of the referent and on whether the referent immediately precedes. The difference in the latter is most obvious when the referent is followed by the two adjectives, the second preceded by the conjunction **e** 'and'.

Table 4.2 Indefinite Noun + Articulated Adjectives

	Masc Sg	Masc Pl
	'nice, quiet boy' ("boy good and quiet")	'nice, well-behaved boys' ("boys good and quiet")
Nom	djalë i mirë e i urtë	djem të mirë e të urtë
Acc	djalë të mirë e të urtë	djem të mirë e të urtë
Dat	djali të mirë e të urtë	djemve të mirë e të urtë
Abl	djali të mirë e të urtë	djemve të mirë e të urtë
Gen	i (një) djali të mirë e të urtë	i djemve të mirë e të urtë
	Fem Sg	**Fem Pl**
	'nice, well-behaved girl' ("girl good and quiet")	'nice, well-behaved girls' ("girls good and quiet")
Nom	vajzë e mirë e të urtë	vajza të mira e të urta
Acc	vajzë të mirë e të urtë	vajza të mira e të urta
Dat	vajze të mirë e të urtë	vajzave të mira e të urta
Abl	vajze të mirë e të urtë	vajzave të mira e të urta
Gen	i (një) vajze të mirë e të urtë	i vajzave të mira e të urta

Table 4.3 Definite Noun + Articulated Adjectives

	Masc Sg	Masc Pl
	'the nice, well-behaved boy'	'the nice, well-behaved boys'
Nom	djali i mirë e i urtë	djemtë e mirë e të urtë
Acc	djalin e mirë e të urtë	djemtë e mirë e të urtë
Dat	djalit të mirë e të urtë	djemve të mirë e të urtë
Abl	djalit të mirë e të urtë	djemve të mirë e të urtë
Gen	i djalit të mirë e të urtë	i djemve të mirë e të urtë
	Fem Sg	**Fem Pl**
	'the nice, well-behaved girl'	'the nice, well-behaved girls'
Nom	vajza e mirë e e urtë	vajzat e mira e të urta
Acc	vajzën e mirë e të urtë	vajzat e mira e të urta
Dat	vajzës së mirë e të urtë	vajzave të mira e të urta
Abl	vajzës së mirë e të urtë	vajzave të mira e të urta
Gen	i vajzës së mirë e të urtë	i vajzave të mira e të urta

4.3 Declension of Adjectives

An adjective may follow the noun or pronoun it modifies; unlike a noun in the position, the adjective does not take a case ending: **pushka e amerikanit** 'the American's gun' vs. **pushka amerikane** 'the American gun'. On the basis of whether they have a preposed adjectival article or not, adjectives in Albanian are divided into two groups: ARTICULATED and UNARTICULATED.

With articulated adjectives the preposed article forms a phonetic and syntactic unit with the adjective stem. As evident in Table 4.2 and Table 4.3, depending on the case, gender, number, and definiteness of the noun it modifies, an articulated adjective will take one of the following preposed articles: **i, e, të, së**. In citing an articulated adjective--e.g., in dictionaries or grammatical discussions--the masculine singular nominative form **i** is traditionally used.

Articulated adjectives include:

1) all those simple adjectives that end in **-ë: i bardhë** 'white', **i mirë** 'good', **i verdhë** 'yellow', **i parë** 'first', etc.;

2) all adjectives formed with the suffixes **-(ë)m(ë), -shëm** and **-(ë)t(ë)**: **i fisëm** 'noble', **i mesëm** 'medium', **i nesërm** 'tomorrow's', **i parmë** 'primary', **i afrueshëm** 'approachable', **i sjellshëm** 'well-behaved', **i hapët** 'open', **i hekurt** 'iron', **i ftohtë** 'cold', **i nxehtë** 'hot', etc.;

3) all adjectives formed directly from participles: **i lexuar** 'read', **i shkruar** 'written', **i hapur** 'opened', **i mbyllur** 'closed', **i ushqyer** 'fed', **i lyer** 'painted', **i thyer** 'broken', **i lënë** 'left-over', **i thënë** 'said', **i vënë** 'placed', **i zënë** 'occupied, busy', etc.;

4) all adjectives composed of the preposed article plus the sequence **pa** + noun: **i pagjumë** 'sleepless', **i papunë** 'unemployed', **i pagjak** 'bloodless', etc;

5) a few simple or derivative adjectives ending in **-ër: i poshtër** 'base, mean', **i shurdhër** 'deaf', **i verbër** 'blind', **i vjetër** 'old';

6) a few other simple adjectives, such as **i ëmbël** 'sweet', **i vogël** 'little', **i keq** 'bad', **i kuq** 'red', **i madh** 'big'.

Unarticulated adjectives are:

1) all adjectives homonymous with autochthonic nouns (those derived from place names): **dibran** 'of, from Dibra', **fierak** 'of, from Fieri', **tiranas** 'of, from Tirana', **vlonjat** 'of, from Vlora', etc.;

2) all adjectives derived by agentive such as suffixes **-ar, -tar, -ik, -ist, -iv, -or, -tor: amtar** 'official', **bankar** 'banking', **djaloshar** 'youthful', **elementar** 'elementary', **lozonjar** 'capricious'; **kombëtar** 'national', **shkatërrimtar** 'destructive', **vendimtar** 'decisive', **alkoolik** 'alcoholic', **heroik** 'heroic'; **komunist** 'communist' **leninist** 'leninist'; **objektiv** 'objective', **edukativ** 'educational', **dimëror** 'wintry', **punëtor** 'working', etc.

3) all adjectives derived with the agentive suffix **-(ë)s** from the participle: **bombardues** 'bombing', **shkatërrues** 'devastating', **goditës** 'striking', **pirës** 'drinking', **shkelës** 'invading', **qortues** 'reprimanding', **vezullues** 'glittering', etc.

4) all compound adjectives (with some rare exceptions like **i shumë-ndrituri Naim** 'the most-illustrious Naim'): **buzëplasur** 'downcast', **ditëgjatë** 'long-lived', **fatmirë** 'fortunate', **ekonomiko-shoqëror** 'socio-economic', **moralo-politik** 'political and moral', etc.

NOTES

1. Adjectives formed from verb citation forms using the dialectal endings **-onj, -enj** by adding **-ës** (**qortonjës** 'scolding', **vezullonjës** 'glittering', **tregonjës** 'indicative') are no longer to be used in standard Albanian; their place has been taken by the adjectives formed from the stem of the dialectal participle that ends in **-ue** (**tregues** 'indicative').

2. Corresponding to some articulated adjectives, there is an unarticulated form which may appear as a predicate complement indicating a transitory condition: **gjallë** 'identical, alive', **sëmurë** 'sick, ill', **shëndoshë** 'healthy, sound', etc.

   Po ai, malësori, mbeti GJALLE? 'But he, the mountaineer, did he stay ALIVE?'

   Hajde udhembarë e na u kthefsh SHËNDOSHË. 'Good-by now, and come back WELL.'

   Edhe SËMURË jam -- i tha. '"I am SICK too," he told him.'

3.   Often, in affective expressions, in place of the word sequence noun + adjective one makes a single word of the sequence in the formation of *ad hoc* constructions. These are momentary creations and do not form permanent lexical items:

Si të shkon tregëtia? -- Ç'TREGËTIZEZA? '"How's business?" "What damn ("black") business?!"'

Ku është Selimi, BURRËZIU? 'Where is Selim, THAT PITIFUL MAN?'

Ne NUSEZEZAT, mbeteshim në shtëpi duke pritur me ankth sa të na ktheheshin burrat. 'We WRETCHED BRIDES remained at home, waiting anxiously for the return of our husbands.'

As in all other compounds, it is the second element that takes all the grammatical markers. There is a normative rule that such constructions are to be written as single words, but the rule is frequently ignored in practice.

4.3.1 Adjective Gender

Adjectives agree in gender with their referent. A given adjective may have different stem forms for masculine than for feminine referents. **laps I KUQ** 'RED pencil', **vijë E KUQE** 'RED line', **djalë TRIM** 'BRAVE boy', **vajzë TRIME** 'BRAVE girl'.

In present-day Standard Albanian, adjective stems distinguish only two forms for gender: masculine and feminine. As for the neuter gender, it is on the way to disappearing completely for adjectives. Unarticulated adjectives have the same form when they modify neuter nouns as when they modify masculine nouns. For articulated adjectives, the article still reflects neuter gender only when the referent is a singular neuter noun derived from an adjective or participle by preposing the article **të,** such as **të ftohtë-t** 'the cold', **të nxehtë-t** 'the heat', **të ecur-it** 'the walking', **të ngrënë-t** 'the eating'; in the nominative case the adjective with such a referent also takes the article **të,** as in **të ecur TË KËNDSHËM** 'PLEASANT walking', except immediately following the modified definite noun, when, following the same general rule as for plural referents, the article has the form **e**:

Nga të qarët E SHUMTË e ndjente kokën si të trullosur. 'From crying A LOT he felt dizzy in the head.'

The use of neuter nouns with adjectives is quite infrequent, because 1) in present-day Standard Albanian there are simply fewer neuter nouns, since those former neuters designating materials or parts of the body have been replaced by masculine forms (see Section 3.2.2 B); and 2) deverbal neuter nouns preceded by an article are usually used without modifying (characterizing) words or are accompanied only by adverbs: **të ecurit SHPEJT** 'walking FAST', **të ngriturit HERËT** 'getting up EARLY', **të ndenjurit VONË** 'staying up LATE'.

The masculine gender form is used as the basic citation form of the adjective. With few exceptions, the feminine gender form can be derived from the citation form by simple rules. These differ for the two classes of adjectives (articulated and unarticulated).

A. Formation of Feminine Articulated Adjectives

Articulated adjectives form the feminine gender:

a) For all articulated adjectives by using the feminine forms of the preposed articles.

Masculine citation form	Feminine citation form
i ve 'widowed'	**e ve** 'widowed'
i gurtë 'stony'	**e gurtë** 'stony'
i njomë 'wet'	**e njomë** 'wet'
i rëndë 'heavy'	**e rëndë** 'heavy'
i vrarë 'hurt, killed'	**e vrarë** 'hurt, killed'

i ëmbël 'sweet'	e ëmbël 'sweet'
i vogël 'small, young'	e vogël 'small, young'
i bukur 'beautiful'	e bukur 'beautiful'
i ftohur 'cold'	e ftohur 'cold'
i pastër 'clean'	e pastër 'clean'
i shkruar 'written'	e shkruar 'written'
i thyer 'broken'	e thyer 'broken'
i verbër 'blind'	e verbër 'blind'
i athët 'tart'	e athët 'tart'
i hapët 'open'	e hapët 'open'
i hekurt 'iron'	e hekurt 'iron'
i pacak 'vagrant'	e pacak 'vagrant'
i pafaj 'innocent'	e pafaj 'innocent'
i pafre 'unrestrained'	e pafre 'unrestrained'
i pafund 'endless'	e pafund 'endless'

b) For stems ending in -m(ë) and a few special, common adjectives, the feminine ending -e is added to the stem:

i afërm 'kin, close'/ e afërme
i djeshëm 'yesterday's'/ e djeshme
i këndshëm 'pleasant, congenial'/ e këndshme
i sotëm 'today's'/ e sotme
i tejmë 'yonder'/ e tejme

As is evident the -ë of the suffix -shëm drops in the feminine form. Also in this group belong the common adjectives i keq 'bad'/ e keqe, i kuq 'red'/ e kuqe, i madh 'big'/ e madhe.

NOTE

The adjectives i ri 'new', i zi 'black, i lig 'bad' are more special yet. These have the following forms: i ri/e re, i zi/e zezë, and i lig/e ligë.

B. Formation of Feminine Unarticulated Adjectives

Adjectives form feminine gender stems:

a) By adding the feminine ending -e to the citation stem form. This group includes some simple adjectives, adjectives derived by certain suffixes, adjectives formed by conversion from various masculine nouns and compound adjectives, the second element of which is a masculine noun, or a construction with the suffix -sh: absolut/absolute, fizik 'physical' fizike, normal/normale, relativ/relative; dinak/dinake 'sly', gjakpirës/gjakpirëse 'bloodthirsty', kyç/kyçe 'key', kokëderr/kokëderre 'pig-headed', sylesh/syleshe 'stupid ("wool-eye")', zemërkatran/zemërkatrane 'black-hearted ("tar-heart")', dhjetëkatësh/dhjetëkatëshe 'ten-story', shumëkëmbësh, shumëkëmbëshe 'multi-legged', shumëkëmbëshe, etc.

b) By using the citation form stem. This group includes all compound adjectives that have as their second element a feminine noun, an adverb, or one of a few masculine nouns designating uncountable substances: bishtgërshërë 'scissor-tailed', flokëgështenjë 'chestnut-color haired, brown-haired', sqepgjilpërë 'needle-beaked', sypishë 'sharp-eyed', zemërhekur' 'merciless, iron-hearted', kokëjashtë 'bare-headed', gojëmjaltë 'honey-mouthed'.

c) For all compound adjectives whose second element is also an adjective, the feminine form has the feminine form of that second element, as in ekonomiko-shoqëror-e 'socio-economic', gojëmbël 'sweet-tongued', shpirtlig-ë 'vile, malicious', zemërkeq-e 'malevolent, bad-hearted', zemërmadh-e 'generous, big-hearted', etc.

NOTE

When the adjective refers to a whole sentence, the adjective is in the feminine gender, implying that the referent is a feminine noun **gjë** 'thing', **punë** 'matter', or demonstrative pronoun **kjo** 'this, she, it', or **ajo** 'that, it, she,':

Nuk është E TEPËRT, po të them se, në lindi një Bilush Rrumbullaku në Këmbëzë, lindi sot, që më pranuat në Parti. 'It is not EXAGGERATED to say that if a Bilush Rrumbullak was ever born in Këmbëzë, he was born there today, when you admitted me into the Party.'

A number of adjectives formed by conversion from nouns, have the same form in the feminine gender as that of the corresponding feminine nouns: **budalla/budallaqe** 'fool(-ish), **merakli/merakleshë** 'caring (person)', **plak** 'old (man)'/ **plakë** 'old (woman)', **punëtor/punëtore** 'industrious', **qefli/qefleshë** 'fun-loving(-er)', etc. Some adjectives have two feminine forms: **trim** 'hero, brave'/ **trime** or **trimëreshë** 'heroine, brave'.

NOTES

1. When the adjective modifies the word **vete/vetja** 'self' it agrees not with this feminine noun, but with the gender of the actual referent. **Ai e ndjeu veten më të lumturin në botë.** 'He felt himself to be THE HAPPIEST man in the world.'

2. Adjectives converted from a few nouns of old formation or from loan words that have kept their foreign form, as well as reduplicated adjectives of the type **maja-maja** 'having many peaks', are invariable in form with respect to number and gender: **allafranga** 'French style' **allaturka** 'Turkish style', **axhami** 'naive', **belik** 'state-owned', **fshaçe** 'peasant-like', **vendçe** 'native style', **gropa-gropa** 'full of holes', etc.

4.3.2 Adjective Number

The adjective in Albanian has two numbers: singular and plural. The structure of the plural form of adjectives depends on gender and on whether the adjective is articulated or unarticulated. All adjectives whose feminine singular form ends in an unstressed **-e** have that same form for the feminine plural stem.

A. Plural Formation of Masculine Articulated Adjectives

The plural stem of articulated masculine adjectives is identical with the singular, with the exception of **i keq** 'bad, evil', **i lig** 'evil', **i madh** 'big', **i vogël** 'small' **i ri** 'new, young', **i zi** 'black':

		Masc Sg	Masc Pl
'nice'		i mirë	të mirë
'long, tall'		i gjatë	të gjatë
'dry'		i tharë	të tharë
'tomorrow's'		i nesërm	të nesërm
'today's'		i sotëm	të sotëm
'accessible'		i afrueshëm	të afrueshëm
'glorious'		i lavdishëm	të lavdishëm
'rough'		i ashpër	të ashpër
'blind'		i verbër	të verbër
'beautiful'		i bukur	të bukur
'juvenile'		i mitur	të mitur
'thin, drawn'		i hequr	të hequr
'near, close'		i afërt	të afërt
'common'		i për bashkët	të për bashkët

'innocent'	i pafaj	të pafaj
'unlucky'	i pafat	të pafat
'mindless'	i pamend	të pamend
'red'	i kuq	të kuq
'foreign'	i huaj	të huaj
'sweet'	i ëmbël	të ëmbël
'widowed'	i ve	të ve
'unnoticed'	i pavënëre	të pavënëre
'bad, evil'	i keq	të këqij
'evil'	i lig	të ligj
'big'	i madh	të mëdhenj
'small'	i vogël	të vegjël
'new, young'	i ri	të rinj
'black'	i zi	të zinj

(**të zinj** now favored over form **të zes**)

The plural formation of the adjectives **i ri** 'new, young' and **i zi** 'black' with the ending **-nj** is like that of masculine nouns and unarticulated adjectives that end in a stressed **i**, as in **bari** 'shepherd', **barinj** 'shepherds', **kalli** 'ear (of grain)', **kallinj** 'ears (of grain)'.

B. Plural Formation of Masculine Unarticulated Adjectives

1. Unarticulated adjectives that are not compound words form the masculine plural:

a) By taking the ending **-ë**. The masculine plural of all unarticulated adjectives that are simple and those derived adjectives with stress on the final syllable are formed in this way: **absurd-Ë** 'absurd', **abstrakt-Ë** 'abstract', **agresiv-ë** 'aggressive', **industrial-Ë, kimik-Ë** 'chemical', **leshtor-Ë** 'hairy', **naiv-Ë** 'naive', **përparimatar-Ë** 'progressive', **relativ-Ë** 'relative', etc. Excepted from this rule are the adjectives that end in stressed **-i** or **-s** and those that have been formed by conversion from nouns (see points b,c,d below).

b) By using the citation form. This group includes all adjectives formed with the suffix **-(e)s**, as in **krijues** 'creative', **lotues** 'tearful', **përkëdhelës** 'flattering, endearing', **pyetës** 'inquiring', **shkelës** 'invader, violator', **veprues** 'active'.

c) By taking the suffix **-nj**. This applies to all adjectives that are of Turkish origin and take a stressed suffix **-li, -çi** or **xhi**, as in **merakli-nj** 'caring, worrying', **inatçi-nj** 'choleric, spiteful', **qejfli-nj** 'fun-loving', **sevdalli-nj** 'loving', etc. These words are used mainly in conversation or in literary texts to express colloquial nuances.

d) By taking the same plural form as the corresponding noun, when the adjective is derived by conversion from a noun: e.g., **fukara** 'poor'/pl. **fukarenj**, **bullafiq** 'fat, fleshy'/pl. **bullafiqër**, **plak** 'old'/pl. **pleq**, **punëtor** 'industrious',/pl. **punëtorë**, **rrugaç** 'hooligan'/pl. **rrugaçë**, **trim** 'brave'/pl. **trima** etc:

Edhe njerëzit BULLAFIQËR si Elez Furka, morën qëndrim të prerë. 'Even CHUBBY people like Elez Furka took a clearcut stand.'
Fshatarët FUKARENJ morën pjesë pa ngurrim në luftën për çlirimin e vendit. 'The POOR peasants participated without hesitation in the struggle for the liberation of the country.'
Populli ynë dhe partizanët e tij TRIMA luftuan me vendosmëri deri në fitoren përfundimtare. 'Our people and its BRAVE partisans fought resolutely to decisive victory.'
Atje rrinë e bëjnë roje dy shelgje PLEQ. 'There two OLD willow trees stand guard.'

NOTE

The adjective **tjetër** 'other' behaves like an unarticulated adjective in the singular. But its plural form **të tjerë** is an articulated adjective.

2. Masculine adjectives that are compound words form the plural:

a) In the same way that their second element forms the plural when it is used by itself. This applies to all compound adjectives, the second element of which is an adjective: **gjakpirës** 'bloodthirsty' pl. **gjakpirës**, **shpirtmadh** 'magnanimous' pl. **shpirtmëdhenj**, **shpirtvogël** 'miserly' **shpirtvegjël**, etc.:

Ne u themi atyre se nuk jemi MENDJEMËDHENJ, por jemi ushtarë të asaj armate të madhe e të fuqishme që po bën revolucionin. 'We tell them that we are not ARROGANT, but soldiers of that great and powerful army that is making the revolution.'

Lavdi, o shokë punëtorë, që dolët FAQEBARDHË. 'Glory to you SUCCESSFUL comrade workers.'

The above rule is also followed by a good many compound adjectives that have a masculine noun as their second element: e.g., **kokëderr** 'pig-headed' **kokëderra**, **kokëkungull** 'block headed ("pumpkin-head")', **kokëkunguj**, **zemërluan** 'lion-hearted' **zemërluanë** etc.

b) By using the citation form. This happens with compound nouns that have a feminine noun as their second element as in **hundëshkabë** 'hook-nosed ("eagle-nosed")', **mjekërfshesë** 'long-bearded ("broom-beard")', **sypishë** 'bright-eyed' ("torch-eye"). The same is true for certain other compound adjectives that have as their second element a masculine noun designating an uncountable substance, e.g., **gojëmjaltë** 'honey tongued', **kokëmish** 'meathead', **zemërçelik** 'stoic ("steel-hearted")', **zemërhekur** 'insensitive ("iron-hearted")'; and for an occasional compound adjective that has as a second element a masculine noun with a special plural form, as in **gjoksshkëmb** 'strong-chested ("rock-chest")', **shpirtlepur** 'fearful, timid ("rabbit-soul")'.

The citation form is also used for the masculine plural for compound adjectives formed of a number (or indeterminate pronoun of quantity, such as **disa** 'several', **shumë** 'many', etc.) plus a noun with the suffix **-sh**, as in **dykatësh** 'two-story', **shumëngjyrësh** 'multi-colored', **tringjyrësh** 'tri-colored':

Në pyjet e vendit tonë ka qindra zogj shumëngjyrësh. 'In the forests of our country there are hundreds of multi-colored birds.'

c) By taking the suffix **-ë**, as in **buzëgaz** 'smiley ("cheer-lips")' pl. **buzëgazë**, **kokëtul** 'fat head' **kokëtulë**, **sylesh** 'stupid ("hair-eye")' **syleshë**.

Ditën e parë u treguam SYLESHË, po kësaj here s'do të na e falte njeri. 'The first day we behaved like FOOLS, but this time no one would forgive us.'

C. Plural Formation of Feminine Articulated Adjectives

Feminine adjectives form the plural stem:

a) By using the same stem as the feminine singular. This group includes all adjectives that end in **-e** in the singular: **e bëshme** 'stout' pl. **të bëshme**, **e djeshme** 'yesterday's' **të djeshme**, **e sotme** 'today's' **të sotme**, **e sjellshme** 'well-behaved' **të sjellshme**, etc. Excepted from this rule are the adjectives **e keqe** 'bad' pl. **të këqia**, **e madhe** 'big' pl. **të mëdha**, **e re** 'new' pl. **të reja**, **e ve** 'widowed' pl. **të veja**.

b) By taking the ending **-a**. This group includes all adjectives that do not end in **-e** in the feminine singular: **e afërt** 'near' **të afërta**, **e mirë** 'nice' **të mira**, **e mundur** 'beaten' **të mundura**, **e qëruar** 'cleaned' **të qëruara**, **e thyer** 'broken' **të thyera**, **e verbër** 'blind' **të verbëra**, **e verdhë** 'yellow' **të verdha**, **e zezë** 'black' **të zeza**, etc.

NOTE

The feminine plural stem form of the unarticulated adjective **tjetër** 'other' is the articulated stem **të tjera.**

D. Plural Formation of Feminine Unarticulated Adjectives

Unarticulated feminine adjectives that are not compounds have the same stem form in the singular and in the plural. This happens because these adjectives take **-e** in the singular, as in **dinake** 'foxy', **malore** 'mountaineer', **trime** 'brave', **shqetësuese** 'upsetting', etc. The adjective **plakë** 'old' forms the plural like the noun from which it is formed by conversion **plakë** 'old woman' pl. **plaka.**

Compound feminine adjectives form the plural in two ways:

a) When the feminine adjective ends in **-e** or in a stressed vowel, or has as its second element a feminine noun that ends in **-ë**, then it has the same form in both numbers: **buzëgaze** 'smiling ("cheery lips")', **kokëderre** 'obstinate ("pig-head")', **faqekuqe** 'rosy-cheeked'; **syqershi** 'bright-eyed ("cherry eye")', **syulli** 'dark-eyed ("olive-eye")', **gërshetëdegë** 'thick-braided ("branch braid")', **sypishë** 'bright-eyed, alert ("torch eye")', etc. This group also includes adjectives that have as their second element a masculine noun designating an uncountable substance: **gojëmjaltë** 'honey-tongued', **zemërhekur** 'insensitive ("iron-hearted")', etc.

NOTE

The adjective **fatkeqe** 'unlucky' and those compound adjectives that have **e madhe** 'big' as their second element form the plural in accordance with the form of the plural of the second element: **fatkëqia** 'unlucky', **shpirtmëdha** 'magnanimous', **hallemëdha** 'much-troubled ("big troubles")', etc.

b) When it has a feminine noun ending in **-ë** as its second element, the adjective forms the plural by taking the ending **-a** (thus forming the plural in the same way as the compound's second element itself): **derëbardhë** 'prosperous, lucky ("white-doored")', pl. **derëbardha, gojëmbël** 'sweet tongued' **gojëmbla, kokëfortë** 'headstrong' **kokëforta, syshkruar** 'variegated-eyed' **syshkruara**, etc.

4.4 Substantivization of Adjectives

As was noted earlier in this chapter, the adjective takes the declensional endings of a noun when it occurs before the noun. The adjective also takes these endings when it appears without a noun. A similar use of substantivized adjectives appears in English in such contexts as "the **meek** shall inherit the earth," "Give me two of the **red** and one of the **blue**." "The **nearest** was only half an hour away by car." In each of these cases, the implied noun is being designated according to a characteristic quality that is relevant and sufficient for identification in a given context.

In Albanian, adjectives become substantivized through the process of conversion; that is, they take on the attributes of nouns (including inflections) without the addition of derivational affixes or a shift in stress (see Table 4.4):

I BARDHI, I VERDHI dhe I ZIU të gjithë kanë të drejtë të rrojnë të lirë. 'THE WHITE, THE YELLOW, and THE BLACK all have the right to live freely.'
Era që vinte nga malet e Moravës sillte me vete TË FTOHTËT e dëborës. 'The wind that came from the Morave mountains brought with it THE COLD of the snow.'
E MIRA dhe E LIGA nuk harrohen 'THE GOOD and THE EVIL are noT forgotten.'

The degree to which the substantivization of adjectives has been established in the lexicon of Albanian varies. In many instances the substantivization becomes fixed, and is now independent of context. These adjectives have passed permanently into the class of nouns. More frequent is the substantivation of adjectives that occurs only within a particular context.

Table 4.4 Substantivized Adjectives	
Indefinite	

	Masc Sg	Masc Pl
	'(a) fiancé (betrothed one)'	'(some) fiancés (betrothed ones)'
Nom	(një) i fejuar	(disa) të fejuar
Acc	(një) të fejuar	(disa) të fejuar
Dat	(një) të fejuari	(disa) të fejuarve
Abl	(një) të fejuari	(disa) të fejuarve
Gen	i (një) të fejuari	i (disa) të fejuarve

	Fem Sg	Fem Pl
	'(a) fiancée'	'(some) fiancées'
Nom	(një) e fejuar	(disa) të fejuara
Acc	(një) të fejuar	(disa) të fejuara
Dat	(një) të fejuare	(disa) të fejuarave
Abl	(një) të fejuare	(disa) të fejuarave
Gen	i (një) të fejuare	i (disa) të fejuarave

Definite	

	Masc Sg	Masc Pl
	'the fiancé'	'the fiancés'
Nom	i fejuari	të fejuarit
Acc	të fejuarin	të fejuarit
Dat	të fejuarit	të fejuarve
Abl	të fejuarit	të fejuarve
Gen	i të fejuarit	i të fejuarve

	Fem Sg	Fem Pl
	'the fiancée'	'the fiancées'
Nom	ë fejuara	të fejuarat
Acc	të fejuarën	të fejuarat
Dat	së fejuarës	të fejuarave
Abl	së fejuarës	të fejuarave
Gen	i së fejuarës	i të fejuarave

In general, then, one can distinguish LEXICALIZED SUBSTANTIVIZATION by means of which new nouns have been formed (as with **e drejtë-a** 'the just', **e mirë-a** 'the good', **e keqe-ja** 'the bad', **e vërtetë-a** 'the true', etc.) from CONTEXTUAL SUBSTANTIVIZATION of adjectives. Words resulting from the first type of substantivization have only genetic ties with adjectives.

Among lexicalized substantivized adjectives, one can distinguish the following groups:

1. Human nouns which designate:
a) persons identified by some particular feature or trait, such as **besnik** 'loyal (one)', **gënjeshtar** 'liar', **i gjallë** 'living (one)', **mëngjërash** 'left-handed (one)', **i ri** 'young (one), **i sëmurë** 'sick (one)' < **i shëndoshë** 'healthy (one)', **shurdh** 'deaf (one)', **i varfër** 'poor (one)', **e ve** 'widow', **vocrrak** 'little (one)';
b) persons identified according to their relations to a thing or phenomenon, e.g. **jugor** 'southerner', **shtatanik** 'prematurely born person ("seven-monther")', **shtëpiak** 'domestic person ("housely")', **ushtarak** 'military (man)', **vjeshtuk** 'autumnal (one)'; **amerikan** 'American' and all other nouns of nationality;
c) persons identified by an action they perform or experience, as indicated by the participial adjective from which the nouns derived: **i ardhur** 'newcomer', **i dashur** 'lovable (one)', **i ditur**

'learned (one)', **i mbytur** 'drowned (one)', **i ngopur** 'satiated (one)', **i njohur** 'recognized (one)', **i pasur** 'wealThy (one)', **i shtypur** 'oppressed (one)', **i vdekur** 'dead (one)', etc.;

The stems of substantivized adjectives in the masculine and feminine gender and in the singular and plural number are identical with the stems of the corresponding attributive adjectives: **i ri** 'young one (Masc Sg)' **e re** 'young one (Fem Sg)', **të rinj** 'young ones (Masc Pl)'/p **të reja** 'young ones (Fem Pl)', **i shëndoshë** 'healthy one (Masc Sg)' **e shëndoshë** 'healthy one (Fem Sg), **gënjeshtar** 'liar (Masc Sg)' **gënjeshtare** 'liar(s) (Fem Sg or Pl)', etc.

NOTE

There are also a few nouns designating mythological beings or animals, which are formed from substantivized adjectives: e.g., **e bukura (e dheut)** 'the beauty (of the earth)' (mythOlogical creature representing the idealized woman), **i paudhi** 'the damned' (the devil), **veshgjati** 'the long-eared' (the donkey).

2. Abstract nouns in the feminine gender, used mainly in the definite form, like **e ardhmja** 'the future ("the coming")', **e bukura** 'the beautiful (in art)', **e drejta** 'the just', **e keqja** 'the bad', **e mira** 'the good', **e reja** 'the new', **e shkuara** 'the past', **e vërteta** 'the true'.

3. Abstract nouns in the neuter gender, like **të errët-it** 'the dark, darkness', **të ftohtë-t** 'the cold, cold (the disease)', **të kuq-të** 'the red', (**të kuqtë e madh** 'erysipelas: a disease characterized by deep-red inflamation), **të ngrohtë-t** 'the warmth', **të thata-t** 'the dry, boils, carbuncles', **të verdhë-t** 'the yellow, jaundice', **të zi-të (e ullirit)** 'hard lot ("the black (of olives)")' In present-day Albanian this method of formation is no longer productive.

4. Collective feminine nouns (*pluralia tantum*) like **të ardhurat** 'income', **të hollat** 'money', **të lashtat** 'crops', **të palarat** 'dirty (unwashed) things', **të vjelat** 'harvest'.

Neuter nouns that designate gerundials have been formed by substantivizing the participle: e.g., **të menduar-it** 'thinking', **të ecur-it** 'walking', **të folur-it** 'speaking', **të hapur-it** 'opening', **të qarë-t** 'weeping', **të vërtitur-it** 'thrusting'. These nouns have the same form as the substantivized neuter adjective which is no longer used in present-day Albanian. This type of formation was productive at one time, but is greatly limited at present, with suffixal formations with **-je** or **im** taking the place of many neuter nouns formed from the substantivized participle (see Sections 3.4.4 and 3.2.2 B on deverbal nominalization). Alongside such nouns, in present-day Standard Albanian one also finds substantivizations of the deverbal adjective in the feminine gender: **të goditur-it** or **e goditur-a** 'the striking', **të shtyrë-it** or **e shtyrë-a** 'the pushing', **të qeshur-it** or **e qeshur-a** 'the laughing', etc. This is in conformity with the general reduction in use of the neuter in modern Albanian.

Contextual substantivization Of the adjective occurs when it functions as a noun only within a specified context. All adjectives in Albanian have the capacity to be so used. This happens when, to refer to a noun used previously (or one known to the addressee in the context), the adjective is used as a noun, and designates not the thing proper but the thing as characterized by the given quality:

Po ti, moj Dafë, e qërove misrin e verdhë kaq shpejt që i je kthyer TË BARDHIT? 'And did you, Dafë, clean up the yellow corn so quickly that you turned to THE WHITE?'
Dy MË TË MËDHATË nuk i kish zënë gjumi akoma. 'The two OLDEST had not yet fallen asleep.'
Dil, moj E BUKURA mbi TË BUKURAT: Të kemi sjellë ujë kroi e luleshtrydhe mali. 'Come out, oh loveliest of the lovely ("THE LOVELY ONE above THE LOVELY ONES"): We have brought you fountain water and mountain strawberries.'
Mimozën nuk e vinin në radhën e TË BUKURAVE. 'They did not put Mimozë in the rank of THE LOVELY ONES.'

This type of substantivization has a purely contextual character. It is a creative act with individual words in specific circumstances. Although these adjectives acquire the meaning of a noun, they lack the lexico-grammatical independence that other nouns have. Outside the given context they no longer designate things, but only features of things. Their gender and number in a given context are independent only in appearance. In essence they are totally dependent on the gender and number of the implied referent:

> **Popullin e kishin marrë tërë jetën nëpër këmbë "TË FUQISHMIT".** 'The people had been kicked around all their life by "THE POWERFUL".'

> **Mentor, na, merri! Ato më të mirat po të jap, TË HEKURTAT.** 'Here, Mentor, take them! I am giving you the very best, THE IRON (ONES).'

Substantivized adjectives are usually used in the definite form or with a qualifying word. But they may also be used in indefinite forms with an indefinite article, **(një, ndonjë, disa, ca)** especially when the noun has been mentioned once within the syntactic unit:

> **Djaloshi, NJË SHPATULLGJERË, NJË VETULLTRASHË, ishte gati të hynte në valle.** 'The boy, A BROAD-SHOULDERED, THICK-BROWED (lad) was ready to get into the dance.'

The concretization of meaning in these adjectives is thus only temporary and conditional; we are therefore dealing here not with the creation of a new word, but rather with the functional use of the adjective in a specific context. Contextual substantivization of the adjective is sometimes used to express a superlative:

> **Bravo, Rako, je I VETMI!** 'Bravo, Rako, you are unique ("THE ONLY ONE").'

> **Për këngë e lahutë e ke TË VETMIN.** 'When it comes to singing and playing the lute, he is in a class by himself ("you have him THE ONLY ONE").'

But examples of substantivized comparatives and superlatives with **më** are not at all uncommon:

> **Partizanët e brigadës IV kryejnë akte nga MË TË GUXIMSHMET në historinë e luftës sonë.** 'The partisans of the IV brigade are carrying out some of the MOST DARING actions ("actions among THE MOST DARING") in the history of our struggle.'

The use of contextually substantivized adjectives with demonstrative and personal pronouns to achieve affective intimacy is very frequent.

> **Karagjozi, ai SHALËGJATI, zbardhte dhëmbët.** 'Karagjoz, that LONG-LEGGED ONE, grinned.'

> **Më vinte keq mua SË GJORËS.** 'I felt sorry, poor me ("it came bad to me THE POOR ONE").'

> **TË ZESTË ne ç "kemi hequr".** 'How we have suffered, us wretches ("BLACK US, what we have drawn")!'

> **Kjo E VOGLA ishte më e bukur nga të tria të motrat e saj.** 'This LITTLE ONE was the most beautiful of her three sisters.'

In many instances the pronoun is not expressed at all, since it is implied:

Ua, ç'e gjeti TË ZIUN. 'Boy, is he in trouble! ("Oh, what he found THE BLACK!").'

Ashtu i hipte se i hante shumë TË SHKRETAT. 'He climbed it like that, because he loved to eat the damn things ("THE FORSAKEN").'

NOTE

In aphorisms and proverbs, before such words as **i burgosur-i** 'the imprisoned', **i dehur-i** 'the drunk', **i gjallë-i** 'the live one', **i ri-u** 'the young', **i sëmurë-i** 'the sick', **i vdekur-i** 'the Dead', etc., and **i lig-u** 'the evil', **i mësuar-i** 'the learned', **i mirë-i** 'the good', **i pasur-i** 'the rich', **i varfër-i** 'the poor', **i vuajtur-i** 'the experienced', etc., it is possible to place a noun, usually the noun **njeri-u** 'person'. The noun is generally only implied. Such usage reflects a mid-way point between adjectives that are substantivized contextually, and those that have been lexicalized as substantives, since the possibility of putting a noun before them is only potential; in practice, it is hardly ever realized. On the other hand, their use only in connection with living beings makes them more restricted than ordinary adjectives. These partially lexicalized forms, conventionalized over the years, now function as ordinary nouns in every context:

TË GJALLËT i kujtojnë shpesh TË VDEKURIT. 'The LIVING think often of THE DEAD.'

Ai sillej si një I SËMURË që s'bën ç'i thonë. 'He behaved like a patient ("SICK ONE") who doesn't do what he's told'.

Mos pyet TË MËSUARIN, po TË VUAJTURIN. 'Don't ask THE LEARNED (person), but rather the experienced one ("SUFFERED ONE").'

In sum, the borderline between total, lexicalized substantivization and partial or, contextual substantivization is not always sharp and clear.

The genitive forms of nouns, for example, may also be used anaphorically to stand for the thing(s) possessed:

Të Skënderit janë atje. 'Alexander's are there.'

Note that unlike substantivized adjectives the adjectival article and the noun form in such examples exhibit a constant genitive form rather than a form that depends on their syntactic function in the sentence.

4.5 Position and Agreement of the Adjective

In Albanian the adjective normally follows the noun it modifies. The adjective stem agrees with the noun in gender and number, but not in definiteness and case.

Ai nxori në fillim ca tinguj TË ÇJERRË, TË THELLË TË NDËRPRERË. 'At first he came out with some RAGGED, DEEP, and DISCONNECTED sounds.'

Drejtoria e spitalit, duke marrë parasysh vëmendjen E MADHE që më kushtonte publiku BOTËROR, u detyrua të lëshonte përditë komunikatë SPECIALE për gjendjen time SHËNDETËSORE. 'The hospital administration, taking into account the GREAT attention that the world public devoted to me, was obliged to issue daily a SPECIAL report on my HEALTH condition.'

Montatori doli në skenë me një çantë në sqetull. Ishte çanta e bashkëpunëtorit SHKENCOR; palltoja dhe borsalina, që bashkëpunëtori SHKENCOR i kishte lënë mbi karrige, dilnin shpesh në skenë. 'The assembly worker appeared on the stage with a briefcase under his arm. It was the briefcase of the SCIENCE associate; the coat and the cap that the SCIENCE associate had left on the chair appeared frequently on the stage.'

The adjective may also appear in positions separated from the noun, e.g., in absolute positions or as a predicate complement:

Sa TË LUMTURA e ndjejnë veten vajzat 'How happy the girls feel.'

E SHIKUAR dhe E BËRË kështu, kjo punë ka një frymë burokratike, zyrtare. 'SEEN and DONE like this, this business has a bureaucratic, official odor.'

Mbeta I KËNAQUR. 'I was pleased ("I remained CONTENT").'

Shpendi ra në tokë dhe po përpelitej I GJAKOSUR. 'The bird fell to the ground and was BLEEDING and convulsing.'

From the examples given above it can be seen that when unarticulated adjectives follow their noun referent in a nominal phrase and when they function as predicate complements, they do not take any case endings, whatever the case of the noun. The same is true of articulated adjectives; but for these, the form of the preposed adjectival article does depend on case. For example, when articulated adjectives are used as the predicate nominative of the subject or the predicate complement of the object, the article appears in the nominative and accusative case form, respectively.

However, when the adjective bears an emphatic or contrastive function it may precede rather than follow the noun:

Pse nuk mendonte kështu edhe për fatin e TË MJERIT Filip? 'Why didn't he think this way about the fate of POOR Philip as well?'

Dhe ju flas me GJYSMAKUN zjarr që mbeti. 'And I speak to you by the (light of the) FLICKERING fire that remains.'

Edhe në gjallje dhe pas vdekjes, po unë do të heq andrallat e atij SHPIRTKRIMBURI burrë. 'Both in life and after death, it is I who shall suffer on account of that ROTTEN (lit: worm-eaten soul) husband of mine.'

In this word sequence, Albanian adjectives become substantivized, that is, they become nouns in form, whereas the noun that follows takes on adjectival characteristics by exhibiting number, but not case agreement. In this position, adjectives are fully declinable (see Table 4.5): unarticulated adjectives take case endings; in articulated adjectives the preposed article as well as the endings on the stem reflects case. Thus, articulated adjectives reflect case both when they precede and when they follow the noun, whereas unarticulated adjectives reflect case only when they precede the noun.

Table 4.5 Substantivized Adjective + Noun		
Indefinite		
	Masc Sg	Masc Pl
	'a wretched ("black") father'	'some wretched fathers'
Nom	një i zi baba	disa të zinj baballarë
Acc	një të zi baba	disa të zinj baballarë
Dat	një të ziu baba	disa të zinjve baballarë
Abl	një të ziu baba	disa të zinjve baballarë
Gen	i një të ziu baba	i disa të zinjve baballarë
	Fem Sg	Fem Pl
	'a miserable girl'	'some miserable girls'
Nom	një e shkretë vajzë	disa të shkreta vajza
Acc	një të shkretë vajzë	disa të shkreta vajza
Dat	një të shkrete vajzë	disa të shkretave vajza
Abl	një të shkrete vajzë	disa të shkretave vajza
Gen	i një të shkrete vajzë	i disa të shkretave vaJza
Definite		
	Masc Sg	Masc Pl
	'the wretched father'	'the wretched fathers'
Nom	i ziu baba	të zinjtë baballarë
Acc	të ziun baba	të zinjtë baballarë
Dat	të ziut baba	të zinjve baballarë
Abl	të ziut baba	të zinjve baballarë
Gen	i të ziut baba	i të zinjve baballarë
	Fem Sg	Fem Pl
	'the miserable girl'	'the miserable girls'
Nom	e shkreta vajzë	të shkretat vajza
Acc	të shkretën vajzë	të shkretat vajza
Dat	së shkretës vajzë	të shkretave vajza
Abl	së shkretës vajzë	të shkretave vajza
Gen	i së shkretës vajzë	i të shkretave vajza

In certain special instances an adjective coming after a noun takes all the substantive grammatical markers of the nominal phrase, with the noun before it unmarked for case. This happens when the speaker wishes to identify the referent by a distinctive attributive feature. In this instance the feature indicated by the adjective has the character of an epithet or title:

Atëhere pse nuk më pyet edhe për dashurinë që ke për këtë Violetë BUKUROSHEN? 'Then why don't you also ask me about your love for this BELLE Violet?'

E nderonin tepër dhe asnjeri (veç ndërgjegjes) nuk i thoshte: Topaz BATAKÇIU. 'They honored him greatly and no one (except his conscience) said to him: Topaz THE CROOK.'

Vocative and evocative expressions of the type

Ama, TË BUKUR NJERI që ka gjetur të pyesë. 'Boy, a FINE GUY he found to ask!'

TË DASHUR SHOKË E SHOQE, motra e vëllezër. 'DEAR COMRADES (male and female) sisters and brothers.'

TË NDERUAR MIQ. 'HONORED FRIENDS.'

are used principally in the nominative and accusative case. Other word sequences that have a formally substantivized adjective, as in:

I ZIU BABA mendonte se edhe kjo ngjarje kishte ndodhur me Memon. 'The wretched ("BLACK") FATHER thought that this incident also had something to do with Memo.'

also occur most often in the accusative and nominative, but show up occasionally in other cases.

On rare occasions calling for a heightened emotional tone adjectives may precede neuter nouns, for the most part in the accusative case:

TË BUKUR të folur që bëri. 'What a BEAUTIFUL speech he gave.'

When the referent is a male, the adjectival article and the adjective stem have their masculine forms, even when the noun designating that male has feminine endings: **hoxha I madh** 'the tall Moslem priest.' Similarly for adjectival article and the adjective stem have their feminine forms: **Sadeti e madhe** 'the tall Sadet (woman's name)'. However, immediately following a feminine genitive, dative or ablative singular definite suffix **-s(ë)** (**-saj** in deictic determiners), the adjectival article has the form **së**: **Shyqos SË shkretë** 'to poor Shyqo (man's name)', **i hoxhës së madh** 'of the tall priest', **ia dhashë dajës së Agimit** 'I gave it to Agim's uncle'.

NOTE

When a single person is addressed in a polite form using the personal pronoun **ju** 'you (pl.)',the predicative adjective, in contrast to the pronoun and the predicative verb, is in singular form: **Ju jeni I QARTË** 'you (Masc Sg) are CLEAR', **JU dukeni shumë I BRENGOSUR** 'you (Masc Sg) seem very WORRIED', **ju jeni E SHPEJTË** 'you (Fem Sg) are fast.'

4.6 Semantic Classification of Adjectives

Along with their morphological classification into articulated and unarticulated types, adjectives may be classified semantically as well. On the basis of the nature of the feature they designate and the manner in which they designate this feature, adjectives in Albanian can be divided into two groups: a) DIRECT QUALIFYING ADJECTIVES:

Iu varën degët E GJELBRA mbi kokë/i dërguan erë limoni. 'The GREEN branches hung over his head/they sent him a scent of lemon.'

and b) MEDIATED QUALIFYING ADJECTIVES, which indicate a quality implicit in the stem from which they are derived:

Shteti ynë i demokracisë SOCIALISTE, në të cilën bëjnë pjesë edhe zgjedhjet për në organin më të lartë të pushtetit SHTETEROR, ka lindur nga revolucioni POPULLOR. 'The state of our SOCIALIST democracy, which also includes elections to the highest organ of STATE power, was born of POPULAR revolution.'

The direct qualifying adjectives designate perceptual or conceptual traits or qualities: color, as in **i bardhë** 'white', **i kuq** 'red', **i verdhë** 'yellow', **i zi** 'black', etc.; space, magnitude, form, as in **i gjatë** 'long' **gjatosh** 'longish', **i gjerë** 'broad', **i hollë** 'thin', **i madh** 'big', **i ngushtë** 'narrow', **i rrumbullakët** 'round', **i thellë** 'deep', etc.; taste, as in **i athët** 'tart', **i thartë** 'sour', **i ëmbël** 'sweet', **i hidhur** 'bitter', **i shijshëm** 'tasty', etc.; physical traits and spiritual states, as in **i butë** 'mild, soft', **i çalë** 'lame', **i dobët** 'weak', **i fortë** 'strong', **i helmuar** 'poisoned', **i kënaqur** 'satisfied', **memec** 'mute', **i mërzitur** 'bored, unhappy', **i njomë** 'wet', **i ri** 'young, new', **i trishtuar** 'sad', **i thatë** 'dry', **i verbër** 'blind', etc.; or character traits and mental qualities, as in **besnik** 'loyal', **budalla** 'foolish', **dinak** 'sly', **intrigant** 'insidious', **krenar** 'proud', **i mprehtë** 'sharp', **i ndershëm** 'decent, honorable', **i turpshëm** 'bashful, disgraceful', **i zgjuar** 'bright, intelligent', etc.

Mediated qualifying adjectives convey the quality of the thing they characterize by designating its relations to another thing, situation, action or number directly by means of their lexical meaning. These adjectives often indicate relations similar to those of the oblique cases of the corresponding nouns from which they have been derived: compare **shall I LESHTË** 'WOOLEN scarf' **shall PREJ LESHI** 'scarf of WOOL', **buzëqeshje FËMINORE** 'CHILD-LIKE smile' **buzëqeshje FËMIJE (FËMIJËSH)** 'smile of a child (of children)', **rreze DIELLORE** 'SOLAR ray', **rreze DIELLI** 'SUN beam', **diell PRANVEROR** 'SPRING sun' **diell PRANVERE** 'sun of spring', **shtyllë E MERMERTË** 'MARBLE column' **shtyllë (PREJ) MERMERI** 'column of MARBLE'. To a certain degree, the examples with nouns in the oblique cases are synonymous with those of the derived qualifying adjectives, but the use of the noun as modifier often implies a specific relationship with that noun rather than a general trait associated with it. Conversely, with mediated qualifying adjectives the relationship is presented as a fixed and abstracted qualifying feature, as a categorial meaning: **rreze DIELLORE** 'solar rays' does not connote simply **rrezet e DIELLIT** 'the sun's rays', but rays having special traits that are characteristic of the sun, as opposed to **rrezet RËNTGEN** 'X-rays', **ULTRAVIOLET** 'ULTRAVIOLET (rays)', etc. Likewise, **dashuri ATËRORE** 'PATERNAL love' does not mean merely **dashuria E ATIT** 'the FATHER'S love', the love of a particular father; rather it designates a general trait that contrasts with other general traits of the same category: e.g. **social, fraternal, human,** etc. love.

The mediated qualifying adjective may express the material of which its referent is made: **rreth I ARTË** 'GOLDEN circle', **kullë E GURTË** 'STONE tower' **derë E HEKURT** 'IRON door', **fustan I MËNDAFSHTË** 'SILK dress', **bluzë E PAMBUKTË** 'COTTON blouse', etc. Or it may express a characteristic property, a thing, person or abstract concept, as in **shtëpi ATËRORE** 'PATERNAL home', **kushte AGROTEKNIKE** 'AGRO-TECHNICAL conditions', **armë ATOMIKE** 'ATOMIC arms', **stili DERADIAN** 'DERADIAN style', **gabim IDEOR** 'IDEATIONAL error', **fenomen NATYROR** 'NATURAL phenomenon', **trup QIELLOR** 'CELESTIAL body', **plan SHTETËROR** 'STATE plan'. But it may also express the relation of the referent 1) to an action, as in **makinë KORRËSE** 'REAPING machine', **makinë MBJELLËSE** 'sowing machine', **qëndrim MOHUES** 'NEGATIVE stand', **trup RREZATUES** 'RADIATING body', **brisk RRUES** 'SHAVING razor', **gisht TREGUES** 'INDEX finger' ; 2) to a moment in time, as in **ngjarja E DJESHME** 'YESTERDAY'S event', **mbledhja E NESËRME** 'TOMORROW'S meeting', **prodhimi I SIVJETSHËM** 'THIS YEAR'S prouction', **gazeta E SOTME** 'TODAY'S paper', **orët E VONA** 'THE LATE hours', etc.; 3) to a spatial point, as in **pamje E JASHTME** 'EXTERNAL view', **ajgensia E KËTUSHME** 'THE LOCAL agency', **kati I POSHTËM** 'the floor BELOW', **dhoma E SIPËRME** 'THE UPPER room', etc.; or 4) to a number, as in **plani I KATËRT** 'THE FOURTH plan', **pranvera E NJËZETË** 'THE TWENTIETH spring', **studenti I PARË** 'THE FIRST student', **radha E TRETË** 'THE THIRD row', etc.

In Albanian the number of direct qualifying adjectives is much smaller than the number of mediated qualifying adjectives. On the other hand, it will be seen below that there are no clear cut boundaries between these two semantic groups. Mediated qualifying adjectives easily become direct qualifying adjectives (in terms of their semantic value), especially when they are used in a figurative sense. The quality that a given adjective designates is always a feature of a named thing from which the adjective derives. It is just this feature that makes possible the figurative use of a given adjective, that is, its use as a direct qualifying adjective. This is also the reason why not every mediated adjective can acquire a direct qualifying sense. Despite the great number of mediated qualifying adjectives, only a relatively small number of them have acquired the ability to designate direct qualifying features as well:

Lëndina dukej e larë nga rrezet E ARTA të diellit pranveror. 'The meadow seemed washed by THE GOLDEN rays of the vernal sun.'

Kyçi i të gjitha fitoreve tona ka qenë dhe mbetet uniteti I ÇELIKTË i popullit me Partinë. 'The key to all our victories has been and remains the STEELLIKE unity of the people with the party.'

Si shumë I LESHTË kërkon të shitesh i pandehur. 'Defendant, you're trying to pass yourself off as very STUPID'.

The modified noun and the rest of the context are helpful in understanding whether the adjective is used in its literal or in its figurative sense, and also which of the qualities has been abstracted in a concrete instance. For example, the adjective **i artë** 'golden' might have the following direct qualifying meanings: 1) **kaçurela TË ARTA** 'GOLDEN curls', **vjeshtë E ARTË** 'GOLDEN autumn', **rreze TË ARTA** 'GOLDEN rays', etc.; 2) 'very good, marvelous', as in **njeri I ARTË** 'wonderful man ("GOLDEN person")', **zemër E ARTË** 'generous ("GOLDEN heart")', **fjalë TË ARTA** 'GOLDEN words', **mot I ARTË** 'GOLDEN year', etc.; 3) 'happy, beautiful,' as in **kohë E ARTË** 'beautiful ("GOLDEN") weather', **ditët E ARTA të rinisë** 'THE GOLDEN days of youth'.

2. GRAMMATICAL TRAITS OF DIRECT AND DERIVED QUALIFYING ADJECTIVES. Direct qualifying adjectives are distinguished from mediated qualifying adjectives not only semantically, but also grammatically. The former have a number of characteristic morphological traits that the latter generally do not have:

1. They may be simple, derivative, or compound words like **i gjallë** 'alive', **i mirë** 'good', **i ngjashëm** 'alike, similar', **guximtar** 'brave, daring', **gjakftohtë** 'cold-blooded, composed', **zemërmirë** 'good hearted'.

2. From them can be formed abstract nouns designating traits, qualities or states, by means of the suffixes **-i, -(ë)si, -(ë)ri, -zi**, etc., as in **bukuri** 'beauty', **lumturi** 'happiness', **bardhësi** 'whiteness', **mirësi** 'goodness'; **gjallëri** 'liveliness'; **marrëzi** 'madness', etc.

3. They may form antonymous pairs, as in **i ri** 'young', **i vjetër/plak** 'old/old (man)', **trim** 'brave', **frikacak** 'cowardly', **i lehtë** 'light', **i rëndë** 'heavy', **i varfër** 'poor'/ **i pasur** 'rich', **i mirë** 'good'/ **i keq** 'bad', **i ëmbël** 'sweet'/ **i hidhur** 'bitter'.

4. With few exceptions, they have the grammatical category of degree. **DJALË I URTË** 'quiet boy'/ **djale MË I URTË** 'quieter boy', **ditë E MIRË** 'nice day'/ **ditë MË E MIRË** 'nicer day';

They are subject to both lexicalized and contextual substantivization: **E BUKURA e dheut** 'THE BEAUTIFUL ONE of the earth', **i gjalli me të gjallët** 'the living (sing.) with the living (pl.)'.

Sokoli kishte blerë dy tablo, MË TË BUKURËN ia dhuroi së motrës. 'Sokol had bought two pictures; he gave THE PRETTIER (one) to his sister'.

Mediated qualifying adjectives 1) are all derived from nouns designating substances or actions from adverbs of time or place, from numerals, or from verbs of action, as in **i bakërt** 'copper(y)', **gëlqeror** 'lime', **kohor** 'temporal', **i djeshëm** 'yesterday's', **i sipërm** 'upper', **i pestë** 'fifth', **i nëntë** 'ninth', **dëftues** 'indicator', **trishtues** 'saddening', etc.; 2) cannot serve as stems to form abstract nouns; 3) cannot form antonymous pairs; 4) are not gradable (except for a few adverbial adjectives like **i afërt** 'near', **i largët** 'distant', **i vonë** 'late') 5) are subject to contextual substantivization only (with the exception of a few adjectives derived from adverbs). When used figuratively, however, mediated adjectives may become direct qualifying adjectives and become gradable.

Both direct and mediated qualifying adjectives may be either articulated or unarticulated.

4.7 Formation of Adjectives

Besides simple adjectives, which cannot be synchronically analyzed into smaller component parts nor shown to be derived by conversion (a shift of a stem from one grammatical category to another without change in form), Albanian has derived adjectives, those whose stems are based on other stems. Albanian adjectives are derived by means of prefixation, suffixation, addition of the preposed article, simultaneous suffixation, and addition of the preposed article, and simultaneous prefixation, suffixation, and addition of the preposed article. In addition to derivation by these morphological devices new adjectives can also be formed by compounding and conversion.

Means of adjective derivation can be further characterized as productive or nonproductive. Knowledge of productive means of derivation is particularly valuable to non-native speakers, since, through these, new adjectives may be formed rather freely. Knowledge of non-productive means of derivation, on the other hand, is valuable mostly for interpreting the meaning of unfamiliar adjectives whose derivational stem is known. Because of this distinction, fully or almost fully productive means of derivation will be kept distinct from marginally productive or non-productive means.

4.7.1 Productive Formation of Adjectives

1. FORMATION BY PREFIXATION.

The most productive prefixes in Albanian for the formation of adjectives are **pa-** and **jo-**, which form adjectives having a negating or privative meaning. These adjectives are ordinarily antonymous to adjectives that serve as their derivational stems. Adjectives with **pa-** are formed from articulated stems, while those with **jo-** are formed from unarticulated stems: e.g., **i paafrueshëm** 'unapproachable', **i pabotuar** 'unpublished', **i pakundërshtueshëm** 'indisputable', **i palavdishëm** 'inglorious', **i pashkruar** 'unwritten'; **jokapitalist** 'non-capitalist', **jonormal** 'abnormal', **jopërparimtar** 'unprogressive', **jozyrtar** 'unofficial'. The prefix **pa-** attaches generally to adjectives formed with the suffix **-shëm** and adjectives formed by articulation of the participle. It also occurs in a few particular formations with other adjectives: e.g., **i paaftë** 'inept', **i padenjë** 'unworthy', **i padrejtë** 'unjust', **i padyshimtë** 'undoubted, certain', **i paplotë** 'incomplete', **i paqartë** 'unclear'.

Adjectives are also productively formed by means of the prefix **ndër-** (similar to English **inter-**), as in **ndërkombëtar** 'international', **ndërluftues** 'at war, belligerent (lit. "inter-fighting")', **ndërsektorial** 'intersectional', **ndërshtetëror** 'interstate'.

The borrowed prefixes **anti-, para-** and **pro-** are also quite productive. With the prefix **anti-** 'anti-' unarticulated adjectives are formed (mostly from unarticulated adjectival stems) that convey the idea of opposition, e.g. **antiajror** 'anti-aircraft', **antifashist** 'anti-fascist', **antifetar** 'anti-religious', **antikombëtar** 'anti-national', **antiamerikan** 'anti-American', **antipopullor** 'anti-popular'. The adjective **antiparti** 'anti-party' has been formed from a nominal stem.

In some instances this prefix has been replaced by the characteristically Albanian prefix **kundër-**, e.g., (mbrojtja) **kundërajrore** 'anti-aircraft (defense).'

The prefix **para- pre-, para- fore-** also serves to form unarticulated (with a few exceptions) adjectives from other adjectives: **parafundor** 'penultimate', **parakapitalist** 'pre-capitalist', **parashkollor** 'pre-school', **paraushtarak** 'para-military', etc.

With the prefix **pro-** 'pro-' a sizable number of unarticulated adjectives are formed, having the meaning of approval or sympathy with, as in **proamerikan, prorevizionist, prosovjetik.**

The prefix **stër** is quite productively used to form both articulated and unarticulated adjectives. Adjectives formed with this prefix have an augmentative meaning: e.g., **stërbujar** 'very noble', **i stërgjatë** 'very long, tall', **i stërlashtë** 'ancient, venerable', **i stërmadh** 'very large'. Compare the **stër-** prefix in kinship terms: (cf. **stërnip** 'great grandson', **stërgjysh** 'great grandfather', etc.)

NOTE

Occasionally an adjective is formed with the borrowed prefix **ultra-**: e.g., **ultramodern, ultrareaksionar.**

THE FORMATION OF ADJECTIVES BY SUFFIXATION

This is one of the most productive methods of formation of adjectives from other parts of speech. Nouns, adjectives, numbers, verbs, and adverbs all serve as derivational stems in the formation of adjectives by means of suffixation.

The most productive suffixes used in the formation of unarticulated adjectives, are **-(ë)s, -ar, -tar, -or, -tor, -ak,** and **-il**. The suffixes **-(ë)s, -ar, -tar, -or, -tor,** originally used only to form agentive nouns (see Section 3.4.1 A), have been extended by analogy to adjectives derived by conversion from such nouns, and now may be considered productive adjectival suffixes as well.

The suffix **-(ë)s** is very productive. These adjectives, much like present participles in English, convey a sense of ongoing action, indicating an active agentive feature, namely, the feature which performs the action designated by the derivational stem. But there are cases when these adjectives have more than one meaning: e.g., **'hot, spicy; combustible'** in spec **DJEGËS** 'hot (burning) pepper' or in **lëndë DJEGËSE** 'fuel (BURNING)'. The derivational stem for this type of adjective is a) the participle stem minus the participle suffix; b) the complete participle stem or c) the verb stem itself.

The stem of the participle (without the suffix **-ur** or **-r**) serves as a derivational stem for adjectives derived from participles of verbs ending in consonants or in **-e**: **grindës** 'nagging', **mbytës** 'suffocating', **ngjitës** 'sticky', **përmbledhës** 'compact, inclusive', **përsëritës** 'recurring', **shkrepës** 'striking', **rrëmbyes** 'impetuous, torrential', **shpërblyes** 'compensatory', **ushqyes** 'nourishing', etc. Note that **-ës** is the form used after consonants, **-s** the form after vowels.

The full stem of the participle serves as a derivational stem in those instances when the participle of the verb ends in **-ë** rather than in **-ur**: **ngrënës** 'eating', **dhënës** 'giving', **marrës** 'taking', **mbjellës** 'sowing', **shirës** 'threshing', **pirës** 'drinking', **prerës** 'cutting', etc.

For the large number of verbs whose participial stem ends in **-ua**, the adjectival suffix **-s** is added to a Gheg form of the participial stem, which ends in **-ue**, e.g., **dallue, gjykue** etc.: **dallues** 'distinctive', **gjykues** 'judicial', **kalues** 'passing', **krahasues** 'comparative', **përfaqësues** 'representative', **plotësues** 'completive', **vazhdues** 'continuous', **veçues** 'separative', **shkrues** 'penman, scribe', etc.

NOTE

Words with **-onjës** such as **dërrmonjës** 'destructive', **drejtonjës** 'managing', **lehtësonjës** 'extenuating', **punonjës** 'working', **qortonjës** 'scolding', are still encountered in standard Albanian, but are increasingly taking on a dialectal character and being replaced by the forms of the **-ues** type described above.

In special cases the suffix **-ë(s)** is added to nominal stems as well. These adjectives attribute a property implied by the derivational stem of the adjective to the referent: **ujës** 'aquatic, water-y', **vajës** 'oil-y, oil bearing', **farës** 'having to do with seeds, seed-y', **rrenës** 'lying (like a liar)'.

The suffix **-ar**, with which adjectives are formed that indicate the relation "of or pertaining to," is also very productive: e.g., **bregdetar** 'coastal', **elementar** 'elementary', **letrar** 'literary', **mesjetar** 'medieval', **djaloshar** 'youthful', **planetar** 'planetary'.

NOTE

In some words this suffix has been used to form adjectives indicating agentive relations with an action expressed by a verb, or implied by an abstract noun: **kundërshtar** 'opposing', (**kundërshtoj** 'I oppose'), **kureshtar** 'curious' (**kureshtje** 'curiosity'). The suffix **-onjar** is an extended form of the suffix **-ar** which has been added to the verb **loz** 'I play' to form the adjective **lozonjar** 'playful'.

The suffix **-tar** formed by analogy with the suffix **-ar** has the same meaning and productivity as that suffix. Adjectives may be formed with this suffix from concrete nouns, as in **amtar** 'maternal' **kombëtar** 'national', **mesdhetar** 'mediterranean', or from action nouns themselves derived from verbs, such as **përfaqësimtar** 'representational', **përfundimtar** 'final, conclusive', **vendimtar** 'decisive'. Another form of this suffix, identical with it in function, is the suffix **-atar**, which likewise has been formed by analogy through the extension of the suffix **-tar**: e.g. **mesatar** 'average', **sqimatar** 'fastidious, dandy'.

The suffix **-or** has been very productive, serving to form adjectives from corresponding nouns: **bimor** 'botanical', **dialektor** 'dialectal', **diellor** 'solar', **dimëror** 'wintry', **ditor** 'daily', **femëror** 'feminine', **foshnjor** 'infantile', **trupor** 'corporeal', **vetor** 'personal', etc. Some of these adjectives are formed from abstract nouns, such as **arsimor** 'educational', **armiqësor** 'hostile', **burrëror** 'manly', **bujqësor** 'agrarian', **burimor** 'of the fountain', **madhështor** 'majestic', **mbretëror** 'royal, kingly', **mjekësor** 'medical', **mjerëzor** 'humane, human', **vajzëror** 'girlish'.

Some of the examples above, with a derivational stem apparently ending in **-ës** or **-ër** may be viewed as having the extended suffixes **-(ë)sor**, or **-(ë)ror**; **gjyqësor** 'judicial', **rrënjësor** 'radical', **paqësor** 'pacific, peaceful'; **botëror** 'world-wide', **shipirtëror** 'spiritual', **shtetëror** 'state', etc.

The suffix **-or** can also derive unarticulated adjectives from verbs, as in **dëftor** 'demonstrative', **kundërshtor** 'contradictory', **lejor** 'concessive', **lidhor** 'conjunctive', **lindor** 'eastern', **mohor** 'negative', **pjellor** 'fertile', where the stems of the respective verbs serve as the derivational stems of the adjectives. A few adjectives in **-or** are formed from other modifier stems as in **madhor** 'adult', **sipëror** 'superlative'.

NOTE

As can be seen, many suffixal formations, derived nominal and adjectival stems are not formally distinct, due in large part to the fact that so many ending in **-ar**, **-tar**, and **-or** have been formed from corresponding nouns through the process of conversion (see Section 4.7.2 F below) that these suffixes may equally well be used to derive adjectives directly as well as nouns. Nonetheless, a certain differentiation has begun between formations with the suffixes **-or**, **-ar**, **-tar**. The suffixes **-ar** and **-tar** are becoming identified more and more with the formation of nouns, whereas the suffix **-or**, is increasingly identified as an adjective formative. Thus, **arsimtar** 'educator' **arsimor** 'educational', **shkencëtar** 'scientist, scholar'/
shkencor 'scientific, scholarly', **shkollar** 'scholar'/ **shkollor** 'scholastic', **shkaktar** 'causal agent'/ **shkakor** 'causative', **vjetar** 'an annual'/ **vjetor** 'annual', **pronar** 'proprietor',/ **pronor** 'proprietory, possessive', **gojëtar** 'glib talker',/ **gojor** 'oral', etc.

A quite productive suffix used in the formation of certain adjectives, some with pejorative connotation, is the suffix **-ak** 'pertaining to ...'. The suffix may be used to derive adjectives from nouns as in **dimërak** 'wintry', **perandorak** 'imperial', **vezak** 'oval', etc.; or from verbs as in **dredhak** 'running', **rrëgjak** 'meager', or from other modifiers, e.g. **hollak** 'slim', **vocërrak** 'small', **zezak** 'black', **zverdhak** 'yellow'.

NOTE

The addition of the suffix **-ak** to stems ending in **-ac**, **-ar**, **-al**, **-at** and **-anj**, as in **burrac-ak** 'cowardly', **frikac-ak** 'fearful', **fushar-ak** 'plainsman' (these words were at first used as nouns, then as nouns and adjectives), led to the formation by analogy of the extended suffixes **-acak**, **-arak**, **-alak**, **-atak** and **-anjak**, which have been used mainly to form nouns, but sometimes also adjectives. The suffix **-acak** has been used to form the adjective **eracak** 'pertaining to smell' (as in **qeneracak** 'dog that has a nose for game'). The suffix **-arak**, which attaches to verb and noun stems, has been used to form the adjectives **luftarak** 'martial, militant', **qesharak** 'laughable', **shtazarak** 'beastly', **vjeshtarak** 'autumnal'. In general such adjectives have a pejorative meaning, but there are also some that do not (e.g., the last example).

The suffixes **-ian** and **-osh** are also quite productive. The suffix **-ian** is used to form adjectives from corresponding proper nouns or adjectives. **drakon-ian** 'Draconian', **shekspir-ian** 'Shakespearian', etc. The suffix is one of those used to form adjectives corresponding to the name of a place or organization, such as **evropian** 'European', **kolkozian** 'communal (pertaining to the kolkhoz)'.

The suffix **-osh** (similar to English **-ish**) serves to form some adjectives that have a clear pejorative meaning, as in **barkosh** 'pot-bellied', others that may be pejorative or ameliorative, as in **bukurosh** 'roguish, handsome', and still others with only an ameliorative or neutral connotation, as in **bardhosh** 'whitish', **gjatosh** 'longish', **ziosh** 'blackish', **thartosh** 'sourish', **larosh** 'spotty'. Adjectival stems serve here as the derivational stems: **i bukur** 'beautiful', **i tharte** 'sour', **i bardhe** 'white', **i lare** 'spotted', **i zi** 'black'. Stems of nouns may also serve for this purpose, as **bark** 'belly' and **dimer** 'winter'.

A. Formation of Adjectives with the Adjectival Article

The preposed adjectival can be viewed as playing a derivational role, in addition to the grammatical role it plays in connection with articulated adjectives as a mark of the agreement between the adjective and the corresponding noun. It may perform this function in conjunction with suffixes, or with suffixes and prefixes simultaneously, but it can also be the sole mark of derivation. Thus, adjectives have been formed from different parts of speech by mere addition of the preposed article. The greatest number of adjectives of this type have been formed from verbal stems and from agglutinated phrases of the form PREPOSITION + NOUN.

This method of forming adjectives has been very productive with the phrase sequence **pa** 'without' + NOUN stem: **i paane** 'endless', **i pabese** 'faithless', **i pacipe** 'shameless', **i pafat** 'unlucky', **i pafund** 'endless', **i pafytyre** 'faceless', **i pashpirt** 'cruel, soul-less', **i pamase** 'immeasurable', **i paparti** 'party-less', **i papune** 'unemployed'. More rarely, a determiner intervenes before the noun stem: **i pandonjemete** 'faultless ("without any defect")'. "Privative" adjectives formed in this way are generally synonomous with adjectives formed with the prefix **pa-** 'without' + stem ending in **-shem**, and are in the process of being replaced by them: **i pander** 'dishonorable'/ **i pandershem; i pafaj** 'blameless, innocent'/ **i pafajshem, etc.**

Similar in meaning with the prefix **pa-**, is the negative prefix **mos-**, generally used with deverbal stems as in **mosmirenjohes** 'ungrateful', **mosperfilles** 'arrogant, inconsiderate'.

Every verb participle can serve as the word-forming stem for a deverbal adjective. In many cases the adjective formed from the participle has developed a specialized meaning, while in others the semantic relationship with the participle is straightforward: **i afruar** 'friendly' (from **afruar** 'approached'), **i besuar** 'loyal, trusted' (from **besuar** 'believed'), **i dredhur** 'twisted', **i hapur** 'open', **i keputur** 'broken', **i nisur** 'started, adorned', **i perdorur** 'used', **i qelbur** 'stinking', **i rrahur** 'beaten', **i syrgjynosur** 'exiled, incarcerated', **i thinjur** 'made gray, gray', **i vendosur** 'placed, decided, resolute', **i vrare** 'wounded, slain', **i zene** 'busy, caught' (from **zene** 'taken, caught').

A certain number of adjectives have participial-like forms, such as **i skamur** 'destitute', **i talentuar** 'talented', even though in fact no corresponding participle nor verb exists in the language.

Semantically, adjectives formed by preposing the adjectival article to a participle usually have a passive sense expressing the result of the action of the corresponding verb. Thus, the adjectives **i hapur** 'open', **i keputur** 'broken' can be interpreted as 'that which has been opened', 'that which has been broken'. But some of them have more than one meaning. For example, **i afruar** 'approachable, friendly, nearing', **i dashur** 'lovable, endearing', **i dëgjuar** 'heard, listening (obedient)', **i ditur** 'known, knowing (erudite)', **i qeshur** 'affable, smiling', **i futur** 'inserted, inserting (eager)', **i kuptuar** 'understood, understanding', **i kënduar** '(well-) read, reading' **i hedhur** 'thrown, adroit' have sometimes a passive and sometimes an active meaning, as in **njeri i ditur** 'educated, learned man' vs. **fakt i ditur** 'known fact'. On the other hand, **i pasur** 'wealthy' has only an active meaning:"that which has".

> **Ajo ishte një plakë punëtore, e urtë dhe E DASHUR, E AFRUAR me çdo njeri.** 'She was an industrious old woman, quiet and LOVABLE ("loved"), FRIENDLY with everyone.'
>
> **TË DASHUR shokë dhe shoqe, motra dhe vëllezër!** 'DEAR (male and female) comrades, sisters and brothers!'

Although teachers warn students against such usages, in the current standard language, these participial adjectives are often used in the place of adjectives derived from the participle with a preposed article and the suffix **-shëm**:

> **NË atë kohë kishte errësim TË DETYRUAR** (instead of **të detyrueshëm**). 'At that time there was OBLIGATORY darkness.'
>
> **Si ai s'ka, të pamundurën e bën TË MUNDUR.** 'There is no one like him; he makes the impossible POSSIBLE.'

B. Formation of Adjectives with Suffixes and Article

In terms of the number of adjectives that are formed with these suffixes, this method is one of the most productive. The productive suffixes involved are **-shëm** and **-(ë)t(ë)**.

The suffix **-shëm** is the most productive of all suffixes in the formation of adjectives in Albanian. An adjective ending in **-shëm** can be formed from almost any verb stem, and to a lesser degree from noun stems, and adverbial stems as well.

A variety of singular stems of common nouns (usually concrete) serve as derivational stems with **-shëm**. Stems that end in **-ë** drop that vowel before the suffix: **i bujshëm** 'noble', **i dëmshëm** 'damaging', **i famshëm** 'famous', **i ligjshëm** 'legal', **i ujshëm** 'watery', **i zakonshëm** 'ordinary'.

Adverbs and various adverbial locutions can also serve as derivational stems, as in **i brendshëm** 'internal', **i djeshëm** 'yesterday's', **i domosdoshëm** 'indispensable', **i gatshëm** 'prompt, ready', **i hershëm** 'ancient, early', **i herëpashershëm** 'periodical', **i këtushëm** 'local', **i mëparshëm** 'former', **i mëtejshëm** 'subsequent, further', **i njëkohshëm** 'simultaneous, contempoary', **i përhershëm** 'perennial', **i përditshëm** 'daily', **i përvitshëm** 'yearly, annually', **i sotshëm** 'today's, contemporary'.

Adjectives formed from verbs that end in a consonant or in **-e**, **-i** or **-ye**, have as their derivational stem the participle without the suffixes **-r(ë)**, **-ur**: **i djegshëm** 'combustible', **i falshëm** 'forgivable', **i kapshëm** 'graspable', **i mundshëm** 'possible', **i përkulshëm** 'flexible', **i rrjedhshëm** 'flowing', **i tretshëm** 'soluble'; **i kapërcyeshëm** 'surmountable', **i lyeshëm** 'paintable', **i pishëm** 'potable', **i shkëlqyeshëm** 'shining', **i thyeshëm** 'breakable', **i ushqyeshëm** 'nourishing'.

As with adjectives with the adjectival suffix **-s** (such as **tregues** 'indicative, pointing') the derivational stem of adjectives derived with the adjectival suffix **-shëm** from verbs whose participial stem ends in **-ua** uses the Gheg form of the participial stem, which ends in **-ue**: **i avullueshëm** 'volatile ("steamable")', **i çmueshëm** 'valuable', **i dëshirueshëm** 'desirable', **i mrekullueshëm** 'marvelous', **i trishtueshëm** 'sad', **bluaj** 'I mill'/ **i blueshëm** 'millable', **shkruaj** 'I write' **i shkrueshëm** 'writeable'.

Some of these deverbal adjectives indicate an active capacity of the thing modified by the given adjective to perform the action designated by the derivational stem of the adjective.

Thus, the adjectives **i habitshëm** 'surprising', **i trishtueshëm** 'saddening', **i ushqyeshëm** 'nutritious' can be synonomous with formations ending in **-(ë)s**, as in **habitës** 'surprising, distracting', **trishtues** 'saddening', **ushqyes** 'nourishing'.

For the most part, however, these deverbal adjectives denote the aptitude, capacity, merit, or necessity of the given thing to submit to the action designated by the derivational stem of the adjective (often corresponding to English -able): e.g., **i admirueshëm** 'admirable', **i besueshëm** 'believable', **i dënueshëm** 'punishable' **i kapshëm** 'graspable', **i lavdërueshëm** 'glorious', **i mendueshëm** 'thinkable', **i përkulshëm** 'flexible', **i thyeshëm** 'breakable', **i zbatueshëm** 'implementable'.

Adjectives formed with this suffix from adverbial stems have for the most part meanings directly corresponding to those of the adverb. Adjectives formed from noun stems can be interpreted as having the property of the noun that comprises the derivational stem, as in **i arsyeshëm** 'reasonable', **i famshëm** 'famous', **i fuqishëm** 'powerful', **i hieshëm** 'graceful', **i logjikshëm** 'logical', **i ndershëm** 'honorable', **i ngeshëm** 'leisurely', **i shijshëm** 'tasty', **i lëngshëm** 'juicy', **i ujshëm** 'watery', etc., or as resulting in that which is designated by the noun as in **i andshëm** 'pleasant', **i dëmshëm** 'harmful', **i dobishëm** 'useful', **i frikshëm** 'fearful', **i frytshëm** 'fruitful', **i turpshëm** 'shameful'. Depending on the situation or context, some deverbal adjectives may have an active or passive meaning: **i dëgjueshëm** 'audible, obedient' (that which hears or can be heard), **i shkueshëm** 'outgoing, approachable', **i shkëlqyeshëm** 'shining, shinable', etc.

NOTE

There is just one instance of an adjective in **-shëm** with a pronominal stem, **i çfarëdoshëm** 'of any kind whatever'.

The suffix **-(ë)t(ë)** is very productive, with derivational stems deriving from a) noun stems, b) adverbial stems, or c) numeral stems.

The meanings of adjectives in **-(ë)t(ë)** formed from noun stems vary. When nouns that designate substances serve as derivational stems, the adjective indicates the corresponding property: **i artë** 'gold, golden', **i bredhtë** 'of fir', **i gurtë** 'stony', **i kristaltë** 'crystalline', etc.

NOTE

A few adjectives of this type are formed from the plural, rather than the singular noun stem, as in **i drunjtë** 'wooden', **i florinjtë** 'gold, golden'.

Adjectives formed from adverbial stems have various meanings more or less directly related to the meanings of the corresponding adverb: e.g., **i afërt** 'close', **i barabartë** 'equal', **i kundërt** 'opposite', **i largët** 'distant', **i rëndomtë** 'ordinary', **i shpeshtë** 'frequent', **i shumtë** 'plentiful', **i tepërt** 'excessive', **i tërthortë** 'indirect', **i veçantë** 'separate'.

An indefinitely large number of adjectives can be formed from number stems yielding the set of ordinal numbers (with the exception of **i parë** 'first'): **i tretë** 'third', **i pestë** 'fifth', **i njëzetekatërt** 'twenty-fourth', **i njëqindtë** '(one) hundredth', **i pesëqindegjashtëdhjetekatërt** 'five hundred and sixty-fourth'. Adjectives that have as their derivational stem an integer that already ends in **-t(ë)** (the ordinals for 6-20, 26-30, 36-40, and so on), do not add another **-të** as suffix: **i gjashtë** 'sixth' (from **gjashtë 'six')**, **i shtatë** 'seventh', **i njëmbëdhjetë** 'eleventh', etc. Since all numbers from **gjashtë** 'six' to **dhjetë** 'ten' already end in **-të**, only the ordinals from **i dytë** 'second' up to **i pestë** 'fifth', **i njëzetenjëtë** 'twenty-first', **i njëzetepestë** 'twenty-fifth', etc. have stem forms with **-të** distinct from those of the corresponding cardinal numbers. For the numbers **njëzet** 'twenty' and **dyzet** 'forty' the ordinal has a single **-t: i njëzetë** 'twentieth' and **i dyzetë** 'fortieth' (see also Section 7.2).

This suffix is also productive with citation form stems of verbs ending in consonants, as in **i çelët** 'clear', **i fshehtë** 'secretive', **i ftohtë** 'cold', **i ngrohtë** 'warm', **i hapët** 'open', **i lagët** 'wet', **i mprehtë** 'sharp', **i nxehtë** 'hot', **i ulët** 'low', **i vakët** 'lukewarm', **i zbehtë** 'pale'.

C. Adjectives Formed by Compounding

A compound adjective is formed from the union of two (sometimes three) stems into a single word. This method of derivation is quite productive for adjectives. The elements of the compound may be in a) coordinate or b) subordinate relationship with one another.

a) COORDINATE ADJECTIVE COMPOUNDING

This method of derivation has become very productive, especially in the literary language of recent times. Constituting the derivational stem are two (sometimes three) adjectives of equal value syntactically and semantically, neither dependent on nor modifying the other, and each complementing the other in meaning: **anglo-amerikan** 'Anglo-American', **agraro-industrial** 'agrarian-industrial', **demokratiko-borgjez** 'bougeois-democratic', **materialo-teknik** 'material and technical', **ekonomiko-shoqëror** 'socio-economic', **sovjeto-anglo-amerikan** 'soviet-anglo-American', **tekniko-shkencor** 'technical and scientific', etc. In speech, the vowel **o** provides a connecting link in these compounds, and in writing this function is additionally performed by the hyphen placed between the component elements, attesting to the relative independence of the parts of the compounds:. e.g., **punë TEKNIKO-SHKENCORE = punë TEKNIKE e SHKENCORE** 'a technical and scientific job'. Some of these formations are not fixed in the vocabulary, but are rather *ad hoc* formations.

b) SUBORDINATE ADJECTIVE COMPOUNDING

This method of derivation is also very productive in the Albanian language. One of the elements of the compound adjective formed, either the qualifying or the qualified element, designates a notion broader than that of the compound as a whole. The qualifying element may come first or in the compound.

In these noun + noun compound adjectives the second element qualifies the first. This type is very common in colloquial language as well as literary. It has its main source in the device of comparison, as in **gërshetë-degë** 'thick-braided' ("branch-braid"). Such a comparison is easily seen in words like **gushpëllumb** 'purple ("throat-pigeon")', **hundëshkabë** 'hook-nosed', **kokëderr** 'stubborn, pig-headed ("head-pig")', **kokëkungull** 'empty-headed ("head-pumpkin")', **sygrifshë** 'variegated-eyed ("eye-jaybird")', **mjekërcjap** 'goat-beard', **zemërkrund-e-gërdhu** 'miserly ("heart chaff-and-bran")', **dor-e-këmbargjendë** 'silver hand-and-footed ("hand and foot-silver")'.

Such adjectives may be composed of: a) two noun stems; b) a noun stem and an adjectival one; c) two adjectival stems; d) a noun stem plus an adverbial stem, or vice versa; e) an adverbial stem and an adjectival stem; f) a number (or pronoun) and an adjective; g) an adjective, a noun and the suffix **-sh**; or h) the reflexive pronoun **vetë** 'self' plus an agentive noun or adjective.

a) Adjectives composed of two noun stems. These adjectives indicate the derived modifying feature indirectly by intersecting the meaning of one thing with that of another, attributing to the first element one of the distinguishing features of the second: e.g., **hundëshkabë** 'hook-nosed ("nose-eagle")', **sylesh** 'stupid ("eye-wool")', **shpirtkazmë** 'malicious, merciless ("soul of a pickaxe")', **vetullsorrë** 'black-browed ("eyebrow-raven")', **zemërgur** 'hard-hearted ("heart-stone")', **zemërlepur** 'faint-hearted ("heart-rabbit")'. In present-day Standard Albanian in poetry, the attributive, second element may itself be double as in **gjuhëhelm-e-thikë** 'bad-mouth ("tongue of poison and knives")', **zemërkrunde-e-gërdhu** 'stingy ("heart of chaff and bran")'. Sometimes, however, comparison does not serve as basis for the formation of the adjective: **sylesh** 'stupid, wooly-eyed', **hundëqurre** 'runny-nose ("nose-mucous")', **këmbëlesh** 'hairy-legged ("leg-hair")', etc.; here the first element is modified by the second element of the composition.

b) Adjectives composed of a noun stem and an adjectival stem.

This is one of the most productive types. In noun + adjective compound adjectives, the second element may serve either as the modifying or modified element. In the first type the first element is composed of a noun designating something belonging to the thing modified by the compound: e.g., **ballëhapët** 'sincere ("forehead-open")', **barkgjerë** 'broad-bellied ("belly-broad")', **belhollë** 'slim-wasted ("waist-thin")', **cipëplasur** 'shameless ("skin-burst")', **derëbardhë** 'lucky ("white-doored")', **ditëgjatë** 'long-lived ("day-long")', **dorëmbarë** 'lucky ("hand-prosperous")', **dritëshkurtër** 'short-sighted ("light-short")', **fatbardhë** 'lucky ("fate-white")', **fijehollë** 'thin-threaded', **fjalëmbël** 'sweet-tongued', **flokëverdhë** 'yellow-haired, blond', **gojëprishur** 'foul-mouthed ("mouth-spoiled")', **kokëprerë** 'beheaded ("head-cut")', **sy-e-vetullzezë** 'black-eyed and -browed', **zemërgjerë** 'generous ("broad-hearted")'.

The second type has become more productive in literary language, but has its source in colloquial Albanian. The first, modifying element may be any kind of noun, while the second, modified element is an agentive noun: **jetëdhënës** 'life-giving', **frytdhënës** 'fruitful', **trup-e-ndotkundërmonjës** 'stinking-bodied', **liridashës** 'freedom-loving', **lotsjellës** 'tear-jerking', **naftëmbajtës** 'oil-containing', **naft-e-gazmbajtës** 'containing oil and gas'.

NOTE

The conjunction **-e-** that we find in the compounds above with more than two derivational stems is still productive as a copulative coordinating conjunction that may be used to avoid repetition:

Kjo ishte vajzë nja 16-vjeçare, SY-E-VETULLZEZË (=syzezë e vetullzezë). 'This was a girl about 16 years old, with dark eyes and brows ("EYE-AND-EYEBROW BLACK") (="eyeblack and eyebrowblack").'

Po sa Lenka kemi njohur ne, ashtu të vogla, FLOKË-E-SYZEZA. 'But we have known many Lenkas, rather small, with dark hair and eyes ("HAIR-AND-EYE BLACK").'

c) Adjectives composed of quantifier plus adjective.

In derivational stems of this type of subordinate compound, any number or one of the quantifiers such as **shumë** 'multi, many' and **disa** 'several' may serve as the qualifying element, while one of a limited group of adjectives serves as the element qualified: **dyvjeçar** 'bi-annual', **njëditor** 'daily', **njëmujor** 'monthly', **njëvjeçar** 'annual', **shumëvjeçar** 'of many years', **treqindvjeçar** 'tri-centennial', **i dyanshëm** 'two-sided', **i njëanshëm** 'one-sided', **i shumanshëm** 'many-sided', **disaditor** 'of several days', **disamujor** 'of several months', **disavjeçar** 'of several years', etc.

d) Adjectives composed of a quantifier plus a noun with the suffix **-sh**.

In derivational stems of this type any number or one of the quantifiers such as **shumë** and **disa** may serve as the qualifying element in the compound, while a noun plus the suffix **-sh** serves as the element qualified: **njërrokësh** 'monosyllabic', **dykatësh** 'two-storey', **dypalësh** 'bilateral', **tringjyrësh** 'tri-colored', **shumëngjyrësh** 'multi-colored', **disaballësh** 'multi-faceted', **disaditësh** 'of several days duration', **disajavësh** 'of several weeks duration', **disakatësh** 'multi-storied', etc. Historically, what has happened here is that the ablative plural case ending **-sh** has become a derivational suffix, converting agglutinated word sequences into single compound words.

NOTE

The suffix **-e** is added to such compounds to form the feminine stem. In adjectives of the type **dyvjeç-e** 'two-year-old', **njëzetvjeç-e** 'twenty-year-old', the consonant cluster **-tsh** has come to be written and pronounced as **-ç: dyvjetsh > dyvjeç.**

PESËMBËDHJETËVJEÇE kish ardhur ajo në kalibe. 'She came to the hut, (when she was) FIFTEEN YEARS OLD.'

Në ballin e saj prej gruaje DYZETEPESËVJEÇE, koha kishte qëndisur gjurmët e veta. 'On the forehead of the FORTY-FIVE YEAR OLD woman, time had embroidered its own footprints.'

Dy vjet më parë, kur qe PESËVJEÇ djalë, kishte edhe ai një njeri për zemër. 'Two years earlier, when he was a FIVE YEAR OLD boy, he too had someone after his own heart.'

e) Adjectives composed of the reflexive pronoun **vetë** 'self' and an agentive noun or adjective.

This derivational type has become more and more productive in recent times. The first element here, the reflexive pronoun **vetë** 'self', serves as the complement of the second element, an agentive noun or adjective: **vetëdashës** 'voluntary ("self-willed")', **vetëmbushës** 'self-filling', **vetëshërbyes** 'self-serving', **vetëshkarkues** 'self-unloading', **vetëvrasës** 'suicidal ("self-killing")', etc.

4.7.2 Non-productive Adjective Formation

A. Adjectives with Prefixes

The negative prefix **a-**, identical in meaning with the prefix **pa-**, is found principally in adjectives of foreign origin: e.g., **asimetrik** 'asymmetric', **apolitik** 'apolitical', **anormal** 'abnormal'. It also appears with an Albanian stem in the formation of the adjective **afetar** 'non-religious'.

The prefix **mbi-**, with a meaning akin to English *super-* or *extra-,* is not very productive in the formation of adjectives: **mbinjerëzor** 'superhuman', **mbitokësor** 'extra-terrestrial', **i mbinatyrshëm = mbinatyror** 'supernatural', etc.,

The prefix **për-**, which conveys the meaning of reinforcement and sometimes comparison, has remained only slightly productive: e.g., **e përdalur** 'tramp' (used of a loose woman) = "thoroughly emerged", **i përkundërt** 'opposite, contrary' (**kundër** 'against'), **i përthimë** '(completely) gray, gray-haired'.

Other prefixes have remained unproductive or only slightly productive. This group includes **ç- (sh-, zh-), an-, in- (i- and im-)** all of which have a negating sense: e.g., **çnjerëzor** 'inhuman', **i çrregullt** 'disorderly', **i shkujdesur** 'careless', **i shndershëm** 'dishonorable', **i zhdrejtë** 'indirect, oblique'; **analfabet** 'illiterate'; **imoral** 'immoral', **impersonal; inorganik, intranzitiv** 'intransitive'.

B. Adjectives with Suffixes

The suffix **-tor** has been only slightly productive in forming unarticulated adjectives. Adjectives formed with this suffix have the meaning "pertaining to" or "having". Noun stems serve as derivational stems: e.g., **baritor** 'pastoral', **leshtor** 'hairy'. A large number of unarticulated adjectives meaning "pertaining to X" have been formed with the suffixes **-ik, -al, -ual, -oz** and **-iv**, and introduced into Albanian from other European languages: **agronomik** 'agronomic', **akademik, atomik, biografik** 'biographical', **diplomatik, fotografik, teorik** 'theoretical', **zoologjik** 'zoological'; **eksperimental, embrional** 'embryonic', **frontal, kontinental, koral** 'choral', **personal; gradual, tekstual; ambicioz** 'ambitious', **luksoz** 'luxurious, deluxe', **nervoz** 'nervous', **poroz** 'porous', **aktiv, edukativ** 'educational', **federativ** 'federal', **objektiv, subjektiv,** etc. For all the examples above, the stem has also been borrowed as a noun. However, among adjectives of this type there are also some whose stem is not otherwise found in Albanian: e.g., **alternativ** 'alternate', **deskriptiv, eruptiv** 'eruptive', **naiv, analitik, brutal.**

Corresponding to noun stems that end in **-ikë**, are adjectives ending in **-ik**: e.g., **agroteknikë** 'agro-technology' / **agroteknik** 'agro-technical', **dialektikë** 'dialectic' / **dialektik** 'dialectal', **teknikë** 'technique' / **teknik** 'technical', etc.

Nouns ending in **-ikë** can also serve as derivational stems for adjectives ending in **-or**: **gramatikor** 'grammatical', **gjimnastikor** 'gymnastic', **muzikor** 'musical', which are formed from noun stems **gramatikë** 'grammar', **gjimnastikë** 'gymnastic' and **muzikë** 'music', plus the adjectival suffix **-or**.

In addition some adjectives have been formed by adding an **-e** suffix to adverbs ending in **-ërisht**, in turn derived from nouns designating human beings: **burrërishte** 'for men', **grarishte** 'for women', **djemërishte** 'for boys', **pleqërishte** 'characteristic of the elderly'.

C. Adjectives with Adjectival Articles

A few adjectives have been formed by simply preposing an adjectival article to adverbial stems, as in **i tatëpjetë** 'downward', **i vonë** 'late'.

D. Adjectives with Suffixes and Articles

The suffix **-ë** has been used to form a number of articulated adjectives from adverbial and noun stems, as in **i drejtë** 'just, right', **i fortë** 'strong', **i kotë** 'vain', **i lartë** 'high', **i mjaftë** 'sufficient', **i plotë** 'full, complete', **i shpejtë** 'fast', **i vërtetë** 'true'.

The suffix **-(ë)m(ë)** is no longer very productive. In the past it has derived articulated adjectives from a) noun stems, b) other adjectival stems, and c) adverbial stems. Noun stems underlie a few adjectives in **-(ë)m(ë)**: **i fisëm** 'noble' from **fis** 'clan', **i mesëm** 'average, middle' from **mes** 'middle'. With other adjevtives as stems, this suffix has also remained largely unproductive: **i epërm** 'superior' from **i epër** 'upper', **i parmë** 'anterior' from **i parë** 'first'.

The **-(ë)m(ë)** suffix has been more productive with simple or compound adverbial stems: e.g., **i andejmë** 'of around there', **i këndejmë** 'of around here', **i këtejmë** 'of here', **i mëtejmë** 'from further', **i mëposhtëm** 'of below', **i nesërm** 'of tomorrow', **i pasmë** 'posterior ("of behind")', **i pastajmë** 'subsequent ("of later")', **i përtejmë** 'over there', **i prapëm** 'last, "of behind"', **i sipërm** 'of above', **i sotëm** 'of today', **i tejmë** 'yonder'.

NOTE

A similar suffix that has remained unproductive in present-day Standard Albanian is the suffix **-ër**. With this suffix, a few articulated adjectives have been formed from various adverbial and nominal stems: e.g., **i poshtër** 'low, vile' from **poshtë** 'below', **i shkurtër** 'short' from **shkurt** 'briefly', **i shurdhër** 'deaf' from **shurdh** 'deaf person'.

E. Adjectives with Suffixes, Prefixes, and Articles

This method of derivation is very limited in yielding articulated adjectives. It involves only the prefix **për-** 'through, throughout, thorough' and the suffixes **-t(ë)** and **-shëm**: e.g., **i përbashkët** 'common', from **bashkë** 'together', **i përfushtë** 'flat' from **fushë** 'plain, field', **i përciptë** 'superficial' from **cipë** 'skin', **i përpiktë** 'precise' from **pikë** 'point', **i përbotshëm** 'worldwide' from **botë** 'world', **i përkohshëm** 'temporary, provisional' from **kohë** 'time' **i përvajshëm** 'lamentable' from **vaj** 'lament', **i përgjithshëm** 'general' from **gjithë** 'all'.

F. Adjectives Formed by Conversion

A number of adjectives are formed by conversion of words (mainly nouns) from other parts of speech into adjectives, without the aid of an affix. As adjectives, these words lose their former syntactic and morphological properties and take on adjectival grammatical properties. Serving as stems to form corresponding adjectives may be simple nouns like **kukull** 'puppet, doll', **kyç** 'key', **bullgar** 'Bulgarian', **freng** 'French(man)', **plak** 'old(man)', **trim** 'hero, brave', etc.; or nouns derived with various suffixes, such as **dorac** 'one-handed (person)', **përtac** 'lazy (person)'; **burracak** 'coward(ly)', **endacak** 'wanderer, nomad(ic)', **frikacak** 'coward(ly)'; **rrugaç** 'hooligan'; **dinak** 'sly(one)', **fluturak** 'flying(one)'; **leckaman** 'ragged (person)', **çalaman** 'cripple, lame (one)'; **dibran** '(inhabitant) of Dibra', **shkodran** '(inhabitant) of Shkodra', **pasanik** 'wealthy (person)', **prapanik** 'backward (one); **shkatërraq** 'sloppy (person)'; **fshatar** 'peasant', **gënjeshtar** 'liar, lying'; **frikash** 'coward(ly)', **qurrash** 'snotty, runny-nose (person)'; **rrëmbyes** 'abducting, predatory', **luftënxitës** 'bellicose (person) warmonger(ing)', **mishngrënës** 'carnivor(ous)', **ndihmës** 'helping, helper', **vartës** 'dependent'; **marksist** 'Marxist', **komunist; grabitqar** 'predator(y)'; **këngëtar** 'singing, singer', **luftëtar** 'fighting, fighter', etc. Under the analogical influence of noun-adjectives like these, the suffixes involved have, in various degrees, become productive in forming adjectives, directly, as discussed earlier in this chapter.

Besides nouns of like those type discussed above, a few adverbs ending in **-çe** have become adjectives by conversion: e.g., **derrçe** 'pig-like, stubbornly', **fshaçe** 'peasant-style', **labçe** 'in the style of Labëri', **vendçe** 'native style'. This is true also of distributive (i.e., with the property that the meaning of the word is distributed more-or-less evenly among the members of the class involved) adverbs formed by noun reduplication (repeating a noun twice): **copa-copa** 'piece by piece, in bits', **fije-fije** 'in threads', **flokë-flokë** 'in flakes', **pika-pika** 'dotted, dappled'. On the analogy of such adjectives, a great number of distributive adjectives have now been formed directly by reduplication such as **katrore-katrore** 'square-shaped', **kllapa-kllapa** 'bracketed', **lara-lara** 'spotted, mottled', **lule-lule** 'flowery', **ngjyra-ngjyra** 'variegated in color', **vargje-vargje** 'verse upon verse, range after range'.

G. Compound Adjectives

a) Adjectives composed of two adjectival stems.

This derivational type is only slightly productive; for the most part the stems are calques: literal translation of words borrowed from foreign languages. In this type of compound the first element is modified by the second, with the meaning correspondingly narrowed down in scope: e.g., **elektromagnetik, electromekanik, gjermanolindor** 'East German', **gjermanoperëndimor** 'West German', **irlandezoverior** 'Northern Irish', **koreanojugor** 'South Korean', **vietnamezojugor** 'South Vietnamese'. Note the role of the vowel **o** here in fusing the two adjectives into a single indivisible word: e.g., **koreanojugor** from **korean jugor** 'South Korean'.

b) Adjectives composed of an adverbial stem plus an adjectival stem.

This type also is not very productive. Here we find the adverbs **gjysmë** 'half (semi-)', **jashtë** 'out (extra-)', **lart** 'high (above-)', **sipër** 'over (super-)', **shumë** 'very, most', and a few others that have united with various adjectival stems: e.g., **gjysmanalfabet** 'semi-illiterate', **gjysmëproletar** 'semi-proletarian', **gjysmëzyrtar** 'semi-official', **jashtëgjuhësor** 'extra-lingual', **jashtëkohor** 'during outside hours', **jashtëshkollor** 'extra-curricular', **i jashtëligjshëm** 'extra-legal', **i jashtëzakonshëm** 'extraordinary'; **i lartpërmendur** 'above-mentioned', **i sipërpërmendur** 'above-mentioned'; **i shumënderuar** 'very-honorable', **i shumëndritur** 'most enlightened'.

> **Pena ime gërvishte në letër dhe përpilonte "materialin" për tezat e studimit të burrit të saj, TË SHUMËNDERUARIT Zylo.** 'My pen scratched on the sheet of paper and compiled "the material" for the study theses of her husband, THE MOST HONORABLE Zylo.'

c) Adjectives composed of an adverbial stem plus a noun (or vice versa).

This type is only slightly productive and not very common in colloquial language. With the adverb coming first, the derivational stem may derive from any adverb plus an agentive: **keqdashës** 'malevolent' ("evil-loving"), **largpamës** 'far-sighted', **largvajtës** 'achiever ("far-goer")', **mirëbërës** 'charitable' ("do-gooder"), etc. The first element modifies the second in the compound.

Still less common and more limited is the type with noun plus adverb, with the noun modified by the adverb, as in **kryejashtë** 'bare-headed ("head-outside")', **kokëjashtë** 'bareheaded ("head-outside")', **hundëpërpjet** 'arrogant ("nose up")'. We may ascribe the origin of this type to agglutination.

CHAPTER 5

Adverbs and Adverbials

5.1 General Information

An ADVERBIAL PHRASE (abbreviated AdvP) is a word or sequence of words which serve the typical functions of an adverb, such as modifying a clause, a verb, an adjective, a noun or another adverb. An AdvP most commonly consists of a single adverb (e.g., **jashtë** 'outside'), adverb group (**jashtëzakonisht keq**, 'unusually badly'), or prepositional phrase (**me gjithë zemër** '"with all heart", sincerely'), but words belonging to other parts of speech may also be used adverbially under certain circumstances: e.g., participial phrases (**duke pritur** 'while waiting', **për të ngrënë** 'for eating, to eat') or noun phrases (**ditën** 'during the day').

The adverb is that part of speech which serves to modify parts of speech other than nouns and pronouns, namely verbs, adjectives, prepositions, and other adverbs. In addition, adverbs may modify phrases, clauses, and even whole sentences. Adverbs are characterized by their lack of any inflectional categories (i.e., they are invariable in form); unlike other invariable parts of speech such as conjunctions and prepositions, they may form a sentence constituent by themselves. As in English, adverbs are somewhat freer in their placement than adjectives, though they most commonly follow the word they modify:

> **Mos SHKEL KËSHTU në dërrasë të kalbur, se s'do të të DALË MIRË.** 'Don't STEP LIKE THIS on a rotten plank, or it won't go ("EMERGE") WELL with you.
> **Ja të mos SHKOJMË LARG, të marrim anëtarët e brigadës kulturale.** 'Well, let's not GO FAR, (and) let's take the members of the cultural brigade.'
> **Pëllëmbën e kish të gjerë, si petë byreku të fryrë si brumë I ARDHUR MIRË dhe të bardhë.** 'He had a broad palm, like a swollen pie leaf, like white, WELL-leavened ("ARRIVED") dough.'

Adverbs are often derived from, and therefore semantically related to, other parts of speech, often by characteristic derivational suffixes; in addition to adverbs so formed, a great number of phrasal locutions also serve as adverbials.

With respect to structure, adverbs may be classified as SIMPLE, such as **mirë** 'well', **keq** 'badly', **bukur** 'lovely'; DERIVED through suffixation such as **trimërisht** 'bravely', **dorazi** 'by the hand', **fluturimthi** 'quickly'; AGGLUTINATED or COMPOUND, such as **kudo** 'everywhere', **kurdo** 'anytime', **gjithnjë** 'always', **këmbadoras** 'hand and foot'; and LOCUTIONARY, such as **sot për sot** 'at present', **ditë për ditë** 'daily', **me të mirë** 'gently', **për së afërmi** 'at close range', **një nga një** 'one by bone', **me ngut** 'in haste'.

Semantically, adverbs extend over a considerable range and designate a wide variety of features and circumstances, as will be seen below.

5.2 Functional Classification of Adverbs

5.2.1 Pro-adverbs

Functionally, one should first distinguish pro-adverbs from all other adverbs. In particular, the interrogative pro-adverbs: **ku** 'where', **kur** 'when', **nga** 'whence, from where', **si** 'how', **qysh** 'how', **pse** 'why', **përse** 'why'--as well as the deictic pro-adverbs: **ashtu** 'like that, that way, thus', **kështu** 'like this, this way, thus', **andej** 'around there, in that direction', **këtej** 'in this direction, around here', **aty** 'right there', **këtu** 'here', **atje** 'over there'--all have the kind of general and abstract meaning associated with pro-forms. In this respect, this group of adverbs resembles pronouns, since, like pronouns, pro-adverbs refer or indicate, rather than name or designate.

Pro-adverbs of manner imply a comparison: **ashtu** 'that way, thus', **kështu** 'this way, like this', **kësilloj** 'this sort of way', **kësisoj** 'like this', **njësoj** 'the same (way)', etc.

The interrogative pro-adverbs, like interrogative pronouns, serve to inquire about the manner or the causal, temporal or locative circumstances of a predication:

Si je? 'How are you?'
Pse shkoni? 'Why are you leaving?'
More, vërtet, KU i kishe gjetur gjithë ato fjalë shkencore në referatin tënd. 'Hey now, WHERE did you find all these scientific words in your lecture?'

The interrogative pro-adverbs of manner **si** 'how' and **qysh** 'how' are used in direct and indirect interrogative clauses. **Si** pervades the entire language, while **qysh** is less common, often having a somewhat rural flavor:

SI i ke punët, shoku Sekretar? 'HOW are things going, comrade Secretary?'
"QYSH e gatuan këtë gjellë?" Drita pyeti plakën fshatare. '"HOW do you prepare this dish?" Drita asked the old peasant woman.'

The interrogative temporal pro-adverb **kur** 'when' is used in direct and indirect interrogative clauses:

KUR lindi Skënderbeu? Asnjë nga historianët e vjetër nuk na e thotë. 'WHEN was Skënderbeu born? None of the old historians tells us.'
S'dihet se KUR ka ndodhur ajo ngjarje që na tregove. 'It is not known WHEN that story you told us took place.'
(For use of the word **kur** as a conjunctive temporal adverb, see Section 5.2.2 B.1.)

Like pronouns, locative pro-adverbs have quite broad meanings. In order to make them more exact, they are followed by another adverb:

ATJE TEJ dëgjohej hingëllimi i dëshpëruar, i mallëngjyer, i ngjirur, i këputur i një kali. 'YONDER was heard the sad, nostalgic, hoarse, broken neighing of a horse.'
Mimozës iu duk sikur goditjet e sahatit të qytetit nuk ranëATJE TEJ, matanë nëbulevard, po sikur gjëmuan ATY BRENDA, në shtëpi të saj. 'It seemed to Mimozë that the chimes of the town clock did not strike WAY OUT THERE, across the boulevard, but as if they thundered RIGHT WITHIN her house.'
This type of adverb can be qualified not only by another adverb, but also by a word sequence, or clause, as seen above.

The interrogative locative pro-adverbs **ku** 'where' and **nga** 'from where' are used in both direct and indirect interrogative clauses. **Ku** and **nga** also serve as conjunctions to connect a main clause to a dependent locative clause.

The pro-adverbs **përse** 'for what, why', and **pse** 'why', are used to inquire about the CAUSE or PURPOSE of an action:

(Cause) **Ja, PËRSE Partia jonë i kushton kujdes edukimit të brezit të ri.** 'Here is WHY our Party devotes care to the education of the new generation.'

Unë thirra dhe nuk e kuptova PËRSE thirrjen time nuk e dëgjova as vetë. 'I called out and did not understand WHY it was that even I did not hear my call.'

(Purpose) **Do të pyeste dy tre vetë, do t'u thoshte nga ishte e PËRSE kishte ardhur dhe me siguri do të dilnin të njohur.** 'He would ask two or three people, he would tell them where he was from and WHY he had come, and assuredly they would find that they knew each other.'

PËRSE të vejë Jani në arat e gjata natën? 'WHY should Jani go to the long fields at night?'

(Ambiguously Cause or Purpose) **Punëtori / PSE sulmon, / PSE sulet ballë brigadës në repart / e i duket puna jo mundim, / po art?** 'The worker / WHY does he attack, / WHY does he dash in front of the detachment's brigade / and feels as if work is not toil / but art?'

Like interrogative pronouns, interrogative pro-adverbs are also used both in sentences with indirect interrogative clauses, and as conjunctions for other types of clauses.

Shko, shko, të lutem, se lajme të tilla, me mirë t'i marr vesh sa më vonë unë, që të kem kohë të mendohem SI t'ia bëj e NGA t'ia kthej. 'Please go, go, because it is better that I learn such news as late as possible, so that I may have time to think HOW to handle it and WHERE to turn.'

As a result of such usage, the adverbs **ku**, **kur, nga,** etc., may now also be considered to be full-fledged conjunctions (see Chapter 10), and depending on their function, may be causal, temporal, or locative conjunctive adverbs:

Kongresi V i Partisë po mblidhet në kohën KUR partia jonë mbushi një çerek shekulli të jetës së saj revolucionare. 'The Fifth Congress of the Party is convening at a time WHEN our Party has completed a quarter century of revolutionary life.'

Grupi komunist i Shkodrës, KU bënte pjesë Qemali, sa vinte e zgjerohej. 'The communist group of Shkodër, IN WHICH Qemal participated, was getting ever larger.'

Like pronouns, pro-adverbs may take prepositions in front of them. The preposition that is most frequently used is **për** 'for': e.g., **për aty** 'for there', **për këtu** 'for here', **për ashtu** 'for that reason', **për kështu** 'for this reason', **për ku** 'for where', **për nga** 'from', **për kur** 'for when'. For more information on the use of prepositions before adverbs of various types, see Chapter 9.

5.2.2 Adverbs Proper

Depending on their meaning and function in the clause, adverbs proper are divided into QUALIFYING adverbs and CIRCUMSTANTIAL adverbs. Qualifying adverbs may be qualitative or quantitative in meaning and are accordingly divided into a) MANNER adverbs and b) adverbial QUANTIFIERS.

Manner adverbs perform the same function with verbs that adjectives perform with nouns:

Bilbili ia thotë BUKUR, lumi vete gjithë VALË. 'The nightingale sings BEAUTIFULLY, the river flows all WAVY.'

Të ngrihemi të gjithë më këmbë dhe atëhere turku do ta ketë KEQ. 'Let us all rise up and then the Turk will be in a FIX ("will have it BADLY").'

Adverbial quantifiers indicate the intensity of an action, or the degree of the quality or circumstance expressed by an adjective or adverb:

(Manner) **Pastaj njëri ia merr këngës LEHTË.** 'Then one of them starts singing SOFTLY.'

(Quantifier) **I ngjan SHUMË s'ëmës.** 'He resembles his mother A LOT.'

There are differences between the two sub-groups in terms of the words they qualify as well (see below).

Circumstantial adverbs designate the settings in which the action of the verb is carried out.

Në fillim shoku Andrea u skuq, PASTAJ u inatos, por më në fund, duke u përtypur, e pranoi gabimin. 'At first comrade Andrea blushed, THEN became angry, but finally admitted his error, squirming ("chewing") all the while.'

ATJE POSHTË, në mes të qytetit, herë-herë ndriçonte ndonjë dritë e zbehtë, ia thoshte një gjel i përgjumur, ngrihej uturima e një motori, lehte një qen dhe PËRSËRI pllakoste heshtja. 'DOWN THERE, in the midst of the city, a pale light shone now and then, a drowsy rooster crowed, the roar of a motor was heard, a dog barked, and AGAIN the silence fell.'

Depending on the condition they refer to, circumstantial adverbs are divided into: a)temporal adverbs, b) locative adverbs, and c) causal adverbs. In contrast to circumstantial adverbs, qualifying adverbs have a closer semantic and syntactic relationship to the words they qualify, the group forming a single constituent of the larger unit of which they are part, while circumstantial adverbs often qualify the whole clause or sentence. With verbs, the usual word order is VERB + QUALIFYING ADVERB, but CIRCUMSTANTIAL ADVERB + VERB. However, for stylistic focus the order for qualifying adverbs may be reversed.

Qualifying adverbs also differ from circumstantial adverbs in formation. As will be seen below, many manner adverbs are formed with a derivational suffix, but very few circumstantial adverbs have been so formed.

A. Manner Adverbs

The term "manner" is used here with a very broad meaning, because in fact the group includes adverbs of many different kinds of meaning. Among those meanings we shall call attention to the following:

A.1 Qualitative Adverbs

Adverbs of the type **mirë** 'well', **keq** 'badly', that correspond to adjective stems (**i mirë** 'good', **i keq** 'bad') modify verbs and indicate something about the action of the verb itself. Other adverbs in this class are **bukur** 'beautifully', **ëmbël** 'sweetly', **hollë** 'thinly', **lehtë** 'easily, lightly', **mbarë** 'well, prosperously', **pastër** 'cleanly', **qartë** 'clearly', **qetë** 'calmly', **shkurt** 'briefly', **shtrembër** 'crookedly', **thjesht** 'simply, purely', **vështirë** 'with difficulty', etc.

Komiteti Qendror i Partisë ka theksuar QARTË se riorganizimi i aparatit shtetëror duhet të shoqërohet me ndryshimin rrënjësor të metodës së punës së tij. 'The Central Committee of the Party has CLEARLY emphasized that the reorganization of the state apparatus must be accompanied by the radical change in the method of its work.'

Asnjë nga sulmet e ushtrisë turke nuk vajti MBARË. 'None of the offensives of the Turkish army succeeded ("went SUCCESSFUL").'

Pasi afroi fyellin në buzë, mënjanoi pak kokën dhe ia mori ËMBËL. 'After bringing the flute to his lips, he tilted his head a bit and began to play it SWEET.'

Për të qenë i thjeshtë teksti, duhet të krihet nga gjërat e panevojshme, që e ngatërrojnë KEQ mendjen e të riut. 'In order that the text be pure, it must be combed of all unnecessary things which BADLY confuse the mind of the young.'

Some manner adverbs may reflect the physical or mental state of the one who carries out a specific action: **fuqishëm** 'powerfully', **furishëm** 'furiously', **gëzueshëm** 'joyfully', **hareshëm** 'merrily', **mendueshëm** 'thoughtfully', **natyrshëm** 'naturally', **shterueshëm** 'dryly', **rrjedhshëm** 'fluently', etc.

> **Me erë e me shira Nëntori kish hyrë / E pylli kish mbetur i shkretë. RRËMBYESHËM Tetori ngado kishte fryrë / E pemëve më s'dukeshin fletë.** 'With wind and rains November had come / And the forest had become desolate. IMPETUOUSLY October had blown from all over / And leaves could no longer be seen on trees.'

> **Një shi i vrullshëm dhe i egër përplasej FURISHËM në muret me plitharë të shtëpisë dykatëshe.** 'A driving, fierce rain dashed FURIOUSLY on the adobe walls of the two-story house.'

> **Ne e sjellim bisedën në një mënyrë të tillë që xha Zariku të tregojë diçka, po ta tregojë NATYRSHËM dhe pa u shtyrë.** 'We bring the discussion around in such a manner that Uncle Zarik may relate something, but relate it NATURALLY and without being pushed.'

A.1a. Spatial Adverbs

Another group of manner adverbs indicate aspects of physical space. Such are the adverbs **cekët** 'superficially, shallowly', **gjerë** 'broadly', **gjatë** 'long', **thellë** 'deeply', **ulët** 'low', etc.

> **Po kujdesi më i madh duhej treguar në mbjellje, se, po u hoth fara THELLË ose CEKËT, e mori lumi.** 'But the greatest care had to be shown at planting, because if the seed were sown (too) DEEPLY or SHALLOWLY, that was the end of it ("the river took it").'

> **Fusha kishte ndjerë vetëm hapjen e themeleve vigane të fabrikës dhe peshën e rëndë të plintave dhe të blloqeve prej betoni, që u ngulën THELLË në trupin e saj.** 'The plain had felt only the digging of the giant foundations of the factory, and the heavy weight of the footstalls and blocks of concrete that were thrust DEEPLY in its body.'

A.1b. Aspectual Adverbs

Some adverbs reflect aspects of the verb in relation to time: **menjëherë** 'immediately', **pak nga pak** 'little by little', **papritur** 'unexpectedly', **papandehur** 'unforeseen' **rëndom** 'commonly, usually', **shpesh** 'often', **vazhdimisht** 'constantly', etc.

> **Hante NGADALË duke fshirë herë pas here buzët e holla dhe dëgjonte lajmet.** 'He ate SLOWLY, wiping his thin lips from time to time, and listened to the news.'

> **Shiu i rrëmbyer i vjeshtës, ashtu siç nis, po ashtu dhe pushon: PAPRITUR e MENJËHERË.** 'The impetuous rains of autumn end the same way they begin: suddenly ("UNEXPECTEDLY") and all at once ("IMMEDIATELY").'

> **Ajo u shtang e u pështet pas furkës së çardhakut, se qoftë fatkeqësia, qoftë lumturia, kur vijnë PAPANDEHUR, të vrasin njësoj.** 'She was stunned and leaned on the pitchfork in the veranda, because, be it misfortune, be it happiness, when they come UNFORESEEN they kill you in the same way.'

> **PAK NGA PAK fytyra e Vitës këmbeu dritë e në këtë këmbim sikur iu mbrujtën disa tipare të reja, të padukura gjer ahere.** 'LITTLE BY LITTLE the face of Vitë changed color ("light"), and in this change it seemed that some new features, invisible until then, took form in her.'

A.1c. Adverbs in -(i)sht

Most adverbs formed with the suffix -(i)sht have meanings with the semantic value of a corresponding sequence containing the adjective or noun stem from which the -(i)sht adverb is formed: "*in a (ADJECTIVE) way*", "*from a (ADJECTIVE) point of view*", "*with (ABSTRACT NOUN)*": **artistikisht** 'artistically' = **në mënyrë artistike** 'in an artistic way'; **besnikërisht** 'faithfully' = **me besnikëri** 'with faith'; **teorikisht** 'theoretically' = **nga pikpamje teorike** 'from a theoretical viewpoint', etc. Other such adverbs are: **ashpërsisht** 'severely, roughly', **bujarisht** 'seriously, nobly', **burrërisht** 'bravely', **djallëzisht** 'devilishly', **dhelpërisht** 'cunningly, foxily', **egësisht** 'fiercely, wildly', **fizikisht** 'physically', **fshehtësisht** 'secretly', **gjallërisht** 'vivaciously', **heroikisht** 'heroically', **hollësisht** 'finely, in detail', **imtësisht** 'finely, minutely', **lehtësisht** 'easily, lightly', **përzemërsisht** 'cordially', **pjesërisht** 'partially', **rastësisht** 'by chance, fortuitously', **teorikisht** 'theoretically', **thjeshtësisht** 'simply, purely', **ushtarakisht** 'militarily', **vullnetarisht** 'voluntarily', **zyrtarisht** 'officially', etc.

> **Kolegjiumi thotë është ca i dobët ARTISTIKISHT.** 'The collegium says it is somewhat weak ARTISTICALLY.'
> **Forca të tjera sulmojnë ASHPËRSISHT fortinën pranë xhamisë së vjetër.** 'Other forces FIERCELY attack the fort near the old mosque.'
> **Nganjëherë Skënderbeu e shikonte këtë çështje edhe me syrin e ushtarit.** 'At times Skënderbeu viewed this matter with the eye of the soldier as well'
> **Atje në luftë gjakun e derdhte populli dhe e derdhte BUJARISHT.** 'There in battle the people shed blood and shed it NOBLY.'
> **Me zhdukjen e klasave shfrytëzuese, si POLITIKISHT ashtu edhe EKONOMIKISHT, u zhduk tek ne përgjithmonë edhe shfrytëzimi i njeriut prej njeriut.** 'With the abolition of the exploiting class, both POLITICALLY and ECONOMICALLY, the exploitation of man by man was likewise abolished forever among us.'
> **Skënderbeu ishte informuar HOLLËSISHT për numrin edhe cilësinë e ushtrisë armike.** 'Skënderbeu was informed IN DETAIL about the number and quality of the enemy army.'

Adverbs formed with the suffix -(i)sht from abstract noun stems may be considered as meaning 'like the concrete noun underlying the abstract stem': **burrërisht** 'bravely' (from **burrëri**, in turn from burrë 'man'), **pleqërisht** 'elderly, like elders', **qenërisht** 'dog-like', **trimërisht** 'heroically', **vëllazërisht** 'brotherly, fraternally', etc.

> **Ndonëse Sulltani i blatonte pasuri dhe nder, i kishte refuzuar të gjitha dhe e vazhdoi luftën TRIMËRISHT.** 'Although the Sultan offered him wealth and honor, he had refused all of them and continued the struggle VALIANTLY.'
> **Që të dyja anët luftuan QENËRISHT, po më në fund ushtria italo-frënge u dërmua krejt prej shqiptarëve të Skënderbeut.** 'Both sides fought DOG-LIKE, but finally the Italo-French army was completely crushed by the Albanians of Skënderbeu.'

Words that indicate particular languages (but not ethnic or national labels like **shqiptar** 'Albanian (masculine)'--see Chapter 3) are also adverbs of this type: **shqip** 'Albanian', **frengjisht** 'French', **rusisht** 'Russian', **anglisht** 'English', **gjermanisht** 'German', **bullgarisht** 'Bulgarian', **rumanisht** 'Rumanian', **turqisht** 'Turkish', etc.

> **Unë flas mirë FRENGJISHT, po RUSISHT s'flas dot.** 'I speak FRENCH well, but I don't speak RUSSIAN at all.'

Notice that these adverbs are used only with verbs of speaking, reading, writing, etc.

A.2 Adverbial Quantifiers

Quantifiers are a class of words that have the function of expressing the degree of intensity of a predicate or the quantity of a noun or other substantive. The quantifiers that will be considered here are adverbial in that they may qualify verbs, adjectives, deverbal nouns, or other adverbs:

Mihali, djali im i madh, e DONTE tokën SHUMË, e punonte me dashuri dhe ia kishte ënda të rrinte gjithmonë përjashta. 'My big boy, Mihal, LOVED the land A LOT, cultivated it with love, and delighted in staying outdoors at all times.'

Aksioni i Federatës s'kishte qenë punë e lehtë, sepse duhej bërë në mes të pazarit në një ndërtesë të ruajtur SHUMË MIRË. 'The action of the Federation had not been an easy job, because it had to be done in the midst of the marketplace, in a building VERY WELL guarded.'

E kishte vënë re se ajo rrinte SHUMË e MËRZITUR, si e hutuar. 'He had noticed that she was going about VERY DEJECTED, as in a daze.'

The class of adverbial quantifiers includes words like **fort** 'much, very, strongly' which are only used adverbially, as well as those like **shumë** 'much, very' which are general quantifiers (e.g., **shumë vjet** 'many years'). The intensity or degree of the realization of an action is expressed by strictly adverbial quantifiers, like: **fort** 'very', **fort e më fort** 'ever so much', **për së tepërmi** 'exceedingly, in excess', **së tepërmi** 'greatly, too much', as well as by general quantifiers in their adverbial role, like **shumë** 'very much', **tepër** '(too) much, very much', etc.:

Një cullufe i kishte rënë mbi ballin e gjerë dhe e hijeshonte PËR SË TEPËRMI. 'A lock of hair had fallen on his broad forehead and graced him EXCEEDINGLY.'

Dhe si e shoh, mallëngjehem FORT sa s'mund të shkruaj, se më njomen sytë. 'And as I look at it, I become so VERY nostalgic that I cannot write, because my eyes get wet.'

Ka qenë një herë e një kohë, ashtu, por kohët e fundit më kanë thënë se është trashur TEPËR në mal. 'He was like that once upon a time, but lately I have heard that he has gotten VERY fat in the mountains.'

Adverbial locutions of the type: **një herë** 'one time', **dy herë** 'two times', **tri herë** 'three times', etc., as well as adverbs of the type: **njëfish** 'once, one-fold', **dyfish** 'twice, two-fold', **trefish** 'thrice, three-fold', etc., are also used to express the intensity of degree of a quality or circumstance:

Kjo ishte një shtëpi gati DYFISH MË E LARTË se fqinja e saj, me të cilën kishte oborr të përbashkët të ndarë me një mur të hollë. 'This was a house nearly TWO TIMES TALLER than its neighbor, with which it shared a common courtyard, separated by a thin wall.'

Mos bir, dëgjomë mua, se kam jetuar TRI HERË MË SHUMË se ti. 'My son, listen to me, because I have lived three times as long as you ("THREE TIMES MORE than you").'

Aq 'so, that much', **kaq** 'so, so much', **mjaft** 'enough', **pak** 'few, a little', **shumë** 'much, a lot' are used both as adverbs and as indeterminate pronouns:

Atëherë derdheshin të tjerët, që u vinin pas, dhe mezi i ngrinin, AQ qenë dobësuar nga udha e të ftohtit. 'Then the others, who followed them, would rush forward, and they could barely lift them up, SO weak had they become from the journey and the cold.'

Dhe ia fillonte, me gishtrinj të dorës, të bënte hesap kaq voza nga AQ KAQ, kaq javë nga AQ KAQ. 'And he would begin, with the fingers of his hand, to calculate so many kegs from THAT MUCH makes THIS MUCH, so many weeks from THAT MUCH makes THIS MUCH.'

B. Circumstantial Adverbs

B.1 Temporal Adverbs

Temporal adverbs designate circumstances having to do with time. As such they typically modify whole clauses, verbs, and deverbal nouns, but they may also modify deverbal adjectives and participles:

> **MBRËME ia mbushi mendjen vetes se Luanin e kishte vetëm mik e asgjë tjetër, kurse SOT, para disa minutave, ato mendime sikur iu tronditën në themel.** 'LAST NIGHT she convinced herself that Luan was merely a friend, nothing more, whereas TODAY, a few minutes before, it seemed that those thoughts were shaken to their foundation.'
>
> **Traga e gjerë, e thelluar VIT PËR VIT nga rrotat e qerres, SOT ishte bërë lumë i vërtetë.** 'The broad track, deepened YEAR AFTER YEAR by the wheels of the wagon, TODAY had become a veritable stream.'

B.1a. Time Relative to Speech Moment

Temporal adverbs are of various kinds. Some implicitly refer to the time of speaking. It is in this sense that one uses the adverbs **dje** 'yesterday', **nesër** 'tomorrow', **pardje** 'day before yesterday', **pasdreke** 'afternoon', **sonte** 'tonight', **sot** 'today', **tani** 'now', **vjet** 'last year', etc.:

> **Por SONTE nga mënyra se si ajo a mbante kokën, të kërrusur e të kthyer pak anash, nga duart që i ngatërroheshin kur lidhnin spangon, Petriti e kuptoi se Lumtoja ishte e lodhur dhe e mërzitur.** 'But TONIGHT, from the way she held her head, bent down and turned a bit sideways, (and) her hands which got mixed up when tying the string, Petrit understood that Lumto was tired and dejected.'
>
> **Domethënë kombinati do ta fillojë punën SIVJET me panxharin tonë.** 'It means that the combine will begin operations THIS YEAR with our beets.'

B.1b. Periods

Some temporal adverbs indicate rather inexact moments of time: **dikur** 'at one time', **njëherë** 'once', **njëditë** 'one day', **njëditë prej ditësh** 'one day ("a day of days")', **një herë e një kohë** 'once upon a time', **një moti** 'one year', **së lashti** 'long ago', **së shpejti** 'soon', etc.

> **Po fyelli i Tanës duhej të shëtiste buzë më buzë dhe shtëpi më shtëpi, që t'u binte brez pas brezi këngëve të reja, për të cilat e kishte gdhendur Miri SË LASHTI.** 'But the flute of Tanë had to promenade from lip to lip and house to house in order to play generation after generation the new songs for which Miri had carved it LONG AGO.'
>
> **Delegatët e zgjedhur për në mbledhjen e madhe kombëtare, që do të mbahej diku SË SHPEJTI, po pregatiteshin për t'u nisur sa më parë.** 'The delegates elected for the great national meeting, which was going to be held somewhere SOON, were getting ready to depart as soon as possible.'

B.1c. Frequency

Other temporal adverbs indicate frequency, such as **gjithmonë** 'forever', **gjithnjë** 'always', **kurdo** 'anytime', **kurdoherë** 'whenever, anytime', **përditë** 'daily', **dendur** 'often', **ndonjëherë** 'sometimes', **nganjëherë** 'once in a while, sometimes', **rrallë** 'rarely', **shpesh** 'often', **shpeshherë** 'often'; or they may indicate continued repetition or extension in time: **ditë për ditë** 'daily, day after day', **javë për javë** 'weekly, week after week', **natë për natë** 'nightly, night after night', **herë pas here** 'time and again, frequently', **kohë pas kohe** 'time after time', **kohë më kohë** 'from time to time', **brez pas brezi** 'generation after generation'.

Partia dhe qeveria jonë kanë mbajtur GJITHNJË një qëndrim të vendosur e parimor, marksist-leninist, ndaj armiqve të paqes e të socializmit. 'Our party and government have ALWAYS maintained a resolute and principled Marxist-Leninist stand toward the enemies of peace and socialism.'

Secili duhet ta shohë veten në pasqyrë dhe ashtu siç lan PËRDITË fytyrën, të pastrojë PËRDITË ndërgjegjen e tij, duke mbajtur një qëndrim komunist ndaj vetvetes. 'Each one must see himself in a mirror, and just as he washes his face DAILY, so should he DAILY clean his conscience by maintaining a communist stand toward oneself.'

Po me Tanën lanë një fjalë: PËRNATË në orën dy, djali do të hipte majë atij ahut më të madh të Çukë Zarës dhe do t'i binte fyellit. 'But they reached accord with Tanë: NIGHTLY, at the hour of two, the boy would climb to the top of the tallest beech tree of Chukë Zarë and play the flute.'

Kështu mendonte Bali NDONJËHERË, por dashuria e tyre e vërtetë nuk ishte punë fëmijësh. 'This is how Bali thought SOMETIMES, but their true love was not child's play.'

DITË PËR DITË majat e maleve që nga Kruja gjer në Qafëkërrabë mbuloheshin nga një mjegull e dendur. 'DAILY the mountain peaks from Krujë to Qafëkerrabë would be covered by dense fog.'

Hante ngadalë duke fshirë HERË PAS HERE buzët e holla dhe dëgjonte lajmet vetëm me një të tundur të kokës. 'He ate slowly, wiping TIME AND AGAIN his thin lips, and listened to the news with only a shake of his head.'

B.1d. Momentary Action

Certain temporal adverbial locutions indicate momentary action: **aty për aty** 'on the spot, right then and there', **hë për hë** 'for now, temporarily', **menjëherë** 'at once, immediately', **njëherë për njëherë** 'once and for all', **tani për tani** 'for the moment, for the present'.

Gjeti ATY PËR ATY edhe arsyen sepse do të shkonte atë mbrëmje, pa tjetër tek Emira. 'He found RIGHT THEN AND THERE the very reason why he would go without fail to Emira's that evening.'

Sidoqoftë, HË PËR HË, Agimi vëndosi të mos bënte zë. 'Anyhow, FOR THE MOMENT Agim decided not to make a sound.'

Meqë e teshtitura s'i la kohë dhe përgjigja e ka lezetin ATY PËR ATY FLAKË PËR FLAKË, Dritani e gjeti të udhës të këmbente fjalë. 'Since the sneezing left him no time, and the reply has relish (only) RIGHT THEN AND THERE and INSTANTANE-OUSLY ("flame for flame"), Dritan found it advisable to exchange words.'

B.1e. Duration

Some adverbs (including those derived from temporal nouns) and adverbial locutions, express, depending on the context, the length of time needed for the completion of a process or the passage of time since the completion of the action, such as **motmot** 'a year', **një copeherë** 'a brief while', **një çikë** 'awhile, a little bit', **një grimë** 'a bit', **një hop** 'for a time, an interval', **gjatë** 'for a long time', **pak** 'a little (while)'

Ai e këndonte këtë këngë me gaz, sepse Tirana, qyteti ku banonte ai, kishte MOTMOT që qe bërë kryeqytet i Shqipërisë. 'He was singing that song with joy, because Tiranë, the city where he resided, had been the capital of Albania for A YEAR.'

E ndoqi NJË COPE HERË vjedhurazi, rrugicë më rrugicë, duke vrapuar. 'He followed her AWHILE stealthily, from alley to alley, running.'

Në të hyrë të oborrit, Lumtoja qëndroi NJË HOP, shikoi fytyrat e njohura të shokëve. 'At the entrance of the courtyard, Lumto stopped FOR A TIME, looked at the familiar faces of comrades.'

Shtrihu, Agim, fli dhe ti NJË ÇIKË, iu lut e motra. 'Lie down, Agim, and sleep A LITTLE BIT, his sister begged him.'
Pa dil NJË ÇIKË këtu. 'Come on out here AWHILE.'

B.1f. Negatives of Time

Some adverbs of time, such as **kurrë** 'never', **kurrën e kurrës** 'never ever', **asnjëherë** 'not once', generally appear only as the second part of a negation, the first part of which can be a particle of negation such as **nuk** 'not', **s'** 'not', **mos** 'don't', **pa** 'without'. The effect of this double negation is to reinforce the negative meaning.

Republika Popullore e Shqipërisë nuk ka lejuar e nuk do të lejojë KURRË t'i preket asnjë e drejtë e saj kombëtare nga kushdoqoftë... 'The People's Republic of Albania has not allowed and will NEVER allow any of her international rights to be impaired by whoever it may be.'
Por këto do të ishin me siguri fjalë pa vend, sepse s'mund të mendohej KURRËN E KURRËS që Turqia e asaj kohe... 'But these would surely be irrelevant words, since it could NEVER have been thought that the Turkey of that time....'

Infrequently, the adverb **kurrë** may also be used in an interrogative clause without a negative particle to mean 'ever':

E pse të qaj? Sa e çuditshme që je, moj Sofikë! Qan KURRË njeriu nga dashuria? 'And why should I cry? How strange you are Sofikë! Does one EVER cry because of love?'
Gabon KURRË Vasili të ta japë plot? 'Does Vasil EVER fail to give it to you full?'

B.2 Locative Adverbs

Locative adverbs indicate the place where an action is carried out or where an event occurs, the place toward which the action of the verb is directed, the place one is traversing or departing from, or the place from which someone or something originated. Locative adverbs are usually found near a verb, a deverbal noun preceded by an article, a deverbal adjective, or a participle. Less frequently, locative adverbs functioning as modifiers can be found near a non-deverbal noun or a pronoun.

Për këtë qëllim gjatë 10-vjeçarit të ardhshëm ne duhet të përpiqemi për mekanizimin maksimal të punimeve bujqësore në fushë, në mënyrë që të lirohet KËNDEJ një numër i madh krahësh pune për të kaluar në male. 'For this purpose, during the coming decade, we must strive for the maximal mechanization of agricultural work in the plains, in order that a large number of working hands FROM HERE may be freed to go to the mountains.'
ATY qëndruan vetëm një natë dhe nuk më kujtohet asgjë prej Podgozhanit, veç babait të Markos. 'THERE they stopped only for one night, and I don't remember a thing about Podgozhan, except Marko's father.'
Rruga gjer në konakët LART qe e shkurtër dhe kështu, kapiten e partizan, nuk patën kohë të thonë gjë tjetër. 'The road to the lodge ABOVE was short, and so captain and partisan did not have time to say anything else.'
Të rendurit LART POSHTË pa u marrë me punë është humbje e kotë kohe. 'Running UP AND DOWN without doing any work is a pointless waste of time.'
Po kjo ngjet dhe në fshatrat RROTULL. 'But this happens also in the SURROUNDING villages.'
Për vashdimësinë dhe shpënien PËRPARA të këtyre problemeve një faktor i madh ka qenë organizimi i kontrollit punëtor. 'A big factor in the continuation and carrying FORWARD of these problems has been the organization of workers' control.

B.2a. Definite Locatives

Locative adverbs may indicate the place where an action is being carried out, or an event occurs, both of them organized around a certain point of orientation. We find this sense in the adverbs **afër** 'near', **atje** 'there', **aty** 'there', **djathtas** 'rightward, on the right', **këtu** 'here', **larg** 'far', **majtas** 'leftward, on the left', **matanë** 'on the other side', **përtej** 'across', **pranë** 'nearby', **rreth** 'around, about', etc.

Xha Selimi, me të thënë këto, ngriti belexhikun LART dhe rrahu nja dy herë kondakun me pëllëmbë. 'Uncle Selim, as soon as he said these words, raised his belexhik [type of rifle] ALOFT and struck the butt with his palm a couple of times.'

Shikon POSHTË e qesh dhe si gjithë të tjerët, duke dëgjuar zëthin e foshnjës që nuk pushon. 'He looks DOWN and laughs like all the rest, as he hears the voice of the baby that does not stop.'

-- I jam qasur vdekjes PRANË me dhjetra herë. 'I have been CLOSE to death tens of times.'

B.2b. Indefinite Locatives

Certain adverbs and adverbial locutions indicate a non-localized place: **diku** 'somewhere', **gjëkund** 'somewhere', **gjetkë** 'elsewhere', **gjetiu** 'elsewhere', **vende-vende** 'here and there'.

Pëshpërisnin, / sikur roniteshin mbi kasolle / lirika të freskëta / shkruar DIKU në qiellin e zi. 'Fresh lyrics, / written SOMEWHERE in the black sky, / whispered, / as if they were crumbling over the hut.'

Çfarë bën tashti, a punon GJËKUNDI? 'What are you doing now; are you working SOMEWHERE?'

Veç kësaj, pranë katedrave e GJETKË duhet të zhvillohet një veprimtari e dendur shkencore? 'In addition, in the curricula and ELSEWHERE an intense scientific activity must be carried out.'

This group also includes the following adverbs and adverbial locutions: **anembanë** 'on all sides, all over', **anë e kënd** 'on all sides, all over', **gjithandej** 'everywhere', **gjithkund** 'everywhere', **kudo** 'everywhere', **ngado** 'anywhere, wherever', **tekdo** 'anywhere, wherever', etc.

Klasat reaksionare dhe imperialistët jo vetëm nuk largohen vullnetarisht nga arena historike, por ata shtypin me forcë NGADO e KUDO revolucionin, jo vetëm nuk i dorëzojnë armët, por po e forcojnë vashdimisht makinën e tyre të shtypjes e të dhunës kundër popujve. 'The reactionary classes and imperialists not only do not depart voluntarily from the stage of history, but they also suppress the revolution by force ANYWHERE and EVERYWHERE; not only do they not surrender their arms, but they are also strengthening constantly their machine of oppression and violence against the peoples.'

Ajo hodhi vështrimin ANEMBANË: pa qiellin e këthjellët e të pafund, pa majat e vargmaleve të Gramozit. 'She looked ALL OVER, saw the clear and infinite sky, saw the peaks of the Gramozi mountain ranges.'

Sofra e jataku i shtrohej TEKDO dhe torba gjithë plot i rrinte çobanit kaçak. 'Food ("the dining table") and shelter were provided for him EVERYWHERE, and the knapsack of the shepherd freedom fighter was always full.'

B.2c. Negative Locatives

As with temporal adverbs, there are certain locative adverbs that are used mainly as rein-forcers in negative clauses, such as: **asgjëkundi** 'nowhere', **askundi** 'nowhere', **gjëkundi** 'any-where, somewhere', **kund** 'anywhere', **kurrkund** 'no place, nowhere'.

Astriti s'kishte për të shkuar ASGJËKUNDI, po u ngatërrua në këtë muhabet e s'dinte si të dilte. 'Astrit wasn't going ANYWHERE, but he had gotten mixed up in this discussion and didn't know how to get out of it.'

Asaj i ishte mbushur mendja se si Grykasi s'kishte GJËKUNDI fshat më të bukur. 'She was convinced that NOWHERE was there a more beautiful village than Grykas.'

B.3 Causal Adverbs

An adverb **prandaj** or **andaj** 'therefore', is used at the head of either an independent or main clause formed as a result of the causative clause, as a restatement or reminder of the cause or reason presented in that first clause. These adverbs are equivalent to the sequences **për këtë shkak** 'for this reason', **për këtë arsye** 'for this reason', and less frequently, **për këtë qëllim** 'for this purpose'. They often function as correlatives of the subordinate causal con-junctions **pse** or **sepse** 'because', **meqënëse** or **me që** 'since'.

Dhe pikërisht pse çështjet nuk paraqiten kështu, PRANDAJ Partia, anëtarët e saj dhe gjithë punonjësit vazhdimisht duhet t'i edukojë politikisht dhe ideologjikisht. 'And precisely because matters are not like this, THAT IS WHY the Party must continually educate its members and all workers politically and ideologically.'

Sepse e ka përdorur kështu Partia këtë armë të fuqishme, PRANDAJ punën tonë nuk e ka prekur ndryshku. 'Because the Party has used this powerful arm in this way, THAT IS WHY the rust has not touched our work.'

Meqënëse ai është i palumtur, prandaj jam i mërzitur. 'Since he is unhappy, I am upset.'

The position occupied by the adverbs **prandaj** and **andaj** in the clause depends on the purpose of the expression. When the speaker desires to emphasize the cause, the causal clause comes at the head of the sentence and the causal adverbs come afterward; but, as mentioned above, in the majority of cases it is the causal adverbs that stand at the head of the sentence. (Quite often, the adverbial role of these words weakens and they become conjunctions. See Chapter 10.)

5.3 Gradation of Adverbs

Manner adverbs may be gradated in quality or intensity by an adverbial quantifier: **shumë** 'very', **mjaft** 'enough', **fare** 'quite, at all', **tepër** 'too much, very much', **krejt** 'completely', **fort** 'strongly, very', **jashtëzakonisht** 'extraordinarily'.

Ata tani e dinë FARE MIRË se lufta e Tiranës do të jetë shumë e vështirë. 'They know now VERY WELL that the battle of Tiranë will be very difficult.'

Nga ana tjetër, merret vesh FARE SHKOQUR që ky bir, cilido që ishte, merrte urdhër më tepër nga Gjon Kastrioti se nga Sulltani. 'On the other hand, one can see VERY PLAINLY that this son, whoever he was, obeyed Gjon Kastrioti more than the Sultan.'

Ajo që Mimozës i dukej e vështirë, bile ndonjëherë e pamundshme ngjau FARE RASTËSISHT. 'That which to Mimozë seemed difficult , at times even impossible, happened COMPLETELY BY CHANCE.'

Ata e dinë FARE MIRË se lufta e Tiranës do të jetë shumë e vështirë, por është dëshira e tyre e zjarrtë që ta godasin armikun në çerdhen e tyre kryesore. 'They know VERY WELL that the battle of Tiranë will be very difficult, but it is their fervent desire to hit the enemy in their principal bases.'

Me lehtësi të madhe, FARE NATYRSHËM, kish lidhur duart plot hir e të hajthme.

'With great ease, VERY NATURALLY, he had tied the graceful and skinny hands.'

Por, me sa di unë, ato nuk shfrytëzohen si duhet ose shfrytëzohen SHUMË PAK'. But, as far as I know, they are not exploited as they should be, or they are exploited VERY LITTLE.'

Vali ndjeu nëpër gjumë se një gjë e fohtë po i kalonte në kokë dhe instinktivisht ngriti dorën, po atëherë qe TEPËR VONË. 'Vali sensed in sleep that something cold was passing over his head and instinctively raised his hand, but then it was TOO LATE.'

Qëndronte aty më këmbë pranë tyre, po i dukej se qe SHUMË LARG. 'He stood there close to them, but felt that he was VERY FAR.'

In the spoken language, and less frequently in the written language, use is made of the adverb **bukur** 'pretty, very' as well.

Po ditë shumë pak kaluan / Dhe BUKUR MIRË e mora vesh / se ç'do të thoshin ato fjalë. 'But only a few days passed / And I understood PRETTY WELL / what those words meant.'

The locution **më së miri** 'best, as well as possible', and less often, in analogy with it, **më së keqi** 'worst, as badly as possible'--both of which are used in this form only--have the sense of a superlative:

Mbrojtja e atdheut dhe sigurimi i fitoreve të revolucionit kërkojnë që ne të kemi edhe në të ardhmen një ushtri të fortë...të armatosur MË SË MIRI me shkencën ushtarake marksiste-leniniste. 'The defense of the fatherland and the assurance of the gains of the revolution demand that we have a strong army in the future as well...equipped AS WELL AS POSSIBLE with the Marxist-Leninist military science.'

Exclamatory constructions with the adverbs **aq** 'so, that much', **kaq** 'this much' and **sa** 'how (much)', not followed by a term of comparison introduced by **sa**, have a strongly intensifying and affective character, expressing the emotions of the speaker (or writer).

Edhe gjithë gjë e gjallë ndjen ne zemër një dëshirë, / Një gaz të ëmbël e të shumë. O! SA BUKUR E SA MIRË! 'And every living thing feels one desire at heart, / A sweet and abundant joy. Oh! HOW BEAUTIFUL AND HOW GOOD!'

Another kind of construction with **aq, kaq,** followed by a clause of consequence, introduced by **sa** also has a somewhat intensified sense:

Ecën AQ SHPEJT, sa dhe ata u habitën se ku i kishte gjithë ato forca. 'He walks SO FAST, that even they were surprised at where he had found all that strength.'

Ishte hera e parë që kundërshtonte KAQ PRERË. 'It was the first time that he objected SO DECISIVELY.'

To give more force, adverbial quantifiers are occasionally repeated, particularly **shumë** or **fare** 'very':

Lumtos, me gjithë armiqësinë e madhe që kishte ndaj Hazmiut, i erdhi SHUMË SHUMË KEQ, aq më tepër kur u bind se ai fliste me sinqeritet. 'In spite of the great hostility he had toward Hazmi, Lumto felt VERY, VERY SORRY, all the more so when he became convinced that he spoke sincerely.'

To indicate a constantly increasing degree of intensity, frequent use is made of the construction: ADVERB + E + MË + SAME ADVERB, as in **fort e më fort** 'ever stronger', **keq e më keq** 'ever worse', **larg e më larg** 'ever father', **mirë e më mirë** 'ever better', **poshtë e më poshtë** 'ever lower', **rrallë e më rrallë** 'ever more rarely', **shpesh e më shpesh** 'ever more frequent', **thellë e më thellë** 'ever deeper'.

Në këtë unitet qëndron garancia për ta ngritur LART E MË LART emrin e lavdishëm të Atdheut tonë, këtu është garancia se çdo vendim që merr Partia, do të bëhet pa tjetër realitet. 'This unity provides the guarantee for raising EVER HIGHER the glorious name of our Fatherland; here is the guarantee that every decision the Party takes will undoubtedly become reality.'

> **Po kjo qëllonte RRALLË E MË RRALLË.** 'But this happened EVER MORE RARELY.'

The degree of comparison can be qualified by placing before the particle **më** one of the adverbs **shumë** 'very, much', **edhe** 'even', **pak** 'a little'.

> **Puna do të shkojë kaq më shpejt më përpara, fronti ynë i luftës po zgjerohet SHUMË MË SHPEJT, armikun do ta mundim EDHE MË SHPEJT.** '(Our) work will progress so much faster, the front line of our struggle is expanding MUCH MORE RAPIDLY, we shall defeat the enemy EVEN SOONER.'
>
> **Kur ai u kthye me fytyrë dhe ajo njohu të atin e Adilit, u trondit EDHE MË KEQ se përpara.** 'When he turned his face and she recognized the father of Adil, she was shaken EVEN MORE than before.'
>
> **Tani e ndjej veten PAK MË MIRË.** 'Now I feel A LITTLE BETTER.'

5.4 Derivation of Adverbs

In their internal structure, adverbs may be simple, derived, or agglutinated words or may be locutions.

SIMPLE adverbs are those not presently perceived by Albanians to be derived from other words. Some simple adverbs consist of a single morpheme: **afër** 'near', **keq** 'bad', **larg** 'far', **mirë** 'well', **pas** 'after', **poshtë** 'below', **prapa** 'behind'. Many simple pro-adverbs have a deictic prefix **kë-** 'near' or **a-** 'remote' (**kë-** drops the **ë** before a vowel): **andej** 'that way, in that direction', **këndej** or **këtej** 'this way, in this direction', **ashtu** 'so, like that', **kështu** 'thus, like this', **atje** 'over there', **aty** 'right there', **këtu** 'here'. Some presently simple adverbs were historically not simple: e.g., **lart** 'above', **sonte** 'tonight', **sot** 'today'.

Far more adverbs in Albanian are derived than are simple. Their derivation has come about in several ways: through direct conversion from another part of speech, through suffixation, by compounding, or by converting prepositional phrases and other sequences into fixed adverbial locutions. The productive generation of non-locutionary prepositional phrases, which are also adverbial, will be covered in Chapter 10 (Prepositions).

5.4.1 Adverbs Formed by Conversion

A. Adverbs Converted from Noun Forms

Certain nouns, usually in the indefinite ablative or accusative indefinite form, but occasionally in other case forms, have come to be used as adverbs by simple conversion: the adverb is or was identical in form to a form of the noun. As adverbs, these words function as modifiers, and their meanings are often quite different from those of the original nouns. Such adverbs differ in the degree to which they still reflect the nouns from which they are derived. The most common group is made up of words that are regularly used as adverbs: **fare** 'very, at all', **krejt** 'totally', **motit** 'long ago', **sheshit** 'openly, in the open' (all originally ablative case nouns); **rrafsh** 'flatly, evenly', **rresht** 'continuously', **rreth** 'about', **rrotull** 'about', **vjet** 'last year' (originally accusative case nouns); **herët** 'early' (originally locative case noun).

As adverbs, they are quite distinct both semantically and grammatically from the corresponding nouns: **farë** 'seed', **herë** 'time', **krye** 'head'. Semantically, some of these adverbs, such as **fare, krejt, herët,** have undergone radical changes. Other adverbs, like **mot** 'next year', **sheshit** 'openly', **vjet** 'last year', have undergone restriction or expansion in meaning.

Words and locutions like the following form a special group: **ditën** 'in the daytime', **natën** 'at night', **një ditë** 'one day', **një natë** 'one night', **një kohe** 'at one time', **një mëngjesi** 'one morning', **një moti** 'one year', **një mbrëmje** 'one evening', **një vere** 'one summer', **një viti** 'one year', **anash** 'sideways'. Because semantically they may still be interpreted as nouns, it must be said that the process of adverbialization has not yet been consolidated in this group of words and locutions. For this reason some linguists treat them as nominal forms, even though syntactically they behave like adverbs.

In the Albanian linguistic literature one finds that a number of linguists do treat such words and sequences as adverbs, since when used as adverbs, they do not have the full range of senses that they have as nouns and cannot take the full range of modifiers: e.g., **ditën** 'in the daytime' (originally accusative definite), **natën** 'at night' (originally accusative definite). It is apparent that such adverbs must be distinguished from corresponding nouns, which may indeed be accompanied by modifiers and prepositions. Compare the examples below in which the words **ditën, natën** serve in a generic sense as adverbs:

> **Nuk shtrihej kurrë NATËN për të fjetur, pa parë qetë në kasollë.** 'He never lay down to sleep AT NIGHT, without seeing the oxen in the hut.'
>
> **Ndryshe nga gjithë njerëzit, punonte NATËN gjer afër të gdhiri dhe flinte DITËN.** 'Unlike all other people, he worked AT NIGHT until near daybreak, and slept IN THE DAYTIME.'
>
> **Mirë, DITËN del për antika, po NATËN ç'kërkon këtej, t'i ruash nga rosat e egra, mos t'i gëlltitin?** 'Granted that IN THE DAYTIME you look for antiques, but what do you seek around here AT NIGHT, to guard them from wild ducks lest they gulp them down?'
>
> **Ditën e djelë ai punonte.** 'He worked Sundays.'

with the following examples in which the same forms are nouns used adverbially, but preserving their non-generic value:

> **DITËN e diel u krye aksioni me goditje të përqëndruar për hapjen e 17 km. kanal.** 'On ("THE DAY of") Sunday the action for the opening of the 17 km. canal was carried out with concentrated blows.'
>
> **NATËN e Vitit të Ri teatri i kukullave dha një koncert shumë të bukur për fëmijët e kryeqytetit.** 'On New Year's Eve ("THE NIGHT of the New Year"), the puppet theater gave a very beautiful concert for the children of the capital'.

A.1 Adverbs Converted from Ablative Nouns

The great majority of nouns in the indefinite ablative case used as adverbs indicate time; only a few indicate place. Singular nouns in both the ablative case and in the accusative case are indefinite, and are accompanied by the article ONE:

> [Accusative] **Unë po vdes, por çështja, për të cilën kam luftuar, do të triumfojë pa tjetër NJË DITË!** 'I am dying, but the cause for which I have fought, will certainly triumph ONE DAY.'
>
> **NJË NATË, kur ranë të flinin, i tregoi të shoqit për këtë.** 'ONE NIGHT, when they went to sleep, she told her husband about this.'
>
> [Ablative] **NJË VITI, plaku u nis si përherë dhe më s'u kthye.** 'ONE YEAR, the old man set out as usual and never returned.'
>
> **Gjer aty NJË MOTI, akoma i kish Jonuz Ranxha në Seltë një palë brirë me njëzet degë.** 'Until about A YEAR AGO, Jonuz Ranxha still had an antler with twenty branches in Seltë.

Expressions of the following type which are used regularly as adverbs, came mostly from a now lost frozen ablative form of substantivized neuter adjectives: **së afërmi** 'near', **së andejmi** 'from there', **së bashku** 'together', **së brendshmi** 'from inside', **së gjalli** 'while alive', **së gjati** 'in length', **së jashtmi** 'from outside', **së këtejmi** 'from here', **së koti** 'in vain', **së largu** 'from afar', **së larti** 'from above', **së mbari** 'felicitously', **së qeti** 'quietly', **së sipërmi** 'from above', **së shpejti** 'quickly, soon', **së tepërmi** 'in excess', **së toku** 'together', **së voni** 'lately'. Some of them, like **së toku, së bashku,** have been formed analogically rather than originating as substantivized neuter adjectives:

Ata u rritën e zemrat e tyre të mësuara SË BASHKU rrahën me forcë për një ndjenjë tjetër të re. 'They grew up and their hearts, accustomed (to being) TOGETHER, beat forcefully to a new sensation.'

Gjetkë, deti ka marrë ngjyrën e reve dhe është i zymtë, i trazuar, saqë, SË SIPËRMI, duket si një fushë e plasaritur. 'Elsewhere, the sea has taken on the color of the clouds and it is gloomy, turbulent, so much so that on the surface ("FROM ABOVE") it looks like a plain full of cracks.'

A.2 Adverbs Converted from Accusative Nouns

As mentioned above, some words which were originally accusative indefinite noun forms are now used regularly as adverbs: **rrafsh** 'flatly, evenly', **rresht** 'continuously', **rreth** 'about', **rrotull** 'about', **vjet** 'last year'. Other nouns in accusative indefinite form may be used adverbially only in certain expressions where the noun is used figuratively: **copë** 'piece, bit, in pieces, clearly', **fluturim** 'flight, flying', **grumbull** 'pile, heap, collectively', **lëmsh** 'ball (of thread), pell mell', **palë** 'pair, fold, pleat', **ujë** 'water, fluidly, fluently', **thikë** 'knife, sharply', **varg** 'range, in a series', **vrap** 'trot, at a trot', etc.

Këmbët u ishin bërë COPË e djersa u kishte dalë mbi rroba. 'Their feet were badly BATTERED, and the sweat had soaked through to the surface of their clothes.'

Marina u mundua e më në fund iu shqit nga duart si një thëllëzë e plagosur që shkëputet nga tufa FLUTURIM. 'Marina struggled and finally tore loose from his hands, like a wounded pheasant that breaks off IN A HURRY ("FLYING") from the flock.'

Mësuesi i fillores i kishte marrë GRUMBULL një ditë dhe i kishte shpënë në spitalin e Tiranës. 'The grade school teacher had taken them COLLECTIVELY one day, and had taken them to the hospital of Tiranë.'

Po edhe sikur ta njihte do të dyshonte shumë kur të dëgjonte të folurit e tij, atë gegërishte të bukur, të cilën tani ai e fliste UJË. 'But even if she recognized him, she would be very doubtful once she heard his way of speaking, that beautiful Gheg idiom which he now spoke fluently ("WATER").'

B. Adverbs Converted from Verb Forms

Adverbs of manner have also been formed by conversion of the participle or the participle preceded by the negative particle **pa**: **dendur** 'often' cf. **dend** 'compress, satiate', **fshehur** 'in a hidden way' cf. **fsheh** 'hide', **hapur** 'openly' cf. **hap** 'open', **kaluar** 'mounted' cf. **kaloj** 'ride a horse', **ndyrë** 'dirtily' cf. **ndyj** 'make dirty', **prerë** 'decisively, precisely' cf. **pres** 'cut', **rrëmbyer** 'rushed' cf. **rrëmbehem** 'I rush', **shkoqur** 'clearly' cf. **shkoqit** 'clarify', **shtruar** 'gently, set' cf. **shtroj** 'set', **padashur** 'unwillingly' cf. **dua** 'want', **pandërprerë** 'uninterrupted' cf. **ndërpres** 'interrupt', **papandehur** 'unexpectedly' cf. **pandej** 'imagine', **papritur** 'suddenly' cf. **pres** 'expect', **papushuar** 'ceaselessly' cf. **pushoj** 'stop', **parreshtur** 'incessantly' cf. **rreshtoj** 'arrest'.

Lumton unë e dua që në fëmini -- u përgjegj PRERË Nazmiu. '"I have loved Lumto since he was in his childhood," Nazmi replied DECISIVELY.'

E shau NDYRË e u derdh të rrëmbente një kopaçe nga sëra e druve që ishin në fund të dhomës. 'He insulted him FILTHILY and rushed over to grab a stick from the pile of wood that was at the end of the room.'

Dhjetë ditë më parë Valdeti hodhi një hap të guximshëm në jetë: PAPRITUR e PAKUJTUAR ishte njohur me një djalë. 'Ten days earlier Valdet took a daring step in life: SUDDENLY and INADVERTENTLY she had met a boy.'

C. Adverbs Converted from Adjective Forms

In present-day Standard Albanian, adverbs with the suffix **-shëm**, are becoming more common: **fuqishëm** 'powerfully', **furishëm** 'furiously', **gëzueshëm** 'joyfully', **hareshëm** 'gaily', **mendueshëm** 'thoughtfully', **natyrshëm** 'naturally', **shterrueshëm** 'exhaustively, drily', **rrjedhshëm** 'fluently'. These adverbs are identical in form with adjectives that end in **-shëm**, e.g., **i fuqishëm** 'powerful', and have no special feminine form.

5.4.2 Adverbs Formed with Adverbial Suffixes

Many adverbs are formed by suffixation. For the most part, suffixes are added to noun and adjectival stems, but in some cases to adverbial stems as well. In present-day Standard Albanian, the most widely used adverbial suffixes are **-(i)sht, -as, -azi**, and **-thi**. To these may be added the suffix **-çe**, which is characteristic of colloquial Albanian.

A. The Suffix **-(i)sht**

The suffix **-(i)sht** is the most productive adverbial suffix in present-day Standard Albanian. In most cases it is added to a derived stem that ends in **-í**, so that the suffix itself appears in the form **-sht**. In analogy with these forms, new adverbs have been formed from derivational stems that do not end in **-i**. This has happened through the extension of the suffix into **-isht**, as in **natyrisht** 'naturally', and **ushtarakisht** 'militarily', all of which have final stress. With this suffix adverbs may be formed prolifically:

1) from feminine abstract noun stems themselves formed with the suffix **-(ë)si**, as in **egërsʹi-sht** 'wildly', **gjerësʹi-sht** 'broadly', **hollësʹi-sht** 'thinly', **imtësʹi-sht** 'finely', **fatmirësʹi-sht** 'fortunately', **fatkeqësʹi-sht** 'unfortunately';

2) from abstract feminine nouns formed with the suffix **-(ë)ri**, as in **besnikëri-sht** 'faithfully', **burrëri-sht** 'in a manly way, bravely', **pleqëri-sht** 'in an elderly way', **trimëri-sht** 'valiantly';

3) from feminine abstract noun stems formed with the suffix **-i**, as in **bujar-i-sht** 'nobly', **dhelpër-i-sht** 'foxily', **njerëz-i-sht** 'humanely'. In this same way adverbs that indicate the language of a people or a dialect have been formed: **arbëri-sht** 'the Albanian spoken in Arbëri (Italo-Albanian)', **bullgari-sht** 'Bulgarian', **çamëri-sht** 'Cham dialect of Albanian' (spoken in Northwest Greece);

4) from masculine abstract noun stems formed with the suffix **-im**, as in **detyr-im-isht** 'dutifully', **gab-im-isht** 'by mistake, mistakenly', **përfund-im-isht** 'finally, definitely', **qëll-im-isht** 'purposely', **shkurt-im-isht** 'briefly', etc. (Note the shift of stress to the final syllable.)

The suffix **-isht** has also been used to form adverbs from a limited number of simple nouns in the feminine and masculine genders, as in **natyr-isht** 'naturally', **rregull-isht** 'regularly', **zakon-isht** 'customarily'.

The scope and frequency of the suffix **-(i)sht** has increased a great deal in present-day Standard Albanian. This increase reflects the increase in the use of suffixal formations in general, and in particular the increasingly frequent formation of abstract nouns with the suffixes **-(e)si, -(e)ri, -i,** and of nouns with the suffix **im**, all of which form canonic stems for adverbs in **-(i)sht**. Furthermore, there have been and are being created a great number of adverbs from stems that do not exist apart from the suffix **-(i)sht**, whose underlying abstract noun stem has no independent use in the language: **bashkarisht (bashkërisht)** 'in common, commonly', **çuditërisht** 'surprisingly, strangely', **denjësisht** 'worthily', **fuqimisht** 'powerfully', **gojarisht** 'orally', **krejtësisht** 'totally', **pjesërisht** 'partially', **plotësisht** 'fully', **posaçërisht** 'especially', **shkencërisht** 'scientifically', **shpirtërisht** 'spiritually', **shprehimisht** 'expressly'. Such analogic formations have given birth to new variants of the suffixes, such as **-arisht, -(ë)sisht** and **-imisht**, which are being used increasingly.

A large number of adverbs have resulted from joining the suffix -(i)sht to adjectival derivational stems. Such are the adverbs **absolutisht** 'absolutely', **arbitrarisht** 'arbitrarily', **artistikisht** 'artistically', **barbarisht** 'barbarically', **mesatarisht** 'on the average', **ushtarakisht** 'militarily'. In adverbial formations of this type, the majority are those that have been constructed upon adjective stems from foreign languages.

At times adverbs have been formed with **-isht** even when there already exist other adverbs formed from the same root, thus giving rise to the creation of doublet, synonymous forms, such as **shkurt** and **shkurtimisht** 'briefly', **së bashku** and **bashkarisht** 'in common, commonly', which are used with different stylistic values, the **-isht** form having a more literary flavor. For the semantic varieties of adverbs formed with the suffix -(i)sht, see Section 5.2.2 A.1c).

B. The Suffix -as or -azi

Another widespread suffix is unstressed **-as, -azi,** which has formed adverbs from simple nominal stems, such as **bárkas** or **bárkazi** 'on the stomach', **brínjas** 'sideways, by the side', **dóras** 'by the hand', **fýtas** or **fýtazi** 'by the throat', **grýkas** or **grýkazi** 'by the throat', **gjúnjas** or **gjunjazi** 'on the knees', **rádhas** or **rádhazi** 'in order'. (Note that the stress remains on the underlying stem.) But it is also added to derived stems, such as in **këmbadóras (-azi)** 'hand and foot, doggedly', **doradóras (-azi)** 'hand in hand', **prishaqéfas** 'killjoy fashion', which are formed simultaneously by agglutination and this suffix:

1   adjectival stems, like **anasjélltas** 'conversely', **djáthtas** or **djáthtazi** 'to the right', **fshéhtazi** 'secretly', **májtas** or **májtazi** 'to the left', **përcíptas** or **përcíptazi** 'superficially';

2)   adverbial stems, like **háptazi** 'openly', **kéqas** 'badly', **lárgas** 'from afar, distantly', **lártas** or **lártazi** 'from on high', **rrëshqánas** 'crawling' **shkúrtas** or **shkúrtazi** 'briefly';

3)   verb stems, like **fálas** 'gratis', **rrëshqítas** or **rrëshqítazi** 'slightly, lightly' **héshturazi** 'silently', **shkárazi** 'superficially, in passing';

4)   participial stems, like **ndárazi** 'separately', **fshéhuras** or **fshéhurazi** 'secretly', **vjédhuras** or **vjédhurazi** 'stealthily'.

C. The Suffix -thi

The unstressed suffix **-thi** is relatively non-productive. It has formed adverbs:

1)   from simple noun stems: **arithi** 'upright' [**ari** 'bear'], **cingëlthi** 'tipcat (kind of game played with peg)', [**cingël** 'peg'], **çapthi** 'step by step', **mullárthi** 'around' [**mullar** 'haystack'], **qirithi** 'sitting up' [**qiri** **tópthi** '(play) ball', **trúpthi** 'bodily'. This type is no longer generally productive except to designate various games;

2)   from derived noun stems, formed with the stressed suffix **-im**: **fluturímthi** 'in flight, in a hurry', **rrëmbímthi** 'hastily', **nxitímthi** 'hurriedly', **kalímthi** 'passing by', **vetëtímthi** 'with lightning speed' etc. In such cases, the suffix together with the stem indicate that the action is caried out in a rapid and sudden manner;

3)   from adjectival stems: **çalamánthi** 'lamely', **qórthi** 'blindly';

4)   from adverbial stems: **përsëprápthi** 'backwardly', **rrëshqánthi** 'creepingly'. The union of the suffix **-thi** with adjectival and adverbial stems is quite limited.

Certain adverbs have been formed simultaneously with the suffix **-thi** and agglutination. Such are the adverbs which indicate various children's games and for this reason are encountered mainly in the speech of children: **brezahýpthi** '(kind of game) [**brezahýp** 'belt-climb'], **pulaqórrthi** 'blindman's bluff' [**pulaqórr** 'blind chicken'], **symbýllthi** 'hide and go seek' [-**symbýll** 'eyes shut'].

D. The Suffix -çe

The suffix -çe, which has its source in Turkish, has been used to form pejorative adverbs from noun stems: **budallallëkçe** 'foolishly', **çapkënçe** 'naughtily', **derrçe** 'pig-like, pig-headed', **fshatarçe** 'peasant-like', **fshaçe (fshatçe)** 'village-like', **hajduçe (hajdutçe)** 'thief-like', **halldupçe** 'Turk-like', **këmbësorçe** 'on foot', **partizançe** 'partisan-like', **qençe** 'dog-like', **vendçe** 'in local style', etc. The pejorative meaning that characterizes some of these constructions is usually also characteristic of the stem with which the suffix unites. In many cases this suffix has been replaced by the suffix **-(i)sht**.

However, the prefix **për-** has formed a number of adverbs from other adverbs, in some cases intensifying the meaning expressed by the other adverb alone. These may be seen as the result of the fusion of the sequence PREPOSITION + ADVERB: **përjashta** 'outside', **përpara** 'forward', **përsipër** 'above', **përkundrejt** 'opposite', **përmbrapa** 'behind'.

5.4.3 Adverbs Formed by Compounding

Only a small number of adverbs appear to have been formed through compounding. The sequences **verë dimër** 'summer (and) winter', **natë ditë** 'night (and) day', **ditë natë** 'day (and) night', for example, though written as two words, are phonologically compounds, having primary stress only on the second constituent.

Adverbial constructions may be formed by reduplicating a feminine singular noun, the nominative definite form followed by the dative definite form. These constructions have a single primary stress (on the second element): **dita-ditës** 'any day now' (**ditë** 'day'), **dora-dorës** 'for the time being' (**dorë** 'hand'), **gryka-grykës** 'at each other's throats' (**grykë** 'throat'), **gjurma-gjurmës** 'hot on the trail' (**gjurmë** 'trail'), **hera-herës** 'at times' (**herë** 'time'), **këmba-këmbës** 'doggedly' (**këmbë** 'foot'), **fundi-fundit** 'after all' (**fund** 'end'), **nata-natës** 'any night now' (**natë** 'night').

A few other adverbs, sometimes classified as agglutinations, seem synchronically to be compounds: **kryekëput** 'entirely', **kryekreje** 'principal', **motmot** 'one year', **shpeshherë** 'often', **rrallëherë** 'rarely'.

5.4.4 Adverbs Formed by Agglutination

A large number of adverbs have been formed by agglutination. The most common types of agglutinated adverbs are formed from the agglutination of a word sequence in which one of the constituent terms is a pro-form. Depending on the constituent elements, we may distinguish several groups of agglutinated adverbials.

a) Agglutinated pro-adverbs, in which the first element is the quantifier **gjithë** 'all', while the second element may be a pro-adverb, a noun, or some other part of speech. Such are: **gjithandej** 'everywhere', **gjithashtu** 'also', **gjithherë** 'all the time', **gjithmonë** 'always' (**-monë** from **mot** 'year' + **-në** [accusative definite singular]), **gjithnjë** 'always'.

b) Agglutinated pronominal adverbs in which the first element is a pro-adverb such as **kur** 'when', **ku** 'where', **nga** 'from', **si** 'how', **qysh** 'how', **tek** 'at, to', and the second element is the verb **do**, (it) wants: **kudo** 'everywhere' ("where it wants"), **ngado** 'anywhere, wherever', **sido** 'anyhow, however', **sado** 'although, however', **tekdo** 'anywhere, wherever'. In construction, this type of adverb is identical with the indeterminate pronouns of the type **kushdo** 'whoever' (see Section 8.8.1 A). The adverb **kurdoherë** 'always, all the time' is the result of three agglutinated elements, and **ngandonjëherë** 'sometimes' has four elements. The word **ndokund** 'somewhere, anywhere' is likewise an agglutinated pro-adverb, in which the more frequent order of constituents is reversed, so that **(n)do** appears as the first term of the agglutination (cf. the indefinite pronoun **ndo-kush** 'anybody, somebody' and the indefinite determiner **ndo-një** 'some, any').

This group also includes agglutinations in which the pronominal adverbs constitute the second term, while the first term is the verb **di** 'know'. Such are: **diku** 'somewhere', **dikund** 'somewhere', **dikur** 'sometime', **disi** 'somewhat'.

c) Agglutinated adverbs in which the second element is the form **-kund** 'where' or **-kundi** 'where', whereas the first element can be a pronoun, an adverb or a particle: **asgjëkundi** 'nowhere', **askund** 'nowhere', **askurrkund** 'nowhere', **kurrkund** 'nowhere', **gjëkundi** 'somewhere', **tjetërkund** 'elsewhere'.

d) Agglutinated adverbs in which the second element is the noun **herë** 'time'. The first element may be a preposition, an adverb, a pronoun or a particle: **asnjëherë** 'not once', **atëherë** 'then', **kurdoherë** 'always', **menjëherë** 'at once', **ngaherë** 'all the time', **nganjëherë** 'sometime', **përherë** 'all the time', **përnjëherë** 'at once'.

e) Agglutinated adverbs formed with an accusative preposition and a noun. This group includes **përballë** 'facing, opposite', **përbri** 'alongside, beside', **përdhe** 'on the ground', **përfundi** 'underneath', **përkrahu** 'by the arm', **përmes** 'through', **përqark** 'round about', **përreth** 'around', **përditë** 'daily, everyday', **përnatë** 'nightly, every night', **përherë** 'all the time', **ngrykë** 'embrace' (**në grykë** 'in throat'), **ndorë** 'handy' (**në dorë** 'in hand'), etc. As we see, the second element of the agglutination, the noun, is always indefinite.

f) Agglutinated adverbs whose constituent elements are two nouns connected by the conjunction **e** 'and' (sometimes realized as **a**). Some other part of speech, most often an adverb, can also be a constituent element in these adverbs. Examples are: **fytafyt** 'at each other's throat, ("throat and throat"), **anekend** 'all over, ("side and corner"), **turravrap** 'hurriedly, ("dashing and speed"), **buzagas** 'smiling ("lip and joy").

g) Agglutinated adverbs formed of a cardinal number + **-fish** (formerly the noun **fije** 'strands, threads' [from **fill** 'thread'] in the indefinite ablative plural with the ending **-sh**): **dyfish** 'two-fold', **trefish** 'three-fold', etc. Formed in analogy to these is the word **njëfish** 'one-fold, single'.

h) Agglutinated adverbs whose constituents come from various parts of speech and whose structure does not fit into the preceding categories. This group includes **ndërkaq** 'meanwhile' ("whilesuch"), **sakaq** 'on the spot, at once', **dosido** 'no matter how, any way ("want as you want")', **njëlloj** 'the same' ("one sort"), **kësisoj** 'in this manner', **kësodore** 'in this manner' ("by this hand"), **sidokudo** 'no matter how, any way, ("however-whenever"), **vetvetiu** 'automatically ("by self-self"), etc.

5.4.5 Adverbial Locutions

An adverbial locution is a sequence of words that has taken on a unitary lexical sense with an adverbial value; unlike compounds or agglutinations, the constituents of locutions keep their stress as individual words and are kept distinct in the orthography: e.g., **herë pas here** 'time after time', **më këmbë** 'on foot'. Their internal immutability as locutions is a matter of degree, but they may be seen as being different from fully free phrases like **në Tiranë**, because they reflect a certain unit status in the way they are learned and manipulated, and may develop meanings that differ to some degree from those of their component parts: **gju më gju** 'sitting down, kneeling' (not simply 'knee to knee' or 'knee on knee').

A. Conjoined Nouns as Adverbials

Adverbial locutions have been formed through the reduplication of the same noun, but connected with the conjunction **e** 'and'. Such are the locutions **anës e anës** 'on the side, sideways', **çift e çift** 'in couples', **palë e palë** 'folded, in pairs', **rreth e rreth** 'around and around', **varg e varg** 'range upon range, verse after verse'.

Adverbial locutions have also been formed from two closely related nouns conjoined by **e** 'and': **copë e çikë** 'in little bits', **ditë e natë** 'day and night', **natë e ditë** 'night and day', **fund e**

krye 'from beginning to end', **hundë e buzë** 'face down', **lesh e li** 'all mixed up', **rreth e rrotull** 'around and about', **orë e çast** 'at any moment', **pikë e vrer** 'incensed, indignant', **tym e flakë** 'all afire', **varg e vistër** 'lined up', **dimër e verë** 'winter and summer'. Locutions of this type function as manner adverbs or as adverbs of temporal circumstance.

5.10.3 Adverbial locutions have been formed through the direct reduplication of a noun in its plural form: e.g., **copa-copa** 'bits and pieces', **copë-copë** 'shattered', **dallgë-dallgë** 'wave upon wave', **fije-fije** 'in strands', **flokë-flokë** 'in flakes', **gropa-gropa** 'full of holes', **grupe-grupe** 'in groups', **herë-herë** 'sometimes', **hove-hove** 'intermittently', **kokrra-kokrra** 'in little bits', **lara-lara** 'mottled', **palë-palë** 'in folds', **pjesë-pjesë** 'in parts', **shkallë-shakallë** 'terraced', **togje-togje** 'in mounds', **tufë-tufë** 'in bunches', **valë-valë** 'wavy', **vende-vende** 'here and there'. Locutions of this type usually function as manner adverbials; less often they function as temporal and locative adverbials. In appropriate contexts they may function as predicative adverbials as well (see Section 3.1).

B. Conjoined Adverbs as Adverbials

Adverbial locutions are also formed from the union of adverbs which have antonymous meanings and which may or may not be connected by the copulative conjunction **e** 'and': **andej-këndej** 'hither and thither, here and there', **tutje-tëhu** 'here and there', **aty-këtu** 'here and there', **posht e lartë** and **lart e poshtë** 'up and down'. In addition they may be formed through the reduplication of the same adverb, connected by the conjunction **e** 'and': **shpejt e shpejt** 'quickly, very quickly', **pranë e pranë** 'nearby, quite nearby', **mirë e mirë** 'well, nice'. Sometimes such reduplication has the effect of intensifying the effect of the single adverb. Adverbial locutions may be formed as well through the reduplication of the same adverb without the use of the conjunction **e**, as in **hollë-hollë** 'very thinly', **rëndë-rëndë** 'very weighty', **shumë-shumë** 'very much'.

NOTE

The adverbial locution **kurrën e kurrës** 'never ever' ("the never of the never"), too, is constructed on the basis of reduplication, with the first term in an apparent accusative case form and the second term an apparent genitive case form.

C. Conjoined Verbs as Adverbials

A limited number of combinations of two antonymous (in a broad sense of the word) imperative verbs, conjoined by the conjunction **e** 'and', have acquired adverbial value in current usage: **shkel e shko** 'superficially' ("step and go"), **çel e mbyll** 'in an open and shut way', **qesh e ngjesh** 'caustically' ("smile and compress").

Note how often the last component of an adverbial locution echoes the sound of the first one, either in whole or in part, resulting in alliteration (**shkel e shko, lesh e li**), consonance (**çel e mbyll, ditë e natë**), rhyme (**qesh e ngjesh**), assonance (**hundë e buzë**) or reduplication of all or most of the first component (**kurrën e kurrës, andej këndej, shpejt e shpejt**).

D. Prepositions in the Formation of Adverbials

As has been noted, prepositional phrases in general may be considered to be adverbial. However, there are certain fixed phrases which may be classified specifically as adverbial locutions, formed of a preposition plus a noun, which together have changed semantically and grammatically into a fixed and inseparable entity that functions as a unitary adverb. Such are the phrases **me hir** 'gracefully, with grace, graciously', **me kohë** 'in time', **me natë** 'nightly', **me ngut** 'under pressure, pressed', **me pahir** 'unwillingly', **me radhë** 'by turn', **me vrap** 'hastily', **për bukuri** 'beautifully', **për turp** 'for shame', **prej kohe** 'since long ago', **prej kohësh** 'times long past', **më këmbë** 'on foot', **në tym** 'in smoke' etc.

Manner adverbial locutions may be productively formed with the preposition **me** 'with' plus a substantivized adjective: **me të butë** 'softly', **me të egër** 'fiercely', **me të keq** 'meanly', **me të mirë** 'nicely', **me të pabesë** 'faithlessly, treacherously', **me të qeshur** 'jokingly', **me të qetë** 'quietly', **me të shpejtë** 'speedily', **me të urtë** 'gently'.

A special type of adverbial locution has been formed with the preposition **për** 'for' plus an adjective with the suffix **-i (u)** and the preposed article **së**: **për së afërmi** 'at close range', **për së gjalli** 'alive', **për së gjati** 'lengthwise', **për së gjeri** 'breadthwise', **për së largu** 'from afar, at a distance', **për së larti** 'from above', **për së shpejti** 'soon', **për së tepërmi** 'excessively, in excess', etc.

Adverbial locutions can productively be composed of a preposition and a number--either **për** + number or **më** + number + **-sh**): **për një** 'for one, apiece', **për dy** 'for two, per pair', **për tre** 'for three'; **më dysh** 'two ways, in two (pieces)', **më trish** 'three-ways, in three pieces', **më katërsh** 'four ways, in four (pieces)', etc.

Adverbial locutions have been formed through the reduplication of the same word and the interposition of prepositions:

1) The reduplication of a noun with the interposed preposition **për** 'for' may serve as a temporal adverbial, as in **darkë për darkë** 'every evening', **ditë për ditë** 'every day', **drekë për drekë** 'every lunch', **javë për javë** 'every week', **mbrëmje për mbrëmje** 'every evening', **mëngjes për mëngjes** 'every morning', **mot për mot** 'every year', **natë për natë** 'every night', **orë për orë** 'every hour', **vit për vit** 'every year' etc.; or as a manner adverbial, as in **ballë për ballë** 'facing', **dorë për dorë** 'hand in hand', **dhëmb për dhëmb** 'tooth and nail', **fjalë për fjalë** 'verbatim', **flakë për flakë** 'fire for fire', **fyt për fyt** 'by the throat', **grykë për grykë** 'by the throat', **kokë për kokë** 'tete a tete, head to head', **krah për krah** 'arm in arm', etc. In all instances the repeated noun is in the indefinite accusative case.

2) The reduplication of a noun with the interposed **më** 'to, at' may function as a locative adverbial, as in **breg më breg** 'hill to hill', **degë më degë** 'branch to branch', **gojë më gojë** 'mouth to mouth', **rrugë më rrugë** 'street by street', **skaj më skaj** 'place to place, corner to corner', **shpat më shpat** 'slope by slope', **shteg më shteg** 'pass by pass', **vesh më vesh** 'ear to ear', etc.; or as a manner adverbial, as in **buzë më buzë** 'on the lips', **gojë më gojë** 'mouth to mouth', **gju më gju** 'sitting down, on the knees', **kokë më kokë** 'head to head', **kurriz më kurriz** 'back to back', etc.

NOTES

1. In reduplications of this type, there are quite a few cases in which the same locution may in different contexts have either its more literal locative value, or a figurative manner value: **degë më degë, shpat më shpat, rrugë më rrugë** may either have their literal locative meanings 'branch to branch', 'slope to slope', 'street to street', respectively, or may mean figuratively 'thoroughly'. Such too are constructions with **pa**: **rrugë pa rrugë** 'cross country' or 'aimlessly'.

2. Such locutions do not characteristically function as temporal adverbials, except for the locution **kohë më kohë** 'from time to time' which is used often.

3) Locutions formed by the reduplication of a noun with the interposed preposition **me** 'with' are rare. They function for the most part as temporal adverbials, and in this respect are similar to reduplications with the interposed preposition **për**: **dita me ditë** 'daily, day by day', **nata me natë** 'nightly, night by night'.

4) The reduplication of a noun with the interposed preposition **pas** 'after, with the first constituent in the indefinite nominative and the second in the indefinite ablative, usually function as temporal adverbials: **brez pas brezi** 'generation after generation', **ditë pas dite** 'day after day', **dorë pas dore** 'hand in hand', **hap pas hapi** 'step by step', **herë pas here** 'time after time', **kohë pas kohe** 'from time to time', **orë pas ore** 'hour after hour', etc.

5) Locutions formed by the reduplication of an adverb with the interposed preposition **më, për,** or **nga** have also been used as manner adverbials: **aty për aty** 'immediately, on the spot',

brenda për brenda 'straight inside', **drejt për drejt** 'directly', **kot më kot** 'in vain', **pak nga pak** 'little by little', **sot për sot** 'at present', **tani për tani** 'for now', **tashti për tashti** 'for now', **vetëm për vetëm** 'solely', etc.

6) Similarly, locutions consisting of the reduplication of a number with the interposed preposition **nga** function as manner adverbials: **një nga një** 'one by one', **dy nga dy** 'two by two', **tre nga tre** 'three by three', **katër nga katër** 'four by four'.

7) Locutions consisting of the preposition **nga** 'from' plus noun in the nominative definite plus the preposition **në** 'to' plus the same noun in the accusative indefinite have been used to form temporal adverbials: **nga dita në ditë** 'from day to day', **nga çasti në çast** 'from moment to mo ment', **nga koha në kohë** 'from time to time', **nga ora në orë** 'from hour to hour', **nga viti në vit** 'from year to year', etc.

CHAPTER 6

Gradation, Comparison and Qualification

All languages have devices for expressing differences of degrees in certain qualities or characteristics, although those devices, qualities, and degrees vary from language to language. In this chapter the devices in Albanian for expressing those differences by comparison and by qualification are examined. COMPARISON treats qualities along a more-less scale, while QUALIFICATION treats them in terms of an absolute base; in English, for example, *warmer* is a compared adjective while *very warm* is a qualified one.

6.1 Comparison

All languages have ways of comparing elements in terms of some implicit or explicit scale. In general, there is some way of indicating that the terms compared are equal in degree (termed EQUIPOLLENT in this book), that one term is greater in degree (termed SUPERIOR), and that one term is lesser in degree (termed INFERIOR). In Albanian the proclitic **më** 'more' enters into most of the kinds of constructions used to signify the superior and inferior degrees and a comparative adverb **aq** 'that much', **kaq** 'this much', **sa** 'as much' or **si** 'as' enters into those signifying the equipollent degree.

Degrees may be compared:

a) for the same quality in something or someone else:

Në shtëpi la t'anë dhe një vëlla MË TË VOGËL se vetja. 'At home, he left his father and a YOUNGER brother ("a brother SMALLER than himself").'

Eliona dukej pak MË E MADHE në moshë dhe MË E PJEKUR nga të tjerat. 'Eliona seemed a little OLDER ("bigger in age") and MORE MATURE than the others.'

b) for the same quality, but at a different time or under different conditions:

Tani dhoma Mimozës i duket MË E PASUR dhe MË E BUKUR se herët e tjera. 'Now the room seems RICHER and PRETTIER to Mimozë than at other times.'

c) for the same quality in respect to the entire class to which the compared term belongs:

Diferenca ekzistuese midis pagës MË të ULËT të punonjësve dhe pagës MË TË LARTË në vendin tonë është nga MË TË VOGLAT. 'The difference existing between THE LOWEST wages of the workers and THE HIGHEST in our country is among the SMALLEST.'

d) for different qualities in the same thing or another thing. **Me Besimin djaloshin e lidhte një histori sa E NDËRLIKUAR aq dhe E PAPËLQYER**. 'The boy was linked to Besim by a history as COMPLEX as it was UNDESIRABLE.'

6.1.1 Comparison of Modifiers

Modifiers are words characteristically used to modify, i.e., to qualify, describe, or classify other words in the phrase or sentence in which they appear. In Albanian, two classes of modifiers, ADJECTIVES and ADVERBS, are distinguishable: adjectives are used to modify nouns or pronouns, while adverbs are used to modify verbs, adjectives, other adverbs, or whole phrases and sentences.

The constructions used in Albanian for comparison are almost identical for adjectives and adverbs. In general, **më** 'more' is placed directly before the modifier to indicate the superior degree, **më pak** 'less (literally, "more little")' to indicate the inferior deqree, and **aq** 'that much (many)' or **kaq** 'this much (many)' to indicate the equipollent degree. The second term of the comparison, when it is made explicit, is introduced by **se, sesa** or **nga** 'than' for constructions corresponding to the English comparative, **sa** 'as much (many)' or **si** 'as' for those corresponding to the English equipollent, and a locative preposition such as **nga** 'from, of' or **në** 'in' for those corresponding to the English superlative.

A large number of modifiers express qualities or characteristics that can be gradated; that is, the intensity or degree of that quality or characteristic in a given instance can be quantified relative to the intensity in others. In comparing the size of two or three balls, for example, one might say in English "This ball is bigger than that one," or "This ball is the biggest of all three," corresponding to the traditional comparative and superlative, respectively. Conversely, one might say "This ball is less big than that one," or "This ball is the least big of all three." Finally, the intensities may be equated, as in "This ball is as big as that one."

Gradable modifiers may be:

1. Adjectives and the adverbs of manner homophonous with them, except that the adverb lacks the adjectival article. These may be used in all degrees (except as indicated below):

a) Simple stems: **(i) ashpër** 'rough(ly)', **(i) bukur** 'beautiful(ly)', **(i) butë** 'soft(ly)', **(i) hollë** 'thin(ly)', **(i) keq** 'bad(ly)', **(i) kthjellët** 'clear(ly)', **(i) lehtë** 'light(ly), easi(ly)', **(i) mirë** 'good, well', **(i) qartë** 'clear(ly)', **(i) rrallë** 'rare(ly)', **(i) urtë** 'quiet(ly), wise(ly)', etc.

Nuk i tha gjë, vetëm i shtërngoi dorën, po në një mënyrë që fliste MË QARTË se çdo fjalë tjetër. 'He didn't say a thing, only shook his hand, but in a way that spoke MORE CLEARLY than any other word.'

b) Modifiers formed from participles: **(i) dendur** 'frequent(ly)', **(i) hapur** 'open(ly)', **(i) shkoqur** 'plain(ly), clear(ly)', **(i) shtruar** 'gent(ly), quiet(ly)', **(i) rrëmbyer** 'driving(ly), rash(ly)', **(i) prerë** 'decisive(ly), exact(ly)', etc.

Ai ka shkuar në treg MË DENDUR se unë. 'He has gone to the market MORE OFTEN than I.'

c) Modifiers with the suffix **-shëm**, **(i) mendueshëm** 'thoughtful(ly)', **(i) gëzueshëm** 'joyful(ly)', **(i) fuqishëm** 'powerful(ly)', **(i) natyrshëm** 'natural(ly)', etc.

Që andej, do të kishte mundësi të qëllonte MË LIRSHËM, pa pasur përpara shkëmbin e kuq. 'From over there, he would be able to strike MORE FREELY, without having the red rock in front of him.'

2. Certain adverbs formed with the suffix **-(i)sht**, such as **hollësisht** 'in detail', **konkretisht** 'concretely', **lirisht** 'freely', **ngushtësisht** 'narrowly', **rastësisht** 'haphazardly, by chance':

Qemali urtë e butë i kërkoi mikut të fliste më qartë e MË KONKRETISHT për të metat e zeshkanit. 'Qemal gently requested his friend to speak MORE CONCRETELY about the faults of the swarthy one.'

A më jepni lejë, të shprehem MË GJERËSISHT, me një figurë më të plotë? 'Will you permit me to expres my self MORE BROADLY, with a better illustration?'

3. Adverbial locutions with **së**, of the type **për së afërmi** 'at close range', **për së largu** 'at a distance', **së mbari** 'happily', **për së mbari** 'in a lucky way, felicitously', **së thelli** 'deeply' which are compared only in the superior degree.

Mori pasqyrën dhe u pa me kujdes MË PËR SË AFËRMI. 'She took the mirror and looked at herself carefully AT CLOSER RANGE.'

Certain locutions of the type **me** + noun are often used as adverbials and may be used in the superior and equipollent degrees: **me gëzim** 'joyfully', **me vrull** 'impetuously', **me vrap** 'speedily', etc:

Ajo ecte përpara, MË ME GUXIM se i shoqi, po dora e vogël i dridhej në dorën e tij. 'She walked ahead MORE COURAGEOUSLY than her husband, but her little hand trembled in his hand.'

Ndërkaq direkët u ngulën dhe ujët u lëshua, në fillim ngadalë e pastaj MË ME RRËMBIM, po porta i bëri ballë. 'Meanwhile, the planks were driven and the water was released, at first slowly and then MORE RAPIDLY, but the gate held out against it.'

Ai e bëri AQ ME TË BUTË sa unë. 'He did it AS GENTLY as I.'

To get the effect of the inferior degree for these locutions the noun is immediately preceded by **më pak**:

Ai rend ME MË PAK SHPEJTËSI se unë. 'He runs LESS SPEEDILY ("with less speed") than I.' (See Section 6.1.2)

4. Adverbs of quantity, such as **shumë** 'many, much, more', **pak** 'few, little', **tepër** 'too much', **fort** 'strongly, very', which occur in the superior and equipollent, but not the inferior degree:

Megjithëkëtë, mendjen nuk e kishte MË SHUMË në ato që po nënvizonte, sesa te shoku që kishte përpiluar raportin. 'Nevertheless, his mind was not MORE on those [things] he was underlining than on the comrade who had compiled the report.'

5. Adverbs of place which are used in all three degrees, e.g., **anash** 'sideways', **andej** 'that way', **afër** 'near', **brenda** 'inside', **djathtas** 'to the right', **këtej (e këndej)** 'this way', **lart** 'above', **larg** 'far', **thellë** 'deep(ly)', **sipër** 'above', **përpara** 'ahead', **prapa** 'behind', **poshtë** 'below', **majtas** 'to the left', **pranë** 'nearby', **tej** 'beyond, over', **tutje** 'yonder, further'.

Aidin Muzhaqi u dërgua prapa në vendin e caktuar, që ta radhiste ushtrinë shqiptare, e cila do të arrinte atje grupe-grupe dhe të mos e linte të shtyhej MË TUTJE. 'Aidin Muzhaq was sent behind to the place specified, so as to line up the Albanian army, which was to arrive group by group, and not let it be pushed FARTHER.'

6. Adverbs of time, such as **para** 'before', **herët** 'early', **vonë** 'late', **shpesh** 'often', which are used in all three degrees:

Sa burra kordhëtarë / Ka nxjerrë Shqipëria / MË PASTAJ E MË PARË / Që i skruan historia. 'How many are the swordsmen / Albania has given birth to / LATER AND EARLIER / that history writes about.'

NOTE **Më parë** 'earlier' is used only in the superior degree.

A. The Superior Degree

The superior degree of the modifier itself in Albanian is formed of the proclitic **më** 'more' plus the modifier. This construction is used both where English would use *more* or *most* + modifier and where English would use the compared form of the modifier itself (usually, modifier + -*er* or -*est*).

më i ëmbël = 'more sweet' or 'sweeter', 'most sweet' or 'sweetest'
më ëmbëlsisht = 'more sweetly', 'most sweetly'
më ushqyes = 'more nutritious', 'most nutritious'
më mirë or **më i mirë** = 'better', 'best' (cf. **mirë** 'well' and **i mirë** 'good')
më pak = 'less ("more little")'

The second or reference term of the construction is: 1) introduced by a conjunction **se** or **sesa** serving the role of English *than* (corresponding approximately to the English comparative); 2) a prepositional phrase introduced by a locative preposition or the preposition **nga**, 3) or a noun phrase in the genitive case. Constructions 2) and 3) both correspond approximately to superlative constructions in English). Since Albanian has only one form, **më**, for both *more* and *most* (or the -*er* and -*est* suffixes, respectively), the interpretation of the construction as comparative or superlative depends on the rest of the construction. As will be seen below, if the modifier is an adjective in a substantivized definite form, or immediately following a definite noun, it usually has a superlative translation in English (e.g., **më i bukuri** 'the most beautiful', literally, "more the beautiful"), whereas in non-substantivized, form it is usually translated as a comparative (e.g., **më i bukur** 'more beautiful').

A comparison with **më** + adjective may appear either in attributive position, directly following the word it modifies:

S'ka gjë MË TË VYER për njeriun se nderi. 'There is nothing MORE VALUABLE to man than honor.'

or in some other position, such as predicate complement:

Teuta dukej pak MË E MADHE në moshë dhe MË E PJEKUR se të tjerat. 'Teuta seemed a little older ("GREATER in age") and MORE MATURE than the others.'

The degree of comparison can be further specified by placing before the particle **më** one of the adverbs of degree **shumë** 'very, much', **edhe** 'even', **pak** 'a little':

Puna do të shkojë kaq më shpejt më përpara, fronti ynë i luftës po zgjerohet SHUMË MË SHPEJT, armikun do ta mundim EDHE MË SHPEJT. '[Our] work will progress so much faster, the front line of our struggle is expanding MUCH MORE RAPIDLY, we shall defeat the enemy EVEN SOONER.'

Kur ai u kthye me fytyrë dhe ajo njohu të atin e Adilit, u trondit EDHE MË KEQ se përpara. 'When he turned his face and she recognized the father of Adil, she was shaken EVEN WORSE than before.'

Tani e ndjej veten PAK MË MIRË. 'Now I feel A LITTLE BETTER.'

Corresponding to the English comparative, generally expressed by **more** + modifier or modifier + **-er** Albanian uses the superior degree expressed by **më** + modifier:

vajzë e bukur 'pretty girl'
vajzë më e bukur 'prettier girl'
Ajo vajzë është më e bukur. 'That girl is prettier.'
Vajza më e bukur është ajo. 'The prettier girl is that one.'

The explicit reference term to which a comparison is being made is introduced by **se** or **sesa** (preferred before verbs) or **nga** (only before a noun phrase), all rendered in English by 'than':

Kjo vajzë është më e bukur se ajo. 'This girl is prettier than that one.'

Corresponding to the English superlative, Albanian again uses the superior degree, indicating by the definite form of the noun or adjective that the superlative is intended, or indicating by the reference term of the comparison the domain over which the superlative extends:

vajza më e bukur 'the prettiest girl (lit. the girl more pretty)'
më e bukura vajzë 'the prettiest girl (lit. more the pretty girl)'
Ajo vajzë është më e bukura në dhomën. 'That girl is the prettiest in the room.'
Ajo vajzë është më e bukur nga të gjitha. 'That girl is the prettiest of all (lit. prettier from all).'

When both sides of a comparison are expressed, the comparative conjunctions used to link them are **se** 'than', **sesa** 'than', and **nga** 'than'. As will be seen below, **nga** is unique in that it may occur as well after **më** + substantivized adjective (or **më** + adjective after a definite noun) in constructions with a superlative sense.

Tani fshati Agimit i duket më i pasur dhe më i bukur SE herët e tjera. 'Now, the village seems wealthier and prettier to Agim THAN other times.'

Kënga qenka më e fortë SE njeriu. 'The song is really mightier THAN man.'

S'ka gjë më të bukur SESA të shohësh Pogradecin. 'There is nothing more beautiful THAN seeing Pogradec.'

Dashke të dalësh më e zgjuar NGA unë. 'So you want to be ("emerge") smarter THAN I.'

Atë mot që Shpiragajt vunë këmbë në Trokth, dimri shtërngoi MË VONË, po MË

RREPTË nga ç'pritej. 'The year that Shpiragajt set foot in Trokth, the winter tightened up LATER, but MORE SEVERELY than (what was) expected.'

Kjo është MË KEQ se të bredhësh maleve dhe të flesh në çadër. 'This is WORSE than roaming ("than that you roam") the mountains and sleeping ("that you sleep") in tents.'

Ajo ndjen: heshtja vret MË KEQ sesa pritja e aq më tepër heshtja për vëllanë atje në mal. 'She feels: the silence hurts WORSE than the waiting, and still more the silence about your brother in the mountains.'

Various adverbs of degree may precede the modifier in the superior degree to indicate different gradations of intensity: **shumë** 'much', **akoma** 'even, still', **edhe** 'even, still', **pak** 'a little', **ca** 'somewhat', **jashtëzakonisht** 'unusually', **absolutisht** 'absolutely', etc.

Po më në fund, ai erdhi në shtëpi AKOMA MË I RRUDHUR, AKOMA MË I VRENJTUR, AKOMA MË I HESHTUR 'But in the end, he came home STILL MORE WRINKLED, STILL MORE GLOOMY, STILL MORE TACITURN.'

Duhet të kishte pësuar cfili EDHE MË TË RËNDA. 'He must have experienced EVEN GRAVER injuries.'

It should be noted that if the second term of the comparison is a clause with conditional or temporal nuances, the conjunction may be implicit rather than explicit.

Shejtan, murmuriti ai, duke menduar me trishtim, se s'kishte gjë më të keqe SESA kur s'të besonte edhe një çamaroke si e motra. 'You devil, he muttered, thinking sadly that there was nothing worse THAN when even a simpleton like his sister didn't believe you.'

When the specific reference term is of no interest, the speaker usually omits the second term and allows the comparison to be defective:

Këngën tonë do ta dëgjonte gjithë fshati dhe për ne s'do të kishte gëzim MË TË MADH. 'The whole village would hear our song, and for us, there could be no GREATER joy.'

In constructions of the superior degree the use of a definite form in the first element (noun or adjective) indicates the superlative, that is the highest degree of the quality involved, in comparison with the same quality in members of the same class:

Ai duhet të ishte ndeshur me rrugët MË të VËSHTIRA të jetës. 'He must have encountered THE MOST DIFFICULT paths of life.'

Gjergj Kastrioti është një nga KRYELUFTËTARËT MË TË MBARUAR, MË FAQEBARDHË dhe MË TË MËDHENJ të botës. 'George Castrioti is one of THE MOST ACCOMPLISHED, MOST SUCCESSFUL, and GREATEST WAR CHIEFTAINS in the world.'

When it occurs immediately after a definite noun, the adjective has the same form as it would in an attributive construction, but is translated as an English superlative:

Popullin tonë edhe në rrethanat MË TË VËSHTIRA, e ka karakterizuar kurdoherë një optimizëm revolucionar. 'Even in THE MOST DIFFICULT circumstances ("the circumstances more difficult"), our people have always been characterized by revolutionary optimism.'

If the adjective itself is substantivized and used in the definite form, it is also translated as an English superlative:

Ky ishte me siguri MË I GJATI në këtë listë. 'This one was surely THE TALLEST ("more the tall") in this list.'

The superlative character of the comparison, may be indicated by a qualifying scope phrase with a noun in case or with a prepositional phrase introduced by a locative preposition (e.g., **në** 'in', **ndër** 'among', **ndërmjet** 'among', **midis** 'among', **prej** 'of, from', **nga** 'from, of'):

Hekurani ishte MË I LUMTURI I NJERËZVE. 'Hekuran was THE HAPPIEST OF MEN.'

Ai ishte MË I GJATI NË ATË GRUP të vogël njerëzish. 'He was THE TALLEST IN THAT small GROUP of people.'

Tirana do të jetë me siguri MË I BUKURI NDËR QYTETET e Shqipërisë. 'Tirana must surely be THE MOST BEAUTIFUL AMONG Albanian CITIES.'

Agimi, si MË I HEDHURI MIDIS TYRE, tha befas... 'As THE MOST ADROIT AMONG THEM, Agim said suddenly...'

MË TË SHËMTUARIT PREJ KËTYRE ishin... 'THE UGLIEST OF THESE were...'

Ai ishte MË I RIU NGA NE, më i miri. 'He was THE YOUNGEST, the best AMONG US.'

Ai është ndoshta zogu MË I BUKUR NË BOTË. 'It is perhaps THE MOST BEAUTIFUL bird IN THE WORLD.'

Kjo është historia MË E VJETËR E SKËNDERBEUT 'This is THE OLDEST history of SKËNDERBEU.'

Vani ishte nga nxënësit MË TË MIRË TË KLASËS. 'Van was among THE BEST pupils OF THE CLASS.'

The locution **më së miri** 'best, as well as possible' and less often, in analogy with it, **më së keqi** 'worst, as badly as possible'--both of which are used in this form only--have the sense of a superlative:

Mbrojtja e atdheut dhe sigurimi i fitoreve të revolucionit kërkojnë që ne të kemi edhe në të ardhmen një ushtri të fortë...të armatosur MË SË MIRI me shkencën ushtarake marksiste-leniniste. 'The defense of the fatherland and the assurance of the gains of the revolution demand that we have a strong army in the future as well...equipped AS WELL AS POSSIBLE with the Marxist-Leninist military science.'

The construction with the modifier preceded by the locution **më se** 'extremely, more than, utterly', which derives from the expression **më tepër se** 'more than', is becoming ever more widespread as a means of intensification:

Këtë që po të them e quaj MË SE TË DOMOSDOSHME. 'I call it UTTERLY INDISPENSABLE, this thing I'm telling you.'

Trajtën "Aranit" e gjejmë dy herë edhe në dokumentet arkivale, por të dy herët janë MË SE TË DYSHIMTA. 'We find the form "Aranit" twice in the archival documents as well, but both are EXTREMELY SUSPECT.'

To express the highest degree possible, the comparative construction **sa + më +** modifier 'as, how', leaving unspecified the scope of the comparison is used--like the unqualified superlative in English:

Shpesh ajo më përkëdhelte dhe më uronte një fat SA MË TË LUMTUR. 'Often she fondled me and wished me THE HAPPIEST lot (possible).'

Ta bëjmë SA MË TË LUMTUR E TË GËZUESHME jetën e popullit. 'Let us make the people's life THE HAPPIEST AND MOST JOYOUS (possible).'

B. The Inferior Degree

A modifier in the inferior degree indicates that the quality designated is less in amount or intensity than another quality, or the same quality in another thing, or in the same thing under different conditions. It is composed of the adjective in the positive degree preceded by the adverb **pak** 'a little, somewhat', in the superior degree **më pak** 'less':

Pse nuk bën si ai shoku yt, që nuk ishte MË PAK I ZGJUAR nga ti? 'Why don't you do like your friend, who was not LESS BRIGHT than you?'

Ajo këndon më pak ëmbëlsisht se tjetra. 'She sings less sweetly than the other one.'

Më pak may in turn be modified by an adverb of degree such as **shumë** 'very, much'.

The conjunctions used in the second part of the comparison are the same ones that are used in the superior degree **se** 'than', **sesa** 'than', **nga** 'than'. Here again the second element may be left unexpressed, when the specific term of reference is assumed to be of no interest to the audience:

> **Vërtet nuk ish më ai Saraga i dikurshëm, që s'pranonte tjetër më të madh e më të mençëm se veten, po edhe më i vogël e MË PAK I MËNÇËM nuk tregohej.** 'True, he was no longer the Saraga of long ago, who did not recognize anyone bigger and smarter than himself, but neither did he pretend to be smaller and LESS SMART.'

Like modifiers of the superior degree, those of the inferior degree may be embedded in the adverbial locution **sa...** 'the (more or less)' **aq...** 'the (more or less)':

> **SA MË TEPËR copëtohet toka, AQ MË PAK PJELLORE bëhet.** 'THE MORE the land is decimated, THE LESS FERTILE it becomes.'

Constructions with modifiers in the inferior degree are mostly limited to literary Albanian due to the infuence of foreign languages and are largely absent in colloquial language. In their place the speaker either negates the equipollent degree or uses the superior degree of the antonymous adjective (or of the same adjective, but with the elements of the comparison switched). Thus, instead of the expression; **Tefta është MË PAK E GJALLË se e motra**. 'Tefta is LESS LIVELY than her sister.', people say, **Teuta s'është AQ E GJALLË sa e motra**. 'Tefta is not AS LIVELY as her sister.', or **Teuta është MË E NGATHËT se e motra**. 'Tefta is MORE SLUGGISH than her sister.', or **E motra është MË E GJALLË se Teuta**. 'Her sister is more lively than Tefta.' Likewise, **Unë nuk jam MË PAK TRIM se ata**. 'I am not LESS BRAVE than they.', becomes **Unë nuk jam MË FRIKACAK se ata** 'I am not MORE FEARFUL than they'; **Ata nuk janë MË TRIMA se unë.** 'They are not BRAVER than I.' or **Unë jam PO AQ TRIM sa ata** 'I am JUST AS BRAVE as they'.

The negation of equipollence uses the constructions **jo aq...sa** 'not so much...as...', or **nuk** (or **s'**) 'not' + verb + **aq** + adverb:

> **Ajo flet JO AQ SHPEJT SA e ëma.** 'She DOESN'T speak AS FAST AS ("speaks not so fast as") her mother.'
>
> **Tani nuk i merrte më punët AQ RRËMBYER.** 'Now he did things less hastily.' ("Now he no longer took things SO HASTILY.")

C. The Equipollent Degree

The modifier in the equipollent degree indicates that the first term of the comparison is equal in degree to the second:

To express this degree the adjective in the first term may be preceded by the comparative adverbs **aq** 'that much, so', or **kaq** 'so, this much', and the second term introduced by **sa** 'as much' or **si** 'as':

> **Duke mbaruar, mund të themi se për Skënderbeun lëvdata është AQ E DREJTË SA EDHE E MERITUAR.** 'In conclusion, we can say that in reference to Skënderbeu, the praise is AS JUST AS IT IS MERITED.'

Sa is used when the two terms are compared in quantity, while **si** is used when they are compared in quality:

> **Vrana Konti ishte AQ TRIM dhe I ZOTI në luftë SA Skënderbeu.** 'Vrana Konti was AS BRAVE and AS CAPABLE at fighting AS Skënderbeu.'
>
> **Ka dhe të tjerë, po jo aq të rrezikshëm SI këta.** 'There are others too, but not so dangerous AS these.'

When the adverb in the first term is missing it may be inferred from the correlative adverb of the second term:

Shumë vjet kishte që e mbaja në sup atë pushkë, po E RËNDË SA asaj dite nuk më ishte durkur kurrë. 'For many years I had carried that rifle on my shoulder, but never before did it feel AS HEAVY AS on that day ("but heavy as on that day it had never seemed to me").'

Besides the order **aq... sa...**, the elements may appear in reverse order **sa... aq...**; the relation of equipollence remains unchanged, but the direction of comparison is reversed:

Duken SA GUXIMTARË AQ EDHE KRENARË. 'They appear to be AS DARING AS they are PROUD.'

Ishte nxehur dhe, SA I BUTË dhe I URTË qe kur nënshtrohej, AQ I EGËR bëhej kur nxehej. 'He was worked up, and as GENTLE and MILD as he was when he quieted down, that WILD he became when worked up.'

When the two terms of comparison are both clauses, **aq** or **kaq** may replace **sa** as the correlative conjunction.

AQ I RREPTË sa është me prindërit ose me shokët e radhës së tij, AQ I SHTRUAR është me anëtarët e partisë. 'AS ROUGH as he is with his parents or with friends of his own rank, THAT MILD he is with party members.'

The second element of the equipollent comparison is sometimes not expressed in the given phrase, because it is implied or is known from what has been said previously. In those instances **aq** or **kaq** establishes the comparison:

Ne krenohemi që kemi një aleat e një mik KAQ BESNIK e TË FUQISHËM. 'We are proud to have SO LOYAL and POWERFUL a friend and ally.'

Këmbët nuk i bindeshin më AQ LEHTË dhe lagështia i kishte depërtuar deri mbi gju. 'His feet no longer obeyed him AS EASILY and the dampness had penetrated (him) up to above the knees.'

The second element of the comparison may also be left unexpressed when the speaker accompanies his speech with gestures, and through them makes the comparison clear:

-- S'ka ditë që të mos shkojnë në zhukë nga tre e katër, na, KAQ TË MËDHENJ, -- dhe preku krahun me dorën tjetër në atë vend ku iu duk se mund të arrinte bishti i qefullit. '"Not a day passes without three or four of them, THIS BIG, going over to the rushes", and he touched his arm with the other hand at the spot where he thought the tail of the mullet might reach.'

A defective comparison often loses the implied connection with the second, unexpressed element and becomes an autonomous form, much like **mjaft** 'enough', which before modifiers corresponds to the *so* or *such* detached from comparisons:

-- Natyrisht që mendoj të shkruaj diçka për të gjitha këto. -- E ke të vështirë? -- Po, -- tha shkrimtari, -- s'është KAQ E LEHTË. -- Ma shpjegoni më mirë, -- tha vajza, -- kjo është një gjë KAQ INTERESANTE. '"Naturally, I'm thinking of writing something about all this." "Do you find it difficult?" "Yes," said the writer, "it's not SO EASY." "Explain it to me better," the girl said. "This is SUCH an INTERESTING thing."'

Ishte hera e parë që kundërshtonte KAQ PRERË. 'It was the first time that he objected SO DECISIVELY.'

The modifier in the equipollent degree may be preceded by the confirmative particle **po**, which takes the place of a second term containing the corresponding predicate being compared:

Po tashti a do ketë të tjerë PO AQ TË VENDOSUR sa Stas Vasili? 'But will there now be others just AS DETERMINED as Stas Vasil.'

Qielli ishte PO AQ I VREJTUR dhe i lartë. 'The sky was JUST AS OVERCAST and high.'

If the second part of the comparison is missing entirely and cannot be inferred from the context, **po** must appear before **aq**.

Compare:

> **Ai hëngri PO AQ NGADALË.** 'He ate JUST AS SLOWLY.'

with

> **Ai hëngri AQ NGADALË SA mundi.** 'He ate AS SLOWLY AS he could.'

In negative clauses the speaker may soften the negative ascription of a modifier by preposing the conjunctive particle **dhe** or **edhe** to **aq** (or **kaq**) plus the modifier:

> **Katerina nuk ishte DHE AQ E BUKUR.** 'Kathryn was not ALL THAT BEAUTIFUL.'
>
> **Nuk ishte EDHE AQ E GJATË koha që ishte strehuar në shtëpinë e tyre.** 'It had not been ALL that LONG a time since he took shelter in their home.'

In a comparison of two clauses, the equipollent construction **aq** (or **kaq**)...**sa** is used as a means of intensifying the modifier involved to such a degree as to produce the result stated in the clause introduced by **sa**:

> **Ecën AQ SHPEJT, sa dhe ata u habitën se ku i kishte gjithë ato forca.** 'He walks SO FAST, that even they were surprised at where he had found all that strength.'
>
> **Tani revizionizmi është bërë KAQ I PAPËRMBAJTUR në vrapin që ka zënë drejt greminës dhe KAQ I PATURPSHËM, sa nuk ngurron të sulmojë edhe materializmin.** 'Revisionism has now become SO IMPETUOUS in its rush towards the ravine, and so SHAMELESS, that it does not hesitate to attack even materialism.'

When the modifier is followed by a negative clause of comparison introduced by **sa**, the adjective may take on a superlative value. Some of these negative clauses have become conventionalized, fixed phraseological expressions: e.g., **sa s'ka më**, 'so much there is no greater', **sa s'ka se ku të vejë** 'the limit, the most (literally, so much that there is nowhere to go).'

> **Gjer tashti u tregova burrë I PJEKUR SA S'KA MË.** 'Until now, I have shown myself to be AS MATURE a man AS CAN BE ("showed myself mature man as there is not more").'
>
> **Nganjëherë më hipën një mërzi E MADHE SA S'BËHET.** 'Sometimes a boredom AS BIG AS THEY COME ("big as is not made") comes over me.'

To indicate proportional comparison of two modifiers, the equipollent and superior degrees are combined, with both modifiers in the superior degree, the first preceded by the conjunction **sa** 'as much' and the second preceded by the correlative **aq** 'that much the ...' or **kaq** 'this much'. The construction corresponds to English constructions with correlatives *the more...the more*:

> **SA MË AFËR vinte, AQ MË QARTË i dukej e qeshura e ëmbël në buzë.** 'THE CLOSER ("more near") he came, THE CLEARER ("more clear") was his sweet smile.'
>
> **-- E SA MË SHUMË që plakem, KAQ MË RËNDOM më vete mendja atje e aq më fort më prishet qejfi.** 'THE OLDER ("The more I am aged") I get, THE MORE OFTEN my mind goes there and the worse I feel.'
>
> **Prandaj, SA MË TË LARTË ta ketë pozitën ndonjë njeri në AMERIKË, AQ MË TË ÇMENDURA dhe TUAFE janë veprat e tij.** 'Therefore, THE HIGHER a person's position in AMERICA, the MORE INSANE and INANE are his actions.'
>
> **SA MË SHUMË çante vapori dallgët drejt lindjes, AQ MË E NGRYSUR bëhej fytyra e doktorit.** 'THE MORE the ship tore through the waves toward the east, THE MORE SOMBER became the doctor's face.'

6.1.1 C. The Equipollent Degree   **241**

6.1.2 Comparison of Nouns

The three degrees of comparison, the superior, the inferior, and the equipollent, are also relevant for comparing nouns. For mass nouns, one amount may be compared to another, and for count nouns, one aggregate may be compared to another:

Unë s'kam më shumë tulla se këto. 'I have no more bricks than these.'
Ai piu më tepër ujë sesa verë. 'He drank more water than wine.'

The superior degree of nouns is formed in the same way as for adjectives, except that **më** must be followed by one of the quantitative adverbs si **shumë 'much, many'** or **tepër '(too) much, many'.** Se 'than' and **sesa** 'than' are used freely to conjoin the second part of the comparison, while **nga** 'than' has a more dialectal flavor characteristic of southern Albania:

Në këtë qytet gjenden më shumë qen se mace. 'In this city are (found) more dogs than cats.'

To get the superlative sense, the substantivized form **të shumtët** 'the most' follows **më**, and the reference group of the comparison is introduced by a locative preposition like **ndër** 'among', **ndërmjet** 'among', **midis** 'among', **prej** 'of', **nga** 'of', **në** 'in'; or the reference group may be indicated by a noun phrase in the genitive case:

Më të shumtët e njerëzve (*or* **prej njerëzve**) **banojnë në ishullin e madh.** 'Most (of the) people live on the big island.'

The inferior degree of nouns is found primarily in literary language and is formed just as it is for adjectives and adverbs with **më pak** 'less fewer' and the same conjunctions as for the superior degree **se, sesa**, and **nga**:

Në këtë qytet gjenden më pak qen se mace. 'In this city are (found) fewer dogs than cats.'

The equipollent degree is formed in the same way as for adjectives and adverbs, with the locution **aq...sa...** 'as many/much...as...':

Në këtë qytet gjenden aq qen sa edhe mace. 'In this city are (found) just as many dogs as cats.'

To add the nuance that, for the example above, there are many dogs and cats or few dogs and cats, **aq** may be followed by **shumë** 'many' or **pak** 'few':

Në këtë qytet gjenden aq shumë (*or* **aq pak**) **qen sa edhe mace.** 'In this city there are just as many/as few dogs as cats.'

6.1.3 Comparison of Other Elements

The comparison of verbs, prepositions or even whole clauses is similar to that of nouns and occurs in all degrees:

Unë notoj më shumë se Skënderi. 'I swim more than Skënder.'
Unë notoj më shumë se Skënderi vrapon. 'I swim more than Skënder runs.'

As for nouns, the superior degree in other parts of speech uses the locutions **më shumë** 'more' and **më tepër** 'more' to indicate the comparison, and may additionally use **më fort** 'more (more strongly)'. In Albanian, this kind of comparison is structurally analogous to adverbial comparisons like **më ngadalë** 'more slowly':

Unë notoj më ngadalë se Skënderi. 'I swim more slowly than Skënder.'

The second term of the comparison may be introduced by the conjunctions **se** 'than', **sesa** 'than', and **nga** 'than' for the sense corresponding roughly to the English comparative; for the sense corresponding to the English superlative the reference group may be introduced by locative prepositions like **ndër** 'among', **ndërmjet** 'among', **midis** 'among', **prej** 'of', **nga** 'of', and **në** 'in', or by simply placing the noun of the comparison group in the genitive case:

Ai qau më fort sesa unë. 'He cried more than I did.'

Prej të tre vëllezërve, ai qau më tepër. 'Of the three brothers, he cried the most.'

As has been noted, the inferior degree is found primarily in literary language. It is formed with **më pak** 'less' and uses the same conjunctions as for the comparative sense of the superior degree:

Agimi vrapon më pak se Skënderi. 'Agim runs less than Skënder.'

The equipollent degree. This degree is formed with the locution **aq sa** 'as much as' in the same way as for other parts of speech:

Ai qau aq sa unë. 'He cried as much as I did.'

Ai qau aq sa qeshi. 'He cried as much as [he] laughed.'

To add the nuance that, for the first example, 'we cried a lot' or 'we cried a little', **aq** may be followed by **shumë** 'much' or **pak** '(a) little':

Ai qau aq shumë (or **aq pak**) **sa edhe unë**. 'He cried as much (or as little) as (even) I did.'

6.2 Qualification of Modifiers

The extent to which the characteristic designated by a modifier (gradable adjective or manner adverbial) is present can be indicated in various degrees. The modifier can be intensified (**ai është shumë i lodhur** 'he is very tired'), minimized (**ai është pak i lodhur** 'he is not very tired'), or approximated (**ai është gati i bardhë** 'he is almost white').

6.2.1 Intensification

The most common means of intensifying a modifier in Albanian is to place an adverb of degree in front of it.

Intensified Adjectives:

Ne jemi ABSOLUTISHT TË BINDUR se lëvizja komuniste dhe kampi socialist nuk mund të forcohen dhe të shkojnë përpara pa luftuar me guxim e vendosmëri Agjenturën më të shkathët e më të rrezikshëm të imperializmit amerikan. 'We are ABSOLUTELY CONVINCED that the communist movement and the socialist camp cannot become strong and march forward without combatting with courage and determination the most agile and dangerous agency of American imperialism.'

Midis reve dukej një copë qielli SHUMË E KALTËR. 'Between the clouds could be seen a DEEP BLUE patch of sky.'

Barkun e kishte MJAFT TË MADH. 'He had A RATHER BIG belly.'

He-he, kjo ka domethënie JASHTËZAKONISHT TË MADHE. 'Heh-heh, this has UNUSUALLY GREAT meaning.'

Po kur bëhet TEPËR I LARTË, murin nuk e mban më toka. 'But when the wall becomes TOO HIGH, the ground won't support it anymore.'

Kam dëgjuar që je FORT DORËSHTRËNGUAR. 'I have heard that you are QUITE TIGHTFISTED.'

Ajo ishte e lagur qull dhe e ngjyer e tëra në baltë, KREJT E BARDHË në fytyrë. 'She was soaking wet and muddy all over, and ALL WHITE in the face.'

Stacioni është FARE I RI. 'The station is COMPLETELY NEW.'

Intensified Adverbs:

Ata tani e dinë FARE MIRË se lufta e Tiranës do të jetë shumë e vështirë. 'They know now VERY WELL that the battle of Tiranë will be very difficult.'

Nga ana tjetër, merret vesh FARE SHKOQUR që ky bir, cilido që ishte, merrte urdhër më tepër nga Gjon Kastrioti se nga Sulltani. 'On the other hand, one can see VERY PLAINLY that this son, whoever he was, obeyed Gjon Kastrioti more than (he obeyed) the Sultan.'

Ajo që Mimozës i dukej e vështirë, bile ndonjëherë e pamundshme ngjau FARE RASTËSISHT. 'That which to Mimozë seemed difficult, indeed at times even impossible, happened COMPLETELY BY CHANCE.'

Ata e dinë FARE MIRË se lufta e Tiranës do të jetë shumë e vështirë, por është dëshira e tyre e zjarrtë që ta godasin armikun në çerdhen e tyre kryesore. 'They know VERY WELL that the battle of Tiranë will be very difficult, but it is their fervent desire to hit the enemy in their principal bases ["nests"].'

Me lehtësi të madhe, FARE NATYRSHËM, kish lidhur duart plot hir e të hajthme. 'With great ease, VERY NATURALLY, he had tied the graceful and skinny hands.'

Por, me sa di unë, ato nuk shfrytëzohen si duhet ose shfrytëzohen SHUMË PAK. 'But, as far as I know, they are not exploited as they should be, or they are exploited VERY LITTLE.'

Vali ndjeu nëpër gjumë se një gjë e ftohtë po i kalonte në kokë dhe instinktivisht ngriti dorën, po atëherë qe TEPËR VONË. 'Vali sensed in sleep that something cold was passing over his head and instinctively raised his hand, but then it was TOO (MUCH) LATE.'

Qëndronte aty më këmbë pranë tyre, po i dukej se qe SHUMË LARG. 'He stood there close to them, but felt that he was VERY FAR.'

The general adverbs used most often in this function are, **shumë** 'very', **jashtëzakonisht** 'extraordinarily, unusually', **mjaft** 'enough, pretty, rather', **tepër** 'extremely, too', **fort** 'very, quite', but also common are **krejt** 'completely, entirely', **fare** 'quite, really', **absolutisht** 'absolutely'. Certain other intensifying adverbs with more particular affective connotations are **thellësisht** 'profoundly', **tmerrësisht** 'terribly', **çuditërisht** 'surprisingly, strangely'. In the spoken language, and less frequently in the written language, the adverb **bukur** 'pretty, very' has this intensifying use as well:

Po ditë shumë pak kaluan / Dhe BUKUR MIRË e mora vesh / se ç'do të thoshin ato fjalë. 'But only a few days passed / And I understood PRETTY WELL / what those words meant.'

An intensifying adverb may be repeated to further intensify the modifier:

Për çudi, tërë ajo lukuni, që pak më parë e tmerroi tashti iu duk SHUMË-SHUMË E VOGËL, e pafuqishme. 'Strangely, that whole pack of wolves that terrified him a bit earlier, now seemed to him to be VERY VERY SMALL and powerless.'

Aktivitetet e saj janë SHUMË E SHUMË TË RRALLA. 'Her activities are few and far between ("VERY, VERY RARE").'

Besides being modified by intensifying adverbs, a modifier may acquire an intensified sense in other ways:

1) A modifier preceded by **sa** 'how (much, many)' acquires an exclamatory function with heightened affect, translating English *how + adjective!*

O, SA E VËSHTIRË ishte për një baba! 'Oh, HOW DIFFICULT it was for a father!'
SA E LARGËT më duket dita e nesërme! 'HOW DISTANT tomorrow seems to me!'
Edhe gjithë gjë e gjallë ndjen në zemër një dëshirë, / Një gaz të ëmbël e të shumë. O! SA BUKUR E SA MIRE! 'And every living thing feels one desire at heart. / A sweet and abundant joy. OH, HOW BEAUTIFUL AND HOW GOOD!'

When the noun modified by the given adjective is present, it is placed between the adverb **sa** and the adjective form, translating English *what (a) + adjective + noun.*, **Sa zakone të** çuditshme që kanë, -- tha vajza. '("HOW MANY") What strange customs they have," said the girl.'

2) The repetition of the modifier, with or without the conjunction **e**, is used with an intensifying function in affective fables and discussions, especially with children, but also in artistic literature:

> **Njëra prej tyre filloi të tregojë një përrallë TË GJATË TË GJATË** or **TË GJATE E TË GJATË**. 'One of them began to tell a LONG, LONG tale.'
>
> **Tani pëllumbat / Rrotull sahatit vërtiten TË BARDHË TË BARDHË** or **TE BADHË E TE BARDHË**. 'Now the pigeons / Whirl around the clock EVER SO WHITE.'

The quality may be further intensified by the prefix **stër-** 'ultra-, super-, over-' on the second adjective:

> **Na ka ardhur gojë më gojë nga moti I LASHTË E I STËRLASHTË.** 'It has come to us mouth to mouth from the OLD and VENERABLE year.'

Repetition of adverbs of degree, particularly **shumë** 'very' or **fare** 'quite' is used quite generally for intensification:

> **Lumtos, me gjithë armiqësinë e madhe që kishte ndaj Nazmiut, i erdhi SHUMË SHUMË KEQ, aq më tepër kur u bind se ai fliste me sinqeritet.** 'In spite of the great hostility he had toward Hazmi, Lumto felt ("came to him") VERY, VERY SORRY, all the more so when he became convinced that he spoke sincerely.'

3) From colloquial language, a number of idiomatic expressions have entered Standard Albanian with special intensive senses:

> **Trupin e ka MASHALLA TË GJATË.** 'He has a WONDERFULLY TALL body.'
>
> **Dhoma ku bëhej konferenca, ishte GOXHA E MADHE.** 'The room where the conference was being held was QUITE LARGE.'
>
> **Duhet të jesh BETER I FORTË.** 'You must be VERY STRONG.'
>
> **Një fshatare meshollë dhe E BUKUR PUNË E MADHE doli te dera.** 'A slender and DARNED PRETTY peasant maiden appeared at the door.'
>
> **I hollë, i gjatë, ashtu siç kish qenë dikur: TRIM MBI TRIMAT.** 'Thin, tall, just as he had been at one time: bravest of the brave ("BRAVE OVER THE BRAVES").'

A few nouns may be used figuratively as if they were unarticulated adjectives expressing a very high degree of a characteristic quality. In such instances, the nouns no longer designate things, but rather one of the features of these things which they possess to a characteristically high degree: **akull** 'ice (cold)', **mjaltë** 'honey (sweet)', **dyllë** 'wax (textured)', **borë** 'snow (white)' etc.

> **Të vegjëlit FLAKË nga fytyra e me buzën në gaz shkonin në shtëpinë tjetër.** 'The children, flush-faced ("FLAME from the face") and with a smile on their lips were going to the other house.'
>
> **Prapa faqeve të tij PRUSH fshihej një shpirt energjik.** 'Behind his rosy-red ("LIVE COAL") cheeks hid an energetic spirit.'
>
> **Drita çante si me shpatë qiellin PUS.** 'The light cut through the limpid ("POOL") heavens like a sword.'

Usually, however, these nouns are used together with an adjective that expressly designates the quality that the noun indicates figuratively. In such cases, the nouns perform the adverbial function of intensification contextually. This "adverbial" function of the noun is confirmed by the fact that such *noun + adjective* constructions can be used as adjectival phrases themselves, expressing a high degree of the quality involved: **akull e ftohtë** 'cold ice, ice cold'; **borë i bardhë, qumësht i bardhë** 'snow white, milk-white'; **mjaltë i ëmbël** 'honey-sweet, sweet honey'; **dyllë, limon i verdhë** ' lemon-yellow wax'; **flakë thanë e kuqe** 'dogberry red flame', etc.

E pse, gjer tërvit nuk e kam mbajtur me grurë QIQËR TË PASTËR, e me misër MJALTË TË ËMBËL? 'Why, until two years ago didn't I keep him in CHICKPEA-CLEAN wheat and HONEY-SWEET corn?'
THANË E KUQE në fytyrë. 'DOGBERRY RED in the face.'

Such constructions may originate in similes:

Ajo u bë E KUQE SI FLAKË. 'She turned RED AS A FLAME.'
Ajo u bë E KUQE FLAKË 'She turned FLAME-RED.'
Ajo u bë FLAKË E KUQE. 'She turned ("became") into A RED FLAME'
Ajo u bë FLAKË. 'She became a FLAME.'

Compare:

Ishte veshur me një fustan TË KUQ SI GJAKU. 'She was dressed in a blood-red ("RED LIKE BLOOD") dress.'
I dukeshin krahët e zbuluar, TË BARDHË QUMËSHT. 'Her bare arms appeared MILK-WHITE.'
Fytyra QUMËSHT E BARDHË e zotit Backa u rrudh papritur. 'The MILK-WHITE face of Mr. Backa frowned unexpectedly.'

4) To indicate a constantly increasing degree in intensity, frequent use is made of the construction *adverb* + e + më + *same*, where English might use a construction with *ever* or with two conjoined comparatives: **fort e më fort** 'ever stronger, stronger, and stronger', **keq e më keq** 'ever worse, worse, and worse', **larg e më larg** 'ever farther, farther, and farther', **lart e më lart** 'ever higher, higher, and higher', **mirë e më mirë** 'ever better, better, and better', **poshtë e më poshtë** 'ever lower, lower, and lower', **rrallë e më rallë** 'ever more rarely', **shpesh e më shpesh** 'ever more frequent', **thellë e më thellë** 'ever deeper, deeper, and deeper':

Në këtë unitet qëndron garancia për ta ngritur LART E MË LART emrin e lavdishëm të Atdheut tonë, këtu është garancia se çdo vendim që merr Partia, do të bëhet pa tjetër realitet. 'This unity provides the guarantee for raising EVER HIGHER the glorious name of our Fatherland; here is the guarantee that every decision the Party takes will undoubtedly ("without other") become reality.'
Po kjo qëllonte RRALLË E MË RRALLË. 'But this happened EVER MORE RARELY.'

6.2.2 Minimization

The degree to which the quality denoted by a modifier is present in a noun can be minimized, even to the point of negation of that quality, by a preceding adverb or adverbial locution: **pak** '(a) little', **shumë** (or **fare**) **pak** 'very little', **aspak** 'not in the least bit', **hiç** 'at all, nothing', **fare** 'not at all' (in clauses, the last three must be used with the negative proclitic **s'** or **nuk** 'not' before the verb):

Ai PAK I ZOTI më duket për këtë punë. 'He seems to me LITTLE suited ("COMPETENT") for this job.' (This has a different meaning from më duket I PAZOTI 'he seems INCOMPETENT to me'.)
Nënokja nuk i ka HIÇ TË MBARA qiqrat. 'Nënokja's chickpeas are not doing well at all ("Nënokja doesn't have chickpeas AT ALL successful").'
Ne nuk jemi ASPAK KOKËFORTË. 'We are not STUBBORN AT ALL.'
Unë pi SHUMË PAK kafe. 'I drink VERY LITTLE coffee.'
Ai ha FARE PAK mish. 'He eats VERY LITTLE meat.'
Sot qielli nuk ka re FARE. 'Today the sky has no clouds AT ALL.'

6.2.3 Approximate Degree

An approximation that tends in the direction of identity with the given feature, is expressed by the positive degree of the modifier accompanied by the approximative adverbs **pothuaj** 'almost', **gati** 'nearly', **gati-gati** 'very nearly', **disi** 'somewhat', etc. E.g.

Skënderi kënaqej tek shikonte gishtat e tyre, GATI TË PADUKSHËM. 'Skënder felt pleased as he looked at their NEARLY INVISIBLE fingers.'

Ishin flakë të mëdha dhe të çuditshme, flakë të zbeta, GATI-GATI TË BARDHA. 'They were big and strange flames, pale, PRACTICALLY WHITE flames.'

Ç'kemi andej nga qyteti -- tha ai DISI I QETËSUAR. '"What's new from the city?" he said, SOMEWHAT RELAXED.'

In the construction **pak a shumë** 'more or less' a lower degree of the given feature relative to the positive degree of the adjective is expressed. E.g. **Sa qeshë me të tjerë, isha PAK A SHUMË E QETË.** 'As long as I was with others, I was MORE OR LESS CALM.' This has become synonymous with **deri diku** 'to a certain extent, up to a point'.

When a continuous increase of the degree of the quality is expressed, the form **më** + modifier is preceded by the adverbial locutions **gjithnjë e** 'forever, always', **gjithmonë e** 'ever, every time', **për ditë e** 'daily' or by the expression **sa vete e** 'more and more':

Revizionistët po e shohin se GJITHNJË E MË E THELLË po bëhet kontradikta e tyre me komunistët e vërtetë. 'The revisionists realize that their division from ("contradiction with") true communists is becoming greater and greater ("EVER DEEPER").

Djali im po bëhet GJITHMONË E më i fortë. 'My boy is becoming EVER stronger.'

Foshnja e saj duket PËR DITË E më e bukur. 'Her baby seems DAILY more beautiful.'

Molla në pemishte SA VETE E po madhohet. 'The apple tree in the orchard is getting EVER bigger.'

CHAPTER 7

Numbers & Numerical Expressions

This chapter deals with the formation and use of cardinal numbers, ordinal numbers, and fractions in Albanian. Strictly speaking, the term **number** is applied specifically to numerical determiners which in a noun phrase precede a noun and are said to be ATTRIBUTIVE to it. Traditionally, the term has also been applied to words which express the correspondence of something to a number that indicates its order relative to other things. These are the so-called ordinal numbers. In grammatical form and meaning these belong to the category of adjectives but are included in this chapter because of their semantic relationships with other numbers.

Numbers, then, are comprised of those words which indicate numerical values within a system of whole numbers and fractions, and words which indicate the order of things and have the grammatical category of adjective: **i parë** 'first', **i dytë** 'second', **i tretë** 'third', etc. Not included as numbers are nouns which indicate imprecise quantities, like **shumicë** 'majority', **pakicë** 'minority', **gjysmë** '(about) half', etc.; nor indefinite quantifiers, such as **aq** 'so many', **ca** 'some', **disa** 'several', **mjaft** 'enough', **pak** 'a little' **shumë** 'a lot', which also appear as determiners in nominal phrases: **pak ujë** 'a little water', etc.

7.1 Cardinal Numbers

CARDINAL NUMBERS are used in counting, in mathematical calculations, and as determiners of entities of certain types. Depending on their structure, cardinal numbers may be classified as *simple, agglutinated, compound* or *locution* (See Table 7.1).

7.1.1 Structure of Cardinal Numbers

A. Simple Numbers

The basic units in the numbering system of Albanian are the SIMPLE NUMBERS: **zero** 'zero', **një** 'one', **dy** 'two', **tre** or **tri** 'three', **katër** 'four', **pesë** 'five', **gjashtë** 'six', **shtatë** 'seven', **tetë** 'eight', **nëntë** 'nine', **dhjetë** 'ten'.

As in English, the number **zero** has a limited usage as a number attributive to nouns: More often, it occurs as an invariable element embedded in sequences of numbers: telephone numbers, decimals, addresses, etc.:

Temperatura në vendet malore do të jetë ZERO gradë celsius. 'The temperature in the mountainous lands must be ZERO degrees Celsius.'
Distanca u përshkua në ZERO minuta e 9 sekonda. 'The distance was covered in ZERO minutes and 9 seconds.'

The only number which reflects gender is the number **tre**, which appears as **tri** when accompanying a feminine noun: **tre djem** 'three boys' / **tri vajza** 'three girls'.

Supi i Mirushit u vra, po ai nuk bërë zë. Ç'po ndodh? -- pyeti S.K. dy TRI HERË, po asnjeri nuk e dinte. 'Mirush's shoulder was hurt, but he kept quiet. "What's happening?" S.K. asked two or THREE TIMES, but no one knew.'
Partia jonë është parti e TRI LUFTËRAVE dhe TRI FITOREVE TË mëdha historike për ne. 'Our party is a party of THREE STRUGGLES and THREE great historical VICTORIES for us.'

Table 7.1 Cardinal Numbers

Simple		Agglutinated		Compound			
0	zero	10	dhjetë				
1	një	11	njëmbëdhjetë	100	njëqind		
2	dy	12	dymbëdhjetë	20	njëzet	200	dyqind
3	tre/tri	13	trembëdhjetë	30	tridhjetë	300	treqind
4	katër	14	katermbëdhjetë	40	dyzet	400	katërqind
5	pesë	15	pesëmbëdhjetë	50	pesëdhjetë	500	pesëqind
6	gjashtë	16	gjashtëmbëdhjetë	60	gjashtëdhjetë	600	gjashtëqind
7	shtatë	17	shtatëmbëdhjetë	70	shtatëdhjetë	700	shtatëqind
8	tetë	18	tetëmbëdhjetë	80	tetëdhjetë	800	tetëqind
9	nëntë	19	nëntëmbëdhjetë	90	nëntëdhjetë	900	nëntëqind

Locutions			
1000	një mijë	1001	një mijë një
3000	tre mijë	3200	tre mijë e dyqind
1,000,000	(1.000.000) një milion	1,000,001	(1.000.001) një milion e një
3,000,000	(3.000.000) tri milion	10,000,000	(10.000.000) dhjetë milion
21	njëzet e një	101	njëqind e një
22	njëzet e dy	220	dyqind e njëzet
142	njëqind e dyzet e dy	999	nëntëqind e nëntëdhjet e nëntë
238	dyqind e tridhjetë e tetë	355	treqind e pesëdhjetë e pesë
.04	(,04) presje zero katër	.027	(,027) presje zero njëzet e shtatë
23,516,798	(23.516.798) njëzet e tri milion e pesëqind e gjashtëmbëdhjetë mijë e shtatë qind e nëntëdhjetë e tetë		

The distinction of gender for even this number is inconsistently maintained, under the influence of the rest of the system which does not recognize gender. There is thus a tendency to generalize the form to **tre** for all genders, though this is contrary to the recommended standard:

> **TRE JAVË para se të shkonte në aksion, Flora u sëmur nga një grip i lehtë.** 'THREE WEEKS before going to the construction project, Flora became ill with a mild case of flu.'

All other numbers are used in the same form regardless of whether they occur with a masculine noun or a feminine or neuter one:

> **Nga gëzimi s'bëj dot NJË PUNË.** 'Overwhelmed by joy I can't do ONE thing.'
>
> **Po njeriu njihet me NJË TË PARË....** 'But a man is known at a glance ("with ONE LOOK").'
>
> **Nga Tirana vjen NJË MINISTËR ose zëvendësministër.** 'From Tirana ONE minister or deputy minister is coming.'
>
> **Porsa erdhën veglat, ai dhe KATËR a PESË MONTATORË të tjerë filluan të punonin me shpejtësi.** 'As soon as the tools arrived, he and FOUR or FIVE ASSEMBLY MEN began to work with rapidity.'
>
> **KATËR KRISMA armësh u dëgjuan njëra pas tjetrës.** 'FOUR gunSHOTS were heard one after the other.'

7.1.1 A. Simple Numbers   **249**

B. Agglutinated Numbers

The AGGLUTINATED NUMBERS 11-19 are formed by adding to the numbers for one through nine, respectively, the morpheme sequence **mbë + dhjetë** (originally, 'onto ten') without an intervening space. **njëmbëdhjetë** '11', **dymbëdhjetë** '12', **trembëdhjetë** '13', **katërmbëdhjetë** '14', **pesëmbëdhjetë** '15', **gjashtëmbëdhjetë** '16', **shtatëmbëdhjetë** '17', **tetëmbëdhjetë** '18', **nëntëmbëdhjetë** '19'.

C. Compound Numbers

Numbers which are multiples of simple numbers and 0 and 100 are COMPOUND: **tridhjetë** '30', **pesëdhjetë** '50', **gjashtëdhjetë** '60', **shtatëdhjetë** '70', **tetëdhjetë** '80', **nëntëdhjetë** '90', **njëqind** '100', **dyqind** '200', etc.

The numbers **njëzet** 'twenty' and **dyzet** 'forty' are formed by compounding **një** and **dy** with the old number **zet** 'score (20)', which is no longer a separate word in the language.

D. Numerical Locutions

As is apparent, NUMERICAL LOCUTIONS differ from agglutinated numbers both in the arrangement of the constituent parts and in the manner of joining them. The numbers 21-29, 31-39, etc., are formed by joining the numbers **njëzet** '20', **tridhjetë** '30', etc., to the numbers 1-9, with the conjunction **e** 'and'. Numerical locutions joined together by that same conjunction are used for the numbers 21-29, 31-39, 41-49, etc., 101-199, 201-299, 1001-1999, etc. When written out, locutions have spaces between their elements: **tridhjetë e një** '31', **dyzet e dy** '42', **njëqind e një** '101, **dyqind e nëntëdhjetë e nëntë** '299', **dy mijë** '2000', etc.

In their singular forms the words **qind** 'hundred', **mijë** 'thousand', **milion** 'million', **miliard** 'billion', **bilion** 'billion', **trilion** 'trillion', etc., function as parts of numbers, except in numerical locutions when preceded by another number: **njëqind e tre mijë** '103,000', **dhjetë milion** 'ten million', **dy miliard** 'two billion', etc.:

> **Vetëm nën këmbët e Tafilit, nja NJËQIND A DYQIND çape nën të, kalonte një përrua.** 'Right under the feet of Tafil, some ONE HUNDRED OR TWO HUNDRED steps below him flowed a brook.'

However, when they indicate an imprecise quantity, they may appear in a plural form, **qind** and **mijë** taking the suffix **-ra**, and the others **-a**. Like the singular forms, these plural forms, when used attributively to a noun, are not inflected for gender, case, or definiteness. Although they indicate inexact quantities, their inexactness has precise limits. Thus, the quantity indicated by **qindra** 'hundreds' approximately extends from 200-1,000; **mijëra** 'thousands' from 2,000-1,000,000; **millions'** from 2,000,000-1,000,000,000, etc.:

> **Tek ju lavdinë e QINDRA e QINDRA vjetëve dhe miqësinë e madhe përshëndesin.** 'In you they salute the glory of hundreds and hundreds of years and our great friendship.'
> **Ëndrat shkojnë e vijnë/Miliona e miliarda janë ato.** 'Dreams come and go/Millions and billions [they are].'

The plural of **dhjetë**, **dhjetëra** 'tens' can also serve this function, covering the range from 20-100:

> **Jo me tetë, po me dhjetëra me qindra krahë.** 'Not with eight, but with tens and hundreds of arms.'
> **Para disa dhjetëra vjetësh këtu shtrihej pylli i ahut.** 'A few decades ("tens of years") ago the beech forest extended out here.'

NOTE

As the second element of numerical locutions after a number greater than one, the nouns **milion, miliard, bilion,** and **trilion** may have a plural form with or without the suffix **-ë**, however, the tendency today is to use them like all the other numbers in an invariable form without **-ë**.

7.1.2 Uses of Cardinal Numbers

A cardinal numbers most commonly occurs with an attributive function, serving to determine the quantity of those countable entities designated by an accompanying noun. **një dritare në ballë** 'one window in front', **një trapezë dhe pesë karrige** 'one table and five chairs', **dy rafte për bibliotekën** 'two shelves for the library', **tri lule në tryezë** 'three flowers on the table', etc. With nouns whose form is the same for singular and plural, as it is for many nouns in the indefinite nominative and accusative cases, the presence of the number may or may not be the only overt mark of plurality in the nominal phrase:

> **KËTO DY IDEOLOGJI nuk mund të bashkekzistojnë në ndërgjegjen e njeriut.**
> 'THESE TWO IDEOLOGIES cannot coexist in the conscience of man.'
> **GJASHTËMBËDHJETË DITË kanë ato lule aty.** 'Those flowers have been there SIXTEEN DAYS.'

When used as determiners before nouns, numbers are not marked for the grammatical categoy of case: In all cases they accompany the noun without undergoing any changes in form:

> **Shokët, që kishin të bënin me Qemalin, nuk ishin më ata të NJË a DY vjetve më parë.** 'The comrades who went around with Qemal were no longer those of ONE or TWO years before.'
> **Shtëpia e Qemalit, ndonëse ishte me DY kate, nuk i nxinte të tërë brenda.** 'Although the house of Qemal had TWO stories, it could not accomodate all of them.'
> **Me një poezi DY strofash këta janë në gjendje të ngrenë në këmbë NJË mëhallë.** 'With a poem of TWO stanzas, they are able to rouse a hamlet.'

But when a number is substantivized, i.e., becomes a noun itself, it may designate or label concrete or abstract entities and take the normal case and definite endings normal for a singular noun. For example a number may be used as the label for a particular year:

> **Anëtar partie i DYZETEDYSHIT je?** 'Are you a member of the party of '42 ("of the FORTY-TWO")?'

The number here appears as the nucleus of a nominal phrase in the genitive case, just like any other noun. In such a use it no longer functions as a number, but rather as a noun which designates a number.

The numbers **një, dy,** and **tre** are substantivized by means of the suffix **-sh: njësh-i** 'the one, the ace', **dysh-i** 'the two, the deuce', **tresh-i** 'the three, the trey':

> **Fiset e sotme të xhunglës afrikane....kanë vetëm tre emra numrash që u korrespondojnë "NJËSHIT," "DYSHIT," dhe shumë".'** 'The contemporary tribes of the African jungle...have only three names of numbers, corresponding to "ONE", "TWO", and "many".'

The substantivized numbers **një, dy, tre,** substantivized locutions and all forms that have these numbers as their last element, are declined as masculine singular nouns: **njësh-i** 'the one', **dysh-i** 'the two', **tresh-i** 'the three', **dyzetetresh-i** 'the foty-third', etc.:

> **Kam qenë disa herë në vitet tridhjetetetë, tridhjetenëntë dhe herën e fundit në mesin e DYZETEDYSHIT.** 'I have been there several times in '38, '39 ("the years thirty-eight, thirty-nine") and the last time in the middle of '42 ("THE FORTY-TWO").'

All other substantivized numbers are declined as feminine singular nouns:

Po megjithëkëtë, edhe pas 1912-ËS, [NJË MIJË E NËNTË QIND E DYMBËDHJETËS] i sunduar nga regjimet antipopullore të bejlerëve dhe borgjezisë reaksionare, populli ynë nuk gëzoi lirinë e vërtetë. 'But despite this, even after 1912 ["THE ONE THOUSAND AND NINE HUNDRED AND TWELVE"], being ruled by the antipopular regimes of the beys and the reactionary bourgeoisie, our people did not enjoy true freedom.'

I shohim fushat dhe qytetet e reja me syrin aq të ri dhe me dëshirën po aq të zjarrtë të 1944-ËS [NJE MIJË E NËNTË QIND E DYZETEKATRËS]. 'We see the plains and the new cities with the same new eyes and the same ardent desire as those of 1944 ["THE ONE THOUSAND AND NINE HUNDRED AND FORTY FOUR"].'

As these last two examples illustrate, four digit numbers in Albanian are not divided into two groups of two, for purposes of pronouncing them--in English, 1912 is pronounced "nineteen twelve"--but are rather pronounced as one large number. In addition, Albanian speakers do not omit the words **qind** or **mijë** in pronouncing large numbers in the way that English speakers omit the corresponding **hundred** and **thousand**, so 36527 in Albanian would either be pronounced **tridhjetë e gjashtë mijë, e pesëqind e njëzet e shtatë** or as a sequence of numbers **tre, gjashtë, pesë, dy, shtatë,** but not grouped as an English speaker might group them into "thirty-six, five twenty-seven".

Other nouns formed by substantivization of numbers develop specialized meanings and uses: for example, **pesë-A** '[THE] five', **dhjetë-A** '[THE] ten', **tresh-I** '[THE] three', **zero-JA** '[THE] zero', etc., are used to indicate grades given in school, playing cards, etc.

Edhe NËNTA edhe DHJETA nota të mira janë. 'Both (the) nine and (the) TEN are good grades.'

Such nouns derived from numbers are used for other purposes as well, like **qindshe-JA** 'THE hundred' which can signify a bill of 100 leks (the Albanian monetary unit), a unit of 100 soldiers, a 100 gram measuring utensil, etc. In most of these nouns the numerical notion of "quantity" is included, but is limited and overshadowed by other meanings. Such nouns no longer indicate the general quantity but rather a particular thing labeled by that number.

A. Numbers in Mathematical Expressions

As in English, numbers used in mathematical calculations express abstractions. In the most common, everyday arithmetical operations--addition, subtraction, and multiplication--the numbers appear in an invariable citation form. In these operations, the verbs **bëjnë** 'they make' (for addition), or **mbeten** 'they leave' (for subtraction) are used to express the result of the operation. The conjunction **dhe** 'and' or the preposition **me** 'with' is used to express 'plus' in addition, the preposition **pa** 'without' to express 'minus' in subtraction, the preposition **nga** 'from' to express 'subtracted from', and the noun **herë** 'time (as in one time, two times, etc.)' to express 'times' in multiplication:

1) Addition:

$1 + 1 = 2$	**Një dhe një bëjnë dy.**
	Njëja me njënë bëjnë dy. (uncommon)
$2 + 3 = 5$	**Dy dhe tre bëjnë pesë.**
	Dyja me trenë bëjnë pesë. (uncommon)

2) Subtraction:

$10 - 1 = 9$	**Dhjetë pa një mbeten nëntë.**
	Një nga dhjetë mbeten nëntë. (alternatively)
$10 - 6 = 4$	**Gjashtë nga dhjetë mbeten katër.**

3) Multiplication:

$1 \times 10 = 10$	**Një herë dhjetë (bëjnë) dhjetë.**
$3 \times 10 = 30$	**Tri herë dhjetë (bëjnë) tridhjetë.**

On the other hand, when more learned expressions are used to express ordinary calculations or when calculations are employed that require formal education, the numbers are used in their substantivized definite forms, with the appropriate case ending. This happens for the mathematical operations of division, subtraction, multiplication, square root, logarithm, etc.):

GJASHTA te (or **ne**) **TRIDHJETA hyn 5 herë.** 'Thirty divided by six is five ("THE SIX in the THIRTY enters five times").'

Po të zbresim nga NJËZETA DHJETË, mbeten DHJETË. 'If we subtract ("lower") TEN from [THE] TWENTY, we have TEN.'

SHTATA e shumëzuar me TETË jep PESËDHJETË e GJASHTË. '[THE] SEVEN multiplied by EIGHT gives FIFTY-SIX.'

Rrënja katrore e KATRËS është e barabartë me DY. 'The square root of [THE] FOUR is equal to TWO.'

Dhjeta në dhjetën hyn një herë. Ten divided by ten equals one ("the ten in the ten enters one time").'

B. Numbers as Pronominals

Numbers are often used in a pronominal sense, taking the place of a noun or nouns contextually "known" to the speaker and hearer. When used pronominally, the numbers for 'two' and above have much the same case forms as plural nouns:

	Masc	Fem
Nom-Acc	dy	dyja
Dat-Abl	dyve	dyjave
Gen	i dyve	i dyjave

These substantivized numbers are used when the speaker does not want to repeat a given noun in the same phrase or when it is not necessary to mention the noun because it is obvious from the context:

Ç'të bënte ai vetë, NJË kundër TREVE! 'What could he do alone, ONE against THREE!'

Jo, jo: NJË kundër KATËRVE me gjithë Skënderin. 'No, no: ONE against FOUR including Skender.'

C. Numbers in Expressions of Time

Cardinal numbers are used in various expressions of time.

C.1 Dates

Numbers may be used to fully abbreviate a complete date. The first part (written in Arabic numerals) indicates the day of the month, the second part (written in Arabic or Roman numerals) indicates the month, and the last part (written in Arabic numbers) indicates the year. The parts are separated by a period. Thus August 20, 1973 may be abbreviated as **20.VII.1973** or as **20.7.1973**.

When the month is written out in full, it is not capitalized and no punctuation mark is used between the parts. August 20, 1973 is thus written: **20 gusht 1973**.

In identifying the place as well as the date, as in dating a letter to someone, the name of the place comes first, then a comma, then the preposition **më** followed by the date:

Tiranë, më 20.VII.1973
Shkodër, më 20 gusht 1973

The preposition **më** 'on (with dates)' is always written out before a date used in a sentence as an adverbial of time:

Kongresi u hap të hënën, MË 20.XI.1972. 'The congress opened (on) [the] Monday, ON 11/20/72.'

Mbledhja bëhet të shtunën, MË 1 shtator 1976. 'The meeting is held (on) [the] Saturday, [ON] September 1, 1976.'

Note that neither the names of the days of the week nor of the months of the year are capitalized in writing. Notice also that while the name of the day of the week is cited in its (feminine singular) nominative form and the name of the month is cited in its (masculine singular) nominative form it is used in the accusative form to mean 'on' that day and 'in' that month. The first day of the week is Monday in Albanian:

e hë në 'Monday'	**të hënën** 'on Monday'
e martë 'Tuesday'	**të martën** 'on Tuesday'
e mërkurë 'Wednesday'	**të mërkurën** 'on Wednesday'
e enjtë 'Thursday'	**të enjten** 'on Thursday'
e premte 'Friday'	**të premten** 'on Friday'
e shtunë 'Saturday'	**të shtunën** 'on Saturday'
e diel 'Sunday'	**të dielën** 'on Sunday'
janar(in) '(in) January'	**korrik(un)** '(in) July'
shkurt(in) '(in) February'	**gusht(in)** '(in) August'
mars(in) '(in) March'	**shtator(in)** '(in) September'
prill(in) '(in) April'	**fetor(in)** '(in) October'
maj(in) '(in) May'	**nëntor(in)** '(in) November'
qershor(in) '(in) June'	**dhjetor(in)** '(in) December'

C.2 Time of Day

Ordinary time is computed in terms of hours and minutes, as in English. The word **orë** means both 'hour' and 'clock, watch'. The word **minutë** 'minute' is usually present if the minutes are expressed before the hour, but absent if they are expressed after the hour. The word **çerek** 'quarter' is used as in English to express fifteen-minute periods before (**pa** 'without') and after (**e** 'and') the hour, while **gysmë** 'half' indicates thirty minutes after the hour only. In writing, the time of day is computed on a 24 hour basis so that 3:00 in the afternoon is indicated as 15.00 (note the period rather than the colon used in English) while 3:30 in the morning is 3.30. Today 'at' some time, the preposition **më** or **në** followed by the accusative singular definite case form of **orë**, while to give the hour, the nominative singular definite form is used:

Ora është tre. 'The time ("hour") is three (o'clock).'
Ishte ora gjashtë. 'It was six o'clock.'
Sa është ora? 'What time is it ("how much is the hour")?'
Ora është tre e pesë. 'The time is 3:05.'
Eshtë tre e njëzet e pesë. 'It's 3:25.'
Eshtë (ora) tre e një çerek. 'It's 3:15.', 'It's a quarter after (or past) three.'
Më orën katër. 'At four o'clock.'
Katër pa një çerek. 'A quarter to (of, till) four, 3:45.'
Në orën dymbëdhjetë e gjysmë. 'At 12:30.'

When used to give the time of day a numerical locution is placed after the noun **orë** 'hour':

Zakonisht qyteti bombardohej në orën NËNTË E GJYSMË të mëngjesit. 'Usually, the city was bombed at HALF PAST NINE in the morning.'

Ky ishte treni i mallrave i orës DY E NJË ÇEREK. 'This was the 2:15 freight train.'

D. Percentages and Ratios

One or more things or beings of a homogeneous group may be related to the rest in the form of a percentage: **Plani i prodhimit industrial u shtua në masën NËNTË PËR QIND.** 'The plan for industrial production was increased to the extent of NINE PERCENT.' Dimensions, ratios, or percentages are also given in decimals which serve like fractions to indicate a part of a whole, **Në rast se shkalla është 1:1000 [një për një mijë], atëherë përpikmëria maksimale e saj është 0,2 m [zero, presje, dy metra].** 'If the scale is 1:1,000 ("one for one thousand") then its maximal accuracy is 0.2 meters ["one, comma, two meters"].'

E. Numbers as Appositives

As in English, cardinal numbers can also be used as identifying appositives to nouns, for example in the numbering of hotel rooms, points on a map, periods of time, etc. The number so used takes no case ending: **gjatë periudhës 1954-1959** 'during the period 1954-1959.'

> **Djathtas në figurën 7 [shtatë] është paraqitur ndryshimi i formës për të njejtën figurë.** 'To the right, in figure 7 [seven] is presented a variation of the form of the same figure.'

F. Numbers in Approximations

Approximate quantities can be indicated in various ways:

a) By giving two cardinal numbers, separated in writing by a hyphen or in speech by **a** 'or', that suggest a particular span:

> **Kur mblidhen tre-katër burra bashkë, nisin e këndojnë.** 'Whenever three (or) four men get together, they start to sing.'
> **Edhe në i prefshin udhën njëzet a tridhjetë vetë.** 'Even if twenty or thirty people cut off his path.'
> With numbers in the hundreds, thousands, millions, etc., the elements **hundred, thousand,** etc., are mentioned only with the second number: **dy-treqind dhen** '200-300 ("two-three hundred") sheep;'

b) By the use of approximative adverbs: **afro** 'almost', **pothuaj** 'almost', **gati** 'nearly', **nja** 'about', **rreth** 'around', **afërsisht** 'approximately':

> **Vjersha ime kishte GATI tridhjetë strofa.** 'My poem had NEARLY 30 stanzas.'
> **Armiqtë patën, veç të plagosurve, AFRO njëmijë të vrarë.** 'The enemy had, besides those wounded, ALMOST a thousand killed.'

c) By the use of plural forms of cardinal numbers for major classes, like **dhjetra** 'tens', **qindra** 'hundreds', etc., to express large quantities:

> **Nga QINDRA xhevahirë njëzë i kishin dhënë.** 'From HUNDREDS of jewels they had given her only one.'

G. Comparative Magnitudes

In order to indicate a quantity greater than that of a given number, it may be preceded by a qualifying word or phrase like **më se** 'more than', **më shumë se** 'more than', **më tepër se** 'more than', **mbi** 'over', or followed by **e ca** (or colloquially **e kusur**) meaning 'over, and then some':

> **Ata kanë bërë MË TEPËR SE dy orë rrugë për të vajtur deri atje.** 'They have been on the road MORE THAN two hours to get there.'
> **Që nga dita e parë e njohjes kanë kaluar MË SE tre vjet.** 'Since our first day of aquaintance MORE THAN three years have passed.'
> **Që prej asaj nate kanë kaluar MË SHUMË SE katër vjet.** 'Since that night MORE THAN four years have passed.'

Ka njëzet E CA vjet që punojmë në kooperativë dhe mendjet tona kanë ndryshuar. 'We've been working at the cooperative for over twenty years ("AND SOME") and our opinions have changed.'

In an analogous way, to indicate an amount less than the given quantity, the expression **më pak se** is used:

MË PAK SE 30 për qind të veprimeve kryesore të punës në minierë e industri. 'LESS THAN 30 percent of the principal work activities in mining and industry.'

H. Numerical Hyperbole

As in English, numbers can be used to indicate an inexact amount of hyperbolic forms, where one deliberately exaggerates by making something either larger or smaller:

Edhe pesëdhjetë vjet ta kërkoje, s'do ta gjejë. 'Even if you searched for fifty years, you wouldn't find it.'
Një minutë, shoku Shkëlqim. 'Just a minute, comrade Shkëlqim.'

Note that in Albanian **një sekondë** is not used the way *a second* is in English in such a locution: instead, **një çast** or **një moment** are used to express the same idea.)

I. Collective Numbers

When preceded by the preposed article **të**, translatable as 'the' or 'all', the numbers for 'two' or more indicate an exhaustive quantity: the number here gives the quantity of things or of beings as a definite totality, as a known and exhaustive whole. In this usage, it will be called a COLLECTIVE number.

Most collective numbers do not show grammatical agreement with the noun they accompany, neither in gender, case nor number:

TË PESË komitët zunë pusi jo si tjetër herë, në Konopishtat,por në Qarr. 'THE FIVE outlaws set ambush not like before, in Konopishtë, but in Qarr.'
Baltë e ujë nga TË KATËR anët. 'Mud and water all over ("from the FOUR sides.")
TË KATËR vajzat e para i martoi Gjon Kastrioti me kryezotër të dëgjuar. 'Gjon Kastrioti married THE first FOUR daughters to renowned chieftains.'
Ai i kish dëgjuar daullen dhe zhurmat e dasmës TË DY herët që kaloi atë natë me trenin e tij të mallrave. 'He had heard the drum and sounds of the wedding both ("THE TWO") times he had passed by that night with his freight train.'

When used as a collective the number **tre** 'three', however, does exhibit agreement for gender:

TË TRI mëmat shkonin mirë. 'THE THREE mothers got along well.'
U qepi nga një fustan TË TRIA çupave. 'She sewed a dress for each of the THREE daughters.'

Used in this way, this number often takes a feminine plural ending **-a**:

Kruja ishte e siguruar prej shkëmbit nga TË TRIA anët. 'Krujë was secured by the rock on ALL THREE sides.'
TË TRIA këto njësi të reja energjitike do të kenë një fuqi prej rreth 100 mijë kw. 'ALL THREE of these new energy units will have a power of about 100 thousand kw.'

When used as a collective the number **dy** 'two' sometimes remains unchanged, while at other times it takes a gender indicator:

Fatmiri i mbulonte sytë me TË DY duart. 'Fatmir covered his eyes with BOTH hands.'
Tani që ishin ndarë TË DYJA shoqet sikur duheshin më shumë 'Now that they were separated, THE TWO women seemed to be much closer.'

TË DYJA brigadat kanë nga pesë batalione. 'BOTH brigades have five battalions apiece.'

Large collective numbers that have **dy** and **tre** as their last constituent element, however, never take the ending **-a** before nouns used in the feminine gender:

Të tridhjetetri ditët kaluan. 'The thirty three days passed.'

To reinforce still more the sense of inclusion, or the definite quantity considered as an exhaustive whole, collective numbers are accompanied by the qualifying particle **që** 'that' (see Section 11.3.1 B), in addition to the preposed article **të**. The idea of precision with regard to the quantity that is indicated by a given number, can be reinforced also by defining particles like **plot** 'full' and **vetëm** 'only, just' (see Sections 11.3.1 B and C).

When used pronominally, numbers take the grammatical category of case; the gender of collective numbers so used depends on the gender of the referent:

Në fund të bisedimeve TË TREVE u qe dukur që kishin bërë një studim të mirë të planit. 'At the end of the talks it seemed to ALL THREE [men] that they had studied the plan well.'

Atëherë në Myzeqe bëhet NJË nga TË DYJA. 'Then ONE of TWO [things] will be done in Myzeqe.'

Po bëjmë një punë TË DY, rrëfejmë nga një përrallë, po të më gënjesh, do t'i jap TË NËNTA, po të të gënjej, do t'i marr TË TRIA. 'Let's both do ("THE TWO [people] we are doing") the same ("one") thing: we each tell a story; if you fool me, I'll give you ALL ("THE") NINE [coins]; if I fool you, I'll take ALL THREE.'

Atëhere po e dredh dhe unë NJË -- i tha inspektori. Fshatari i zgjati qesen e duhanit. '"Then I'll light ONE up, too," the inspector said to him. The peasant handed him the tobacco pouch.'

DY nga punëtorët e komunales pinin cigare, i treti thithte çibukun. 'TWO of the municipal workers smoked cigarettes, the third puffed on the pipe.'

The collective numbers for 'two' and above, when used pronominally, have the same case forms as plural nouns, except that they are declined with the article **të**:

	Masc	Fem
Nom-Acc	**të dy**	**të dyja**
Dat-Abl	**të dyve**	**të dyjave**
Gen	**i të dyve**	**i të dyjave**

Note that the collective number **të dyja** 'the two (fem.)', but not **të tria**, has -j- inserted after the stem in the feminine gender:

Që TË TRIA u shtypën njera pas tjetrës. 'ALL THREE were trampled, one after the other.'

Pajën e TË TRIAVE do ta trashëgosh ti. 'You shall inherit the dowery of ALL THREE.'

Më tutje gjen tri gra, nga TË TRIA njera tha. 'Further on he finds three women, one of THE THREE said.'

7.2 Ordinal Numbers

Ordinal numbers are simply adjectives formed from numbers and used to indicate the relative position of the members of a group or series. In general, the ordinal numbers in Albanian are formed by attaching a preposed adjectival article to the corresponding cardinal number and, with the exceptions noted below, adding the derivational suffix **-të** (see also Section 4.7.1 B).

The ordinal numbers in Albanian from 1st to 10th are: **i parë** 'first', **i dytë** 'second', **i tretë** 'third', **i katërt** 'fourth', **i pestë** 'fifth', **i gjashtë** 'sixth', **i shtatë** 'seventh', **i tetë** 'eighth', **i nëntë** 'ninth', **i dhjetë** 'tenth'. All but **i parë,** which has been formed by suppletion, have a cardinal number as their root. Note that cardinal numbers that already end in -të (**i gjashtë** through **i dhjetë**) do not add an additional -të suffix. In accordance with the general rule that prevents two successive occurrences of **ë** in a word after the stressed syllable (see rule 2) of Section 1.2.4 B), **i katërt** has no final **ë** and **i pestë** has only the final **ë**. Unlike its corresponding cardinal number, **i tretë** does not have a form derived from **tri**.

The ordinal numbers from 11th to 19th are: **i njëmbëdhjetë** 'eleventh', **i dymbëdhjetë** 'twelfth', **i trembëdhjetë** 'thirteenth', **i katërmbëdhjetë** 'fourteenth', **i pesëmbëdhjetë** 'fifteenth', **i gjashtëmbëdhjetë** 'sixteenth', **i shtatëmbëdhjetë** 'nineteenth'. As is evident, all these are regularly formed merely by placing a preposed adjectival article before the corresponding integer.

The ordinal numbers, 30th, 50th, 60th, 70th, 80th, and 90th are likewise formed through the simple addition of the preposed article: **i tridhjetë** 'thirtieth', **i pesëdhjetë** 'fiftieth', etc. The ordinals **i njëzetë** '20th' and **i dyzetë** '40th' prepose the article and add -**ë** (historically -të, with subsequent simplification of the geminate **tt** cluster thus formed). The ordinals 100th, 200th,..., 900th, however, require both the article and the suffix -**të**: **i njëqindtë** 'hundredth', **i dyqindtë** 'two hundredth', etc., as do 1,000th, 2,000th, etc.; 1,000,000th, 1,000,000,000th, etc.: **i njëmijtë** 'thousandth' (note that stem final -**ë** of **mijë** drops), **i njëmiliontë** 'millionth', etc.

The ordinal numbers 21th, 31, ... 91st, 101st, etc., whose corresponding cardinal has the final digit **një** are formed by adding the suffix -**të** to **një** 'one' instead of using the suppletive form -**parë**: **i njëzetenjëtë** 'twenty-first', **i tridhjetenjëtë** 'thirty-first', **i njëqindenjëtë** 'hundred and first' (note here and below that ordinal numbers are written as a single word, regardless of their length, unlike their corresponding cardinals. Compare: **dyqind e nëntëdhjetë e një** 'two hundred ninety-one' vs. **i dyqindenëntëdhjete një të** 'two hundred and ninety first'. Note also that when the number is collapsed orthographically in this manner, every stem final -**ë** is deleted before the conjunction **e**).

The numbers 22nd, 23rd,...29th; 32nd, 33rd,...39th, etc., are formed by taking the ordinal form of the last digit for the corresponding integer, and, as noted above, writing the whole thing as one word, preceded by a preposed article: **i njëzetedytë** 'twenty-second', **i tridhjetenëntë** 'thirty-ninth', **i gjashtëqindedyzetekatërt** 'six hundred and forty-fourth', **i pesëmijeshtateqindetetëdhjetetretë** 'five thousand seven hundred and eighty-third'.

As noted above, ordinal numbers are adjectives grammatically, and the preposed article varies according to gender, number, and case just as it does for other adjectives. Like other adjectives, they may be substantivized: e.g.,: **i pari** 'the first', **i dhjeti** 'the tenth' (see Section 4.4).

7.3 Fractions

Fractions occupy a special place among numbers. Fractions in Albanian are locutions composed of a cardinal number as first element and a substantivized ordinal number in a feminine form as second element. Fractions that have as their first element the number **one**, have their second element in the singular: **një e dyta** 'one half', **një e treta** 'one third', **një e katërta** 'one fourth', etc. Fractions that have as their first element the number **dy** 'two' or a higher number have their second element in the plural: **dy të tretat** 'two thirds', **katër të pestat** 'four fifths', **gjashtë të nëntat** 'six ninths', etc.

Fractions with **një** 'one' as their first constituent element are used and declined only in the singular number:

	'one fourth (1/4)'	'one tenth (1/10)'
Nom	një e katërta	një e dhjeta
Acc	një të katërtën	një të dhjetën
Dat Abl	një të katërtës	një të dhjetës
Gen	i një të katërtës	i një të dhjetës

Those fractions that have as their first element the number *two* or a number above *two*, are used and declined only in the plural number;

	'two fourths (2/4)'	'three eighths (3/8)'
Nom-Acc	dy të katërtat	tri të tetat
Dat-Abl	dy të katërtave	tri të tetave
Gen	i dy të katërtave	i tri të tetave

NOTES

1. In mathematical contexts, indefinite forms of such fractions may occur, but only in Nom-Acc form (with no final **-t**).

2. As can be seen in the table above, the second parts of fractions are declined like substantivized adjectives of the feminine gender, except for the one difference that for fractions with **një** as first element, the article in the Dat—Abl and Gen cases has the form **të** rather than the **së** of non—substantivized adjectives: **i një të tretës** 'of one-third'.

The second element (the denominator) of fractions used in abstract mathematical expressions are sometimes in the definite and sometimes in the indefinite form: **NJË TË DYTË** 'ONE HALF', **NJË TËKATËRT** 'ONE FOURTH', **TRI TË TETA** 'THREE EIGHTHS', **DY TË KATËRTA** 'TWO FOURTHS', **NJË TË TRETË** 'ONE THIRD', **SHTATË TË TETA** 'SEVEN EIGHTHS', **TRI TË KATËRTA** 'THREE FOURTHS', **PESË TË TETA** 'FIVE EIGHTHS'.

Tri të dyta mbi një të katertën janë baras me tri të katërta mbi një të tetën. 'Three halves over one fourth equal three fourths over one eighth.'
Shtatë të dymbëdhjeta plus një e treta plus një e katërta. '7/12 + 1/3 + 1/4.'

In mathematical operations, even when the first element of a fraction is a number greater than two, a fraction is syntatically treated as a noun in the singular rather than plural number, since it is thought of as a single number, in apposition with **thyesë** 'fraction':

Thyesa 5/4 [pesë të katërta] tregon se çdo njësi është ndarë në 4 [katër] pjesë të barbarta dhe prej këtyre janë marrë 5 [pesë] pjesë. 'The fraction 5/4 indicates that every unit is divided into 4 equal parts, and that 5 parts have been taken from these.'

Decimal numbers are written with a comma, rather than a decimal point. They are read sometimes as compound numbers, expressed as integers, and sometimes as fractions (in which the second element is a substantivized feminine adjective): **të dhjeta** 'tenths', **të qindta** 'hundredths' or **të mijëta** 'thousandths'. Thus 0,5 can be read as **zero pesë**, 'zero five', **zero presje pesë** 'zero comma [point] five', or **pesë të dhjeta** 'five tenths'. Note that Albanian follows the international tradition of indicating the decimal point by a comma, rather than by the period that Americans use. The period is then available to be used in large numbers in places where Americans place commas: 15.037,30 = 15,037.20.

A noun indicating the unit of measurement appears in the accusative indefinite case after a fraction.

Një nxënës, duke u pregatitur në shtëpi për mësimet e ditës së nesërme, harxhoi 3/4 [TRI TË KATËRTA] ORË për mësimin e matematikës dhe 1/2 [NJË GJYSMË] ORË për mësimin e historisë. 'Preparing himself at home for the lessons of the following day, a pupil spent THREE FOURTHS (of an) HOUR on the mathematics lesson and A HALF HOUR on the history lesson.'
1/4 [NJË E KATERTA] PJESË e këtij shiriti është mbuluar me viza të pjerrëta. 'A FOURTH ("1/4 PIECE") of this ribbon is covered with sloping lines.'

Other nouns or pronouns must be in the genitive case following a fraction:

Investimet për zhvillimin e dy degëve kryesore të ekonomisë sonë -- të industrisë dhe të bujqësisë -- do të zenë më shumë se 2/3 [DY TË TRETAT] E INVESTIMEVE të përgjithshme. 'Investments for the development of the two main branches of our economy--industry and agriculture--will account for more than TWO THIRDS OF ALL INVESTMENTS.'

TRI TË KATËRTAT e këtyre ishin nga principata atërore e Skënderbeut. 'THREE FOURTHS of these were from the paternal principality of Skënderbeut.'

Ishin vënë njëra mbi jetrën voza të mëdha djathi, që zinin pothuaj TRI TË KATËRTAT e gjithë vendit. 'Placed on top of one another were great kegs of cheese, that occupied nearly THREE FOURTHS of the entire place.'

The fractions **një e dyta** or **një e dytë** 'one-half (1/2)' and **një e katërta** or **një e katërt** 'one-fourth (1/4)' are frequently replaced by the **(një) gjysmë** 'half' and **(një) çerek** 'quarter'. When they are used as nouns--and declinable as such--these two words may be followed by another noun in the genitive case: **GJYSMA e shekullit** '[THE] half of the century', **ÇEREKU i punës** 'One ["THE"] QUARTER of the work.' But when they are used as determiners, and thus not declinable, the following noun--unlike after whole numbers--is always in the ablative indefinite case, except for nouns designating measuring units: **gr(am)**, **k(ilo)g(ram)**, **m(etër)**, **k(ilo)m(etër)**, **h(ekt)a(r)**, etc., which may be in the accusative indefinite case instead:

Padashur i kujtohej dasma e tij e largët, gati GJYSMË SHEKULLI më parë. 'Involuntarily, he recalled his distant wedding, nearly HALF [OF](A) CENTURY earlier.'

Pas NJË ÇEREK ORE maqinat e tyre ecnin me shpejtësi drejt Tiranës. 'After a QUARTER OF AN HOUR, their vehicles drove rapidly toward Tiranë.'

Beleva GJYSMË KILE djathë. 'I bought HALF [OF](A) KILOGRAM of cheese.'

When **gjysmë** and **çerek** are used in a numerical locution composed of a whole number plus a fraction, the fraction part of the locution appears after the noun being quantified:

Që nga stacioni i ri gjer këtu rruga më këmbë nuk mban as DY ORË E GJYSMË. 'The road on foot from the new station up to here does not take even TWO HOURS AND A HALF.'

When the numerator of the fraction is larger than one, the plural forms **gjysma** and **çerekë** will normally be used: **tre çerekë** 'three quarters'.

CHAPTER 8

Pronouns and Other Pro-forms

The characteristic semantic function of PRO-FORMS is to refer rather than designate. While nouns, adjectives and numbers have specific, independent and fixed meanings, pro-forms indicate their referents as to certain categorical properties, so that a given pro-form may refer to quite different referents in different contexts:

Vetëm njëri, Harilla Lluka, porsa më pa, hoqi borsalinën gjithë respekt dhe përkuli koën dy-tri herë në drejtimin tim. KY ishte frikacaku më i madh i lagjes. 'Only one, Harilla Lluka, took off his hat very respectfully, as soon as he saw me, and bent his head two-three times in my direction. He ("THIS ONE") was the biggest coward of the neighborhood.'

Përmbysjen e qeverisë zogiste KÇN do ta arrinte me anën e një kryengritjeje të armatosur të POPULLIT, kur KY të ishte i organizuar mirë. 'The NLF would achieve the overthrow of the Zog government by means of an armed rebellion of THE PEOPLE, when THE LATTER was well organized.'

Depending on their meaning and function, pro-forms in Albanian may be classified as follows (See also Section 5.2.1 Pro-Adverbs):

1. Personal Pronouns
2. Reflexive Nouns
3. Demonstratives
4. Deictic Adjectives
5. Pronominal Adjectives
6. Interrogative Pronouns
7. Relative Pronouns
8. Indeterminate Pronouns
9. Reciprocal Pronouns
10. Indefinite Quantifiers

8.1 Personal Pronouns

PERSONAL PRONOUNS may serve as the sole constituents of nominal phrases; they indicate an ANTECEDENT in terms of the grammatical categories of person and number, irrespective of gender:

Person	Sg	Pl
1st	**unë** 'I'	**ne** 'we'
2nd	**ti** 'thou, you'	**ju** 'you'

For the third person, Albanian uses demonstratives to indicate the gender, number, and perceived nearness of third person antecedents. Demonstratives may also be used as determiners in NP's (see Section 3.1.2).

	Near	Remote
Masc Sg	**ky** 'this, he'	**ai** 'that, he'
Fem Sg	**kjo** 'this, she'	**ajo** 'that, she'
	Near	Remote
Masc Pl	**këta** 'these, they'	**ata** 'those, they'
Fem Pl	**këto** 'these, they'	**ato** 'those, they'

Do ta fitojmë luftën, -- u tha mjeku të plagosurve të tjerë dhe ATA pohuan me kokë pa e ditur se kjo frazë ishte si përfundim i një mendimi shumë të gjatë të doktorit. 'We're going to win the war--the doctor said to the other wounded men, and THEY nodded in agreement without knowing that this phrase was the result of a very long deliberation by the doctor.'

First and second person personal pronouns distinguish gender neither in the singular nor in the plural: **unë, ti, ne, ju** 'I', 'you', 'we', 'you' are used both for masculine and for feminine referents. Both the first and second persons have different words for singular and plural. Just as the pronoun **ne** 'we' is not the plural of the pronoun **unë** 'I' in the sense of indicating a plurality of speakers, but rather indicates the speaker together with one or more other persons, the plural form **ju** 'you' indicates that the persons addressed include the singular second person **ti** 'you'.

NOTES

1. Not infrequently, especially in scientific writing, an "anonymous" plural first person form is used instead of the singular form:
NE mendojmë se ky është një problem serioz. 'WE think that this is a serious problem.'
Me shqyrtimin e materialeve dialektologjike të mbledhura në atë krahinë NE i vumë vetes si detyrë hartimin e një skice dialektologjike informative përshkruese. 'Having examined the dialectal materials collected in that region, WE set ourselves the task of drafting a descriptively informative dialectal sketch.'

2. As a mark of honor or courtesy, a plural form of the second person pronoun is used to address a single person:
-- JU jeni drejtori i punimeve? '"ARE YOU the director of the operations?"'
JU bile u nisët i pari -- vazhdoi Kujtimi duke sjellë ndër mend të kaluarën. '"Indeed YOU were the first one to depart," Kujtim continued as he recalled the past.'
Kam dëgjuar për JU po s'JU kam parë. 'I have heard of YOU, but I have not seen YOU.'

8.1.1 Declension of Personal Pronouns

Personal pronoun forms reflect the grammatical category of case. Table 8.1 gives the declension (i.e., the set of case forms) of the first and second person pronouns, and Table 8.2 the declension of the third person pronouns.

Table 8.1 Declension of 1st and 2nd Person Pronouns				
	1st Sg	2nd Sg	1st Pl	2nd Pl
Nom	**unë**	**ti**	**ne**	**ju**
Acc	**mua**	**ty**	**ne**	**ju**
Abl	**meje**	**teje**	**nesh**	**jush**
Dat	**mua**	**ty**	**neve**	**juve**
Gen	**i mua**	**i ty**	**i neve**	**i juve**

Table 8.2 Declension of 3rd Person Demonstratives			
Remote			
	Masc Sg	Fem Sg	Masc Pl	Fem Pl

	Masc Sg	Fem Sg	Masc Pl	Fem Pl
Nom	ai	ajo	ata	ato
Acc	(a)të		(a)ta	(a)to
Abl	(a)tij	(a)saj	(a)tyre	
Dat	atij	asaj	atyre	
Gen	i(a)tij	i(a)saj	i(a)tyre	

Near			
	Masc Sg	Fem Sg	Masc Pl	Fem Pl
Nom	ky	kjo	këta	këto
Acc	këtë		këta	këto
Abl	këtij	kësaj	këtyre	
Dat	këtij	kësaj	këtyre	
Gen	i këtij	i kësaj	i këtyre	

NOTES

1. The rarely used genitive case form of the first and second persons singular and plural appears mainly in the spoken language, principally before appositive constructions as in:

Si do të vejë halli I MUA (I TY) të gjorit, I NEVE, (I JUVE) të shkretëve? 'What is going to become OF poor ME (OF YOU), OF US (OF YOU) unfortunates?'
Ky të përket ty, pse je kryetari I gjithë NEVE. 'This pertains to you, because you are the chief of all of US.'

2. In the spoken language, and less frequently in the written, the dative forms of the first and second person plural pronouns **neve** and **juve** are sometimes used instead of the standard forms of the nominative **ne** and **ju**, as well as in place of the standard accusative forms **ne** 'us' and **ju** 'you', especially when preceded by prepositions:

I kemi parë pasqyrat NEVE (NE). 'WE have seen the mirrors.'
Ajo që bëri princi, ose që i thanë të bënte, nuk ka ndonjë rëndësi PËR NEVE (PËR NE) tani për tani. 'What the prince did, or was told to do, is of no importance TO US for the present.'

3. Instead of the contemporary standard forms listed in TABLE 8.2, older Albanian, particularly in poetry, has third person ablative forms like **asi** and **si** for masculine singular, **asish** for masculine plural; **aso** and **soje** for feminine singular, **asosh** and **sosh** for feminine plural; and **syresh** for both genders:

Sulejman Tafili u ul e mori nja dy SYRESH. 'Sulejman Tafil bent down and took a couple OF THEM.'
Nëna ime, zoti gjeneral, është mësuar me të këtilla ndarje; nuk largohem SOJE për të parën herë, as që do të jem unë i pari bir që i bëhet kurban Atdheut. 'My mother, General, is used to such partings; it is not the first time that I am going away FROM HER, nor will I be the first son that is sacrificing himself for the Fatherland.'

The use of such old ablative forms increases when the deictics are used as determiners rather than as pronouns.

4. As objects of accusative and ablative prepositions, third person pronouns are usually used without the deictic prefix **a-** or **kë-**:

Unë kam folur gjerë e gjatë me TË. 'I have spoken with HIM at length.'

I bëhet se ajo kullë e tillë ka për të mbetur përherë për TË, e largët, e huaj, e ftohtë. 'He feels that for HIM that tower is forever to remain distant, foreign, cold.'

Trimëria e partizanëve në luftën kundër pushtuesve e tradhtarëve, sjelljet shembullore me popullin, ngjallën admirimin dhe dashurinë për TA. 'The bravery of the partisans in the struggle against the occupiers and traitors, their exemplary conduct toward the population, aroused admiration and love for THEM.'

Në ato çaste tendosjeje Spiro Shtegu vuri re se regjimenti fashist ishte ngritur në këmbë dhe po kundërsulmonte drejt TYRE. 'In those tense moments, Spiro Shteg noticed that the Fascist regiment was on its feet and was counterattacking toward them.'

8.1.2 Use of Personal Pronouns

In Albanian, unlike English, pronominal subjects of finite verbs are usually indicated by the ending on the verb rather than by a separate personal pronoun. A first or second person personal pronoun will be used for the most part only when the pronominal subject is emphasized or contrasted, or when the pronominal subject is one part of a compound subject. A third person pronoun will, in addition, sometimes be used to identify the gender of the subject, where that gender is ambiguous in the given context:

Megjithatë, ai ishte i zoti i punës dhe ç'thoshte AI, bënim NE. 'Nevertheless, he was in charge and WE did what HE said.'

E ç'tju tregoj më parë për atë udhëtim të këndshëm që bëmë gjatë dy javëve nëpër vendin tonë! 'And how can I begin to tell you about that pleasant two-week trip we took in our country!'

Atë e dimë edhe NE, jo vetëm TI. 'Not only YOU, but WE also know that.'

Mos jeni JU më trima se ata? Mos janë ATA më budallenj se ju? 'Are YOU braver than they? Are THEY more stupid than you?'

ATA luftonin dhe asgjë e keqe s'na ka ardhur deri më sot prej tyre. 'THEY were fighting, and to this day no harm whatsoever has come to us from them.'

However, a pronominal subject may be expressed by a personal pronoun even when there is no special reason to do so:

-- Ti thua, -- e mori prapë fjalën Skënderi, -- të vemi prapë atje vetëm sepse TI do që t'u thuash atyre një fjalë të vetme. '"You say," Skënder spoke up again, "we should go back there just because YOU want to say a single word to them?"'

Pronominal direct and indirect objects of verbs are always marked by pronominal object clitics for first and second person objects; for third person objects the appearance of the object clitic depends on discourse conditions discussed elsewhere (see Section 2.1.1 A). In addition, accusative and dative case personal pronouns may be used to express emphasized, contrasted or compounded direct and indirect objects of a verb.

Personal pronouns in the accusative case may also appear as objects of prepositions:

Prandaj edhe për NE çështja e teksteve shkollore në të gjitha këto lëndë, dhe veçanërisht në ato të letërsisë, brenda dhe jashtë shkollës, duhet t'i nënshtrohet një analize dhe një kontrolli të vërtetë në prizmin e filozofisë sonë. 'Therefore, for US as well, the question of school textbooks on all of those subjects, and especially literature, must submit both within and without the school to a true analysis and control, in the context of our philosophy.'

Po për kë? -- pyeti Memoja. -- PËR TY! -- tha mësuesi. PËR MUA? -- pyeti ai -- Nuk e prisja nga ju, zoti mësues! -- shtoi Memoja me sarkazëm. '"But for whom?" Memo asked. "FOR YOU!" said the teacher. "FOR ME? he asked. "I did not expect it from you, mister teacher!" Memo added with sarcasm.'

Personal pronouns are almost exclusively used in the ablative case only as objects of prepositions:

Përpara MEJE një mori instrumentesh. 'In front of ME a multitude of instruments.'
Po pse luftoni kundër NESH. 'But why are you fighting against US?'
Ja ç'kërkoj prej JUSH. 'Here is what I ask of YOU.'

8.2 Reflexive Nouns

A pro-form in a clause identifies its antecedent as being the same as the subject of the verb in the clause. The feminine nouns **vetja** 'self' and **vetvetja** 'self' serve as reflexive pro-forms in Albanian.

Atëhere e përmblodha VETEN, i vajta afër dhe i vura dorën në sup. 'Then I gathered MYSELF together, approached him and placed my hand on his shoulder.'
-- Lumi s'ngrin kollaj, -- iu përgjegj VETES së tij Rrapi. '"The river does not freeze easily," Rrapi replied TO HIMSELF.'
I dhimset VETJA. 'He pities HIMSELF.
Në fillim u trondit, por pas pak e përmblodhi VETEN, ektheu traktorin dhe dalëngadalë filloi të zbriste nga rruga më e shkurtër, përmes vreshtave. 'At first he was shaken, but after a while he collected HIMSELF, turned the tractor around, and slowly began to descend by the shortest road, through the vineyards.'
Rina! tha me VETE Stavri duke vështruar një fotografi që ndodhej mbi tryezë. 'Rina! said Stavri to HIMSELF, while looking at a photograph that was on the table.'

The feminine singular definite form may have as antecedent a subject of any person, gender, and number:

-- Nuke e di -- tha Vera, -- po mua nuk më duket e drejtë që gratë ju t'i vini përherë në punët më të rënda, kurse për VETE të silleni rrotull hijeve. '"I don't know," said Vera, "but I don't think it's fair to put your wives to work always on the hardest jobs, while for YOURSELVES you loaf in the shade.'
Ç'thua more, je në VETE ti apo jo? 'What are you saying, fellow; are you in your right mind ("in SELF") or not?'
Agimit iu duk i fortë, shumë më i fortë se VETJA. 'Agim felt that it was strong, very much stronger than HIMSELF.'
Mund ta shpëtojmë vetë VETEN. 'We can save OURSELVES by ourselves.'
Prandaj ato e ndjejnë VETEN në Zhamë sikur të ishin në shtëpinë e tyre, në Gruz a në Shkretë, në Bruz a në Nojë. 'That is why in Zhamë they feel [THEMSELVES] as if they were in their own home in Gruz or in Shkretë, in Bruz or in Nojë.'

The reflexive nouns in Albanian are declined like other definite feminine singular nouns:

Nominative	vetja	vetvetja
Accusative	veten	vetveten
Dative	vetes	vetvetes
Ablative	vetes	vetvetes
Genitive	i vetes	vetvetes

The only indefinite reflexives used are the accusative indefinite forms **vete** and **vetvete** when they are objects of the accusative prepositions, **në** 'on', **me** 'with', **mbi** 'on', **për** 'as for, for', etc.:

Ajetit për VETE të tij i dukej si shumë absurd ai mendim. 'As for his OWN SELF, Ajet felt that that thought was much too absurd.'
Mbase as vetë nuk e dinin, po ata ishin duke shembur kullat e padukshme që kishin në VETE. 'Perhaps they themselves did not realize it, but they were smashing the invisible towers that they carried on THEMSELVES.'

Ti ke me VETE pasaportën e Republikës, krenarinë dhe dinjitetin që të jep atdheu socialist. 'You have on your person the passport of the Republic, the pride and dignity that the socialist fatherland gives you.'

Even after these prepositions, the reflexive pronoun is used in the definite form when followed by a modifier:

Kur kishte ardhur nga Lazi e Fushë-Kruja, kishte ndjerë në VETEN e tij forcën e madhe që i kishte lënë jeta që kishte kaluar midis punëtorëve. 'When he had come back from Lazi and Fushë-Krujë, he had felt in HIMSELF the great force that the life he had led among the workers had given him.'

Ikën nga një krahinë në tjetrën dhe të duket çudi, -- tha Rrapi Gjini -- e sidomos, kur shkon në ndonjë vend malor, thua me VETEN tënde: ç'njerëz të mrekullushëm e punëtorë! '"You go from one region to another and you marvel," said Rrapi Gjini, "especially when you go to some place in the mountains, and you say to YOURSELF: what wonderful and industrious people!"'

NOTE

1. Reflexives usually refer to animate beings, but sometimes one does refer to something inanimate:

Edhe këtë radhë po i fliste nëna, zëri i saj s'kishte ndryshuar, ai zë sillte me VETE jehonën e largët të shumë ninananave. 'This time, too, his mother was speaking; her voice had not changed and carried with IT the distant echo of many lullabyes.'

2. From the viewpoint of its derivation, the stressed, intensive adverb **vetë** 'self, alone' is related to the reflexive noun. Its most frequent use is to intensify the subject, which may have been expressed by a noun or pronoun:

Në fillim UNË VETË isha në gjendje më të keqe se ajo dhe s'mund të bëja asgjë për të. 'In the beginning, I MYSELF was in a worse position than she, and could not do a thing for her.'

Kaloi më tutje pa u ndaluar e desh u pengua te një hu, që e kishte ngulur mu pranë kosheres dikur AI VETË. 'He went further without stopping, and almost tripped over a stake that HE HIMSELF had driven at one time right near the beehive.'

Në grindej nganjëherë, grindej se i kishte fajet VETË KRYETARI. 'If he quarreled sometime, he quarreled because THE PRESIDENT HIMSELF was to blame.'

Shpesh më ka qëlluar rasti të dëgjoj fshatarët që duke lëruar këndojnë; VETË ia marrin, VETË ia presin. 'I have often by chance heard the peasants sing as they plow; they do it all themselves ("ALONE they take it up, ALONE they cut if off").'

Besides the subject, **vetë** may intensify other nouns or pronouns in the sentence, either preceding or following the word so intensified:

U dukej një gjë e çuditshme -- si atyre ashtu edhe VETË ISMAILIT -- që të rrinim e të vazhdonim mësimet, ashtu siç bënin më parë. 'It seemed such a strange thing--both to them and to ISMAIL HIMSELF--to stay and continue their studies just as they used to.'

ATË VETË e kishin nxjerrë në tabelën e të dalluarve të ndërmarrjes. 'HIM HIMSELF they had put on the list of the distinguished members of the enterprise.'

8.3 Demonstratives

DEMONSTRATIVES point to things, living beings or features of these things or living beings in terms of their perceived distance from the speaker. The demonstratives for 'this' **ky**, **kjo** and 'that', **ai, ajo** point to someone or something perceived to be close to or away from the speaker, respectively.

> **Qeveria e popullit, me dekret, do të zhdukte tapitë e të zotërve të çifliqeve dhe KËTO do t'u ndaheshin jo vetëm fshatarëve pa tokë, po edhe malësorëve dhe fshatarëve me pak tokë.** 'The government of the people would, by decree, abolish the title deeds of the landlords, and THESE would be distributed not only among landless peasants, but also among the highlanders and peasants possessing a little bit of land.'

Demonstratives in Albanian have the grammatical categories of gender, number and case. They have special forms only for the masculine and feminine genders. Standard Albanian has not maintained the neuter demonstrative. In place of older neuter forms, masculine demonstrative pronouns are used as determiners before neuter nouns, as in **ky të ecur** 'this kind of walking', **ky të folur** 'this kind of speaking' etc. When the reference is to something unidentified by gender, feminine pronouns are used:

> **KJO s'më pëlqen.** 'I don't like THIS.'
> **Ç'është KJO që po bëni?** 'What's THIS you're doing.'

For the declension of the demonstratives see Table 8.2. In a sequence of *demonstrative + noun*, both elements are declined: thus, **ky djalë** 'this boy', **i këtij djali** 'of this boy', **këtij djali** 'this boy', **këtë djalë** 'this boy', etc.; **ato vajza** 'those girls', **i atyre vajzave** 'of those girls', **atyre vajzave** 'those girls', **ato vajza** 'those girls', etc. In this sequence the noun most often appears in an indefinite case form, but not infrequently it is used in a definite form:

> **-- Dëgjo Halit, i tha -- do të marrësh katër kaçile misër dhe do ta shpiesh në shtëpinë e KËTIJ MIKUT që na erdhi sot këtu.** '"Listen Halit," he said to him, "you will get four baskets of corn, and you will take it to the house of THIS FRIEND who came here today."'

Under the influence of the nominal declension, the forms of the ablative in demonstrative pronouns have been replaced nearly everywhere by forms of the dative. The ablative forms **kësi** 'this (m.)', **këso** 'this kind (f.)', **kësish** 'these (m.)', **kësosh** 'these (f.)', **sish** 'those (m.)', **sosh** 'those (f.)' are now quite rare:

> **Me këtë sjellje ajo po bëhej një shembull shumë i mirë edhe për vajzat e tjera, që mund t'u ndodhnin KËSO punësh.** 'With this sort of conduct she was setting a very good example for the other girls as well, to whom THESE KINDS of things might happen.'
> **Gjimnazi i Tiranës ASO kohe, si gjimnazi i vetëm i kryeqytetit, dallonte nga shkollat e tjera.** 'The gymnasium of Tiranë in THOSE days, being the capital's only gymnasium, stood out from the other schools.'

8.4 Deictic Adjectives

The deictic adjectives **i këtillë** 'such as this', **e këtillë** 'such as this (f.)', **i atillë** 'such as that', **e atillë** 'such as that (f.)', **i tillë** 'such (m.)', **e tillë** 'such (f.)', usually appear, like other articulated adjectives, after a noun in a NP, but for various stylistic effects, they may also appear before a noun:

> **Në hetim e sipër, midis feldfebelit dhe Qamilit, u nde një gjendje E ATILLË, që e detyroi Qamilin të tundej mbi këmbën e shëndoshë dhe të heshte një copëherë.** 'In the course of the investigation, there was SUCH a tense situation between the sergeant-major and Qamil, that Qamil was obliged to sway on his sturdy foot and to be quiet for a while.'
> **TË TILLA ritme zhvillimi të prodhimit industrial nuk njeh absolutisht asnjë vend kapitalist.** 'Absolutely no capitalist country has even known SUCH rates of development in industrial production.'

The declension of the **i këtillë, i atillë, i tillë** is identical with the declension of any other articulated adjective: e.g., Nom. **një djalë I këtillë** 'a boy such as this', Gen. **i një djali TË këtillë** 'of a boy such as this', Acc. **një djalë TË këtillë** 'a boy such as this', Abl. **prej një djali TË këtillë** 'by a boy such as this.' Notice that in English the *such* often comes at the beginning of the noun phrase, so that *a boy such as this = such a boy as this.*

Like other adjectives, the deictic adjectives are usually used together with nouns:

Por, pikërisht një qëndrim I TILLË i Sofikës kundrejt burrit të saj e shtynte atë të tregohej më e vëmendshme. 'But precisely SUCH an attitude by Sofikë toward her husband induced her to appear more attentive.'

And like other adjectives, when they are not accompanied by nouns, they are used mainly in the nominative and accusative cases:

E TILLË është fytyra antimarksiste, antisocialiste e kundërrevolucionare e revizionistëve hrushoviane. 'SUCH is the anti-Marxist, anti-socialist and counter-revolutionary face of Khrushchevian revisionists.'

TË TILLA janë qëllimet e tyre strategjike tradhtare. 'SUCH are their traitorous strategic goals.'

Fëmijët duhen rritur të guximshëm e të fortë. Prindët kërkojnë t'i bëjnë TË TILLË. 'Children should be raised up to be daring and strong. Parents seek to make them SUCH.'

Like other adjectives **i atillë, i këtillë, i tillë** may form NP's, with a preceding determiner. In such cases, they have the value of a noun, and can be used in all cases usually in the indefinite form, but less frequently in the definite as well:

-- Tashti u fute sërish në temë. -- Pa më thuaj, a mund të gjendet NJË I TILLË? '"Now you are back on the subject." "Tell me, now, can SUCH A ONE be found?"'

8.5 Pronominal Adjectives

PRONOMINAL ADJECTIVES characteristically indicate to whom something or someone belongs: **oborri IM** 'MY yard', **vajza JOTE** 'YOUR girl', **qëndrimi YT** 'YOUR stand', **shoku I TIJ** 'HIS friend', **mësuesi YNË** 'OUR teacher', etc. Although they often indicate possession, pronominal adjectives are used to express much of the same range of associative relations as exhibited by the genitive case in nouns:

Treni IM niset në orën 4. 'MY train departs at 4.'

Tema JONË nuk është aq interesante sa JUAJA. 'OUR theme is not as interesting as YOURS.'

Çdo film, roman a pjesë teatrale ka heronjtë E VET. 'Every film, novel or play has ITS OWN heroes.'

Pronominal adjectives usually appear after the nouns they modify, except that singular first and second person adjectives may follow *or* precede the following kinship nouns: **atë** 'father', **bijë** 'daughter', **bir** 'son', **dhëndër** 'groom', **ëmë** 'mother', **emtë** 'aunt', **gjysh** 'grandfather', **gjyshe** 'grandmother', **kunat** 'brother-in-law', **kunatë** 'sister-in-law', **kushëri** 'cousin', **kushërirë** 'cousin (f.)', **mbesë** 'niece', **motër** 'sister', **nip** 'nephew', **njerkë** 'step-mother', **shoq** 'husband', **shoqe** 'wife', **ungj** 'uncle', **vëlla** 'brother' and **zot** 'lord, master'.

Erdhën dhe herë të tjera në këto anë dhe doradorës dhe unë u binda që IM atë kishte të drejtë. 'They came this way temporarily at other times as well, and I became convinced that MY father was right.'

Siç më rrëfente IME gjyshe, kështu e ka pasur YT atë edhe YT gjysh. 'The way MY grandmother told me, this is the way YOUR father and YOUR grandfather had it.'

Ç'ke që i thërret kështu SAT bije, more Met? 'Why are you yelling like this at YOUR daughter, Met?'

Third person pronominal adjectives cannot precede nouns. However, the kinship nouns listed above can be preceded by an adjectival article with the same value for the third person:

I gjyshi e hipte në vithe të kalit dhe e merrte në mal. 'HIS grandfather would mount him on the buttocks of the horse and would take him to the mountain.'

Maja e ndjente se I ati po bëhej më i vendosur. 'Maja sensed that HER father was becoming more determined.'

Vajzës i ra udha nga E ëmta kur po shkonte te një shoqe. 'The girl's path ran by HER aunt's house, as she headed toward a girl friend.'

E ëma do t'i derdhej në qafë dhe do ta bënte qull me lotët e saj të ngrohtë. 'HER mother would embrace her and would drench her with her warm tears.'

E mbesa, pa ditur gjë, ia lexoi fjalë për fjalë. 'HER niece, not knowing anything, read it to her word for word.'

Kjo qe E kushërira e xha Dalipit. 'This was uncle Dalip's cousin.'

NOTE

In this regard, **i zoti / e zonja** '(his, her, its, their) master / mistress', with "kinship" nouns preceded by articles with the value of pronominal adjectives, must be distinguished from the adjectives **i zoti / e zonja** 'capable'.

8.5.1 Grammatical Distinctions in Pronominal Adjectives

Pronominal adjectives each consist of a preposed adjectival article plus a pronominal stem, but over a period of time these two parts have become joined together in many of the first and second person forms to make it impossible in many forms to distinguish the two parts today. When the parts are distinguishable, the generalization can be made that the adjectival article reflects the case, gender, and number of the word modified by the adjective; the root of the adjective indicates the number and person of the antecedent; as with other adjectives, a derivational suffix **-e** (if any) on the stem indicates that the word modified is feminine, while a derivational suffix **-a** on the stem indicates that the word modified is feminine plural. The first and second person pronominal adjectives are quite irregular in form (see Table 8.3). Note that the natural gender (sex) of the antecedent overrides its grammatical gender (declensional type), if the two are in conflict in determining agreement with the pronominal adjective (as in the first example below):

Një ditë DAJOJA IM kish ardhur te ne. 'One day MY UNCLE had come to our house.'

-- Është fqinji YNË -- u përgjegj Rina. '"It's OUR neighbor," replied Rina.'

Është i bukur fshati YT? 'Is YOUR village pretty?'

Do të na gëzojë së tepërmi vizita JUAJ. 'YOUR visit will please us no end.'

NOTE

The first person singular pronominal adjective forms **e mi** and **e mia** 'my (f.)', decline in the same way as do articulated adjectives, while the first person plural pronominal adjectives **tanë** and **tona**, like unarticulated adjectives, are invariable in different cases. Similarly, the second person singular pronominal forms **e tu** and **e tua** are declined like articulated adjectives, while the second person plural pronominal adjectives **tuaj** and **tuaja**, like unarticulated adjectives, are invariable in different cases.

In contrast with the first and second person, the preposed adjectival article of third person pronominal adjectives has its usual forms, depending on the word modified (see Section 4.2). The stems **tij** 'his', **saj** 'her', and **tyre** 'their' may be preceded by the deictic prefixes **a-** 'remote' or **kë-** 'near'. When they modify feminine plural referents, **tij** and **saj** add the feminine plural suffix **-a**, like any other adjective whose stem ends in a consonant.

A pronominal adjective (**i tij, i saj, i tyre**) may have as referent:

a) any noun or pronoun in the clause of which it is part:

Table 8.3 Declension of 1st and 2nd Person Pronominal Adjectives				
	Antecedent Person			
	1st Sg 'my'	2nd Sg 'thy'	1st Pl 'our'	2nd Pl 'your'
Word Modified				
Singular				
Masculine				
Nom	im	yt	ynë	juaj
Acc-Dat-Abl-Gen	tim	tët	tonë	tuaj
Feminine				
Nom	ime	jote	jonë	juaj
Acc	time	tënde	tonë	tuaj
Dat-Abl-Gen	sime	sate	sonë	suaj
Plural				
Masculine				
Nom-Acc	të (e) mi	të (e) tu	tanë	tuaj
Dat-Abl-Gen	të mi	të tu	tanë	tuaj
Feminine				
Nom-Acc	të (e) mia	të (e) tua	tona	tuaja
Dat-Abl-Gen	të mia	të tua	tona	tuaja

Kara Mahmut Bushatlliu kujtoi se ngjarjet ndërkombëtare po zhvilloheshin në favor TË TIJ. 'Kara Mahmut Bushatlli thought that international affairs were developing in HIS favor.'

Pra, disfata E TIJ qe fitore e drejtpërdrejtë e Ali Pashës, triumf I TIJ personal mbi armiqtë E TIJ. 'Therefore, HIS fiasco was Ali Pasha's straight victory, HIS personal triumph over HIS enemies.'

Kësisoj u ndodh befas para Hamzait, pa pasur kohë të sillte në mendje fjalët që kishte bërë gati prej kohësh për t'i thënë Skënderbeut kur ta takonte, apo cilitdo në vend TË TIJ. 'He thus appeared suddenly before Hamza, with no time to bring back to mind the words he had long prepared to say to Skënderbeu when he met him, or anyone else in his place.'

Trupin e madh të vëllait TË TIJ e vendosën në mes të dhomës. 'They placed HIS brother's big body in the middle of the room.'

Bukuria E SAJ atë ditë mund të këndohej vetëm me çifteli. 'That day one could sing the praises of HER beauty only with the **çifteli** [a two-stringed mandolin].'

Po ai i foli me respekt të madh babait TË TYRE. 'But he spoke to THEIR father with great respect.'

Kurveleshi është një vend malor, domethënë pjesa më e madhe e sipërfaqes SË TIJ është me male. 'Kurvelesh is a mountainous place, that is to say, the greater part of ITS surface consists of mountains.'

b) a noun or pronoun in a preceding clause or one understood from the context:

Skënderbeu e zhveshi pallën. Llamburitjet E SAJ erdhën gjer te ne e na hapën sytë. 'Skënderbeu unsheathed his sword. ITS glitter reached all the way over to us and opened our eyes.'

Kjo është lopata e Sadik V. E sheh shenjën që është prishur? Ka qenë emri I TIJ. 'This is the shovel of Sadik V. Do you see the defaced mark? It was HIS name.'

The three third person pronominal adjectives above contrast with the third person reflexive adjective **i vet**, '(his, her, its, their, one's) own'. The most likely antecedent of the **i vet** is the third person subject of the verb in the clause, if there is one, or some other plausible third person referent in the sentence if there is no plausible third person subject.

Kolektivi kujdesin E VET për këta shokë nuk duhet ta tregojë duke u fërkuar krahët. 'The collective should not show ITS concern for these comrades by pampering them.'

Gjithkush lëvdon pjellën E VET. 'Everyone praises HIS OWN offspring.'

-- Pse erdhe? -- nguli këmbë Zana, e tmerruar dhe e çuditur nga zëri I VET. '"Why did you come?" Zana insisted, terrified and amazed by HER OWN voice.'

Third person pronominal adjectives are used much more frequently than the third person reflexive adjective **i vet**, which has become common only in recent years. The potential use of either now makes it possible to avoid ambiguity in many sentences in which there are at least two third persons, either of which is a plausible antecedent of a third person adjective. In the following sentences the choice of **i tij** rather than **i vet** or vice versa makes clear which of the available third person referents is the antecedent.

Mbase ky ishte gëzimi I TIJ, pse ajo vajti në hekurudhë. 'Perhaps this was HIS joy, because she went to work on the railroad.'

Barleti e përshkruan gjerë e gjatë fushatën e Skënderbeut në Itali, po s'na jep motin e vajtjes SË TIJ. 'Barletius describes at length Skënderbeu's campaign in Italy, but he does not give us HIS [Skënderbeu's] motive.'

The same is true, on occasion, for the reflexive pronoun:

Kryetari i thërriste në emër, si shokut TË VET. 'The chairman called him by name, as to HIS OWN friend.'

E mori djalin pranë, duke e tërhequr për zverku me dorën e rrudhur, i mbështeti kokën në gjunjët E VET dhe nisi t'i lëmonte flokët. 'He drew the boy close to him, dragging him by the neck with the wrinkled hand, placed his [the boy's] head on HIS [own] knees, and began to stroke his [the boy's] hair.'

8.5.2 Constructions with Pronominal Adjectives

In most NP's with a noun and a pronominal adjective, the noun precedes the adjective. If preceded by an indefinite determiner and followed by a pronominal adjective (itself preceded by an adjectival article), the noun may be in either a definite or indefinite case form. If not preceded by an indefinite determiner, the noun will always be in a definite case form. A noun preceding a 1st or 2nd person pronominal adjective form without an intervening adjectival article must be in a definite case form, even when an indefinite determiner precedes. Table 8.4 gives the normal, non-contrastive forms for saying 'my male friend' (**shoku im**), 'my female friend' (**shoqja ime**), 'our male friend' (**shoku ynë**), 'our female friend' (**shoqja jonë**), 'thy male friend' (**shoku yt**), 'thy female friend' (**shoqja jote**), 'your male friend' (**shoku juaj**), 'your female friend' (**shoqja juaj**), with the noun followed by the pronominal adjective. Table 8.5 shows the definite case forms of the noun after the indefinite determiner **një** 'a'. The sense of these indefinite constructions is like English 'a male friend of mine' (**shoku im**), and 'a female friend of yours' (**shoqja juaj**).

Table 8.4 Definite Noun + 1st or 2nd Person Pronominal Adjective

Nom	shoku	im	shoqja	ime	shoku	ynë	shoqja	jonë
Acc	shokun		shoqen	time	shokun		shoqen	tonë
Dat-Abl	shokut	tim	shoqes	sime	shokut	tonë	shoqes	sonë
Gen	i shokut		i shoqes		i shokut		i shoqes	
Nom	shoku	yt	shoqja	jote	shoku	juaj	shoqja	juaj
Acc	shokun		shoqen	tënde	shokun		shoqen	tuaj
Dat-Abl	shokut	tënd	shoqes	sate	shokut	tuaj	shoqes	suaj
Gen	i shokut		i shoqes		i shokut		i shoqes	

Table 8.5 Indefinite Noun + 1st or 2nd Person Pronominal Adjective

Nom	një shoku	im	një shoqja	juaj
Acc	një shokun		një shoqen	tuaj
Dat-Abl	një shokut	tim	një shoqes	suaj
Gen	i një shokut		një shoqes	

For a small class of kinship nouns, the 1st and 2nd Sg pronominal adjectives commonly precede the noun, and both the adjective and the noun have their indefinite case forms. The form of the adjective will reflect the gender of the noun (see Tables 8.6 and 8.7):

Table 8.6 1st Sg Pronominal Adjective + Kinship Noun

	Masc		Fem
	'my brother'	'my father'	'my sister'
Nom	im vëlla	im atë	ime motër
Acc	tim vëlla	tim atë	time motër
Dat-Abl	tim vëllai	tim eti	sime motre
Gen	i tim vëllai	i tim eti	i sime motre

Table 8.7 2nd Sg Pronominal Adjective + Kinship Noun

	Masc 'thy brother'	Fem 'thy sister'
Nom	yt vëlla	jot motër
Acc	tët vëlla	tët motër
Dat-Abl	tyt vëllai	sat motre
Gen	i tyt vëlla	i sat motre

NOTES

1. Átë is the only noun in Albanian whose dative-ablative-genitive case form has a stem (et-) different from that used in the nominative and accusative cases (see Table 8.6).

2. Most of the forms of the 2nd Sg pronominal adjective are different when they precede a feminine kinship noun than when they follow one. Compare Tables 8.3 and 8.7.

3. The relative order of noun and pronominal adjective in a noun phrase makes it possible to distinguish kinship nouns from ordinary nouns: while kinship nouns may appear in constructions like those in Tables 8.6 and 8.7, ordinary nouns may not. Notice the difference between the ordinary noun **shok** 'comrade, companion, friend' and the kinship noun **shok** 'mate, (male) spouse, husband'. **Im shok**, with **im** preposed, means 'my husband', im contrast to **shoku im** which means 'my friend'. In this respect, compare **shok** with **mik,** both of which have possible English translations 'friend': **shok** is friend in

the sense of companion, while **mik** is friend as opposed to enemy. The contrast is not so apparent when the possessor is postposed: **shoku im** and **miku im** are synonymous as 'my friend'. But **im shok** occurs (as a kinship term), as we have just seen, while ***im mik** does not.

8.5.3 Substantivized Pronominal Adjectives

Unlike other substantivized adjectives, substantivized pronominal adjectives can be used only in the definite case forms, whose number and gender are determined by their specific referent.

Table 8.8 Substantivized Pronominal Adjectives				
		Referent		
Person		Masc Sg	Fem Sg	Masc Pl	Fem Pl
1st	'mine'	**imi**	**imja**	**të mitë**	**të miat**
	'ours'	**yni**	**jona**	**tanët**	**tonat**
2nd	'thine'	**yti**	**jotja**	**të tutë**	**të tuat**
	'yours'	**juaji**	**juaja**	**tuajt**	**tuajat**
3rd	'his, its'	**i tiji**	**e tija**	**të tijtë**	**të tijat**
	'hers, its'	**i saji**	**e saja**	**të sajtë**	**të sajat**
	'theirs'	**i tyre**	**e tyrja**	**të tyret**	**të tyret**
	'one's own'	**i veti**	**e veta**	**të vetët**	**të vetat**

Unë kisha etje, po edhe ai kishte etje, po një etje të ndryshme nga IMJA. 'I was thirsty, and he was thirsty also, but it was a different thirst from MINE.'
Si të gjithë aksidentet, edhe YNI kishte ngjarë fare kot. 'Like all accidents OURS also had happened entirely without reason.'
Do të kesh një punë më të bukur se JONA. 'You will have a better job than OURS.'
Si duket TANËT na pandehnin të mbaruar. 'Apparently OURS thought that we were finished.'
Miku im dhe JUAJI të dërgon të fala. 'My friend and YOURS send you regards.'
T'u rritshin TË TUTË. 'May YOURS grow up [to adulthood].'
Ai kishte kaluar në një rrugë të ndryshme nga E TYRJA. 'He had passed by a different road from THEIRS.'
Si la nja dy të vrarë nga TË TIJTË, u detyrua të shtrihej barkazi. 'After leaving two OF HIS [soldiers] dead, he was forced to lie down on his belly.'
Ata sy iu duken si TË SAJTË. 'Those eyes seemed to her like her own ("HERS").'
Agimi në TË TIJAT, ata në TË TYRET. 'Agim to HIS, they to THEIRS.'

A pronominal adjective may be substantivized:

a) following a demonstrative pronoun:

Kështu ka bredhur AI IMI, më këmbë, këtyre anëve. 'This is how THAT [ONE] OF MINE has roamed about these parts, on foot.'
Po KËTË TONIN, ç'u hipi në kokë që e kanë mbushur me makina si mizë lisi? 'But THIS [ONE] OF OURS, what possessed them to fill it with machines like oak tree flies?'
Kishte një këmishë burrash, ngjyrë mjalti që nuk ndryshonte nga AJO E TIJA. 'He had a honey-colored man's shirt that did not differ from [THAT OF] HIS OWN.'

NOTE

When the pronominal adjective is preceded by *demonstrative + noun*, if the focus of the sequence is on the demonstrative, the noun is in the definite form and the pronominal adjective is substantivized:

Krahasimi me Darvinin e forcon edhe më tepër KËTË MENDIMIN TONIN. 'The comparison with Darwin strengthens even more THIS IDEA OF OURS.'

Unë s'jam dakort me KËTË MENDIM TËNDIN. 'I am not in accord with THIS IDEA OF YOURS.'

Here it is understood that the addressee has other thoughts from which the speaker is consciously isolating the thought in question; the focus is on **KËTË mendim** 'THIS idea'. This construction is different semantically from constructions of the type **KY DJALI YT është shumë i zellshëm.** 'THIS BOY OF YOURS is very zealous.', in which the speaker is making a straightforward statement, not contrasting *this boy* with other boys of yours (you may not have others), but rather *your* boy with other people's boys.

b) in the nominative and accusative cases, when preceded by an indefinite noun in turn preceded by a general determiner like **çdo** 'any, every', **asnjë** 'not any, no', **tjetër** 'other', **ca** 'some', **cilido (cilado)** 'anyone', **njëri (njëra)** 'one' **akëcili** 'such and such', **pak** 'few', **mjaft** 'enough':

Ideja e zhvillimit dhe përparimit të skencës dhe jo lavdia personale duhet të udhëheqë në punën e vet ÇDO shkencëtar TONIN. 'The idea of the development and progress of science, and not personal glory, should guide EVERY scientist [of] OURS in his work.'

Mbrëmë kur mbaroi shfaqja Agimi doli pa ASNJË përgjigje TIMEN. 'When the performance ended last evening Agim went out without ANY answer from me ("MINE").'

c) when preceded by an indefinite noun in turn preceded by a number:

Pasi çarmatosën ushtrinë e Duçes gjermanët në udhëheqje vunë nga NJË ushtar TË TYREN. 'After disarming Duce's army, the Germans placed their own soldiers one by one in positions of leadership ("in leadership placed EACH soldier THEIRS").'

NOTE

When a pronominal adjective modifies a noun that is preceded by the indefinite article **një**, two possibilities exist (contrast English *a friend of mine* and *one of my friends.*):

1) The noun is in a definite form, while the possessive adjective remains indefinite:
NJË SHOKU YNË në Uzinën e traktorëve, ka shkruar një pjesë me një akt. 'A FRIEND OF OURS at the tractor plant has written a one-act play.'
Dua t'ju them NJË MENDIMIN TIM për librat që botohen. 'I want to express A THOUGHT OF MINE about the books that are being published.'

2) The noun remains indefinite, while the possessive pronoun becomes substantivized:
Atje ishte NJË BATERI JONA. 'There was A BATTERY OF OURS.'
Ata kishin NJË ZAKON TË TYREN. 'They had A CUSTOM OF THEIR OWN.'
Kisha harruar nën jastëk të hotelit një gazetë shqipe, që përmbante NJË VJERSHË TIMEN. 'Under the pillow at the hotel I had forgotten an Albanian newspaper which contained A POEM OF MINE.'

d) when it serves as a PREDICATE COMPLEMENT or as part of the PREDICATE NOMINATIVE:

Ai ishte nga toka ime e largët, ishte IMI. 'He was from my far off land; was one of my own kind ("was MINE").'

Por, siç ka thënë një i vjetër, "atdheun e duam jo se është i madh, por sepse është YNI." 'But, as an old timer has said, "We love our country not because it is big, but because it is OURS."'

Do të të kem TIMIN vazhdimisht. 'I will constantly regard you as MINE. ("I will have you MINE continuously").'

e) usually when another adjective intervenes between the noun and the pronominal adjective. This happens especially when the pronominal adjective is in the first person and the noun is definite:

Nisim që atje të bujmë, që të marrim ushqim të ri për udhën e largët TONËN. 'Let us begin to lodge right there, in order to get fresh food for OUR distant journey.'

Qeshte me zemërimin e kotë TIMIN. 'He laughed at MY vain anger.'

In these instances normal usage has the usual order *noun + unsubstantivized pronominal adjective + adjective.* But if a determiner (rather than an adjective) appears after the noun, the only correct possibility is the order: *noun* (definite or indefinite) + *determiner + substantivized possessive pronoun:* **Një kompani TJETËR JONA pret një kolonë armike në afërsitë e Shijakut.** 'ANOTHER company [of] OURS is waiting for an enemy column in the vicinity of Shijak.'

8.6 Interrogative Pronouns

The interrogative pronouns in Albanian are **kush** 'who' and **cili** 'who' in various case forms, **ç** 'what', **çfarë** 'what (kind of)', **sa** 'how much, how many' **se** 'what', and **i sati** 'which (in numerical order)' and **i sejtë** 'of what, from what (something is made)' in various case forms. They replace noun phrases in direct and indirect questions:

Po KË të dëgjoja? 'But WHOM should I have heard?'

Doktori e merrte me mend se Ç'kishte ngjarë. 'The doctor surmised WHAT had happened.'

The referent of the interrogative pronoun may be unknown to the speaker, to the listener or to both of them:

Është gabim i madh të mbahet qëndrim burokratik dhe liberal kundrejt të metave dhe gabimeve, pavarësisht se KUJT i takojnë ato. 'It is a great mistake to take a bureaucratic and liberal stand toward defects and errors, no matter TO WHOM they pertain.'

KUSH erdhi dje këtu? 'WHO came here yesterday?'

Interrogative pronouns can be used as objects of prepositions:

ME CILIN mbante lidhje tipografia juaj? 'WITH WHOM did your printing plant maintain ties?'

In addition, most interrogative pronouns can also be used in determiner position (before a noun) in noun phrases:

Kur ka ndodhur ndonjëherë dhe në Ç'VEND është parë që pleqtë dhe plakat të ngrihen, të flasin e të vendosin kundër fesë? 'When has it ever happened, and in WHAT COUNTRY has one seen old men and women rise up and speak out and make judgments against religion?'

Ç'mosmarrëveshje keni? 'WHAT disagreements do you have?'

Interrogative pronouns will be discussed below in three groups, according to their variability of grammatical form.

1. Interrogative pronouns whose forms reflect case only: **kush** 'who' and **sa** 'how much, how many'.

a) The interrogative pronoun **KUSH** 'who'.

The interrogative pronoun **kush** presupposes an animate referent.

KUSH po troket në derë? 'WHO is knocking at the door?'

Whether its antecedent is masculine, feminine, singular, or plural, it has the same forms, and it always agrees with finite verbs in the singular.

Kush has the following case forms:

Nom	kush	'who'
Acc	kë	'whom'
Dat-Abl	kujt	'to whom'
Gen	i kujt	'whose'

The interrogative pronoun **kush** may be the object of various prepositions. For example:

Me KË ke ardhur? 'With WHOM have you come?'

In the genitive case only, it may modify a noun:

E di ti bija e KUJT je? 'Do you know WHOSE daughter you are?'

b) The interrogative pronoun **SA** 'how much, how many, to what extent'.

The antecedent of the interrogative pronoun **sa** is a measurement of quantity or extent:

SA është? 'HOW MUCH is it?'
SA jeni? 'HOW MANY of you are there ("how many you are")?'

The pronoun has the following case forms:

Nom-Acc	sa
Dat-Abl	save
Gen	i save

In practive the case form **save** is very rarely found in standard Albanian. Instead, the invariable determiner form **sa** is used, followed by a noun in the appropriate case:

SA vetave u tha sot? 'HOW MANY persons did he tell today?'
Prej SA vetave ke marrë letra? 'From HOW MANY persons have you received letters?'

As a pronoun, **sa** may theoretically be the object of any preposition, but in practice it is replaced by the determiner construction except after nominative and accusative prepositions:

Me SA erdhi? 'With HOW MANY did he come?'

2. Interrogative pronouns whose forms reflect the grammatical category of gender, number, and case: **cili** 'which, who', **i sati** 'which (in numerical order)', and **i sejtë** 'of what (is made)'.

a) The interrogative pronoun **CILI** 'which, who'.

In contrast with **kush**, **cili** picks out its antecedent from a specific set, whether that set consists of animate or inanimate living beings and objects:

CILI qe ai i huaj që ia pa hairin kësaj toke? 'WHO was the foreigner who profited from this land?'
CILËT janë ata tiranë / Që të prenë e që të vranë? 'WHO are those tyrants / THAT cut you and killed you?'

The set from which **cili** picks a member may be indicated by a noun or pronoun object of the preposition **nga** or **prej**:

CILI PREJ tyre nuk e kuptonte rëndësinë e çlirimit të Tiranës? 'WHO AMONG them did not understand the significance of the liberation of Tiranë?'
CILI NGA ne nuk u gëzua? 'WHICH OF us did not rejoice?'

The forms of the interrogative pronoun **cili** reflect the grammatical category of gender, number, and case:

	Masc		Fem	
	Sg	Pl	Sg	Pl
Nom	cili	cilët	cila	cilat
Acc	cilin	cilët	cilën	cilat
Dat-Abl	cilit	cilëve	cilës	cilave
Gen	i cilit	i cilëve	i cilës	i cilave

Cili normally appears at the front of its interrogative clause, sometimes acting as determiner of a following noun:

CILËT bij të tradhëtuan / Dhe të dogjën dhe të shuan. 'WHICH sons betrayed you / And burned and annihilated you.'
Nuk dimë nga CILA përgjigje do të ishte më i kënaqur. 'We don't know WHICH reply would have pleased him more.'

b) The ordinal interrogative **I SATI** 'which (in numerical order)'.

The substantivized adjective **i sati** is used as an interrogative in direct and indirect questions about numerical order:

I SATI ditar është ky që gjejmë? 'WHICH [first, second...] diary is this that we find here?'

This interrogative consists of the preposed article **sa** + the derivational suffix **-të** + singular definite case ending, in analogy with the forms of ordinal numbers: compare **pesë** 'five' / **i pestë** 'fifth'. The interrogative **i sati** resembles ordinal numbers not only in formation, but also in grammatical and syntactic characteristics. For example:

	Masc		Fem	
	'which'	'first'	'which'	'first'
Nom	i sati	i pari	e sata	e para
Acc	të satin	të parin	të satën	të parën

As a pronoun, **i sati** is used--like the ordinal numbers--only in the nominative and accusative, in the capacity of a predicate nominative, or of a predicate complement of the subject or object:

I SATI është Sokoli? 'WHICH [number] is Sokol?'
I SATI doli Sokoli? 'How did Sokol place ("THE HOW MUCH did Sokol come out")?'
TË SATIN e klasifikuan Sokolin? 'What rank (or rating) did they assign Sokol ("the HOW MUCH did they classify Sokol")?'

The pronoun **i sati** differs from ordinal numbers only in that it is always used in the definite form.

c) An interrogative pronoun **i sejtë** 'of what, from what' has been formed of a preposed article + **se** + the suffix **-të**:

E sejtë është kjo unazë? 'OF WHAT is this ring [made]?'

3. Interrogative pronouns which are invariable in form: **ç** 'what', **çfarë** 'what (kind of)', and **se** 'what'.

a) Like the English word *what* the proclitic interrogative **ç'** may serve as a pronoun meaning 'what', or as an interrogative determiner (see Section 3.1.2) meaning 'what, which' in a noun phrase. When it is not followed by a noun, it is an interrogative determiner asking for identification of the noun:

Ç'deshi të thosh Skënderi me ato fjalë? 'WHAT did Skënder mean by those words?'
E di që s'kanë ç'të më japin sot. 'I know that they don't have anything ("WHAT") to give me today.'
E marr me mend ç'gëzim po më pret. 'I can imagine WHAT joy awaits me.'

The pronoun **ç'** is voiced before voiced stops and voiceless before all other sounds, except before affricates and apical and laminal fricatives, in which case **çfarë** is used instead. As a

Me ÇFARË lajmi më vjen? 'WHAT (SORT OF) news do you come (to me) with?'
Armiku u përpoq të merrte vesh ÇFARË personash kishkin ftuar komunistët në konferencë. 'The enemy tried to find out WHAT (KIND OF) people the communists had invited to the conference.'

c) The interrogative pronoun **SE** 'what'.

A prepositional phrase with **se** as object of an accusative preposition may be used as an interrogative in a variety of direct and indirect questions:
Me SE do të shkojmë? 'How ("with WHAT") will we go?'
Dhe mbi SE nuk u foli. 'But about WHAT he did not speak to them.'

8.7 Relative Pronouns

A RELATIVE PRONOUN indicates that the dependent clause that it introduces belongs to a nominal phrase. In some respects relative pronouns are like conjunctions, but they differ from other conjunctions in that they serve at the same time as a pronoun in the clause they introduce. Furthermore, unlike conjunctions, some of them have variable forms.

Relative pronouns are either *definite* or *indefinite*.

The relative pronoun is definite when it follows a nominal phrase and has that NP as its antecedent. The rest of the dependent clause modifies the NP. The DEFINITE RELATIVE PRONOUNS are **që** 'that' and **i cili** 'which':

BARDHYLI, QË heroizmin e shikonte vetëm në luftë me armë, ishte në grindje me QAMILIN, I CILI i jepte rëndësi luftës së nesërme. 'BARDHYL, WHO saw heroism only in armed struggle, quarreled with QAMIL, WHO emphasized the battle of tomorrow.'

The relative pronoun is indefinite when the dependent clause it introduces serves as a NP itself, as the object of a verb or a preposition. The INDEFINITE RELATIVE PRONOUNS are **kush** 'who(ever)', **cili** 'which (ever), who(ever)', **ç** 'what(ever)', **çfarë** 'what(ever)', and **sa** 'how(ever) many, how(ever) much':

Bishat naziste rrënuan Ç'gjetën përpara. 'The Nazi beasts destroyed WHAT(EVER) they found in front of them.'

The case of the definite relative pronouns **cili** and **kush** is determined by its function in the clause, whereas its number and gender are determined by the gender and number of the noun or pronoun to which it refers.

E kush nuk e pret me buzë në gaz këtë MUAJ të ëmbël, I CILI, posi një dhëndër, e sjell për dore natyrën e qeshur. 'And who does does not await with a smile this sweet MONTH [Masc Sg Acc] WHICH [Masc Sg Nom], like a bridegroom, brings forth smiling nature by the hand.'

The other relative pronouns are invariable in form.

8.7.1 Definite Relative Pronouns

a) The definite relative pronoun **QË** 'that'.

The definite relative pronoun **që** is invariable in form for human and non-human antecedents of whatever gender and number, and for any case required by its syntactic role in the clause it introduces:

Kjo ishte Tirana jonë, Tiranë e lirisë QË partizanët do ta çlironin. 'This was our Tiranë, the Tiranë of liberty THAT the partisans were going to liberate.'

Revolucionar i vërtetë është ai QË fjalën e bashkon me veprën. 'The true revolutionary is he WHO joins word with deed.'

Janë gjurmët e lotëve rrëke, QË ranë gjatë shekujve. 'They are the tracks of torrents of tears THAT fell in the course of centuries.'

Usually, as a relative pronoun **që** serves in the clause it introduces as a subject or direct object:

Këtë e kuptonte edhe mjeku, QË hëpërhë, ishte larg zonave të betejës. 'The doctor, too, WHO for the present was far from the battle zones, understood this.'

Po unë isha shumë i sigurtë se ata i dëgjuan fare mirë ato QË tha halla. 'But I was quite sure that they heard very well the things ("those") THAT auntie said.'

Under the influence of colloquial language, however, the relative pronoun **që** is sometimes also used without official sanction in the standard language as an indirect object.

Si ato mizat e dheut, QË u është prishur foleja, shumë ushtarë armiq ua mbathën këmbëve. 'Like ants whose ("THAT") nest has been destroyed, many enemy soldiers took to their heels.'

When its antecedent is a temporal noun, **që** serves frequently as a complement of time in the clause it introduces:

Si i gjithë kokektivi, ashtu edhe unë vajta në aksion ditën QË duhej vajtur. 'Like the whole collective, I also went into action the day THAT one was supposed to go.'

In colloquial Albanian, it also serves occasionally as a locative complement.

b) The definite relative pronoun **I CILI** 'who, which'.

Using **i cili** as a relative pronoun distinguishes literary from colloquial Albanian, which uses only **që**. In function, **i cili** is synonymous with the pronoun **që** 'that', but both in function and form, allows greater specificity than the latter, since **i cili** has distinct case forms for masculine and feminine, singular and plural:

	Masc		Fem	
	Sg	Pl	Sg	Pl
Nom	i cili	të cilët	e cila	të cilat
Acc	të cilin	të cilët	të cilën	të cilat
Dat-Abl	të cilit	të cilëve	së cilës	të cilave
Gen	i të cilit	i të cilëve	i së cilës	i të cilave

8.7.2 Indefinite Relative Pronouns

Indefinite relative pronouns, like definite relative pronouns, play a grammatical role in the clause they introduce; unlike definite relative pronouns, they have no specific nominal or pronominal referent. a) *The indefinite relative pronoun* **KUSH** 'who(ever)'.

Kush presupposes some animate antecedent. As an indefinite relative pronoun, **kush** exhibits the same grammatical forms that it has as an interrogative pronoun; it can be used in any case required by the clause it introduces, and may serve as object of a preposition:

Le ta marrë KUSH të dojë, veç ta çelë. 'Let WHOEVER wants to, take it, just so he opens it up.'

Ballistët rrethonin fshatin dhe kërcënonin KË mundnin. 'The Ballists surrounded the village and threatened WHOMEVER they could.'

Hajde me KË të duash. 'Come with WHOMEVER you wish.'

Merre prej KUJT të duash. 'Get it from whomever you like.'

b) *The indefinite relative pronoun* CILI 'who(ever)'.

Cili may have an animate or inanimate antecedent. Like the corresponding interrogative pronoun, its form reflects the gender and number of its antecedent, and the case required by its role in the clause it introduces; in the genitive case it is replaced by **i kujt**:

Të ngrihet CILI të dojë. 'Let WHOEVER wants to, rise.'
Ndihmoji CILIT të duash. 'Help [to] WHOMEVER you wish.'
Puno me CILIN të duash. 'Work with WHOMEVER you wish.'

c) *The indefinite relative pronoun* Ç' 'what'.

As a relative pronoun the invariable **ç'** may have both animate and inanimate indefinite antecedents of any gender and number, or it may refer to an indefinite abstract "it". It may serve as the subject or direct object of the clause it introduces, and that clause itself becomes a NP that can serve, for example, as object of a preposition or, preceded by **se**, as object of a verb. Note that the verb in the clause is in the third person and agrees in number with the antecedent of **ç'**:

Ç'ishin djem, kishin hequr tani edhe kanatieret. 'ALL ("WHAT") that were boys had now taken off even their underwear.'
Donin të dëgjonin se Ç'po ngjiste rreth tyre. 'They wanted to hear WHAT was happening around them.'
Ne Ç'kemi këtu e themi. 'WHATEVER we have [in mind], we say it here.'
Atëherë vetullat e tij u dukën më të zeza NGA Ç'i kishte në të vërtetë. 'Then his eyebrows seemed blacker than ("FROM WHAT") they were ("he had them") in reality.'
Fshatarët e dy katundeve ndihmuan me Ç'u erdhi për dore. 'The peasants of two villages helped out with WHATEVER was at hand ("came to them by hand").'

d) *The indefinite relative pronoun* SA 'as much (many) as'.

To a limited extent, the pronoun **sa** is used as an indefinite relative pronoun. When used as such, it has an invariable form and is used only as a subject or object, mostly with animate antecedents, but sometimes with inanimate ones as well:

SA lindin, aq do të vdesin. 'AS MANY AS are born, that many shall die. = What is born will die.'

It is used mainly to introduce NP clauses that function as objects of the prepositions **nga** 'from', **me** 'with', and **për** 'for':

Dhe, pasi ishte ndezur e bërë tym NGA SA dëgjoi e NGA SA pa, nuk mori dot vesh mirë se si përfundoi kuvendi. 'But, being all fired up ("after he had been ignited and made smoke") FROM what ("AS MUCH AS") he heard and what he saw, he did not at all understand clearly how the convention concluded.'
ME SA dukej, Rrapi s'e priste këtë pyetje. 'Apparently ("WITH AS MUCH AS seemed"), Rrapi did not expect this question.'

NOTES

1. The frequent use of the indeterminate pronouns **gjithë** 'all', **tërë** 'all', has led to the formation of the compound pronouns **gjithë sa** 'all that', **tërë sa 'all that'**, **gjithë ç** 'whatever, all that', which are used in place of **sa** 'what', **ç'** 'what', when one desires to emphasize the idea of entirety. **Nxori andej GJITHË Ç'duhej: pambuk, jodio, fasho.** 'He took out ALL THAT was necessary: cotton, iodine, bandages.'

2. Combining an indeterminate pronoun with a relative pronoun has given rise to the formation of the pronominal locutions **cilido që** 'whoever, whichever', **çfarëdo që** 'whatever', etc. in usages like:

Çlirimi i popujve nga skllavëria koloniale është bërë në rrugë të ndryshme, por CILATDO QË të kenë qenë këto rrugë, baza e çlirimit të tyre ka qenë e mbetet lufta e masave të popullit. 'The liberation of peoples from colonial slavery has taken many roads, but WHICHEVER roads these may have been, the basis of their liberation has been and remains the struggle of the popular masses.'

ÇFARËDO QË të ngjiste, Rina do të luftonte edhe me pushkë po të ishte nevoja.
'WHATEVER MIGHT happen, Rina would fight even with a rifle if necessary.'

3.   **Sa** 'as much' is also used as a determinal with a following noun.

I ra me SA fuqi pati. 'He hit him with ALL the strength he had.'

8.8 Indeterminate Pronouns

An INDETERMINATE PRONOUN like **dikush** 'someone' or **secili** 'each one' has a referent presumed to be unidentifiable by the audience, unlike determinate (personal) pronouns like **ti** 'you', **ai** 'he', **ky** 'this one' etc., which denote particular referents--e.g., **Agim, Petrit**, 'a stone, a boy'--in particular contexts.

The indeterminate pronouns include: **kush** 'who(ever)', **dikush** 'someone', **ndonjëri** 'someone, anyone', **askush** 'no one', **kurrkush** 'no-body', **asgjë** 'nothing', **gjë** 'thing, anything', **gjëkafshë** 'something, anything', **diçka** 'something', **seç** 'something', **hiçgjë** 'nothing', **secili** 'each one'.

The relatively large number of indeterminate pronouns is related to the variety of meanings they express. Some of them indicate a class of animate referents: e.g., **dikush, kush, njëri**. Some indicate a class of inanimate referents: **gjë, gjëkafshë, diçka**, etc. Still others indicate that the class of their referent is empty: **askush, asgjë, asnjë**, etc. But all of them have in common the property that they do not presuppose that the audience is familiar with the referent.

In terms of their internal structure, most indeterminate pronouns are agglutinated words, at least one of whose elements is fossilized. The following types are distinguishable according to the fossilized element(s) involved:

1. Indeterminate pronouns with the suffixed element **-do**, originally the second person singular form of the verb **dua** 'I want': **kushdo** 'anybody ("who you want")', **cilido** 'anyone ("which you want")', **çfarëdo** 'any ("what kind you want")'.

2. Indeterminate pronouns with the prefixed element **di-**, originally the second person singular form of the verb **di** 'know': **dikush** 'someone ("you know who")', **diç** 'something ("you know what")', **diçka** 'something ("you know what there is")', **disa** 'several ("you know how much")'.

3. Indeterminate pronouns formed with the prefixed element **ndo-**, originally **n-** from **në** 'if' + **do** 'you want': **ndokush** 'somebody, anybody'.

4. Indeterminate pronouns formed with the prefixed element **se-**, originally the subordinating conjunction **se-**: **sekush** 'everyone', **secili** 'each(one)', **seç** 'something'.

5. Indeterminate pronouns formed with the prefixed element **akë-**, which exists only in the following agglutinated words: **akëkush** 'so and so', **akëcili** 'so and so', **akësh** (from **akë** + **ç**) 'such and such a thing, a certain thing'.

6. Indeterminate pronouns formed with the prefixed element **as-**, which otherwise appears as the negative proclitic **as** 'not (a), nor, not even': **askush** 'nobody', **asnjë** 'none', **asnjeri** 'no one', **asgjë** 'nothing'.

7. Indeterminate pronouns formed with the prefixed element **kurr-**, which has its source in the adverb **kurrë** 'never'. Thus **kurrkush** 'nobody', **kurrgjë** 'nothing'.

8. Indeterminate pronouns formed with the prefixed quantifiers **gjithë-** 'all', **tjetër-** 'other' or **shumë-** 'many': **gjithëkush** 'everyone', **gjithësekush** 'everyone', **tjetërkush** 'someone else', **shumëkush** 'many'.

9. Indeterminate pronouns formed from two synonymous nouns: **gjëkafshë** 'anything, something', **gjësendi** 'anything, something'.

Morphologically, some indeterminate pronouns are variable, such as **kush, dikush, secili**, etc., and some are invariable: **gjë, diçka**, etc.

The majority of indeterminate pronouns may serve a variety of syntactic functions, such as subject, object, and various kinds of complements, but others perform only limited syntactic functions: for example, **gjë** 'thing, and **gjëkafshë** 'anything' are limited to use as direct object or subject of verbs.

8.8.1 Semantic Classification of Indeterminate Pronouns

Semantically indeterminate pronouns can be divided into those with animate or inanimate referents presumed to be unknown to the audience and those that indicate indefinite quantities.

A. Indeterminate Pronouns with Animate Referents

Indeterminate pronouns indicating a class (or a null class) of animate referents are: **kush** 'somebody', **dikush** 'someone', **sekush** 'everyone', **ndokush** 'anybody', **njeri** 'someone', **askush** 'nobody', **asnjeri** 'no one'.

With the exception of the pronouns **njeri** and **asnjeri**, pronouns in this class have been formed with the stem **kush**. The indeterminate pronoun **kush** differs from its interrogative homonym in semantic and syntactic traits. As an indeterminate, its meaning is like that of other indeterminate pronouns, such as **njeri** and **dikush**. It usually comes at the end of the clause and is not accompanied by prepositions. As an interrogative, its meaning is like that of the interrogative **cili**, it comes at the beginning of the clause, and it may be accompanied by prepositions:

> **Ata venin e vinin midis tyre, herë qëndronin në një krah, herë në krahun tjetër, sikur trembeshin se mos ua rrëmbente KUSH.** [indeterminate pronoun]. 'They went back and forth among each other, stopping now on one side and now on the other, as if they were afraid that SOMEBODY might grab it from them.'
>
> **KUSH** [interrogative pronoun] **do të fitojë, ne apo ato?** 'WHO will win, we or they?'

Repetition of the indeterminate pronoun **kush** often has the meaning 'one...another' or 'some...other':

> **Njerëzit zbritën, ndreqën KUSH kapelën e KUSH gravatën dhe po mateshin të hynin brenda.** 'The people descended, SOME adjusting their hats, OTHERS their ties, and were attempting to come inside.'

It is also used with a kind of distributive application, like English 'each one', in which case the pronouns are connected by the coordinating conjunction **e**:

> **Njerëzit kishin filluar të vraponin, KUSH E KUSH të hynte më parë në stadium.** 'The people had begun to run, EACH ONE trying to be first to enter the stadium.'

As an indeterminate pronoun, **kush** is used mainly in the nominative and dative cases:

> **Ecnin ngadalë që të mos i dëgjonte KUSH.** 'They walked slowly so that they might not be heard by ANYBODY.'
>
> **Mos i thuaj KUJT për këtë gjë.** 'Don't tell ANYBODY about this matter.'

A special accusative case form **kënd** is used very rarely, except in compounds formed with **kush**.

While **kush** itself as an indeterminate pronoun is relatively infrequent and limited in use, the indeterminate pronouns **dikush** 'someone', **ndokush** 'anybody', which are formed with **kush** and are similar to it in meaning, are commonly used and, unlike **kush**, used freely in any case, including the genitive, accusative, and ablative:

U dëgjua zëri i Agimit dhe i DIKUJT tjetër. 'The voice of Agim and SOMEONE else was heard.'

Gjatë atyre ditëve me shi, ajo rrinte në dritare dhe DIKË kujtonte. 'During those rainy days she would stay by the window and remember SOMEONE.'

Babai më zgjati dorën dhe ra në karrike si i shtyrë prej DIKUJT. 'Father gave me his hand and fell into the chair as if pushed by SOMEONE.'

Unlike **kush**, these pronouns can also be used with prepositions:

Kishte lexuar diku, ose kishte dëgjuar nga DIKUSH, s'mbante mend mirë. 'He had read somewhere, or had heard from SOMEONE, he didn't remember well.'

Pastaj, po ajo grua, pasi shkëmbeu nja dy fjalë me DIKË, shkoi të çilte portën. 'Then, that same woman, after she exchanged a few words with SOMEONE, went to open the door.'

The indeterminate pronoun **njeri** 'anyone' is derived from a noun. As an indeterminate pronoun **njeri** has a very general meaning like that of other indeterminate pronuns such as **ndokush** 'anybody', **ndonjë** 'any', with which it can often be interchanged. It is used mainly in negative or interrogative clauses, or in antecedent clauses of hypothetical sentences:

Ajo u çudit se si kishte kaluar kaq rrugë e rrugica dhe, sikur ta pyeste NJERI (=ndonjë, ndokush), nuk do të ishte në gjendje t'i përgjigjej. 'She was amazed at how she had passed so many paths and bypaths, and if ANYONE had asked her, she would not have been able to answer him.'

The indeterminate pronoun **njeri** 'anyone' is clearly distinguished semantically and grammatically from the noun **njeri** 'man, person'. Thus, while it can be used in all cases, except the genitive, and can also be used with different prepositions, as an indeterminate pronoun, it no longer reflects distinctions of definiteness and number:

Sikur ndiqej nga NJERI. 'As if he were chased by SOMEONE.'

The negative indeterminate pronouns **askush** 'nobody' and **asnjeri** 'no one', unlike the corresponding pronouns **kush** 'who' and **njeri** 'someone', are used in all cases. The accusative form of **askush, askënd** has a limited use.

B. Indeterminate Pronouns with Inanimate Referents

Indeterminate pronouns indicating a class (or null class) of inanimate referents are: **diçka** 'something', **seç** 'something', **diç** 'something', **gjë** 'anything', **gjëkafshë** 'anything', **gjësend** 'anything', **asgjë** 'nothing', **hiçgjë** 'nothing', **hiçmosgjë** 'nothing', **kurrgjë** 'nothing', **asgjësend** 'nothing', **asgjëkafshë** 'nothing', **çfarëdo** 'any(thing)'.

The pronouns **diçka, diç,** and **seç** indicate something of a small, but positive indefinite quantity:

Ju dini DIÇKA dhe nuk flitni. 'You know SOMETHING and are not speaking.'

Myzeqari i erdhi pranë dhe qëndroi më këmbë sikur DIÇ kërkonte. 'The man from Myzeqe approached him and stood by as if he were searching for SOMETHING.'

Gjatë udhës, vetëm dy arsimtarët SEÇ bisedonin vazhdimisht. 'Along the way, only the two educators were continuously discussing SOMETHING.'

The indeterminate pronoun **gjë** 'anything, not a thing' differs from the noun **gjë** 'thing' from which it is derived, both semantically and grammatically. As an indeterminate pronoun it is used only with negative and interrogative clauses, and with dependent conditional clauses, and no longer reflects the grammatical distinctions made by the noun (gender, number, case and definiteness), and is used in an invariable form:

Unë i di këto punë e ti nuk di GJË. 'I know these matters, while you don't know a THING.'

8.8.1 B. Indeterminate Pronouns with Inanimate Referents   **283**

The noun **gjë** 'thing' has also served in the formation of pronouns **gjësendi** 'something' and **gjëkafshë** 'something':

Përsëri përmendej, hidhej si ta kish pickuar GJËSENDI dhe lëshonte ndonjë britmë. 'Again he would regain consciousness, jump up as if SOMETHING had pricked him and let out a scream.'

Po të më duash për GJËKAFSHË, shoku Thanas, në zyrë jam. 'If you should need me for SOMETHING, comrade Thanas, I am in the office.'

Inanimate indeterminate pronouns are invariable in form, whether serving as subjects or objects of clauses, or as objects of prepositions:

Edhe sikur t'u ndodhë GJË atyre, do të lajmërohemi me kohë. 'Even if SOMETHING should happen to them, we shall be informed well in advance.'

Po ty nuk të tha GJË? 'But didn't he say ANYTHING to you?'

The negative pronouns in this group are: **asnjë** 'not one, none', **hiçgjë** 'nothing', **hiçmosgjë** 'nothing', **mosgjë** 'nothing', **kurrgjë** 'nothing', **asgjësend** 'nothing', **asgjëkafshë** 'nothing':

Ç'kishte të keqe ai trakt? ASGJË. 'What was wrong with ("what bad did it have") that tract? NOTHING.'

Grindja kish ardhur për HIÇMOSGJË. 'The bickering had come over NOTHING.'

Ata s'dinë KURRGJË. 'They know ("don't know") NOTHING.'

The indeterminate pronouns **asnjë** 'not one, none', **çfarëdo** 'anything' are the only pronouns in this group that may also be used as determiners (the latter only before a noun in the indefinite ablative singular):

Nuk mbulohet me ÇFARËDO velënxe. 'It is not to be covered with just ANY KIND of blanket.'

As a pronoun **çfarëdo** is usually followed by a modifying clause:

Agimi është në gjendje të bëjë ÇFARËDO QË T'I THONË. 'Agim is in a position to do ANYTHING THEY MAY TELL HIM.'

None of the other pronouns of this group is used as a determiner in NP's. With the exception of **diç** 'something' and **seç** 'something', they may, however, all be used as objects of prepositions.

C. Indeterminate Distributive Pronouns

Indeterminate pronouns that indicate all the members of a set considered separately are **secili** 'every one, each one', **gjithkush** 'everybody, everyone', **gjithsecili** 'everyone', **gjithsekush** 'everybody, everyone', **kushdo** 'anybody, anyone':

Ato i thanë njëra tjetrës ç'kishin për t'i thënë dhe SECILA shkoi në punën e vet. 'They told each other whatever they had to say and EACH ONE went her way.'

In general all these pronouns have quite similar meanings:

SECILA i thoshte edhe diçka mënjanë. 'EACH ONE would tell her something aside as well.'

Ja, kjo ishte harmonia vëllazërore, që dëshironte GJITHËSECILI të kishte, së pari në shtëpinë e tij. 'Well, this was the fraternal harmony that EACH ONE desired to have, first of all, in his own house.'

However, they cannot replace each other in every context:

Janë masat e gjera ato që krijojnë, që ndërtojnë dhe transformojnë botën e shoqërinë dhe, kur e bëjnë këtë, do të thotë se çdo meritë, pa nënvleftësuar meritën e

GJITHËSECILIT, e vënë në shërbimin e përgjithshëm të shoqërisë. 'It is the broad masses that create, that construct and transform the world and society, and when they do this it means that they put every talent to the general service of society, (yet) without underestimating the merit of EVERY INDIVIDUAL.'

Njeriu që e mban në dorë atë fletë, CILIDO qoftë e ndjen menjëherë veten pjesëtar të kësaj lufte. 'The man who holds that sheet in his hand, WHOEVER he may be, feels himself to be a participant in this struggle.'

GJITHËKUSH përpiqej të arrinte i pari. 'EVERYBODY was trying to be the first to arrive.'

The scope of the pronouns **kushdo** 'anybody' and **cilido** 'anyone, anybody' is usually restricted by a modifying relative clause or prepositional phrase introduced by the preposition **nga** 'from' or **prej** 'from':

Skënderbeu doli në shesh dhe ftoi në duel CILINDO prej oficerëve që rrethonin Sulltan Muratin. 'Skënderbeu stepped forth and challenged to a duel ANYONE of the officers who surrounded Sultan Murad.'

Ai kishte borxh t'ia tregonte CILITDO që vinte për herë të parë. 'He was obligated to show it to ANYONE who came for the first time.'

The pronouns **secili, gjithësecili**, and **cilido** have forms that exhibit gender and case distinctions, while the forms of **kushdo** and **gjithkush** exhibit case distinctions only, reflecting the underlying forms of their constitutive elements **cili** and **kush**, respectively:

	'each one'	'anybody'
Nom	secili	kushdo
Acc	secilin	këdo
Dat-Abl	secilit	kujtdo
Gen	i secilit	i kujtdo

D. Indeterminate Alternative Pronouns

The indeterminate pronoun **tjetërkush** 'someone else, something else', composed of the determiner **tjetër** 'other' + the indeterminate pronoun **kush**, has case forms like **kush**:

	'someone else, something else'
Nom	tjetërkush
Acc	tjetërkënd
Dat-Abl	tjetërkujt
Gen	i tjetërkujt

8.9 Reciprocal Pronouns

RECIPROCAL indeterminate pronouns have been formed by combining nominative definite forms of the pronoun **një** 'one' with substantivized forms of **tjetër** 'other' in the same gender. The nominative form of the reciprocal pronoun thus formed is used only as object of the preposition **nga** 'from' or **te** 'to, at':

	'one another, each other'	
	Masculine	Feminine
Nom	njëri-tjetri	njëra-tjetra
Acc	njëri-tjetrit	njëra-tjetrën
Dat-Abl	njëri-tjetrit	njëra-tjetrës
Gen	i njëri-tjetrit	i njëra-tjetrës

Another reciprocal pronoun composed of the singular nominative definite form **shok** 'comrade' (feminine **shoqe**) plus the singular oblique (i.e. non-nominative) forms of the same word is more limited in use, since it has no nominative form:

'friend-to-friend, one friend to another'

	Masc	Fem
Nom	---(Non-existent)	---(Non-existent)
Acc	**shoku-shokun**	**shoqja-shoqen**
Dat-Abl	**shoku-shokut**	**shoqja-shoqes**
Gen	**i shoku-shokut**	**i shoqja-shoqes**

Uleshin e rrinin në lëndinë, i këndonin NJËRI-TJETRIT vjersha. 'They would sit down in the meadow, reciting poems to EACH OTHER.'
I ka marrë malli për SHOKU-SHOKUN. 'The comrades have missed each other ("Nostalgia for FRIEND-TO-FRIEND has taken them.")'

8.10 Indefinite Quantifiers

In contrast with numbers, which are definite quantifiers, indefinite quantifiers denote indefinite amounts:

DISA ishin të lehta e me ngjyra të ndezura. 'SEVERAL were woolen and in bright [lighted] colors.'
SHUMË syresh e kishin të afërt. 'MANY of them were related to him.'
E kush t'i ka sjellë GJITHË këto lajme interesante? 'And who has brought you ALL these interesting news items?'

On the basis of what they can quantify, quantifiers can be classified as DETERMINAL or GENERAL. Unless otherwise specified, all indefinite quantifiers, like the definite ones, can be used pronominally, i.e., as the nucleus of a nominal phrase: **ca** 'some', **disa** 'several, some', **pak** 'few', **një** 'one', **një palë** 'a few, several', **ndonjë** 'some(one, thing)', **shumë** 'much, many', **mjaft** 'a fair amount, enough', **plot** 'plenty', **kaq** 'this much', **aq** 'that much'.

8.10.1 Determinal Quantifiers

Determinal quantifiers are those which may quantify only a nominal referent. The noun may follow the quantifier in the NP, in which case the quantifier serves as a determiner; or the noun may be absent, in which case the quantifier itself serves pronominally, as the nucleus of the NP. The major determinal quantifiers are **një** 'a,an', **ndonjë** 'some, any', **ca** 'some', **disa** 'several, some', and **një palë** 'a few, several'.

The indefinite quantifier **një** is obviously related derivationally to the number **një** 'one', but differs from it in that it does not serve for numbering, but rather to indicate some animate or inanimate referent not presumed to be familiar to the audience. Used as a determinal in a NP, this **një** is the indefinite article, which is followed in the NP by an indefinite singular noun:

Mund të gdhend NJË njeri që t'i ngjajë heroit. 'I can chisel A man that would resemble the hero.'

Used pronominally, **një** is usually followed by a modifier, such as an adjective, a prepositional phrase introduced by **nga** 'from' or **prej** 'from', or by a relative clause:

Dje takova NJË nga Vlora. 'Yesterday I met SOMEONE from Vlorë.'
U takova me NJË që s'e kisha parë ndonjëherë. 'I met SOMEONE I had never seen before.'

The indefinite quantifier **ndonjë** is used pronominally to mean 'someone, something', without requiring an explanatory complement as the pronoun **një** does:

Por pati edhe NDONJË që u shqetësua. 'But there was also SOMEONE who was upset.' Compare English "I know one" **(një)** with "I know someone' **(ndonjë).**

In their indefinite forms **një** and **ndonjë** are invariable. In their definite forms, however, **njëri** '(the) one, one (of them)', **ndonjëri** 'a certain one', they reflect the categories of gender and case.

	Masc		Fem	
Nom	njëri	ndonjëri	njëra	ndonjëra
Acc	njërin	ndonjërin	njërën	ndonjërën
Dat-Abl	njërit	ndonjërit	njerës	ndonjërës
Gen	i njërit	i ndonjerit	i njërës	i nondjërës

In the following examples note the use of the definite form to imply that the referent is part of a group known to the audience: **NJËRI qeshte lehtë me ironi.** 'ONE (masc.) (of them) was laughing lightly with irony',

-- Moj vajza -- tha NJËRA -- ç'po ndodh kështu? '"Hey, girls," ONE (fem.) (of them) said, "what's going on?"'

In the next example, that partitive relationship is made explicit:

-- Na falni i tha NJËRI prej tyre. 'Excuse us, ONE of them said to him.'

Note the use of the definite form also when the indeterminate pronoun is used correlatively with the substantivized adjective **tjetri**:

T'i biesh NJËRËS faqe, i pëlcet TJETRA. 'If you strike him on (THE) ONE cheek, THE OTHER ONE bursts.'

Një and **ndonjë** may also serve as objects of prepositions:

NË katin e dytë të hotelit kishte disa dhoma bosh, në NJËRËN flinte një i njohuri im. 'On the second floor of the hotel there were some empty rooms; in ONE (of them) slept an acquaintance of mine.'

When **një palë** 'a few, several' is used pronominally as a subject, it is semantically equivalent to **disa** 'several' or **ca** 'some' and its predicate is in the plural number:

NJË PALË mbetën prapa, të tjerët arritën më shpejt. 'SEVERAL fell behind, the others arrived sooner.'

Otherwise, we would be dealing with the noun **palë** 'pair', preceded by the number **një** 'one' denoting a single entity made up of two identical parts as in **një palë pantallona** 'a pair of pants' or **një palë çorape** 'a pair of socks'.

The indefinite quantifier **disa** 'several' supplies the plural case forms corresponding to the singular forms provided by **një**:

Nom	disa
Acc	disa
Dat-Abl	disave
Gen	i disave

Këta që i afroheshin Mimozës, nuk ishin të gjithë djemtë e klasës, por DISA. 'Those that approached Mimozë were not all the boys from the class, but (only) SOME.'

8.10.2 General Quantifiers

The quantifiers **shumë** 'much, many, very, quite', **pak** 'a little, little, few, a few', **mjaft** 'enough, a fair amount, quite a bit, plenty, quite', **plot** 'plenty, completely', **kaq** 'this much, this many, so much, so many, so', and **aq** 'that much, that many, so much, so many, so' range in function over many areas of quantification, as indicated partially by the possible English translations. If the referent is clear in the context, they may even be used pronominally as subjects or objects:

Kanë vdekur SHUMË. 'MANY have died.'
Pruri KAQ. 'He brought THIS MUCH [indicating the amount by a gesture].'

CHAPTER 9

Prepositions and Prepositionals

The PREPOSITION in Albanian as in English is an invariable part of speech that indicates the semantic and syntactic relationship of a following word or phrase, called the "object" of the preposition, to some other constituent in a sentence: **luaj ME top** 'I play WITH a ball', **e njoha NGA të folurit** 'I recognized him BY his speech', **rreshtohuni PËR dy**line up BY two', **udhëtimi RRETH botës** 'the journey ROUND the world', **lapidari BUZË rrugës** 'the obelisk BY the road', **një letër PËR mua** 'a letter FOR me', **i shpejtë NË punë** 'fast AT work', **i dashur ME të gjithë** 'friendly WITH all', **dy PREJ nesh** 'two OF us', **larg NGA qyteti** 'far FROM the city'. In these examples it is evident that the word or phrase which the prepositional phrase relates to its object may be verbal, nominal, adjectival, pronominal, adverbial, or numerical, but in the majority of cases prepositions connect a nominal with a verb.

Usually the object of the preposition is nominal or pronominal, but in certain cases the object is adverbial: **u nis PËR këtu** 'he set out FOR here', **u nis PËR atje** 'he set out FOR there', **e dua PËR sivjet, jo PËR mot** 'I want it FOR this year, not FOR next year', **PËR më vonë** 'FOR later', **PËR ku je nisur** 'where are you headed FOR', **PËR këtej** '(THROUGH) this way', **PËR andej** '(THROUGH) that way', **kritika NGA poshtë lart** 'criticism FROM below to above', **nuk u dëgjua as PËR mirë, as PËR keq** 'He was not heard from either FOR good or FOR bad', etc. The adverbial in such constructions is usually one of the pro-adverbs **ku** 'where', **kur** 'when', **nga** 'whence, thence', **ashtu** 'in that way', **kështu** 'in this way', **këtej** 'over here', **andej** 'over there', **këtu** 'here', **atje** 'there', whose meaning is like that of a pronoun (see Section 5.2.1). But the group also includes certain adverbs which in these constructions are equivalent to nominals (e.g., **për mirë**= "**për të mirë**" 'for the better', **për keq** = "**për të keq**" 'for the worse', **për nesër** = "**për ditën e nesërme**", 'for tomorrow = for the following day'), or which serve as designations of loss, e.g.,: **nga brenda jashtë** 'inside out, from within to without', **nga jashtë brenda** 'from without to within', **nga poshtë lart** 'from below to above', **nga lart poshtë** 'from above to below', **për mot** 'for next year', **për sivjet** 'for this year'.

NOTE

The preposition may have an entire phrase as its object when the phrase is substantivized, i.e. when it is used as a noun:

Po tregtari e priste dhe e përcillte ME "eja pazarin tjetër". 'But the merchant received and saw him off WITH "come back the next shopping day".'

Trupi m'u mbush si me gjilpëra, sa u bëra PËR hapu dhe të futem. 'My body felt so prickly that I was ready to commit suicide ("ready FOR open up and that I get in"; from the expression **Hapu o varr të futem brenda.** "Open up oh grave and let me in.")'

To strengthen the meaning or make it more precise, sometimes two prepositions are used together: **për në** 'for in', **për nga** 'for by', **për e të** 'for to', **prej nga** 'from'. With frequent use, in time such sequences of prepositions may be agglutinated, as has happened with **nëpër** 'among', **përmbi** 'over', **përveç** 'except, besides'.

As in English, in introducing complements of particular verbs, the choice of a given simple preposition often seems quite arbitrary in terms of the usual meaning of the preposition: **mendoj për...** 'I think about...', **flas për...** 'I speak about...', **shndërrohet në...** 'it changes into...', **shpresoj në...** 'I hope for...' etc.

The object of most prepositions is in the ablative or accusative case. The use of nominative case objects with the prepositions **te(k)** 'to, at' and **nga** 'by, from', is believed to stem from the origin of these prepositions as conjunctions; i.e., **shkova te pusi** 'I went to the well', **vij nga lumi** 'I come from the river' may well have come from constructions such as, **shkova te është pusi** 'I went over to where the well is', **vij nga është lumi** 'I come from where the river is'.

9.1 Prepositional Classes

The syntactic classification of prepositions divides them according to the case of their object, when that object is a nominal phrase (NP). As a rule, in Albanian the NP object of a preposition is in one specific case. Apparent exceptions to this rule are the prepositions **ndaj** 'toward' and **për** 'for', both of which may have special NP objects in a case other than the usual one.

The preposition **ndaj** 'toward' is normally used with ablative objects, as in: **ndaj meje** 'toward me', **ndaj shokëve** 'toward comrades', etc. Its only accusative objects are neuter nouns formed from participles: **ndaj të gdhirë** 'toward dawn', **ndaj të ngrysur** 'toward dusk ("darkening")'.

Vetëm NDAJ të gdhirë të ftuarit shkuan në shtëpi. 'Only TOWARD dawn ("dawning") did the guests go home.'

The preposition **për** 'for' is normally use with accusative objects; its only ablative objects belong to a limited category of nouns that designate attachments to or parts of the body of living beings: **për dore** by the hand', **për krahu** 'by the arm', për **flokësh** 'by the hair' etc.

Dy burra të fuqishëm e hiqnin PËR litari, një tjetër e kishte zënë PËR bishti. Po lopa nuk donte në asnjë mënyrë të çapitej. 'Two powerful men pulled it BY the rope, another had gotten hold of it BY the tail. But the cow did not want to budge under any circumstances.'

9.1.1 Prepositions with Nominative Objects

The prepositions that are used with objects in the nominative case are **nga** 'toward, of, by, from' and **te(k)** 'to, at'.

a) A prepositional phrase introduced by the preposition **nga** may indicate:

1) place: most often the origin of an action, less often the place toward which the action is directed or where it happens, the place where something is found or from which it derives, etc.:

NGA bjeshkët e Veriut, me lulen e trimave, Lekë Dukagjini rendi në ndihmë të vëllezërve. 'FROM the mountains of the North, with an elite of brave men, Lek Dukagjin ran to the aid of his brothers.'
Seiti me të tjerët rrinin strukur prapa gardhit dhe vështronin NGA kodra. 'Seit and the others huddled behind the fence and looked TOWARD the hill.'
Manifestuesit kaluan pastaj NGA sheshi "Skënderbej". 'The demonstrators then passed BY Skënderbeu square.'
Pranë meje ia ka marrë këngës një vullnetar NGA Skrapari. 'Near me a volunteer FROM Skrapar has begun to sing.'

2) cause:

Dëbora ishte shkrirë NGA shiu që kishte rënë gjatë natës. 'The snow had melted FROM the rain that had fallen during the night.'

3) time:

NGA pasdrekja zunë bubullimat e vetëtimat. 'Toward afternoon thunder and lightning began.'

4) scope:

> **E dua Nënën, se është e bukur, e fortë...e madhe NGA zemra.** 'I love Mother, because she is beautiful, strong...(and) big OF heart.'

5) agency:

> **Banesat e ndërtuara NGA vullnetarët ishin zbukuruar me flamurë të kuq.** 'The dwellings built BY volunteers were decorated with red flags.'

Note that **nga** may mark the logical subject of a passive. **Vetura është larë NGA unë.** 'The car has been washed by me.'

6) the whole of which something forms a part:

> **Kjo vajzë ishte një NGA dallëndyshet e para që lajmëronte ardhjen e një pranvere të re.** 'This girl was one OF the first swallows to announce the arrival of a new spring.'

NOTES

1. The preposition **nga** is in some senses synonymous with the preposition **prej** 'from' (see below).

2. Unless preceded by a determiner a noun object after **nga** is normally used in the definite form, even when its referent is indefinite: **nga fshati** 'from the (or a) village', **nga gëzimi** 'from [the] joy', **nga ethet** (pl.) 'from [the] fever' etc. When preceded by a determiner, it may be used in the indefinite form:
Deda ishte nga një fshat i largët i Mirditës. 'Deda was from a distant village of Mirditë.'

b) The prepositional phrase introduced by the preposition **te** 'to, at' (before vowels the variant **tek** is generally used instead), indicates the place where something is located or is occurring, or the place toward which movement is directed thus combining part of the senses of both 'at' and 'to':

> **Afërdita, fytyrëqeshur, qëndron një copë herë TE pragu i shkollës.** 'Afërdita, with a smiling face, stands a while AT the threshold of the school.'
> **Shikoj diellin, që po mbytet në det dhe më shkon mendja TEK anija, TE shokët.** 'I look at the sun that is sinking in the sea and my mind goes TO the boat, TO my comrades.'

NOTE

As object of the preposition **te(k)**, a noun is always in the definite form, whether or not its referent is definite, unless it is preceded by a modifying word: **te shtëpia** 'at [the] home', **te lumi** 'at the (or a) river', **tek ura** 'at the (or a) bridge'.

9.1.2 Prepositions with Accusative Objects

The most frequently used prepositions take accusative case objects: **në** 'in, on', **me** 'with', **për** 'for', **pa** 'without', **më** 'in, on', **mbi** 'over', **nën** 'under', **ndër** 'among', **nëpër** 'among'. Considerable use is also made of prepositional locutions ending in **me** or **në** (such as **bashkë me** 'together with, along with', **tok me** 'together with', **brenda në** 'inside'), and those composed of NË + noun + ME, as in **në krahasim me** 'compared with', **në lidhje me** 'in connection with', **në pajtim me** 'in compliance with', **në përshtatje me** 'in agreement with', etc. Common noun objects of accusative case prepositions often appear in an indefinite form, even sometimes when English treats the noun as definite: **në lum** 'to the river'.

a) The prepositional phrase introduced by the preposition **në** may indicate:

1) the place where something is located or moves, as well as the place toward which is is directed, thus combining part of the senses of English 'in', 'on', and 'to':

Lirinë e kishit kudo, NĚ krahëror, NĚ ballë, NĚ shpatë dhe NĚ ushtat. 'Freedom was manifest in you all over, ON your chest, ON your forehead, IN your sword and IN your spears.'

NĚ fshatrat tona janë ngritur shkolla të pajisura më së miri me 'IN our villages, schools have been built very well provided with teaching equipment.'

E shikoja çdo mëngjes, kur shkoja NĚ punë. 'I used to see him every morning, when I went TO work.'

2) a place, in a figurative sense:

I zhytur NĚ mendime ai nuk i dëgjoi fjalët e shokut. 'Plunged IN thought, he did not hear the words of the comrade.'

3) the time when something happens or an action is completed:

Kanalin e mbaruam NĚ ditët e para të shtatorit. 'We completed the canal IN the first days of September.'

Ndryshe nuk do të derdhej ashtu si burimi NĚ pranverë, pa pyetur në e pi apo s'e pi kush. 'Otherwise, it would not have been poured out like a well IN spring, without first inquiring whether someone would or would not drink it.'

4) the reference topic:

Ai është i kursyer NĚ fjalë. 'He is stingy WITH words.'

5) the result of the passage of a thing from one situation to another:

Zbatimi në jetë i kësaj vije bëri që shqipëria të shndërrohet nga një vend i prapambetur e thellësisht bujqësor, NĚ një vend bujqësor-industrial të përparuar. 'The implementation of this line led to Albania's changing from a backward and fundamentally agrarian country, TO an advanced agrarian-industrial country.'

6) a quantitative limit:

Rënia e Shkupit shënonte një fitore të rëndësishme ushtarake të forcave kryengritëse shqiptare, të cilat ishin rritur NĚ 30 mijë vetë. 'The fall of Skoplje marked a significant military victory of the Albanian rebel forces, which had grown to 30 thousand bodies.'

b) A prepositional phrase introduced by the preposition **me** 'with' may indicate:
1) accompaniment, association, or combination:

Agimi ME Perlatin po afroheshin drejt nesh me hapa të shpejta. 'Agim AND [WITH] Perlat were approaching us quickly.'

Tri ditë rresht guzhinieri na gatoi mish ME fasule. 'Three days in succession the cook cooked a meat dish WITH beans for us.'

Thuaji se nuk i ka hije të mbajë mëri ME shoqet. 'Tell her that it does not behoove her to hold a grudge AGAINST her friends.'

2) the means, instrument, or tool with which something is done: **Populli shqiptar e ka çarë rrugën e historisë ME shpatë në dorë.** 'The Albanian people have hacked their way in history WITH the sword at hand.'

Fshiu djersën ME shami dhe u ul të ndizte një cigare. 'He wiped off the sweat WITH a handkerchief and sat down to light a cigarette.'

3) the manner in which an action is expressed: **Pionierët e pritën ME gëzim të madh këtë lajm.** 'The pioneers received this news WITh great joy.'

4) time: **Kur fillonin shirat, rrinte ME ditë pa ardhur në shtëpi.** 'When the rains began, he would not come home FOR days.' In this use it often performs functions of manner adverbs ending in -ly in English: *joyfully, sincerely, quickly,* etc.

5) the reference topic: **Nuk donte të ndahej nga ne, sadoqë, ME moshë ishte më i vogël.** 'He did not want to be separated from us, even though he was younger IN years.'

6) the material of which something is made or with which it is filled: **Xhenierët po ndërtonin ME shpejtësi një urë ME trungje pishash.** 'The engineers were building in a hurry (WITH speed) a bridge WITH trunks of pine trees.'

Kur u kthye nga fshati, Bardhyli na solli një shportë të madhe ME rrush të zi. 'When he returned from the village, Bardhyl brought us a big basket WITH black grapes.'

7) cause: **Rilindasit ishin të bindur se Shqipëria ME pasuritë e saj natyrore, në kushtet e një administrate tjetër, mund të ishte e sigurtë për një përparim të shpejtë.** 'The men of the Reawakening were convinced that under a different administration, Albania, WITH her natural wealth, could be certain of making rapid progress.'

Të gjithë gajaseshin ME shakatë e xha Kadriut. 'All were amused AT the jokes of uncle Kadri.'

8) a feature or quality: **Pyjet ME dushk dhe lajthishtet kishin marrë një ngjyrë të kuqe.** 'The forests OF oak and hazelnut trees had taken on a reddish hue.'

9) a condition: **Kjo arrihet në radhë të parë ME pjesëmarrjen e gjerë të grave në ndërtimin e socializmit, në punët e arsimit dhe të kulturës.** 'This can be achieved primarily WITH the broad participation of women in the building of socialism, (and) in matters of education and culture.'

NOTE

Locutions that have as their last element the preposition **ME**, such as **bashkë me** 'together with', **në krahasim me** 'in comparison with', **në kundërshtim me** 'in opposition to, in contrast to', **në lidhje me** 'in connection with', **në pajtim me** 'in conformity with', **tok me** 'together with', **në përputhje me** 'in conformity with', **ballë për ballë me** 'face to face with', etc., also fundamentally indicate some kind of relationship of association or combination.

c) The preposition **pa** 'without' is the antonym of the preposition **me**; it generally indicates the lack, absence, or exclusion of someone or something. The prepositional phrase introduced by the preposition **pa** may indicate:

1) the opposite of accompaniment or combination:
Liliana nuk dilte kurrë shëtitje PA Entelën. 'Lillian would never go out strolling WITHOUT Entelë.'

Liria nuk e dinte që gjyshi i Aliut e pinte kafen PA sheqer. 'Liria did not know that Ali's grandfather did not drink coffee WITHOUT sugar.'

2) lack of means: **Çuditesh kur mendon se si i kanë ndërtuar këto mure PA mjetet e teknikën e sotme.** 'You wonder how they built these walls WITHOUT the tools and technology of today.'

3) absence of a characteristic:
Likja tha se kishte ardhur koha që gratë të dilnin në mbledhje e në punë PA drojtje, PA frikë nga askush, se asnjeri nuk mund t'i pengonte. 'Likja said that the time had come for women to attend meetings and work outside WITHOUT hesitation, WITHOUT fear of anyone, because no one could obstruct them.'

4) absence of a feature:
Deti nuk dukej, se nata ishte PA hënë e PA yje. 'The sea could not be seen, because the night was WITHOUT moon and WITHOUT stars.'

5) a condition:
Në një kohë të tillë, PA mushama, PA çizme është vështirë të punosh me çekiç në dorë përjashta. 'WITHOUT a raincoat, WITHOUT boots it is difficult to work outside in such weather with a hammer.'

d) A prepositional phrase introduced by the preposition **për** 'for' may indicate:

1) aim or purpose:
Lëvizja PËR shkollën dhe PËR shkrimin shqip ishte një lëvizje me karakter politik. 'The movement FOR Albanian schools and literature was a movement that had a political character.'

Piloja atë mëngjes do të shkonte PËR kashtë në Grizë. 'That morning Pilo was going to go to Grizë FOR straw.'

2) cause:

PËR një pe, PËR një gjilpërë, vajti dëm një gunë e tërë. 'Because of ("FOR") a thread, because of ("FOR") a needle, a whole cloak was ruined.'

3) time (duration, limit):

Diktatura e proletariatit do të eksistojë PËR aq kohë sa do të ekzistojë edhe rreziku i restaurimit kapitalist. 'The dictatorship of the proletariat will exist FOR as long as the danger of capitalist restoration exists.'

Punën e sotme mos e lër PËR nesër. 'Do not put off today's work FOR tomorrow.'

4) place (mainly the end of directed movement):

Unë e kopjova kanunoren dhe e mora me vete kur shkova PËR Kolonjë. 'I copied the by-laws and took it with me when I left FOR Kolonjë.'

Aty-këtu shihte armiq të shtrirë PËR tokë e të fshehur pas kaçubesh. 'Here and there he saw enemies lying ON the ground and hidden behind bushes.'

When used to indicate direction of movement, the preposition **për** is usually followed by the preposition **në** 'in':

Në mbrëmje baresha mblodhi patat dhe u nis PËR NË shtëpi. 'In the evening the shepherdess gathered the geese and set out FOR home.'

5) attribution:

E megjithatë ai shquhej PËR lëvizje të gjalla si të një të riu, PËR zërin kumbues e për sjelljen e tij të dëlirë. 'And nonetheless he was distinguished FOR his lively movements as befits a youth, FOR his ringing voice and for his clean conduct.'

Për këngë e PËR lahutë e ke të vetmin. 'For singing and FOR (playing the) lute he has no equal.'

NOTE

When used to mean something like "as if to be", the preposition **për** may be used not only with the accusative case, as in **Saliu i kishte marrë patat PËR ROSA** 'Sali had mistaken ("taken") the geese FOR DUCKS,' but with the nominative as well, as in **Ai mbahet PËR TRIM.** 'He pretends TO BE BRAVE.'

e) The prepositional phrase introduced by the preposition **më** 'on, in' may indicate:

1) place:

Një tank në bulevard vente e vinte me shpejtësi duke qëlluar MË të dy anët. 'A tank in the boulevard went back and forth quickly, shooting ON both sides.'

2) time:

Inxhinieri e rregulloi turbinën për dy ditë dhe MË 29 Nëntor, ditën e festës së lirimit, ne bëmë përurimin e dritës elektrike në fshat. 'The engineer fixed the turbine in two days, and ON November 29, the feast day of Liberation, we greeted the (arrival of) electric light in the village.'

NOTES

1. In time expressions the preposition **më** is now used mainly with dates, or in clusters of the type **më të ngrysur** 'at dusk ("at darkening")', **më të perënduar** 'at (sun) set[ting]', etc.

2. In general the preposition **më** is encountered much more frequently in the language of the authors of the National Awakening and in colloquial language than in current literary language. Its place is being taken over by the expanded use of the preposition **në** 'in, on'.

f) A prepositional phrase introduced by the preposition **mbi** 'over, above' may indicate:

1) the place above or on which an action occurs or something exists:

Aeroplani këtë radhë fluturoi fare ulët MBI kokat tona. 'This time the airplane flew very low OVER our heads.'

Drapri i artë i hënës shkëlqente MBI malin e Dajtit. 'The golden crescent of the moon shone ABOVE Mount Dajti.'

2) the object of speech, thought, feelings, etc, corresponding to the English words *about, on,* or *concerning:*

Sidoqoftë, pikëpamjet e tua MBI jetën e njerëzit, MBI paqen e luftën, -- tha Besimi, -- shpeshherë janë të thata. '"Anyway, your views ABOUT life and people, ON peace and war," Besim said, "are often dry."'

g) The preposition **nën** 'under, below', is the antonym of **mbi** when used in its locative sense:

Çdo gjë dukej e heshtur dhe e ftohtë si dëbora që kishin NËN këmbë. 'Everything seemed to be silent and cold, like the snow they had under [their] feet.'

In journalistic and scientific writing, the preposition **nën** is also used with causative value:

Armiku u detyrua të tërhiqej NËN grushtët e fuqishme të dy batalioneve partizane. 'The enemy was obliged to withdraw UNDER the powerful blows ("fists") of the two partisan battalions.'

When used in this sense, its object is limited to nouns like **ndikim** 'influence', **drejtim** 'direction', **pretekst** 'pretext', **udhëheqje** 'leadership', **veprim** 'activity': **NËN drejtimin...** 'UNDER the direction...', **NËN udhëheqjen...** 'UNDER the leadership...', often followed by a nominal in the genitive, as in the sentence above.

h) A prepositional phrase introduced by the preposition **ndër** 'among, between' often indicates the universe used as the reference for comparison:

Detyrat revolucionare nuk e pengonin Qemalin që të ishte një NDËR më të dalluarit në mësime. 'Revolutionary tasks did not prevent Qemal from being one OF the most distinguished ones in his studies.'

Saranda dhe Pogradeci janë dy NDËR qytetet më të bukura të Shqipërisë. 'Sarandë and Pogradec are two OF the prettiest cities of Albania.'

Megjithëse është NDËR vjershat e para të poetit, ajo shquhet për idenë e për vlerën programatike që ka. 'Although it is among the earliest poems of the poet, it stands out in terms of the idea and programmatic value it possesses.'

NOTES

1. This preposition is occasionally used to express locative relations indicating a part of the body or a personal pronoun as object: **ndër duar** 'in the hands', **ndër dhëmbë** 'between the teeth', **ndër sy** 'to one's face'; **ndër ne** among us', **ndër ju** 'among you', **ndër ta** 'among them'.

2. The object of the preposition is always in the plural.

i) A prepositional phrase introduced by the preposition **nëpër** 'through, throughout' may indicate:

1) an extended location:

Brigada IV vazhdon presionin natë për natë në sektorin e saj, duke e gozhduar armikun NËPËR llogore. 'The 4th brigade keeps up the pressure night after night in its sector, pinning the enemy down in ("THROUGHOUT") the trenches.'

Në vjeshtë, mbasi mbaronin punët NËPËR ara, myzeqarët u suleshin kënetave. 'In autumn, after finishing their work IN the fields, the Myzeqarë [farmers] attacked the swamp lands.'

2) a particular place through which or in which movement occurs:

Së shpejti do të fillonin shirat e vërteta të vjeshtës dhe era do të ulërinte NËPËR maz-gallat dhe oxhakët. 'Soon the real rains of autumn would begin, and the wind would howl AMONG the crags and chimneys.'

Duke ardhur rrotull NËPËR qytet, gjetën një taksi. 'Roaming ("coming around") THROUGH the city, they found a taxi.'

9.1.3 Prepositions with Ablative Objects

Taking ablative case objects are the simple prepositions **prej** 'from, of, by', **ndaj** 'toward', and **për** 'by'; prepositions derived from nouns, such as **anë** 'beside', **majë** 'atop', **buzë** 'along the edge of'; prepositions derived from adverbs, such as **afër** 'near', **krahas** 'alongside', **larg** 'far'; agglutinated prepositions like **përveç** 'except' and **sipas** 'according to'; and locutions such as **me anë** 'by means of', **në mes** 'in the midst of'.

a) A prepositional phrase introduced by **prej** may indicate:

1) the place from which something or someone originates:

PREJ asaj ane vinin jonet e një kënge të fuqishme burrash. 'FROM that side came the melodies of a powerful men's song.'

Tefiku ishte bir i një bujku PREJ Malaseji. 'Tefik was the son of a farmer FROM Malasej.'

2) the material of which something is made:

Ne po ngroheshim pranë zjarrit, kur dëgjuam hapat e saj të shqetësuar nëpër shkallët PREJ druri. 'We were warming ourselves by the fire, when we heard her distressed footsteps on the wooden stairs ("stairs OF wood").'

3) a feature or quality represented by the object:

Nuk shkoi shumë dhe në dhomë u fut një burrë nja dyzet vjeç, me pamje PREJ kapa-daiu. 'Not long after, there came into the room a man of about forty, with a swash-buckler look ("look OF swashbuckler").'

4) the set from which the referent is selected:

Shumë PREJ nesh gjatë kësaj kohe u thinjën. 'Many OF US became greyhaired during this time.'

5) the agent of an action:

Usta Vangjeli heshti, i mundur PREJ të tjerëve. 'Master Vangjel became quiet, defeated BY the others.' Note that **prej** is used to indicate the logical subject of a passive: **Vera u pi PREJ nesh**. 'The wine was drunk BY us.'

6) the starting time of an action):

Për herë të parë e ndjeu me të gjitha fuqitë e veta se aty kishte lënë zemrën, kishte lënë atë që dashuronte PREJ vjetësh. 'For the first time he felt with all the strength of his being that he had left his heart there, he had left her whom he had loved FOR years.'

7) quantity:

Robert Guiskardi organizoi një ushtri PREJ 30 mijë vetësh dhe një flotë PREJ 30 ani-jesh. 'Robert Guiscard organized an army OF 30 thousand troops and a fleet of 30 ships.'

8) cause:

Demali kishte një natyrë të çelur, të sinqertë, dhe kur ish puna për të mbrojtur parimet e tij, nuk trembej PREJ asgjëje. 'Qemal had an open, sincere face, and when it came to defending his principles, he was not afraid OF anything.'

NOTE

In locative, causative, and agentive uses the preposition **prej** is synonymous with the preposition **nga** (see above), and in recent times seems more and more to be replaced by it for those uses.

b) The preposition **ndaj** 'toward, in respect to' is used to express orientation or comparison:

Jeta e re i ka zgjeruar shpirtrat e njerëzve, i ka bërë më të ndjeshme NDAJ së bukurës, më të thella, më të pastra. 'The new life has broadened peoples' lives; it has made them more sensitive TOWARD beauty, deeper, purer.'

Ti, NDAJ këtij, je sa një gurneckë vetë. 'COMPARED TO this one, you are only the size of a fish.'

c) The preposition **për** may be used before noun objects in the indefinite ablative case which designate a part of the body on which the action of the verb falls:

Ato dukeshim si duar dëshmitarësh të heshtur, që donin ta mbërthenin PËR fyti. 'They seemed like hands of silent eye-witnesses that wanted to grab him BY the throat.'

d) A prepositional phrase introduced by the preoposition **sipas** 'according to' may indicate:

1) manner:

Ti i shikon gjërat SIPAS vetes sate. 'You see things in your own way ("ACCORDING TO your own self").'

2) basis:

Specialistët thoshin se, SIPAS projektit, duheshin së paku dy javë e gjysmë për ta bërë këtë gjë. 'The specialists were saying that, ACCORDING TO the projection, at least two and a half weeks were needed to do this job.'

e) Other ablative prepositions derived from nouns, (e.g., **majë** 'atop', **midis** 'between, among', **buzë** 'along the edge of', **rrëzë** 'at the foot of') or adverbs (e.g., **afër** 'near', **larg** 'far', **përtej** 'beyond, across', **sipër** 'above') generally express relationships of place more often than time, corresponding to the meaning of the nouns and adverbs from which they have been derived. Other prepositions in this category include: **anembanë** 'all over', **anës** 'beside', **ballë** 'in front of', **bri** 'beside' (an apocopated form of **brinjë** 'rib'), **faqe** 'at the cheek of', **brenda** 'inside', **drejt** 'straight', **gjatë** 'along, during', **jashtë** 'outside', **këtej** 'this way', **krahas** 'alongside', **kundër** 'against', **kundrejt** 'across, opposite', **larg** 'far', **matanë** 'on the other side', **mes** 'in the middle of', **ndanë** 'beside', **ndërmjet** 'among', **nëpërmes** 'through', **nëpërmjet** 'by means of, through', **para** 'in front of, before', **pas** 'behind, after', **përballë** 'opposite', **përbri** 'beside', **përkrah** 'alongside', **përmes** 'through', **përpara** 'before', **përposh** 'below', **përreth** 'round about', **përsipër** 'above', **poshtë** 'below', **pranë** 'near', **prapa** 'behind', **rreth** 'around', **rrotull** 'around', **sipër** 'above', **tatëpjetë** 'down(ward)', **tutje** 'beyond', **veç** 'only, just, except'.

Most prepositional locutions ending in a noun have objects in the genitive case (see below), but some are used with the ablative as well, e.g.,: **me anë kursesh** 'by means of courses', **në bazë fshati** 'on a grass-roots basis ("on base of village")', **në mes dy zjarrësh** 'between two fires', **për punë inati** 'for reasons of spite'. The locution **me anë** 'by means of' has the same meaning with ablative as with genitive objects, except that the noun object in the ablative is in the indefinite:

Në këto kushte çështja e kufirit greko-turk mbeti për t'u zgjidhur ME ANË bisedimesh. 'In these circumstances, the issue of the Greek-Turkish border remained to be solved BY MEANS OF negotiations.'

The prepositional locution **në mes** 'in the middle of' may indicate a place:

NË MES grurit që kish hedhur shtat, dukej një pemë. 'AMIDST the wheat that had shot up, a tree appeared.'

The same locution may also indicate a set from which a member is selected:

Dhe zgjodha më trimin NË MES tyre. 'And I chose the bravest FROM their MIDST.'

However, the preposition **ndër** is usually found for this use.

A number of adverbial locutions formed from words that are more or less synonymous are also used as prepositional locutions: **anë e kënd** 'everywhere', **anë e përqark** 'round about', **anë e qark** 'round about', **rreth e rrotull** 'round and about', **rreth e përqark** 'round about', **rreth e qark** 'round about'. Under this category also come adverbial locutions formed through the repetition of a word, connected by **e** 'and' or **për** 'for'; **rreth e rreth** 'all around', **tej e tej** 'right through', **ballë për ballë** 'face to face', **mes për mes** 'through the middle.'

9.1.4 Prepositional Locutions with Genitive Objects

The prepositional locutions **me anë** or **me anën** 'by means of', **në drejtim** 'with regard to, toward', **për punë** 'by reason of', **në sajë** 'thanks to', **për shkak** 'because of', and most others ending in a noun are used with objects in the genitive case. The meaning of these locutions is usually transparent from the meaning of the component parts.

a) A prepositional phrase introduced by the locution **me anë, me anën**, indicates a means:

Kontrolli punëtor është mjeti i sigurtë, ME ANËN e të cilit klasa punëtore mban në duart e veta diktaturën e proletariatit. 'Workers' control is the certain means THROUGH which the working class keeps in its hands the dictatorship of the proletariat.'

ME ANË të Frontit Partia grumbulloi rreth vetes në mënyrë të organizuar shumicën dërrmuese të popullit. 'BY MEANS of the Front the Party gathered around itself in an organized manner the overwhelming majority of the people.'

NOTE

This locution is not used before nouns designating a physical instrument: a tool like **kazmë** 'pick', **lopatë** 'shovel', **sharrë** 'saw', or beasts of burden like **gomar** 'donkey', **kalë** 'horse', **qe** 'oxen'.

b) The locution **në drejtim** 'in the direction of, with regard to' is usually used in journalistic style in the sense of orientation or goal:

Gjatë këtij pesëvjeçari janë arritur suksese të dukshme edhe NË DREJTIM të përmirësimit të gjendjes materiale dhe të ngritjes së nivelit kulturor të masave punonjëse. 'During this five-year plan tangible successes have been achieved also TOWARD the improvement of the material situation and the raising of the cultural level of the working masses.'

But it can be used also to indicate physical direction:

Brigada të nesërmen do të nisej për të kaluar Shkumbinin NË DREJTIM të Veriut. 'The brigade was going to leave the next day to cross the Shkumbini TOWARD the North.'

c) A prepositional phrase introduced by the locution **në sajë** or **në saje** 'owing to, with the aid of, thanks to' generally indicates the cause or means that makes something possible:

Çlirimi i atdheut, triumfi i revolucionit popullor dhe gjithë realizimet e ndërtimit socialist në vendin tonë janë arritur, në radhë të parë, NË sajë të udhëheqjes së urtë dhe vijës së drejtë të PPSH. 'The liberation of the fatherland, the triumph of the popular revolution and all attainments in socialist construction in our country have been realized WITH THE AID, first of all, of the wise leadership and correct line of the Albanian Labor Party.'

Forcat e armatosura mbaheshin NË sajë të kontributeve të mëdha vullnetare në të holla, që jepte popullsia. 'The armed forces were maintained THANKS TO the large voluntary contributions of money by the population.'

d) A prepositional phrase introduced by the locution **në vend** 'in place of, instead of', indicates substitution or replacement:

Eja me mua se të kam në vend të vëllait. 'Come with me because you are like a brother to me ("I have you in place of the brother").'

e) The locutions **për arsye** 'by reason of, owing to' and **për shkak** 'on account of, because of' may be considered synonymous, but the sense of active causation is somewhat stronger in the second:

Kongresi që mbani sot, ka një rëndësi të madhe për vendin, PËR ARSYE të situatës në të cilën e zhvilloni këtë kongress dhe për detyrat që do t'u caktoni masave të gjera të grave. 'The congress that you hold today is of great importance to the country, OWING TO the conditions under which you are holding this congress, and the tasks that you will set for the broad masses of women.'

f) Other prepositional locutions governing the genitive include: **me përjashtim** 'with the exception of', **me rastin** 'on the occasion of', **në bazë** 'on the basis of', **në mes** 'in the midst of', **për hir** 'for the sake of', **nga ana** 'on the part of', **nga shkaku** 'because of'. This class of locutions is being enriched continually with new formations. The following sequences are on the way to becoming prepositional locutions: **me ndihmën** 'with the help of', **në dëm** 'to the detriment of', **në dobi** 'to the benefit of', **në fushën** 'in the field of', **në lëmë** or **në lëmin** 'in the area of' etc.

9.2 Formation of Prepositionals

Morphologically, prepositionals may be single or agglutinated words or they may be locutions. In the class of single words are all the simple prepositions **mbi** 'over', **me** 'with', **më** 'in, on', **ndaj** 'toward', **ndër** 'among', **nën** 'under', **pa** 'without', **për** 'for', **prej** 'from', **te(k)** 'to, at', and a number of derived prepositions formed by conversion from single-word adverbs and nouns: **afër** near', **brenda** 'inside', **gjatë** 'during', **jashtë** 'out', **kundër** 'against', **larg** 'far', **lart** 'above', **para** before', **pas** 'after', **tutje** 'beyond', **veç** 'except'; **anë** 'side', **ballë** 'in front of', **bri** 'side', **buzë** 'at the edge of', **faqe** 'facing', **majë** 'atop', **mes** 'in the middle of', **rrëzë** 'at the foot of'. Nouns that have been converted into prepositions are all single words, so that the corresponding prepositions are likewise simple words.

In the category of agglutinated words are prepositions formed from the agglutination of two separate words: **nëpër** 'among', **përmbi** 'over', **përveç** 'except, besides', **sipas** or **simbas** 'according to, in accordance with', **ndërmjet** 'among', **nëpërmjet** 'by means of, through'; as well as those formed by conversion from agglutinated adverbs, such as **matanë** 'on the other side of' (from **më atë anë**), **përballë** 'facing, opposite', **përbri** 'alongside, beside', **përkrah** 'alongside, beside', **përmes** through', **përpara 'in front' përreth** 'around'.

A PREPOSITIONAL LOCUTION is an invariable sequence of two or more separate words that functions like a single preposition. Included in this categoy are adverbial locutions like **ballë për ballë** 'face to face with', **rreth e qark** 'around', **rreth e rrotull** 'round about', etc., as well as those clusters of adverb + preposition, preposition + noun, preposition + noun + preposition like **bashkë me** 'together with, along with', **tok me** 'together with', **me përjashtim** 'with the exception', **nëbazë** 'on the basis', **për arsye** 'by reason, because', **në kundërshtim me** 'contrary to', **në lidhje me** 'in connection with', etc. As a rule, in a prepositional locution, after a preposition which governs the accusative case, the noun is indefinite. The only exceptions are the locutions **me anën** 'by means', **me rastin** 'on the occasion'. The former has an alternate, indefinite form **me anë** 'by means'.

After the preposition **nga** 'by, of', the noun used is in the definite form: **nga ana** 'from the side', **nga shkaku** 'because', **nga puna** 'from work'.

A change of form from the indefinite to the definite signals that the locution is being used as a regular word sequence: e.g., **me përjashtim** 'except for' / **me përjashtimin** 'with the exception', **në bazë** 'based on' / në bazën 'on the basis', **në mes** 'among' / **në mesin** 'in the middle', **në vend** 'instead of' / **në vendin** 'in the place', etc.

CHAPTER 10

Conjunctions and Clauses

10.1 Conjunctional Phrases

A CONJUNCTIONAL phrase (abbreviated ConjP) is a word or sequence of words which serve the typical functions of a conjunction, joining together two or more words or phrases with the same syntactic function or marking a following word or phrase as a modifier or complement to another element.

A CLAUSE is a phrase that contains a finite verb form. Every full sentence contains at least one syntactically INDEPENDENT clause, i.e. a clause whose function is not to act as subject, object, complement, or modifier of some part or all of another clause. In addition to its independent or MAIN clause, a sentence may contain one or more DEPENDENT clauses, clauses which do serve in one of those functions.

CONJUNCTIONS are invariable words or word sequences that join clauses or clause constituents to one another. Unlike prepositions, conjunctions do not govern (i.e. limit) the case of a following nominal phrase. On the basis of their syntactic function conjunctions are traditionally divided into two groups: coordinating and subordinating. Coordinating conjunctions serve to link two clause constituents or two clauses of the same type (e.g., two nouns, two nominal phrases, two dependent clauses), while subordinating conjunctionals serve to introduce a dependent clause. Among the subordinating conjunctions, only **sa** 'as, as much as', **se** 'than, because', **sesa** 'than', **si** 'like', and **porsi** 'like, just like' may also serve to link constituents of clauses.

Morphologically, conjunctions of either type may be simple words, (consisting of a single morpheme), agglutinated words or locutions. Simple conjunctions are those like **dhe** 'and', **në** 'if', **o** 'or', **por** 'but', as well as conjunctions that derive from other simple words (pronouns, adverbs, particles), such as **sa** 'as', **ku** 'where', **kur** 'while', **nga** 'whence', **si** 'as', **tek** 'as', **a** 'whether'. Agglutinated conjunctions are single words resulting from the union of two or more separate words, such as **derisa (gjersa)** 'inasmuch as', **porsa** 'since', **sesa** 'than', **kurse** 'whereas', **nëse** 'if', **sikurse** 'as', **ndonëse** 'although', **pasi (mbasi)** 'after', **meqë** 'since', **mirëpo** 'even though', **megjithatë** 'nevertheless', as well as conjunctions formed by conversion from other agglutinated words, such as **ngado** 'wherever', **kudo** 'wherever', **kurdo** 'whenever', **sado** 'however much', **sido** 'no matter how'.

CONJUNCTIONAL LOCUTIONS are invariable sequences of two or more words that function as a conjunction. They may be continuous sequences like **në qoftë se** 'if', **me qëllim që** 'so that', **edhe pse** 'even though', or discontinuous, correlative sequences **qoftë...qoftë** 'whether ("be it")..or ("be it")', **jo vetëm që... por edhe** 'not only...but also' etc.

Certain particles may function as conjunctionals in particular environments. Such are the interrogative particles **a** 'whether or not' and **mos** 'lest' which in indirect questions serve to connect the dependent clause with the main clause:

Tashti të të shoh A je trim. 'Now I shall se IF you are brave.'
Vetëm se kam frikë MOS nuk e gjejmë atje dhe na vete rruga kot. 'Only I'm afraid THAT we won't find him there, and our trip will be wasted.'

Certain adverbs may also be used as conjunctionals: **përkundrazi** 'conversely', **gjithashtu** 'as well as'. Conjunctionals may also be composed of complete phrases, such as **domethënë** 'that is (to say)', **bie fjala** 'such as', **fjala vjen** 'for instance', **për shembull** 'for example'.

NOTE

In colloquial speech, in folklore, and for special effects in literature as well, the coordinating conjunctions **e, dhe**, and **edhe**, are used to join verbs in what appear to be subordinate relationships:

Për të ngrënë di E ha (= di të hajë),/po si shkaba takat s'ka. 'As for eating he knows how AND eats (= knows how to eat)/but lacks the power of the eagle.'
Dil E shih (=të shohësh) një herë jashtë. 'Go AND look outside once (=to look).'
Ha një çikë dhe ti, se njeriu s'ka rrënjë E ta mbajë (=që ta mbajë), kjo bukë na mban gjallë. 'Eat a little bit, now, because man does not have root to hold him up ("AND hold him" = 'sothat it hold him'); this food keeps us alive.'
Bjer E fli (=të flesh). Go to sleep ("fall AND sleep" = 'that you sleep').'
Mëmë, mëmë, me ç'mend e le ti njerinë e panjohur DHE më hyri (=që të hynte) brenda? 'Mother, mother, whatever possessed you to go and let the stranger enter my home ("with what mind did you let the unknown person AND he entered me" = 'that he would enter')?'

10.2 Types of Conjunction

10.2.1 Coordinating Conjunction

Depending on the type of relationships they express, coordinating conjunctions may be additive, disjunctive, contrastive, consequential, expository or expansive. A coordinating conjunction (except the first element in a correlative conjunction) always joins the constituent it introduces to a preceding constituent, even if the latter is unexpressed in the sentence.

a) ADDITIVE conjunctions: **as** 'not, not even', **dhe** 'and', **e** 'and', **edhe** 'and, yet, still', **si (e)dhe** 'as well as', **hem...hem** 'both...and', **si...si** 'both...and', **si...ashtu (e)dhe** 'like...also'. The conjunctions **hem** and **si** are used only in repeated correlative constructions. The conjunctions **as, dhe**, and **edhe** may also be repeated as correlative conjunctions: **as...as** 'neither...nor', **dhe...dhe** 'both...and', **edhe...edhe** 'both...and'.

Additive conjunctions are typical coordinating conjunctions in that they join constituents or clauses of the same type by simple addition:

Retë, të përhime E të palëvizshme, qëndronin lart në qiell, sikur kishin ndaluar për të kundruar botën. 'The clouds, grey AND still, hovered high in the sky, as if they had stopped in order to observe the world.'
Ecte nga e shpinin këmbët DHE s'ish i zoti as të mendonte se ç'duhej të bënte. 'He went wherever his feet took him, AND was not able to even think what he should do.'
Ushtria SI nga numri, SI nga artileria, nuk ishte më e vogël se ajo që rrethoi DHE mori Stambollin tre vjet më vonë. 'The army ,BOTH in size AND artillery strength, was not smaller than that which besieged AND captured Istanbul three years later.'

The conjunction **as** has a negative sense that is reinforced when it is repeated:

Dhe këtë pamje AS e pikturon, AS e fotografon, AS e përshkruan dot. 'And this scene, you can NEITHER picture, NOR photograph, NOR describe at all.'

NOTE

Of the three synonymous additive conjunctions **dhe, e**, and **edhe, e** is the most frequent and **edhe** the least frequent by far. Although synonymous, these conjunctions may not be used freely in place of one another. For example, **e** cannot be replaced by **dhe** or **edhe** in certain fixed phrases, including all repetitive constructions like the following: **ec e ec** 'walk and walk', **keq e mos më keq** 'from bad to worse', **rreth e rrotull** 'around and about'. On the other hand, **dhe** and **edhe**, but not **e,** may be repeated before correlative constituents:

edhe...edhe... 'both...and', **dhe...dhe...** 'both...and'.

b) DISJUNCTIVE conjunctions: **a** 'or', **apo** 'or', **o** 'or', **ose** 'or', **daç...daç...** 'either...or...', **ja...ja...** 'either...or...', **ndo...ndo...** 'either...or, whether...or...', **qoftë...qoftë...** 'whether...or..., be it...or be it...'. The conjunctions **o** and **ose** may also be repeated before correlative constituents: **o...o...** 'either...or...', **ose...ose...** 'either...or':

O do të shpëtojmë të dy bashkë, O do të mbetem edhe unë këtu, bashkë me ty. 'EITHER we will be saved together, OR I too shall remain here with you.'

Do të ikni prapë, APO do të rrini përgjithnjë? 'Are you going again, OR are you going to stay permanently?'

-- Ndoshta nuk vjen këndej, -- thashë unë, -- OSE ndoshta shpartallohet prej partizanëve shqiptarë. '"Perhaps it won't come this way", I said, "OR perhaps it will be smashed by Albanian partisans.'

Qindra e mijëra ishin ata që merrnin pjesë në këtë luftë, QOFTË duke bërë akte heroike, QOFTË duke shpërndarë traktet e Partisë. 'Hundreds and thousands took part in this struggle, EITHER by performing heroic acts, OR by distributing Party tracts.'

c) CONTRASTIVE conjunctions: **kurse** 'on the other hand, in contrast, while, whereas', **megjithatë** 'nevertheless, despite that, in spite of that', **megjithëkëtë** 'nevertheless, in spite of this, despite this', **mirëpo** 'even so', **ndërsa** 'but even so, while, whereas', **teksa** 'just as', **po(r)** 'but', **porse** 'yet, on the other hand', **veç** 'except', **veçqë** 'except that, only', **veçse** 'except that, only', **vetëm** 'only', **vetëm se** 'only that', etc.:

Ditën kulloste qetë, KURSE natën, në pranverë, bashkë me djem të tjerë të fshatit, shkonte kulloste kuajt. 'During the day he grazed oxen, WHEREAS at night in the spring, he and other boys in the village grazed horses.'

Nuk kemi shumë kohë që jemi njohur, MEGJITHATË jemi bërë miq. 'We have not been acquainted very long, NEVERTHELESS we have become friends.'

Ajo e vështronte me vëmendjë, NDËRSA ai vazhdonte punën i menduar. 'She looked at him attentively, WHILE he continued to work preoccupied.'

Lirinë s'jua solla unë, PO e gjeta këtu në mes tuaj. 'I did not bring you freedom, BUT rather found it here in your midst.'

Jemi të rrethuar, PORSE çdo problem ka një zgidjhe. 'We are surrounded, BUT every problem has a solution.'

Po ajo pamje e bukur e mëngjesit, VEÇ dielli ndriste më shumë. 'It was the same beautiful morning scene, EXCEPT that the sun was shining more brightly.'

Haxhi Xhafa nuk kishte ndryshuar, VEÇSE mbante sot një palë dylbi të mëdha, të varuara në qafë. 'Haxhi Xhafa had not changed, ONLY today he had a big pair of field glasses that dangled from his neck.'

d) CONSEQUENTIAL conjunctions: **andaj** 'that is why, so', **ndaj** 'hence, so', **pra** 'so', **prandaj** 'therefore, so'. The clauses which these conjunctions introduce indicate something which is either a conclusion from or a consequence of an antecedent clause:

Duket sikur horizontet e hapura u vrisnin sytë këtyre kullave, NDAJ i kanë zvogëluar fare dritaret. 'It seems as if the open spaces hurt the eyes of these houses, SO they have made the windows very small.'

Më erdhi rëndë ta shihja në sy, PRANDAJ vështrova dallgën e rrëmbyer, që u përplas pas bregut. 'I could not bring myself to look him in the eye, SO I looked at the tumultous wave that crashed against the shore.'

E dinte të vrarë, PRA u martua me një tjetër. 'She thought him killed, SO she married someone else.'

e) EXPOSITORY conjunctions: **domethënë** 'that is to say', **bie fjala** 'let us say', **për shembull** 'for example', **apo** 'or rather', **ose** with the meaning of 'in other words' or 'otherwise', **si** or **siç** with the meaning of 'for example'. These conjunctions serve to link clauses or constituents of clauses that clarify, specify, or expand the meaning of another clause or constituent:

Komitetet e Partisë duhet t'u kushtojnë një vëmendje më të madhe çështjeve organizative të Partisë, OSE më mirë, zbatimit të politikës organizative të saj. 'The Party committees should pay greater attention to the organizational matters of the Party, IN OTHER WORDS, the implementation of its organizational policy.'

Botëkuptimi marksist-leninist duhet formuar gjatë procesit të shkollës, dhe me të gjitha format e përshtatshme, DOMETHËNË jo vetëm nëpërmjet mësimit të veçantë teorik të marksizëm-leninizmit. 'The Marxist-Leninist worldview ought to be formed during the educational process, and in all relevant forms, THAT IS TO SAY not merely through the special theoretical learning of Marxism-Leninism.'

Disa pemë, PËR SHEMBULL portokajtë, limonat, mandarinat, i pjekin frutat në dimër. 'Some fruit trees, FOR EXAMPLE, orange, lemon, tangerine trees, ripen their fruit in winter.'

NOTE

Some conjunctions, mostly coordinating, but some subordinating (**dhe** 'and', **e** 'to, and', **por** 'but', **mirëpo** 'however', **megjithatë** 'nonetheless', **ose** 'or', **po** 'and', **se** 'because', **sepse** 'because'), are used to introduce afterthoughts:

Vendi ynë po zhvillon një revolucion të thellë kulturor. DHE ajo që ka më shumë rëndësi është se arsimi dhe kultura jonë e re bazohet në shkencën e marksizëm-leninizmit. 'Our country is carrying out a profound cultural revolution. AND what is more important is that our new education and culture are based on the science of Marxism-Leminism.'

Tërë punët na i prish Rako Ferra, E ferrë vërtet na është bërë! 'All our work is ruined by Rako Nettle, AND a real nettle he has become to us.'

Të rrosh do të thotë të jesh, të lëvizësh, të veprosh! PO sidomos të veprosh! 'To live means to be, to move, to act! BUT especially to act!'

A di ndonjë vend ku nuk të zë era o Agron? SE këtu ku kemi qëndruar të pret thëllimi. 'Oh, Agron, do you know a spot where the wind doesn't blow? BECAUSE here where we stopped the freezing wind cuts right through you.'

f) SUPPLEMENTING conjunctions are all correlative: **jo që...po...**' 'not only...but...', **jo që...po(r) edhe...** 'not only...but also...', **jo veç (që)...por edhe...** 'not just (that)...but even...', **jo vetëm (që)...por edhe...** 'not only (that)...but also...', **jo vetëm që...por as...** 'not only that...but not even...', **jo vetëm (që)...por...** 'not only (that)...but...', **jo vetëm (që)...porse...** 'not only (that)...but yet...', **le që...por...** 'let alone (not to mention)...but...', **le që...por as (që)...** 'let alone...but not even (that)...', **le që...por edhe...** 'let alone...but even...'. The locutions, which may link both clauses and constituents of clauses, are usually used with an additive, and only rarely with a contrastive sense:

Pirroja përpara fakteve nuk u tund: JO VETËM QË i pohoi me kryelartësi, POR EDHE e mbrojti vijën e tij si të drejtë dhe të pagabueshme. 'Pirro did not budge before the facts: NOT ONLY did he admit them proudly, BUT he EVEN defended his line as correct and infallible.'

Uji te Këneta e Zezë JO VETËM QË s'ish shterur, PO EDHE qe shtuar. 'The water at the Black Swamp NOT ONLY had not dried up, BUT had EVEN increased.'

In the semantics of these locutions, the emphasis is on the second element, as if to say: not only X but more so Y. A gradational relationship is thus established between the two clauses or constituents, whether that relationship is additive or contrastive. On the whole, supplementing conjunctions are newer than the other coordinating conjunctions, but today they are used quite frequently:

Nxënësit dhe studentët duhet të dalin nga bangat e shkollës JO VETËM me njohuri teorike, POR EDHE me njohuri praktike. 'Pupils and students should come out of school NOT ONLY with theoretical knowledge, BUT ALSO with practical knowledge.'

Po Bardhi, përkundrasi JO VETËM QË s'tregoi asnjë shenjë shqetësimi, PO bëri edhe diçka që e hutoi fare gruan. 'On the contrary, Bardhi NOT ONLY showed no sign of concern, BUT did something which stunned the woman completely.'

LE QË dhelpra i fluturoi nga duart, PO i fluturuan edhe çarqet. 'It was not enough ("LET ALONE") that the fox escaped from his hands, BUT even the traps got away from him.'

10.2.2 Subordinating Conjunction

According to the type of relationship they express, subordinating conjunctions are classified as complementive, locative, temporal, causative, intentional, comparative, conditional, consequential, concessive, and oppositional conjunctions.

a) COMPLEMENTIVE conjunctions: **se** 'that', **që** 'that', **(në)se** 'whether'. These conjunctions do not express explicit semantic relationships, but only link a following complement (subject, predicate, or object) clause to its controlling clause, much as *to* (before an infinitive) or *that* (before a clause) function in English:

Ti mendon, SE ka shkuar kot tërë ajo punë që është bërë këtu? 'Do you think THAT all that work that has been done here was in vain?'

Por detyra ime si komunist është QË ta shpejtoj këtë ditë, QË të ndihmoj sadopak që drita të shkëlqejë këtu. 'But my duty as a communist is to accelerate ("THAT I speed") this day, to help no matter how little so that the light may shine here.'

When the dependent clause is an indirect question, **në** or **nëse** is used rather than **se**:

Se mos e dimë ne NË ishte vetëm apo jo. 'We don't know WHETHER he was alone or not.'

S'është puna NËSE e njoh apo jo, more shok. 'It's not a matter of WHETHER or not I know him, comrade.'

Sometimes, when the dependent clause is presented as a comparison or supposition, the conjunction **sikur** 'as when, as if' may also be used as a complementive conjunction:

Unë ndjeva papritur, SIKUR një pelerinë e akullt më mbuloi me kujdes të gjitha pjesët e trupit. 'I felt unexpectedly AS IF an icy cloak covered carefully all the parts of my body.'

Blertës iu bë befas SIKUR qe zhdukur kufiri që i ndante njerëzit nga njeri-tjetri. 'Suddenly it seemed to Blertë that ("AS IF") the border that separated men from one another had disappeared.'

b) LOCATIVE conjunctions: **ku** 'where', **tek** 'where (at)' **nga** 'from where, towards where', **kudo** 'wherever', **ngado** 'from wherever', **tekdo** 'wherever', **deri ku** 'up to where', **gjer ku** 'up to where', **nga ku** 'from where', **që ku** 'from where', **kudo që** 'wherever', **ngado që** 'from wherever', **tekdo që** 'to wherever', etc.:

Ku ka zemër, ka dhe krahë. 'WHERE there is heart, there are also wings.'

'Ballistët u thyen keq dhe zunë të ikin NGA i shpinin këmbët. 'The Ballists were beaten badly and fled TO WHERE their feet took them.'

TEK dhemb dhëmbi, vete gjuha. 'WHERE the tooth aches, the tongue goes.'

Kishte njohur me rrënjë dhembjen e madhe të popullit, kasollë më kasollë, shtëpi më shtëpi, KUDO QË e çonte puna. 'He had known in depth the great suffering of the people, from hut to hut, from house to house, WHEREVER his work took him.'

NGADO QË shkonte, populli i dilte përpara dhe e përgëzonte. 'WHEREVER he went, the people went out to meet him and to greet him.'

c) TEMPORAL conjunctions: **kur** 'when', **sa** 'as long as', **si** 'after', **tek** 'while, as', **që** 'since', **gjersa** 'until', **pasi (mbasi)** 'after 'afterward)', **ndërsa** 'while, as', **po(r)sa** 'as soon as', **qëkurse** 'since', **sapo** 'as soon as', **teksa** 'just when, no sooner...than', **kurdo që** 'whenever', **kurdoherë që** 'whenever that', **para se** 'before', **posa që** 'inasmuch as', **që kur** 'since when', **që se** 'since', **qysh se** 'from the time that', **sapo aqë** 'just as', **sa herë (që)** 'every time (that)', **sa kohë (që)** 'as long as', etc.:

Kjo do të fillojë, KUR gjendja e armikut të jetë bërë kritike. 'This will begin WHEN the situation of the enemy becomes critical.'

SA jam me ty, nuk bëhem merak. 'AS LONG AS I am with you, I'm not worried.'

SI e hoqi pak mënjanë, ia shtërngoi dorën fort dhe ashtu shfaqi gjithë ç'i vlonte ato ditë në shpirt. 'AFTER he drew him a little to the side, he shook his hand firmly and so expressed all that was then agitating his soul.'

Mirëpo një ditë prej ditësh gjahtari ra e vdiq, se i shkau këmba nëpër karpa, TEK po ndiqte ca dhi të egra. 'However, one day the hunter fell and died, when his foot slipped on a rock AS he was chasing some wild goats.'

Sa vite kishin kaluar QË nuk i kish parë kështu yjet. 'How many years had passed SINCE he had [not] seen the stars like this.'

Unë e ndiqja me sy, GJERSA humbiste në kaltërsinë e qiellit. 'I used to follow it with my eyes, UNTIL it got lost in the blue sky.'

Më treguan se, NDËRSA po mundohej të hapte kapakun, e qëlloi tanku tjetër. 'They told me that, WHILE he was trying to take the top off, the other tank hit him.'

Ai ta tregon vendin ty, POSA të kthehet tashti nga ushtria. 'He will put you in your place, AS SOON AS he returns from the army.'

Mësuesja, PARA SE të fillonte nga regjistrimi, u mundua që të familjarizohej me fshatarët. 'The teacher began to familiarize herself with the villagers, BEFORE starting with the registration.'

SA HERË QË thyhet një normë ose një koncept i vjetër, do të ketë kundërshtarë. 'WHENEVER an old norm or concept is broken, there will be opponents.'

d) CAUSATIVE conjunctions: **se** 'for', **sepse** 'because', **si** 'since', **pasi (mbasi)** 'due to, owing to', **derisa** 'being that', **gjersa** 'since', **përderisa** 'since, insofar as', **kur** 'when', **që** 'in order that', **sapo** 'since', **meqënëse** 'inasmuch as', **meqë** 'since', **ngaqë** 'on account of', **ngase** 'from what', **prejse** 'from what', **duke qënë se** 'being that', **nga frika se** 'fearing that', **nga shkaku që** 'because', **për arsye se** 'because, for the reason that', **për shkak se** 'because, for the reason that' **posa që** 'considering that', **sapo që** 'being that':

Vendi dridhej, ai mbeti/SE s'tronditej nga tërmeti. 'The ground shook, he remained, FOR he did not fear the earthquake.'

Plaku eci me kujdes, SEPSE në çdo çap i dukej sikur do të pengohej në shinat. 'The old man walked carefully, BECAUSE at every step he felt as if he would stumble on the tracks.'

SI s'kishte kamzhik, i ra kafshës me grusht. 'Not having ("SINCE he did not have") a whip, he hit the animal with his fist.'

Jo, unë dashurinë time e mendoj ndryshe: PËRDERISA e dashuroj me tërë mend një vajzë, duhet ta lidh jetën me të. 'No, I conceive of my love differently: INSOFAR AS I love a particular girl without reservations, I should bind my life with hers.'

Beu e kishte hequr nga toka e tij dhe e kishte kredhur këtu në kënetë, PËR SHKAK SE, në kohën e Fan Nolit, Koz Dynjaja pati ngritur bujqërinë më këmbë. 'The bey had removed him from his land and had plunged him into this swamp, FOR THE REASON THAT during the time of Fan Noli, Koz Dynjaja had roused up the peasantry.'

I dukej sikur nuk vlente asgjë, POSA QË kish frikë të shfaqte haptazi mendimin e saj. 'He felt as if he were not worth anything, CONSIDERING THAT he was afraid to speak his mind openly.'

e) INTENTIONAL conjunctions: **që** 'so that', **me qëllim që** 'with the aim that', **në mënyrë që** 'in order that':

Ne mësojmë dhe kërkojmë të flasin masat e gjera lirisht, të kritikojnë të metat dhe njerëzit, ME QËllim QË këta të edukohen dhe të ndreqen. 'We teach and want the broad masses to speak freely, to criticize defects and individuals, IN ORDER THAT these may be educated and straightened out.'

QË të kishin qetësi dhe të mësonin shok me shok, dilnin kodrave të qytetit, ku rrinin gjersa ngrysej. 'So that they might have peace and learn together as friends, they would hike to the city's hills and stay there until dusk.'

Në vatrat tona të ndezura do t'u rrëfejmë fëmijëve për jetën e zezë, që kemi bërë, NË MËNYRË QË ata të mos harrojnë për asnjë çast se revolucioni ishte i shtrenjtë dhe se ai duhet mbrojtur me gjak. 'At our lighted hearths we shall tell the children about the bleak life we have lived, SO THAT they may not forget even for a moment that the revolution is dear and must be defended with blood.'

f) COMPARATIVE conjunctions include: **sa** 'as much as', **se** 'than', **si** 'like, as', **sesa** 'than', **po(r)si** 'like, as', **sikurse** 'as, like', **sikundërse** 'as, like', **ashtu si(ç)** 'just like, as', etc.:

Kurrë nuk e kam ndjerë veten të bashkuar me ty kaq SA sot. 'Never have I felt myself to be united with you AS MUCH AS today.'

SA më shpejt të mbarojë shirja, aq më pak humbje do të ketë. 'The sooner ("AS MUCH more soon") the threshing ends, the fewer ("so much less") the losses will be.'

Gjer atëherë kish kujtuar se do të hante me kënaqësi të madhe, po kujtimi i fëmijëve e turbulloi dhe bukën tjetër e hëngri më shumë prej turpit SE prej urisë. 'Until then, he had thought he would eat with great pleasure, but the memory of the children troubled him, and he ate the other bread more out of shame THAN out of hunger.'

Gojë më gojë, SI vetëtimë, u hap fjala dhe arriti në çdo pozicion të partizanëve: "Tirana duhet çliruar me çdo kusht!". 'From mouth to mouth, LIKE lightning the word spread, and reached every battle station of the puritisans; "Tiranë must be liberated by all means".'

E ku ka gjë më të bukur SESA të plakesh me dyfek në dorë! 'What is more beautiful THAN to grow old with rifle at hand!'

Fliste me zor, SI KUR i çelte grykën vullkanit të dëshpërimit. 'He spoke with difficulty, AS IF he were loosening up the mouth of a volcano of despair.'

Le ta thoshte troç atë që kish bërë, të pranonte gaimin e të mos kërkonte t'i bënte dredha plumbit, ASHTU SI e kishte zakon. 'Let him tell bluntly what he had done, admit his error and not seek to evade the bullet, AS was his habit.'

NOTE

Related to its use as a comparative conjunction, **si** 'as' can be used before a NP to indicate the capacity (e.g., job, relationship, duty or function) in which someone or something is being considered:

Tani ai punonte SI traktorist. 'Now he was working as a tractor driver.'

g) CONDITIONAL conjunctions: **në** 'if', **po** 'if', **nëse** 'if', **kur** 'when, if', **sikur** 'if', **në qoftë se** 'if (it be that)', **në është se** 'if (it is the case that)', **në rast se** 'in case (that)', **po qe se** 'if (it be that)', **me kushte që** 'on condition that, provided that', etc.:

NË doni të ruani veten dhe fëmijët, farkoni arma të forta. 'IF you want to defend yourselves and your children, forge powerful weapons.'

Atij që nuk të do, PO t'i japësh majëzën e thoit, të rrëmben gishtin, NË i dhënç gishtin, të merr dorën, PO i dhe dorën, të merr trupin, dhe, PO të kapi trupin, të mori edhe shpirtin. 'IF you give the tip of your fingernail to him who does not like you, he will take your finger; IF you give him the finger, he will take your hand; IF you give him the hand, he will take your body, and IF he seizes your body, he will take your soul.'

Pikërisht për ta, për lumturinë e tyre bëhet lufta. KUR të mos marrësh pjesë ti, kush të marrë? 'It is precisely for them, for their happiness that the war is being fought. If ("WHEN") you don't take part in it, who shall?'

SIKUR ta shohësh nga aeroplani, fshati do të duket si një unazë gjelbërore me një gur në mes. 'IF you see it from an airplane, the village will seem like a greenish ring, with a stone in the center.'

Haram të qoftë qumështi im, NË RAST SE armikut i tregon shpinën! 'Accursed be the milk I fed you if ("IN CASE") you turn your back on the enemy!'

PO QE SE edhe ajo të do, unë gëzohem, gëzohem shumë, që gjeti një djalë si ti. 'IF IT

BE THAT she loves you too, I'm glad, I'm very glad that she found a boy like you.'

h) RESULTATIVE conjunctions: **sa** 'so much that', **saqë** 'so much that', **(k)aq sa** 'so much that', and **kështu që** 'so that':

Takimi me shokun e tij të dashur e tronditi AQ shumë, SA iu mbushën sytë me lot. 'The meeting with his dear friend shook him up so much THAT his eyes filled with tears.'

Burri, gruaja dhe plaku ishin, siç duket, KAQ të lodhur e të këputur, SAQË nuk na vinin re fare. 'The man, the woman and the old man apparently were so tired and exhausted THAT they didn't pay any attention to us.'

Shtrëngoi pusullën, AQ SA ndjeu dhembje në gishta e në kyçet e krahut. 'He squeezed the note SO MUCH THAT he felt pain in the fingers and arm joints.'

Karrike s'kishte për të gjithë, KËSHTU QË një pjesë e spektatorëve u shtrua këmbëkryq. 'There were not enough chairs for everybody, SO THAT a portion of the spectators sat down crosslegged.'

i) CONCESSIVE conjunctions: **megjithëse** 'although', **megjithëqë** 'although, even though', **ndonëse** 'even though, although', **sado (që)** 'however much', **sido (që)** 'no matter how, however', **edhe në** 'even if', **edhe në qoftë se** 'even if', **edhe po** 'even if', **edhe pse** 'even though, despite the fact that', **edhe sepse** 'granted that', **edhe sikur** 'even if, notwithstanding':

MEGJITHËSE armiku përdor tanke, autoblinda dhe të gjitha armët që disponon, sulmi i partizanëve është i pandalshëm. 'ALTHOUGH the enemy is using tanks, armored cars and all the arms at his disposal, the offensive of the partisans is unstoppable.'

Shqipëri! O mëma ime! NDONËSE jam i mërguar,/dashurinë tënde kurrë zemëra s'e ka harruar. 'Oh, my mother Albania! EVEN THOUGH I am abroad, my heart has never lost its love for you.'

Kjo ishte një provë e madhe për organizatën, EDHE PSE aksioni nuk paraqitej shumë i vështirë. 'This was a big test for the organization, EVEN THOUGH the operation was not very difficult.

j) OPPOSITIONAL clauses corresponding to those in English introduced by *whereas* and *while* are introduced in Albanian by the conjunctions **nëse, në qoftë se** 'provided that', **ndërsa** 'whereas', **në** 'while, although', **në vend që** 'instead of'.

An oppositional dependent clause bears a similar semantic relationship to its controlling clause as a contrastive coordinate clause bears to the clause it is coordinate with. However, the two differ in position: the dependent clause precedes the opposed main clause, while the coordinate clause must follow the clause it is contrasted with.

All the oppositional conjunctions have other uses as well: **në, nëse,** and **në qoftë se** are also used as conditional subordinate conjunctions, **ndërsa** and **në vend që** as contrastive coordinate conjunctions: As coordinate conjunctions the latter two generally appear between the clauses that they join, whereas as oppositional subordinating conjunctions they often appear at the beginning of the sentence.

NËSE ju dëshironi të ikni shpejt që këtej, ne dëshironim që të mos kishit ardhur fare këtu. 'WHILE you [for your part] want to leave early, we [for our part] did not want you to come here at all.'

NË QOFTË SE në vitin 1938 jeta mesatare e njeriut në vendin tonë ishte rreth 38 vjet, sot ajo ka arritur në 69 vjet. 'While ("IF") in 1938 the average life span in our country was about 38 years, today it has reached 69 years.'

Kështu NDËRSA në mbarim të vitit 1955 kooperativat përfshinin vetëm 14,5 për qind të tokës së punueshme të fshatarësisë, pas një viti ato kishin 30,8 për qind. 'Thus, WHEREAS at the end of 1955 the cooperatives included only 14.9 percent of the arable peasant land, a year later they accounted for 30.8 percent.'

Po vajza, NË e kishte qëruar nga krandet, nuk e qetësoi dot nga "mizat" e

nëndheshme, që ia ngacmoi më keq me ato fjalë. 'But while ("IF") the girl had cleared it of brushwood, she did not pacify its underground "flies" which provoked it even worse by those words.'

Eh! bre xha Hasam, NË VEND QË të shkosh përpara, po ecën prapa. 'Hey, uncle Hasam, INSTEAD of going forward, you are walking backward.'

CHAPTER 11
Particles

11.1 Characterization of Particles

PARTICLES are invariable words that affect the meaning or affective value of the phrases in which they are used, but which do not conveniently fit into any of the traditional grammatical parts of speech.

Ja PO dalin te Zaranka. 'Look, they ARE comING out at Zarenkë.'
Ata NUK i kap dot në befasi. 'You can NOT take them by surprise.'
Po me se lave PA? 'But what EVER did you wash with?'
Shokë, SEÇ na mori malli! 'HOW nostalgic we've become, comrades!'

Unlike prepositions and conjunctions, particles do not relate the phrase syntactically to the rest of the sentence. And unlike adverbs and interjections, particles may not stand alone as lexical constituents of a sentence. Some particles are homonymous with words which may stand alone as other parts of speech. For example, the momentive particle **po** and the negative particle **jo** are homonymous with the interjections **po** 'yes' and **jo** 'no', respectively:

Po kështu, -- i tha, -- as kështu nuk të zuri? -- JO. '"Well, what about this way," he said to her, "didn't he even grab you this way?" "NO."'
-- Të jenë tanët? -- NDOSHTA. '"Might they be ours?" "PERHAPS."'

11.1.1 Position and Stress of Particles

There are two kinds of particles, depending on whether the particle occupies a fixed position in the clause or is movable.

Fixed particles must either always stand at the beginning or always at the end of the phrase they are in: (Initial) **nuk** 'not', **nja** 'or so, approximately', **desh** 'almost', **sapo** 'as soon as, just, hardly', etc.; **de** 'expression of impatience', **dot** '(cannot) at all', etc. The number of phrase-initial particles is very limited in comparison with the phrase-final ones.

Free particles such as **bile** 'indeed', **ndoshta** 'perhaps', **vallë** 'I wonder' may be used in phrase-initial, -medial, or -final position:

Kush të jetë, VALLË, ky që u gjet tani? 'Who can it be, I WONDER, this one that was found now?'
VALLË, kush do t'i marrë erë? 'I WONDER who will smell it ("take wind from it")?'
Kush do të jetë ky komisar, VALLË? 'Who can this commissar be, I WONDER?'

Particles may be stressed words or unstressed clitics. Polysyllabic particles are usually stressed: **vetëm** 'sole, just, only', **sidomos** 'especially', **ndoshta** 'perhaps', **vallë** 'I wonder', etc. Monosyllabic particles used as interjections, such as **ja** 'here, there', **jo** 'no', etc., are also stressed. Typically however, monosyllabic particles are unstressed clitics: **nja** 'approximately', **nuk** 'not', **le** 'let', **de** 'expression of impatience', etc.

Certain monosyllabic words are unstressed as particles but stressed as interjections: Compare: (unstressed **a** 'question particle')

-- A mund të qëndrojnë këtu? 'Can they stop here?'

(stressed **a** 'hunh?')

-- Alo, më jep Lizën. A? Liza je? Ka ardhur këtu një grua nga fshati. 'Hello, give me Liza. HUNH? Are you Liza? A woman from the village has come here.'

(unstressed **mos** 'negative particle')

-- Si të MOS vija! -- tha ai dhe buzëqeshi. '"How could I NOT come! he said and smiled."'

(stressed **mos** 'don't!')

-- MOS --...dhe nuk fola. U largova prej shokut pa e përshëndetur. '"DON'T"...and I did not speak. I left my friend without saying goodbye.'

Most particles composed of more than one word are unstressed: **as që** 'not even, nor', **e po** 'well', **si nja** 'about', etc. But locutions containing stressed particles have stress on that particle: **po që PO** 'definitely, for sure', **jo që JO** 'positively no', **po se PO** 'definitely', etc.

11.2 Structure and Derivation of Particles

Particles may be simple words like **bash** 'exactly', **bile** 'indeed', **ja** 'here', **jo** 'no', **nuk** 'not', **po** 'yes', **s'** 'not', **vallë** 'I wonder'; agglutinated words like **posi** 'as, as if', **siç** 'as', **thuajse (pothuajse)** 'nearly', **kushedi** 'who knows?'; or locutions like **as që** 'not even, neither', **ja që** 'well now', **pa le** 'let alone', **se mos** 'as if', **vetëm që** 'its just that', **vetëm e vetëm** 'simply because, solely', etc.

When they become particles, words converted from other parts of speech lose or weaken their original lexical meaning and lose the grammatical functions and variable forms they may have had previously. In some cases they even lose their phonological stress properties they may have had originally. Thus, the invariable jussive particle **le** (from the imperative singular form of the verb **le** 'let') has not only weakened the meaning of the full verb, but has lost the stress, syntactic functions, and other grammatical forms of the verb. Likewise, when the adverb **vetëm** 'only, just' is used as a particle, it no longer has the meaning 'alone' that it has when it is a separate constituent of a clause, and may no longer bear phrase stress in phrase final position, as the adverb can. Compare:

(Particle)

Kemi një punë të madhe për të bërë dhe këtë VETËM populli mund ta kryejë. 'We have a big job to do, and ONLY the people can do this (job).'

(Adverb)

Erdhe, more Thanas? Mirë bëre që erdhe, se edhe ne mërzitemi VETËM. 'Have you come, Thanas? You did well to come, because we are bored by ourselves ("ALONE").'

11.3 Functions of Particles

For convenience in discussion, particles can be roughly divided into four groups on the basis of their function: 1. definitive particles, 2. modal particles; 3. expressive particles; and 4. verbal particles.

11.3.1 Definitive Particles

DEFINITIVE PARTICLES further define the semantic value of the phrase. This group includes: a) The deictic particle **ja** 'here' b) delimitive particles, c) emphatic particles, and d) approximative particles.

A. The Deictic Particle **ja**

Ja 'here! there!' is used frequently and in a variety of nuances, both in colloquial and written Albanian. It serves to call attention to someone or something, usually close at hand:

JA, këtu afër është: një, dy, tre, i katërti në të djathtë. 'HERE he is close by: one, two, three, the fourth from the right.'

-- Vajzat? Ku janë? -- JA një grumbull, në të djathtë të kullës së dytë. '"The girls? Where are they?" "THERE'S a bunch, to the right of the second house.'

The particle is also used to indicate the approach or fullfullment of something that is desired or expected to happen:

JA, rashë e vdiqa, ç'do të bësh ti? 'Suppose I dropped dead ("THERE I fell and died"), what would you do?'

Kërkon përsëri të gjejë një vend tek unë, kur JA diçka e papritur. 'He tries again to find a spot over at my place, when suddenly ("THERE!") something unexpected (happens).'

The particle **ja** is often used to start a story or tale, or when something unexpected happens to the speaker:

JA si i tregonte vetë disa ngjarje të vegjëlisë së tij. 'WELL NOW, HERE'S how he himself used to tell some stories about his childhood.'

JA si ndodhi puna. 'WELL HERE'S how the thing happened.'

NOTE

The particle **qe** is synonymous with the particle **ja**; its use is limited mainly to Gheg speakers:

Kuptoj, shoku Agim, kuptoj. Do të punojmë, si kurrë. QE dorën. 'I understand, comrade Agim, I understand. We shall work as never before. HERE'S my hand (on it).'

B. Delimitive Particles

DELIMITIVE PARTICLES delimit the semantic scope of the phrase to which they belong. The particle **mu** 'just, right, exactly' is usually used before words or word sequences that serve as locative, modal or comparative modifiers:

Kur ike ti, yt atë plak, të puthi MU në ballë. 'When you left, your old father kissed you RIGHT on the forehead.'

Por sa e bukur je lëndinë, / Kur vesa zë shkëlqen mbi bar, / Kur rrezet derdhen MU si ar. 'But what a lovely meadow you are, / When the dew glistens on the grass, / When the sunbeams pour just like gold.'

The particles **plot** 'fully' and **rrumbullak** 'roundly, in full measure' accompany integers:

Kanë kaluar PLOT dy orë që nga koha kur erdha. 'FULLY two hours have passed since I came.'

Dhe vërtet, Petrushi kishte mundur në përleshje RRUMBULLAK tre. 'And in fact, Petrushi had defeated FULLY three (of them) in fights.'

The particles **pikërisht** 'precisely', **tamam** 'exactly', **bash** 'exactly, smack' are usually initial in a phrase serving as subject or object, or as a locative, comparative or temporal modifier:

Dhe PIKËRISHT kjo shoqe e ndihmoi vajzën përfundimisht. 'And PRECISELY this comrade helped the girl decisively.'

PIKËRISHT gjatë koncertit shoqja Gjeraqinë -- sqaroi Muhameti. '"RIGHT during the concert, comrade Gjeraqinë," explained Muhamet.'

Po BASH në këtë Tiranë jetonte ai popull, që shkroi një kapitull të tërë në historinë tonë të lavdishme. 'But RIGHT in this Tiranë lived that people which wrote an entire chapter in our glorious history.'

The particle **pikërisht** is especially common with pronouns and adverbs:

Ku PIKËRISHT? 'PRECISELY where?'
Kush PIKËRISHT? 'PRECISELY who?'
Çfarë (cilin) PIKËRISHT? 'PRECISELY what (which)?'

The class of delimitive particles also includes the particles **po porsa, sa, sapo, që, qysh, deri** or **(gjer)**, which narrow the scope considered in the action or process of the verb that follows in the phrase.

The momentive particle **po** is placed before verbs in the present or imperfect tense of the indicative or admirative mood in order to express actions going on at a particular moment (see Sections 2.3.1 A and B.1).

Shkrep në shkrep Dajtit bujar PO na vjen një gjeraqinë. 'From rock to rock on noble Mount Dajti a hawk IS comING to us.'
PO mbusheshin dy vjet që Sokoli s'kish bërë një rrugë kaq të largët. 'It was going on two years ("two years WERE fillING up") that Sokol had not taken such a long trip.'
Po kush turmenë PO e çaka? 'But who IS splitING up the mob?'

The particles **porsa** (or **posa**), **sa, sapo**, all of which can be translated as English *'just'* are usually placed before verbs, in one of the indicative mood past tenses (except the imperfect), to indicate that the action of the verb was completed slightly before the moment of reference:

Dukej sikur PORSA kishte dalë nga lumi. 'He looked as if he had JUST emerged from the river.'
Xhoda SA u kthye. 'Xhoda JUST returned.'
Partia SAPO qe krijuar, po çetat e saj shpartallonin batalione me milicë. 'The Party had JUST been created, but its guerrilla units were smashing battalions of irregulars.'

The particles **që, qysh, deri**, and **gjer** are placed before temporal or locative adverbial phrases. The particles **që** and **qysh**, pinpoint the beginning of an action in time or space, like English *(right) from* or *since*, whereas the particles **deri** and **gjer** serve to pinpoint the time or place where the action of the verb terminates, like English *(right) up to, until, till*:

Këtë Partia jonë e kishte të qartë QYSH në fillim, prandaj në këtë çështje veproi drejt. 'This Party of ours was clear about it RIGHT FROM the start, that is why it acted correctly in this matter.'
Thellë nga shpirti, QË nga fundi, / më pushton një mall i lehtë. 'From deep in my soul, FROM the VERY bottom / a light longing seizes me.'
Atëherë i ungji, sa mbajti udha QË nga Fieri GJER në Trokth, rrëfeu fije e për pe të ngjarat. 'Then his uncle related in detail all the happenings, for the duration of the journey ALL THE WAY FROM Fier TO Trokth.'
Dhe ashtu, për krah ushtarëve, QË nga 10 qershori e DERI më 20 korrik, të dy oficerët, morën pjesë në shërbimet kulturore që iu bënë bimëve. 'And so, alongside the soldiers, THE WHOLE TIME FROM June 10 UNTIL July 20, both officers took part in plant cultivation work.'

Before the articulated indefinite determiners **gjithë** 'all' and **tërë** 'entire', or collective numbers (those preceded by the preposed article **të**), the particle **që** is also used to emphasize the sense of an exhaustive, definite totality:

U puthëm buzë më buzë QË të tre. 'ALL three of us kissed one another on the mouth.'
Masat janë marrë QË të gjitha. 'All the measures have been taken.'
Të quheni vërtet bijtë e Skënderbeut, QË TË TËRË. 'You ought truly to be called the sons of Skënderbeu, ALL (OF YOU).'

C. The Emphatic Particles

EMPHATIC PARTICLES serve to emphasize a phrase. This class includes the particles **vetëm** 'only, solely', **veç** 'except', **veçse** 'except, but', **sidomos** 'especially', **veçanërisht** 'specially', **edhe** or **dhe** 'even', **madje** 'furthermore, in fact, moreover', **bile** 'indeed', and others. According to the type of emphasis they give, emphatic particles may be divided into separative and augmentative particles.

C.1 Separative Particles

SEPARATIVE PARTICLES include **vetëm, veç, veçse, sidomos, veçanërisht**, etc. These particles get their emphatic effect by stressing differences:

Armikut nuk i zihet besë, nuk i zihet besë imperializmit, VEÇANËRISHT imperializmit amerikan. 'The enemy cannot be trusted, imperialism cannot be trusted, ESPECIALLY American imperialism.'

VETËM ca njerëz kishte parë. 'He had seen ONLY a few people.'

Mbi ty tek-tuk VEÇ ndonjë varr / si kaktus i çuditshëm i kohës sonë / ka mbirë. 'Here and there over you ONLY a grave / like a strange cactus of our time / has taken root.'

Nuk kishin kaluar VEÇSE pak ditë që ishte ndarë nga ai dhe nuk pandehte kurrë ta takonte kaq shpejt. 'There had passed ONLY a few days since he had separated from him, and never imagined he would meet him again this soon.'

Dhe vërtet shumë fshatarë, SIDOMOS pleq, e quajtën të domosdoshme të venin dhe ata. 'And truly many villagers, ESPECIALLY old men, considered it essential that they go too.'

When repeated, the particle **vetëm** 'just, simply, only, solely' is even more emphatic. Single or double, it is often followed by the conjunction **që** or **se** to form a locutionary particle:

Përmbys dheun VETËM E VETËM që t'ia shkulë fjalën nga goja. 'He raises hell ("overturns the world") JUST so he can get the word(s) out of his mouth.'

Ai VETËM QË është i sëmurë, sepse vullneti nuk i mungon. 'It's SIMPLY that he is sick, because he does not lack the will.'

Included as an emphatic particle is **sa** 'so much', when followed by the preposition phrases introduced by **për** 'for':

SA për ditë kemi mjaft. 'AS for days, we have enough.'

SA për mua mos u shqetësoni, kush e nis vallen, di ta dredhë vetë! 'AS for me, do not concern yourselves; he who begins the dance knows how to twist it himself.'

Kaq SA për sonte. Po vete ora dy. 'So MUCH FOR tonight. It's going on two o'clock.'

This particle is also used with verbs, especially before non-finite forms of the type **për të punuar** 'to work', in a benefactive, modifying or predicative function. In this construction it is often preceded by the particle **vetëm**:

I duhej dhënë fund prodhimit SA PËR TË PRODHUAR, me qëllim që të realizohet vëllimi global. 'It was necessary to put an end to production JUST FOR THE SAKE OF PRODUCTION, in order to achieve the required overall volume.'

Në heshtjen që ra pas fjalës së agronomit, ajo u kollit pak, SA PËR TË DHËNË të kuptohej se ish aty. 'In the silence that fell after the agronomist's speech, she coughed a bit, JUST TO LET it be known that she was there.'

Nuk ka asnjë kuptim të mësuarit e teorisë marksiste-leministe, në bangot e shkollës ose jashtë shkollës, VETËM SA PËR TË SHKUAR radhën. 'There is no sense at all in learning Marxist-Leninist theory, at school desks or outside of school, MERELY TO go through the paces ("TO PASS the line").'

C.2 Augmentative Particles

The AUGMENTATIVE PARTICLES are **dhe** or **edhe** 'even', **bile** 'in fact, indeed, even', and **madje** 'furthermore, in fact, moreover', which get their emphatic effect by stressing an augmentation:

Kur s'patën plumba, shtinë DHE me gurë! 'When they lacked bullets, they attacked EVEN with stones!'

EDHE këtu nuk hoqi dorë nga dasmat ky? 'EVEN here this guy did not give up weddings?'

MADJE, ai qysh tashti na e ka nevojën. 'WHAT'S MORE, he has need of us even now.'

Ta merr mendja që ke ndryshuar, shumë BILE. 'Of course you have changed a lot, IN FACT.'

BILE, fanatizmi është trashëgim nga e kaluara. 'TO BE SURE, fanaticism is a legacy of the past.'

The particle **bile** can be repeated for additional emphasis:

BILE-BILE, do të jetë mirë, që të zotohemi të qëndrojmë përgjithnjë në fshat. 'YES INDEED, we would do well to pledge to remain in the countryside all the time.'

The class of augmentative reinforcing particles also includes the particle **as** 'not even, neither', which may be used before any part of speech:

Atëhere AS ti nuk do të shkosh. 'Then you NEITHER will go.'

Po ti AS duhanin s'ke kohë të na dredhësh. 'But you don't have time even to roll a cigarette ("to roll EVEN tobacco").'

D. Approximative Particles

Included as APPROXIMATIVE PARTICLES are **afro** 'nearly, about', **aty-aty** 'thereabout', **nja** 'or so, approximately', **si nja** 'in the vicinity of, something around', **gati** 'almost, practically', **rreth** 'around', **thuajse (pothuajse)** 'practically, so to speak', **desh** 'nearly, almost', **mend** 'almost', which are used initially in a phrase to convey approximation.

The particles **afro, aty-aty, nja, si nja, gati, rreth, thuajse (pothuajse)** are used before numbers:

Para Çlirimit në vendin tonë numëroheshin RRETH 380 kuadro me arsim të lartë, RRETH 1600 mësues dhe një numër shumë i kufizuar teknikësh të mesëm etj. 'Before the Liberation there were AROUND 308 cadres with advanced education, AROUND 1,600 teachers and a very limited number of middle-rank technicians, etc.'

Ndenji aty AFRO një orë. 'He remained there NEARLY an hour.'

Dhe m'u kujtua një natë e tillë GATI tre vjet të shkuar. 'And I recalled such a night ALMOST three years ago.'

NJA njëzet kokë dele, që i kishin shpëtuar përmbytjes, blegërinin e kërkonin shoqet majë pullazit. 'ABOUT twenty head of sheep that had survived the flood were bleating and looking for their friends on top of the roof.'

Një plak SI NJA gjashtëdhjetë vjeç, nuk i kishte hequr akoma dhentë nga fshati. 'An old man ABOUT sixty years old, had not yet withdrawn his sheep from the vllage.'

Që prej asaj nate që kish arritur aty, kishin kaluar THUAJSE dy muaj. 'PRACTICALLY two months had gone by since the night he had arrived there.'

The particles **thuajse** (or **pothuajse**) and **gati** are used before other words besides numbers:

Rruga nuk dukej POTHUAJSE fare. 'The road was PRACTICALY invisible.'

GATI të gjithëve ju pashë në shfaqjen e fundit. 'I saw NEARLY all of you at the last performance.'

Kur u afrua, nga fytyra m'u duk GATI fëmijë. 'When he drew near, he seemed to me, because of his face, ALMOST a child.'

The particle **gati** can be repeated to emphasize the closeness of the approximation:

GATI-GATI nuk mbaj mend fare. 'I remember ALMOST nothing at all.'

Asgjë s'do ta kishte nevrikosur Ilirin më tepër se kjo fjalë e lëshuar GATI-GATI kot. 'Nothing could have upset Ilir more than this word that was dropped ALMOST for no reason AT ALL.'

The particles **desh** and **mend** are used only before action verbs in the past definite with the meaning 'barely missed doing something', indicating an action that was not actually carried out, but which was almost carried out:

Lena DESH u ngrit, po e mbajti veten. 'Lena ALMOST stood up, but restrained herself.'

Kaloi më tutje pa u ndalur e DESH u pengua te një hu, që e kishte ngulur mu pranë kosheres. 'He went further without stopping, and JUST MISSED tripping over a post that he had driven right by the beehive.'

MEND e morën djalin në qafë. 'They BARELY MISSED ruining the boy ("took the boy in the neck").'

The particle **sa** is also used with the meaning of the approximative particles **desh** and **mend**, when placed before negative verbs in the indicative mood (those preceded by a negative particle **s'** or **nuk** 'not'). In such cases the particle **gati** may precede the particle **sa**:

Kur mbeti vetëm, ai SA s'fluturoi nga gëzimi. 'When he was alone, he PRACTICALLY flew off with joy.'

Tefiku SA nuk kish shkalluar nga mendtë. 'Tefik NEARLY went crazy.'

Në rrugën e vogël ai pa shokun, që GATI SA nuk vraponte. 'In the little street he saw his comrade, who was PRACTICALLY running.'

Aha, pasnesër është festa e tyre kombëtare, GATI SA s'më doli nga mendja. 'Aha, the day after tomorrow is their national festival; I almost forgot ("it ALMOST went out of my mind").'

11.3.2 Modal Particles

MODAL PARTICLES serve to express the attitude of the speaker toward the truth value of an event or the manifestation of an objective reality. This class includes particles that are: a) affirmative, b) negative, c) interrogative, d) dubitative, and e) softening.

A. Affirmative Particles

AFFIRMATIVE PARTICLES include: **po** 'yes' and **posi** 'certainly', as well as **po që po** 'definitely yes', **po se po** 'definitely yes', etc. All of these may also be used as independent interjections.

The particle **po** has broad use, and appears with many semantic nuances. It serves to affirm or approve an idea, or permit an action:

-- Me gjithë mend e ke? -- PO. '"Are you serious?" ("Do you have it with all mind?") "YES."'

-- Mos të thanë gjë? -- pyeti një nga shokët. -- PO, më thanë -- ia priti Qemali buzagaz, duke hyrë brenda në vendin e mbledhjes. '"Did they tell you anything?" one of the comrades asked. "YES, they did," replied Qemal, smiling, as he went in to the meeting place.'

The particle **po** is used as well when the speaker unexpectedly remembers something he has forgotten:

Tjetri, ah, PO, tjetri është gjeolog. 'The other, ah, YES, the other is a geologist.'

To reinforce the affirmation, the particle **po** is repeated or replaced or accompanied by reinforcing words like **sigurisht** 'certainly', **natyrisht** 'naturally', etc.:

-- Repart me dy veta? -- thoshte me duf tjetri. -- Lërmë, aman! -- PO, PO, bile shumë i rëndësishëm. '"A unit of two people?" the other was saying angrily. "Please don't bother me!" "YES, YES, indeed a very important one."'

Affirmation may also be strengthened by the particle **posi** and the locutions **po e po, po që po**, or **po se po**. These are used especially when the speaker affirms something that is doubted:

-- SIGURISHT! -- iu përgjigj Çuçi. -- Po ju? '"CERTAINLY!" Çuçi replied to him. "What about you?"'

-- Ne PO E PO. Ju çfarë vendi zutë? '"We DEFINITELY YES. What sort of a place did you get?"'

Djemtë PO SE PO, por edhe shumica e pleqve vendosën të mos punonin asnjë ditë angari për beun. 'The boys DEFINITELY YES, but even the majority of the old men decided not to put in a single day of obligatory work for the bey.'

NOTE

The locution **si urdhëron** (plural **si urdhëroni**) 'as you command' is used to express the full approval of the speaker, his readiness to accept what is expressed:

-- Ti e ke bërë këtë? -- SI URDHËRON. '"Did you do this?" "YES."'

SI URDHËRONI! -- ia nise ti me gjakftohtësinë më të madhe. '"AS YOU WISH!" you began with the greatest self-composure.'

In some cases--depending on the context--all affirmative particles, and in particular the particles **po, posi** interweave their affirmative meaning with some affective nuance (disbelief, surprise, irony, scorn, etc.)

Nga që nuk dinte ç'të bënte tjetër, shfrynte. -- POOOO...POOOO...do t'i mburret nuses ai! 'Since he didn't know what else to do, he snorted. "Oh yes ("YESSS... YESSS..."), he's going to boast to the bride!"'

Që ta merrje nuse për mua? POSI! Ti të gjitha vajzat e Korçës kërkon t'i marrësh nuse për mua. 'To take her as my bride? Oh sure ("CERTAINLY")! You want every girl in Korçë to be my bride.'

NOTE

Colloquial affirmative particles like **e** 'yeah', **ëhë** 'unh-hunh', etc. are commonly used in speech:

-- Nesër thuaj! -- E, nesër! -- bëri me dorë Arifi. '"Say tomorrow!" "Okay, tomorrow!" Arif gestured with his hand.'

-- Të pëlqen? -- ËHË. '"Do you like it?" "Unh-hunh."'

B. Negative Particles

NEGATIVE PARTICLES include **jo, nuk, s', mos, jo që jo, jo se jo, as që, dot**.

The particle **jo** 'no' serves as a negative reply to a question, statement, or request:

-- A i ke thënë njeriu se do të vije këtu? -- JO. Nuk i kam thënë njeriu. '"Have you told anyone that you were coming here?" "NO, I have not told anyone."'

Cilin do të thërresë në mes të natës në raport Tursun pashai? Mos vallë Kurdishxhiun, apo plakun Tavzha, apo komandantët e tjerë? JO. Do të thërresë këtë kokë. 'Whom will Tursun Pasha ask to report in the middle of the night? Kurdishxhi, perhaps, or old man Tavzhë, or other commanders? NO. He will ask for me ("this head").'

Often the particle **jo** is used in place of a verb with a negative particle, or in place of a whole negative VP:

> **Burokratët kanë frikë nga masat, revolucionarët JO.** 'Bureaucrats are afraid of the masses; revolutionaries (are) NOT.'
>
> **Prindërit tuaj jemi, apo JO?** 'We're your parents, aren't we? ("your parents we are, or NOT?")'

The negative particles **nuk** 'not' and **s'** 'not', which are synonymous in meaning and interchangeable in use, serve to negate totally what is expressed by the verb, giving the entire clause negative force. Either may appear before any finite verb form in the indicative conditional and admirative mood:

> **-- NUK lejoj, -- ia priti i xhindosur.** '"I will (do) NOT allow (it)," he shot back in rage.'
>
> **Historiani frëng ka thënë me të drejtë: "Sikur të kishin luftuar mbretërit e Bizantit si Skënderbeu, Stambolli NUK do të kishte rënë në duar të turqve."'** 'The French historian has rightly said: "Had the kings of Byzantium fought like Skënderbeu, Istanbul would NOT have fallen into the hands of the Turks."'
>
> **Ore po të thonë që po vinë, ti S'marrke vesh! -- ia priti plaku që rrinte para Elit.** '"Look, I am ("they are") telling you they are coming, but you just DON'T listen!" retorted the old man who stood in front of Eli.'

The negative particle **mos** 'don't, not' is used with finite verb forms in the subjunctive, optative, and imperative moods, and with non-finite verb forms in gerundive and infinitive constructions. In subjunctive and infinitive forms it follows the particle **të**, and in gerundive forms it follows the particle **duke**:

> **MOS u bëni merak, kapiten DANI.** 'Don't worry, Captain Dan.'
>
> **Atëherë do të luftonte dhe nuk do të pushonte gjersa të MOS kishte më armiq.** 'Then he would fight and would not stop until there wouldn't be ("until to NOT have") any more enemies.'
>
> **Ç'nuk kishim bërë për të MOS e marrë, po ku dëgjonte ai.** 'What didn't we do in order NOT to take him (along), but he wouldn't listen.'
>
> **'Ata i dëndësuan në mënyrë të pabesueshme sulmet e tyre, duke MOS marrë parasysh asgjë.** 'They intensified their assaults in an incredible manner, NOT taking anything into consideration.'

This particle can also be used by itself as an interjection taking the place of a whole negative clause. In that case, its negative meaning is intermixed with an emphatic affective value, especially sorrow: **-- Është vrarë Kajoja! -- MOS!** '"Kajo has been slain!" "OH NO!"'

To strengthen the negation, the negative particles **jo** and **mos** can be repeated. In such cases, the negative takes on an affective nuance, such as surprise or sorrow. The particles **nuk**, **s'**, and **jo** can be reinforced by certain adverbs or made more precise by complementary negative words: **kurrë** 'never', **as** 'not even', **dot** 'not at all', **para** 'hardly', and all words with the negative prefix **as-** (**asnjë** 'no one, not a', **asgjë** 'nothing' etc.):

> **JO! JO! Më mirë t'ua them, se sa të më turpërosh.** 'NO NO! It's better that I tell them about it than that you should disgrace me.'
>
> **MOS, MOS! Unë tokën si njerkë KURRË S'e kam parë, po e kam parë si nënë.** 'NO DON'T! I have NEVER [NOT] considered the land a stepmother, but rather a mother.'
>
> **Afrohuni, shokë, pa frikë dhe kini për të parë se ASGJË NUK do të ndodhë.** 'Come closer, comrades, without fear, and you will see that NOTHING will [NOT] happen to you.'
>
> **A do ta lëmë të vazhdojë në këtë rrugë? SIGURISHT JO.** 'Are we going to let him continue on this path? CERTAINLY NOT.'

Locutionary particles like **jo që jo** 'definitely not', **jo se jo** 'definitely no', **as që** 'nor' are used especially when the speaker denies something over which some doubt has been cast:

Unë JO QË JO, por edhe babai im s'ka vënë dorë kurrë në ta. 'CERTAINLY NOT I, but even my father has never laid hands on them.'

Kjo nuk është një punë e thjeshtë, shokë, dhe AS QË mund të kryhet nga një ose dy persona. 'This is not a simple job, comrades, NOR can it be done by one or two persons.'

While two negative particles in a single clause reinforce the negation, a negative subordinate clause may logically cancel out a negation in its controlling clause, theoretically yielding a logically positive sentence:

S'është e mundur që tërë ky rreth të MOS ketë qoftë edhe një talent të vetëm! 'It's not possible that this entire district should NOT have even one solitary talent! (=This district must have at least one talented person.)'

Të MOS mendojmë se NUK kemi të meta dhe gabime. 'Let us NOT think that we do NOT have any faults of deficiencies. (=Let's admit our mistakes.)'

The particle **jo** is sometimes used before the preposition **pa** 'without'. In such cases, too, the clause as a whole is logically equivalent to a positive:

Pas këtyre fjalëve, që i shqiptoi JO pa dhimbje, ai heshti, bëri një pauzë të gjatë. 'After these words, which he pronounced NOT without pain (=with pain), he became silent and made a long pause.'

In interrogative clauses, negative particles have an affirmative, often affective value:

NUK dalim pakëz në ballkon, se m'u mërzit kjo dhomë e murrme. 'Why DON'T we step out ("Do we NOT go out?") on the balcony for a while; I'm tired of this grey room.'

Kush NUK e kujton çastin e lumtur, kur u nisëm për herë të parë në hekurudhë. 'Who does NOT recall the happy moment when we first set out for the railroad.'

-- Si JO -- u përgjegj. Në mënyrë shkencore, bile. '"Certainly ("how NOT?")," he answered. Indeed, in a scientific manner.'

Pse të MOS vija?! 'Why wouldN'T I come?!'

The particle **dot** expresses impossibility, rendered in English often as '(not) at all'. In interrogative or conditional clauses with overt or implied negatives it often corresponds to English *can't* or *couldn't*:

Po këtë ç'e keni? Nuk e shitët DOT? 'But what is this you have? COULDN'T you sell it?'

Vasalët tanë nuk dalin DOT nga kështjellat e tyre -- vazhdoi kryeveqilharxhi. '"Our vassals can't leave their castles AT ALL," continued the chief deputy.'

C. Interrogative Particles

INTERROGATIVE PARTICLES include: **a**, **ë**, **e**, and **apo**. The interrogative sense of these particles is usually mingled with other semantic nuances, espcially affective ones.

The interrogative particle **a** introduces an interrogative phrase asking for a choice between alternatives; if there is only one such clause, the implied choice is between the alternative suggested by the interrogative phrase and its opposite. That is, the choice is essentially between *yes* and *no*:

A s'jemi edhe ne të gëzuar? 'Are we not happy, too?'

A mos më ke kërkuar në shtëpi? 'Have you looked for me at home?'

If the other alternatives are included in the sentence they are introduced by the particle **apo**. In some ways, then, **a...apo** correspond to English *whether...or*.

The interrogative particles **a** and **ë** are used as interjections at the end of a sentence to ask for confirmation. Such sentences sometimes have affective nuances such as *scorn, irony, or rebuke*:

Kështu janë burrat, A? 'Men are like this, are they?'

Po si thua ti, këput fiq dhe ha, Ë? 'What do you think, [as easy as] picking off figs and eating them, HUH?'

These particles also are often used by themselves as interjections to ask for the repetition of something that the speaker failed to hear:

-- A? -- ia bëri portieri, që iu bë se ajo diçka pështpëriti. -- Fol më fort, se më kanë lënë veshët. '"WHAT'S THAT?" went the gate keeper, who thought that she had whispered something. "Speak louder, because I'm deaf ("the ears have left me").'

-- Kot pyes. Më tërhoqi vëmendjen fizionomia e tij -- tha Memoja. -- E? -- Fizionomia! '"I'm just asking. His physiognomy attracted my attention," said Memo. "HOW'S THAT?" "His physiognomy!"'

The interrogative particle **e** is widely used as an interrogative interjection:

-- E? -- pyeti përsëri ai me padurim. -- Vajte? '"WELL?" he asked again impatiently. "Did you go?"'

-- E? -- pyeti Memua. '"WHAT?" asked Memo.'

D. Dubitative Particles

DUBITATIVE PARTICLES, including **ndoshta** 'maybe', **mbase** 'perhaps', **kushedi** 'who knows', **sikur** 'it's as though', **vallë** 'I wonder' are used to express attitudes like doubt, distrust, or uncertainty. The particles **vallë** and **gjë** are used only in interrogative clauses, whereas the three synonymous particles **ndoshta, mbase, kushedi** and the particle **sikur** are used in non-interrogative clauses as well:

-- Përse më thirrën VALLË? -- mendonte Malaj, -- apo përsëri për atë punën e vjetme? 'Why did they call me, I wonder," Malaj was thinking, "is it about that business of last year, again?"'

Shiko mirë se NDOSHTA e gjen. 'Look well and MAYBE you will find it.'

MBASE unë ekzaltohem, MBASE unë e teproj, por para këtyre njerëzve mahnitem. 'PERHAPS I get carried away, PERHAPS I overdo it, but I am awe-struck in the presence of these people.'

KUSHEDI mendoi, -- mund të ketë gjetur ndonjë tjetër. '"Maybe ("WHO KNOWS")" he thought, "she may have found someone else."'

Ty SIKUR të shoh pak si të çuditur. 'You seem to me ("IT IS AS IF I see you") slightly surprised.'

The dubitive particles **ndoshta, mbase, kushedi** can be used as interjections by themselves:

-- U ndeshët me Skënderbeun? -- pyeti jeniçeri. NDOSHTA. '"Did you clash with Skënderbeu?" asked the Janissary. "PERHAPS."'

Mos janë vëllezër? -- KUSHEDI. -- S'e mbaj mend. E mbaj unë. -- MBASE. '"Aren't they brothers?" "Maybe ("who knows")." "I don't remember." "I do." "MAYBE."'

The particle **mos** can introduce an interrogative clause as a negative dubitative particle to ask for confirmation, much as tag questions are used in English:

MOS do të thuash që i fsheh unë? ngriti zërin Lulzimja. '"You DON'T mean that I hide them, DO YOU?" Lulzimja raised her voice.'

MOS është e fortë? 'She isN'T strong, IS SHE.'

The particle **mos** is also used with another dubitative particle **ndoshta, vallë, kushedi, gjë** to emphasize the uncertainty:

Të pritni se MOS KUSHEDI gjendet ndonjë peshk budalla. 'Wait, because WHO KNOWS MAYBE there's a stupid fish around.'

MOS VALLË ia rrëmbeu zemrën Skënderi? 'I WONDER if MAYBE Skënder stole her heart?'

Kishte frikë se MOS qe GJË sëmurë, por më tepër e hante meraku se MOS i kishte ndodhur ndonjë e papritur. 'He feared that MAYBE he was POSSIBLY ill, but he was even more worried that something unexpected had PERHAPS happened to him.'

The locutionary particle **se mos** 'as though, as if' is used in afterthoughts to express doubt, together with affective nuances, especially scorn:

-- Shiko, shiko. Na marrshin të keqen! SE MOS ne i pëlqyem. 'Look, look. The plague take them! ("may they take the evil"; i.e. the evil that would befall us) AS THOUGH we liked them.'

Ai kështu e ka. SE MOS nuk e njeh. 'That's how he is ("this way he has it"). AS THOUGH you don't know him.'

E. Softening Particles

SOTENING PARTICLES serve to soften or lessen the effect of the phrase to which they apply. This class includes the particles **pa, as, le, para, dot**, etc.

The particles **pa** and **as** are used before verbs in the imperative mood to soften the command into a wish or suggestion. In English the same effect is created by putting the request into question form:

Zemër, PA më thuaj, emrin si e kanë, / se për kokën tënde seç po vij vërdallë! 'Sweetheart, WOULD YOU tell me, what are they called, / because I swear I am going around in circles.'

PA shih dhe ti një herë, Agim. ' WOULD YOU just take a look, Agim.'

AS na këndo, ti o vashë, një këngë me zë të trashë. 'WOULD YOU sing us, oh maiden, a song in a thick voice.'

The particle **le** 'let' is used before verbs in the third person singular or plural, and in the first person plural, of the present tense of the subjunctive mood to create a jussive mood, a kind of softened imperative. Followed by verbs in other tenses of the subjunctive mood, for any person or number, it also expresses a kind of permissiveness on the part of the speaker:

Le të shkojnë dhe fëmijët e tu, se kjo rrugë për ta po ndërtohet. 'LET your children go too, for it is for them that this road is being built.'

Më mirë LE të kalbesha unë në burg sesa të burgosej gjithë Shqipëria. 'It were better that I rotted ("better LET me have rotted") in prison than that all of Albania be imprisoned.'

Dhe ç'ti gjente, LE t'i gjente me shokët bashkë. 'And whatever their fate, they SHOULD have shared it with their comrades. ("And whatever found them LET it have found them together with their comrades.")'

The particle **para** is used only after the negative particles **nuk** 'not' and **s'** 'not' to soften the negation. In English such softening is expressed by 'hardly', 'barely', 'not (so) much', etc.:

Dhoma S'PARA ishte e madhe. 'The room was NOT SO VERY big.'

NUK PARA del në fshat. 'He does NOT go out MUCH in the village.'

11.3.3 Expressive Particles

EXPRESSIVE PARTICLES serve to emphasize the affective side of speech and to augment its expressive force. This class includes the particles **ç', de, pa, pra, se, seç**.

The particles **ç'** and **seç** are similar in meaning and use; they usually appear at the beginning of an indicative verb phrase or at the beginning of a series, to convey the immediacy of the action to the speaker:

Brenda në Tiranë, / mu afër spitalit, / Ç'u vra Qemal Stafa, / një trim nga të malit.
'Inside Tiranë, / right near the hospital, / Qemal Stafë was JUST killed / a tremendously brave ("from the mountain") man.'
Një ujk i uritur SEÇ na la folenë. 'A hungry wolf NOW ("for us") leaves his lair.'

The particles **de** and **pra** are also similar in meaning and use, they serve to express the speaker's impatience, in the way that a mild impersonal curse emphasizes the meaning or that afterthoughts like 'after all' make comments in English. They are often used in the proximity of other particles, particularly **ja, jo,** and **po**:

Ruaj zërin DE, se do ngjiresh prapë dhe na mori lumi! 'Take care of your voice DARN IT, or you will get hoarse and then we're sunk ("the river took us").'
Merre PRA! 'SO take it!'
-- **Ja PRA, këto direktiva nuk i dinë këta tanët, prandaj bien në gabime, -- tha Petro Paskali.** '"Well NOW, these (men of) ours do not know these directives, so they fall into error," said Petro Paskal.'

The particles **pa** and **se** are synonymous in interrogative clauses. They are normally used at the end of an interrogative clause as afterthoughts, much like English *actually, really, anyway.*

-- **E si e mori vesh PA?** 'And how did he find out, ACTUALLY?'
Dhe përse PA, për një lëkurë ujku. 'And for what I ask you ("ACTUALLY"), for a wolf's hide.'
-- **Sa hije të paska SE?! -- tha halla. Mirëpo, kush e besonte SE?** '"How well it REALLY fits you ("how much shade it actually has for you")?!" said the aunt. But who believed her, ANYWAY.?'

Locutionary particles like **e po** 'well', **ja që** 'it's just that', **le që** 'conceding that', **pa le** 'no less!' have a variety of affective uses, hinted at but not defined by their English glosses here.

-- **E PO, të na trashëgohen, o Ramiz!** 'WELL, best wishes to the newlyweds ("may they have heirs for us") Ramiz.'
-- **E mirë është, po JA QË ajo fiket.** 'It is good, but IT's JUST THAT it dies out.'
Gjersa të mbarojë kjo punë...LE QË s'ka për të mbaruar dot shpejt. 'Until this job is finished...THOUGH it is not going to get finished soon at all.'
Edhe roje, PA LE! Ç'të duhej roja ty, bre Bim! 'guard duty, NO LESS! What do you need guard duty for, Bim!'

11.3.4 Verbal Particles

Some linguists include as particles a group of formatives derived from various parts of speech, which have lost their original lexical and grammatical characteristics and their independence as words, and have long ago changed into markers of certain grammatical forms of verbs. These VERBAL PARTICLES are: **u, do, të, me, për, pa,** and **duke**.

The particle **u** serves to mark a large number of the verb forms in the reflexive, middle, and passive voices: **U lava** 'I washed myself', **lahU** 'wash yourself', etc.

The particle **do** serves to mark future tense and conditional mood verb forms: **DO të lexoj** 'I will read', **DO të punoja** 'I would have worked', etc.

The particle **të** serves to mark verbs in the subjunctive and subjunctive-admirative mood: **TË jem** 'that I be', **TË paskësha** 'may I have' etc.;

The particles **pa** and **duke** plus the participle, form the privative (**PA punuar** 'without working') and gerundive (**DUKE punuar** 'by working, while working') verb forms.

The particles **për** and **me** plus the particle **të** and the participle form infinitives like **ME të shkuar** 'upon going' and **PËR të shkuar** 'to go, for going'. The particle **me** plus the Gheg form of the participle forms infinitives used by Gheg speakers, of the type **ME shkue** 'to go'.

CHAPTER 12

Interjections and Interjectional Phrases

12.1 Interjectional Phrases

An INTERJECTIONAL phrase (abbreviated IjP) is a word or sequence of words that is syntactically independent of other phrases; it serves to express the speaker's attitude towards the audience or towards the rest of the sentence or discourse in which it is embedded. Vocative expressions, parenthetical comments, and interjections are the most common types of interjectional phrases, but any full word or phrase may be used interjectionally, for example, to express emotions like surprise, anger, or sorrow, to announce a topic, or to express agreement or disagreement.

The interjection is an invariable part of speech that serves to express rather than refer to, the feelings, desires, and will of the speaker.

Spoken Albanian is characterized by a wealth of interjections whose meaning is often clarified by the particular intonations, facial expressions and gestures which accompany them. In speech, the intonations suffice to give us the value of an "ah!" or an "oh"; in the written language, interjections are interpretable only by taking the context into account. Contextual interpretation of interjections is not always certain, especially when they stand in isolation. That is why, for example, in the text of a play written for the stage, the author often finds it necessary to make more exact, by means of text enclosed in parentheses, the value he wishes to give to a vocative and its corresponding facial expression:

Gëzimi -- Njëri nga ata më tha: -- S'e kafshon dot këtë mollë se je plak e të mbeten dhëmbët.
Pullumbi -- (me habi) -- A!
'Gëzim: One of them told me, "You can't bite this apple, because you are old, and your teeth would get stuck."
Pullumb: (with amazement): OH!'
Mrika -- Sikur nuk pate edhe ti dëshirë të rrije me të!
Dom Gjoni (shikon me inat Mrikën) HE...HE....
'Marika: It appears that you had no desire to stay with her.
Don Juan (eyes Marika with anger): Well...Well....'

Interjections may be simple or derived. Simple interjections may be single phonemes (mostly vowels), but the majority of them are longer phoneme sequences: **a, e, ë, i, o, u, y, sh, au, eu, oi, ou, ua, ba, he, moj, sus, sha, ama, ohu, ore, more, obobo, ububu**, etc.

These interjections may also be reiterated:

U! U! Pse pak të duket ty? 'OH! Do you think it's such a trifle? ("why, does it appear little to you?")'
Unë të hyj më në qytet? BA-BA-BA! Ku ka me çetën! 'Me enter the city again? UNTHINKABLE! There's nothing like the guerrilla life!'

The class of simple interjections also includes a small number of interjections that have been borrowed from other languages: **alo** 'hello', **aman** 'please', **bis** 'encore!', **hajde** 'come along, come on', **marsh** 'march!', **urra** 'hurrah' etc. Ordinarily, borrowed interjections have limited use, or use in specific fields.

Some derived interjections are formed from other parts of speech which lose or weaken their primary lexical meaning, are pronounced with an affective intonation, and are used solely to express the feelings, desires of will of the speaker. Compare:

a)   **QYQJA hap krahët, ngrihet nga dega e thatë e ahut, fluturon drejt në Jutbinë.** 'THE CUCKOO spreads its wings, takes off from the dry branch of the beech tree, and flies straight to Jutbinë.'

b)   **QYQJA! E shkreta Shegë, ç'ka për të hequr me të!** 'HEAVENS! Poor Shegë, how she will suffer with him!'

Other derived interjections have been formed from the agglutination of phrases, by virtue of their long and continuous use as stereotyped formulas of congratulations or greetings: **falemnderit** 'thanks', **lamtumirë** 'goodbye', **mirupafshim** 'goodbye', **tungjatjeta** 'hello, goodbye' etc. In these former word sequences, the constituent parts have lost completely their former grammatical functions, and in part have also undergone phonetic changes.

Certain fixed phraseological locutions occupy a special place among derived interjections: **djall o punë** 'damnation', **hej dreq** 'you devil', **më qafsh** 'I beg you ("may you weep for me"), **punë e madhe** 'big deal ("big work")', etc. Such conventional locutions function as interjectional phrases in that they are reproduced as complete, syntactically autonomous units used as wholes to express the speaker's feelings:

DREQI TA HAJË, mirë thonë arabët: njerëzit verën e dërgojnë në bark, kurse ajo u shkon në kokë. 'THE DEVIL TAKE ["eat"] IT, the Arabs say well: people send the wine to their stomach, yet it goes to their head.'
PUNË E MADHE nuk shikon? 'BIG DEAL, don't you see?'
Eja me mua, eja, MË QAFSH, mos i fol babait dhe vëllait. 'Come with me, come, I BEG YOU, don't talk to father and brother.'

derived interjections include certain fixed noun forms, some given a kind of imperative force by a preceding particle **o**, some by a verbal 2nd person plural ending **-ni**, and some by both together: **o burra** or **o burrani** 'onward!' [**burra** 'men'], **forca** or **forcani** 'heave-ho!' [**forca** 'powers'], **korba** 'woe is me!, oh no!', **qyqja** 'woe is me!, oh no!', etc. This group includes also certain invariable forms of substantivized adjectives: e.g., **të keqen** 'bless you' (short for **të keqen tënde e marrsha unë** 'may I take your evil upon myself').

NOTE

The ending **-ni** is found also in a number of other interjections, simple and derived that are used to express the speaker's desire or will: **hadje/hajdeni** 'come on', **hë/hëni** 'let's go', etc. It may also be used to express various greetings, such as, **mirëmëngjes/mirëmëngjesni** 'good morning', **mirëmbrëma/mirëmbrëmani** 'good evening', **mirëdita/mirëditani** 'good day', **tungjatjeta/tungjatjetani** 'hi, hello,' etc. The ending **-ni** indicates that these imperative interjections are addressed to a plural "you" or politely to a singular "you". Such forms with the ending **-ni** are not standard. They are only rarely encountered in the spoken language, and still more rarely in the written language. The form without **-ni** are usually used instead to address even a plural "you".

12.2 Classification of Interjections

According to how they are used, interjections are classified as 1) *affective interjections*, which express emotions, and 2) *imperative interjections* which express the desire or the will of the speaker. Each of these classes is further subdivided. Of course the dividing lines between these classes and sub-classes are not hard and clear and the same interjection can serve a variety of functions.

12.2.1 Affective Interjections

AFFECTIVE INTERJECTIONS serve to express joy, satisfaction, dissatisfaction, surprise, fear, sorrow, pain, disappointment, anger, threat, scorn etc. Depending on the desire or aim of the speaker, the same interjection may express quite different feelings through intonation, gesture, and facial expression. Thus, the interjection **oh** can be used to express joy, despair, anguish, distress, surprise, regret, disbelief, etc.:

Despair: **-- OH, po sikur të mos ndodhë? -- mendoi i dëshpëruar dhe shikoi me kujdes orën.** '"OH, but what if it doesn't happen?" he thought dejectedly and looked carefully at the watch.'

Joy: **-- OH, sa mirë! Mua më pëlqen byreku me djathë, -- tha ai me gëzim, duke u hedhur në tokë.** '"OH, how nice! I like cheese pie," he said cheerfully, as he jumped on the ground.'

Anguish: **Shpresa, që e kuptoi menjëherë ç'kërkonte, i foli: -- Na e vranë, Ylli, na e vranë! -- OH!** 'Shpresa, who understood at once what he was looking for, spoke to him: "They killed him, Yll, they killed him!" "OH!"'

Distress: **-- OH! -- thonë vashat të pikëlluara, -- gjersa të shkrijë lumi dhe të hapen krojet, do të na ngordhë gjithë gjëja e gjallë.** '"OH!" say the distressed maidens, "by the time the river thaws out and the water fountains open up, our entire livestock will die."'

Surprise: **-- OH, -- shpërtheu një britmë habie. -- Më mbeti çizmja.** '"OH," escaped a cry of surprise. "I'm stuck with the boot."

Regret: **OH, si s'durove deri të enjten.** 'OH, how is it you couldn't wait until Thursday.'

Disbelief: **-- Do t'ia mbushim mendjen edhe xha Rexhepit. -- OH, e ku i mbushet mendja atij!** '"We will persuade Uncle Rexhep as well." "OH, you can't persuade him."'

The facial expressions and gestures that sometimes accompany these interjections can only partially express what the interjection expresses. In writing, punctuation marks, repetition of individual letters or of the entire interjection are devices that attempt to reflect intonational characteristics of the interjection, but succeed only to a small degree:

A! A! Kush qenka! 'O ho! Look who's (here)!'

AA, tashti filloi avazi i gjatë. 'AAHH, now the long melody has begun.'

OH...OH...OH... -- kënaqej Kasemi. -- Kjo është jetë! '"OOHHH," sighed Kasem with pleasure, "This is the life!"'

PA-PA-PA, ç'njerëz! 'PHEW, what (mean) people!'

Depending on the context, the same interjection can express different feelings but the opposite also happens: different interjections can express the same feelings, so long as they have the same intonation. Thus, to express a sense of surprise, one can use any of the interjections **a, ah, bobo, korba, more, oj, pupu, qyqja, u, ua, uh,** etc.

A, kush qenka, çuni i Janit! 'WELL, look who's here, Johnny's kid!'

AH! Ti qenke! Ku të kam parë unë ty? 'OH! It's you! Where have I seen you (before)?'

-- MOOORE! Qenkam vrarë, jo shaka! Nikollaqi. '"HEYYY! I've been wounded, no joking, Nikollaq!"'

-- OJ, ishin, thotë. Sa të duash. 'AND HOW there were," he says. "All you want."'

PUPU, sa e bukur! Shiko, shiko si ndrit "fap, fap". 'WOW, how beautiful! Look, look how splendiferous she shines.'

-- U, mësuesi, mezi të njoha, -- thirri ai dhe u përqafuan. '"MY GOODNESS, teacher, I barely recognized you," he cried out, and they embraced.'

UA, si të shihte ai ty! 'BOY, the way he looked at you!'

UH! -- tha e habitur. '"HUH!" he said, surprised.'

Besides interjections of variable meaning, whose value is determined by context and intonation, Albanian has some interjections with a more or less fixed meaning: **bobo, bubu, obobo, ububu** to express fear or despondency; **u, ua, oj** to express surprise, etc. The interjections with the most fixed, and definite meaning are the imperative interjections: **hë, hop** to hurry someone up; **sus, shët** to request calm or silence; **ore, moj** to call someone's attention, etc.

On the basis of the feelings they are associated with most often, the affective interjections may be divided into sub-groups:

a) *Interjections that express joyful feelings* 'joy, satisfaction, enthusiasm, admiration, etc.): **o, oh, oho, hoho, ohoho, të lumtë** 'bravo', **urra** 'hurrah', etc.:

Zyloja u ngrit e hapi derën. -- O, hajde, Hodo Allamani, hajde -- thirri. 'Zylo got up and opened the door. "OH, come in, Hodo Allamħan, come in," he yelled.'

Sa mirë, OH, sa mirë që na erdhi përsëri! 'How nice, OH, how nice that he came to us again.'

OHO, OHO! Dolën! Dolën -- brohoritën të rinjtë sa i panë. 'HEY, HEY! They've left! They've left!" the young people shouted, as soon as they saw them.'

OHOHO! klithi përsëri Iliri dhe zuri të fërkonte duart i gëzuar. 'OH HO! Ilir screamed once again, and began to rub his hands, joyfully.'

b) *Interjections that express surprise*: **au, eu, oj, ou, pa (pah), u, ua, uh**, etc.

-- AU! Si, qenke memec e ditke të flasësh? '"WELL! How's this, you are dumb and can still speak?"'

-- EU, si qenka djegur! '"GEE, how it's burned!"'

-- OJ, pa dale! u çudit ai duke e shtyrë me sa fuqi atë që deshi të hynte i pari. '"WHOA, take it easy!" he (said) amazed, as he pushed with all his strength the guy who tried to get in first.'

-- OU, paskeni ardhur edhe ju sonte këtu? '"WELL, WELL, you've come here tonight, too?"'

PAH, sa i shijshëm qe bërë! 'WHEW, how delicious it turned out to be!'

U! Po ti nga na dole? Na i bëre sytë ujë. 'WELL, and where have you been? We've been dying to see you ("you made our eyes water".'

-- UA, ne jemi shumë të gëzuar, tha Alma. '"IN FACT, we are very happy," said Alma.'

Marina -- UH, po atë e dinë të gjithë. 'Marina--WELL MY DEAR, everybody knows who she is.'

c) *Interjections that express worry or fear*: **bobo, bubu, korba** ("raven"), **kuku, obobo, qyqja** ("cuckoo") **ububu**, etc.:

Tina doli nga dhoma e menduar dhe e dëshpëruar: BOBO, do të jetë gënjyer korba! 'Tina emerged from the room preoccupied and dejected: GOOD GRIEF, she must have been deceived, the wretch!'

Dera e udhës trokiti. -- KORBA! u drodh plaka dhe u gjet në këmbë. 'There was a knock on the street gate. "MY GOD!" the old woman trembled and stood up.'

QYQJA, ç'bëmë ne, QYQJA! Therëm kaun! 'HEAVENS, what have we done! We slaughtered the ox!'

UBUBU! Mirë bëra që ika. 'HORRORS! I did well to leave.'

d) *Interjections that express indifference or contempt*: **ama, ahu, ehu, ohu, ptu, y**, etc.;

AMA, kryetar paskeni! 'HMPF, some president you have!'

AHU! Ti, shoqja agronome thua të numërojmë edhe thelat e bostanit. 'TSK TSK! you, comrade agronomist want us to count even the melon slices.'

-- EHU, ti, xha Osman, ke llafe. '"REALLY! uncle Osman, you're a big talker."'

IIII, sa i keq je! 'UGH, you're terrible!'

-- OHU, unë kam njëzet vjet që e di, -- tha pa e prishur gjakun Nazmija. '"HMPF, I've known that for twenty years," said Nazmija without getting upset ("ruining the blood").'

Ai ka qenë patriot, kurse ti...PTU! 'He was a patriot, while you...PTOOEY [spits]!'

Y, shpifaman! 'SHAME ON YOU, you liar!'

e) *Interjections that express dissatisfaction, regret, or distress:* **a, ah, e, eh, of, oi, uf, vaj,** etc.:

Ai shtyu dorën fort, sikur të ishte trembur nga diçka dhe më tha: -- A! Të lutem! Të lutem! Ne nuk pranojmë. 'He pushed his hand hard, as if he had been frightened by something, and said to me: "OH! Please! Please! We can't accept."'

AH, more shokë, sa e rëndë qenka vdekja! 'AH, my friends, how difficult it is to die.'

-- E, mor vëlla! tha ai. -- Më lëndohet zemra kur i sjell ndër mend ato ngjarje. '"EH, brother!" he said. "My heart aches when I recall those events."'

EH, të ishte Kristofori. Sa qejf i ka këta pëllumbat i gjori. 'OH, if only Christopher were here. How he delights in these pigeons, the poor guy.'

OF, i gjori unë, i varfri unë. Pse s'e dëgjova vëllanë? 'OH, wretched me, poor me. Why didn't I listen to my brother?'

-- OIIII, moj Olimbi, sa më ka ardhur keq. 'OOH, dear Olimbi, how sad I felt.'

UF, unë e mjera! Gjallë qenka? 'OH my ("desolate me")! Is he alive?'

12.2.2 Imperative Interjections

IMPERATIVE INTERJECTIONS express the desire or will of the speaker. They can be divided into three sub-groups:

a) *Interjections that call out:* **ej (hej), o, ore (or, mor, more), moj (ori, mori), pst,** etc.;

-- Gati? Gati? EJ, ju! Më vonë bisedohet! '"Ready? Ready? HEY, you! It will be discussed later."'

-- Ngadale, O se na shurdhove! -- tha Guri. '"Easy THERE, you're making us deaf!" Guri said.'

Barinjtë qenë zgjuar dhe kishin dhënë alarmin: "Ujku, ORE, ujku, në kope!" 'The shepherds were awake and had given the alarm: "The wolf, MAN, the wolf, in the fold!"'

-- MOJ, me ty po flas! 'HEY YOU, I'm talking to you!'

-- MORE, mos ka ndonjë rrezik kjo punë? '"SAY, is this job dangerous?"'

The interjections **ej, o,** and **pst,** etc., are used without reference to sex; **or, ore, mor, more** are used for addressing males, while **moj** is used for addressing females.

NOTE

In nominal phrases the interjections **o, ore, or, mor, more, moj** normally serve as pre-determiners before nominative case nouns, thus making a kind of VOCATIVE case for Albanian:

O shqipëri, për ty ç'më merr malli. 'O Albania, how I long for you.'

-- O shoko, O partizan, na ndrit pak me atë pishë. '"O comrade, O partisan, give us a little light with that torch."'

ORE ti, sa ma shet këtë qilim? 'HEY you, how much would you sell this rug to me for?'

MORE Miti, po këtë të ma kishe thënë në krye fare. 'SAY Miti, you should have told me this right from the start.'

Ah! MOJ Tanë, më turpërove në pleqëri. 'Ah! DEAR Tanë, you've disgraced me in my old age.'

b) *Interjections that express command, encouragement or request:* **o burra, forca, hop** (or **hopa**), **hë na, sus, sët, të keqen,** etc.:

-- FORCA, jepi! -- thërritnin dhe djersët u shkonin çurg. '"HEAVE-HO, at it!" they yelled and their sweat streamed down.'

Duke i dhënë levës me sa mundte, Nikoja thërriste: -- O, HOP...Edhe një

herë...HOPA! 'Pushing the lever as hard as he could, Niko shouted: "Okay, WHOOP...Once more...WHOOP!"'

-- HË, -- më nxiste xhaxhoja. Ai donte që unë të haja tri lugë dhe ai një. '"Go ON," my uncle kept urging me. He wanted me to eat three spoonfuls to every one of his.'

-- NA, lexoje. Shto ndonjë gjë, që të duket e arsyeshme dhe pregatitu të flasësh. '"HERE, read it. Add something that might seem reasonable to you, and get ready to speak."'

-- SUS, ti atje, s'e kam me ty! -- ia preu shkurt plaku. '"HUSH, you over there, I'm not addressing you!" the old man said curtly to him.'

Pak ujë, motër, TË KEQEN! '"A little water, sister, BLESS YOU."'

NOTE

A special place among imperative interjections is occupied by interjections spoken to animals: to call them, frighten them off, or give them commands. In this category are: çit, ish, pis, tik-tik, ush, yja, etc.:

ÇIT, moj lanete, se më dukesh si paguri i rakisë. '"SCRAM, you devil, 'cause you look like a whiskey canteen to me."'

'"ISH," deshi t'i përzinte ai, po pulat s'lëvizën nga vendi. '"SHOO," he tried to chase them off, but the chickens did not budge.'

PIIIS! -- e ndillnin edhe mëma me Blertën. Po macja e vogël ishte lart në akacje. '"KITTYY!" mother and Blertë called out to her. But the little cat was up in the acacia tree.'

Unë vete te ajo ditë për ditë, i thërres pulat e saj "TIK-TIK-TIK" dhe u hedh për të ngrënë. 'I go there every day, call out "CHICK-CHICK" to her chickens, and feed them.'

-- U bë tamam si karroca e Çapajevit! YJA! -- ia bëri ai kalit. '"It's become exactly like the carriage of Chapayev! WHOA THERE!" he shouted to the horse.'

3. *Interjections that express different greetings, gratitude, congratulations* etc.: **falemnderit** 'thank you', **lamtumirë** 'good bye', **mirëmëngjesi** 'good morning', **mirëdita** 'good day, hello', **mirëmbrëma** 'good evening', **mirupafshim** 'see you later, so long', **mirë se erdhe** 'welcome', **mirë se vjen** 'welcome', **mirë mbeç** 'goodbye', **ditën e mirë** 'good day, goodbye', **natën e mirë** 'good night', **tungjatjeta** 'hello, goodbye', **udha e mbarë** 'goodbye, farewell', etc.

Jo, FALEMINDERIT. Me punë shkoj mirë tashti. 'No, THANK YOU, I'm doing fine at work now.'

Ai mori borsalinën, e vuri në kokë, hapi derën dhe tha: -- LAMTUMIRË! 'He took the hat, put it on his head, opened the door, and said: "GOODBYE!"'

MIRUPAFSHIM, gjyshi i Meremes. 'SEE YOU LATER, Mereme's grandpa.'

-- MIRËDITA, u përgjegj Besniku. '"GOOD DAY, replied Besnik."'

MIRË SE ERDHE tha Sokoli dhe u ngrit e shkoi i dha dorën. 'WELCOME, said Sokol, and he got up and shook hands with him.'

Although normally these interjectional words and expressions have not lost entirely the lexical meaning of their constituent elements, they are pronounced with strong emotional tones, are used purely as greetings, and resemble the group of interjections that express commands or encouragement.

12.3 Syntax of Interjectional Phrases

Interjectional phrases are most commonly found at the beginning of the sentence, but they often appear in the middle or the end of the sentence as well. They are separated from other parts of speech by an intonation break or by a comma, suggesting that their role is parenthetical to the rest of the sentence. When pronounced forcefully, they normally stand by themselves, indicated in writing by a following exclamation point, but it is permissible in Albanian to write an exclamation point and question mark next to one another whenever the feeling (especially surprise) that is expressed by the interjection is accompanied by an interrogation:

> **Ki kujdes, mos fol shumë Afroviti -- UA!** 'Be careful, Aphrodite, don't talk too much--OOPS!'

> **-- Ju na keni lënë vetëm, -- tha Besniku me zë të shurdhër. A!? ia bëri i habitur tjetri. -- Vetëm?** '"You've left us alone," Besnik said in a muffled voice. "HUH!?" went the other, amazed. "Alone?"'

Interjections. can be used as an independent interjectional phrase, or as a syntactically unrelated unit within the sentence. In both cases they express the feelings, desires or will of the speaker.

Since the context of interjectional phrases is not clearly defined, they are often accompanied by some other phrase that spells out the idea or feeling of the speaker:

> **OHO! Doli thëllënza nga çerdhja.** 'OHO! The pheasant has come out of the nest.'

> **-- SHËËËT! -- ia bëri ngadalë, -- mos kthe fjalë!** '"SHHHH!" he went slowly, "don't talk back."'

Interjections are often used with the value of a word within a clause, but syntactically unrelated to it, indicated in writing by attaching it to the other words in the clause with a comma, and in speaking by including the interjection in the same intonation contour as the word(s) adjacent to it. Affective interjections are used in just this manner:

> **-- AH, ç'ia ke punuar një herë Salih Protopapës në atë mbledhje.** '"BOY, you really fixed Salih Protopapë good at that meeting."'

> **-- OH, sa më është bërë qejfi!** '"OH, how delighted I was!"'

Similarly interjections followed by vocatives may share their intonation contour:

> **Ai i mori me mend e me vete nisi të dëshpërohet duke thënë: "AH, Gëzim, Gëzim!"** 'He guessed it and began to feel disappointed with himself, saying: "AH, Gëzim, Gëzim, Gëzim!"'

Parenthetical interjections are sometimes found within the clause:

> **Pse i lëviz ashtu buzët, AH, të shkreta?** 'Why do you move your poor--(SIGH!)--lips like that?'

In general, interjections are not syntactically related to the other constituents of a clause, and for this reason are not regarded as clause constituents. However, occasionally an interjection is used as if it were a clause constituent, most often a verb, but sometimes also as if it were a verbal complement:

> **-- Ke frikë se mos i bie zjarri dhe HAJT pastaj t'i gjesh në mes të gërmadhave.** 'You are afraid it will catch fire, and then just you try ("SCRAM!") to find them in the midst of the ruins.'

> **Ngarkohuni dhe MARSH në brigadë! -- urdhëroi Agimi.** '"Load up and march ("MARCH!") in the brigade!" Agim ordered.'

> **HOP nis e gumëzhin tërë pylli.** 'Suddenly ("WHOOP!") the whole forest begins to rumble.'

> **Ua mbledh unë edhe burrave edhe djemve. SUS rrinë.** 'I tell them off, men and boys alike. They keep MUM.'

Interjections are often contextually substantivized, and then serve like other nouns as clause constituents, especially as subjects and objects of verbs, as objects of prepositions, as nucleus of a nominal phrase, and with different number and case forms. In such cases, they refer to, rather than express feelings:

> **Sepse një AH dhe një brengë, u mbushi zemrat me hidhërime.** 'Because a sigh ("AH") and a grief filled their hearts with sorrows.'

> **Lëri AHET dhe UHET po ulu aty se je mirë, tha Arapi.** 'Forget about ("leave them") the AH's and UH's, and sit down there, because you are well off, said the Negro.'

12.4 Onomatopoeic Words

Onomatopoeic words are closely related to interjections. Like interjections, they tend to be single syllables or repetitions of single syllables; they express rather than refer; they are fixed in form; they do not have derivational elements in their composition; they are usually syntactically unrelated to other words in a sentence; and they are usually pronounced with their own intonation contour. Even so, onomatopoeic words differ from proper interjections because they do not directly express the feelings, desires or will of the speaker, but rather initiate the sounds, voices, noises, yells, screams, etc. of various objects and phenomena in the real world. As a result, unlike interjections, the intonation with which onomatopoeic words are pronounced does not depend on the speaker's emotions, but rather on the speaker's conventionalized notion of the sounds he is attempting to reproduce, and the sounds of the onomatopoeic word do not bear an entirely arbitrary relation to what is represented by the word.

Onomatopoeic words imitate the sounds:

a)   of people:

-- SA ftohtë bën! BËRR! -- tha burri me kapele kashte. '"How cold it is! BRRR!" said the man with the straw hat.'
Nënë, moj, nënë, HA-HA-HA! -- qeshi e thirri ai me zë gazmor. '"Mother, hey mother, HA-HA-HA!" he laughed and shouted in a joyful voice.'

b)   of birds:

'**Në oborr, në degët e dendura të një portokalli, ia thoshte përvajshëm një kumri: GU-GU-GU.** 'In the yard, in the dense branches of an orange tree, a turtledove sang plaintively: coo-coo-coo.'

c)   of animals:

MIAU-MIAU -- bëri macja e bardhë. '"MEOW-MEOW", went the white cat.'

d)   of the objects and phenomena of nature:

Gjylet fluturonin mbi qytet dhe pëlcisnin matanë me një zhurmë të llahtarshme: -- BËZZ-BUM! BËZZZ-BUM. 'The shells flew over the city and burst on the other side with a terrifying noise: "BZZZ-BOOM! BZZZ-BOOM!"'
Era hidhte valle, vërtitej dhe ulërinte: -- VUU! VUUU! 'The wind danced, flurried, and wailed: "WOO! WOOO!"'

Different onomatopoeic words may be used to imitate the theoretically same original sound, partially because the "same" sound, even produced in identical circumstances, may be perceived and imitated in different ways by different people. Thus, for example, to imitate the coughing of a choking person, onomatopoeic formations like the following are used in Albanian: **khu-khu, kuh-kuh, kum-kum, ku-ku-ku,** etc.

Plaku i Hyskës kollitej në një qoshe: KHU-KHU...KHU-KHU... -- KUH-KUH! -- u kollit plaku. KUM, KUM, KUM e mbyti kolla. E shkuli kolla, Ku-KU-KU! KU-KU-KU! 'The old man of Hyskë coughed in a corner: "HOUGH-HOUGH...HOUGH-HOUGH!" coughed the old man. HUGH, HUGH, HUGH, the cough choked him. The cough tore him up. COOH-COOH-COOH! COOH-COOH-COOH!"'

In some cases, the difference in the phonetic composition of onomatopoeic words for the "same" sound is supposed to reflect differences actually found in the real world. For instance, depending on the type of laughter represented, quite a few onomatopoeic formations are used in Albanian: **he-he-he, hi-hi-hi, ho-ho-ho, ku-ku-ku,** etc.

Compare: **-- HE-HE-HE! qeshi me zor plaku. Dhe qeshte duke treguar nofullat e tij pa dhëmbë: -- HI-HI-HI!** '"HEH-HEH-HEH-!" the old man laughed with difficulty. And laughing, he showed his toothless ("without teeth") jaws: "HEE-HEE-HEE!"'
-- HO-HO-HO! -- qeshi Guri me të madhe. '"HO-HO-HO!" Guri roared ("laughed greatly") with abandon.'
Çupëzat qeshën KU-KU-KU dhe u turpëruan e u skuqën si ato mollët në degë. 'The

little girls laughed TEE-HEE and were embarrassed, and they turned red like apples on the twig.'

On the other hand, certain onomatopoeic words have a fairly consistent phonemic and graphemic representation in Albanian: **ciu-ciu** (bird), **fiu** (whistling), **ga-ga-ga** (goose), **ka-ka-ka** (chicken), **ku-ku** (cuckoo), **kuak-kuak** (duck), **miau** (cat), **mu-mu** (cow), **krra-krra** (raven), **ham-ham** (dog), **bërr** (cold shiver), **tik-tak** (watch), **dang-dang** (bell), **ty-ty** (bugle), **tak-tak** (knocking), **vu-vu** (wind), etc.

Certain onomatopoeic words, especially those that accompany physiological activities and actions (shivering, laughter, whistling, snoring, etc.), are often used to suggest feelings like fear, scorn, irony, etc.:

> **Plaku i ra kokës me grushte. -- KUKU? thirri. -- E nga e more këtë qelbësirë, ore Rushit?** 'The old man hit his head with (his) fist. "WHA?" he yelled. "Where did you get this rotten thing, Rushit?"'
> **-- PTU, sa i pështirë qenka.** '"PHOOEY, how disgusting it is."'

In these examples, **ku-ku** and **ptu** are not onomatopoeic words, but interjections; words, that is, with which we express feelings. Strictly speaking, they are onomatopoeic only when used to imitate directly the voice of the cuckoo or spitting by a human being:

> **Vetëm qyqja e kuqe kukat në një rrem të thatë dhe kënga e saj kumbon kobshëm lugjeve: KUKU, KUKU!** 'Only the red cuckoo cries out on a dry oar, and her song resounds dreadfully through the valleys: CUCKOO, CUCKOO!'
> **-- PTU, -- pështyu Qazimi në hajat pa asnjë shkak.** '"PTOOEY," Qazim spit on the porch without any reason.'

Onomatopoeic words are usually used in isolation. They do not engage in normal syntactic relations with other parts of the clause, and are therefore not clause constituents:

> **DANG-DANG! DANG-DANG-DANG! -- Kjo e rënë e çangës i kujtoi që duhej të nisnin punën.** '"DING-DONG! DING-DING-DONG!" The ringing of the gong reminded them that they should start working.'
> **BU, BU, BU...! Ja ku pas pak na duket që po vjen një re sterrë e zezë.** 'WHOOSH...! And shortly after we see a pitch-black cloud coming.'

But, like interjections, they can occasionally be used in the role of a clause constituent, especially as verbs or verbal complements:

> **Sa merrja veten nga dasma, BAM një gjë tjetër.** 'No sooner did I recover from the wedding when something else hit me ("when BANG something else").'
> **Pse nuk e thoshte BRAM atë që kishte për të thënë?** 'Why didn't he come right out and say ("say BAM") what he had to say?

Like any other words, onomatopoeic words may be contextually substantivized. In such cases, they take on the usual lexical and grammatical characteristics of a noun, and are especially frequent in NP's as subject or object of a verb:

> **TIKTAKËT monotonë të sahatit të murit ia shtonin harmoninë.** 'The monotonous TICK-TOCKS of the clock on the wall added to its harmony.'
> **Mori velenxën dhe u mbulua kokë e këmbë, që të mos dëgjonte më PËSHPËSHET e kushërinjve.** 'He took the blanket and covered himself from head to foot, so as not to hear the WHISPERINGS of his cousins.'

Index

Index

Index